Promotional Strategy

**Managing the Marketing
Communications Process**

The Irwin Series in Marketing

Consulting Editor
Gilbert A. Churchill
University of Wisconsin, Madison

Promotional Strategy

Managing the Marketing Communications Process

JAMES F. ENGEL
Graduate School, Wheaton College (Illinois)

MARTIN R. WARSHAW
The University of Michigan

THOMAS C. KINNEAR
The University of Michigan

Fifth Edition · 1983

RICHARD D. IRWIN, INC.
Homewood, Illinois 60430

ISBN 0-256-02846-X

Library of Congress Catalog Card No. 82–84060

Printed in the United States of America

1 2 3 4 5 6 7 8 9 0 K 0 9 8 7 6 5 4 3

Preface

As a basic text, *Promotional Strategy: Managing The Marketing Communications Process* differs somewhat from many similar works. It builds on a rigorous base of consumer behavior and then proceeds to treat advertising, sales promotion, reseller stimulation, personal selling, and other communication tools as part of an overall promotional mix. In other words, various communication methods are treated as variables for use alone or in combination to communicate the want-satisfying attributes of products and services. The approach throughout is to develop fundamental considerations as background and then to focus on managerial issues and problems. Much of the usual descriptive content in books on advertising and promotion has been condensed and integrated into a discussion of the theory and rationale of the various topics that are covered.

Problems are viewed through the eyes of the promotion manager, and major emphasis is placed on understanding the factors that affect promotional decisions and mold managerial strategy. Simple answers to problems that defy simple rule-of-thumb solutions are avoided. No attempt is made to build this degree of certainty into the discussion when, in fact, such certainty seldom exists in the "real" world.

In short, it is our belief that a keen understanding of the variables affecting decisions, an awareness of sources of information pertaining to these variables, a knowledge of the strengths and limitations of methods and strategies, and a grasp of the fundamentals of managerial decision making should be the basic subject matter in a modern marketing textbook. Actual decision rules and practices usually are unique to specific problems within the firm, and it is a futile exercise, for the most part, to document endless lists of possible strategies that usually have only a relatively limited application. It would be wishful thinking to maintain that this or any other text can cover all that needs to be known about communication methods in marketing. An attempt has been made, instead, to provide a balanced overview of pertinent topics and thereby provide sufficient background for the student to perform well in advanced courses and on the job as one gains experience and insight.

For those who have had a prior course in consumer behavior, Part Two of the text may be covered rapidly or perhaps omitted altogether. It has been our experience, however, that students without a background in this area cannot comprehend the deeper issues of promotional strategy.

Some schools retain separate courses in advertising and sales management. Although we have integrated appropriate topics in this text, the material is readily adaptable to a more limited course in advertising through omission of Part Five. We strongly recommend that the integrated point of view be taken whenever possible, however, for it is becoming increasingly common in promotional practice.

This edition contains a great deal of new material. The consumer behavior section has been completely rewritten reflecting the latest research in the area. Of special import is the consideration of low-involvement behavior. The chapter on market segmentation has also been extensively revised and all of the remaining material has been checked to make sure that it reflects the current state of knowledge. In addition, we have not hesitated to express ourselves freely on broader social issues. We are especially concerned when poor business practice results in under-informing or misleading the consumer. Our goal is to educate students of marketing and promotion to take the marketing concept as a guide to action. Finding out what consumers want or need and then aiding in the satisfaction of those needs is not only socially beneficial; it is good business practice.

Once again we wish to thank all of our many colleagues and friends who have contributed comments and criticisms in response to the first four editions. Rather than name them all we wish to thank them as a group and to recognize two persons who provided formal and extensive reviews of the fourth edition. They are: Cynthia J. Frey of Boston College and Linda L. Golden of the University of Texas at Austin. We believe that the fifth edition has been much improved because of their input.

Special thanks are also due Bernard Guggenheim of Campbell-Ewald, to John Barbie and Joe McGowan of Leo Burnett Company, Inc. and to Parker Llewellyn of Foote, Cone & Belding.

Finally our thanks go to our patient families who have put up with us through the hectic times of book revision.

Of course, no one acknowledged here is responsible for any errors or omissions in the manuscript. The blame is entirely ours, although each author continues to assign the blame to the others.

JAMES F. ENGEL
MARTIN R. WARSHAW
THOMAS C. KINNEAR

Contents

cessing under Low Involvement: *The Stages in Information Processing. The Boredom Barrier.* The Issue of Manipulation. Summary.

PART ONE
Overview

Part One is devoted to introductory concepts in order to provide a foundation and framework for the chapters to follow. Chapter 1 reviews the subject of marketing management and clarifies the role of promotion within the marketing mix. To many readers, these topics will be quite familiar. Taking promotion as the communication function of marketing, Chapter 2's analysis of the nature of communication discusses various theoretical perspectives and draws a sharp distinction between the problems presented in face-to-face communication and those arising from the use of mass media. Chapter 3 gives an overview of promotional strategy through an actual case history and provides an outline of the stages in promotional planning and strategy which serves as the rationale for the organization of succeeding chapters.

CHAPTER 1

Introduction

One can just imagine the satisfaction with which management received the 1980 sales figures—a total of $2.8 billion compared with just $1.2 billion in 1976. By anyone's standards this represented an enviable sales growth. In fact it led to a brave claim in its annual report that the company has "demonstrated resistance to adversity."[1] This demonstrated resistance did not last long, however. In fact, most of the top management team was no longer present in 1981 to face the shock of a 23 percent earnings decline and a most pessimistic short-run future. Total net income dropped more than 20 percent.

How could such adversity hit, *especially with the great name of Levi Strauss?* This brand name had become virtually a household word for many decades. With such a steady growth of sales and income it would be a strong temptation to diversify into related lines and make maximum promotional mileage out of the Levi name, especially given the onset of a multiplicity of new brands in the blue jeans market and the tendency for retailers to offer Levi's at a discount—something unheard of in earlier times. So diversification began in earnest.

Medium-priced men's, women's, and children's slacks.

Higher fashioned lines such as the "David Hunter" line of men's jackets and dress slacks.

A new line of "activewear" which included skiwear and warm-up suits.

---

[1] "It's Back to Basics for Levi's," *Business Week,* March 8, 1982, p. 77.

These, in turn, are only a few components of the 24 separate product categories in which Levi Strauss has chosen to compete. While nonjean lines reached about 33 percent of total revenue by 1981, many of the new lines failed to make the grade—especially the David Hunter line. This forced Robert D. Haas, the new chief operating officer, to conclude: "We've realized that just putting the Levi's name on something isn't enough to gain instant marketing acceptance."[2] Another executive added, "The Levi's brand is our strongest asset, but it's not all powerful."[3]

What went wrong here? No doubt there were many considerations,[4] but there are signs that management lapsed into a *selling* or a *promotional orientation*. As Kotler puts it:

> The *selling concept* is a management orientation that assumes that consumers will either not buy or not buy enough of the organization's products unless the organization makes a substantial effort to stimulate their interest in its products.[5]

It is based on the assumption that a high level of advertising or sales fire power will somehow work to move the product. It almost endows promotion with a kind of magic through which the consumer can be maneuvered in almost any direction management desires.

No one denies the potential impact from skillful use of media, but a selling orientation tends to ignore an absolute fact of business life—*consumer sovereignty*. The consumer tends to see and hear what he or she wants to see and hear, and the firm can do little to overcome this basic human charactertistic! We intend to demonstrate in detail just how consumer sovereignty works and what it means for promotional management, but one thing is clear—if the consumer does not want the product or service, the firm is pretty much powerless to do anything about it except to change what it is offering to the market.

What this boils down to is that promotion is only one part, albeit an important one, of a total mix of marketing efforts. It cannot, for example, move an unwanted product, one which is overpriced, and so on. It simply does not possess that so-called magic referred to above.

Now, returning to Levi Strauss, it is obvious that its lessons were painful ones. Realizing that its name and promotion firepower are not sufficient, it has returned to concentration on what it does best—production and marketing of its basic line of jeans. It has not withdrawn from most of its areas of diversification, but its efforts are now being placed effectively where they are likely to produce greatest results. In other

---

[2] Ibid., p. 77.

[3] Ibid., p. 78.

[4] For further commentary see, "Levi Strauss to Sell its Brand Products Through J. C. Penney," *The Wall Street Journal,* December 17, 1981, p. 26.

[5] Philip Kotler, *Principles of Marketing* (Englewood Cliffs, N.J.: Prentice-Hall, 1980), p. 22.

words, it is in the process of shifting back from a promotion orientation to a *marketing orientation.*

PROMOTIONAL STRATEGY AND THE MARKETING CONCEPT

"If you don't know where you're going, any road will take you there. We have a pretty good idea of our basic course, and we try to hew to that line. . . . We don't force a product on the market just because it's state of the art."[6] This is the philosophy stated by Charles S. Grill, manager of marketing communications for the Sharp Electronics Corporation. Development of the Carousel Convection Microwave oven (CCM) exemplifies the way this philosophy finds its way into day-to-day practice.[7]

Extensive marketing research revealed that consumers were looking for a total cooking device. Microwave ovens could not match traditional convection ovens in some respects, so both were combined into one range, the CCM. Research findings showed clearly that $700 was the absolute maximum possible price, so that suggested retail price for the CCM was set at $639.95. "The Unbeatable Combination" was the promotional theme, and it registered the benefit of an oven that can both bake and brown food using metal appliances. The product itself, the price, and the promotional messages all were subjected to extensive market research before details were finalized.

Introductory ads with the Unbeatable Combination theme broke on network and spot television. Some use also was made of print. Advertising, in turn, was backed up by point-of-sale material and a training videotape designed to educate retail salespersons in how to demonstrate, explain, and sell the CCM.

Sharp recognized the headaches which poor quality control would bring in the form of customer dissatisfaction and complaints. Therefore, quality control was given highest priority.

The company launched the CCM on the expectation that it would pass General Electric and Litton and find itself in second place in the industry behind Amana. It was recognized at the outset that displacement of Amana from its number one slot would be totally unrealistic, at least at this point in time.

Sharp's business philosophy lies squarely on the *marketing concept* defined in this way by Kotler:

The *marketing concept* is a management orientation that holds that the key to achieving organizational goals consists of the organization's determining the needs and

---

[6] "Marketing, Technical Research Lead Sharp From Pencil Pushing to $2 Billion in Electronics Sales," *Marketing News,* March 6, 1981, p. 1.

[7] This discussion is based on ibid., pp. 1 and 4.

wants of target markets and adapting itself to delivering the desired satisfactions more effectively and efficiently than its competitors.[8]

It starts from the premise of consumer sovereignty and moves from there. The product itself, its promotion, its price, and its distribution all are adapted to consumer motivations in such a way as to attract and hold their loyalty. There is clear recognition that failure to adopt a marketing orientation can be followed in short order by a marked drop in market standing.

Marketing, then, encompasses a broad mix of efforts (product, price, promotion, and distribution) through which the firm adapts its offerings to a changing environment. No single element of this mix can be managed in isolation apart from the others without some potentially disastrous outcomes.

Promotion as a Part of Marketing Strategy

Promotion is a term which has assumed many meanings over the years. The original connotation in Latin was "to move forward." More recently the meaning has narrowed so that it refers to communication undertaken to persuade others to accept ideas, concepts, or things. As used in this book, promotional strategy is a *controlled integrated program of communication methods and materials designed to present a company and its products to prospective customers; to communicate need-satisfying attributes of products to facilitate sales and thus contribute to long-run profit performance.* The tools of promotion include:

1. *Advertising*—any paid form of nonpersonal presentation of ideas, goods, or services by an identified sponsor, with predominant use made of the media of mass communication.
2. *Personal selling*—the process of assisting and persuading a prospect to buy a good or service or to act upon an idea through use of person-to-person communication.
3. *Reseller support.*
4. *Publicity*—any form of nonpaid commercial significant news or editorial comment about ideas, products, or institutions.
5. *Sales Promotion*—those marketing activities, other than personal selling, advertising, and publicity, that stimulate consumer purchasing and dealer effectiveness, such as displays, shows and exhibitions, demonstrations, and various nonrecurrent selling efforts not in the ordinary routine.[9]

---

[8] Kotler, *Principles of Marketing*, p. 22.

[9] *Marketing Definitions: A Glossary of Marketing Terms,* compiled by a committee of the American Marketing Association under the direction of Ralph Alexander (Chicago: American Marketing Association, 1960).

Promotion, then, is the communication function of marketing. It is multifaceted and complex in its own right. No single textbook could treat all of these topics in detail. Our focus here is mostly on consumer goods, because the whole industrial market raises unique and specialized issues. Therefore, greatest attention is paid to advertising, stimulation of support in the trade, and personal selling. Activities of a more supplementary nature such as sales promotion and public relations and publicity also are covered but in less depth.

Marketing Management

Readers know by now that the first chapter of every text must have lots of definitions, and we certainly do not want to disappoint you. So, let's tighten up a bit on just what is meant by marketing. One of the best definitions states that it is "the process in society by which the demand structure for economic goods and services is anticipated or enlarged and satisfied through the conception, promotion, exchange, and physical distribution of such goods and services."[10] The demand structure and other elements in the environment therefore define the opportunity for the firm which, hopefully, is capitalized upon through skillful use of marketing efforts.

These concepts can be grasped more clearly in the form of the diagram presented as Figure 1-1. It shows (1) the elements of the environment; (2) the marketing mix; and (3) outcomes.

The environment. Certain factors must be accepted more or less as given in that they are beyond the immediate and direct control of management. Most of these are external—demand, competition, marketing law, the wholesale and retail structure, and the advertising media. Others are internal, including resources, facilities, and policies. Some of these really are profit inhibitors in that they restrict ability to gain competitive advantage. An example would be "marketing myopia," where management loses sight of its real business and fails to change its product offerings as the world around the firm changes.[11] These are basic management issues, however, and they are beyond the scope of discussion here. Thus, we will confine our attention to the external environment.

Demand. Demand, of course, refers to aggregate of needs, desires, and potential responses for the product or service in question. Researchers for the Sharp Corporation, for example, found that people were looking for a "total cooking device" which could achieve the best of both worlds, so to speak, in terms of the microwave and convection ovens. This under-

---

[10] Statement of the Philosophy of Marketing of the Marketing Faculty of The Ohio State University, Bureau of Business Research, Ohio State University, 1964, p. 2.

[11] Theodore Levitt, "Marketing Myopia," *Harvard Business Review,* July–August 1960, pp. 45–56.

FIGURE 1–1
Marketing Management

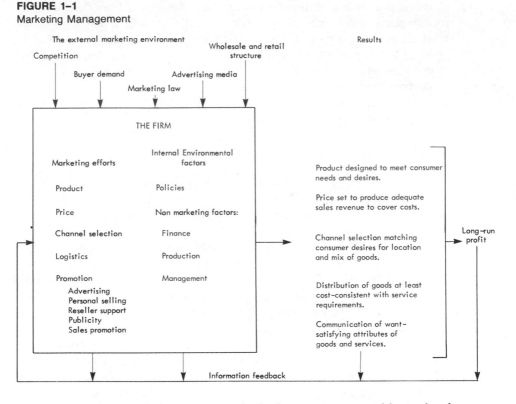

scored a good opportunity which the company quickly took advantage of.

Sound marketing is based on the premise that loyal customers are built, by and large, only if the product, package, price, selling appeals, retail outlets used, and so on are geared to factors which motivate the buyer's behavior. A sale will not take place if the price is thought to be too high, regardless of the promotional firepower. Similarly not many people were ready to accept Levi Strauss as a fashion marketer through its David Hunter line. In short, consumers cannot be manipulated as many marketing critics are apt to allege. They still retain the final vote.

Competition. The Levi Strauss people found to their sorrow that the jeans market attracted competitors in droves, some of whom moved beyond the Levi image into high fashion. Very few Americans, for example, could fail to identify Brooke Shields and her Calvins. After all that, who would want to be seen in anything less? This created a formidable challenge for Levi Strauss, to say the least.

Obviously a marketing manager cannot directly control the actions of competitors short of outright collusion. So, marketing strategy must be designed with a wary eye toward what they probably will do. It becomes necessary to assess the firm's strengths and weaknesses to capitalize upon what it does best while shoring up potential areas of vulnerability.

Marketing law.   The framework of law defines the marketing playing field. The Robinson-Patman Act, to mention just one example, specifies that retail advertising allowances must be made available to competitors on proportionally equal terms. Other laws center in on false and misleading advertising and place some real limits on managerial discretion. The importance of marketing law is obvious, and it is the subject of a later chapter.

The wholesale and retail structure.   If a product is ever to reach the consumer, it usually must pass through the hands of such marketing intermediaries as wholesalers and retailers, although some firms have their own wholly owned distribution system. But the majority of available wholesalers and retailers are independent, and the manufacturer has the challenge of building an effective channel of distribution. One of the greatest problems faced by Levi Strauss arose when Gap Stores, Inc., an independent chain and Levi's largest single customer, reduced its total dependence on Levi's to around 35 percent in 1981.[12] Management was quickly forced to seek new outlets, but that gave rise to a new set of problems to be discussed later.

The important point to note here is that these resellers can be an absolutely essential component of the total marketing effort. Without their support and cooperation, trouble is inevitable.

Advertising media.   Advertising media also are independently owned, and the producer faces the challenge of making an appropriate choice from among what is available. Reference here is to those physical vehicles designed to carry a message to a mass market. The challenges of media selection are demanding indeed as later chapters will reveal.

The marketing mix.   Figure 1–2 effectively illustrates the components of marketing strategy, often referred to as the "Four P's:" (1) product; (2) price; (3) place (distribution); and (4) promotion.

The objective is to unite these working tools of the marketing manager into an organized and integrated program of action. Each variable contributes in its own unique fashion to the overall objective of maximizing long-run return on investment.

Each area of marketing activity, in itself, is a *submix* of efforts within the broader program. For example, most firms produce more than one product, and the entire product line is referred to as the *product mix.*

Product.   When Levi Strauss & Company introduced its new line of athletic apparel in 1979, it generated only $9 million in sales and was soon dropped as being unprofitable. On the other hand, Sharp Electronics Corporation has had a recent succession of highly successful new introductions. What is the essential difference? As Charles Grill, marketing com-

---

[12] "It's Back to Basics for Levi's," p. 78.

FIGURE 1–2

The Marketing Mix

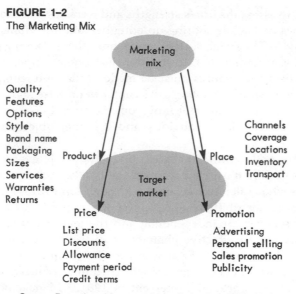

Quality
Features
Options
Style
Brand name
Packaging
Sizes
Services
Warranties
Returns

Channels
Coverage
Locations
Inventory
Transport

Product

Place

Target
market

Price

Promotion

List price
Discounts
Allowance
Payment period
Credit terms

Advertising
Personal selling
Sales promotion
Publicity

Source: Reproduced by special permission from Philip Kotler,
Principles of Marketing (Englewood Cliffs, N.J.: Prentice-Hall, 1980),
p. 90. Copyright 1980 by Prentice-Hall, Inc.

munications manager, puts it—a Sharp product is not produced until "a
gap in the market is perceived."[13] In other words, it will not act without
some real evidence that a new product will satisfy consumer needs and
desires. This is the first requirement of sound marketing thinking. Moreover, the product must be created and marketed with full awareness of
competing brands, legal restrictions such as the laws prohibiting product
adulteration, and probability estimates of a favorable economic climate.

Price. The product or service must, of course, be offered to the buyer
at a price which will produce an acceptable return on investment over
the long haul. A target return usually is established which then serves
as the guideline for price policy.

The consumer once again exerts sovereignty, however. The Sharp CCM
oven probably would never be a market success if it were priced over
$700. That figure appears to be the upper limit of what people will pay,
and there is little the company can do about that except to live with it.

Potential actions by competitors also are an important consideration,
especially when a limited number of firms offer highly similar products.
A price change by one is certain to be matched by others, and a price
war is an ever-present danger. The chaos resulting from price deregulation
in the U.S. airline industry stands as a classic contemporary example of
what ruinous price competition can do.

---

[13] "Marketing, Technical Research Lead Sharp," p. 1.

Finally the laws pertaining to pricing are quite specific; the Robinson-Patman Act and the Federal Trade Commission Act, among others, provide real constraints on pricing policy.

Promotion.   As has been pointed out above, promotion encompasses a system of communication tools designed to present a company, its products, and its services to consumers. Because it is the subject of this book, nothing more need be said at this point.

Place (distribution).   Finally, products must be made available when and where the potential buyer dictates. There are two important areas of decision related to this issue: (1) channel selection; and (2) actual physical distribution (logistics).

Levi Strauss management has made the decision to distribute its branded products through J. C. Penney in the hopes that this switch in distribution strategy will broaden its consumer base.[14] It no doubt is hoped that consumer demand for ready product availability will be met by this move, and management may have made a sound decision. On the other hand, it has shifted from a policy of selective distribution through department stores and specialty chains such as The Gap. In so doing, it has reduced retailer incentive for instore promotional push. Whether or not the Levi's brand name can overcome this limitation is yet to be seen. There always is the tension, then, between the need for retail display and sales effort and the need to meet consumer desires for product availability. This is discussed in detail in later chapters focusing on reseller promotion and support.

The second aspect of distribution strategy, now often referred to as logistics, focuses on the activities required to assemble, store, and ship products to middlemen in the channel of distribution. Logistics management is concerned primarily with two activities: (1) movement of goods from one place to another, including storage when necessary; and (2) coordination of customer demand with the supply of goods. Transportation, inventory control, warehousing, and supply scheduling are all integral components of a logistics system.

Results.   Refer once again to Figure 1–1 and notice that each element of the marketing mix is managed to attain objectives specific to that policy area. The goal of pricing policy is to set a price to produce sales revenues sufficient to cover costs and contribute to return on investment. These and other goals are also summarized in Figure 1–1. Long-run profit is the final result of the proper blending of all marketing efforts into an integrated and coordinated marketing program.

Profit thus far has been referred to only as long-run earnings. Short-run profit can be a meaningless criterion of marketing success, for it is possible to make a quick profit while threatening long-run survival. To

---

14 "Levi Strauss to Sell its Brand Products Through J. C. Penney."

take an example, a well-known food processing company could capitalize on its name, long the leader in the industry, and sell a stock of adulterated cranberries which otherwise would be discarded at a loss. Immediate losses could be averted and profits enhanced, but it goes without saying that an adverse consumer reaction to such an ill-advised decision would damage the company's hopes of continuing in business on a profitable basis. Most large firms today are publicly owned corporations which must be managed to assure long-term survival, and marketing efforts can be justified only to the extent that a positive contribution is made to this objective.

Information feedback. As Figure 1–1 illustrates, information plays two important roles in marketing management: (1) determination of the basic facts about the environment; and (2) measurement of effectiveness.

Information on the environment. Management cannot adapt to the environment without information on the opportunities and limitations that will be faced. Imagine the difficulties, for example, in designing a new product without information on consumer needs and desires, the availability of similar products by competitors, and the capabilities of the firm to produce and market the item. Feedback of this type is indispensable, and it receives attention throughout much of this book.

Information on performance. Management also must know the results when marketing action is undertaken. A record of success or lack of success is essential to avoid repeating previous mistakes and to permit further capitalization on actions that have worked in the past.

Further dangers of viewing promotion in isolation. While we have stressed this point before, its importance can scarcely be overestimated—promotion cannot be managed without full coordination and integration with other aspects of marketing strategy. To illustrate the dangers inherent when this is not done, assume that the advertising manager has reported a strong surge of purchases of a dishwashing detergent resulting from a short-term price promotion. Assume further that this rise in demand is reflected in increased orders from the trade and strongly optimistic reports from the sales staff. While it would appear that advertising has been unusually successful with its price appeal, it also is possible that it has been counter-productive from the total perspective of company operations.

This advertising outcome could have stimulated consumers to purchase the product sooner than they would have without the price reduction, and many may have stocked up for the future without a substantial gain in new users. Retailers, in turn, build inventories in anticipation of increased demand, and a surge of orders is received at the plant. Meeting the orders may, in turn, have required the addition of new shifts of workers, substantial overtime, and changes in prices or margins.

Once buyers have redeemed the coupons, if few new users actually have been added, a sales slump inevitably will result from the fact that consumer demands are satisfied for the time being. In turn, retailers must of necessity cut back on inventories, and the resources added by the manufacturer to meet the surge in orders, such as additional production workers, must be withdrawn. In this case advertising has accomplished basically only one thing: *a disruption of normal flows* of sales revenues, dealer orders, capital investment, production scheduling, and work force planning.[15]

In this example, admittedly somewhat limited in that it is explicitly assumed that advertising primarily borrowed sales from the future, the false success of advertising management has created disequilibriums and has disrupted the functioning of the entire firm. The advertising manager was guilty of *suboptimization*—maximization of response to one activity without regard to others. Advertising response was sought with little or no consideration of its effects on other elements of the marketing or production programs of the firm.

SUMMARY

The nature of marketing management has been reviewed briefly to provide a perspective for realistic consideration of the role of promotion in the marketing mix. While it is necessary to abstract promotion from the total program in order to study it in detail, long-run profit can be maximized only when all types of marketing efforts are undertaken, with full realization of the interdependent relationships which exist in the marketing program.

Review and Discussion Questions

1. Compare and contrast promotion and marketing. How does promotion differ from advertising? From personal selling?
2. What is the task of marketing management? What is meant by the term *marketing mix?* Describe and discuss the major elements of the marketing mix, stressing the nature of the interrelationships involved.
3. Consumer demand is cited as a factor to which marketing efforts must be adapted. To what extent can demand be regarded as a *constraint* or limitation on the marketing program? To what extent can it be regarded as presenting an *opportunity* for marketing?
4. Discuss the other factors which comprise the marketing environment, showing the manner in which they define the opportunities and limitations for feasible marketing action.

---

[15] This example is similar to one discussed by Jay Forrester to illustrate the application of industrial dynamics to advertising problems. See "The Relationship of Advertising to Corporate Management," *Proceedings: Fourth Annual Conference* (New York: Advertising Research Foundation, 1958), pp. 75–92.

5. What is a marketing strategy? How might one go about comparing different marketing strategies?

6. What is a promotional strategy? How does it compare with a marketing strategy? How might one describe a specific type of strategy?

7. What types of information feedback are needed for successful management of the marketing function?

8. What is meant by the term *suboptimization*? Why is the danger of suboptimization so great in the management of the promotional efforts of the firm? Can suboptimization be eliminated in designing promotional strategies?

9. The goal of marketing activity is often stated as being to maximize long-run profit. Why is short-run profit not emphasized? Should the marketing goal always be long-run profit maximization?

10. Why is an understanding of consumer behavior so vital to the development of an effective marketing and promotional strategy?

CHAPTER 2

The Nature of Communication

It was an unforgettable moment in the great history of the Zappo Company. All members of the executive committee sat in hushed silence as the chairman of the board, Zebbulon T. Zappo, Jr., made this electrifying announcement. "Gentlemen, we've done it! We have come up with a new line of pots and pans that will last forever, but that's just the start. Bring them in!"

All eyes turned as Z. Tyrone Zappo III, the director of marketing, opened the curtains and showed the new product line. "It's hard to believe," he exclaimed, "but this new line will last forever in normal use, and if the consumer ever wants to get rid of it, perish the thought, it's biodegradable. Not only that, it's clear as crystal, and you can see everything as it cooks. But nobody has to watch for long, because it concentrates heat so much that it cuts cooking time by 85 percent."

As crescendo of applause began around the room, the senior Zappo silenced them and said, rapturously, "There's even more. Go on son." "Dad's right," his son responded. "The best part of all is that it never has to be washed. It cleans by itself with high heat if it sits for 15 minutes or so."

"It's a miracle," intoned a quiet voice in the corner, "a miracle!" "That's it," exclaimed Zebulon Zappo. "We're going to call this line the Zappo Miracle," and all eyes looked upward.

"But we've got to communicate it to the world," the younger Zappo noted with enthusiasm, reflecting the wisdom gained from his MBA coursework. "It will never succeed if we don't communicate." Ideas now

FIGURE 2–1
A Symbolic Representation of the Communications Process

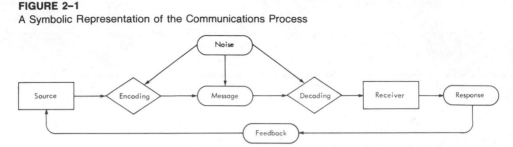

gushed to the surface around the table. "10,000 salespeople—hit every home!" "Let's sponsor our own television special." "How about buying all of the time on the superbowl." *"This story has to be told."*

Maybe this scenario is a bit far fetched, but there is no question that *communication* is the latest of the "in" words. One does not have to turn very far to find books on communication as the key to marriage, sales success, and so on. Few ever analyze, however, just what is meant by this term and the real complexities inherent in the whole communication process.

Promotion, of course, is the communication function of marketing, and it is the purpose of this chapter to delve into the complexities of this process. We intend to return to the Zappo Miracle, but first it is necessary to lay some important groundwork from communication theory.

WHAT COMMUNICATION IS ALL ABOUT

Communication can be said to happen whenever an individual attributes significance to message-related behavior.[1] It is important to note at the outset that communication does not take place if the recipient fails to attend to and process the message. Communication, then, is much more than *sending*.

It is helpful to visualize the communication process through use of a model which appears in Figure 2–1. This model is a composite of many perspectives and theories which have appeared in the vast literature on this subject. Although writers may differ on details, most agree on the essence of what takes place.[2]

---

[1] C. David Mortensen, *Communication: the Study of Human Interaction* (New York: McGraw-Hill, 1972), p. 14.

[2] See, for example, Mortensen, *Communication;* Cassandra L. Book, *Human Communication: Principles, Contexts, and Skills* (New York: St. Martin's Press, 1980); John C. Merrill and Ralph L. Lowenstein, *Media, Messages, and Men,* 2d ed. (New York: Longman, Inc., 1979); Werner J. Severin and James W. Tankard, Sr., *Communication Theories Origins, Methods, Uses* (New York: Hastings House, 1979); Melvin L. DeFleur and Sandra Ball-Rokeach, *Theories of Mass Communication,* 4th ed. (New York: Longman, 1982); and Robert Hopper and Jack Whitehead, Jr., *Communication Concepts and Skills* (New York: Harper & Row, 1979).

Source

The communicator may be an individual or an impersonal entity of some kind. Communication begins when words are selected which are arranged in a pattern or sequence to be communicated. This is referred to as *encoding*. The encoded message, which may or may not be an accurate representation of intended content, is transmitted through some form of *channel,* most frequently the spoken word.

Receiver

The person who is the target of the communicated message usually attempts to *decode* its contents and uncover the meaning. The actual effect, however, is dependent upon his or her perception of that message, not the intent of the message itself or its actual physical content.

Message

Although a variety of nonverbal signal systems also may be used, most messages are consciously phrased in either spoken or written language.[3] All languages are composed of *signs* and *symbols*. As one authority authority points out:

Signs may be divided into two major types, natural and conventional. A natural sign is an event in our experience which refers to some other event because our experience has taught us that the two events are associated or connected in some fashion. Thus, a Kansan sees a dark cloud on the horizon, and he interprets what he sees as the sign of an approaching tornado. The cloud is a natural sign of the tornado. A conventional sign, which we shall call a "symbol," is an artificial construct made by human beings for the purpose of referring to something. A symbol is a sign which is deliberately employed in order to convey a meaning. Symbols become a part of a language when human beings agree that they shall "stand for" given referents. Symbols are signs, but not all signs are symbols.[4]

A symbol thus acquires a more or less unique meaning through social consensus.

Learning a language means far more than just developing proficiency in grammar and vocabulary.[5] Language introduces a child to the rules regulating social relations and morality. In addition, one learns the roles one must play in later life through becoming aware of one's own identity as a person and as a member of groups in which one seeks status.

---

[3] See Mark L. Knapp, *Nonverbal Communication in Human Interaction,* 2d ed. (New York: Holt, Rinehart & Winston, 1978).

[4] Lionel Ruby, *An Introduction to Logic* (Philadelphia: J. B. Lippincott, 1950), p. 18.

[5] For a more extensive discussion see Erwin P. Bettinghaus, *Persuasive Communication* (New York: Holt, Rinehart & Winston, 1968), chap. 6.

Newborn children are initially incapable of symbolic communication. Although they notice people and phenomena of various types, all interaction with others is nonverbal, consisting of a motley collection of sounds. These sounds, which may serve as signs of their physical state, can be roughly understood only in terms of intensity, pitch, and duration. Soon they begin to imitate some of the sounds they hear and they repeat them, with the result that children start to associate words with objects. After a time one can use the word *ball,* for example, without the physical object being present. The object and the word have become associated, so that the child behaves toward the word in much the same manner as one behaves toward its referent.

When the point is reached that a word calls forth the same responses as the original stimulus, the word is said to have attained *denotative meaning.* The word now stands for or denotes the object. The individual's own unique feelings and psychological predispositions also affect the meaning of words, however. The meaning that is unique to the individual is referred to as *connotative meaning.*[6] The child who is frightened by a dog, for example, will have a very different connotative meaning when hearing the term *dog* than will a child who has a friendly pet, even though the denotative meanings attributed by the two children to this term may be identical.

The real distinction between denotative and connotative meaning is of real significance in persuasive communications. Consider these advertising appeals:

> The Zappo Miracle Uses Space Age Technology to Let You Cook in an Instant
>
> The Zappo Miracle uses the latest technology to let you cook in an instant.

The denotative meaning of each appeal is identical, but the connotative meanings are quite different. The advertiser probably would receive greatest response to the first message.

Noise

The fidelity or accuracy of communication is greatly influenced by noise which enters into the message itself, the communication channel, and the encoding process. Noise refers to any extraneous factors which can interfere with reception of the message.[7] Examples might be use of extraneous appeals in the message, actual physical noise or interference

---

[6] David K. Berlo, *The Process of Communication* (New York: Holt, Rinehart & Winston, 1960), p. 209.

[7] For a helpful discussion of the problem of noise in communication, see John Parry, *The Psychology of Human Communication* (New York: American Elsevier, 1968), pp. 83–126.

at any stage, distractions, and so on. In addition, there can be a variety of competing stimuli which distract the recipient and inhibit grasp of the full impact of the message.

Feedback

Feedback occurs when there is some type of response (or nonresponse) from the recipient. This subject is of considerable importance and is discussed in detail later. Let it simply be noted now that feedback must be monitored before any evaluation can be made of message effectiveness. The fact that the message was *sent* implies nothing about its impact.

Insights from Information Processing Theory

Any communicator initiates communication with some kind of goal or intent for the message. But, as we have stressed, intended effect does not necessarily equal actual effect. The receiver must respond in terms of his or her own background and psychological processes. The words or other message symbols only serve to activate learned responses stored within memory.

It is known from the literature on information processing to be reviewed later that humans perceive selectively; communication undertaken without regard to another's motivational influences is doomed to failure unless the communicator has phenomenal luck. This is the principle of audience sovereignty referred to earlier. Humans have full power to expose themselves to messages selectively. Unwanted messages may be avoided completely even if they are exposed, or it is possible that the recipient will intentionally miscomprehend and distort message content. Finally, we are quite selective as to what we let into memory storage. In short, we see and hear what we want to see and hear, often to avoid having our beliefs and attitudes changed.

This perceptual selectivity is perhaps the greatest obstacle any communicator must face. One notable example is mentioned here to illustrate this point. Propaganda often was used in World War II on the theory that exposure would generate response—a badly mistaken notion. Some change in strategy soon became necessary. One of the greatest surprises came when it was found that propaganda designed to induce Nazi surrenders became effective only after the Wehrmacht had disintegrated and the war cause appeared hopeless to the individual soldier.[8] Prior to that time Nazi group morale remained high, and propaganda messages fell on deaf ears.

---

[8] Edward Shils and Morris Janowitz, "Cohesion and Disintegration in the Wehrmacht in World War II," in *Process and Effects of Mass Communication*, ed. Wilbur Schramm (Urbana: University of Illinois Press, 1954), pp. 501–16.

INTERPERSONAL COMMUNICATION

Let's return now to the legendary story of the Zappo Miracle. A few months have elapsed and quite a salesforce has been recruited. "You Can Double Your Income by Selling a *Miracle* in Your Spare Time." Ads appeared everywhere featuring Zebulon T. Zappo urging upwardly mobile married couples to "fullfill their dreams" with a Miracle. In the process America began to hear the story right in its own homes.

Now we join salesperson Sam James talking with Laura Ellis, a recent high school graduate who is about to be married. Sam demonstrated the Miracle by cooking a complete meal and is now about to close the sale. "Can't you just visualize how it will be every night? Your husband will worship at your feet and hold you high as his queen. You will be the wife of his dreams." Laura frowned, however, and objected, "But the price." (Naturally a miracle will be priced far higher than a competitor's product). "Oh never worry," Sam said in a soothing voice. "It's the best investment of your life. And because I really want to help you, we have a special price for tonight only—10 percent off. But you must decide now. What do you say?" Laura hesitated but signed and Sam exited in victory.

A Model of Interpersonal Communication

Now, what happened in the interaction between Sam and Laura? The interpersonal communication process is depicted in Figure 2–2.

The communicator.   Sam James began with both an intended content for his sales messages and an intended effect. In order to encode this intent into a meaningful message for Laura, he must attempt to understand what is motivating and influencing her at that point in time. This ability to place oneself in another's shoes, referred to as *empathy,* is a requirement for effective face-to-face communication.

Empathy begins early in life, through learning to take the role of another. The child in play imitating his or her father or mother is an example. As the child matures there is a steady development of acquaintance with

FIGURE 2–2
Interpersonal Communication

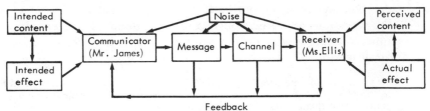

FIGURE 2–3
Overlap of Psychological Fields in Communication

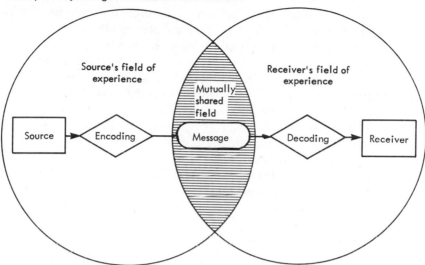

the social heritage and expectations of others. Sooner or later he or she acquires a common set of meanings and definitions by which people regulate their lives. Taking the role of others becomes commonplace at this point, and effective communication is facilitated.

The message. For Laura Ellis to receive and grasp the point of Sam James' message, two requirements must be met: (1) the message should be designed to attract attention, and (2) it should employ symbols that give rise to common meanings. This requires that the message be oriented as closely as possible to Laura's background, interests, needs, and psychological predispositions. The visions provided of marital bliss no doubt were well conceived from this perspective if one can put aside for now some real ethical issues raised by his sales approach.

Communication is facilitated when Mr. James and Ms. Ellis are as much alike as possible in terms of background, stored information and experience, needs, social influences, and so on. In other words, they should experience an *overlap in psychological fields*—that is, an overlap in the sum total of influences on their behavior. Imagine the confusion that might result if there were no overlap whatsoever. Anyone who has visited a foreign country is well aware of the difficulties two individuals face when they attempt to communicate in entirely different languages. The consequence is likely to be noise rather than communication. Figure 2–3 illustrates the importance of mutually shared psychological fields in communication.

Social norms (expected uniformities in behavior) at least partially come to the communicator's rescue. Norms provide approximate uniformities in behavior and ways of thinking which result from the pressures of others. In most situations Ms. Ellis and Mr. James are probably subject to certain common social influences. Assume, for example, that they both are from the same Chicago suburb, both members of the same church denomination, graduates of the same high school, and members of the same tennis club. Both are expected to behave in a relatively similar manner in the groups to which they belong, and they also are exposed to similar environmental influences. Thus they should be able to anticipate each others' reactions and communicate with relative ease.

The channel. The channel signifies the medium through which the message is sent. Thus usually consists of the spoken words, although various forms of writing can be used. The importance of nonverbal signals coming through these channels should not be overlooked, however. Such forms as body movement (kinesic behavior), paralanguage (voice qualities, laughing, yawning), use of dress, and so on all enter into the communicative act.

Noise. The fidelity or accuracy of communication is greatly influenced by noise which can affect both message and channel. Noise, as we have stated earlier, refers to any extraneous factors which interfere with message reception. If the television is playing in the background at the high moment of one of today's soaps, James may be hard-pressed to close the sale. Another important source is illness or stress which can obviously distract either of the parties. When this happens, especially, if the source is external, there may be nothing the communicator can do to break through.

The receiver. For effective communication to occur, the content of the message as perceived by Laura must closely correspond to the actual content transmitted by James. Obviously this may not occur because of selective information processing. For example, she may have extreme skepticism that the Miracle will perform as claimed, even though James has performed a full demonstration. Her only reaction may be, "Oh yeah?" If she feels this strongly, persuasion will not occur. In a sense, she erects a strong filter in such situations that cannot be circumvented short of outright deception or use of short-run manipulation techniques mentioned in the next paragraphs.

Feedback. The model of interpersonal communication shows the importance of feedback from the receiver. In effect, Laura now becomes sender and James the receiver. In this sense, communication always is a circular process unless no opportunity is given for feedback (a very real problem in mass communications as we will demonstrate shortly).

A smile, an affirmative reply, a frown, or some other response (such as no reaction at all) provide the basis to determine whether or not Laura is getting the message. If the message appears to be off target, James can try again and modify what he says and does to get his points across.

FIGURE 2–4
Mass Communication

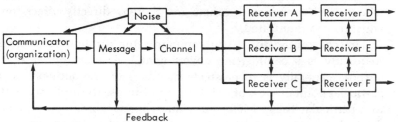

Feedback

James also receives feedback from the message and the channel. As he sees or hears the signals being used, he may detect that the form is not appropriate, in which case changes are made. Similarly, he may detect noise in the channel providing undue distraction and try to avoid it.

The factor of instantaneous feedback makes face-to-face communication highly efficient. Both sender and receiver are able to keep trying until effective contact is made. This factor, however, gives rise to the ever present danger of manipulation defined as *"Any persuasive effort which restricts another's freedom to choose."*[9] Manipulation occurs when techniques are used which somehow bypass another's filter and induce a response which might not occur if time were given for reflection. James did this quite skillfully with his strongly emotional "marital bliss" pitch accompanied by a special discount if the decision is made now. He can use outright deception, pressure tactics, strongly emotional appeals, and so on to induce an instant decision without allowing for deeper reflection. Unfortunately, many "miracles" have been sold in that way in past years and have resulted in a high level of consumer dissatisfaction. Most states now have cooling off laws which permit a period of time to elapse before such a sales contract becomes final. The consumer, in other words, is permitted to have second thoughts.

In the long run, this kind of manipulation becomes exceedingly difficult. Consumer sovereignty still is a fact of life. What we are referring to here is short-term, hit-and-run tactics which, in effect, inhibit the normal processes of audience sovereignty.

Mass Communication

Mass communication requires a process in which the message is transmitted to a large group of individuals (mass) at roughly the same point in time. The basic model of mass communication is illustrated in Figure 2–4.

It will be noticed that the communicator now is designated as an organi-

---

[9] Em Griffin, *The Mind Changers* (Wheaton, Ill.: Tyndale, 1976), p. 28.

zation, because the message is the output of many individuals. In addition, the audience consists of an interconnected group of receivers, each of whom may interact with others and thereby directly affect the content which is communicated.

The communicator. The communicator through mass media most frequently is a commercial, governmental, or educational agency. The purpose generally is to persuade members of the audience to accept a particular point of view or to inform and educate the audience with respect to a particular topic. Many individuals interact in a complex process to determine message content. As a result, speed in the preparation of the message for communication usually is drastically reduced by the necessity for collective decisions.

One can just imagine Zappo, Jr., and Zappo III going after each other to come up with an acceptable advertising campaign. Others would be in the act also, to say nothing of a similar gang in the advertising agency. By the time they are all through, who knows what will emerge? Maybe Mrs. Zebbulon T. Zappo, Jr., will have to make the final decision (This is how the name Edsel was chosen two decades ago). Whatever the outcome, a message created by committee may reflect compromise more than persuasive power, although this by no means has to be the case if the managerial procedures discussed at length in later chapters are followed.

The message. The message format does not differ greatly from that in interpersonal communication because it comprises both verbal and nonverbal symbols. The primary difference is that it generally must be more impersonal than the message transmitted through face-to-face channels because it is directed to a group rather than to an identified individual. As a result it is difficult to orient its content to achieve maximum impact on a given person. This inflexibility is one of the primary disadvantages faced when the mass media are used.

Determination of message content for a large group presents obvious problems in that one message must be suitable for many individuals, each of whom differs in certain ways. Direct role-taking is impossible and the function of social norms becomes especially significant, as Berlo points out:

Knowledge of a social system can help us make accurate predictions about people, without the necessity of empathizing, without the necessity of interaction, without knowing anything about the people other than the roles that they have in the system. . . . For every role there is a set of behaviors and a position. If we know what the behaviors are that go with a role, we can predict that those behaviors will be performed by people who perform that role. Second, if we know what behaviors go with a given rank or position, we can make predictions about people who occupy that position.[10]

---

[10] Berlo, *The Process of Communication* (New York: Holt, Rinehart & Winston, 1960), p. 149. Copyright 1960 by Holt, Rinehart & Winston. Used by permission.

The channel.   The channel includes such media as radio, television, magazines, daily and weekly newspapers, films, books, and so on. These media generally are published, aired, or viewed at regular intervals, with the result that speed and flexibility of communication are further hindered. In addition, communication is indirect because of the fact that the communicator and the recipients are not simultaneously present in space or time. These disadvantages are counteracted, however, by the fact that many people can be reached relatively quickly at a much lower cost than would be possible through the face-to-face channel.

The receivers.   The audience is best conceived as a group, no member of which is directly known to the communicator. Each member perceives selectively in that he or she retains full powers to screen out unwanted communication through selective exposure, distortion, and retention. Selective screening is especially pronounced with mass media because of the necessity to design the message to be acceptable to many people. As a result it may be off target for many of the intended recipients and thus become ignored, distorted, or forgotten. This is perhaps the key problem encountered in advertising strategy.

It also must be recognized that communication through the mass media is a social process in the sense that individuals interact with others regarding the message content. Word-of-mouth communication can either enhance or hinder the communicator's objectives. Favorable word-of-mouth can be an asset, because the message is disseminated and reinforced to a much greater extent than usually is possible through the mass media. The opposite, of course, can also be true in that unfavorable word-of-mouth can almost totally counteract anything the mass communicator attempts to say. Also evidence is strong that personal recommendations/ communications are more cognitively vivid, more easily retrieved from memory, and more salient to the receiver.[11]

Feedback.   The fact that communicator and recipient are physically separated means that effective feedback is difficult. At the very least it is quite delayed, because resort usually must be made to some type of audience survey. Readership of a magazine article or the viewing audience of a television program can be determined by asking people what they have read or seen. Standardized techniques for this purpose are discussed in Chapter 15.

Audience surveys are expensive and time-consuming, and the results may not be known for weeks or months. Obviously, feedback is too late to permit altering the message during initial contact between communicator and audience. Feedback in the sense discussed here is used primarily to determine the messages to be transmitted in the future.

---

[11] Amos Tversky and Daniel Kahneman, "Judgment under Uncertainty: Heuristics and Biases," *Science* 185 (1974), pp. 1124–31.

FIGURE 2–5

Comparative Advantages and Limitations of Interpersonal and
Mass Communication

Factor	Interpersonal communication	Mass communication
Reaching a large audience		
Speed	Slow	Fast
Cost per individual reached	High	Low
Influence on the individual		
Ability to attract attention	High	Low
Accuracy of message communicated	Low	High
Probability of selective screening	Relatively low	High
Clarity of content	High	Moderate to low
Feedback		
Direction of message flow	Two-way	One-way
Speed of feedback	High	Low
Accuracy of feedback	High	Low

Interpersonal versus Mass Communication

The comparative advantages and disadvantages of interpersonal and
mass communication are summarized in Figure 2–5. The mass media suffer
from delayed feedback, inflexibility, and a greater likelihood of selective
screening by audience members. These disadvantages are substantial and
present real problems that must be dealt with in promotional strategy.
The costs of reaching an individual through the mass media, however,
are substantially lower. In addition the accuracy of the message communicated to a large audience is likely to be high because the message does
not change, as it might if it were passed from one individual to the
next through face-to-face channels.

Because individuals are so prone to screen out the content of mass
media, it is quite difficult to achieve major changes in attitudes and predispositions. The result is more likely to be stimulation of interest or awareness and reinforcement of present views. The greater flexibility and feedback permitted in interpersonal communication allow the communicator
to counter objections and comments and thereby achieve changes in attitudes and predispositions more readily.

In a practical situation, it is necessary to compare the communication
advantages with the cost advantages of using a particular channel. When
the audience is large it usually is necessary to accept the inefficiencies
of mass communication because of the distinctly lower cost per individual
contacted.

COMMUNICATION IN MARKETING

At one time all promotion was undertaken on a face-to-face basis
through personal selling, and in terms of total expenditures, personal

selling still is of greater importance than the mass media. From a communications point of view, personal selling involves one person interacting directly with another person. The advantage is that bargaining can take place as the salesperson feels out the prospect and thereby determines the proper communication content in view of the customer's background and psychological influences.[12] The seller then can phrase the message so that effective communication results, and if the message somehow misses its mark, the availability of direct and immediate feedback permits one to try again. The customer, in turn, can readily express needs and thereby procure necessary information in a direct and expeditious fashion. Both parties therefore engage in mutual role taking, and the communication difficulties, while they are never to be minimized, are less than those presented when the mass media are used. The communication process in personal selling is discussed in greater detail in Chapter 17.

Because managers of promotion in most firms, especially those in the consumer goods market, must contend with large groups of buyers, the mass media must also be utilized. The resulting problems in communication are significant. Those of special importance are: (1) the need to isolate market segments, (2) the selection of appropriate communication media to reach target segments, (3) the design of persuasive messages for groups rather than one individual, and (4) the delay in response feedback. Figure 2–6 illustrates some of the types of interpersonal and mass communication information flows (plus product and money flows) that take place in marketing products.

Isolation of Market Segments

Because mass media messages must be aimed at many individual recipients, direct mutual role taking cannot occur. Fortunately, however, it is possible to isolate relatively homogeneous *segments* of a total audience who have enough in common through shared social roles that communication can take place. An advertising campaign, for example, might be directed to young, midwestern mothers in the middle social classes who are junior executives with college degrees. Each of these demographic factors (young, midwestern, mother, middle class, college educated, junior executive) implies certain modes of behavior, and messages framed in these terms can reach desired targets and communicate without any direct interaction between source and recipient.

The way to adapt to this communication situation is to define the target market and to study the backgrounds and motivational influences

---

[12] For a more thorough discussion see Frederick E. Webster, Jr., "Interpersonal Communication and Salesman Effectiveness," *Journal of Marketing* 32 (July 1968), pp. 7–13, and Allen L. Pennington. "Customer-Salesman Bargaining Behavior in Retail Transactions," *Journal of Marketing Research* 5 (August 1968), pp. 255–63.

28

FIGURE 2–6
Examples of Communication Flows

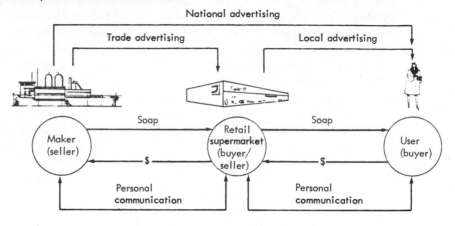

A complex flow–an appliance case

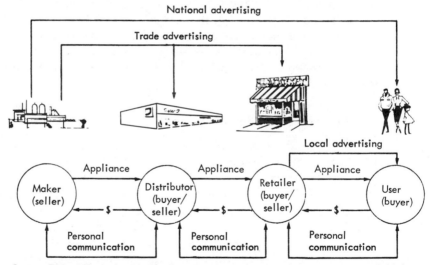

Source: Federal Trade Commission, Hearings, Fall 1971; written testimony by A. A. Achenbaum, senior vice president, J. Walter Thompson Co.

of its members *before* communication is undertaken. Such an analysis is advisable also when reliance is placed on personal selling, but it is a necessity when the mass media are used.

How should segmentation be undertaken? This subject is discussed in detail later, but for now it is sufficient to point out that the most obvious and least troublesome classification is along such demographic dimensions as geographical location, age, income, social class, occupation, or education. These data usually can be obtained rather easily and inexpensively with the tools of marketing research.

It is also necessary to segment buyers in terms of the influences that motivate them to buy or not to buy. For instance, skillful use of research will permit classification of consumers as heavy, moderate, light, or nonusers of a product or brand. In addition, the reasons for placement into each of these classifications should be determined, such as differences in underlying motives, styles of life, pressures from friends or relatives, and so on.

By no means, however, are demographic and usage classifications the only distinctions that are valuable in segmentation. The growing tendency in the United States to greater human diversity and rapid changes in attitudes and values makes it necessary to be alert to segments which are distinguished by commonly held attitudes and interests but which may include a cross section of demographic classifications. In any case, the objective is to isolate homogeneous groups and to determine the factors that members have in common with respect to the product being promoted. Efforts, then, are directed at segments where the probability of successful communication and persuasion appears to be greatest. Without segmentation analysis it is unlikely that a successful promotional campaign can be undertaken on a mass scale.

Selection of Communication Media

A mass market can be reached through a variety of media, including the usual mass media (such as television, magazines, or newspapers), direct mail, display of a product on a shelf, and point-of-sale advertising. These media all share the common characteristic that one message or appeal is used to reach more than one prospect.

As will become apparent later, selection of appropriate media is a difficult task. Fortunately, there are now many sources of data which document the characteristics of the audience reached by a given medium, say a men's magazine. If market segments are properly defined and classified, it is possible to select media which reach the desired target audience. The objective is to minimize waste coverage insofar as possible. This topic is discussed in Chapters 12 and 13.

Design of the Persuasive Message

Promotion through mass media requires that the story be told in such a way that it will communicate to groups of prospects an inflexibility that may cause the message to miss the mark with some individuals. The salesperson, on the other hand, is free to vary the message to meet each situation; this is the powerful advantage of personal selling.

If the market has been properly segmented the probability of successful communication is increased. From the point of view of promotion, the goal of segmentation is to achieve homogeneity so that one message will be suitable for many individuals. Success is further enhanced by pretesting the message so that the probability of effective communication can be gauged before funds are invested in the campaign and modifications can be introduced when they are found to be appropriate or necessary. This topic is discussed in Chapters 14 and 17.

Feedback of Response

Feedback is delayed when the mass media are used, whereas the salesperson has the advantage of instantaneous feedback through gestures or verbal reactions. The advertiser must use measures to analyze readership, message comprehension, attitude change, or other forms of response. Feedback of these types is useful, however, only to measure effectiveness and to permit postmortem analysis of the reasons for success or failure. Management can gauge the performance of its advertising department or agency as such, but feedback comes too late to save a sale if the message has been off target. This topic is discussed in Chapter 15.

The Paradox

It is obvious that the mass media present some significant communication problems. Advertising and publicity through the mass media will always represent inefficient communication, even with precise definition of market target, motivation research, and feedback of results through various media. This is because of the very nature of the communication process. Nevertheless, a mass market generally can be reached economically *only* with mass media. This leads to the seeming paradox that advertising provies *efficient promotion through inefficient communication.*

SUMMARY

This chapter has explored the fundamentals of the communication process. A model of interpersonal communication was presented which comprised the communicator, the message, the channel, the receiver, noise, and feedback. The model was modified slightly for mass communication to show that the communicator is an organization, the message is sent through mass channels, and the audience consists of many receivers who are connected by interpersonal channels.

The mass media, of course, are of greatest significance in modern marketing. Stress was placed on the problems presented by the inflexibility of the message sent through mass channels, delayed feedback, and difficulties of audience identification. These disadvantages generally are offset by the low cost per person reached. Thus the marketer usually cannot avoid use of the mass media, although a distinct role remains for interpersonal communication in the form of personal selling.

Review and Discussion Questions

1. What is meant by the term *empathy?* What role does it play in the communication process?

2. Describe how a child might have learned meaning for the following terms: *cow, mother, ugly, Republican,* and *snow.*

3. Describe what kinds of connotative meaning most people have for the following terms: *affection, love, fondness, tenderness, attachment, endearment, liking, devotion.* How might the connotative meanings differ from the denotative meanings?

4. What are the requirements which should be met if one person is to communicate effectively with another person? What is the function of social norms?

5. What is meant by noise in communication? What types of noise can enter when a salesperson talks with a customer? What types of noise can enter when a commercial for a brand of deodorant is aired during an afternoon soap opera on television? What, if anything, can be done to reduce noise in marketing communication?

6. It is frequently said that "human beings see and hear what they want to see and hear." What is the effect of this perceptual selectivity when one person attempts to communicate with another person? Do the effects differ when the person receiving the message is a member of the audience exposed to a television commercial?

7. What types of feedback are received by the salesperson who attempts to sell aluminum cookwear to a new bride? How does feedback change when the sales message is communicated to its market through use of television commercials?

8. Is advertising more efficient or less efficient than personal selling?

9. Given the problems of communication with a mass market, how can advertisers still experience success through use of the mass media?

10. Explain the importance of market segmentation in promotional strategy.

CHAPTER 3

Promotional Strategy: An Overview

It isn't often that a newly introduced product achieves such popularity that it is out of stock most places just a few months after it is introduced. But that was the case with Aapri, a cleansing facial skincare item launched by the Gillette Company in June 1981.[1]

Gillette purchased Aapri Cosmetics, a company located in Orange Grove, California, in the fall of 1980. Previously Aapri cosmetics had been marketed only in health food stores and failed to make much of a dent in the market. Gillette was soon to change all that, however.

Aapri is described as an "apricot cosmetic facial scrub." It makes use of finely ground apricot pits to remove dead skin scales. The results? It ". . . leaves your face baby soft and smooth, not tight and dry."[2] This product proved to be such a success that it had gathered 14.2 percent of the facial cleanser market by October 1981—quite an achievement!

The success of Aapri, of course, was not an accident. Rather, it was the outcome of some carefully conceived promotional strategies. It is the purpose of this chapter to provide an overview of what is involved in promotional decision making. After a brief general discussion of the stages involved in the process, we will return to this case example to show what is involved in moving from concept to action. This chapter, then, provides the format for the content and ordering of the topics introduced in the chapters which follow.

---

[1] This example is based on Carol Poston, "Aapri Scrubs Up on Sales," *Advertising Age,* March 1, 1982, p. M–22; and Pat Sloan, "Gillette: Aapri 'Sold Out,'" *Advertising Age,* October 12, 1981, pp. 1 and 92.

[2] Poston, "Aapri Scrubs Up," p. M–22.

THE STAGES IN PROMOTIONAL PLANNING AND STRATEGY

Figure 3–1 provides a summary of a systematic approach to promotional planning and strategy. The approach encompasses the following stages: (1) situation analysis, (2) establishment of objectives, (3) determination of budget, (4) management of program elements, (5) measurement of effectiveness, and (6) evaluation and follow-up.

Figure 3–2 presents the same sequence graphically. Note, however, that it is depicted as an "adaptive" process in that it specifically encompasses systematic procedures for gathering information which then can lead to needed program adaptations. For example, advertising message

FIGURE 3–1
Stages in Promotional Planning and Strategy

   I. Situation analysis
      A. Demand
          1. Cultural and social influences
          2. Attitudes
          3. Individual differences
          4. Decision processes
      B. Competition
      C. Legal considerations
      D. Internal organizational considerations
          1. Personnel
          2. Monetary
          3. Established policies and procedures
          4. Operational distinctives
  II. Establishment of objectives
      A. Definition of market targets
      B. Communication message
 III. Determination of budget
 IV. Management of program elements
      A. Advertising
          1. Analysis of media resources
          2. Selection of advertising media
          3. Message determination
              Personal selling
      B. 1. Analysis of resources
          2. Selection, motivation, and deployment
      C. Stimulation of reseller support
          1. Analysis of reseller resources
          2. Stimulation of performance
          3. Improvement and augmentation of performance
      D. Sales promotion
      E. Supplemental communications (public relations)
          1. Assessment of relevant publics
          2. Determination of media and message
  V. Coordination and integration
      A. Achievement of proper balance between program elements
      B. Scheduling of execution
      C. Utilization of personnel and outside services
 VI. Measurement of effectiveness
VII. Evaluation and follow-up

34

FIGURE 3–2
Decision Sequence Analysis of Promotional Planning and strategy

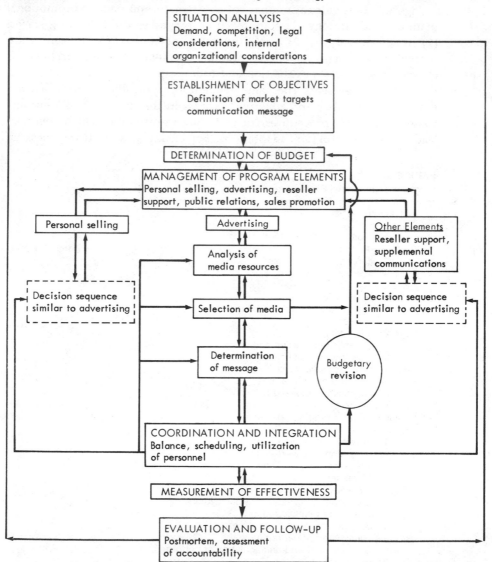

Note: This is similar in certain respects to the diagram utilized by Michael Ray which in turn was adapted from the sequence suggested in earlier editions of this text. See Michael L. Ray, "A Decision Sequence Analysis of Developments in Marketing," *Journal of Marketing* 37 (January 1973), p. 31.

and media decisions are interrelated. The decisions in one area can lead to modifications in another, as the two-way arrows indicate. Furthermore, a feedback loop represents the fact that the initial budget may have to be modified as planning proceeds. Evaluation and follow-up are shown as providing vital new input to the situation analysis for succeeding planning periods. Thus the continual and ongoing nature of planning is graphically portrayed.

Situation Analysis

The starting point always is analysis of the environment, with special focus on (1) demand; (2) competition; and (3) legal considerations. These forces, of course, are external to the firm, but there also is an internal environment that affects everything which is done in promotional strategy. This refers mostly to the human and financial resources which are available and the framework of established policy. Now, let's examine how these factors were weighed and evaluated in Gillette's decision to buy Aapri Cosmetics and introduce this product nationally.

Demand. So-called scrub products for the skin have been available on the market for some time. Many are marketed to the under-35 segment for treatment of acne. Aapri contains nothing which would be specially beneficial for this purpose over and above currently available products. Rather it contains ground apricot pits and emollients in a detergent emulsion. Hence it is a cleansing agent designed to enhance beauty.

Women, especially those over 30, make use of quite a range of soaps, cleaners, astringents, and masques. Indeed, the health and beauty aid market has been one of the economic bright spots in recent years. Now where does Aapri fit in this product range? A test market in Phoenix and Tucson, Arizona, answered this question. Aapri was found to compare favorably with similar products offered principally in large department stores at a very high price, whereas Gillette mass merchandised Aapri at a low competitive price, backed up with substantial advertising and sales promotion. According to executives, "This item is perceived as a good quality treatment which is mass marketed."[3]

The test market demonstrated that women under 30 tried Aapri but did not repurchase in substantial numbers. This was not true for the over-30 segment, however. They proved to be much more loyal, but it is interesting to note that Aapri has not replaced any other health and beauty item. Its primary effect is to reduce the frequency of face washing to about three times a week rather than daily. Aapri, in turn, is used an average of four times per week.

Aapri, then, is positioned to appeal to the 30-and-over market as a high-quality but low-priced "treatment" item which enhances beauty of the skin. It is nonabrasive and leaves the face feeling smooth. Its strong acceptance both in test market and then nationally illustrates the magnitude of the potential market.

Competition. There are two main competitors which also sell through food and drugstores—Noxell's Noxzema and Chesebrough-Pond's Pond's.

---

[3] Ibid., p. M–22.

Interestingly, both also have gained in sales, indicating that Aapri primarily is picking up customers who were using bar soaps or those buying more expensive preparations in department stores. The major difference between Aapri and the other two mass merchandised items is that the latter two are formulated from polyethylene granules which "become like glass when they are ground so small" according to Dola Hamilton, product manager for Aapri.[4] Once again, however, competitive comparison between these three does not seem to be a major issue given their common market growth. Rather, there may be no real competitive product. One analyst said that, "It's much as when Pampers were introduced. The success of the original product is being measured by the consumer takeover."[5]

Legal considerations. Laws pertaining to marketing cannot be disregarded in planning by any firm. Prohibition of false and misleading claims is just one of the many legal restrictions which Gillette management must heed. More specific legislation in the Pure Food and Drug Act pertains directly to product formulation and marketing. These laws need not be elaborated here (see Chapter 9).

Internal considerations. Obviously Gillette management saw virtue in taking over a smaller company which had pioneered a product Gillette previously had not had. What was the advantage for Gillette? It could make use of its unique mass distribution through food and drug outlets. This really is its competitive distinctive here. Also, it possesses a well-known and respected company name which would launch this otherwise unknown brand into national prominence. Gillette, then, was using its skills and distinctives in both distribution and promotion.

Gillette functions under a brand management system of organization with a management team responsible for this brand within the larger personal care division. The company does not try to have all possible promotional skills in house and follows the usual practice of using an advertising agency—N. W. Ayer.

The company is adept at marketing research. It made wise use of a test market, for example. This is yet another area of management skill which helped make this product a success.

All things considered, Gillette possesses a great deal of marketing muscle as a company, and internal considerations affecting this product can only be evaluated as favorable and not as a profit inhibitor (see Chapter 1).

Establishment of Objectives

Based on the situation analysis, what could the company reasonably anticipate once the product was introduced nationally? First, the market

---

[4] Ibid., p. M–22.
[5] Ibid., p. M–22.

target seems crystal clear—the over-30 woman who has at least a normal concern for the health and appearance of her skin. The younger market seems more attracted to other options, especially those with medicinal qualities.

There apparently is some concern about the use of soaps and stronger agents on the skin and a receptivity to a product which both cleanses and soothes. This, then, leads to the obvious positioning of Aapri as a gentle cleanser. Stress is placed on quality, availability, and low price.

The whole program of communication clearly was designed to register these benefits, and this would be an example of a cognitive goal. While there is no evidence of the precise statement of goal, the general intent is quite clear. Notice how clearly it picks up the benefits uncovered through market research.

There also was a sales or market share goal in this introductory period. It seemed reasonable from the test market to strive for at least a 6 percent market share in the first 10 to 12 months.

Determination of Budget

Once objectives have been established it is necessary to determine a preliminary promotional budget. This is a difficult task as later chapters indicate. The initial estimate usually can be only tentative, and modifications generally are required as the planning process proceeds.

As we will illustrate in Chapter 11, the best approach is to begin with promotional objectives and then "build up" costs to reach the needed budget level. In this situation, the strategy calls for achievement of a hefty market share in a large segment over a relatively short period of time. It seems obvious that there must be an intensive advertising campaign backed up by point-of-sales support, and this would demand a large budget. Indeed that proved to be the case with a total marketing budget of nearly $17.5 million in the introductory period, with $9.5 million allocated to television in the major metropolitan markets. By anyone's standards, this is a heavy expenditure level, and it appears to be quite realistic in view of projected levels of market share and sales.

MANAGEMENT OF PROGRAM ELEMENTS

Among the various communication resources available to the firm are advertising, resellers (wholesalers and retailers), personal selling, sales promotion (packaging, price offers, and so forth), and supplemental communication support such as public relations. Decisions must be made with respect to the best promotional mix making use of these elements as they are seen to be appropriate.

Advertising

Gillette wisely placed the lion's share of its introductory marketing budget in advertising. Two primary decisions had to be made: (1) what message should be featured and (2) what media should be used?

Media. Achievement of a strong market share in a large market over a short time period requires the use of media which can reach a broad market target on a repetitive basis. Television, radio, newspapers, and possibly consumer magazines are a possibility. Television probably is most appropriate given the opportunity for high repeat exposure and visual and emotional impact allowed through use of both sight and sound. Also, some markets can be hit harder than others through a spot TV campaign. This, of course, was the strategy used, and its success speaks for itself.

Message. It is clear that the cleansing and beauty benefit must stand out loud and clear in all that is done. The TV campaign coordinated by the N. W. Ayer advertising agency featured a head and shoulders presenter, in her bathroom, speaking about these product benefits (see Figure 3–3). Apparently the message came through as intended.

FIGURE 3–3
The Presenter in Aapri TV Ads

Source: Reprinted from Carol Poston, "Aapri Scrubs Up on Sales," *Advertising Age*, March 1, 1982, p. M–22. Reprinted with special permission of Crain Communications, Inc.

Reseller Support

Wholesalers and retailers frequently are in a position to provide meaningful promotional assistance. Although personal selling long has been the main form of communication in the retail store, its importance has diminished in recent decades as manufacturers presell through advertising. Therefore, the main task of the retailer is to provide display, shelf space, and so on. Often it is difficult to achieve this type of support, since the objectives of resellers and manufacturers can conflict. As a result, it is necessary to use various means both to stimulate their backing and to supplement what they can do.

Gillette, of course, has long had a strong market position, and few distributors would ignore this fact. Furthermore, the strong introductory advertising campaign is a real plus in that the likelihood of consumer traffic is high. Therefore, achieving distribution proved to be no problem, and, in fact, was the key to the success of this product. Gillette followed a "pull strategy" in which its advertising virtually guaranteed both distribution and point-of-sales support. In addition, over 15 million free samples were distributed. Retailers would not be reluctant, then, to do their part.

It is not known exactly what was done in the way of point-of-sale display and advertising. No doubt Gillette provided a number of special displays, shelf talkers, and so on which would benefit both manufacturer and retailer.

If this type of support is not forthcoming, the campaign probably will not succeed. Advertising, in effect, plants seed which are then activated at point-of-sale. What happens there can never be left to chance.

Personal Selling

Aapri is not a product which has to be demonstrated or explained. This was done entirely through preselling. If that were not the case, mass distribution through drugstores and supermarkets never would have been possible. In addition, there would have been the necessity both to motivate and train retail sales personnel to do what is necessary, and that never is easy to accomplish.

Sales Promotion

Sales promotion is a kind of catch-all term for "short-term incentives to encourage purchase or sales of a product or service."[6] Most often it includes packaging, sampling, premiums and coupons, and price incentives.

---

[6] Philip Kotler, *Principles of Marketing* (Englewood Cliffs, N.J.: Prentice-Hall, 1980), p. 500.

Gillette felt two steps were necessary in this situation. First, the package was brightened with more use of the orange color, and the package itself was streamlined. The objective, of course, was to make it stand out on the retail shelf so it would be noticed. More than one product has died because this commonsense step was not taken.

Its second strategy was to distribute more than 15 million samples in major markets during July, 1981. This is wise only if there are real and demonstrable product benefits. The intent, of course, is to build a degree of consumer interest and loyalty, and it apparently succeeded.

Supplemental Communications

Sometimes it is necessary and valuable to supplement the normal advertising and selling efforts with public relations. This is the function which "evaluates public attitudes, identifies the policies and procedures of an individual or an organization with the public interest, and executes a program of action to earn public understanding and acceptance."[7] The public could include employees, shareholders, resellers, suppliers, the educational community, government, consumer groups, and the public at large.

Gillette would not have as much to gain with public relations in this situation as they would if the product were a truly significant technical breakthrough such as the new Kodak film disk cameras. The public already had quite a high level of awareness before Kodak even began its own marketing support. Public relations also is warranted if, for some reason, it is necessary to fight a negative public image. Various companies, for example, have come on strong with nutritional benefits in the face of adverse publicity.

On the other hand, Gillette could benefit from widespread product announcements through the trade press. The primary target here would be retailers in the hopes of generating interest and sales support.

Coordination and Integration of Efforts

Coordinated management of various components of the promotion mix obviously is essential. Advertising, for example, cannot be overemphasized relative to other types of communication unless the problem calls for dominant use of mass media. Too often one phase is allowed to get out of balance, with the result that profit opportunities are lost.

Coordination also requires skillful use of managerial talent. Decisions must be made regarding the necessity of using outside services such as

---

[7] Bertrand R. Canfield and H. Frazier Moore, *Public Relations Principles: Cases, and Problems* (Homewood, Ill.: Richard D. Irwin, 1973), p. 4.

advertising agencies, research suppliers, and media buying services. Because the advertising agency is in such widespread use, the decision may focus on division of responsibilities between management within the firm and agency personnel.

It appears that Gillette management did a very good job in this respect, but there was one unexpected outcome. Demand was so high that it was not possible to keep retailers' shelves supplied during the months of September and October 1981.[8] Therefore, ads were run during October in 75 newspapers covering 50 major markets apologizing for a temporary situation. The ads ran adjacent to the food day sections of newspapers and headlined "Sold Out by Popular Demand."[9]

Measurement of Effectiveness

Contemporary marketing management places high premium on measurement of effectiveness. In this situation, the initial market share projection of six percent was substantially exceeded. In reality, Gillette achieved a market share of 14.2 percent and a dollar share of 15.3 percent by October 1981.[10]

The effectiveness of the advertising campaign, of course, is reflected by this sales level, but that never is a sufficient measure in and of itself. Was the message delivered to the target audience as specified? This question requires measurement of communication performance such as brand name awareness, recall of major benefits, ad viewership, and so on. No doubt this type of measurement was done routinely by the company and its agency.

Evaluation and Follow-Up

Every effort should be made to assess the strengths and weaknesses of the promotional plan with the objective of cataloging experience for use in future planning. Given that management turnover is a way of life in many organizations, it is not surprising that past mistakes are repeated continually. Part of the problem lies in the fact that records are not kept, perhaps for the reason that managers are avoiding accountability for performance. Whatever the reason, failure to use the results of experience in future planning is inexcusable, and a formal postmortem analysis should be a routine part of the management process.

In the case of Gillette, we have followed the company only through its introductory period, and certainly there is every reason for optimism

---

[8] Sloan, "Gillette: Aapri 'Sold Out' " p. 1.

[9] Ibid., p. 1.

[10] Poston, "Aapri Scrubs Up," p. M–22.

in the short run. One unanswered issue is just why distribution failed to keep up with demand. This level of interest could have been predicted from test markets. Will it happen again? And, what is competition going to do? The health and beauty market is highly volatile, and brand loyalty can be a very temporary thing. In other words, this initial sales success, while notable, is no guarantee of the future. Management will have to keep their ears to the ground if it is to be maintained.

A LOOK AHEAD

The remainder of the book roughly follows the outline in Figures 3–1 and 3–2. Part Two is devoted to the first topic, situation analysis, with most of the part centering on analysis of demand. A sophisticated understanding of buyer motivation and behavior is perhaps the greatest key to promotional success. Some emphasis also is given to legal constraints.

Part Three covers basic considerations in planning, including the second and third topics, determination of objectives and establishment of the budget.

Part Four, "Management of Advertising and Sales Promotion Efforts," is the core of the book. Topics covered include analysis of media resources, selection of media, design of the advertising message and measurement of advertising effectiveness. Management of sales promotion will also be covered.

Part Five continues in the same vein by considering personal selling as a promotional tool and the management of the personal selling resources of the firm.

Part Six deals with gaining promotional suppport from resellers through various policies aimed at improving or supplementing their performance and with supplemental communications such as public relations and publicity.

Part Seven is devoted to the last topic, that of organizing and coordinating the promotional program. The last chapter in this part deals with the extremely important economic and social dimensions of promotion in our modern society.

It should be stressed that the issues faced in the management of promotion are too complex to allow pat answers. Certain decision routines are developed later, but they are intended only to discipline thinking and to guarantee systematic and rigorous analysis. It is human nature to give way to a "quest for certainty" (a search for concrete and definite answers where none exist). The proper attitude of inquiry, however, calls for an awareness of the state of knowledge and an appreciation of the need for research in areas where knowledge is scanty or missing. A keen appreciation for research and a certain sophistication in its use are central to promotional success.

Review and Discussion Questions

1. In what ways can the internal environment of the business firm affect promotional planning and strategy?

2. What reasons can you give for the fact that "preselling" through advertising has largely precluded the role of personal selling at the retail level? Will this trend continue? In what areas does a role for personal selling remain? Why?

3. Given the decline in the need for retail personal selling, what forms of promotional support can the retailer be expected to offer?

4. Analyze the Aapri case history in terms of the outline given in Figure 3–1 and answer the following questions
   a. Was the situation analysis sufficiently complete to permit realistic planning?
   b. Were the objectives for the campaign reasonable? Did they adequately reflect the findings of marketing research?
   c. Did the emphasis of the television campaign seem appropriate in view of the demand analysis?
   d. Would it be reasonable to use local newspapers, spot radio, Sunday, supplements, or other forms of local media rather than spot television?
   e. What do you think the future holds for Aapri? Why?

5. What is the "quest for certainty?" Why is it such an ever-present danger? Can it be avoided?

PART TWO
Situation Analysis

The first stage in the model of promotional planning and strategy presented in Chapter 3 is the situation analysis, covering demand, competitive response, legal constraints, and considerations internal within the firm. These determinants of promotional strategy are discussed in this section, with the exception of competition and internal considerations referred to elsewhere at various points.

In the analysis of the promotional problem, the inquiry, of necessity, focuses first on demand. Four chapters are devoted to this important subject. The first (Chapter 4) centers on information processing and thus clarifies the manner in which an audience responds to persuasion. Chapter 5 goes on to describe "high-involvement" decision-process behavior, and it presents the variables only from the perspective of the individual. Chapter 6 extends this subject by clarifying social influences from the points of view of culture, social class, reference groups, and family. Chapter 7 then gives an overview of "low-involvement" consumer behavior, and it points up the differences required in promotional strategy. Chapter 8 concludes the discussion of demand with a discussion of market segmentation.

The remaining factor in the situation analysis, legal constraints, is discussed in Chapter 9. Legal issues are growing in importance, so the review of pertinent legislation and judicial rulings is of considerable significance.

CHAPTER 4

Information Processing

Totally disgusted with the poor performance of his 1980 U.S.-made car, Sam James (remember him?) said, "Never again." His disillusionment was complete because he had felt his highly touted front-wheel-drive would be just the answer. He found himself quite interested in the heavy copy two-page spread for the 1981 Peugeot 505, introduced by the French manufacturer to get a stronger toehold in the U.S. market.[1] In fact, he found himself quite interested in the ads for most imports, whereas he quickly turned away from anything labeled Detroit. After a few days, he found himself rereading the Peugeot ads and especially their selling points such as graduated power assist steering, supple ride, and unusual handling characteristics. Soon, he visited a local dealer and paid $14,000 to be one of the growing number of 505 owners (Peugeot sales ran 75 percent ahead of the previous year, after the 505 introduction).

Laura Ellis (our beleaguered Miracle customer), on the other hand, responded quite differently to advertising for the new Andrew Jergens product, Aloe & Lanolin Skin Conditioning Lotion. While she could not recall seeing any of the nationwide spot television ads run on a saturation basis, she found herself recognizing this product when she saw a special display encouraging her to give Aloe & Lanolin a try.[2] She was attracted by a 1.5-ounce bottle offered at the low price of 39 cents, used it for a

---

[1] "Peugeot Marketing Campaign Treats Car Buyers as Intelligent: Sales Soar," *Marketing News,* December 25, 1981, pp. 1–2.

[2] For details, see " 'Thoroughly' Researched Aloe & Lanolin Stirs Competition in Hand Care Markets," *Marketing News,* December 25, 1981, p. 4

few weeks, and became a loyal customer. Advertising must have had some effect, but she certainly was not aware of it.

What's happening here? To find the answer it is necessary to probe into the complex subject of cognitive processes—the way in which information is "transformed, reduced, elaborated, stored, recovered, and used."[3] In marketing circles, *information processing* is the in term for all of this, and it will be necessary to understand something of how memory functions and what this means for promotional strategy.

Information processing, however, took two different tracks in the examples used. In the first place, Sam was actively searching for information, monitoring various sources to learn about the imports, while pretty much ignoring what Detroit had to say. If he had been queried at any stage, no doubt he could have given very accurate recall of advertising, especially the newspaper copy for Peugeot.

Why the difference? The explanation lies largely in the extent of *consumer involvement.* Involvement, as used here, refers to personal relevance and the necessity to be certain the right choice is made. No doubt Sam was pretty cautious before putting $14,000 down for the Peugeot, so he consciously acquired and used much information. Laura, on the other hand, was not actively searching yet still was influenced by advertising to recognize Aloe & Lanolin in the store. Probably her response was, "Why not try it? What have I got to lose for 39 cents?" She did no real decision making per se and waited until after the purchase to evaluate the product, rather than before as Sam did.

So, information processing varies substantially from one type of purchasing situation to the next, depending upon the degree of involvement. It is necessary, of course, to sharpen what we mean by involvement and the ways it effects decision processes. But first, it is important to understand something about the functions of memory. Then it is possible to provide some pretty definitive insight into that all-important subject of consumer sovereignty.[4]

MEMORY

There are a number of theories on memory organization and function, but there is a growing consensus now that there is one basic memory system with three distinct components or functions: (1) sensory memory; (2) short-term memory; and (3) long-term memory.[5]

---

[3] Ulrich Neisser, *Cognitive Psychology* (New York: Appleton, 1966), p. 4.

[4] The literature on the subjects discussed here is voluminous. Rather than footnote many original sources here, the reader will frequently be referred to the extensive literature review in James F. Engel and Roger D. Blackwell, *Consumer Behavior,* 4th ed. (Hinsdale, Ill.: Dryden Press, 1982).

[5] For an excellent summary, see James R. Bettman, *An Information Processing Theory of Consumer Choice* (Reading, Mass.: Addison-Wesley, 1979), especially chap. 6. Also see Engel and Blackwell, *Consumer Behavior,* Chap. 9.

Sensory memory. Any type of incoming stimulus receives an initial analysis for meaning through physical properties such as loudness or pitch. This analysis takes place largely instantaneously, and the outcome is preliminary classification as to what the input is.

Short-term memory. Once it has received sensory processing, the stimulus enters a short-term memory, and this is where it is assigned meaning. In some manner, it is compared against contents of long-term memory (existing beliefs, attitudes, and so on) so that it is categorized and interpreted.

Short-term memory is limited in capacity to six or seven "chunks" or items of information at a time. So obviously some stimuli will never even achieve entry because of capacity limits. Furthermore, it takes from about three to 10 seconds to move an item into long-term memory. If it is merely to be stored for later *recognition,* less time is needed, whereas recall demands *longer* processing.

What seems to be going on in short-term memory? Current theory now contends that new information is related to the content of long-term memory through message-relevant thoughts generated through *rehearsal* (silent, inner speech). Material admitted into long-term memory normally receives support arguments (agreement with its content and positive evaluation). Existing beliefs can be held intact, however, through counterarguments (refutations of the message and resistance) or source derogations (negative evaluation of the sender). When the latter two cognitive responses appear, long-term memory is, for the most part, left unaffected. As we will stress later, it is precisely here that consumer sovereignty is most clearly demonstrated. To a high degree, people see and hear what they want to see and hear.

Long-term memory. This is best viewed as an unlimited, permanent storage. In a sense, it provides each person with a "map of the world." However it is organized, one element is logically related to another in such a way that the individual can assimilate new information with existing values and previous experience.

Much could be said about various memory control processes such as retrieval. While this is helpful for general background, we now have a sufficient foundation to probe more deeply into the way in which involvement affects consumer information processing.[6]

INFORMATION PROCESSING UNDER HIGH INVOLVEMENT

High involvement is defined here as *the activation of extended problem-solving behavior when the act of purchase or consumption is seen by the decision maker as*

---

[6] For more detail see Bettman, *An Information Processing Theory.* A summary of his book appears in James R. Bettman, "Memory Factors in Consumer Choice: A Review," *Journal of Marketing* 43 (Spring 1979), pp. 37–53.

having high personal importance or relevance.[7] It is a direct sign that the purchase is important to the individual in terms of his or her basic values, goals, and self-concept. By extended problem solving we mean the classical model of rational decision making defined more than 70 years ago by John Dewey.[8] As applied in consumer behavior, it may be conceived as encompassing these stages:[9]

1. *Problem recognition.* What occurs to begin the process?
2. *Search.* What sources of information are utilized to reach a decision, and how important is each source?
3. *Alternative evaluation.* What factors are used by consumers to evaluate each alternative, and what is the relative importance of these factors?
4. *Choice.* What is actually selected from available options?
5. *Outcomes.* Does the choice result in satisfaction or doubt?

Because the right choice must be made, there is active information search and use. This information then is processed and stored in memory so that it may be readily recalled during alternative evaluation. Usually a number of product attributes are evaluated and weighed to determine whether or not expected benefits are offered. The outcome is development of *beliefs* about each alternative, an *attitude* for or against the purchase or each, and purchase *intentions.* In short, *thinking leads to feeling which leads to action.*[10] This is all shown pictorially in an abbreviated model appearing in Figure 4–1.

High involvement is most often present when one or more of these conditions hold:

1. The product is seen as related to or reflecting upon one's self image (jewelry, clothing, etc.).
2. The product is costly and the risks of a wrong decision are high.
3. There is strong social influence to conform, accompanied by motivation to acquiesce to such norms.

It is apparent that purchase of a Peugeot qualifies. To some degree an unusual and expensive car may reflect on self image. There is no question of its costs and the risks of getting a lemon. Finally, purchase of an unusual and different car may be the in thing to do in a given social setting. Not surprisingly, extended problem solving would be expected.

Extended problem solving is discussed in detail in the next two chapters, and little more need be said here. From this brief introduction, the heavy

---

[7] Engel and Blackwell, *Consumer Behavior,* p. 24.

[8] John Dewey, *How We Think* (New York: D. C. Heath, 1910).

[9] This book draws upon what has come to be known as the EKB (Engel, Kollat, Blackwell) model. See Engel and Blackwell, *Consumer Behavior.*

[10] The extensive research on involvement leading to this conclusion is summarized in Engel and Blackwell, *Consumer Behavior,* chaps. 2 and 19.

FIGURE 4–1
A Summary Model of the Extended
Problem-Solving Decision Process

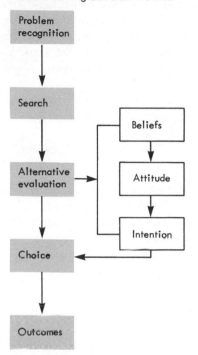

Source: Adapted from James F. Engel
and Roger D. Blackwell, *Consumer Behavior*, 4th ed. (Hinsdale, Ill.: Dryden Press,
1981), p. 33. Used by special permission.

information campaign used by Peugeot makes sense. The objective was
to give facts upon which the customer could form solid beliefs about
the benefits offered by this largely unknown make and model, hopefully
followed by positive attitude and intention to buy. Advertising, in turn,
is backed up by personal selling which no doubt is needed by the consumer
to resolve any remaining questions.

The Stages in Information Processing

Under high involvement, there is motivated information search and
a good deal of resulting information processing. It is interesting to note
that most of this appears to take place in the left hemisphere of the
brain, the sector now felt to be the seat of problem-solving activity.[11]

---

[11] For a review of contemporary research, see Flemming Hansen, "Hemispheral Lateralization: Implications for Understanding Consumer Behavior," *Journal of Consumer Research* 8 (June 1981), pp. 23–36. Also Engel and Blackwell, *Consumer Behavior*, chap. 9.

Moreover, print information is much more likely to be processed here, and that says something about the value of this medium when it seems that involvement is likely to be an issue for most consumers. Television, on the other hand, is processed mostly in the right hemisphere in the form of visual images. Finally, that information which winds up in the left brain is processed in such a way that it can be *recalled,* thus validating recall measurement as a worthwhile measure of advertising effectiveness under these conditions.

Now, what happens as that promotional stimulus (perhaps a print ad for the Peugeot) reaches the consumer? The various stages are shown in Figure 4–2.

Although each is discussed in detail below, it is important to define each stage precisely at the outset:

1. *Exposure*—achievement of proximity to a stimulus so that there is opportunity for activation of one or more of the senses.
2. *Attention*—allocation of information-processing capacity to a stimulus.
3. *Comprehension*—the meaning attributed to a stimulus.
4. *Yielding/acceptance*—reinforcement and/or modification of existing beliefs and cognitive structures by a stimulus.
5. *Retention*—transfer into long-term memory.

FIGURE 4–2
Information Processing under High Involvement

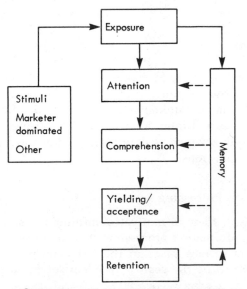

Source: James F. Engel and Roger D. Blackwell, *Consumer Behavior* (Hinsdale, Ill.: Dryden Press, 1982), p. 274. Reproduced by special permission.

There are some profound ramifications for promotional strategy, because memory can act as a filter and, in effect, stop the process at any stage. Assuming the odds of success are 50 percent at each stage (half are exposed, half attend, and so on), the probability of a message making it into long term memory and actually affecting some change is only .03125 ($E.5 \times A.5 \times C.5 \times Y/A.5 \times R.5$). If anyone thinks this cannot happen, just check out the data in Figure 4–3 for products which are likely to have a degree of involvement for most people.

It all comes down to this essential point, as Engel and Blackwell put it:

What this all says is that consumers are actively monitoring the environment for *relevant* information under high involvement, accepting that which is felt to be pertinent and rejecting that which is not. Furthermore, they will tend to resist influence attempts which are perceived as going against the grain. Anyone who ignores these facts will find his or her marketing effort to be fruitless, thus placing a premium on careful research.[12]

Exposure

Exposure happens when one or more of the five senses is activated and transforms stimulus energy into the sensations of sight, smell, touch, taste, and hearing. This comes about only through good media selection— the message has to reach people where they are. Media planners, however, must contend with evidence documenting that people can *selectively expose* themselves when they have some advance warning that unwanted messages are coming. This is what we envisioned Sam James doing if he had some inkling that the "latest word from Detroit" was about to cross his path. Katz argues that it happens this way:

(*a*) . . . An individual self-censors his intake of communications so as to shield his beliefs and practices from attack; (*b*) . . . An individual seeks out communications which support his beliefs or practices; and (*c*) . . . The latter is particularly true when the beliefs or practices in question have undergone attack or the individual has otherwise been made less confident of them.[13]

Not everyone agrees with Katz, and there is some contradictory evidence. Yet, everyone no doubt has found themselves doing exactly this at times. So, it should be accepted as yet another fact of life of audience sovereignty.

---

[12] Engel and Blackwell, *Consumer Behavior*, p. 275.

[13] Elihu Katz, "On Reporting the Question of Selectivity in Exposure to Mass Communication," in *Theories of Cognitive Consistency: A Sourcebook*, ed. R. P. Abelson et al. (Chicago: Rand McNally, 1968), p. 789.

FIGURE 4–3
Registration of Featured Idea—Recall after 24 Hours

	Magazines		Television	
	Number of ads	Recall range (percent)	Number of ads	Recall range (percent)
Tires				
	13	0– 3.9	13	0– 3.9
	21	4– 7.9	5	4– 7.9
	11	8–11.9	5	8–11.9
	2	12–15.9	4	12–15.9
	3	16–19.9		
	2	24–27.9		
	2	28–31.9		
Automobiles				
	20	0– 1.9	49	0– 1.9
	33	2– 3.9	29	2– 3.9
	47	4– 5.9	19	4– 5.9
	27	6– 7.9	6	6– 7.9
	12	8– 9.9	4	8– 9.9
	7	10–11.9	2	10–11.9
	7	12–13.9	2	12–13.9
	1	14–15.9	4	14–15.9
	1	16–17.9	1	16
	1	18–19.9		
	3	20–21.9		
	3	22–23.9		
	1	24		
Life insurance				
	24	0– 1.9	8	0– 1.9
	23	2– 3.9	13	2– 3.9
	10	4– 5.9	7	4– 5.9
	2	6– 7.9	5	6– 7.9
	1	8– 9.9	3	8– 9.9
			1	10–11.9
			1	14–15.9
			1	18–19.9
			1	20–21.9
TV sets				
	5	0– 1.9	6	0– 1.9
	6	2– 3.9	9	2– 3.9
	4	4– 5.9	4	4– 5.9
	4	6– 7.9	3	6– 7.9
	3	8– 9.9	1	8– 9.9
	1	10–11.9	3	10–11.9
	2	12–13.9	2	12–13.9
	1	14–15.9	1	14–15.9
	1	18–19.9	3	16–17.9
Aftershaves, colognes				
	2	0– 3.9	7	0– 3.9
	10	4– 7.9	4	4– 7.9
	3	8–11.9	3	8–11.9
	1	12–15.9	2	12–15.9
	1	16–19.9	1	16–19.9
	1	20–23.9	3	24–27

Source: *Advertising Age,* April, 12, 1971, p. 52. Reprinted with permission of *Advertising Age.* Copyright 1971 by Crain Communications, Inc.

Attention

Once exposure takes place, information-processing activity is allocated to the stimulus, and it can be said that attention is attracted. One of the first effects is triggering of the *orientation reaction*. This may take the form of turning in direction, a sense of alertness, and so on.[14] Its function is to prepare the organism to cope with novel stimuli, and it serves to arouse the central nervous system.

Selective attention.   As we have stressed, some stimuli move from short-term memory into long-term, and others do not. Here are some of the factors which are known to affect attention.

The influence of need states.   It is reasonable to expect that an aroused bodily need will affect attention. It has been shown, for example, that hungry people are more likely to give food-related responses when ambiguous stimuli are seen or heard.[15] In addition, psychological motives can have the same effect, as was demonstrated in one experiment in which those with a strong affiliation motive identified a greater number of pictures of persons as standing out most clearly in a larger grouping of pictures than did those with a weaker affiliation motive.[16]

There are some obvious implications for promotional strategy. The hungry consumer, for example, will more readily notice food advertisements. An appeal to greater social acceptance through avoidance of body odor will in all probability be more effective with those who fear social rejection. Many other examples could be given.

Perceptual defense and vigilance.   Further documentation of the fact that people see and hear what they want to see and hear has been provided, initially through a series of experiments undertaken to analyze the influence of personal values on the speed of perception for value-related words. It has been found rather consistently that words connoting important values to the individual are perceived more readily. This selective influence of values has come to be called *perceptual vigilance.*[17] Although this area of research has been plagued with methodological problems, it is now generally accepted that vigilance can occur under properly controlled conditions.

---

[14] R. Lynn, *Attention Arousal and the Orientation Reaction* (Oxford: Pergamon Press, 1966).

[15] See, for example, R. N. Sanford, "The Effects of Abstinence from Food upon Imaginal Processes: A Further Experiment," *Journal of Psychology* 3 (1937), pp. 145–59; J. W. Atkinson and D. C. McClelland, "The Projective Expression of Needs: II, The Effect of Different Intensities of the Hunger Drive on Thematic Apperception," *Journal of Experimental Psychology* 38 (1948), pp. 643–58; and R. Levine, I. Chein, and G. Murphy, "The Relation of the Intensity of a Need to the Amount of Perceptual Distortion," *Journal of Psychology* 15 (1942), pp. 283–93.

[16] J. W. Atkinson and E. L. Walker, "The Affiliation Motive and Perceptual Sensitivity to Faces," *Journal of Abnormal and Social Psychology* 53 (1956), pp. 38–41.

[17] See, for example, L. Postman and B. Schneider, "Personal Values, Visual Recognition, and Recall," *Psychological Review* 58 (1951), pp. 271–84.

It seems reasonable that perceptual vigilance might be manifested through enhanced speed of perception for preferred brand names. This hypothesis was confirmed in one study where it was found that consumers recognize preferred brand names significantly more readily than they do nonpreferred brand names.[18]

The opposite of perceptual vigilance is *perceptual defense,* a process in which perception of threatening or low-valued stimuli is delayed or avoided. The evidence is extensive that barriers can be raised which prevent or inhibit perception.[19] Undoubtedly consumers at times avoid attention to and perception of promotion for nonpreferred brands in this manner.

Maintenance of cognitive consistency. The elements within the consumer's memory interact to provide a "map of the world," and attitudes are particularly important in this context. A demonstrated human tendency to resist changes in this map is referred to as maintenance of cognitive consistency.[20] It is now known, for example, that attitudes are change resistant to the extent that:

1. They are strongly held.
2. They are embedded in a set of related and supportive values and beliefs.
3. They are related to a person's conception of self relative to others.
4. The system of which they are a part is not complex and differentiated, thereby causing one to respond in terms of "all black or all white."
5. They are associated with important needs or personality traits.

Selective attention to promotional messages. As we have stressed before, data from a variety of sources indicate that the typical advertising message is attended to by only a fraction of the potential audience. On the average, for example, the 30-second television message will be attended to by fewer than 30 percent of those who are exposed. As Leo Bogart points out, "Advertising research data accurately reflect the fact that many messages register negative impressions or no impressions at all on many of the people who are exposed to the sight or sound of them.[21]

---

[18] Homer E. Spence and James F. Engel, "The Impact of Brand Preference on the Perception of Brand Names: A Laboratory Analysis," in *Marketing Involvement in Society and the Economy,* ed. P. R. McDonald (Chicago: American Marketing Association, 1970), pp. 267–71.

[19] See, for example, F. H. Nothman, "The Influence of Response Conditions on Recognition Thresholds for Taboo Words," *Journal of Abnormal and Social Psychology* 65 (1962), pp. 154–61, and E. Zigler and L. Yospe, "Perceptual Defense and the Problem of Response Suppression," *Journal of Personality* 28 (1960), pp. 220–39.

[20] See Shel Feldman, ed., *Cognitive Consistency* (New York: Academic Press, 1966); and Abelson et al., *Theories of Cognitive Consistency.*

[21] Leo Bogart, "Where Does Advertising Research Go from Here?" *Journal of Advertising Research* 9 (March 1969), p. 6.

Selective inattention to advertising can happen, of course, when there is high involvement and the message tends to go against the grain. Consider the problem faced by Renault as they begin another assault on the U.S. market, this time in cooperation with American Motors.[22] Renault made a serious blunder with its Dauphine in the late 1950s and left many with a sour taste. Add to this the research evidence that some American consumers consider French cars as being too odd for American tastes, and we can understand the risks faced in introducing the brand-new Renault Fuego. It is entirely possible that some never will process the introductory ads, regardless of their firepower. Only time will tell.

Comprehension

At the next stage of information processing, the individual now attempts to arrive at some meaning for the incoming message. Hopefully the message as comprehended will be close to the intent of the communicator, but this often is not the case. Often people miss the point as a way of keeping existing beliefs intact; other times noise in the communications process interferes. Jacoby and associates, for example, discovered that nearly everyone miscomprehends at least some of the things they see on television.[23] In another illustrative study, only 16 percent of those exposed to television commercials could identify a sponsor later, and for every two persons who correctly named a brand, at least one named a competitor.[24] So attention by no means guarantees comprehension.

Yielding/Acceptance

All persuasion has change of cognitive structure and/or behavior as its ultimate goal, but this may or may not happen. Let's take as our example the National Rifle Association ad appearing in Figure 4–4. Obviously the objective here is to change the attitudes of those who are negative to the NRA. In some cases, this may indeed happen, depending upon strength of underlying beliefs. The probability of change is inversely related to belief strength—the more they are imbedded, the less the likelihood of change.

For those who are open to change, yielding and acceptance will occur through the process of rehearsal (silent inner thoughts) referred to before. The greater the percentage of support arguments, the better the prospects.

---

[22] Douglas R. Sease, "American Motors Is About to Blot Itself Out to Build New Image around Jeep, Renault," *The Wall Street Journal*, April 8, 1982, pp. 23 and 41.

[23] Jacob Jacoby, Wayne D. Hoyer, and David A. Sheluga, *Miscomprehension of Televised Communications* (New York: American Association of Advertising Agencies, 1980).

[24] Harry W. McMahan, "TV Loses the 'Name Game' but Wins Big in Personality," *Advertising Age*, December 1, 1980, p. 80.

FIGURE 4–4
The National Rifle Association Campaign: What Will its Impact Be?

JANICE SCHULER: Eighteen years old. High school senior and
National Scholastic Shooting Champion.
Member of the U.S. Shooting Team and Life Member
of the National Rifle Association.

"I've been shooting competitively since I was seven years old.
It's been a sacrifice, but it's been worth it because I've had the chance
to travel, meet people and learn a lot about myself.
I practice about nine hours a week in the range at school because I want to make
the Olympic Team and try to get a shooting scholarship for college.

My dad bought me a NRA Life Membership when I was fourteen,
and I'll always be grateful to all the members for promoting competitive shooting
and giving me the chance to do well
at something I enjoy so much." **I'm the NRA.**

The NRA is the national governing body for the shooting sports.
It raises money, selects and trains the people who represent America in shooting competitions
around the world, including the Olympics. If you would like to join the NRA and want
more information about our programs and benefits, write Harlon Carter, Executive Vice President,
P.O. Box 37484, Dept. JS-10, Washington, D.C. 20006.
Paid for by the members of the National Rifle Association of America.

Source: Reproduced by special permission from the National Rifle Association.

Such a person might evaluate what is said and conclude, "These people aren't so bad. They've gotten a bad deal from the media." This is an example of a support argument generated during rehearsal, and it is a sign that beliefs and attitudes will be affected positively.

On the other hand, it doesn't take much imagination to think what the responses might be from those who are opposed. "What a bunch of baloney. These people still are a bunch of rednecks no matter what they say" (counterargument). Or, "What would you expect from the National Rifle Association? Certainly not the truth" (source derogation). When counterarguments and source derogations are detected, this is pretty firm evidence that the message is being actively resisted and hence will have little or no impact on the individual.

So, who determines the outcome—the communicator or the recipient? One could perhaps argue that the communicator has a good deal of power in a personal selling situation such as we discussed in Chapter 3 or perhaps through use of outright deception. But this certainly will not generate a repeat customer. In the final analysis, the consumer still is sovereign and controls what actually enters into long-term memory.

Retention

The mechanics of memory need not be discussed further here other than to restate that storage in long-term memory is the last stage of information processing and a necessity if lasting change is to take place. The message now has survived quite a process, and it is likely that it has been shaped and fitted along the way. Hopefully, it still bears some resemblence to the communicator's intent.

So, Can Promotion Ever Succeed?

The reader by now may be wondering just what impact, if any, can be made through communication. If the intent is to change strongly held contradictory beliefs and attitudes, there is reason for some dismay, because consumer sovereignty still is alive and well. At the very least this would imply that mass marketers would be well advised to avoid those who have some opposing tendencies and concentrate on those who are already neutral or even sympathetic toward what is being said. This is really the underlying rationale for market segmentation. It also is possible to search out those who are wavering in beliefs for one reason or another. Perhaps they have become disillusioned with their brand for one reason or another. If there are enough people in this category, this could signal a valuable market opportunity.

When high involvement is there, the communicator is best advised to begin with research and try to understand the nature of the individual's information search. Messages can get through if (1) they are directed meaningfully toward the dispositions and need states of those in the target market and (2) are oriented toward reinforcing these tendencies and showing how the product or service offered is a valid alternative.

INFORMATION PROCESSING UNDER LOW INVOLVEMENT

In most buying actions, quite frankly, the purchase is not of sufficient importance to activate motivated search and information use. Leo Bogart has some helpful insights here:

A cornerstone of communications research has long been the notion of selective perception, the idea that people tend to pay attention to messages that support their predispositions and to block out incongruent messages . . . The problem must be posed quite differently in the case of messages that arouse no contradictory prior judgments, simply because they arouse no reactions at all. Perhaps the main contribution that advertising research can make to this study of communications is in the domain of inattention to low-key stimuli, as exemplified by the ever-increasing flow of unsolicited and unwanted messages to which people are subjected in our overcommunicative civilization.[25]

When involvement is low, not much is at stake, and the consumer is not motivated either to search for or to reject information. As was the case in purchase of Jergens Aloe & Lanolin, a product is tried and evaluated *after* purchase. Now *action leads to thinking which leads to feeling* (see Figure 4–5.)

The Stages in Information Processing

Even though motivated search is largely absent, it should not mistakenly be assumed that promotion has no impact on decision, for that is not the case. Attention now is *involuntary* and occurs as the consumer is using media for purposes such as entertainment. It is becoming increasingly clear that a selling message can be processed and stored in long-term memory *without having an apparent effect on cognitive structure at that point in time.*[26] It seems to take place mostly in the right brain hemisphere in the form of visual images which enter memory and bypass the yielding/acceptance stage.[27] So that stage now is removed; other than that a model of information processing is identical in other respects (Figure 4–6).

This information stored in the right brain hemisphere can have a later effect on a buying decision, even though there is no recall of its content. This happens when there is some kind of reminder at point-of-sale such

---

[25] Bogart, "Advertising Research," p. 6.

[26] See Engel and Blackwell, *Consumer Behavior,* Chap. 9 for a review of pertinent evidence.

[27] Hansen, "Hemispheral Lateralization."

FIGURE 4–5
The Low-Involvement Decision
Process

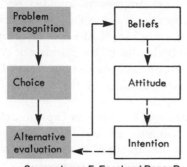

Source: James F. Engel and Roger D.
Blackwell, *Consumer Behavior*, 4th ed.
(Hinsdale, Ill.: Dryden Press, 1982), p. 37.
Used by special permission.

as a display, special offer, or so on. Then, memory is activated in the form of *recognition* which could induce a "why not try it" response. The earlier message, then, has built a degree of awareness which is later activated, and this is an essential point. There has been an unfortunate tendency recently to downgrade the selling power of television which of all media is most processed as visual images in the right brain. The conclusion has been that lack of recall signifies lack of impact, whereas recognition would seem to be a much more appropriate measure.

FIGURE 4–6
Information Processing Under Low Involvement

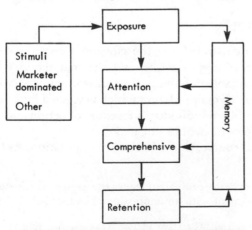

Source: James F. Engel and Roger D. Blackwell, *Consumer Behavior*, 4th ed. (Hinsdale, Ill.: Dryden Press, 1982), p. 38. Used by special permission.

The Boredom Barrier

Probably the main reason why so many filter out unwanted messages is that advertisements in particular are frequently avoided because of sheer disinterest and boredom. People really don't care about what is said. This is further complicated by a high level of noise resulting from vast numbers of competing appeals. Estimates of the number of commercial messages coming at us during an average day range from 300 to as many as 2,000. Is it any wonder that so many of them are lost in the noise?

Given a high level of noise, what can be done to capture attention? This is discussed in more depth in Chapter 14, but it is worth pointing out here that something must be done to break through the boredom barrier. Recourse is frequently made to novelty, catchy headlines, unusual graphics, color, and other such means of attracting attention. The ads in Figures 4–7 and 4–8 are unusual and probably would capture attention simply because they stand out and utilize visual gimmicks. Figure 4–9 uses a shock headline to attract attention. This does not necessarily mean that these are good ads, however. That judgment must be reserved pending evidence on response.

Another problem is to make sure that the message registers the brand name. This is especially crucial under low involvement, because the brand name probably will be lost if it does not visually dominate. This cannot be left to chance. Another helpful clue is to develop a central character signifying nearly all the message is trying to convey.[28] Examples are Rusty Jones and Ronald MacDonald. Point-of-sale tie-ins building on that character will readily trigger recognition and, hopefully, a "why not try it" response.

THE ISSUE OF MANIPULATION

We have tried to demonstrate how the consumer remains sovereign through selective information processing and the manner in which its functions provide a formidable defense against unwanted persuasion. Yet there always is the danger of manipulation which is viewed here as strategies which somehow inhibit an individual's freedom of action and encourage a response they otherwise would not make.[29]

Outright deception, of course, is one form of manipulation. As Gardner puts it:

If an advertisement (or advertising campaign) leaves the average consumer within some reasonable market segment with an impression(s) and/or belief(s) different

---

[28] Harry W. McMahan, "Do Your Ads Have VI/P?" *Advertising Age,* July 14, 1980, pp. 50–51.

[29] Em Griffin, *The Mind Changers* (Wheaton, Ill.: Tyndale, 1976).

FIGURE 4–7
Use of Unusual and Striking Layout to Attract Attention

Courtesy Artistic Brass

FIGURE 4–8
Use of Contemporary Art Forms to Attract Attention

Source: Reproduced with permission of the American Telephone and Telegraph Company.

FIGURE 4–9
Use of Shock Headline to Attract Attention

Crumple up this ad.

Then take it to your local Xerox office.

Tell a sales representative that if the new Xerox 5400 copier is so terrific, let's see if the ball of paper in your hand will go through its document feeder.

Chuckle to yourself as he smooths out the ad and carries it to the 5400. After all, you've never seen a document handler that could handle a problem like this.

Then he may pause to tell you how the 5400 can automatically copy on two sides of a sheet of paper. He may even point out its uncanny self-diagnostic systems and lightning-fast automatic bi-directional sorter.

But you both know why you're there.

At last, he slides the crumpled page towards the document handler and pushes the button. And…and…and…

Sorry. But what happens next is between you and your local Xerox representative. So pay him a visit, soon.

And find out if the original goes in.

And if it does, how the copy comes out.   **XEROX**

XEROX® and 5400 are trademarks of XEROX CORPORATION.

Source: Reproduced with permission of the Xerox Corporation.

from what would normally be expected if the average consumer within that market segment had reasonable knowledge and that impression(s) and/or belief(s) is factually untrue or potentially misleading, then deception is said to exist.[30]

This is not the most readable definition (it was prepared for lawyers), but it makes the point that people are deceived if their *comprehension* of a message is something other than the literal truth, no matter what the message itself said. At the bottom line, then, it is not the message content per se that makes it misleading but the comprehension of it. There have been many examples of ads which were truthful on the surface but left quite another impression.

Another dimension of deception is the use of various means which dominate the message content and stimulate a response just because they were used. Examples would be appeal to a strong but irrelevant emotion, use of distractions such as music or loud sound, and so on. Fortunately, people soon catch on to such gimmicks and rarely are a repeat customer if they have been had. That is quite a powerful deterrent.

There also has been fear of manipulation through use of so-called subliminal perception. One of the raging controversies of the 1950s and the 1960s was over the question of whether or not people could be influenced to act almost hypnotically without awareness on their part. This implies a complete circumvention of the perceptual filtering process. This whole matter was triggered by an alleged advertising test in which the words DRINK COKE and EAT POPCORN were flashed on a movie screen at such speed that no one knew they were there. Sales of both products supposedly increased sharply. These findings have been unanimously dismissed as being methodologically invalid, and nearly all attempts at replication have failed.

The issue was brought to light more recently through the influential book by Dixon in which he demonstrated that subliminal perception can occur.[31] Moreover, there is some evidence that it might work as an advertising strategy.[32] We need to evaluate how this takes place, however. A stimulus is flashed so quickly that there is not full conscious awareness, but yet there is still some registration on memory. The days of big brother and magic persuasive powers are not here, fortunately, because there is no proof that selective information processing is circumvented and people are induced to act without any defenses. There still is full power to screen out unwanted messages, and consumer sovereignty remains intact.

There are some good reasons why subliminal advertising makes little

---

[30] David M. Gardner, "Deception in Advertising: A Receiver Oriented Approach to Understanding," *Journal of Advertising* 5 (November 1976), p. 7.

[31] Normal F. Dixon, *Subliminal Perception—The Nature of the Controversy* (Maidenhead-Berkshire, England: McGraw-Hill, 1971).

[32] See especially, Joel Sagert, "Another Look at Subliminal Perception," *Journal of Advertising Research* 19 (February 1979), pp. 55–58.

sense as a strategy. At best, only a fractional or brief stimulus is presented. It is hard enough to break through with use of all the persuasive firepower at one's disposal without recourse to such a brief stimulus that it probably is all the more prone to become lost in the noise. Hopefully this will put the whole issue to death.

SUMMARY

This is the first of four chapters on the subject of consumer demand, and it addressed the important issue of information processing. First it was necessary to distinguish between high-involvement and low-involvement decision-process behavior. Under high involvement it is important for the consumer to make the "right choice," because of the high personal relevance attached to the buying action. This gives rise to extended problem-solving behavior complete with information search and considerable alternative evaluation prior to purchase. When high involvement is present, the consumer actively monitors the environment for relevant information and is resistant to that which is not. The following steps in information processing then were discussed: (1) exposure, (2) attention, (3) comprehension, (4) yielding/acceptance, and (5) retention.

When the buying and consumption action has less personal relevance, it is said that this represents low involvement. In such situations consumers often purchase with little or no prior thought, largely based on a why-not-try it reaction. Yet, promotion can still have an impact though registration of a visual stimulus which lies dormant until activated at point-of-sale. Here there is little motivated information search or active resistance to appeals designed to induce changes in beliefs and behavior.

Throughout the chapter, it has been demonstrated that the consumer is sovereign, controlling the information which is received and processed. Because of this, promotion cannot succeed without accurate research into motivating influences and an understanding of how information is processed.

Review and Discussion Questions

1. Differentiate between high involvement and low involvement. What difference do these factors make in the way in which information is processed and used by the consumer?
2. Distinguish between sensory memory, short-term memory, and long-term memory. What role does "rehearsal" play?
3. Try, if you can stand it, to pay close attention to a series of television commercials and monitor your own thoughts. In what way do you detect source derogation, counter-argumentation, and support argumentation?
4. Assume that a teenager cannot remember seeing advertisements for any brand

of deodorant other than her preferred brand, even though she has finished paging through a consumer magazine replete with competitive ads, one of which was a two-page, four-color spread. What explanations can be given?

5. Under what conditions might you expect perceptual defense to affect the perception of brand names?

6. A leading critic of advertising contends that advertising has the power to influence people to buy unwisely—to act in a way that they would not otherwise. What would your response be?

7. Under what circumstances, if any, would you expect to encounter consumer avoidance of attitude-discrepant advertisements?

8. What is the boredom barrier? How does it affect response to advertising?

9. Charles Green, 29-year-old printer, has just finished watching the New York Jets lose to the Cincinnati Bengals on television. The score was 47–6. Charles has a 10th-grade education, is married, makes $19,500 a year working a 24-hour week, and has four children. A researcher comes into his home asking him which commercials telecast during the game he can recall. When questioned he could not remember a single one, even though he was exposed to 39, including 6 at one stretch during four station breaks. All he could remember was that the Bengals intercepted four of the quarterback's passes and caught him 14 times for a total loss of 136 yards. Upon deeper questioning he did remember seeing one beer commercial and could relate the brand name and some of the content of the message. What explanations can you give for the apparent failure of advertising to influence Charles?

CHAPTER 5

The High-Involvement Decision Process

Now it is necessary to return to the high-involvement decision process which we have only examined in barest detail. What happens to initiate the process? What sources are used in search? What does the consumer do in alternative evaluation, and what is the role of promotion in changing beliefs and attitudes? How is choice actually made, especially in today's world in which in-home shopping is becoming more commonplace? These questions are examined in this chapter which is the first of two on the subject. Social influence is the subject of the next chapter.

The model used previously is now considerably expanded (see Figure 5–1). It may seem pretty hard to follow at this point, but we will take it stage by stage, and hopefully it will all fit together in a very logical and reasonable pattern by the end of this and the following chapters. So bear with us as we flesh out the so-called EKB model of consumer behavior.[1]

PROBLEM RECOGNITION

Problem recognition occurs when there is a *perceived difference between the ideal state of affairs and the actual situation sufficient to arouse and activate the decision*

---

[1] This is one of the two models used in James F. Engel and Roger D. Blackwell, *Consumer Behavior*, 4th ed. (Hinsdale, Ill.: Dryden Press, 1982).

FIGURE 5–1
A Model of High-Involvement Decision-Process Behavior (the EKB Model)

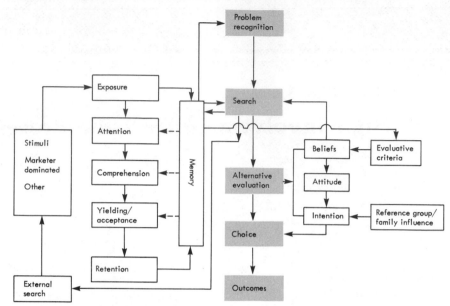

Source: James F. Engel and Roger D. Blackwell, *Consumer Behavior,* 4th ed. (Hinsdale, Ill.: Dryden Press, 1982). This is a slight modification of the abbreviated model appearing on p. 33; the complete model appears on p. 500. Used by special permission.

process. [2] Once this occurs the human system is energized, and goal orientation commences in the form of purposeful activity. Problem recognition can be influenced, then, by a focus on either the ideal state or the actual state.

Determinants of the Ideal

People are motivated to act if somehow they catch a glimpse of what might be as compared to what is. This ideal or "might be" is affected by four determinants: (1) motive activation; (2) reference group influence; (3) the effects of other decisions; and (4) promotional efforts.

Motive activation. Motives are best viewed as enduring predispositions to strive to attain specified goals. Thus, they comprise the ideal state and, if activated, give rise to a feeling of discomfort known as drive which, in turn, energizes behavior. Maslow has hypothesized that motives are organized in such a way as to establish priorities and a hierarchy of importance ranging from (lowest to highest): (1) survival; (2) motives related to human interaction, love, and involvement; and (3) motives

---

[2] Engel and Blackwell, *Consumer Behavior,* p. 301.

related to competency and self.[3] Each higher order of motive will not be activated until lower orders are relatively satisfied. Some motives, of course, are virtually insatiable, such as striving for status, and serve as a continued source of problem recognition. Knowing this can provide the clues to some effective promotion. Hart Schaffner & Marx, for example, stresses that a handsome suit is the key to success for the man on the way up.

Reference group influence.   While this is the subject for the next chapter, other people can set a stringent standard for behavior in some social settings. When this is the case, then their norms may function as the major determinant of the ideal state.

Other decisions.   Sometimes one action leads to another. For example, fresh paint on a wall can make the carpet look shabby. Once the carpet is replaced, something else may have to go, and on it progresses. Nearly everyone has had this happen at one time or another.

Promotional efforts.   Sometimes advertising and personal selling can have the effect of showing an all-new concept of what might be. This certainly was the case with the Sharp CCM oven (discussed in Chapter 1) combining the advantages of both convection and microwave. Here, then, is a brand-new solution to an old problem. For this to succeed, however, the benefits offered must be consistent with underlying consumer motives. Yet it should be recognized that motive activation and the other factors are likely to play a much greater role than marketing efforts in stimulating problem recognition in most situations, although there can be exceptions where the solution offered really does provide an altogether new standard.

Dissatisfaction with Actual State

There are two major ways in which the actual state can be seen as falling short of the ideal. The first is changed circumstances. One common cause is depletion of an existing stock of goods. In other situations existing products are seen as being unsatisfactory. Perhaps the washing machine has failed to complete its full cycle, and it is found that repair is impossible without excessive cost. Finally, changes within the family also can have this effect. Birth of children gives rise to perceived need for new furniture; changes in income (hopefully upward) can open or close a range of decision options.

Sometimes marketing efforts show existing solutions to be inadequate. On occasion this is tried by direct comparative advertising, but it is doubtful that this has much effect on problem recognition. No doubt a new

---

[3] A. H. Maslow, *Motivation Personality* (New York: Harper & Row, 1954).

solution such as the CCM oven will be more effective in that no existing option now is seen as adequate.

Some Clues for Promotional Strategy

Consider the obstacles faced by a firm selling swimming pools for home installation. This may appeal to such basic motives as status and prestige, but an initial desire to buy can be opposed by many factors such as cost and safety, with the result that a problem will not be recognized and acted upon. No amount of promotion is likely to change matters.

Advertising and selling can serve to bring a product to the buyer's attention, thereby triggering some initial interest prior to problem recognition. This, in effect, qualifies the product for the finals. Product awareness is thus stored in memory for later use, and this can be significant.

Most authorities now agree that efforts designed to stimulate problem recognition are destined for low payout, because some degree of problem recognition usually must exist before consumers are even interested in what the marketer has to say. What this says, is essence, is that the greatest opportunities exist when primary demand (favorable attitude toward the product class) is at a high level. Prior to that point the product is not seen as a feasible alternative, and the message will not have a great deal of effect. Much so-called primary demand advertising tends to have a low return for this reason. The sporadic campaigns of the milk producers are a case in point.

SEARCH

After problem recognition, the individual may or may not search for additional information. At times *internal search* (a memory scan) will be entirely sufficient, but most likely it is not, in which case external search is activated. A model of what is involved is shown in Figure 5–2. This should look pretty familiar, because all it shows is that external information is gathered which then is processed as discussed in Chapter 4.

Whether search will take place or not depends entirely upon the tradeoff between the perceived benefits and perceived costs. These issues are discussed first, followed by a review of the various sources which can be used and the overall importance of each.

The Perceived Benefits of Search[4]

The expected rewards from external search are affected by (1) the quantity and quality of presently stored information; (2) ability to recall

---

[4] The quantity of underlying research is quite large here, and the reader is referred to Engel and Blackwell, *Consumer Behavior*, chap. 11 for a detailed review.

FIGURE 5–2
The External Search Process

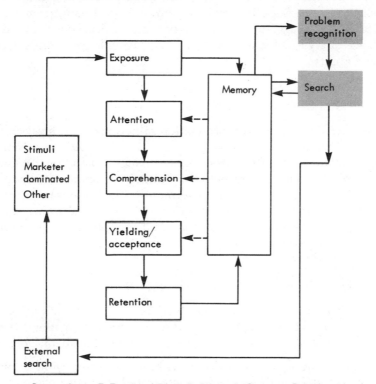

Source: James F. Engel and Roger D. Blackwell, *Consumer Behavior*, 4th ed.
(Hinsdale, Ill.: Dryden Press, 1982), p. 322. Used by special permission.

and use that information; (3) the degree of perceived risk; and (4) confidence in decision-making ability.

The individual learns from past experience to become more proficient over time and hence possesses a great deal of information. Therefore, the longer various products and brands have been purchased and used, the less the tendency to search. But stored information, no matter how extensive, may be perceived as being of low quality. This is especially likely to be the case when there has been dissatisfaction with previous purchases, a long time lapse since the last decision, and changes in the benefits offered by various competitors.

Ability to recall relevant information is another determinant of search, because memory fades over time. It is strengthened, of course, if relevant behavior has been undertaken in the recent past. Recall also is greater when a current problem is seen as being similar to one faced previously.

The extent of perceived risk is another major determinant of whether or not search will take place. Search increases with (1) the perceived importance of the action; (2) the price of the product; (3) the length of time the consumer is committed to using the product; (4) the degree to which the item is socially visible; (5) physiological dangers such as side effects of drug usage; (6) the number of separate decisions required (such as choice of style, color, and brand); and (7) confidence in one's decision-making ability.

The Costs of Search

It is often overlooked that information gathering has both psychological and monetary costs. In the first place, search delays purchase. Moreover, visits to retailers are often associated with such frustrations as finding a parking place and interacting with indifferent or incompetent sales personnel. Finally, doing such things can cost money. The result is that consumers often limit search, especially those in the lowest educational strata, by focusing attention on a familiar brand and by opting to pay an average (as opposed to lowest) price.[5]

Search from the Perspective of Consumer Welfare

Some concerned with consumer welfare argue that rational decision making requires exhaustive search—the more the information the better. For example, Federal Trade Commission member Elizabeth Dole stated:

Many of the trade regulation rules currently being considered by the Commission have as their unifying theme the disclosure of full and accurate information to consumers about competing goods and services. . . . It is essential that such information be available to consumers in order for them to compare products and determine what is best for their needs.[6]

There are undeniable consumer benefits resulting from such actions as improved nutritional labels on canned foods, but there also are some important unanswered questions. First, how much information is enough? Is it possible to overload the information-processing ability of the consumer? Research increasingly is showing that this can occur, and, when it does, it is not in the consumer's best interests.[7] Also, quantity does not signify quality. In the final analysis this whole question must be resolved on the basis of the information the consumer both *needs* in deci-

---

[5] J. W. Newman and R. Staelin, "Prepurchase Information Seeking for New Cars and Major Household Appliances," *Journal of Marketing Research,* 9 (1972), pp. 249–57.

[6] Elizabeth Hanford Dole, "In the Consumer's Interest," speech before the Southeastern Conference on Family Economics and Home Management, University of North Carolina at Greensboro, February 4, 1977.

[7] For the most recent among many published studies see Debra L. Scammon, " 'Information Load' and Consumers," *Journal of Consumer Research* 4 (September 1977), pp. 148–55.

sion making and *is willing to use.* Industry and other sources must meet legitimate consumer expectations in this respect.

INFORMATION SOURCES USED IN SEARCH

What are the sources used when consumers engage in external search? The alternatives may seem to be endless, but as Figure 5–3 indicates, there are several basic categories: (1) general sources (word-of-mouth influence and general content media), and (2) marketer-dominated sources (personal selling, advertising, point-of-sale influence, and publicity.

FIGURE 5–3
Categories of Consumer Information Sources

	Face-to-face	Mass media
General	Word-of-mouth influence	General content media
Marketer-dominated	Personal selling	Advertising point-of-sale influence and publicity

Obviously the importance of any given source may vary from one type of decision to the next, and here is a helpful typology to use when comparing importance:

1. *Decisive effectiveness*—a major or even dominant impact on decision.
2. *Contributory effectiveness*—some role such as stimulating awareness or interest but not decisive.
3. *Ineffective*—exposure but no particular role in the decision.

From the growing body of evidence comparing the relative impact of various sources, here are some generalizations that emerge.[8]

1. The various media are *complementary* rather than competitive. People usually do not rely on one exclusive source.
2. The mass media, whether marketer-dominated or not, perform a largely *contributory* role of providing such information as brand features and availability.
3. Print appears to play a greater role than television advertising under high involvement because it is processed in the left hemisphere of the brain which also is the seat of problem solving.

---

[8] The sources are too numerous to detail. See Engel and Blackwell, *Consumer Behavior,* p. 337.

4. The nonmarketer-dominated sources, especially word-of-mouth, tend to play a *decisive* role because their greater credibility and clarity assume a legitimizing function.

Obviously, generalizations such as these are subject to exceptions, but they provide a good foundation on which to proceed.

General Sources

General content media. Often the general media, especially those which include product comparisons, have quite an impact. An example is the negative effect on sales of some running shoe manufacturers and positive effects on others after publication of the 1980 shoe comparison in *Runner's World.*[9] Here is a situation where consumers have little else on which to base a decision. On the other hand, a widely used product-ratings source, *Consumer Reports,* seems to be declining in importance, presumably because of greater buyer sophistication.[10]

The mass media also can provide information on trends. *Better Homes and Gardens* and other magazines in the "shelter" group are widely used sources on furnishings and decorating trends. Similarly, *Cosmopolitan* and *Playboy* are deliberately written to provide information on all aspects of lifestyle.

Word-of-mouth. Personal influence, operating through word-of-mouth, is a major information source in consumer decision making. Those who serve the important role of information dissemination through this channel are referred to as *opinion leaders,* although this term can be misleading. They tend to be pretty much like those whom they influence with one major difference—they have information or expertise that the other person does not.[11] It is a well-known fact that the neighbor with the most children is among the most frequently consulted sources for advice on minor childhood ailments.

Word-of-mouth emerges as a major information source in a variety of consumer studies. Just to take two illustrations, advertising stimulated initial interest in the purchase of Contac (an over-the-counter cold remedy) when it was first introduced, but word-of-mouth communication was the most significant factor in product trial.[12] And friends and relatives giving their recommendations was found to be the most important reason

---

[9] Sam Harper, "Athletic Shoe Surveys Run into Industry Dispute," *Advertising Age,* September 22, 1980, p. 48.

[10] J. L. Engledown, R. D. Anderson, and H. Becker, "The Changing Information Seeker: A Study of Attitudes Toward Product Test Reports—1970 and 1976," *Journal of Consumer Affairs* 13 (Summer 1979), pp. 75–85.

[11] There is a great deal of research on the characteristics of opinion leaders. See Engel and Blackwell, *Consumer Behavior,* pp. 361–65.

[12] Unpublished findings, Ohio State Studies in Self-Medication, 1970.

for choosing a physician.[13] Not surprisingly, people turn to others because of their high perceived credibility—they are seen as not trying to persuade anyone.

How does interpersonal influence work?   For a couple of decades it was felt that there was a two-step flow of communication. Specifically, this hypothesis stated that influences and ideas flow from mass media to opinion leaders and then to others.[14] This infers, then, that the mass media exert their greatest influence on the opinion leader who passes their content on. The two-step flow is no longer felt to be accurate because it assumes that the audience is merely a passive recipient of influence. The truth is that up to 50 percent of word-of-mouth communications are initiated by people seeking information.[15] In reality, then, the mass media stimulate word-of-mouth from both opinion leaders and recipients.

Implications for promotional strategy.   The toughest problem is to reach opinion leaders who can exist in all strata of society and not form a distinct segment. When this is possible, there are several interesting strategies. First, ads can be directed to them in the hopes that they will use the product and talk with others. Second, opinion leaders tend to be innovators, so monitoring of their behavior can be an advance notice of consumption trends. Third, products can be given or loaned to them in the hopes that others will be attracted. Finally, known opinion leaders can be hired by manufacturers or retailers as sales persons or perhaps as a Vice President of Community Affairs or some other such title to capitalize upon their influence.

When opinion leaders cannot be identified as a distinct segment (as is usually the case), the alternative strategy is to stimulate information seeking through word-of-mouth. Sometimes this can be very direct—"Ask your friends," or "Ask the person who owns one." A more indirect way is to use clever or intriguing advertising to stimulate people to talk about a product. The Alka-Seltzer "Try it, you'll like it" campaign has a deserved place in advertising history for the way it triggered conversations of this type (although it didn't seem to move much product judging by the fact that the advertising agency was fired shortly thereafter).[16]

Whatever the strategy, it always must be kept in mind that this channel can have real impact in that most buyers assume that other people have

---

[13] Roger D. Blackwell and W. Wayne Talarzyk, *Consumer Attitudes Toward Health Care and Malpractice* (Columbus, Ohio: Grid Publishing, 1977).

[14] Paul F. Lazarsfeld, Bernard R. Berelson, and Hazel Gaudet, *The People's Choice* (New York: Columbia University Press, 1948).

[15] This type of finding has emerged in many studies beginning with those by Donald Cox at Harvard in the 1960s. For one of the most recent, see Jagdish N. Sheth, "Word-of-Mouth in Low-Risk Innovations," *Journal of Advertising Research*, June 1971, pp. 15–18.

[16] See J. R. Mancuso, "Why Not Create Opinion Leaders for New Product Introductions?" *Journal of Marketing* 33 (1969), pp. 20–25.

no commercial ax to grind. On the other hand, friends and neighbors may be perceived as lacking the competence to provide the detailed product information available through advertising. One never can be sure what type of information is likely to pass through one channel relative to another, so it is always necessary to monitor the content of word-of-mouth. If it is positive, then this is a real promotional boost. If it is negative, it may be possible to provide some redirection through advertising or publicity.

Marketer-Dominated Sources

Media advertising. Once a problem has been recognized, the buyer becomes more receptive to information from all sources, including advertising. Real help can be given to the consumer, first of all, by understanding motivations and expected product benefits. Then it is beneficial to both buyer and seller to stress the way in which the product or service stands out in terms of desired benefits. The effect can be a distinct change in beliefs, attitudes, and intentions (this is discussed in more detail later).

Point-of-sale influence. Personal selling plays a large role in many high-involvement decisions. Some information can be given only through conversation and demonstration. Unfortunately, retail selling often seems to be a forgotten art today, and the result all too often is a lost sales opportunity.

All good salespeople know that preferences and intentions are least stable immediately prior to a purchase. Most readers can recall examples of impatience to buy once they have made a decision to do so. Many people are willing even to accept substitutes rather than return home empty-handed. The buyer, therefore, is subceptible to suggestion at this point, and the opportunity is bright for the salesperson who correctly sizes up prospects and directs his or her desires skillfully. Personal selling is discussed in more depth in a later chapter.

Sometimes point-of-sale advertising and display also is useful in high-involvement decisions, although its greatest use is in the low-involvement situation. The consumer can benefit from displays, shelf talkers, brochures, and so on.

Publicity. Publicity is general interest information submitted to and used by mass media at no charge. The usual objectives are to influence sales, to gain acceptance of company policies, and to enhance the understanding between the public and a business. Publicity often takes the form of press releases and other means of information on product discoveries, scientific advances, company news, and so on. Sometimes this will be of help to the consumer in decision making, especially when the news is about a new product. This certainly proved to be the case when Eastman Kodak reaped extensive media publicity on its new disk camera long before any advertising or retail promotion appeared. No doubt the product already was presold to some degree.

ALTERNATIVE EVALUATION

Let's return once again to Sam James and his contemplated purchase of the Peugeot 505. No doubt he has searched rather extensively for relevant information. Now, what does he do with it? He began with a set of product attributes or benefits which no doubt were refined a bit during search. More technically, these attributes or benefits are referred to here as *evaluative criteria* because they provide the foundation on which various alternatives are compared. As information is processed, different makes of cars are compared in these terms, and the outcome is change of existing *beliefs* or formation of new beliefs about each car, including the Peugeot. For example, will the 505 really give unusually good steering and handling as it claims? The sum total of beliefs about each make along the various relevant evaluative criteria represent an *attitude*, either favorable or unfavorable, toward the act of purchasing and using each make.

All things being equal, the prospect purchases the make toward which the attitude is most positive, and this normally leads to an *intention* to act. Intentions, in turn, usually culminate in purchase unless some unexpected circumstance intervenes.

This illustration has given the essence of a fairly complex process of alternative evaluation shown in Figure 5–4. It shows the functional relationship among evaluative criteria, beliefs, attitudes, intentions, and choice. Each of these elements is discussed in the following sections.

FIGURE 5–4
Alternative Evaluation

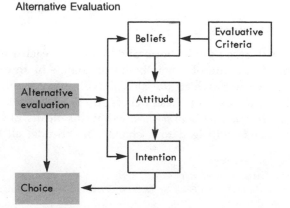

Source: James F. Engel and Roger D. Blackwell, *Consumer Behavior*, 4th ed. (Hinsdale, Ill.: Dryden Press, 1982), p. 415. Used by special permission.

Evaluative Criteria

Put more formally, evaluative criteria are *"desired outcomes from choice of use of an alternative expressed in the form of the attributes or specifications used to compare various alternatives."*[17] Or, stated more simply, they are desired attributes or benefits. They can either be *objective* (price, durability) or *subjective* relating to symbolic values (youthfulness, status). In the most basic sense, they are a product-specific expression of underlying goals, motives, and lifestyle.

When there is high involvement, consumers usually follow what has come to be known as a *compensatory strategy* in alternative evaluation.[18] This means that consumers generally process information by brand (CPB), in a somewhat holistic fashion, rather than comparing various brands one attribute at a time (CPA).[19] A given brand, in turn, will not be rejected just because it doesn't fully deliver in terms of one desired attribute or benefit; rather weakness on one dimension may be compensated for by strength on others.

There are two possible forms of the compensatory strategy. In the first, the *expectancy-value* approach, it is assumed that more than one attribute will be used in the evaluation process, and six or seven may be the maximum. A judgment is made on whether or not the brand actually fills the bill in terms of each attribute and whether or not this is a good or bad thing. The total brand evaluation is the sum of these ratings for each attribute. In the *attribute-adequacy* approach, on the other hand, the consumer proceeds in pretty much the same manner, with the exception that there is an explicit assessment of the difference between ideal benefit expected on each attribute and the actual extent to which the brand measures up. Hence, this probably is the ultimate of extensive problem solving.

Beliefs, Attitudes, and Intentions

As the consumer evaluates a product or brand in terms of each attribute, the outcome is either formation of a new belief or change in an existing belief specifying the extent to which the alternative measures up to the expected benefit. The sum total of these beliefs, then, represents *attitude toward purchasing the particular alternative in question.* What this means, of course, is that a change in beliefs will lead to a change in attitude, all things

---

[17] Engel and Blackwell, *Consumer Behavior,* p. 414.

[18] See James R. Bettman, *An Information Processing Theory of Consumer Choice* (Reading, Mass.: Addison-Wesley, 1979), pp. 132–33.

[19] See Bettman, *An Information Processing Theory,* pp. 179–85; Also Flemming Hansen, "Psychological Theories of Consumer Choice," *Journal of Consumer Research* 3 (December 1976), pp. 132–37.

considered. But the payout is yet to come, because a change in attitude leads to an *intention to act* which (again assuming all other things to be equal) then leads to purchasing action. A change in beliefs and attitudes, therefore, is a totally valid marketing goal.

The Fishbein Model.   What we have done thus far is to give a verbal statement of what has come to be known as the Fishbein Behavioral Intentions Model. In its more extended form, it specifies that a person's intention to perform a given behavior will give an approximate prediction of behavior.[20] Intentions, in turn, are calculated on the basis of attitude toward a given action plus the influence of social pressures, and the general formula appears as follows:[21]

$$B \approx BI = w_1(A_B) + w_2(SN)$$

where:

$B = $ Overt behavior
$BI = $ Behavioral intention
$A_B = $ Attitude toward performing a given behavior
$SN = $ Subjective norm
$\begin{matrix} w_1 \\ w_2 \end{matrix} = $ Empirically determined importance weights

This may all seem a bit abstract, but this model has come to assume some real importance in the study of consumer behavior. Furthermore, there is payout in promotional strategy if these concepts and variables are taken seriously.

Measurement.   Although Fishbein specifies that both attitude toward the behavior (A_B) and social influence (SN) be measured, we will concentrate only on the former and save the latter topic for the next chapter. There are many possible approaches to measurement, but we will follow the book, so to speak, to show how it might work out using a practical example.

A_B quite literally measures the expectancy-value approach to alternative evaluation discussed above. First of all, A_B should be viewed as attitude toward purchasing and using a given brand in a product class, and it is computed from beliefs which measure the consumer's assessment of whether or not this brand possesses a desired attribute. An evaluation also is made the importance of each attribute. Here, then, is its computational form:

$$A_B = \sum_{i=1}^{n} b_i e_i,$$

[20] Martin Fishbein and Icek Ajzen, *Belief, Attitude, Intention and Behavior: An Introduction to Theory and Research* (Reading, Mass.: Addison-Wesley, 1975).
[21] Ibid., p. 301 and following.

where:

A_B = Attitude toward performing the behavior
b_i = Belief that performing behavior B leads to consequence i
e_i = The person's evaluation of consequence i
n = The number of beliefs

Now, let's focus on what might happen in the selection of a moving company. This certainly is an apt high-involvement example because of high perceived risk on what will happen to the furniture once choice is made. Research must begin by inquiring about which evaluative criteria or attributes enter into choice. Assume that the following are listed by most people in a given market segment (notice how precisely they are stated): (1) guaranteed prices; (2) on-time pickup and delivery; (3) insurance giving full replacement value if goods are damaged; (4) availability of packing service; (5) friendly employees; and (6) clean vans.

The next step now is to measure how important each benefit is to the consumer. Technically this is known as "attribute salience," and it gives the e score in the above formula. Here is how it is measured using a six-point scale for each attribute:[22]

The total price must be guaranteed in advance

	+3	+2	+1	−1	−2	−3	
Very good	___	___	___	___	___	___	Very bad

This would be done for each of the six attributes, and the higher the positive score, the more important it is that an alternative measure up on that dimension.

The belief that a given company (say company A) actually fills the bill for a given attribute is measured this way:

Company A guarantees total price in advance

	+3	+2	+1	−1	−2	−3	
Very likely	___	___	___	___	___	___	Very unlikely

This, then, measures b_i, and the higher the score in the positive direction, the better the evaluation of a particular company.

The A_B score now is computed by multiplying the e and b components for each belief and then summing across the total number of beliefs (n). This is done for each company, one at a time. Figure 5–5 shows what the resulting data might look like.

The total A_B score for each company was gotten by multiplying e_i by b_i for each company, one attribute at a time, and then adding up

---

[22] These questions follow closely the guidelines given in Fishbein and Ajzen, *Belief, Attitude, Intention, and Behavior.*

FIGURE 5–5
Attitudes (A_B) Toward Three Moving Companies

Attribute	Evaluation (e_i)	Beliefs (b_i)		
		Company A	Company B	Company C
1. Guaranteed prices	+3	−3	−3	−3
2. On-time pickup and delivery	+3	+1	−2	−3
3. Damage replacement insurance	+3	+1	−1	+1
4. Availability of packing service	+3	+3	+3	+3
5. Friendly employees	+1	+1	−1	−3
6. Clean vans .	+1	+3	+1	+1
Total score (A_B)		+10	−9	−10

the total. The score of +10 for company A was arrived at, for example, by starting with guaranteed prices and multiplying +3 by −3, noting the score of −9, and then moving on to on-time pickup and delivery, doing this once again, summing all values.

We can learn a great deal from this table. First, guaranteed prices is an important expected benefit, and no company is seen by consumers as providing what they want. Company A rates reasonably well on the other important attributes, but B and C are not seen as offering on-time service. All three have apparently stressed the availability of packing service in their advertising, so there is no problem there. The last two attributes (friendly employees and clean vans) are much less important. People seem to be saying, "Do what I want on the first four and I won't worry about friendliness or cleanliness." Therefore, the ratings given each company are not of any particular importance with respect to cleanliness or friendliness.

Implications for Promotional Strategy

Figure 5–5 pulls together everything we have been trying to say in this section, so it is helpful to evaluate what the companies might do given their overall evaluations. There are two possibilities: (1) try to change the consumers' evaluative criteria and (2) try to change beliefs.

Changing evaluative criteria (e_i). Company C faces the greatest problems of any of its major competitors. It is evaluated negatively on two important criteria and positively on one which really doesn't matter (clean vans). Perhaps it could try to convince people that a price guarantee really is not that important: "Our estimates are accurate, so don't worry." Or, "It's not reasonable for us to get it there on the exact day. Use our packing service and count on our clean vans to do the job."

Such a strategy is destined for failure. Evaluative criteria have their roots in basic motives and lifestyle. Hence, they can be highly resistant to change when high involvement is present. After all, guaranteed prices and on-time service are not unreasonable to expect, and the industry has been seriously deficient in these respects. It is naive to expect people to change, and it is far better to take these criteria as a given and move from there.

If the frontal attack is tried by company C, one could just imagine the selective information processing which would occur. "Trust your price estimates—who is kidding who? And what do you mean it's not reasonable to expect you there when you promise? Get lost!" The best conclusion is that no amount of advertising or selling can save a product which is improperly positioned with respect to salient evaluative criteria.

This should not be interpreted to mean, however, that people always buy wisely and that their criteria are above reproach. There are times, for example, when subjective criteria such as reputation of manufacturer are substituted for more objective and potentially more valid considerations. Some consumers have come to realize that the chemical formulation of aspirin is guaranteed by government regulation to be essentially the same. Unfortunately many, if not most, buy aspirin on the basis of brand reputation and pay a substantial price premium. Here a strong case can be made for consumer education.

Unfortunately some companies still are fighting consumer education, or at least are hoping that it will go away. What possible objection, for example, can there be to posting octane ratings on the gasoline pump? The manufacturer will be hurt if the consumer uses this objective criterion *only* if it has failed to meet usual industry standards by hiding under the guise of its brand name. It is a poorly kept trade secret that one major company did exactly this in the past while its advertising trumpeted an unsubstantiated claim of quality. Is it any wonder that pressures for consumerism continue to grow?

Changing beliefs (b_i). Coming back now to company C, it needs to assess why it received such low ratings on guaranteed price and on-time performance. Maybe it fails to make the grade in these terms. If so, this is a product problem, not a promotion problem. Assuming the package of services offered really is deficient, it cannot sit back and hope that things will get better. Rather, now is the time to change and make that fact known.

It also is possible that company C just has not told its story. If it can offer these benefits, let that fact be known. If it has changed its service mix as suggested above, advertise that fact. This is precisely the strategy followed by Allied Van Lines to combat a sluggish moving market.[23] They started offering guaranteed prices and guaranteed on-time

23 "Tough Market Forces Allied Pledge," *Advertising Age,* April 12, 1982, p. 12.

pickup and delivery in May 1982 and announced that fact with radio spots run in 200 major markets featuring such celebrities as retired UCLA basketball coach, Johnny Wooden. One wonders, however, why it took a depressed market to force this change.

Company C could, as we suggested earlier, try to make a big thing out of its clean vans. Or company A could have two-page ads showing their friendly employees. Perhaps beliefs can be changed in this way, but what difference would it make on attitude and intention? Probably very little because these benefits are not important.

There is an important lesson to be learned here. *Promote benefits, not product attributes.* Too many firms want to tell their story, building the selling points on what executives think is important. This may make everyone, especially an advertising agency, feel good when it is displayed across the country. But what difference will it make? People are interested only in what it means to them in terms of their expectations. If this point could be grasped and implemented, it is our opinion that promotional effectiveness would double overnight.

Finally, company A is in a relatively strong position, but it may not stay that way forever. It is perceived very well on three of the four determinant attributes, and it can strengthen its market position by reinforcing positive belief levels and beginning to guarantee prices. Simply continue to let the market know what a good job it is doing in providing on-time service and so on, and every other competitor will be playing catch up. By the way, this firm apparently has been doing a fairly good job of knowing what people want and providing it. In short, they are good marketers.

CHOICE AND ITS OUTCOMES

The last two stages of the high-involvement decision process (Figure 5–1) are *choice* and *outcomes* of choice (especially satisfaction or dissatisfaction).

The Choice Process

As Figure 5–1 shows, people usually make their final choice in a manner consistent with purchase intentions, but there are unanticipated circumstances such as lack of funds which could lead to contrary behavior. In-store influences also can have this effect.

Most buying is done in a retail setting, and there is little that need be said about this now, because the subjects of personal selling and sales promotion are covered thoroughly in later chapters. What is of interest here is the growing incidence of in-home buying. Bob Stone estimates that about 12 percent of all consumer purchases were made this way in

1976 and that the total sales volume represented will exceed $120 billion by the end of 1981.[24]

Strategies used to reach consumers in their homes are now referred to as *direct marketing,* defined in this way:

Direct (response) marketing is the total of activities by which products and services are offered to market segments in one or more media for informational purposes, or to solicit a direct response from a present or prospective customer or contributor by mail, telephone, or other access.[25]

So consumers can make use of telephone, mail order, catalogs, door-to-door salespeople, or television. The latter is especially interesting, because it will soon be possible to reproduce any information the consumer wants on a television screen with opportunity for direct response. The generic name for this service is videotex, and one of the most interesting tests has been undertaken in several markets by Warner Communications. It has taken the form of interactive cable television marketed under the trade name QUBE which gives people the opportunity to purchase immediately by pushing a button as an item is displayed on the screen.[26] We are confident that this form of buying will grow rapidly in the future.

No doubt all forms of direct marketing will grow as well. As Stone has noted, changing consumer lifestyles place greater emphasis on leisure time and the desire for convenient shopping.[27] Added to this are growing problems of congested parking lots, uninformed sales personnel, and other irritations encountered at the retail level. Now the technology is available to permit tight market segmentation and personalization, so a whole new era may be opening.

Satisfaction/Dissatisfaction

The extended problem solving undertaken when high involvement is present understandably leads to the expectation that the product or service will perform as intended. When this does not prove to be the case, this expectation is shattered and dissatisfaction results, followed by complaints, diminished brand loyalty, and so on.[28] On the other hand, a confirmed expectation strengthens the probability that the same choice will be made in the future, and this is a valuable asset for any firm.

---

[24] Bob Stone, *Successful Direct Marketing Methods,* 2d ed. (Chicago: Crain Books, 1979), p. 3.

[25] Ibid., p. 3.

[26] Bernard F. Whalen, "Videotex: Moving From Blue Sky to Black Ink," *Marketing News,* October 3, 1980, p. 1.

[27] Stone, *Successful Direct Marketing,* p. 4.

[28] The literature on the issue of satisfaction has burgeoned in recent years. See especially Richard L. Oliver, "Theoretical Bases of Consumer Satisfaction Research: Review, Critique, and Future Direction," in *Theoretical Developments in Marketing,* ed. Charles W. Lamb, Jr., and Patrick M. Dunne (Chicago: American Marketing Association, 1980), pp. 81–84.

The words of Thomas A. Murphy, chairman of General Motors Corporation, are worthy of careful note:

Public sentiment is clearly against big business . . . It has been building for many years, and for a number of reasons—but principally, in my judgment, because business has been falling short of customer expectations. And today's customer dissatisfaction is both the sorry evidence and the sad result. . . . We simply are not being believed . . . We move in the right direction every time we emphasize quality as well as quantity in our products, every time we focus on service as well as sales, every time we welcome criticism and act upon it rather than avoid it and condemn it.[29]

A sober warning is sounded for management. All advertising and selling messages must create realistic expectations consistent with product performance. Unless this is done, the consumer will quickly cast a negative future vote. The Whirlpool Corporation has done this in a new corporate advertising campaign designed to avoid superlatives and exaggerated claims.[30] It says, simply, "We promise to build and sell only good quality, honest appliances designed to give you your money's worth. And we promise to stand behind them."[31]

WHAT DOES IT ALL MEAN FOR PROMOTIONAL STRATEGY?

This has been a long chapter, and the reader understandably may be experiencing some difficulty fitting all the pieces together. So, there is benefit in reviewing the major implications:

1. The best strategy is to focus on people who already are experiencing problem recognition because they will be receptive to what you have to say.
2. Sometimes advertising and selling can help trigger problem recognition, but this is true only when there is an offering of something so new that it provides an altogether different concept of "what might be."
3. An understanding of the sources used by consumers in search behavior is the key to effective media strategy.
4. When high involvement is likely, the print medium offers special benefits because of its processing in the left brain hemisphere. And there is no reason to be afraid of long copy.
5. All things being equal, a change in consumer beliefs about the benefits offered by a product or brand leads to an ultimate change in behavior.

---

[29] Thomas A. Murply, "Businessman, Heal Thyself," *Newsweek,* December 20, 1976, p. 11.

[30] "Whirlpool Promises Quality, Value, Honesty, Service to 'Make Your World a Little Easier,'" *Marketing News,* February 5, 1982, p. 10.

[31] Ibid., p. 10.

6. Advertising should feature benefits, not product attributes per se.
7. A loyal customer is one of the greatest assets, and loyalty can be enhanced by avoiding exaggerated claims which can only lead ultimately to a reaction of dissatisfaction.
8. Attempts to change consumers' evaluative criteria are likely to end in failure.

SUMMARY

This chapter has covered an abbreviated version of the EKB extended problem solving model, and a wealth of material has been covered. All stages were discussed including: problem recognition, search, alternative evaluation, choice, and outcomes of choice (especially the problem of satisfaction). A great many implications for promotional strategy were highlighted, some of which were summarized in the immediately preceding section. Others will be highlighted in later chapters.

Review and Discussion Questions

1. Assume that you are the director of marketing planning for a large cosmetic manufacturer that recently has become the leader in the market for women's electric hair-setting machines. Your product consists of a number of electrically heated curlers which allow the woman to set her hair in 30 minutes or less. Management has suggested that it is necessary to stimulate problem recognition in a larger proportion of the market. What are your recommendations concerning (a) the desirability of stimulating problem recognition, (b) the techniques that should be used for this purpose, and (c) the probability of success?
2. The majority of high-involvement purchases are preceded by external search. Why is this so?
3. An argument can be made for use of long copy advertising in the print media when the purchase has a high degree of involvement. What is the rationale?
4. What is an opinion leader? Do they differ from those they seek to influence? What role do they play in the search process as opposed to consumer advertising and personal selling?
5. What is the two-step hypothesis? Is it an adequate model for the word-of-mouth process? Why or why not?
6. What are evaluative criteria? How are they formed? What is the role they play in decision process?
7. A product which used a synthetic substance as a substitute for leather failed in test market. Consumers said it could not possibly have the same properties as leather. Could this belief be changed through advertising?
8. Before World War II the Customer Research Department of the General Motors Corporation asked consumers to appraise the relative importance

of various product attributes. Dependability and safety usually came out on top followed by price and styling. What uses, if any, can be made of these data?

9. What are the causes of the so-called consumer movement which is leading to current emphasis on consumer education? What role does the business firm play in helping the consumer to buy wisely?

10. There are growing levels of reported consumer dissatisfaction today. What implications does this have for marketing management?

CHAPTER 6

The High-Involvement Decision Process: Social Influences

Thus far high-involvement decision process behavior has been viewed only from the perspective of the individual, but this obviously is incomplete. A person could survive only with great difficulty if forced to cope with the environment without the help and support of others. We exist in a cultural context, and these norms and values affect what we do. Furthermore, people in close contact for extended periods of time have remarkably related preferences and behavior. Their actions are correlated, and this has real significance for the planning of promotional strategy.

This chapter begins with an analysis of social systems which, in effect, provide the setting for behavior: culture, subcultures, and social class. Then the focus shifts to the impact of face-to-face relationships in the form of reference groups and the nuclear family.

THE CULTURAL CONTEXT

The term *culture* is used here to refer to that complex of ideas, values, attitudes, and other meaningful symbols created by people to shape human behavior and the artifacts of that culture as they are passed from one generation to the next.[1] It thus provides a set of norms and shared beliefs

---

[1] Alfred L. Kroeber and Talcott Parsons, "The Concepts of Culture and of Social System," *American Sociological Review* 23 (October 1958), p. 583.

that mold and shape much of what the consumer does. Cultural norms are learned early in life and hence are very resistant to change. Thus, the marketer can do little other than to understand these values and behavioral patterns and adapt to them accordingly.

The Dangers of Ethnocentrism

Some of marketing's greatest blunders have occurred when moving from one culture to another. To take just one example, a canned fish manufacturer naively aired advertising in Quebec showing a woman in shorts golfing with her husband who served canned fish for the evening meal. This effort was a complete flop because of the fact that all three of these activities violate norms of the French-Canadian culture.[2]

Now, why did this happen? Executives wrongly assumed that their understanding of human behavior would hold in another culture. This is referred to as *ethnocentrism,* and it plagues everyone who must work in a culture other than his or her own. Do not assume that this happens only when national boundaries are crossed, because it soon will become evident that it is a very real problem in understanding different generations within the United States.

Understanding the American Culture

The core values of American culture are usually thought to encompass such ideals as achievement and success, efficiency and practicality, progress, material comfort, individualism, freedom, external conformity, humanitarianism, and youthfulness. But these values are not held uniformly in all subgroups, and they are in rapid flux. Understanding the causes of these dynamics is an essential for creative marketing today.

Two different forces must be analyzed to understand the basic values in a total society or subgroup. The first source of values is referred to as the *institutional triad*—families, religious institutions, and schools. The second source is *early lifetime experiences,* including such diversified influences as war, social disturbances, family upheaval, and so on. In turn, institutions such as the media play a vital role in transmitting these values. The way in which values pass from one generation to the next is shown in Figure 6–1, and it is important to understand some of the important trends and their impact on behavior.

Institutional influences.   As long as the institutional triad shown in Figure 6–1 is stable, values will be stable. But when these institutions change, as they have in recent decades, the effects can be dramatic.

---

[2] See David A. Ricks, Jeffrey S. Arpan, and Marilyn Y. Fu, *International Business Blunders* (Columbus, Ohio: Grid Publishing, 1975).

FIGURE 6–1
The Transmission of Values From One Generation to the Next

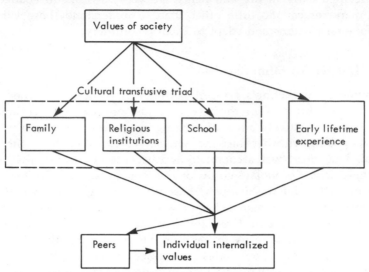

Source: James F. Engel and Roger D. Blackwell, *Consumer Behavior*, 4th ed. (Hinsdale, Ill.: Dryden Press, 1982), p. 195.

Declining family influence. In many societies the extended family is the basic social unit—grandparents, uncles and aunts, and so on. The net effect is that values tend to be stabilized and resistant to change. In Western society, however, the extended family has nearly ceased to exist, with the result that one source of value stability has disappeared.

Even the nuclear family has declined in its influence on children as they are growing up. Over 50 percent of children are now enrolled in preschool or day-care facilities and do not spend formative years with their parents. In addition, about 45 percent of all children will spend at least part of their childhood in a one-parent household. Finally, over 50 percent of wives are now working, and many fathers are employed in professional occupations which have extensive time demands. The result is the rapid increase in "weekend parents." Collectively, these changes have resulted in reduced parent-child involvement and less opportunity for parents to instill their values in offspring. It is small wonder that the values of today's consumers differ from those of their parents.

The changing role of religion. Judeo-Christian religious institutions have traditionally played an important role in shaping American life, but this influence now is a declining one as measured by church membership and attendance. In this same context it should be noted, however, that a rejection of the institution does not necessarily imply diminished interest in the divine or the supernatural. Quite the opposite is true as is indicated by upwards of 40 percent of high school youth engaged in Bible study, interest in occult and eastern religions, and so on.

The decline of the religious institution is best explained by its secularization or loss of function. Francis Schaeffer convincingly argues that religion historically has provided the foundation of values by which justice, science, the arts, and all other cultural dimensions are assessed.[3] Now, he contends, religion has become compartmentalized to the spiritual and has lost its impact on life as a whole. The historic sense of right and wrong thus becomes quite relative, with the ultimate result that anything goes.

The increased role of the educational institution. The vacuum left by these two is increasingly being filled by the schools. First of all, contact with people has been increased through rising preschool and post high school enrollments. Of greater significance, however, are changes within educational methods. The teacher of today is no longer a product of the upper-middle class as once was the case, with the result that a wider spectrum of perspectives and values is communicated. Second, there is a decreased emphasis on description and memorization in favor of analytical approaches questioning old solutions and formulating new ones. Often there are no correct answers, and rigid definitions of right and wrong are viewed as outmoded.

The outcomes. Of the three institutional determinants of value transfusion, two are losing their influence, and the educational institution assumes a more profound role. Traditional value stabilizers have been undermined, with the result that change must be accepted as a way of life.

Intergenerational motivating factors. People are a product of their environment, and they frequently are motivated to achieve as adults what they feel they were deprived of earlier. For this reason, early lifetime experiences become important and explain some important differences between generations.

The pre-World War II generation. About 80 percent of those alive today were not even born during the Great Depression of the 1930s, and most were born even after World War II. But those who lived through these events were profoundly shaped by them. The relative economic deprivation of the Depression and the war led to emphasis on values such as job security, individualism, patriotism, and material achievement. As such, these values undergird strivings to help fill the void of what people lacked as children. The typical American way of life, epitomized in the so-called core American values mentioned earlier, describes this generation, who will respond to products and services compatible with their motivations. Yet, *this generation is a minority,* and their values cannot

---

[3] Francis A. Schaeffer, *How Should We Then Live?* (Old Tappan, N.J.: Fleming H. Revel Company, 1976).

be assumed to apply to generations which follow. Unfortunately, this mistake often is made by senior marketing executives who come from this generation and respond to others in an ethnocentric fashion.

The "interpersonal" generation. This generation experienced their childhood during the 1950s and the 1960s. Their critical lifetime experience was shaped by such factors as the nuclear age, the civil rights movement, the paradox of continued poverty in an economy of affluence, ecological concern, the divisive effects of the Vietnam War, and a revolution in communication technology. The influence of these events has been accentuated by the declining influence of the family and a deprivation centering around the absence of love and meaningful relationships. Thus, for many in this generation, current life motivation centers on love, community, and understanding, as opposed to material achievement and a high standard of living which is *assumed* rather than sought. Marketing appeals based on their parents' values will be rejected as "OK for them but irrelevant for me."

The emerging "me" generation. Those currently in high school and on the college campus show quite a different pattern because their crucial lifetime experiences have been affected by the energy crisis, massive inflation, growing tax burdens, and feminism. Whereas the concern of the generation just before them was how to help others achieve the good life, their concern has shifted to one of *maintaining the good life.* Here are some of the findings from a study by Yankelovich, Skelly & White:

The cornerstone of the new values is a shift from the concept of self-denial to a new focus-on-self . . . The new focus-on-self subsumes, "I have a duty to myself;" and more specifically: self-understanding, self-expression, self-fulfillment, concern with physical self, etc. It means putting yourself either on par with or a little above the others that perhaps you once considered before you yourself.[4]

Hence students have turned back to the study of business and engineering and are placing a premium on achievement and success.

In many ways, this generation parallels the pre-World War II generation, but there are differences. Some of the previous taboos expressed in the traditional rights and wrongs are now accepted as being OK as long as no one gets hurt.

A changing scene. Contemporary American values clearly represent modifications of more long-standing traditions. Some emerging values described here include (1) creative eroticism, (2) the leisure life, (3) the theology of pleasure, and (4) youthfulness. Many other trends could be identified, of course, but space is limited.[5]

---

[4] Florence R. Skelly, "Emerging Attitudes and Life Styles," paper presented to American Association of Advertising Agencies Annual Meeting, White Sulphur Springs, W.Va., May 16–19, 1979.

[5] See especially Arnold Mitchell, *Consumer Values: A Typology* (Menlo Park, Calif.: SRI, 1978).

Creative eroticism. Contemporary society is characterized by a lifting of constraints, especially concerning sex. While this does not necessarily signal great change in behavior, there undeniably is a much greater willingness to talk openly about previously taboo issues.

In a very real sense, contemporary advertising can be characterized as in the midst of a sexual revolution. The type of advertisement presented in Figure 6–2 is now commonplace in even middle-of-the-road magazines. Not surprisingly, the appeal to sex has generated considerable controversy. Some assert that it can only contribute to declining standards of morality.[6] Others justify the emphasis as long as it sells the product. Unfortunately, many who take this latter position never stop to question whether sex is a *relevant* appeal for the product in question. Is it relevant, for example, to sell sun tan lotion on the basis of a sexual suggestion as opposed to featuring such product benefits as protection from burns and moisturizers? There is no doubt that attention will be attracted, but it is an open question whether or not sales will be affected. Unfortunately, sex can become a misused creative gimmick.

Recent evidence suggests that decorative female models in print ads only affect memory of model-related information. This has the positive benefit of increasing the recognition of the entire ad. The sexual stimulus in the ad achieves a greater degree of cognitive processing and therefore, is more likely to be stored and retrieved at a later time. However, associated brand names are processed independently, with the result that they are not more likely to be remembered than brand names in ads not featuring a decorative model.[7] Without looking back at Figure 6–2, can you name the brand in the ad, or its main feature or selling point?

It is incorrect, however, to claim that the use of sex in advertising, in itself, is contributing greatly to moral decline. It must not be overlooked that this appeal was almost totally unused in earlier decades for the reason that social values were greatly different. Any sexually related advertisements probably would meet with selective attention, comprehension, and retention. On the other hand, there is no question that uninhibited sexuality is given endorsement when it is so widely seen in the mass media, and this may serve to accentuate what many view as a socially deleterious decline in morals. Thus it should be used only where it is appropriate to the product in question, and then with discretion.

The leisure life. One major change is less emphasis on the values of hard work and long hours and a correspondingly greater emphasis upon leisure. Justin Voss offers this insightful comment: *"Leisure* is a period of time referred to as *discretionary time.* It is that period of time when an

---

[6] See for example Kathy McNeel, "You Dirty Old Ad Men Make Me Sick," *Detroit News,* November 25, 1969.

[7] Robert W. Chestnut, Charles C. Lachance, and Amy Lubitz, "The 'Decorative' Female Model: Sexual Stimuli and The Recognition of Advertisements," *Journal of Advertising* 6, no. 4 (1977), pp. 11–14.

FIGURE 6–2
An Appeal to Sex

Announcing the Sensuous Tan.
Its secret is Tropic Sun with Aloe.

You want a deep, dark sensuous tan. And you want it fast. But first you must know the secret: Tropic Sun™ with Aloe.

Smooth it on all over. Its deliciously rich coconut scent is only a hint of what's to come. Feel your skin drink in the luscious tropical oils of coconut, sweet almond and eucalyptus. Now feel the soft, smooth touch of aloe. You're on your way to the Sensuous Tan. You and Tropic Sun with Aloe.

TROPIC SUN with ALOE

In lotion, oil, butter and after tanning moisturizer

Sea & Ski Corporation
a SmithKline company

©Sea & Ski Corp. 1978

Courtesy Sea & Ski Corporations

individual feels no sense of economic, legal, moral, or social compulsion or obligation nor of physiological necessity. The choice of how to utilize this time period is solely his."[8]

Thus the budget of time available for leisure may be a more significant factor in buying and consumption than the budget of available money. Time-saving appliances, for example, assume a new importance, and consumers are prepared to pay the monetary cost in return for increased leisure. Longer vacations, earlier retirement, more holidays are becoming more common, as is the four-day work week. Henry Ford said in 1926 that, "It is the influence of leisure on consumption which makes the short day and the short week so necessary."

The theology of pleasure.   Traditionally, the American religious heritage has emphasized the worth of an individual, and values have developed which condone consumption of products for reasons of self-interest and fulfillment of reasonable physical needs. It has been stressed that the ways to achieve these goal objects are hard work and the accumulation of wealth. It is this set of values, often identified as the Puritan ethic, which is under increasing challenge in today's culture.

The Puritan ethic is being replaced with a theology of pleasure, which releases prohibitions on pleasure and challenges the legitimacy of delayed gratification. The demand for leisure, of course, is just one expression of this new theology. It also is manifested in such things as the general acceptance of bright and sensual colors, and cosmetics which emphasize bodily pleasure (Figure 6–3 is an example). Also products for personal use which previously would not even be hinted at in intimate conversation, now appear in the mass media. Male and female hygiene products are noteworthy examples.

Youthfulness.   At one time, the aged were objects of veneration and prestige. Experience with life brought respect and considerable social influence. Today the primacy of experience has been usurped by education and creativity, so that the educated college graduate may receive greater prestige and influence than the seasoned senior executive. The result is that the young are increasingly being given responsibility for running society in general, as well as its institutions.

The social rewards for youthfulness generate powerful motivations to appear as youthful, regardless of chronological age. Figure 6–4 shows an advertisement which capitalizes on this desire. Another illustration is provided by the market acceptance of a sporty compact car with an image of racing and sensuality. Although this car was introduced as a direct appeal to youth, the age of the typical buyer turned out to be 46!

Marketing and the question of values.   Since our discussion has only been suggestive of the basic values of American culture and their influence

---

[8] Justin Voss, "The Definition of Leisure," *Journal of Economic Issues* 1 (1967), pp. 91–106.

FIGURE 6–3
An Appeal to Bodily Pleasure

Courtesy the Adidas Company

FIGURE 6–4
An Appeal to Youthfulness

Courtesy Palmer & Lord, Ltd.

on buyer behavior, the reader is encouraged to explore this subject more deeply.[9] Up to this point it has been assumed that the business firm must adapt to culture and that an individual organization is powerless to bring about much change. This assumption is sharply challenged by some critics, however. Some allege that marketing is largely responsible for certain adverse aspects of the world as we know it today. Advertising, in particular, is identified as the villain that has brought undue emphasis on materialism, youthfulness, and so on. It cannot be denied that the sheer volume of marketing stimuli will have some influence in this manner, but it is quite another matter to argue, for example, that marketing *causes* materialism.

It must be remembered that consumers retain the powers to screen out unwanted appeals through selective perception. Given this pervasive human response to unwanted stimuli, it is fallacious to claim that advertising and other forms of promotion have caused materialism. Striving for a high and rising standard of living is a basic motivation, and promotional efforts are only a reflection of the fact that this is basic to our way of life. In the most basic sense, *marketing reflects the values of a society.* If present consumption patterns and emphases may lead to long-run adverse effects, the primary blame lies in the area of human values, not in the practices of business firms.

SUBCULTURES

Within society as a whole there are many subcultures or groups with a distinct set of values and norms shaped by nationality, religion, geographical areas, or race. Often these form important markets in their own right. Geographic segmentation is discussed in Chapter 8, and it is helpful here to describe briefly the consumer motivations and behavior found in the fastest growing minority group in America—the Hispanic market.

In the early 1970s, people of Spanish extraction (Spanish-Americans, Cubans, and Puerto Ricans) comprised about 4 percent of total population and were not looked upon by many firms as being a viable market segment. But high fertility and immigration levels have caused total numbers to grow to about 17 million or 7 percent of the population. In fact, Hispanics outnumber blacks in 18 states and represent more than one out of five in both Texas and California.[10]

---

[9] For a thorough review, see Engel and Blackwell, *Consumer Behavior,* chaps. 4 and 7.

[10] Reid T. Reynolds, Bryant Robey, and Cheryl Russell, "Demographics of the 1980s," *American Demographics* (January 1980), pp. 11–19 and Supplement to *American Demographics* (April 1981), p. 2. For additional demographic materials, see Roberto Anson, "Hispanics in the United States: Yesterday, Today, and Tomorrow," *The Futurist* (August 1980), pp. 25–31 and Stephanie Ventura and Robert Heuser, "Births of Hispanic Parentage," *Monthly Vital Statistics Report* (March 20, 1981).

Most Hispanics are bilingual, but it is a great mistake to assume that they may be communicated with adequately in English. About 94 percent speak Spanish in the home, and most think in Spanish. Thus, marketers must use both the Spanish language and its thought forms.[11]

Some products have been successfully adapted to this market, although this never should be tried without prior testing. Cudahy, for example, introduced a premium bacon under the brand name Rex, and it was marketed on the premise that a lean, premium product could be offered in a 12-ounce package at a price comparable to the largest competitor's 16-ounce package. The package bannered the message, "Valo Su Peso En Carne." And Gillette razors have been promoted with Spanish models in appropriate Hispanic settings. The appeals used generally are educational in nature, involving a simple but direct hard sell.[12]

Hispanic values and motivations present some pitfalls to the unwary, however. While others might be interested in the health benefit touted by Colgate toothpaste, the Hispanic is more interested in personal appearance. Similarly, Best Foods found that Mazola corn oil cannot be marketed with a health claim as it is elsewhere because those in this segment are more interested in how it tastes rather than low cholesterol.

Other lessons have been learned as well. Bulova achieved a 40 percent market share by positioning its watch through Hispanic media as an expensive but affordable piece of jewelry. In so doing, it positioned itself squarely on target with the desires of the newly emigrated to acquire status symbols which show that they have arrived. These same people are not especially receptive to coupons and price appeals. They run directly counter to the motivations of those who are now making a better living. Understandably they do not want to use coupons which are "for people who can't afford to pay the full price."[13]

SOCIAL CLASS

One of the useful ways to stratify a society is in terms of social class. Social classes are large and relatively permanent groupings within society which have the function of transmitting cultural patterns in such a way that family members have a more or less clearly defined set of expectations about life. People within a class, in other words, *tend* to behave in like manner. Although America is often thought of as being classless, quite the opposite is true, and the differences between classes offer some insights for promotional strategy.

---

[11] Jim Sondheim, Rodd Rodriguez, Richard Dillon, Richard Paredes, "Hispanic Marketing—the Invisible Giant," *Advertising Age,* April 16, 1979, S–2.

[12] "Hispanic Marketing," *Advertising Age,* April 16, 1981, pp. S–1 to S–24.

[13] These examples come from Luiz Diaz-Albertini, "Brand-Loyal Hispanics Need Good Reason for Switching," *Advertising Age,* April 16, 1979, pp. S–22 and S–23.

Social Classes in America

Broadly speaking, an individual's social position is determined by (1) occupational prestige; (2) performance within occupational class as evaluated by others; (3) social interaction and acceptance; (4) possessions; (5) value orientations; and (6) class consciousness. Of these factors, occupation is now felt to be the most accurate predictor. After all, what is the first question people usually ask of one another? "What do you do for a living?" And there is a definite hierarchy of occupational prestige. Income, by the way, no longer is a valid measure in and of itself. This is not surprising when a driver for the Chicago Transit Authority (CTA) can make more than a full professor at a local college or university.

Here are some rough and reasonably accurate indications of the social class structure in America:

1. *Upper-upper*—roughly 1 percent. This is the social elite characterized by inherited wealth.
2. *Lower-upper*—1 to 2 percent. Often called the *nouveaux riches,* members of this class have earned their wealth and position and hence do not have the prestige of those in the upper-upper stratum.
3. *Upper-middle*—10–21 percent. Comprised largely of successful professionals and businesspersons, members of this class have a way of life centered around career, education, and consumption of quality items.
4. *Lower-middle*—28–30 percent. This group is most often described as the typical Americans. The home is very important; occupation is usually white collar.
5. *Upper-lower*—35–45 percent. This is the largest segment; it is characterized by blue-collar occupations and lack of change in life. This group is discussed in more detail below.
6. *Lower-lower*—10–25 percent. These are the true "forgotten Americans"—the slum dwellers with poor educations.

While class consciousness is probably less in the United States than in some parts of the world, it is by no means absent, especially among those in higher classes. This suggests that firms with market targets in the upper classes must base what they do on knowledge of lifestyle. Members of the working class are not likely to respond positively to the ad in Figure 6–5. One could not imagine very many who wear a tux and toss around terms such as "Leroux Creme de Cassis."

Social Class and Consumer Lifestyle and Behavior

There have been a number of studies demonstrating differences between various classes in consumer decision-making and behavior.[14] Be-

---

[14] See Engel and Blackwell, *Consumer Behavior,* chap. 5.

FIGURE 6–5

Courtesy General Wine & Spirits Co.

cause of space limitations the working class is used as an illustration.[15]

In earlier decades the working-class housewife traditionally was characterized as one who centered her values and social life on the home. A feeling of uncertainty and reluctance to think for herself often was manifested in reliance on national brands and other buying patterns which gave a greater sense of certainty. The home orientation, in turn, was reflected in the high premium placed on the latest in labor-saving appliances and ways to make otherwise dull surroundings as attractive as possible.

More recent findings show some dramatic changes in this pattern. First, the working-class wife shows a new confidence in her ability as a consumer and will not accept advertising she feels is trying to disparage her. Second, the emphasis is now on a much smaller family, which reflects a modification of the traditional orientation toward the home. Women in this class appear to have been influenced by the liberation movement to the extent that they are not willing to be enslaved by the home. This does not mean, however, that children and the home are unimportant; rather it is a sign that horizons have broadened.

The market for convenience foods and labor-saving appliances is even greater now than it was in the past, but the reason is that these products facilitate the expanded role of the woman both inside and outside the home. Furthermore, she is now more concerned with personal care and grooming, and here is another market opportunity.

Careful attention must be paid to media choice. *Cosmopolitan* or *The New Yorker* reaches a class segment which is totally different, whereas *True Story* may be quite appropriate.

This short example should make it clear that buyers can be affected by social class in ways which are important for promotion. This has ramifications both for media and creative strategies.

REFERENCE GROUPS

A reference group is any interacting aggregation of people *that influences an individual's attitudes or behavior.* The use of the term *group* may be misleading, because a single individual can perform this function, so we really are focusing on social influence in a more general sense. A reference group may either be primary, secondary, or aspirational. A primary group is one that is small enough so all members can communicate with each other face-to-face. Secondary groups are social organizations where less

---

[15] Adapted from Lee Rainwater, Richard P. Coleman, and Gerald Handel, *Workingman's Wife* (Dobbs Ferry, N.Y.: Oceana Publications, 1959) and updated by a 1973 study by Social Research, Inc., reported in *Advertising Age,* October 8, 1973, p. 33. Although this information is dated, the lifestyle described has not changed much in the following decade.

face-to-face interaction takes place (union, church, profession). Finally, an aspirational group is one to which an individual aspires to join or associate.

Normative versus Comparative Reference Groups

Sensitivity to the reactions of others may take a variety of forms. First, an individual may be motivated to conform when others are in a position to exert rewards or punishments. Some church groups perform this role, for example. Other people then serve as a *normative reference group.* This is the type of social influence depicted in the model of consumer behavior appearing in Figure 5–1. At other times, the group may be used simply as evidence about reality. The buyer of a new suit may observe what others are wearing in order to discover the latest styles, while feeling perfectly free to buy what he likes. In this example, other people serve as a *comparative reference group.*

How can we detect whether such influences exist and the form they take? It is helpful to refer back once again to the Fishbein Behavioral Intentions Model. Thus far it has been used only with respect to belief, attitude, and intention; but Fishbein has postulated that attitude toward behavior (A_B) and subjective norms (SN) must be taken together before it is possible to predict a person's intentions to act.[16] The reader will recall that this formula is used:

$$B \approx BI = w_1 (A_B) + w_2 (SN)$$

where:

B = Overt behavior
BI = Behavioral intention
A_B = Attitude toward performing the behavior
SN = The subjective norm
$\begin{matrix} w_1 \\ w_2 \end{matrix}$ = Empirically determined weights

The subjective norm component represents the person's evaluation of what other people think he or she should do. Thus, it is a function of their *beliefs* about others' expectations and their motivation to *comply*. SN is computed in this way:

$$SN = \sum_{j=1}^{n} NB_j MC_j$$

---

[16] Martin Fishbein and Icek Ajzen, *Belief, Attitude, Intention and Behavior: An Introduction to Theory and Research* (Reading, Mass.: Addison-Wesley, 1975), p. 301 and following.

where:

SN = Subjective norm

NB_j = Normative belief (belief that others think he or she should or should not perform the given behavior)

MC_j = Motivation to comply with the influence of referent j

n = Number of relevant groups or individuals.

Here is how SN might be measured using the example of selection of a moving company, the example we followed in the previous chapter:[17]

My closest friends think I

	+3	+2	+1	−1	−2	−3	
should	___	___	___	___	___	___	should not

use company A when I move.

Motivation to comply is assessed in this way:

In general

	+3	+2	+1	−1	−2	−3	
I want to do	___	___	___	___	___	___	I want to do the opposite of

what my closest friends think I should do.

These scores would be multiplied and summed for all potential reference groups which might apply in this situation.

There is little reason, by the way, to suspect that SN will have much influence on the selection of a moving company. Even if friends have an opinion, the majority of people probably would make their decision on the other factors measured with respect to A_B (referring back to the discussion in Chapter 5).

Practical Implications

Figure 6–6 provides an interesting set of reasons as to why there might be reference group influence on a particular buying decision. In probably the most influential study undertaken on this topic to date, however, Burnkrant and Cousineau found that people are most likely to accept the views of others as being relevant when they are unable to assess product attributes and performance from direct observation and experience.[18] They may conform, not to avoid punishment, but rather to acquire what they conceive to be a good product. Hence, it is most probable that comparative reference group influence is of the greatest marketing significance.

---

[17] Ibid., p. 301 and following.

[18] Robert Burnkrant and Alain Cousineau, "Informational and Normative Social Influence in Buyer Behavior," *Journal of Consumer Research,* December, 1975, pp. 206–15.

FIGURE 6–6
Ways in which Reference Groups Influence Brand Decisions

Informational Influence
1. The individual seeks information about various brands of the product from an association of professionals or independent group of experts.
2. The individual seeks information from those who work with the product as a profession.
3. The individual seeks brand-related knowledge and experience (such as how Brand A's performance compares to Brand B's) from those friends, neighbors, relatives, or work associates who have reliable information about the brands.
4. The brand which the individual selects is influenced by observing a seal of approval of an independent testing agency (such as Good Housekeeping).
5. The individual's observation of what experts do influences his choice of a brand (such as observing the type of car which police drive or the brand of TV which repairmen buy).

Utilitarian Influence
1. To satisfy the expectations of fellow work associates, the individual's decision to purchase a particular brand is influenced by their preferences.
2. The individual's decision to purchase a particular brand is influenced by the preferences of people with whom he has social interaction.
3. The individual's decision to purchase a particular brand is influenced by the preferences of family members.
4. The desire to satisfy the expectations which others have of him has an impact on the individual's brand choice.

Value-Expressive Influence
1. The individual feels that the purchase or use of a particular brand will enhance the image which others have of him.
2. The individual feels that those who purchase or use a particular brand possess the characteristics which he would like to have.
3. The individual sometimes feels that it would be nice to be like the type of person which advertisements show using a particular brand.
4. The individual feels that the people who purchase a particular brand are admired or respected by others.
5. The individual feels that the purchase of a particular brand helps him show others what he is, or would like to be (such as an athlete, successful businessman, good mother, etc.).

Source: C. Whan Park and V. Parker Lessig, "Students and Housewives: Differences in Susceptibility to Reference Group Influence," *Journal of Consumer Research*, September 1977, p. 105. Used by special permission.

Nevertheless, the expectations of others still can be an important factor in the choice decision. Sometimes a certain product or brand is used simply because it is the in thing to do. This is especially likely when the product is highly visible and when its use may say something to others about the individual. In this sense, it refers in some way to a sense of self-esteem. When this is known to be the case, the promotional strategy is pretty obvious. Witness the success of Michelob, deliberately positioned as a premium beer to be served on those "special occasions," putting a "little weekend in your week." (See Figure 6–7.)

The above example, of course, assumes a degree of normative influence, and the marketer is well-advised to capitalize upon that fact. But what is the best strategy when the influence is only comparative? Here there

108

Courtesy Anheuser Busch, Inc.

is an informational vacuum, and others' opinions are used mostly as just another information source. Other than making reference to the fact that "everyone's doing it," the advertiser is better off stressing primary benefits and making them the main appeal. Remember, there is no particular motivation here to follow social influence, so it is difficult to argue that this then should be the source of a primary promotional appeal.

FAMILY INFLUENCES

The family, in contrast to most of the larger social systems discussed in this chapter, is a *primary group,* characterized by face-to-face association and cooperation. It is a special reference group. This means that the family is uniquely important in determining individual personality and attitudes. The family also differs in that it is both an earning and a consuming unit. Finally, it serves to filter the norms and values of larger social systems so that these influences upon the individual often are altered.

In this section, the significance of the family in the decision process is the primary consideration. Two aspects in particular are relevant: (1) effects on individual predisposition and (2) family role structures in household decision making.

Effects on the Individual

The family is a primary group with continuous person-to-person interaction. As a unit it shares financial resources and has common consumption needs. Thus, motives of family members become more homogeneous than do those of members of other groups. At times, however, there will be conflict in motives of individual members, with the result that purchase decisions will generate conflict. For promotional planning it is necessary to know which motives are operative and the degree to which they are unique to the individual or common to family members. When they are unique to the individual, of course, appeal will be made only to that person. Where motives are shared without conflict, appeal is made to all members in common. The problem arises when conflict exists, as it might, for example, when one spouse prefers cultural activities for recreation and the other prefers sports. The best promotional strategy might be to legitimize the motive of each member (for example, the husband needs golf to relax) and communicate this to the family as a whole.

A considerable degree of attitude convergence exists in most families as individuals interact with each other. Moreover, attitudes may exist in harmony or in conflict. In some situations the attitudes of other family members will not be taken into account; in others, they will be highly relevant. It appears that the extent to which one individual considers others' attitudes in a given purchase is a function of: (1) the individual's decision-making competence, (2) cultural norms clarifying which members should dominate, (3) the individual's needs for power and affiliation, and (4) the extent to which others contribute economic and social resources to the family.

Unfortunately, the process of family decision making has not been extensively investigated, and it is difficult to generalize how conflict situations become resolved. There are a number of purchases, however, in which the family functions as a unit, in which case promotional strategy must be based on evidence concerning the interaction process.

Family Role Structures

Role structure refers to the behavior of family members at each stage in the decision process. There are the following possibilities: (1) autonomic—equal number of decisions made by each spouse; (2) husband dominant; (3) wife dominant; and (4) syncratic—most decisions made by both partners.[19] Of course, these may vary from product to product.

Bases of role structure variations. All societies have different roles for men and women, and it is common for the male to take leadership in task fulfillment, whereas the wife more often functions to bring about family cohesion and morale.[20] But these general role specifications differ in such subcultures as the black market, where the mother often must serve as family leader. Moreover, the role of each member changes throughout the family life cycle. As the length of a marriage increases, for example, the degree of joint decision making decreases as each member gains competence.[21] Other factors also intervene, such as social class and geographical location.[22] Also, in American society women are more and more taking equal positions with men. However, there are still significant role positions in purchase decisions.

Variations by product and stage in decision. Figures 6–8 and 6–9 contain material in summary form documenting how role structures vary by product and by stage in the decision process. The figures are based upon research done by Davis and Rigaux.[23] They distinguished three phases in purchase decisions: (1) problem recognition, (2) search for infor-

---

[19] See P. G. Herbst, "Conceptual Framework for Studying the Family," in *Social Structure and Personality in a City*, ed. O. A. Oeser and S. B. Hammond (London: Routledge and Kegan Paul, 1954).

[20] See Bernard A. Berelson and Gary A. Steiner, *Human Behavior* (New York: Harcourt Brace Jovanovich, 1964), p. 314.

[21] Elizabeth H. Wolgast, "Do Husbands or Wives Make Purchasing Decisions?" *Journal of Marketing* 23 (October 1958), pp. 151–58.

[22] See Engel and Blackwell, *Consumer Behavior*, chap. 6.

[23] Harry L. Davis and Benny P. Rigaux, "Perception of Martial Roles In Decision-Processes," *Journal of Consumer Research* 1 (June 1974), pp. 51–61.

FIGURE 6–8
Marital Roles in 25 Decisions

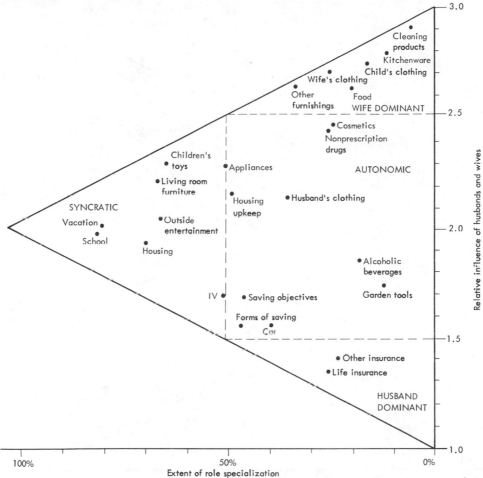

mation, and (3) final decision. Figure 6–8 shows roles at the problem recognition stages. Comparison of Figure 6–8 and Figure 6–9 shows clearly how roles change through the phases of a purchase decision. The latter figure shows how roles change between the search and the decision stages. By examining the two figures one can follow the role structure for the various products. For example, a car is autonomic in problem recognition, husband dominant in search, and syncratic in final decision, whereas food is wife dominant at all stages.

Some generalizations are possible. It seems that the greater the price

FIGURE 6–9
Changes in Marital Roles between Phases 2 and 3

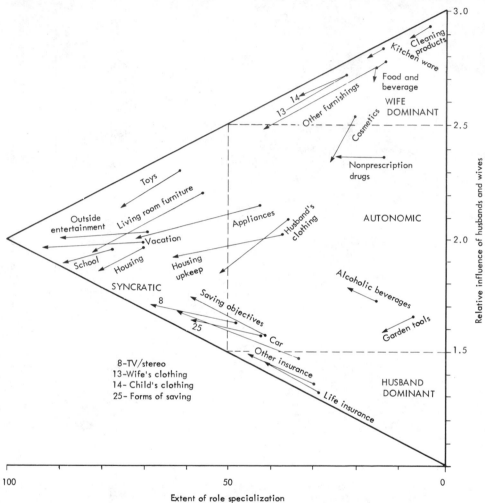

Source: Harry L. Davis and Benny P. Rigaux, "Perception of Marital Roles in Decision Processes." *Journal of Consumer Research* 1 (June 1974), p. 54. Reprinted with permission from the *Journal of Consumer Research.*

of the item, the greater the tendency for the husband to be involved. Automobiles and insurance are examples. Also, the extent of involvement seems to vary according to cultural norms of specialization, such as, in our culture, the interest of the husband when the product is technically or mechanically complex. Wives' participation seems to vary less across products than does the participation of husbands.

Husbands are more involved in evaluation of alternatives when the product attains some complexity. Yet in absolute terms wives are more involved in this stage of the decision process than are husbands.

Finally, the wife is most frequently involved in the actual purchase, and it is not uncommon for her to be designated as the *household purchasing agent*. This designation does vary substantially from product to product, however, as is indicated by the data in Figure 6–8.

It should be stressed that the results in Figures 6–8 and 6–9 are only rough indicators, and it is probable that there is wide interfamily variation. Stage in lifecycle, for example, is a variable which will account for a number of differences. The biggest problem with these results is that over the next decade, the changing roles of men and women in the family may change these research findings to a great degree.

Implications of family role structures. Family role structures are of importance in determining, first, who should be the primary recipient of promotional messages. Second, the type of information featured will vary depending upon the role each member assumes. The wife may be more interested in the convenience features and space in the automobile, and advertisements with this type of emphasis should be designed with female influence in mind. The husband, on the other hand, will generally be more concerned with performance and should be appealed to in these terms. Many other examples could be given.

SUMMARY

This chapter has analyzed the nature and effects on social influence which evolve from culture, social class, reference groups, and family. A promotional program cannot disregard these factors because social influence often is of major importance in the purchasing decision.

This chapter could, of course, only highlight some of the major generalizations from a wealth of research findings. The serious student of consumer behavior will find a vast literature on this subject. Moreover, no direct attention has been paid to the methodological problems which plague research in this area. These difficulties, however, are not sufficient to prevent collection and use of information on social influences. The major strategic implications discussed here should provide the framework for part of the research inquiry underlying every program of promotional strategy.

Review and Discussion Questions

1. A well-known business executive made the following statement: "Oh the youth of today are no different from when I was a kid. They will take their place in the business world, and things will carry on. All this stuff about a youth market is just a bunch of bunk." Evaluate.

2. Assume that you are in the position of explaining the traditional Judeo-Christian view of creation to a group of high school seniors today. This viewpoint stresses that God created the world and that evolution is, as yet, an unproved hypothesis. Would you approach the youth of today in a manner different from the approach used for the youth of another generation? If so, how and why?

3. The manufacturer of a new brand of soft drink wishes to gain a high degree of acceptance among black consumers in large cities. An advertising strategy is contemplated which will be directed specifically at this group. Is this advisable? What policy recommendations would you make?

4. What variables determine social class? How should they be ranked in importance?

5. The manufacturer of a nationally distributed washday detergent has asked you, as his director of marketing research, to evaluate possible social class influences on use of the product. Would product preferences and consumption patterns vary between social classes? Why, or why not?

6. The operator of a large discount chain is contemplating opening a store in the inner-city area. What precautions would you recommend she take?

7. The manufacturer of a well-known make of electric range is introducing a new model. This model is improved by the addition of a new automatic timing system and a dual oven which allows the user to bake at two different temperatures at the same time. Unfortunately, the price is $200 higher than existing models. It is believed, therefore, that promotion should be aimed toward upper-middle-class families. Do you concur? Why, or why not?

8. For which of the following products is reference group influence most likely? (a) canned peaches; (b) diet cola; (c) color television; (d) men's suits; and (e) dining room furniture.

9. Assume that a manufacturer is interested in assessing the influence of reference groups in evaluating why a new automotive diagnostic center has been unsuccessful. The center features a process whereby an automobile is diagnosed mechanically and an objective indication is given of necessary repairs. The price for diagnosis is $9.95. What would your hypothesis be regarding the probable influence of reference groups on consumer choice?

10. From an individual's point of view, how does family influence differ from other groups' influence?

11. A manufacturer of wallpapers observes that in many families the attitudes of several family members are operative but incompatible during the purchase process. Why might this be? How will this affect promotional strategy?

CHAPTER 7

The Low-Involvement Decision Process

"Like the snapped fingers of a hypnotist, Aloe & Lanolin Skin Conditioning Lotion, marketed by Andrew Jergens Company, Cincinnati, awakened the hand care market in 1981 after several years of deep sleep." So read a glowing trade report of this new Jergens product first mentioned in Chapter 4.[1]

The company faced a dilemma, because Vaseline Intensive Care and Jergens Lotion dominated the market prior to 1981, followed by Procter & Gamble's Wondra and many others. What can it do to gain market share? Probably Jergens Lotion was in a relatively stationary position, but a new product might cannabilize sales from it. Therefore, it would be necessary to appeal to a different segment to minimize this danger. Aloe & Lanolin was designed to lean more toward a therapeutic benefit, as opposed to the cosmetic appeal of the parent product.

Aloe & Lanolin was subjected to three years of test markets. One experiment showed that it was preferred over Vaseline Intensive Care on 18 of 18 product attributes after two weeks of use. Later it was introduced nationwide on a mass basis backed by a national television spot campaign supported by newspaper ads offering a coupon. Along with this was extensive point-of-sale promotion. The result? There is every

---

[1] " 'Thoroughly' Researched Aloe & Lanolin Stirs Competition in Hand Care Market," *Marketing News*, December 25, 1981, p. 4.

reason to expect that the product will exceed the number three competitive position it attained in test market.

This product category is low involvement for most people. In other words, they use what's available as long as it does the job. The promotional strategy required here differs sharply from that discussed in the previous two chapters. It is the purpose of this chapter to provide an overview of decision making under low involvement and to stress the marketing implications. Fortunately much of the foundation was previously laid in Chapter 4; therefore this chapter will be relatively short.

POINTS OF DIFFERENCE

What makes low involvement different? First, it is not a routinized or habitual decision which takes place after brand loyalty has been established through a previous extended decision process. This, of course, does happen, in which case the decision process takes the form of the model in Figure 7–1. Here problem recognition immediately leads to choice for the reason that there is high loyalty surrounding a preferred alternative that is continually reinforced through satisfactory use.

Olshavsky and Granbois put their finger on the real issues here:

A significant proportion of purchases may not be preceded by a decision process. This conclusion does not simply restate the familiar observation that purchase behavior rapidly becomes habitual, with little or no pre-purchase processes occur-

FIGURE 7–1
A Routine Decision Process
Based on High Involvement

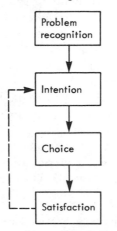

Source: James F. Engel and Roger D. Blackwell, *Consumer Behavior,* 4th ed. (Hinsdale, Ill.: Dryden Press, 1982), p. 34. Used by special permission.

FIGURE 7–2
The Low-Involvement Decision Process

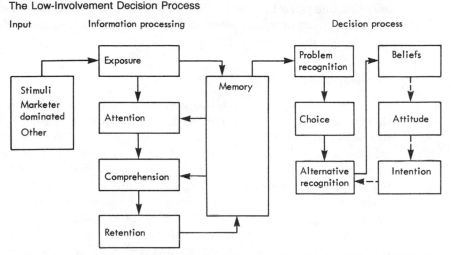

Source: James F. Engel and Roger D. Blackwell, *Consumer Behavior*, 4th ed. (Hinsdale, Ill.: Dryden Press, 1982), p. 543. Used by special permission.

ring after the first few purchases. We conclude that for many purchases a decision process never occurs, not even on the first purchase.[2]

What the authors are saying is that problem recognition leads directly to choice oftentimes with no intervening alternative evaluation. This is precisely what happens under low involvement as the model in Figure 7–2 shows.

Why is a product such as Aloe & Lanolin low involvement for many consumers? The fact is that the whole product class is not one characterized by high personal relevance for many people.[3] So the brand doesn't perform as claimed? So what? There is little perceived risk that there will be severe consequences if the product does not live up to expectations,[4] nor are there greater anxieties about the outcome.[5] Finally, it is not likely that hand lotion is intimately related to one's self concept so that just the "right" purchase must be made (except perhaps for those

[2] Richard W. Olshavsky and Donald H. Granbois, "Consumer Decision-Making—Fact or Fiction?" *Journal of Consumer Research,* 6 (September 1979), p. 93.

[3] Richard E. Petty and John T. Capicoppo, "Issue Involvement as a Moderator of the Effects on Attitude of Advertising Content and Context," in *Advances in Consumer Research,* vol. 8, ed. Kent B. Monroe (Ann Arbor, Mich.: Association for Consumer Research, 1981), pp. 20–24.

[4] Richard Vaughn, "The Consumer Mind: How to Tailor Ad Strategies," *Advertising Age,* June 9, 1980, pp. 45–46.

[5] John L. Lastovicka and David M. Gardner, "Components of Involvement," in *Attitude Research Plays for High Stakes,* ed. John C. Maloney and Bernard Silverman (Chicago: American Marketing Association, 1979), pp. 53–73.

who see their hands as being the key to youthfulness and hence use only that one perfect brand of dish detergent).[6] There will be no extensive problem solving here, and alternative evaluation will take place *after* purchase rather than *before.*

Information Processing

It is necessary only to restate the main conclusions of Chapter 4. First, there is no active search, with the result that attention to marketing stimuli is *involuntary.* Perceptual barriers are not high, and information enters into memory without having much effect on cognitive structure. It seems to be stored in the right brain hemisphere rather than the left which is the seat of rational problem solving.[7] Therefore, the information is stored in the form of holistic and largely visual impressions without the individual having awareness that this is taking place. What happens is that there is passive low-level learning which bypasses the yielding/acceptance stage which is so important in high involvement. The outcome is stored information which may become activated at a later time and serve as a trigger on product trial.

Problem Recognition

It is doubtful that problem recognition occurred when the consumer first saw ads for Aloe & Lanolin. Rather, it is more likely that some evidenced low-level interest stating "this might be worth looking into." In fact, that is about the most that can be expected.

For most people, problem recognition is triggered by depletion of the existing stock of hand lotion. A mental note is made to pick up something the next time there is a chance.

Choice

Choice more often than not occurs when the product is seen at retail through display or other means intended to serve as a remainder and trigger for trial. The risk is low so why not try the product?

Alternative Evaluation

The brand is evaluated during its use. Probably only one or two major attributes or evaluative criteria are used, and it is likely that one of the

---

[6] Vaugh, "The Consumer Mind."

[7] Flemming Hansen, "Hemispheral Lateralization: Implications for Understanding Consumer Behavior," *Journal of Consumer Research* 8 (June 1981), pp. 23–26.

so-called *noncompensatory* methods of alternative evaluation will be followed.[8] In the noncompensatory approach weakness in one attribute is not compensated for by strengths of another as tends to happen in extended problem solving. In other words, Aloe & Lanolin might be rejected if the consumer thinks it does not leave her hands feeling soft, no matter what other benefits it offers. Here are the major variations in this approach to alternative evaluation:

1. *Conjunctive.* Minimum acceptable levels are established for each important attribute, and a brand is rejected if it falls below on any attribute.
2. *Disjunctive.* Select the first alternative to exceed the minimum specified level on any attribute.
3. *Lexicographic.* The brand that dominates on the most important criterion is the winner.
4. *Sequential Elimination.* One attribute is selected for use and alternatives falling below minimum cutoff point are eliminated. Then processing proceeds to the next attribute.

The outcome is change of an existing belief or formation of a new belief that the product fills the bill in terms of the most salient attributes. This then is followed by a favorable attitude and an intention to repurchase once the supply is used up. Apparently this is what has happened with Aloe & Lanolin judging by the market position it has attained.

Jergens' management should not rest on their laurels, however, because brand loyalty is pretty shaky under low involvement. The consumer may repurchase for now, but there is nothing stopping her from trying something else tomorrow if it promises even greater benefits. Brand switching is commonplace, and it often is triggered by couponing, price reductions, and so on.

PRECHOICE INFLUENCES THE DECISION

Advertising and sales promotion emerge as the two best strategies. The latter subject is covered in much more detail in a later chapter, so the discussion here is brief.

Advertising

Advertising plays a very clear role—to register the brand name and perhaps some information on one or at most two salient attributes. It may not matter so much what is said as the very fact that awareness is

---

[8] Vaughn, "The Consumer Mind." Also, James R. Bettman, *An Information Processing Theory of Consumer Choice* (Reading, Mass.: Addison-Wesley, 1979), pp. 179–85.

FIGURE 7–3

The Relationship between Market Share and Awareness

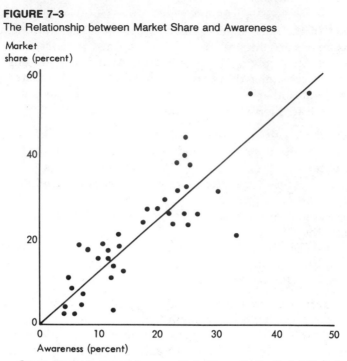

Source: "Brand Awareness Increases Market Share, Profits: Study," *Marketing News*, November 28, 1980, p. 5. Used by special permission from the American Marketing Association.

both attained and maintained. In a very interesting recent study of sales of food products, there was found to be an amazingly direct correlation between awareness and market share.[9] This is very clearly seen in Figure 7–3 reporting the results of another study. In short, unknown brands do not move from the shelf.

The visual media. Because there is more right brain information processing when low involvement is present, this argues for at least some use of the visual media. Remember that images are stored in the right brain in visual fashion. Television is an especially appropriate option because no other medium offers the unique combination of sight and sound. Whatever the case, long copy is *not* recommended. The consumer is not weighing selling points now as would be the case in extended problem solving.

Name registration. Eminent advertising analyst Harry W. McMahan has always contended, "The name of the game is the name . . . Here is where all advertising starts and where so much of television advertising

---

[9] *Project Payout. A Review and Appraisal of the Pilot Study in Milgram's Store #40* (New York: Advertising Research Foundation, 1980).

misses."[10] No doubt the form of the brand name itself has much to do with this. "Aloe & Lanolin" is a name which states exactly what the product is, and it builds upon growing use of the aloe vera plant to soothe skin irritations. Suppose Jergens had chosen something innocuous (and meaningless) such as "Nature Fresh?" There is no peg on which to hang this name, and it should not be expected that advertising will do much given involuntary exposure. This is why the brand name must stand out if anything is to happen.[11] Why advertise if at least this degree of awareness is not established?

Memorability.   We have previously discussed the problem of information overload and the extent to which many ads simply get lost in the "noise." Yes, the name must be registered, but this may not happen unless the ad is memorable and stands out in some way.

What to say and how to say it—this question will plague us later in this book, because there is no good answer. The problem is especially acute under low involvement, because there really isn't much to say in the way of brand uniqueness. What can Coca Cola say that hasn't already been said? In 1979 the Company began running its "Have a Coke and a Smile" campaign, but that was dropped in 1982 in favor of "Coke Is It!" As its commercials say, "Coke is it! The Biggest taste you've ever found. Coke is it! The most refreshing taste around." And on it goes.

Why the change? Here are the words of John Bergin, President, McCann-Erickson USA and head of the Coca-Cola account worldwide:

We have not talked taste or refreshment except perhaps as a throwaway line for years, and no one really knows why. So what we've really done with this lyric is restate for the consumer precisely what the consumer thinks of our product anyway."[12]

So, use is being made of comedian Bill Cosby, the Grambling University Marching Band, and a pep rally at Rice University to mention only a few variations. One TV spot (Figure 7–4) shows a farmer toiling in the fields while family and friends are waiting at home with a surprise birthday party.

Frankly, we think Coca Cola could say about anything as long as it keeps its name forward in the consumer's mind. Whether it is "Coke is it!" or "I'd like to buy the world a Coke" probably makes little difference. It does matter how it is said, however, and the various spokespersons and "slice of life" commercials may well break through and keep the Coke name before the public.

---

[10] Harry W. McMahan, "TV Loses the 'Name Game' but Wins Big in Personality," *Advertising Age,* December 1, 1980, p. 54.

[11] Ibid.

[12] Nancy Giges, "New Coke Ads Reflect a New Aggressiveness," Advertising Age, February 8, 1982, p. 82.

122

FIGURE 7–4
The "Coke Is It!" Campaign

Courtesy the Coca Cola Company

It must not be assumed, by the way, that the role of advertising is merely to entertain. Far from it! When people were asked to list the ads they thought were most outstanding, a large proportion could not even remember the name of the product being advertised.[13]

Repetition. Most of those who have written on the subject of low involvement agree that a repetitive advertising campaign is a key to success.[14] Given the odds of breaking through the noise barrier and the fractional exposure which occurs under the best of circumstances, it may

[13] Dave Vadehra, "Coke, McDonald's Lead Outstanding TV Commercials," *Advertising Age,* May 25, 1980, p. 37.

[14] Michael L. Rothschild, "Advertising Strategies for High and Low Involvement Situations," in Maloney and Silverman, *Attitude Research Plays,* pp. 74–93. This is a good summary of the thinking.

take a great many exposures to register the name and its principal benefit. More is said on this subject later, but it should be noted here that "wearout" is always a problem. The theme must be repeated with variation if it is to succeed. This, in fact, is one of the stated reasons for the change in the Coke campaign.[15] Some themes can survive for a long period of time as is evidenced by the Gillette "Dry Look" campaign first introduced about 1968.

Sales Promotion

The Aloe & Lanolin campaign was given a substantial boost by print ads featuring a 25-cent coupon, run in newspapers in the top 100 markets. This amounted to about 35 million coupons, and even a small redemption will move a great deal of product and induce trial. A point-of-sale display with a large trial bottle and special small size bottle offered for 39 cents also helped.

Stimulation of trial, then, is a primary objective. Once the consumer can see what the product has to offer, there is at least a chance of winning repeat patronage. This can be accomplished through sampling, package design, point-of-purchase display, price dealing, couponing, in-store advertising, and contests and premiums. All of these are discussed in Chapter 16.

It is interesting that the fast food industry has chosen, at least in part, to compete with sales promotion. Even though McDonald's changed ad agencies presumably to increase its mass media firepower, the new agency chose to run the "You Deserve a Break Today" theme in conjunction with a sweepstakes-type contest tied in with a "Quality—It's in the Bag" theme.[16] Image advertising is not especially effective when major competitors offer basically the same service mix.

Product Policy

The fast food industry provides a good illustration of the incentive to improve product or service mix when low involvement is presented. If this is not done, there always is the risk of lagging in market share as someone moves ahead with a minor change. This, of course, is the greatest problem McDonald's and other "pioneers" face. In recent years, a whole host of competitors have entered the market offering more attractive outlets, salad bars, specialty food items, and so on. What should the major competitors do? Match others item for item or what? Sometimes this is a rapid route to loss of distinction. A much better strategy is to

---

[15] Giges, "New Coke Ads."

[16] Bill Meyers and Richard Morgan, "Old McDonald's Ads Haunt Burnett," *Adweek,* April 5, 1982, p. 1ff.

monitor customers continually to see what changes they might like and then to make changes when it seems appropriate. This, of course, provides an all-new message for advertising which, in turn, serves to keep the name in the public eye.

Some will argue that product innovations coming through this route are minor indeed. There is some truth to this claim, but a wider view should be taken. Toothpaste manufacturers are currently battling on the issue of taste. This may not be important in the long run, but look at the changes which have occurred over time—fluoride, better packaging, whitening agents, and so on. Some might contend that the consumer can get the same benefit from using soda bicarbonate on the toothbrush. If this is so, why don't more people do it? Apparently the industry has offered something the people find to be of benefit.

SUMMARY

This chapter has added to our previous understanding of low-involvement consumer behavior which occurs for these reasons: (1) lack of high personal relevance; (2) low perceived risk; (3) no particular effect on one's self-concept; and (4) low anxiety about outcomes. When these situations hold, alternative evaluation follows purchase rather than preceding it. Therefore, the greatest need is to stimulate trial. Advertising can help by registering the name and stimulating interest, but the various methods of sales promotion assume greatest importance.

Review and Discussion Questions

1. Assume you have been called in as a marketing consultant to suggest a strategy to advertise a new brand of bread and sweet-rolls. Would this be a high-involvement or a low-involvement product line? Why?

2. If you consider the new line to be low involvement for most people, what suggestions would you have for an advertising campaign?

3. Would extensive couponing be advisable in the situation discussed above? Why or why not?

4. On what basis can it be said that repetition is a good strategy for some products?

5. What role does advertising play in attracting people to a fast food chain such as Wendy's or Kentucky Fried Chicken?

6. Why is recognition now being seen by more and more researchers as the best measure of the attention-attraction power of a television ad?

7. Would print advertising be an effective strategy when low involvement is present? Why or why not?

8. If low-involvement ads tend to be processed in the right brain with little or no consumer awareness, does this imply that we now have a new tool of consumer manipulation? Comment.

CHAPTER 8
Market Segmentation

In 1978 the tape recorder division of Sony was in the doldrums and had to generate new business to regain its former profitability. Then a new idea was spawned—a portable tape recorder. After considerable brainstorming and some informal market testing, the Sony Walkman was born.[1] It is nothing more than a pocket-size cassette player connected to a set of featherweight headphones, and it was first introduced in 1979. By the end of 1982, it will be selling at the rate of 3.5 million units annually. Why the success? First, the company identified a sizable market of active consumers mostly in their teen years who want to take music with them wherever they go without unnecessary weight and bulk. Then, it selected these people as a market target and developed the highly successful Walkman.

Here Sony was following a deliberate policy of *market segmentation—". . . dividing a market into distinct and meaningful groups of buyers who might merit separate products and/or marketing mixes.''*[2] Market segmentation requires, first of all, that some basis be found to identify those groups or segments of the market who are likely to respond differently to a product and its marketing mix. The second stage then is target marketing—the selection of a segment

---

[1] Shu Ueyama, "The Selling of the 'Walkman,'" *Advertising Age*, March 22, 1982, pp. M–2 ff.

[2] Philip Kotler, *Principles of Marketing* (Englewood Cliffs, N.J.: Prentice-Hall, 1980), p. 294.

or segments offering the best opportunity and developing an appropriate strategy for each. This requires a careful analysis of buyer motivation and behavior as discussed in the previous chapters and, in a sense, is one of the most practical payoffs in marketing research.

THE CONCEPT OF SEGMENTATION

Until the post-World War II era, market segmentation was not an especially vital consideration in planning. Although there may have been heterogeneity in the market in terms of desires and product preferences, it frequently was possible to ignore these differences. This was permissible because the environment often was one characterized by an excess of demand over supply. The manufacturer of the first electric refrigerator could, for example, sell its entire output without consideration of preferences for colors, freezer size, left- versus right-hand door opening and so on.

In today's market the situation is quite changed. The buyer has both the time and the affluence to shop for items which suit preferences. For their part, manufacturers are competing for this sale, and the winner will be that firm whose marketing mix most closely matches the consumer's desires. It is small wonder, then, that companies now recognize the heterogeneity inherent within most markets and closely tailor their offerings to these demand variations.

It should not be assumed that all markets are highly segmented. It is doubtful that demand for such staples as salt varies much from one individual to the next. In other situations, quite the opposite is true. The essential point is that promotional planning requires a factual basis of the extent to which segmentation is present.

Criteria of Usable Segments

Frequently segmentation analysis will produce results which are not of much use in promotional planning. Three criteria should be met: (1) the segment should be of sufficient size and market potential to warrant expenditure of marketing funds; (2) it must be possible to reach the segment through available media; and (3) the segment should show clear variations in market behavior in comparison with other segments.

Sufficient size. If a total market consisted of 1 million persons, it is probably true that there are 1 million segments. Obviously such a conclusion is of no use, because a segment must offer sufficient size and market potential if it is to be of any significance. A leading manufacturer of paper products was confronted by this problem when a new and demonstrably different crayon was introduced in 11 test markets. While the product appealed to a certain segment of users more than to others, it appeared that only 2 percent of a $30 million market could be captured. In turn, sales revenue did not warrant the necessary expenditures to produce and market the product.

Reachability.   It often is found that consumers differ in personality or other attributes but that the segments thus isolated cannot be reached feasibly through promotional efforts. An excellent example is provided by a series of studies on the personality trait "persuasibility."

It has been established experimentally that some people are more resistant to communication influence than others, and this has led to a series of studies on the correlates of persuasibility.[3] It has been demonstrated that women are more persuasible than men; intelligence and persuasibility are not related; feelings of social inadequacy underlie persuasibility; behavior is guided by external standards; and conformity is the rule.[4] Self-esteem is the personality trait most frequently correlated with persuasibility,[5] although others have offered alternative explanations.[6]

These data are intriguing, but their relevance for promotional planning is questionable.[7] First, it is by no means clear that those low in self-esteem and hence high in persuasibility possess unique needs to which appeals can be directed. Of even greater importance, there is no reason to expect differences in media exposure patterns among those who are persuasible and those who are not. Hence, there is no good way to reach the persuasible without considerable waste. Persuasibility as a segmentation variable, therefore, has not proved to be a way to isolate *reachable* segments.

Behavioral variations.   Many attempts have been made to use personality and other attributes to predict variations in behavior using the first method of segmentation analysis discussed earlier. Later discussion will indicate, however, that the resulting relationship between attribute and behavior more often than not is quite tenuous. This means that the data really have little applicability in planning.

---

[3] Irving L. Janis and Peter B. Field, "A Behavioral Assessment of Persuasibility: Consistency of Individual Differences," in *Personality and Persuasibility*, ed. Carl Hovland and Iriving Janis (New Haven, Conn.: Yale University Press, 1958), pp. 29–54.

[4] Irving L. Janis and Peter B. Field, "Sex Differences and Personality Factors Related to Persuasibility," in ibid., pp. 55–68; also Harriet Linton and Elaine Graham, "Personality Correlates of Persuasibility," in ibid., pp. 68–101.

[5] Carl I. Hovland, Irving L. Janis, and Harold H. Kelley, *Communication and Persuasion* (New Haven, Conn.: Yale University Press, 1953), p. 187.

[6] Arthur B. Cohen, "Some Implications of Self-Esteem for Social Influence," in Hovland and Janis, *Communication*, p. 119; also Donald F. Cox and Raymond A. Bauer, "Self-Confidence and Persuasibility in Women" (Harvard Business School, 1962), mimeographed.

[7] See James W. Carey, "Personality Correlates of Persuasibility," in *Toward Scientific Marketing*, ed. Stephen A. Greyser (Chicago: American Marketing Association, 1964).

Using Segmentation Analysis in Promotional Planning

The selection of mass media requires such information as the age, income, and location of those in each segment. Fortunately, there now is a wealth of data on media audiences in these same terms and the result is that media can be selected with a minimum of waste. Therefore, clear-cut demographic data must be collected for each segment.

Lifestyle, preferences, attitudes and other similar psychological variables provide useful insights in designing the promotional message. Assume, for instance, that heavy users of Maxwell House coffee base their preference on the fact that coffee is one significant way for a housewife to demonstrate her expertise in cooking. A good cup of coffee, in other words, says something to her family and to the world about her as a housewife. The product, in turn, meets her desires. Given this information, an advertisement might well feature the coffee being consumed at the table with obvious expressions of satisfaction by family members. Quite a number of other illustrations could be given, and it is clear that a rich basis is provided for creative imagination.

BASES FOR SEGMENTATION

A great variety of factors can be used to segment a market and many of these are itemized in Figure 8–1. Bases in this figure are classified as being geographic, demographic, psychographic or behavioristic in nature. The first two of these classifications describe the consumer's "state of being" while the third is related to the consumer's "state of mind."[8]

Not all of the bases listed have proven to be of equal usefulness in developing promotional strategies. Bases of a demographic or geographic type together with selected psychographic and behavioral bases such as product usage rate, attitude toward brand and preferred values and benefits are the most widely used in current practice. Thus the discussion of bases for market segmentation will be limited to these with particular attention being paid to the problems associated with measurement and analysis. Market segmentation is not difficult to understand conceptually but very real problems may arise when attempts are made to apply the concepts in practice.

Geographic Variables

Peugeot Motors of America has located most of its dealers for this premium-priced, French-made car on the East and West coasts, including

---

[8] Ben M. Enis, *Marketing Principles: The Management Process* (Pacific Palisades, Calif.: Goodyear, 1974), p. 281.

FIGURE 8–1
Major Segmentation Variables and Their Typical Breakdowns

Variables	*Typical Breakdowns*
Geographic:	
Region	Pacific, Mountain, West North Central, West South Central, East North Central, East South Central, South Atlantic, Middle Atlantic, New England
County size	A, B, C, D
City or SMSA size	Under 5,000, 5,000–19,999, 20,000–49,999, 50,000–99,999, 100,000–249,999, 250,000–499,999, 500,000–999,999, 1,000,000–3,999,999, 4,000,000 or over
Density	Urban, suburban, rural
Climate	Northern, southern
Demographic:	
Age	Under 6, 6–11, 12–19, 20–34, 35–49, 50–64, 65+
Sex	Male, female
Famly size	1–2, 3–4, 5+
Family life cycle	Young, single; young, married, no children; young, married, youngest child under six; young, married, youngest child six or over; older, married, with children; older, married, no children under 18; older, single; other
Income	Under $3,000, $3,000–$5,000, $5,000–$7,000, $7,000–$10,000, $10,000–$15,000, $15,000–$25,000, $25,000 and over
Occupation	Professional and technical; managers, officials, and proprietors; clerical, sales; craftsmen, foremen; operatives; farmers; retired; students; housewives; unemployed
Education	Grade school or less; some high school; graduated high school; some college; graduated college
Religion	Catholic, Protestant, Jewish, other
Race	White, black, oriental
Nationality	American, British, French, German, Scandinavian, Italian, Latin American, Middle Eastern, Japanese
Psychographic:	
Social class	Lower lowers, upper lowers, lower middles, upper middles, lower uppers, upper uppers
Lifestyle	Straights, swingers, longhairs
Personality	Compulsive, gregarious, authoritarian, ambitious
Behavioristic:	
Purchase occasion	Regular occasion, special occasion
Benefits sought	Economy, convenience, prestige
User status	Nonuser, ex-user, potential user, first-time user, regular user
Usage rate	Light user, medium user, heavy user
Loyalty status	None; medium; strong; absolute
Readiness stage	Unaware, aware, informed, interested, desirous, intending to buy
Marketing factor sensitivity	Quality, price, service, advertising, sales promotion

Source: Philip Kotler, *Principles of Marketing* (Englewood Cliffs, N.J.: Prentice-Hall, 1980), p. 297. Reprinted by permission of Prentice-Hall, Inc.

53 (out of 330) in the state of California.[9] The midwest, on the other hand, remains as a "domestic car bastion," and Peugeot has only three dealers in the state of Michigan (and a brave lot they are!). Obviously this is a reflection of geographic variation in receptivity to this somewhat unusual and previously largely unknown import, and this provides a useful example of how geography can provide a basis for determination of marketing strategy.

It is necessary to determine the *relative sales possibilities* from one geographic area to the next. For example, if a product is sold nationwide, should twice as much effort be placed in the Chicago market as compared with Ann Arbor, Michigan? Should Ann Arbor receive an equivalent or proportional allocation of promotional funds? Such questions as these can be answered only when *market potentials* are computed, for, as a general rule, efforts are allocated in proportion to potential, all other things being equal.

Several different potentials might be computed for a given product: (1) volume attainable under ideal conditions, i.e., if all efforts were perfectly adapted to the environment; (2) the relative capacity of a market to absorb the products of an entire industry such as the major appliance industry; (3) the relative size of market for a company's type of product, i.e., sales of color television sets versus stereo sets; and (4) the actual sales a company can expect. The last category, of course, is the equivalent of the sales forecast for a firm, or the sales volume which can be expected if the firm continues on its present course. Potential, on the other hand, refers to sales possibilities rather than expected sales, and it is of greater significance for purposes of demand analysis. Although forecasting is necessary in determining allocations and budgets, it is beyond the scope of this book.[10]

The measure of potential which is generally found to be most useful comprehends either category two or category three—market strength (capacity) for industry products rather than the products of a firm. This is not to say, however, that potential is the sole basis for allocation of resources, because potentials for industry sales do not reveal the competitive structure of a market or the firm's ability to make inroads. Ann Arbor, for example, might appear to offer high potential, whereas, in reality, competitors are so entrenched that inroads would be impossible. Ideally, then, potentials must be augmented with information about the competitive structure as well as the firm's previous experience in the market. The goal, of course, is to make an optimum allocation of resources

---

[9] "Peugeot Marketing Campaign Treats Car Buyers as Intelligent; Sales Soar," *Marketing News,* December 25, 1981, pp. 1–2.

[10] See *Forecasting Sales,* Business Policy Study no. 106 (New York: National Industrial Conference Board, 1963).

to alternative markets, and this never can be done with great precision without a reliable estimate of the impact of a given level of promotional expenditure on market share. Nevertheless, an array of markets in terms of potential provides a workable estimate of the probability of response to sales efforts. The methods used to compute potentials will be discussed in Chapter 11.

Demographic Characteristics

The market potential for any product is determined by people who want or need that alternative and who have the necessary resources. Motivation to buy to some extent is both determined and revealed by the demographic life position of the person (age, education, income, sex, and so on), as is ability to pay. There are many possible demographic bases for segmentation itemized in Figure 8–1, but those which are most widely used are age, income, and sex.[11]

Age. Buyer wants and abilities to buy obviously change as they age and pass through various stages in their life cycle, and this provides useful clues for marketing strategy. Jergens' Aloe & Lanolin, a product discussed thoroughly in an earlier chapter, proved to be most appealing to women over the age of 35. This is not surprising given preference of younger consumers for a medicated skin conditioner. Furthermore, there would have been little to gain if the younger market segment had been the target of efforts to change their preferences. The logical strategy, therefore, is to target for the somewhat older segment and capitalize upon the opportunity which is there.[12]

Age can be a surprisingly difficult variable to work with, however, as some manufacturers have found. The original target of the X car Citation (the first General Motors model with front wheel drive) was the so-called "new value buyer" between the ages of 24 and 35. Nevertheless, the older generation responded much more heavily and, for a time, generated a demand which exceeded supply.[13] Soon sales started to lag, and GM decided to try once again for the younger market in its 1982 campaign. A series of cartoon-style commercials featured "Working Woman," "Family Man," and two other groups within the 24–35 segment in the hopes that these people finally will believe that "Chevy makes good things happen."[14] We find it somewhat surprising that executives feel their ads

---

[11] For a much more thorough discussion, see James F. Engel and Roger D. Blackwell, *Consumer Behavior*, 4th ed. (Hinsdale, Ill.: Dryden Press, 1982), chap. 3.

[12] " 'Thoroughly' Researched Aloe & Lanolin Stirs Competition in Hand Care Market," *Marketing News*, December 25, 1981, p. 4.

[13] Jay McCormick, "Chevy Splits Citation Target Audience," *Advertising Age*, November 9, 1981, pp. 10ff.

[14] Ibid.

alone will change what appears to be an established set of preferences. While this may happen, such a strategy reflects more of a promotional orientation relying on sales firepower than it does careful market segmentation based on a realistic demand assessment.

Income. Income segmentation long has been used by marketers with generally favorable results. For example, the 1982 Jaguar is targeted to those making about $100,000 per year, and the media used include mostly national magazines and Sunday newspaper supplements appealing to this affluent segment.[15] These, in turn, are confined largely to the two coasts, reflecting the geographic segmentation of the market.

One must be cautious in assuming that income is a reflection of the consumer's social class. This obviously is not the case given the high wages now earned by those in the trades and various blue-collar occupations. Therefore, income by itself usually is not an accurate basis for segmentation unless one takes account of this consideration.

Sex. It is obvious that some products appeal more to men than they do women, and vice versa. With the emergence of the working wife and greater female initiative through the equal rights movement, the woman often becomes a most viable market segment. Witness the success of Virginia Slims cigarettes ("You've come a long way baby!").

Demographics as a clue to lifestyle. It is sometimes overlooked that demographic data can provide some interesting insight into lifestyle differences between segments. For example, the heavy buyers of Kentucky Fried Chicken has the following demographic profile:

Both spouses work.

More children than average.

Significantly higher family income than average.

Average educational attainment.

Middle-class occupational status.[16]

It is not difficult to conclude that time is at a premium for members of this household. Undoubtedly they are willing to incur the extra cost of purchasing prepared food in return for the gains in leisure time. Given the relatively high income status, it is also probable that they would be responsive to buying with a credit card and so on.

Psychographic Characteristics

In psychographic segmentation, consumers are differentiated on the basis of differences in patterns by which people live and spend time

---

[15] Gay Jervey, "Jaguar Pays the Price to Get Back in Hunt," *Advertising Age,* April 12, 1982, p. 91.

[16] D. J. Tigert, T. R. Lathrope, and M. J. Bleeg, "The Fast Food Franchise: Psychographic and Demographic Segmentation Analysis," *Journal of Retailing* 47 (1971), pp. 86–87.

and money. These patterns represent consumer lifestyle. Some include social class as a part of lifestyle (see Figure 8–1), whereas others will classify it as a demographic variable. For the most part, reference is made here to consumer activities, interests, and opinions (often referred to as AIO measurements) and the way in which these affect buying activities.[17]

Here is an example of what we mean. Consider the heavy users of eye makeup. Demographically they are younger and better educated than average, more likely to be employed outside the home, and they tend to live in metropolitan areas.[18] This tells us something, but notice how much is added when users are differentiated from nonusers in psychological graphic terms:

Highly fashion conscious.

Desirous of being attractive to men.

Oriented to the future.

Interested in art and culture.

Interested in world travel.

Not home centered.

Relative rejection to the traditional.

These data, of course, say nothing about awareness or attitudes toward specific brands or types of eye makeup. The usefulness in promotional strategy enters in providing clues about the type of person the prospects are and the way they should be depicted in the message.

One could use this psychographic profile in a mechanical way and depict an overdressed woman with a man worshipping at her feet as they sit in an art institute in Paris with a letter from mother crumpled on the floor. Needless to say this is absurd, but an appeal to the wrong type of person in contradictory settings will have the effect of activating selective screening of the message by the prospect. Therefore, the key is to utilize people and settings in such a manner that they are consistent with and not contradictory to the psychographic profile.

The two advertisements in Figure 8–2 should be examined to determine whether these models and settings are psychographically appropriate. Are these women likely to be the types that are cosmopolitan in tastes, oriented toward fashion, and interested in men? Probably most will give an affirmative answer. If so, it can be concluded that proper use has been made of psychographic data.

The makeup example above is an example of product *specific* AIO analy-

---

[17] There was a period in which attempts were made to measure consumer personality and use these data to predict product and brand choice. This has proved to be a hopeless deadend, however, and we do not discuss it here. For details, see Engel and Blackwell, *Consumer Behavior*, pp. 214–22.

[18] William D. Wells and Douglass J. Tigert, "Activities, Interests, and Opinions," *Journal of Advertising Research* 11 (1971), pp. 27–35.

134

Helena Rubinstein creates Long Lash.

© 1973 HELENA RUBINSTEIN, INC.

Available with wand or brush applicator.

Now... mascara that conditions as it waterproofs.

Long Lash is more than just a mascara. It's a whole beauty treatment for your delicate, hard-working lashes.

Now you can darken them, lengthen them, thicken them, waterproof them, with no fear of drying them out.

For it has an oil base that softens. Proteins that condition. And emollients that make lashes a snare of silk.

Dermatologist tested and approved.

Helena Rubinstein

Courtesy Helena Rubenstein

FIGURE 8–2 (*continued*)

Source: Reproduced with permission of the Almay Company.

sis. That is, the AIO scales were tailormade for the product. Another type of AIO scale is based on *general patterns* of lifestyle (family orientation, self confidence). Figure 8–3 presents a description of eight male psychographic segments that were defined by applying statistical procedures to this type of AIO scale.

There are times in which psychographics provides important clues for creative strategy. For many years Merrill Lynch, Pierce, Fenner & Smith, Inc., a major stock broker and investment firm, featured its well-known "Bullish on America" advertising campaign. Psychographic research showed that most of the middle and upper class could be characterized as being (1) belongers (motivated by acceptance); (2) emulators (copying the rich and successful); and (3) achievers (success oriented). The "Bullish on America" theme was distinctly patriotic and was found to appeal mostly to the belongers. This segmentation was reinforced by showing a single bull moving into a herd, communicating safety in numbers— also a belonger theme. The agency taking over this account saw more promise in targeting to the achievers, and the message was modified to show a single bull, hopefully connoting, "Like you, Mr. Achiever, we are a breed apart."[19]

Evidence to date indicates that lifestyle segmentation is most appropriate when the following circumstances are present:

The product offers primarily psychological gratification.

Product performance cannot be evaluated objectively.

High involvement is present with most buyers.

Advertising is the major tool in the marketing mix.

Consumers are willing to switch brands when not completely satisfied.

The product category is not dominated by one or two brands.

The product is not purchased primarily on the basis of price.

Many conceptual and research issues remain with respect to the usefulness of lifestyle in promotional strategy. Wells, Kinnear and Taylor, and Bernstein give the use of lifestyle measures a mixed report.[20] But, for now, it appears to be a useful addition to business practice.

Behavioristic Variables

In this method of segmentation, buyers are differentiated on the basis of knowledge, attitude, use, or response to a product or its attributes. It

---

[19] Nancy Giges, "Why Y&R Took Bull out of the Herd," *Advertising Age*, November 9, 1981, p. 82.

[20] William D. Wells, "Psychographics: A Critical Review," *Journal of Marketing Research* 12 (May 1975), pp. 196–213; Thomas C. Kinnear and James R. Taylor, "Psychographics: Some Additional Findings," *Journal of Marketing Research* 13 (November 1976), pp. 422–25; and Peter W. Bernstein, "Psychographics Is Still an Issue on Madison Avenue," *Fortune*, 97, no. 1 (1978), pp. 78–84.

FIGURE 8–3
Eight Male Psychographic Segments

Group 1. *"The Quiet Family Man"* (8% of total males)

He is a self-sufficient man who wants to be left alone and is basically shy. Tries to be as little involved with community life as possible. His life revolves around the family, simple work, and television viewing. Has a marked fantasy life. As a shopper he is practical, less drawn to consumer goods and pleasures than other men.

Low education and low economic status, he tends to be older than average.

Group II. *"The Traditionalist"* (16% of total males)

A man who feels secure, has self-esteem, follows conventional rules. He is proper and respectable, regards himself as altruistic and interested in the welfare of others. As a shopper he is conservative, likes popular brands and well-known manufacturers.

Low education and low or middle socio-economic status; the oldest age group.

Group III. *"The Discontented Man"* (13% of total males)

He is a man who is likely to be dissatisfied with his work. He feels bypassed by life, dreams of better jobs, more money and more security. He tends to be distrustful and socially aloof. As a buyer, he is quite price conscious.

Lowest education and lowest socio-economic group, mostly older than average.

Group IV. *"The Ethical Highbrow"* (14% of total males)

This is a very concerned man, sensitive to people's needs. Basically a puritan, content with family life, friends, and work. Interested in culture, religion, and social reform. As a consumer he is interested in quality, which may at times justify greater expenditure.

Well educated, middle or upper socio-economic status, mainly middle aged or older.

Group V. *"The Pleasure Oriented Man"* (9% of total males)

He tends to emphasize his masculinity and rejects whatever appears to be soft or feminine. He views himself a leader among men. Self-centered, dislikes his work or job. Seeks immediate gratification for his needs. He is an impulsive buyer, likely to buy products with a masculine image.

Low education, lower socio-economic class, middle aged or younger.

Group VI. *"The Achiever"* (11% of total males)

This is likely to be a hardworking man, dedicated to success and all that it implies; social prestige, power and money. Is in favor of diversity, is adventurous about leisure time pursuits. Is stylish, likes good food, music, etc. As a consumer he is status conscious, a thoughtful and discriminating buyer.

Good education, high socio-economic status, young.

Group VII. *"The He-Man"* (19% of total males)

He is gregarious, likes action, seeks an exciting and dramatic life. Thinks of himself as capable and dominant. Tends to be more of a bachelor than a family man, even after marriage. Products he buys and brands preferred are likely to have "self-expressive value," especially a "Man of Action" dimension.

Well educated, mainly middle socio-economic status, the youngest of the male groups.

Group VIII. *"The Sophisticated Man"* (10% of total males)

He is likely to be an intellectual, concerned about social issues, admires men with artistic and intellectual achievements. Socially cosmopolitan, broad interests. Wants to be dominant, and a leader. As a consumer he is attracted to the unique and fashionable.

Best educated and highest economic status of all groups, younger than average.

Source: William D. Wells, "Psychographics: A Critical Review," *Journal of Marketing Research,* 12 (May 1975), p. 201. Reproduced with the permission of The American Marketing Association.

is finding widespread use. Our discussion here is confined to benefit segmentation and segmentation by product usage rates.[21]

Benefit Segmentation

Considerable attention was focused in earlier chapters on the attributes used (or benefits desired) by consumers in the process of alternative evaluation. In benefit segmentation the first step is to determine these desired benefits and then assess, from the consumer's perspective, whether or not available products fill the bill. If not, there may be a market niche which can be filled by careful product design and marketing strategy. In effect, then, the consumer sets the agenda.

Benefit segmentation was followed with unusual success by Libby, McNeill & Libby in introduction of the Libby's Lite brand. Sales of the total canned food category were in a slow decline, and some action was necessary. Low-sugar canned fruit had been introduced in the 1960s but was withdrawn from the market with the ban on cyclamates. Consumer research showed, however, that consumers still desired a low-sugar product with a natural, fresh taste. Libby was able to develop such a product in 1979, and it was introduced to the market. Soon Libby's 10 percent share of the total market was evenly split between syrup-packed and Lite, and this brand achieved about 65 percent of the market category of all light fruit. As one executive stated, "Lite has rejuvenated a mature business, and there's room for still more growth."[22]

Product Usage Rates

It often proves useful to segment the market in terms of consumer usage rates for a specific product category. Different strategies then are required for those in various usage categories.

Nonusers of product category. It is important to determine whether or not nonusers offer a potential market. Frequently the problem is only lack of awareness. If this is the case, an opportunity may exist to build familiarity through promotion and thereby lay the groundwork for later sales.

In other instances, a basically favorable attitude may exist but may be constrained by opposing forces from the environment. For example, if the problem is concern over financing, advertising or personal selling possibly could stimulate sales by promoting availability of easy credit.

Most likely the analysis of nonusers will document segments that will not respond, regardless of the strategy. There may be basic conflict be-

[21] See Kotler, *Principles of Marketing,* chap. 10, for more detail.
[22] Janet Neiman, "Another Lite Success Story," *Advertising Age,* October 12, 1981, p. 43.

tween the company offer and evaluative criteria, lifestyles, and so on. Every attempt should be made to avoid such segments if possible, because the probable return from the effort is not likely to be worth the expense.

Users of product but not the company brand. The purpose of this inquiry is to assess the probability of making inroads into competitors' markets. If their offerings or images are weak in certain respects or fail to satisfy important evaluative criteria, it may be possible to increase market share. On the other hand, competitors may be found to be invulnerable in certain segments, especially if there is brand loyalty based on psychological commitment or centrality. The best strategy always is to *appeal to the waverers* (those whose commitment is diminishing) rather than to attack an entrenched competitor head-on.

Regardless of competitive market shares, many feel that the best strategy is to appeal to heavy users of the product class, often referred to as the *heavy half.* For example, the so-called heavy half of the beer drinkers' market (in actuality this is 17 percent of the total market) consumes 88 percent of all beer; the heavy half in the market for canned soup (16 percent of the total) consumes 86 percent of the product sold.[23] The assumption is that the heavy half is the most productive segment, and there probably is some merit for this viewpoint. Certainly the propensity to respond will be higher. Concentration on this segment has been made more feasible through use of data provided by syndicated research services which show the extent of product consumption by audiences of various advertising media.

Efforts should not be concentrated on the heavy half, however, unless there is evidence documenting that it is not feasible to turn nonusers into users and light users into heavy users. There should be an inquiry into why they buy or do not buy, what the product means to them, and other related questions. It may be found that sales increases are a possibility.

Users of product and company brand. The greatest asset possessed by any organization is its core of satisfied users, and the present user cannot be overlooked in promotional strategy. It is of particular importance to monitor brand image and to clarify that the company offerings are still satisfying salient evaluative criteria better than the perceived offerings of a competitor. Any deficiencies should, of course, be remedied.

In addition, it is useful to monitor awareness of the company brand and competitive brands. In a highly volatile market, eroding awareness can be followed by a sales decline. A frequent advertising objective is just to maintain "share of mind"—that is, relative awareness vis-à-vis competitors.

---

[23] Norton Garfinkle, "How Marketing Data Can Identify Your Target Audience," address given to Eastern Regional Convention of the American Association of Advertising Agencies, October 1966.

It also may be possible to assess the potential for increasing brand loyalty among light to moderate users, stimulating new product uses, encouraging switching from competitive brands, and preventing inroads by competitors, to mention only a few of the many possibilities.

Undertaking Segmentation Analysis

Many bases for segmentation have been analyzed in this section, none of which are applicable in every situation. Thus it is impossible to generalize with respect to the ideal approach. What emerges is the wide variety which is possible and the ways in which research imagination and creative planning can identify groupings which lie beneath the surface of the market. It is apparent that promotional strategy requires a probing analysis to determine whether or not viable segments exist. If they are present and unrecognized, a profitable opportunity may be lost.

Usually it will be necessary to use a wide battery of measures of both consumer attributes (age, lifestyle, and so on) and behavior. In that way the analysis itself can uncover segments. If one begins with preconceived bases, one might miss the properties that are within the data. This is not to say, of course, that background and experience are irrelevant in determining possible bases for segmentation. The point is that this is only a start.

It is essential that correct statistical techniques be employed in data analysis. A wide variety are applicable including cross classification and chi square analysis, multiple regression, multiple discriminant analysis, factor analysis, canonical correlation, and nonmetric scaling to mention only a few. Each makes different assumptions about underlying properties of the data, but further discussion is beyond the scope of this book.[24]

THE MARKET TARGET DECISION

Once the market has been segmented along relevant dimensions, the firm now has three options: (1) undifferentiated marketing; (2) differentiated marketing; and (3) concentrated marketing.[25]

Undifferentiated Marketing

If this strategy is followed, segments, in effect, are ignored, and one marketing mix is offered for everyone. All efforts are poured into building

---

[24] For a useful introduction, See James H. Myers and Edward Tauber, *Market Structure Analysis* (Chicago: American Marketing Association, 1977).

[25] These options, broadly speaking, were first suggested by Wendell R. Smith, "Product Differentiation and Market Segmentation as Alternative Marketing Strategies," *Journal of Marketing*, July 1956, pp. 3–8.

a superior image which will overcome these demand variations. Certainly there are cost advantages which are undeniable as Henry Ford found when the Model A Ford was introduced in any color you want "as long as it is black." Ford, of course, had a near monopoly on the market, but few firms enjoy that advantage today. As a result, undifferentiated marketing is exceedingly rare.

One variation seen more commonly is to produce only for the largest segment of the market, perhaps using the heavy half concept. The problem is that this strategy appeals to most competitors who concentrate in similar fashion and ignore smaller segments. The outcome often is that they are sitting ducks for competitors who differentiate and provide the desired option ranges.

Differentiated Marketing

In differentiated marketing, a firm operates in two or more segments and offers a unique marketing program for each. This strategy has become quite common in larger corporations as is reflected in a trend toward multiple product offerings. It certainly offers the advantage of recognizing the demand variations which are there and capitalizing upon them, in contrast with the strategy discussed above.

Differentiated marketing is not without its disadvantages, however, as the Chevrolet Division of General Motors has found.[26] Traditionally Chevrolet offered only a few models and represented a distinct image of basic transportation at a low price. Over the years, however, a multiplicity of models has been offered, and the distinctions between Pontiac, Oldsmobile, Buick, and Cadillac have progressively become blurred. In addition, its traditional price advantage has virtually disappeared. As one competitor said, "I wonder if people know what the heck a Chevy is anymore. Motherhood and apple pie don't fly very far these days."[27] The division's traditional first-time and low-income buyers have switched to imports in large numbers, and company attempts to fight this trend have been a flop. The most notable example is the failure of the ballyhooed import fighter, Cavalier, to gain a market foothold. Even more distressing is the fact that Chevy has lost its position as the top-selling domestic division to Ford.

What this example demonstrates is that differentiated marketing, first of all, is more costly. Chevrolet lost its price advantage and became vulnerable to the imports. Moreover, there is the danger of blurring the traditional product image in core markets unless great care is taken. No firm can be all things to all people.

---

[26] Robert Simison, "Chevy, GM's Leader, Sustains Worst Slump in U.S. Auto Industry," *The Wall Street Journal,* January 4, 1982, pp. 1 and 4.

[27] Ibid., p. 1.

Concentrated Marketing

In the above strategies the firm goes after the whole market, but often it is wise to concentrate on one segment or at most a very few. The objective is to establish a larger share and focus resources on excellence in a more limited market. There are numerous examples which could be cited. One of the most notable is the success the Tandy Corporation has had with its Model 80 Radio Shack home computers. While there are a great many competitors, the Model 80 has held top position through continued product innovation, intensive distribution, and availability of service and softwear help.

The danger of concentration, of course, is that a market can dry up with amazing rapidity. Therefore, some diversification may be a wise policy to follow, especially if there is a high rate of product change.

SUMMARY

This chapter has been addressed to the all-important subject of market segmentation. The objective is to isolate homogeneous groups within the market so that promotional efforts can be more closely oriented to demand variations within each segment. The result ideally is a reduction of waste and an increase in productivity.

A number of segmentation bases were discussed, including demographic, geographic, product usage, and attitudes. None is ideal for all purposes, and it was suggested that the best procedure is to collect a wide variety of data on attributes and behavior and analyze the data in a variety of ways. The result frequently is an uncovering of segments which might otherwise have been overlooked.

Review and Discussion Questions

1. What is the general procedure in establishing market targets?
2. Ideally one would consider each individual buyer as a market segment and tailor the promotional mix accordingly. Since this seldom is practical, what is the goal of market segmentation?
3. List and describe the most common dimensions of demographic classification. What can analysis along these dimensions reveal?
4. The blue-collar class was discussed in Chapter 5. What uses can be made of knowledge of this class in promotional planning?
5. Survey data reveal that the market for a line of name brand stereo units selling for a minimum of $200 is concentrated among males under 35, bachelors, located on the east and west coasts, college graduates, earning $12,000 and over. How can these findings be used in promotional strategy?
6. Assume that researchers in a large New York advertising agency devise a valid measure of persuasibility. Critically evaluate whether or not this mea-

sure can and will prove useful in planning the advertising campaign for a large household detergent account. Would the account director for a line of refrigerators and freezers use this measure differently than his counterpart on the detergent account?

7. What is geographic market potential? What is the goal of analysis of potential? What are the primary methods used for this purpose?

8. You are the marketing manager for a firm which makes a line of electric hair curlers. When using this product, a girl can set her hair in 15 to 30 minutes. What segments would you expect to find in the market?

9. Would your answer to question 8 be different if you were selling the product in West Germany? In Kenya?

10. How might the bases of market segmentation differ in the industrial market?

11. Why are there no specific rules to follow in determining the best base for segmentation?

12. What is the difference between segmentation making use of demographics and segmentation based on psychographics? What advantage does the latter have over the former?

13. What is the probable psychographic profile of the market segment described in question 8? What implications would this have for the promotional campaign.

14. Distinguish between undifferentiated, differentiated, and concentrated marketing. Under what circumstances should each be used?

CHAPTER 9

The Regulation of Promotion

The creative process which is the basis of effective promotional strategy by definition requires discipline. One of the areas of discipline is to see that there are no violations, intentional or unintentional, of laws and regulations controlling the content or mode of delivery of promotional communication.

The legal constraints on marketing in general and promotion in particular have multiplied rapidly over the years. Congress has been especially busy over the past decade and a half. Although it is necessary to review the major restrictions on promotion in this text, this review cannot be exhaustive. Enough detail is provided, however, to enable the reader to sense the current direction of governmental regulatory policy and to establish whether or not a proposed promotional campaign meets the legal requirements set by Congress and the various regulatory agencies.[1]

---

[1] For a more detailed background on legislation see John S. Wright, Daniel S. Warner, Willis L. Winter, Jr., and Sherilyn K. Ziegler, *Advertising,* 4th ed. (New York: McGraw-Hill, 1977), chap. 20; Earl Kintner, "How Advertising Has Policed Itself," in *Advertising Today, Yesterday and Tomorrow* (New London, Conn.: Printers' Ink, 1962), pp. 408–11.; "How Government Regulates Advertising," *Advertising Age,* November 21, 1973, pp. 144–55; "How the U.S. Regulates Advertising," *The World of Advertising* (Chicago: Advertising Publications, 1962), p. 182 ff.; the monthly publication *Washington Report* (Washington, D.C.: American Advertising Federation); and Joe Welch *Marketing Law* (Tulsa, Okla.: Pennwell Publishing Company, 1980).

PERTINENT LEGISLATION

Federal Legislation

Prior to the 20th century the doctrine of *caveat emptor* prevailed, with little or no buyer protection against false and deceptive methods of sale. Post Office fraud laws were adopted in 1872 to provide remedies against the use of the mails to defraud, but effective legal curbs awaited passage of the Pure Food and Drug Act in 1906 and, most significantly, the Federal Trade Commission Act of 1914.

The Pure Food and Drug Act. A series of articles was published by Samuel Adams in 1906 to expose quackery and unfair practices in the sale of patent medicines. Shortly after this exposé, the Pure Food and Drug Act was passed by Congress. This act was intended from its inception to have limited applicability; it served only to require correct description of contents on the package of drug items. It was superseded in 1938 by the Federal Food, Drug, and Cosmetic Act, to be discussed later.

The Federal Trade Commission Act. The Pure Food and Drug Act did little to prevent advertising and selling abuses, and the first truly effective legislation passed was the Federal Trade Commission Act of 1914. While the prevention of deceptive advertising was only a secondary purpose, Section Five prohibited unfair methods of competition in interstate commerce where the effect is to injure competition. The Federal Trade Commission (FTC), strengthened by key Supreme Court decisions, began to move against false and misleading advertising, and 70 percent of the cases processed by the Commission fell into this category by 1925.[2] Enforcement efforts, however, were severely limited by the Raladam case of 1931, in which the Supreme Court held that the Commission lacked jurisdiction over false and misleading advertising in the absence of proof of substantial competitive injury.[3]

In 1936 Congress passed the Robinson-Patman Act, a law designed to give the FTC broad powers to control discriminatory pricing practices. Sections 2d and 2e of the act prohibit the offering by sellers or the seeking by buyers of advertising allowances and promotional services which are not available on a proportionately equal basis to all firms selling the same product or service in competition with one another.

The Wheeler-Lea Amendment to the Federal Trade Commission Act in 1938 added significantly to the Commission's powers.[4] Congress provided that intent to defraud no longer needed to be proved before action

---

[2] See Kintner, "How Advertising Has Policed Itself," p. 409.

[3] Ibid.

[4] Public Law 447, approved March 21, 1938, 75 Cong., 3d Sess., U.S. Stat. L., vol. 52.

could legally be taken, thereby giving the Commission broader jurisdiction. Other fundamental changes were as follows: (1) "unfair methods of competition" was expanded to encompass deceptive acts or practices, (2) the Commission was empowered to issue cease and desist orders which become binding after 60 days, (3) the Commission was given jurisdiction over false advertising of foods, drugs, and cosmetics, and (4) the Commission was permitted to issue injunctions to halt improper food, drug, or cosmetic advertising when it appeared the public might be harmed.

The years following the Wheeler-Lea Amendment have been marked by a series of congressional actions aimed at requiring certain industries to provide special disclosures of information through their labeling and advertising activities, to prevent consumer deception and to facilitate consumer comparison of alternate product or service offerings. The specific laws which have given the FTC greatly increased powers over the promotional activities of firms in these industries include the following six laws, the names of which indicate the nature of their applicability: the Wool Products Act (1939), the Fur Products Labeling Act (1951), the Textile Fiber Products Act (1958), the Fair Packaging and Labeling Act (1966), the Truth in Lending Act (1969) and the Fair Credit Reporting Act (1970).

The Commission staff continually monitors all forms of interstate advertising. For example, television networks are required to submit typed scripts covering one broadcasting week each month. Also a substantial number of complaints from individual citizens are processed and acted upon yearly.

A preliminary investigation is held if it appears that action is required. Minor complaints may be turned over to the Division of Stipulation for an informal nonpublicized settlement, but more serious cases result in a formal complaint issued by the Bureau of Litigation upon the approval of the full Commission.[5] A respondent has 30 days to answer a formal complaint, after which a hearing is held before an examiner. The examiner's decision may be appealed to the Commission by either side, and, in turn, Commission decisions may be appealed through the federal courts. A consent order may be issued by the Commission whereby actions are enjoined but no guilt is admitted by the respondent. A finding of guilty after formal proceedings, however, culminates in a cease and desist order. Both consent orders and cease and desist orders are binding.

The Commission on its own volition or at the request of an industry group occasionally will call a trade conference to establish a code of fair practice. The codes thus established may cover activities deemed to be

---

[5] The issuance of the formal complaint may not be necessary in situations specified in the Magnuson-Moss Act of 1975 which will be discussed in a later section of this chapter.

illegal by the Commission, such as the use of fictitious list prices, or unethical practices which technically are within the law.

In late 1973, the FTC was further strengthened by passage of legislation appended to the Alaska Pipeline Bill. The law authorizes the FTC to institute its own court actions if the Justice Department does not act within 10 days on an FTC request; increases penalties for violation of cease and desist orders from $5,000 to $10,000; and permits the FTC to obtain preliminary injunctions against unfair or deceptive advertising. In addition, the bill grants all federal regulatory agencies, including the FTC, far-reaching information-gathering powers.[6]

In 1975 Congress passed the Magnuson-Moss Warranty—Federal Trade Commission Improvement Act.[7] This law is composed of two parts; the first of which deals with ways of clarifying and strengthening product warranties to improve the protection of consumers. The second part of the act which is of special interest to managers of promotion broadens the jurisdiction of the FTC and extends its rule-making authority.

Certain changes such as the derivation of expanded powers for the FTC from statute rather than from judicial review are readily understood. The impact of other changes is less clear. For example, under Magnuson-Moss the FTC was provided with rule-making authority permitting the establishment of trade regulation rules that specify unfair or deceptive acts or practices that are prohibited. It is of interest that the term *unfair* was neither defined or clarified.

In 1980 because of criticism of the way the "unfairness" doctrine was applied (to be discussed later), another FTC Improvements Act was passed. This statute forbid the promulgation of any rule by the FTC to regulate commercial advertising on the basis of unfairness for the three-year period 1980–82.[8] Hearings were to be held during that period to ascertain whether or not the FTC should regain its full range of powers in the area of "unfairness."

The Federal Food, Drug, and Cosmetic Act.   The earlier act of 1906 was supplanted in 1938 by the Federal Food, Drug, and Cosmetic Act. The Food and Drug Administration (FDA) is empowered to investigate and litigate advertising claims appearing on the label or package of food, drug, and cosmetic items. The FTC monitors all other forms of advertising for these products.

As a result of increasing pressures for more effective efforts to protect the consumer, the Hazardous Substance Labeling Act was passed in 1960. This law requires special disclosure on the label for household products

---

[6] Public Law 93–153 (1973).

[7] Public Law 93–637 (1975).

[8] Federal Trade Commission 1980, *Improvements Act of 1980*, Public Law 96–2532.

that have toxic, corrosive, irritant, or similar characteristics.[9] In 1962 still more regulatory power was granted the FDA with the amendment of the 1938 act to give the FDA authority to establish "comprehensive procedures providing for pre-marketing approval of claims and labels for prescription drugs, as well as provisions which assure that advertising is consistent with permissible labeling claims."[10] This legislation was especially aimed at gaining the full disclosure of side effects and complications that might be associated with prescription drugs.

The Truth in Packaging Act (1966) granted the FDA additional powers to require disclosure of information on labels of food, drug, and cosmetic products and to regulate packaging procedures which might tend to confuse consumers or make product comparisons difficult.[11]

The FDA has the power to seize shipments of goods upon receipt of evidence that its regulations have been violated. Notable examples of seizure in recent years include shipments of frozen orange juice allegedly containing misrepresentation of contents and shipments of coffee containing false price information.[12] Of course, in the situations where consumer health is endangered the FDA has recalled entire batches of canned tuna, mushrooms, and soups where the threat of botulism appeared to exist.

For many years the FDA and the FTC were antagonists because of the overlapping nature of their jurisdictions. It is important to note that in recent years the two agencies have become close collaborationists rather than rivals. The FDA with its vast scientific resources does the testing of product efficacy. Although the FDA is limited to what goes on the label (with the exception of prescription drugs where it also controls advertised claims), the results of its experimentation are used by the FTC as the basis of its charges of misrepresentation or fraud.

In 1962, with the advent of the new legislation, the FDA undertook a study of the effectiveness of all prescription drugs then on the market. Findings announced 10 years later resulted in the removal from the market of several products which were deemed to be ineffective. At that time the FDA began a similar study of over-the-counter products such as analgesics and antacids.

With a markedly increased budget in recent years, with vast scientific resources, and with a new era of cooperation with the FTC, the FDA is a potent force in the regulation of product development and promotion by members of the food, drug, and cosmetics industries. Insofar as firms

---

[9] The 1972 law which created the Consumer Product Safety Commission transferred to it from the FDA the responsibility for enforcing the 1960 law.

[10] "How Government Regulates Advertising," p. 148.

[11] Ibid.

[12] See "How the U.S. Regulates Advertising," p. 182.

in these industries are among the largest spenders for promotion, the influence of the FDA on American marketing practices is formidable.

State and Local Regulation

The inadequacies of the Pure Food and Drug Act passed in 1906 led to demands for regulation within the advertising industry itself, and *Printers' Ink* responded by proposing its "model statute" in 1911. This has since been adopted in whole or in modified form by the great majority of states. The provisions of the model statute specify clearly what practices constitute deceptive advertising, and it undergoes occasional modification to reflect changing standards of practice.

The variety of local laws pertaining to advertising truly defies description. Some legislation strongly parallels the *Printers' Ink* model statute. Other laws regulate house-to-house selling, advertising appeals, and the use of such media as billboards and signs.

Self-Regulation

In 1971 the advertising industry in cooperation with the Council of Better Business Bureaus (CBBB) established an ambitious program of self-regulation. The goal of the program was to enable the members of the industry to respond more effectively to public complaints about national advertising. The coverage of the program was broad and in addition to matters of truth and accuracy it was also concerned with matters of taste and social responsibility.

The mechanics of the program are quite complicated and are, therefore, illustrated in Figure 9–1. It can be seen that complaints about advertising are received by the National Advertising Division (NAD) where they are evaluated. The complaint is either dismissed at this point or the advertiser is requested to provide substantiation for its claims. Once again the complaint may be dismissed or if the substantiation is not acceptable, the advertiser can be requested to discontinue its message. If the advertiser agrees to cease and desist the case is terminated. If not, the matter can be appealed to a National Advertising Review Board (NARB) by either the advertiser or the NAD.

The NARB is composed of a chairman and 50 members representing various segments of the industry and the public at large. In response to an appeal the chairman may appoint a five-person panel to consider the case. If the panel finds in favor of the advertiser the case is closed. If the panel finds that the ad in question is misleading the advertiser is requested to modify or terminate use of the message. Refusal on the part of the advertiser to obey the findings of the panel results in the referral of the complaint to the appropriate governmental agencies and the making public of the findings of the NAD and NARB panel. Figure 9–2 illustrates the responses of four companies to challenges from the NAD.

FIGURE 9–1
A Flow Diagram of the NAD and NARB Self-Regulatory Process

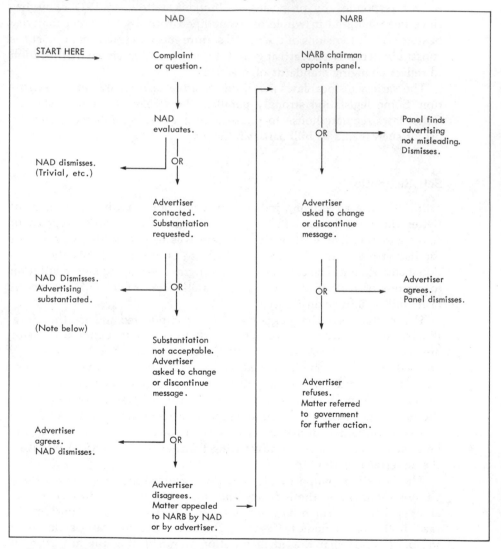

Note: if the original complaint originated outside the system, the outside complainant at this point can appeal to the chairman of NARB for a panel adjudication. Granting of such appeal is at the Chairman's discretion.
Source: The National Advertising Review Board: 1971–1976, Published by the NARB, 1977.

FIGURE 9–2

An Example of Company Responses to Challenges from the National Advertising Division

---

FOUR BOW TO CHALLENGE FROM NAD

NEW YORK—Air Florida, Borden, Maybelline and Ragold's Velamints came in for copy modification requests from the National Advertising Division in March. Eight other advertisers substantiated their ad claims when challenged by the NAD, the Council of Better Business Bureaus' unit that initiates and processes ad challenges as part of the advertising community's self-regulatory system.

Advertising that was modified or discontinued following an NAD inquiry.

Air Florida (Romann & Tannenholz, New York) was challenged for print ads that stated, "But nobody beats Air Florida at its own game. We've always given you the best price to Florida . . . For years, Eastern, Pan Am and TWA have been the most expensive airlines to fly." A rival airline gave NAD information that indicated its fares to Florida matched, or were lower than, Air Florida's at times in 1981. The airline noted that the campaign had run its course and there were no plans to repeat it.

Borden Inc. (Bozell & Jacobs) for Bama peanut butter ran afoul of NAD with copy that claimed, "Peanut Butter lovers say, 'You can't beat Bama! Jif can't! Peter Pan can't! Skippy can't!'" Copy added that in a taste test, children "who love peanut butter found Bama peanut butter unbeatable! None of the leading brands beat the delicious taste of Bama." Substantiation was requested and conflicting data led NAD to rule that it was "inappropriate to make the parity claim vis-a-vis all three competitive brands." Borden indicated the claims would no longer be used unless it develops "further test data."

Schering-Plough's Maybelline Co. (Ted Bates & Co.) for Colors That Cling eyeshadow ran a tv spot that said Colors That Cling is creaseproof "even eight hours later." A competitor's challenge provided results of a panel test. Before the matter could be resolved, Maybelline advised that the ad had been discontinued "for reasons unrelated" to the NAD inquiry.

A Bates magazine ad for Maybelline's Fresh Lash mascara that claimed "24 hours later . . . your mascara looks fresh" was substantiated by Maybelline.

Ragold Inc. (Don Tennant Co.) for Velamints' vacation offer used a print ad stating, "Velamints invites you to save $500 on a vacation to the French Riviera." The ad indicated the savings was based on a trip with a retail value of $1,499 for $999. NAD sought an explanation as to how the retail value was derived and then questioned the information Ragold presented since lower air fares would be available to travelers who booked direct. During the back-and-forth process, Ragold said the ad had run its course and NAD closed the case.

Source: Reprinted with permission from the April 19, 1982, issue of *Advertising Age*. Copyright 1982 by Crain Communications, Inc.

IMPORTANT AREAS OF REGULATION

The vigor of regulatory activity by the federal government with respect to the promotional activities of business has increased steadily over the past decade and a half. The special message sent to Congress by President John F. Kennedy in 1962 entitled "Strengthening of Programs for Protection of Consumer Interests"[13] can be said to have marked the beginning

---

[13] *Congressional Record,* March 15, 1962, pp. 108, 3813–3817.

of an era. Certainly the years since the early 1960s have been marked with legislation and administrative actions aimed at promoting a fuller realization of the rights of consumers. In his special message Kennedy enumerated the following four basic rights:

1. *The right to safety*—to be protected against the marketing of goods which are hazardous to health or life.
2. *The right to be informed*—to be protected against fraudulent, deceitful, or grossly misleading information, advertising, labeling, or other practices and to be given the facts he needs to make an informed choice.
3. *The right to choose*—to be assured, wherever possible, access to a variety of products and services at competitive prices, and in those industries in which competition is not workable and government regulation is substituted, an assurance of satisfactory quality and service at fair prices.
4. *The right to be heard*—to be assured that consumer interests will receive full and sympathetic consideration in the formulation of government policy, and fair and expeditious treatment in its administrative tribunals.

As noted in the preceding sections, the Federal Trade Commission and the Food and Drug Administration are the major but by no means the only recipients of power to regulate promotional activity by business. We will discuss briefly some of the regulatory efforts of these two agencies and the philosophy underlying their actions.

Content of Advertisements

A large proportion of present and proposed regulation involves restriction or control of the content of the advertisement. These questions of content include whether or not the advertisement is truthful, in bad taste, invades the reader's right of privacy, and so forth. The FTC has been especially concerned with cases of deception, while the legislative branch of the federal government has passed laws which actually forbid the advertising of certain products in selected media.

Misleading representation. Many of the complaints issued by the FTC were aimed at stopping such overt deceptions as the misrepresentation of foreign merchandise as having domestic origin or claiming in the absence of proof that a wheat germ oil improves heart action.[14] A more important issue from the viewpoint of the mass communicator, however, has arisen from a series of complaints issued by the FTC pertaining to the representation of products in television commercials.

The so-called sandpaper case stands as a landmark. The Ted Bates

---

[14] Advertising Alert no. 8, August 30, 1963.

Advertising Agency claimed in a series of television commercials that Palmolive Rapid Shave would soften sandpaper sufficiently to permit shaving the sand grains from the paper.[15] To illustrate this claim on television a sheet of plexiglass covered with sand was substituted for sandpaper. The Commission held that such a representation was false and misleading, but the respondents answered that the technical requirements of television present such difficulties that substitutes often must be made for materials used in commercials. They went on to point out that there was no intent to deceive and that such substitution in no way misrepresented product qualities. The FTC ruled as follows, however:

The argument . . . would seem to be based on the wholly untenable assumption that the primary or dominant function of television is to sell goods, and that the Commission should not make any ruling which would impair the ability of sponsors and agencies to use television with maximum effectiveness as a sales or advertising medium. . . . Stripped of polite verbiage, the argument boils down to this: "Where truth and television salesmanship collide, the former must give way to the latter." This is obviously an indefensible proposition. . . .[16]

As a result of this decision, *both the client and the agency were prohibited from making any type of deceptive claim in the future.* Notice that the order issued was so broad as to prohibit future deception, although criteria defining deception were not in existence. The courts held that such a broad order was improper and remanded the FTC to reconsider the case. A revised order was later issued.[17] The Commission was upheld by the federal courts, and it was a final decision that the sandpaper mock-up used was deceptive. This finding does not mean that mock-ups and other artificial devices are prohibited; rather, it constrains the advertiser from using demonstrations which are likely to mislead.

The courts have traditionally held that advertising must be written so as not to deceive "the trusting as well as the suspicious, the casual as well as the vigilant, the naive as well as the sophisticated."[18] In the sandpaper case the product did not remove grains from sandpaper in the manner claimed in the television commercial. Doubts have been expressed, however, as to whether such a presentation really misrepresents product features in such a manner as to be harmful to the consumer. The problem is, of course, one of defining where puffing stops and misrepresentation begins.

Since the sandpaper case the FTC has handled several similar situations. In one case the FTC accepted an assurance of voluntary compliance from Lever Brothers Company, Inc., to discontinue certain TV commercials

---

[15] Advertising Alert no. 1, January 12, 1962.

[16] Ibid.

[17] Advertising Alert no. 6, June 28, 1963.

[18] "How the U.S. Regulates Advertising," p. 184.

advertising its laundry detergent, All. The TV spots in question showed an actor wearing a stained shirt being immersed in water up to his chin. As the water rose the actor added the detergent and expounded on its efficacy. As the water receded the actor showed off his stainfree shirt. The FTC ascertained that the shirt had been washed in the interim by means of a standard washing machine and had not been cleaned by the immersion process.

Voluntary compliance rather than more formal means of procedure was accepted in this use by the FTC because it was held that the commercial in question was of a "fanciful or spoofing" variety. The FTC held, however, that even these types of commercials can be misleading and suggested that any advertiser in doubt as to whether its commercial had the capacity to deceive should make application to the FTC for an advisory ruling prior to the dissemination of the commercial for broadcast.[19]

A recent action against misleading advertising occurred in March 1970 when the FTC issued a consent order prohibiting the Colgate-Palmolive Company and its advertising agency from using "deceptive tests, experiments or demonstrations to sell its products." The FTC specifically challenged the truthfulness of a water demonstration TV commercial for Baggies, the company's brand of plastic bag wrap.[20]

It should be noted that "consent orders differ from orders in litigated cases only in that they do not constitute a finding or an admission that respondents have violated the law."[21] They are fully as binding in forbidding respondents to engage in the practices prohibited by the order. Consent orders cannot be appealed to the courts. Sixty days after their issuance they become enforceable by fines up to $10,000 per violation.

Unfairness. In a 1972 decision by the Supreme Court (*FTC* v. *Sperry & Hutchinson*)[22] the FTC was encouraged to apply the doctrine of unfairness to protect consumers. When the FTC was founded in 1914 Congress granted the FTC the power to proceed against "unfair methods of competition." In the Wheeler-Lea amendment (1937) the powers of the FTC were extended beyond unfair methods of competition to "unfair or deceptive acts or practices." This was the first attempt to extend the jurisdiction of the FTC in this area from manufacturers and competitors to include consumers as well.

The Magnuson-Moss Act (1975) as noted previously supported the unfairness doctrine and its extension to rule development for consumer protection. The FTC wasted little time in exercising its new powers and proceeded to develop rules to regulate the advertising of opthalmic goods

---

[19] Advertising Alert no. 3, March 31, 1969.

[20] Ibid.

[21] Ibid.

[22] *FTC* v. *Sperry & Hutchinson Co.* (1972), 405 U.S. 233.

(1978), vocational schools (1978), the funeral industry (1979), credit (1979), used cars (1979).

In 1978 the FTC staff report on regulation of television advertising to children was published.[23] The public outcry was so vociferous that in 1980 Congress passed the FTC Improvement Act which put the use of the unfairness doctrine on hold for three years while a study was made to determine the desirability of using unfairness as a factor in regulating advertising. Nothing in the legislation prevented the FTC from continuing to monitor advertising and to use the doctrine of "deception" to make a case against an advertiser who, in the opinion of the FTC, was guilty of misleading the consumer. The status of the use of "unfairness" in the regulation of promotion remains uncertain at the time of writing this chapter.

Health claims.   The FTC is also using its regulatory powers to control advertised health claims. In March 1969 the FTC made public its "Proposed Guides for Advertising Over-the-Counter Drugs." Although advisory, these guides were aimed at assuring that: (1) the benefits, efficacy, or safety of these drugs are not misrepresented, (2) advertising is consistent with labeling, and (3) untruthful claims of superiority of one product over another are not made.[24] These guidelines follow a long series of complaints such as those the FTC has lodged against the J. B. Williams Company because of certain advertised health claims made for the company's product, Geritol. In 1965 the FTC issued a cease and desist order requiring that Williams and its advertising agency stop misrepresenting the effectiveness of Geritol. The company appealed the order to the federal courts, and in August 1967 the U.S. Court of Appeals for the Sixth Circuit upheld the Commission's order with minor modifications. In 1968 the FTC claimed that its modified order was being violated again and threatened Williams with punitive action unless the offending commercials were promptly withdrawn.[25]

Obscenity and bad taste.   It is difficult to define what is obscene or what is in bad taste. Generally, advertisers and the media have policed themselves to avoid advertising which might prove to be illegal or offensive, given present-day community standards. Because of many complaints about receipt of "sexually provocative" direct mail advertisements, a law was passed by Congress in 1967 entitled "Prohibition of Pandering Advertisements in the Mails."[26] This act allows a householder to file a notice with the local postmaster requesting that certain advertisements not be delivered to his or her address. When notified by the postal authori-

---

[23] *FTC Staff Report on Television Advertising to Children (1978)*, submitted to the Federal Trade Commission, February, 1978.

[24] Advertising Alert no. 3, March 31, 1969.

[25] Advertising Alert no. 8, December 31, 1968.

[26] Title III of the 1967 Postal Revenue and Federal Salary Act.

ties, the advertiser must remove the householder's name from the mailing list and make certain that no future mailings are sent to that address. A U.S. Supreme Court decision of May 1970 upheld the 1967 law and interpreted it so broadly that a citizen of the United States has the right to prevent a direct mail advertiser from sending anything at all one does not wish to receive.

Type of Product Advertised

There are social conventions which prevent certain types of products from being advertised. For example, hard liquor is not as yet advertised on television, and only in recent years have women been seen in printed media advertisements for liquor. Social objection to advertising is diminishing, with the result that more freedom is being exercised not only with respect to what is being advertised but also with respect to how it is presented.

The most important restriction upon the promotion of a product in the history of advertising occurred on January 1, 1971. After that date the FTC was empowered to ban the advertising of cigarettes on radio and television. The amount of revenue lost by the broadcast industry has been enormous, and although some of the funds used for broadcast advertising have been shifted to other media, in total the cigarette industry has drastically cut back on advertising expenditures. In addition to the ban on broadcast advertising, the legislation also required that the cigarette label contain the statement, "Warning, The Surgeon General has determined that cigarette smoking is dangerous to your health."

The FTC also acquired the authority to monitor the cigarette industry's other advertising activities to see if a large buildup of promotion in non-broadcast media would occur. As noted above, there was no such buildup, and this part of the law has remained inoperative.

In February 1978 the FTC issued a staff report which recommended that advertising on television aimed at young children be restricted sharply.[27] The rule as proposed by the FTC's Bureau of Consumer Protection would: (1) ban all advertising on television shows seen by substantial audiences of children under age 8, (2) ban advertising of sugary foods on television shows seen by significant numbers of children between the ages of 8 and 11, and (3) allow continued advertising on TV of "less hazardous" sugared foods to the 8–11 group, but only if such advertising were "balanced" by advertiser-funded nutritional and health disclosures.

Vertical Cooperative Advertising

Advertising in which the manufacturer shares the cost with resellers is called vertical cooperative advertising. This type of promotion is big

---

[27] "Report by the FTC's Staff Recommends Major Strictures on Children's TV Ads," *Advertising Age*, February 27, 1978, p. 1.

business; estimates have been made that over $1 billion is spent annually in this country on co-op advertising. Because payments for co-op advertising may be used as disguised price discrimination, a practice which is illegal under the Robinson-Patman Act, the FTC is quite vigilant in monitoring co-op programs to ensure their legality. On June 1, 1969 the latest revised guidelines for the use of co-op advertising were issued by the FTC. These guidelines are reviewed in some detail in Chapter 21. At this point it is sufficient to recognize that the use of cooperative advertising programs is subject to considerable legal constraint.

Advertising and Competition

An opinion held by an increasing number of governmental officials is that the excessive use of advertising can have a harmful effect on competition. This opinion received a great deal of impetus from the U.S. Supreme Court's decision in 1967 to uphold the FTC's order that Procter & Gamble divest itself of the Clorox Company which it had acquired 10 years earlier.[28] One of the principal considerations involved in this decision was the fact that the huge advertising outlay of Procter & Gamble and the advertising expertise it had at its disposal substantially reduced competition in the liquid bleach industry.

In February of 1971, the FTC accused four major cereal manufacturers of having a joint market monopoly. Kellogg, General Mills, General Foods, and Quaker Oats were alleged to have engaged in "actions or inactions" over a period of 35 years that have resulted in a highly concentrated, noncompetitive market for ready-to-eat cereals. The FTC stated that this had been accomplished by "proliferation of brands and trademark promotion, artificial differentiation of products, unfair methods of competition in advertising and promotion, and acquisition of competitors."[29]

In attempting to set new legal precedents through the application of antitrust law to oligopolies as well as monopolies, the FTC is facing years of litigation. The four companies cited filed formal denials of the charges stating that competition in their industry is "vigorous, substantial and effective."[30] After over 10 years of legal skirmishing and the expenditure of millions of dollars by both sides, the case was dropped by the Reagan administration in 1982. Thus, the FTC's foray into the application of antitrust law to oligopolies may be blunted for some time to come.

Although strong arguments have been made to support the view that advertising adds to the competitive nature of our economy rather than subtracting from it, it seems clear that for the foreseeable future govern-

---

[28] "A High Court Backs FTC; Orders P & G to Drop Clorox," *Advertising Age*, April 17, 1967, p. 1.

[29] *Washington Report*, May 12, 1972, pp. 5–6.

[30] *Washington Report*, July 26, 1972, p. 8.

mental antitrust actions will be a constraining influence on larger users of advertising.[31] This issue is discussed further in Chapter 25.

Remedial Alternatives

Various remedies for consumer protection have been classified by Cohen into three categories: prevention, restitution, and punishment.[32] Examples of preventive remedies would be the FTC's Codes of Conduct or Trade Regulation Rules as well as the disclosure of information requirements in written consumer warranties as mandated by the Magnuson-Moss Act.

Another type of preventive remedy is "advertising substantiation" a program developed by the FTC in 1971. The goal of advertising substantiation is to ensure that advertisers use only those claims for their product or service offerings which can be supported by fact. Since the inception of the program, companies in a variety of industries have been required to submit proof of stated claims or to terminate or modify the advertising message in question.[33]

For several years following the introduction of the program complaints were settled by either the furnishing of acceptable proof by advertisers or by signing a consent decree under which the advertiser agreed to modify or terminate his claim. As part of the consent decree in some cases the FTC required that the advertiser devote a portion of its future advertising to what has been termed "corrective advertising." In such advertising the consumer had to be informed as to the true status of the product or service and any misleading claims had to be corrected or modified.

In 1975, the FTC found that claims made for Listerine mouthwash by its manufacturer, Warner-Lambert Company, were false. The company had advertised for almost 50 years that Listerine could prevent common colds or lessen their severity. These claims could not be substantiated and the FTC required that their use be terminated. In addition, Warner-Lambert was ordered to insert in the next 10 million dollars of their advertising the statement, "Contrary to prior advertising, Listerine will not help prevent colds or sore throats or lessen their severity."

Warner-Lambert tested the findings of the FTC and its authority to order corrective advertising in the federal courts. In two cases brought before the Court of Appeals for the District of Columbia Circuit in 1977 the FTC was upheld both on its original finding that the advertising claims were false and on its authority to order corrective advertising.

---

[31] See Jules Backman, *Advertising and Competition* (New York: New York University Press, 1967).

[32] Dorothy Cohen, "Remedies for Consumer Protection: Prevention, Restitution, or Punishment," *Journal of Marketing* 39 (October 1975): 24–31.

[33] "How Government Regulates Advertising," p. 147.

The corrective statement, however, was modified slightly in that Warner-Lambert was allowed to drop the phrase "Contrary to prior advertising" from the corrective statement.[34]

Warner-Lambert took the case to the Supreme Court which in 1978 refused to review the findings of the appeals court. Thus the powers of the FTC in both the area of claim substantiation and corrective advertising have been upheld. In the classification schema previously noted the FTC at this date has a powerful preventive remedy in claim substantiation and can order a form of restitution through corrective advertising.

Other remedies classified under the heading of restitution include those which require advertisers to make affirmative disclosure about their products or services indicating the weak points of their offerings as well as the strong ones. Refunds to customers who have been mislead and subsequently harmed, limitations of contracts and cooling-off periods for consumers who buy from door-to-door salespeople are additional forms of restitution which are remedies for consumer protection.

The final category of remedies include punishments. The FTC has the authority to levy fines of up to $10,000 per violation of a cease and desist order. A defendant who refuses to obey an injunction may be found in contempt of court and sentenced to jail. Although the punishment remedy has been used sparingly in the past, it is an effective alternative that can be applied if attempts to protect the consumer through prevention and restitution remedies fail.

SUMMARY

This chapter provided a brief review of some of the more pressing legal restrictions on promotion. The focus was on advertising because it is the communication tool most often singled out for control by state and federal governmental authorities. Content of advertising, type of product being advertised to specific audiences, and the impact of advertising on competition are all areas that require special attention by management if legal problems are to be avoided. Finally, a discussion of the various types of remedies for consumer protection centered around the classification of prevention, restitution, and punishment.

Review and Discussion Questions

1. What have been the major turning points in the historical development of state and federal laws to protect the consumer against false and deceptive methods of sale in the United States since the turn of the century?

2. Explain briefly the original role of the Federal Trade Commission in prevent-

---

[34] *Warner-Lambert Co.* v. *Federal Trade Commission,* CCH #61,563 (CA-D.C., August 1977), and CCH #61,646 (CA-D.C., September 1977).

ing advertising and selling abuses. How has this role expanded since the turn of the century?

3. What is a Printer's Ink model statute?

4. What is meant by the term *misleading representation?* What happened in the famous "sandpaper" case?

5. What is meant by "voluntary compliance"? What is a consent order?

6. Explain how the FTC program of advertising substantiation works?

7. How is the concept of "corrective advertising" linked to the claim substantiation program?

8. Discuss some of the recent changes in the type of product that can be advertised to certain audiences or in specific types of media.

9. What are the implications of the FTC suit against the cereal manufacturers?

10. What is the importance of the Listerine case?

11. What is the difference between remedies such as refunds, limitations of contracts and claim substantiation?

12. In your opinion, is it still possible to develop viable and effective promotional programs given the extent of government regulation?

PART THREE
Determination of Objectives and Budget

Determination of objectives and utilization of the organization's basic financial resources comprise the second and third stages in the framework for promotional planning introduced in Chapter 3. These considerations are discussed jointly in this part because many of the issues overlap and are relevant to both areas. Chapter 10 presents a discussion of (1) the importance of setting promotional objectives, and (2) the difficulties of doing so. Chapter 11 considers procedures to be followed in arriving at a financial budget.

At this stage the promotional program is viewed in its broadest terms; the topics covered are those that can precede detailed consideration of each element of the promotion mix. Subsequent parts pertain specifically to the management of advertising (Part Four) and personal selling, reseller support, and other elements (Part Five). Part Six summarizes the remaining stages of the promotional planning framework with a discussion of how the program is coordinated and evaluated.

CHAPTER 10
Promotional Objectives

This chapter continues discussion of the process of planning promotional strategy and begins at determination of objectives—the second stage following completion of the situation analysis (see Figure 3–1). Good management obviously requires objectives (i.e., a clearly stated desired end-result), and this fact has always been recognized by those engaged in promotional strategy. Communication and persuasion, however, are still understood imperfectly at best, and it is not surprising that it often is difficult to clarify the function of these variables in the marketing mix. In fact, these difficulties have caused many to avoid setting objectives altogether, with the result that promotion frequently falls short of its potential.

Objectives must be specified for advertising, personal selling, reseller support programs, and public relations. The greatest problems are most frequently encountered in planning advertising strategy, so determination of advertising objectives is the major subject of this chapter. The concluding section focuses more briefly on objectives for reseller support programs and public relations, but discussion of personal selling is reserved for Part Five.

DETERMINING ADVERTISING OBJECTIVES

Two types of objectives are required if persuasive communication through the mass media is to have optimum effectiveness: (1) definition of market targets and (2) objectives for the communication message. Definition of market targets was the subject of Chapter 8 and does not require much additional discussion here. Quite a different set of problems is encountered in establishing message objectives. Objectives must, first of all, specify basic message content (sometimes referred to as the purchase proposition). In addition, the desired end result must be stated with precision. This requires: (1) an objective, quantitative determination of the present status concerning awareness, attitude, behavior, and so on (referred to as the benchmark); (2) the specified change in awareness, attitude, or behavior; and (3) specification of measurement methods and criteria.

Communication versus Sales Objectives

It is interesting to ask executives to indicate what the objectives for their advertising actually encompass. The answer is likely to be, "to increase sales 10 percent," "to make a greater penetration in the Midwest," or "to increase buyer preference," to mention several typical responses. On careful analysis it is apparent that these statements encompass an entire marketing program rather than advertising. It is unreasonable to ask advertising to carry the whole burden *unless* advertising is the only variable in the marketing mix.

A debate has arisen over the appropriate form for advertising objectives. Some maintain that success can only be measured in terms of sales. Others contend that each element in the marketing mix has a more specific role and that a change in sales is the result of each component working together with the others. According to this view, advertising performs the function of persuasive communication through use of mass media, with the result that objectives should be stated in *communication* terms.

This whole argument is tied into the *hierarchy of effects hypothesis,* that advertising and promotion work to stimulate awareness, which leads to attitude change, which leads to behavior change. The hierarchy of effects is basically a model of consumer response to promotional activity. The response may be at a cognitive, affective, or behavioral level. Figure 10–1 presents a graphic representation of the model. This model hypothesizes that the consumer passes through the stages of awareness, knowledge (cognitive), liking and preference (affective), intention-to-buy or conviction, and purchase (behavioral). This assumed relationship has been severely challenged in recent years, however, and both positive and negative evidence has been produced.

The case for communication objectives.   The association of National Advertisers focused industry attention on the case for communication objectives through its influential position paper authored by Russell Colley.[1] Colley's thesis was that advertising should be managed to attain

---

[1] Russell H. Colley, ed., *Defining Advertising Goals* (New York: Association of National Advertisers, 1961).

FIGURE 10–1
Hierarchy of Effects Model

Stage	Response
Cognitive	Awareness ↓ Knowledge
Affective	Liking ↓ Preference
Behavioral	Intention-to-buy ↓ Purchase

clearly stated communication goals so that success and failure can be measured. This philosophy has since become known as DAGMAR (Defining Advertising Goals, Measuring Advertising Results). It is argued that sales cannot serve as the objective because *all* marketing efforts blend imperceptibly to increase volume and profits. In Colley's words: *"Advertising's job purely and simply is to communicate, to a defined audience, information and a frame-of-mind that stimulates action. Advertising succeeds or fails depending on how well it communicates the desired information and attitudes to the right people at the right time and at the right cost."* [2]

The NICB study on setting advertising objectives referred to above disclosed that the minority of companies that do set advertising objectives for the most part state them in communication terms. Many embrace this approach for the reasons mentioned by Colley and for the additional reason that communication objectives are more workable. The argument is that communication response can be measured using existing tools, whereas advertising efforts usually cannot be related to sales short of full-scale market experiments in which all other marketing variables are held constant, while advertising varies. Few firms can afford this type of research on a continuing basis.

The case for sales objectives.   There have been some vigorous attacks on the DAGMAR concept. One leading critic maintains that it is a philosophy of despair:

. . . as a goal for advertising, communication is not superior to sales because it is no longer exclusively caused by advertising. Both communication *and* sales are caused by many factors. In either case, it would be very pessimistic to believe

---

[2] Ibid., p. 21.

that weather or competition or other uncontrollable factors bias the future one way today and another way tomorrow. As Einstein once put it: "Nature may be obscure, but she is not devious." We assume, in other words, the basic stability of enough of the phenomena we *cannot* control or measure to permit the successful prediction of an effect from a few causes we *can* measure and control. Since both sales and communication studies require this assumption, why not measure sales?[3]

Thus, according to this view, it is erroneous to assume that communication is a more precise measure than sales.

Other critics have maintained that promotion can indeed accomplish communication goals yet have no influence whatsoever on sales. It will be recalled that communication is effective only to the extent that it predisposes a prospect to buy at some future point or reinforces an existing preference. But if communication fails in this sense, it is not the fault of the *type* of objective used but the *determination* of the objective.

Assume, for example, that research discloses 60 percent of potential customers who are not aware of a new soap product. Assume further that an advertising campaign then intervenes and communicates product benefits to 50 percent of this group. Does this mean that advertising has been successful? The answer may be no, because communication can implant facts without having any influence in terms of persuasion. In fact, recipients can even be made *less likely to buy* after awareness is stimulated. The point is that the message which is communicated can be irrelevant and totally ineffective in stimulating the necessary predisposition to buy.

On the other hand, the case for sales objectives advanced by the critics of DAGMAR is not especially convincing. They have not refuted the fact that *all* marketing efforts influence sales in most situations. How, then, can advertising be related to sales in such a way that concrete objectives can be established and performance measured at reasonable cost? The fact that needed answers have not been forthcoming virtually necessitates the establishment of communication goals except in those situations where sales is more appropriate as a measure, as is discussed in the section below.

A recommended approach. It is apparent that there is a division of opinion on the question of communication versus sales. However, this is not an irreconcilable issue, because there are situations where communication objectives are required and others where specified sales response is more appropriate.

It will be recalled that some buying situations can be classified as

---

[3] A. J. Vogl (quoting Charles A. Ramond), "Advertising Research—Everybody's Looking for the Holy Grail," *Sales Management,* November 1, 1963, p. 43.

extended decision making in which the buyer proceeds through various stages until the purchase is made. The process begins with problem recognition and extends through such other stages as alternative evaluation and search. It is clear that an individual in the early stages of problem recognition most likely will not be stimulated to make a purchase by being exposed to an advertisement, especially when the planning period for purchase is relatively long, as it might be with such products as major appliances. All that advertising can legitimately be expected to do is to affect one's *propensity to buy* through stimulation of awareness or initial interest. Exposure to communication hopefully should have some effect, therefore, in moving one closer to a purchase at some future point. Stimulation of an immediate sale, on the other hand, is not an appropriate aim.

However, what if the potential buyer has already decided to purchase and is engaging in search. At this point an advertisement or other promotional stimulus may succeed in triggering a sale. Various forcing methods such as price reductions may well be advised for this purpose. In this situation, a sales objective is quite appropriate.

Sales objectives also are acceptable when the planning period for purchase is relatively short—perhaps even a matter of seconds. Relatively little thought, for example, will precede trial of a new soft drink. Similarly, a sales objective was chosen for the Goodyear Christmas Album campaign in which the objective was to present the album at its $1 price so forcefully that consumers would make a special visit to their Goodyear tire dealers to obtain it. It is reasonable to expect that advertising exposure would have this effect.

From these three different situations, it is clear that *the form of the objective depends on the stages of consumer decision making found in the target market segments.* Stimulation of a purchase is, on occasion, proper, but it must not be overlooked that this is accomplished through communication of a persuasive message. Therefore, all promotion goals, in the final analysis, are communicative goals; the only real difference lies in the nature of the expected response.

DAGMAR MOD II

Aaker and Myers in their book, *Advertising Management* propose the use of what they named DAGMAR MOD II. This approach was developed to deal with the serious questions that were raised to challenge one fundamental aspect of the hierarchy of effects model to which DAGMAR is tied. This aspect is the assumption that the consumer always passes through the levels of the hierarchy in the specified order.

Research summarized by Ray has identified circumstances where the order of responses in the hierarchy of effects seems to hold and other circumstances where a different order seems more descriptive of consumer behavior.[4] He identified three situations:

1. Situations where the consumer is highly involved with the purchase process and where high product differentiation exists. Ray called this a *high-involvement learning approach* situation and found that the hierarchy holds. Specifically, awareness learning takes place that leads to knowledge learning that leads to affective learning and so on.

2. Situations where the consumer is highly involved with the purchase process, and where little product differentiation exists. This is called a *cognitive approach* situation. Here the flow is awareness ⟶ action ⟶ attitude. That is, the attitude change follows purchase in order to bring it into a consistent pattern with behavior. This pattern is tied to the reduction of cognitive dissonance associated with selecting from among products with little differentiation.

3. Situations where the consumer has low involvement with the purchase decision process. This is the *low-involvement learning approach*. It is based upon a theory proposed by Krugman to explain the power of television advertising. Krugman hypothesizes that perceptual defenses are absent or reduced when the consumer has low involvement with the promotional message, as one would while watching television commercials. As a result, a change in cognitive structure takes place surrounding the brand being advertised. This change in cognitive structure is not attitude but may relate to knowledge or beliefs. This change affects behavior and then attitude will change to be consistent with the behavior. In other words, in a low-involvement situation, attitude change is not necessary to cause behavior change. The flow is: promotional stimulus received under low involvement (TV commercial) ⟶ shift in cognitive structure other than attitude ⟶ behavior ⟶ change in attitude to be consistent with behavior. (See Chapter 7.)

DAGMAR MOD II instructs the users to determine the nature of the hierarchical model that will apply in the particular circumstances at hand. The hierarchical model should be expected to be situation specific, and research efforts should be expanded to understand each unique circumstance. Second, DAGMAR MOD II puts emphasis on broader analytical models of consumer behavior, in order to better understand the links between variables such as attitude and behavior. The whole focus of Part Two of this book has been to present such a broad analytical focus. Indeed both communications and sales objectives should be set with a good understanding of the relevant consumer behavior.

---

[4] Michael L. Ray, "Consumer Initial Processing: Definitions, Issues, Applications," in *Buyer/Consumer Information Processing*, ed. G. David Hughes and Michael L. Ray (Chapel Hill: University of North Carolina Press, 1974).

Criteria of Workable Objectives

A statement of objectives for the promotional mix should meet five basic criteria: (1) proper definition of market target, (2) clear statement of message content, (3) quantitative statement of benchmarks, (4) specification of appropriate measurement methods and criteria, and (5) designation of time allowed.

Definition of market target.   As has been noted, it is necessary to know both the demographic characteristics of target segments and their media exposure patterns. Fortunately, it now is possible to utilize syndicated research services which provide extensive demographic data on audiences of various media. Thus, the objective of media strategy is to select media which reach the desired audience with a minimum of overlap and waste.

Proper media strategy obviously requires that the target market be defined *specifically*. Examples where sufficient specificity was attained include the following:

1. Research showed that purchasers of Hamilton watches are 35 and older and are in the upper-income and education brackets. Media were then selected to reach this segment.
2. The media objectives for the Shell Oil "racing" campaign for premium motor oil were (1) to reach a mass male audience and (2) to emphasize the 18–49 age group in which racing interest is highest.
3. Bostonian shoes range in price from $29.95 to $60.00, with the result that greatest appeal is to higher-income segments. Thus the objective of a campaign was to direct emphasis to adult males, 18 years of age and over, in middle- and upper-middle-income groups.

In each of these instances, research was undertaken to isolate the demographic characteristics of the target market so that media could be selected to reach the target segment with a minimum of waste.

Consider this statement, however. Arrow shirts were advertised with the objective of reaching both men and women, with special emphasis on "younger readers." Who are "younger readers"? And what is meant by "special emphasis"? This fuzzy objective gives the media analyst no real guidance.

Fortunately, the growing use of the computer in media selection has forced management to be more precise in its thinking, because the computer permits storage of vast amounts of information about media audiences. Therefore there is no excuse for failure to match target audience and media in precise demographic terms.

Clear statement of message content.   At some point it is necessary to specify the basic substance of the communication message. This usually is stated in fairly general terms, with specific details of execution left to artists and writers. As such, this statement is often referred to as the creative platform or purchase proposition. An acceptable creative platform must first of all be based on consumer research which documents the fact that the product features emphasized are an important motivating influence. In addition, it must be stated with sufficient clarity to provide meaningful guidance to those who must execute the concept in a finished advertising campaign.

A good example of a well-stated creative platform is provided by a campaign for White/Westinghouse electric ranges. The objective was to establish White/Westinghouse as the "best buy." Market surveys disclosed that advertising should feature the new "No-Turn Speed Broil," an exclusive product feature that was well received by those surveyed. The following creative platform was specified: "Only White/Westinghouse has the new "No-Turn Speed Broil" for superior broiling. It seals in juices for finest flavor. It broils in half the time and is cleaner, safer, and easier—no smoke—no spatter—no flame—no turn." Notice that judicious use was made of information on consumer motivation (a desire for a clean and smokeless broiler) and information on product characteristics.

On the other hand, consider the difference in this statement of objective: Diet-Rite will be promoted for ". . . its real old-time Cola taste and refreshment." This is little more than a general creative philosophy which lacks the specificity necessary to be of any operational value.

Quantitative benchmark statement. Effectiveness cannot be measured unless there is a quantitative indication of present status concerning awareness, market share, attitude, or other response criteria which form the basis for a statement of objectives. Measurement of effectiveness requires a thorough before-and-after study which documents present status before the campaign and then isolates changes which have taken place. For example, consumers might be asked, "Which brand first comes to mind when you think of typewriters?" Assume that brand A receives an awareness level of 35 percent and that the objective for advertising is to raise this figure to 55 percent. An identical study after the campaign has ceased will indicate whether or not the increase in awareness was achieved.

The Shell Oil campaign mentioned earlier fell short of this criterion because its advertising was undertaken to (1) increase awareness of Shell Oil among the total male audience and (2) obtain greater awareness of product benefits among present customers. Benchmarks are lacking as well as specified percentages of change, with the result that it would be impossible to measure advertising effectiveness. Similarly, Exxon set out to (1) win new customers, (2) increase station sales volume, and (3) increase the sales ratio of premium lead-free gasoline compared with regular lead-free. Once again there are no benchmarks or projected percentages of change.

Contrast the following objectives listed in the NICB study on objectives to those mentioned above:

1. Increase the percentage of heavy family flour users from 20 percent of the total market to 25 percent.
2. Increase the number mentioning brand A when asked, "What brand of all-purpose flour claims it gives you a feeling of confidence when you use it?" from 35 percent to 45 percent.
3. Increase the number mentioning brand A when asked, "What brands of all-purpose flour have you seen or heard advertised recently?" from 60 to 90 percent.[5]

Assuming that the responses specified are valid for purposes of the campaign, this statement of objectives is an ideal illustration of the proper use of benchmarks and expected percentages of change.

Statement of measurement methods and criteria. In appraisals by management the proof of success of a promotional campaign is all too often unrelated to campaign objectives. For example, the goal of a campaign for Welch's grape juice was to convince parents that this product is the best drink for their children because of its nutritious value and good taste. Although increased awareness and conviction comprised the objective, success was measured in terms of a sales increase for which many other factors may have been responsible. There was no measurement whatsoever in terms of awareness or conviction. Similarly, a sales increase was cited as proof of advertising success for Betty Crocker potato products, even though the stated objective was to show how these products can make meals more varied and interesting. While a sales increase is gratifying, it is an irrelevant measure of advertising effectiveness, because a change in sales was not the objective.

A better approach is illustrated by the advertising undertaken for the Aero Commander Division of the Rockwell-Standard Corporation. An objective of increasing awareness was measured by the number of inquiries to the company resulting from the campaign. It was specified initially that the number of inquiries received would be presumed to reflect the awareness that was generated.

In summary, if an increase in sales is desired, then changes should be measured in sales. If an increase in awareness is the objective, changes in awareness *and only awareness* are the proof of success or failure.

Designation of time allowed. Objective statements should also include a provision of the time period in which they are to be accomplished.

---

[5] National Industrial Conference Board, *Setting Advertising Objectives*, 1967.

This would specify the point in time at which the post-campaign measurement would take place.

The Process of Setting Objectives

As mentioned previously, promotional objectives must be consistent with overall marketing objectives, and the task is to define the role for communication within this broader framework. Unfortunately, there is no simple way to translate the marketing goal into communication terms. Suppose it has been determined that the marketing program for an airline is to increase customer traffic 20 percent within the next year. What is the role for communication?

The logical approach, of course, is to begin with the problem analysis. The answer might lie in stimulating traffic among present customers, among light users, or perhaps among nonusers. Is there any area where buyers feel that the company is failing to meet their needs? It is possible, for example, that scheduling problems in the past have discouraged some potential travelers, or perhaps previous delays in arrival are at fault. Whatever the case, valuable clues should emerge from the problem analysis, and, if so, the role for communication should be clarified.

Assume that the difficulty indeed lies in buyer dissatisfaction with delays in arrival and resulting inconveniences. It may be that this situation can be remedied; if so, communication of this fact to prospective travelers may be a key to increasing sales. Obviously, however, an increase in sales will be the result of a properly tuned marketing program consisting of product, services, price, and so on.

The key, therefore, lies in a careful situation analysis, especially in the area of consumer demand. The following aspects are of particular importance: (1) the rating received by the product according to evaluative criteria; (2) the information base of those in the target market—i.e., awareness of the product and its features; (3) the nature of the search process, if any, and the sources of information which are used; and (4) strength of preference and attitude.

In the survey of engineers' attitudes toward relay brands conducted by the Sigma Instruments Company, the company received a good overall rating along evaluative criteria with the exception of two aspects: (1) breadth of line and (2) competitive prices. Apparently prospective buyers were unaware that the company was quite competitive in these respects. To build awareness an advertising campaign was undertaken which featured a four-page insert in a limited number of publications. Advertisements featured both competitive prices and breadth of line; and a free relay was offered for trial. The results were higher ratings along the dimensions of price and breadth of line as well as a strong pattern of increase in sales. The campaign thus featured relevant information which, when communicated effectively, resulted in increases in both awareness and sales.

Obviously it is impossible to provide a general formula to be followed in setting objectives. It is useful to describe one example in detail because it offers a good illustration of effective use of background analysis, to say nothing of highly analytical promotional planning.[6]

General Motors Corporation: A case history. The General Motors Corporation has modified the DAGMAR approach to fit the unique needs of its various divisions. The basic research instrument used is a relatively standardized questionnaire which covers many of the points previously discussed in Part Two. A prospective buyer is first asked to indicate brands he or she considers to be competitive for the business, regardless of whether or not they are regarded favorably or unfavorably. Then those brands that receive favorable consideration are determined, and the respondent is run through a product-image battery of questions consisting of 35 different image items for each brand included in the buying class. The general format of the questionnaire is indicated in Figure 10–2.

FIGURE 10–2
Content of Questionnaire to Establish Advertising Goals
for GM Products

```
     I.  Preference levels by brand by series of brand
         1.  Awareness
         2.  "Buying class"
         3.  "Consideration class"
         4.  First choice
    II.  Product image
   III.  Message registration
         1.  Specific product attributes
         2.  Pricing structure of the market
         3.  Familiarity with the market
         4.  Slogans
    IV.  Market behavior
         1.  Shopping behavior, dealer visits
         2.  Intentions
         3.  Purchases
     V.  Product inventory
         1.  Content and condition
    VI.  Demographics
   VII.  Media consumption (hours per week)
         1.  Television by selected programs
         2.  Magazines by selected magazines
         3.  Radio by time slot
         4.  Newspapers by type
```

---

[6] "How G.M. Measures Ad Effectiveness," *Printers' Ink,* May 14, 1965, pp. 19–29. Facts and figures are reproduced with special permission.

The heart of the GM approach is measurement of advertising goal accomplishment through a series of matched independent surveys. The benchmark wave of interviews leading to objectives for the campaign is followed by five subsequent waves throughout the year. If the campaign is not progressing as planned, changes are made in objectives and plans.

Using this procedure, it is possible to place a value on each of the preference levels isolated through consumer interviews. In one example, given the fictitious name "Watusi," the data in Figure 10–3 resulted.

Five percent of those studied considered Watusi their first choice. Subsequent interviews indicated that 84 percent will actually visit a dealership, and 56 percent will purchase the automobile. Thus it is possible to relate preference and awareness to later buying action and to *assess the economic worth of moving a prospect from one preference level to another.*

Assume that a decision is made to aim promotional efforts to people in the "buying class" with the objective of moving them to include Watusi in their "consideration class." To move a person from one preference level to another it is necessary to modify one's attitude toward the product

FIGURE 10–3
Value of Preference Levels for Watusi in Terms of Probability of Purchase and Dealer Visitation

	Preference level (percent) March 19—	Probability will visit Watusi dealer	Probability will buy Watusi
Watusi first choice	5%	0.840	0.560
Watusi in consideration class	7	0.620	0.220
Watusi in buying class	8	0.400	0.090
Aware of Watusi	14	0.240	0.050
Not aware of Watusi	66	0.015	0.004
Total	100%		

so that the person regards it favorably. At this point the research data on various components of the product image become useful. In the Watusi example, the findings in Figure 10–4 were reported.

Thus the image of Watusi was available for two target groups. If no difference is detected in opinion regarding a feature, it has little significance at this level of preference. While Watusi had a poor reputation for gas economy, there was no difference between the two preference levels on this issue, and this factor was of little relevance. The feature where the difference was greatest is trade-in value. While this make, in fact, did offer the highest trade-in value, this point had not registered with a certain market segment. So the advertising goal was to improve the Watusi reputation for trade-in value, and the statement of objectives outlined in Figure 10–5 was used.

The strategy used to attain these goals was not specified, but a measure-

FIGURE 10-4
Item Average Ratings of Watusi by Those Considering It to Be in Their
Buying Class (on scale of 1-100)

	Will not give it favorable consideration	Will give it favorable consideration	Difference
Smooth riding	88	91	3
Styling	76	89	13
Overall comfort	81	87	6
Handling	83	86	3
Spacious interior	85	85	0
Luxurious interior	79	85	6
Quality of workmanship	80	83	3
Advanced engineering	77	83	6
Prestige	73	82	9
Value for the money	76	79	3
Trade-in value	59	77	18
Cost of upkeep and maintenance	63	67	4
Gas economy	58	58	0

ment of results showed a change from 59 to 75 in evaluation of trade-in value of the Watusi by those who previously would not give it favorable consideration, a sharply favorable increase.

The method used here, of course, is by no means suggested for every problem. But it illustrates how one company grappled with the issues and established concrete and measurable research-based objectives, even though they did not establish a target level that the rating of the Watusi was expected to reach.

Problems in Determination of Objectives

It should by no means be inferred that determination of objectives is an easy process. Several difficulties can assume major importance: (1) determining a realistic expected result stated in quantitative terms, and (2) setting up before-and-after studies to measure effectiveness.

FIGURE 10-5
Advertising Goal Statement for Watusi

Division	Series or product—Watusi
Advertising objective	To increase rating of Watusi regarding trade-in value
Target market	All male heads of new car-owning households
Size of target market	19,100,000
Dates goal is to be in effect	October to following September

Determining a realistic expected result. A realistic expected result can be discussed in the context of an actual problem—promotion of sales in the tea industry.[7] An association of importers and producers recognized that tea consumption was lagging behind the growth of population and total food sales. The 10 percent who were steady tea drinkers consumed over 50 percent of the total; those who drank it occasionally totaled another 40 percent. A large remaining segment regarded it as a "sissy" drink. The industry agreed to attempt to change the image and make tea a more popular drink, and the marketing goal was to increase tea consumption an average of 5 percent per year.

How does one move from this overall marketing goal to a realistic promotion objective? In this situation, it was obvious that consumers regarded tea as something for the "sick, weak, or elderly" and did not view it as a preferred mealtime drink. Therefore, the role for communication was to change this basically unfavorable image through stressing regular home consumption and associating the product with such positive terms as "cheery," "friendly conversation," and so on.

Assuming that $2 million is available to spend and that only 20 percent now view tea favorably, the question is how much change can be accomplished through this expenditure. This is an extremely difficult question. In this example the goal was to raise the image to a rating of 40 percent after five years, and there is every indication that it was achieved. How the specified 20 percent increase was determined is not known.

Determination of a realistic expected result usually must begin with past experience, and this can be an invaluable guide. Ideally, records have been kept over time so that the response from past campaigns has been logged. Postmortems are particularly valuable in determining what works and what does not work. Unfortunately, records of this type are seldom kept in usable form. No doubt the growing insistence by management on more precise objectives and accountability for performance will do much to remedy this deficiency in the future.

Another possibility is to undertake experimentation to ascertain the amount of change that can reasonably be expected. Sometimes this can be done in a laboratory, although expensive test market experiments may also be required. The artificiality of the former approach and the costs of the latter make experimentation the distinct exception rather than the rule. This may change as computer simulation becomes more commonplace, because it is possible to simulate the behavior of a market segment and thus gain some rough insight into possible response to promotional efforts.

Setting up before-and-after studies. While measurement of effectiveness is the subject of later chapters, it is worth pointing out here

---

[7] Colley, *Defining Advertising Goals*, pp. 74–76.

that measurement methods can present some real obstacles. One problem is to select matched samples on a before-and-after basis. Even more critical is the need to isolate what would have happened in any event had no advertising been undertaken.

Implications of Objective Setting

The many issues in the setting of objectives for advertising make it clear that objectives cannot be established through automatic use of checklists or rules of thumb. There is no substitute for research into the problem, with proper market segmentation at the heart of the inquiry.

Selection of the best or optimum strategy probably is an illusive goal. It is more realistic to anticipate that careful attention to objectives will, at the very least, help management to avoid gross misallocation of resources. In addition, establishment of a research tradition within a business firm which insists upon postmortems of campaigns and collection of records documenting success or failure should lead to an accumulation of invaluable experience. The base is then provided for growing precision in promotional strategy.

OBJECTIVES FOR OTHER AREAS OF THE PROMOTIONAL MIX

Personal selling objectives are discussed in detail in Chapter 19 and hence are not discussed here. Therefore, this section focuses first of all on determination of objectives for reseller support programs and concludes with a similar discussion for the public relations function. Although the predominant part of this chapter is devoted to advertising, this is not meant to indicate that the use of mass media is necessarily of greatest importance in the promotional mix. Advertising was discussed in greater depth primarily because much that was said about objective setting there is fully applicable in this section as well.

Reseller Support Programs

Although communication with consumers is direct in the form of mass media messages, goods are physically distributed to these same consumers in more indirect fashion. The channels of distribution often are long and may include many intermediaries such as wholesalers and retailers. When these intermediaries or resellers assume title to goods, manufacturer control over how these goods are resold is sharply restricted. As a result, the manufacturer may encounter great difficulty in encouraging resellers to cooperate in the overall promotional strategy through personal selling support, retail advertising, display, and so on. Because the potential selling power inherent within the reseller organization is so great, few companies can neglect seeking support for their lines regardless of the difficulties which are presented.

As the discussion in Part Six will indicate, there is much the manufacturer can do to stimulate reseller support through pricing strategy, inventory policies, controlling the competition by others who sell the same product, training programs and other devices intended to improve selling performance, and supplemental activities such as missionary salespersons and provision of selling aids. Each of these activities, in turn, must be based on objectives which specify the anticipated end result in quantitative terms.

Unfortunately, the area of reseller support programs has suffered from lack of attention to properly defined and stated objectives. Usually programs are undertaken with no statement of objectives. In addition, those which are used frequently are nothing more than general policies or philosophies as is illustrated by the following example.

The International Nickel Company, Incorporated (Inco) developed a comprehensive program to stimulate the sales of stainless steel products in department stores. An in-store program was instituted with the objective of spotlighting stainless steel, creating sales excitement at the retail level, generating a sales playback to manufacturers of stainless steel products, and stimulating larger purchases of nickel by the steel companies, Inco's major customers. There is no possible way that Inco can determine whether or not its program succeeded because there are no benchmarks. Even if sales of stainless steel items increases, how much of an increase is necessary to justify the costs? "Creating excitement at the retail level" is nothing more than an unmeasurable platitude.

Consider, on the other hand, the reseller strategy underlying the Goodyear Christmas Album campaign discussed earlier. One of the objectives was to persuade 80,000 dealers to stock the Christmas Album and to promote it locally. A clear-cut target is presented, and it is possible to assess success or failure in terms of dealer orders and retail promotional activity.

These two illustrations reinforce the point that objectives are useful *only* when they are stated with sufficient precision to provide guidance for strategy as well as benchmarks for measurement of effectiveness. The reseller promotional program is not an exception to this general rule.

Public Relations

Public relations is defined as the communication function "which evaluates public attitudes, identifies the policies and procedures of an individual or an organization with the public interest, and executes a program of action to earn public understanding and acceptance."[8]

---

[8] Bertrand R. Canfield and H. Frazier Moore, *Public Relations: Principles, Cases, and Problems,* 8th ed. (Homewood, Ill.: Richard D. Irwin, 1981), p. 4.

The role for its most frequently utilized tool, publicity, is to present "information designed to advance the interests of a place, person, organization, or cause and used by mass media without charge because it is of interest to readers or listeners."[9]

Since public relations and publicity represent a communication function, all that was said earlier pertaining to advertising objectives is applicable here. To provide greater insight into the unique problems of public relations management, however, it is useful to discuss briefly the target markets for public relations efforts and the goals which can be accomplished.

Target markets and objectives.   Figure 10–6 provides an overview of the target markets for public relations and some of the tasks which can be accomplished through this form of communication.

FIGURE 10–6
Target Markets and Representative Objectives for the Public Relations Function

Ultimate consumers
  Disseminate information on the production and distribution of new or existing products
  Disseminate information on ways to use new or existing products

Company employees
  Training programs to stimulate more effective contact with the public
  Encouragement of pride in the company and its products

Suppliers
  Providing research information for use in new products
  Dissemination of company trends and practices for the purpose of building a continuing team relationship

Stockholders
  Dissemination of information on: (1) company prospects; (2) past and present profitability; (3) future plans; (4) management changes and capabilities; and (5) company financial needs

The community at large
  Promotion of public causes such as community fund-raising drives
  Dissemination of information on all aspects of company operations with the purpose of building a sense of unity between company and community

Notice that the emphasis is on dissemination of information with the intent of creating a more favorable image for a company and its products. Thus the expected results often are intangible and difficult to measure. Nevertheless, public relations is a communication function, and it should be undertaken to accomplish specific communication goals. The fact is, however, that only a few leaders seem to have grasped the essence of goal-oriented management which insists upon accountability for performance. As a result, public relations all too frequently is not phased into the promotional mix on the same basis as advertising and other forms

---
[9] Ibid.

of communication. There is no reason why this state of affairs should continue, because it primarily reflects questionable management rather than unique difficulties inherent in the public relations function.

Interrelationship among Objectives

Objectives assigned to the various promotional activities are complementary to each other. In combination with objectives for other elements of the marketing mix they yield the overall marketing objectives, which in turn combine with objectives for finance, production, and so forth, to yield overall company objectives. Figure 10–7 represents this hierarchical relationship among objectives. For simplicity, other marketing mix objectives and objectives for other departments have been omitted from the figure.

SUMMARY

While all would agree that promotional strategy should be based on objectives, determination of objectives is a demanding task. Only a minority of firms actually take this step, with the result that it often is impossible to measure success or failure in meaningful terms. This can lead to perpetuation of ineffective promotional strategy.

All of the elements of the promotional mix, in essence, are communication functions. As such they should be managed to attain communication goals which have been discovered by a research-based situation analysis.

It was stressed in this chapter that communication objectives should

FIGURE 10–7
Relationship of Promotional Objectives to Other Objectives

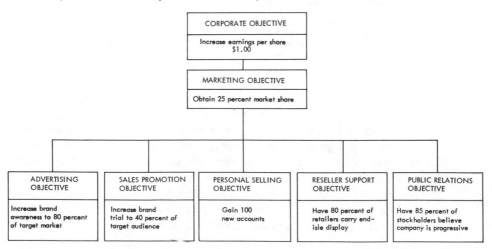

encompass the target market, message content, the desired effect, and measurement methods and criteria. Many examples were given to illustrate varying degrees of success or failure in meeting these criteria. Enough is now known, however, to refute any justification for management not being goal oriented, and it is anticipated that the growing insistence by management on accountability will lead to a sharp increase in goal orientation.

Review and Discussion Questions

1. Briefly explain the differences between different hierarchy of effects orderings, and how these affect promotional objectives.

2. In one sense it can be said that stimulation of a sales increase is a communication objective. Elaborate.

3. Under what circumstances is a sales objective appropriate? Under what circumstances would it be more appropriate to attempt to stimulate changes in awareness, attitude, or other so-called communication responses?

4. A leading manufacturer of camping trailers based its advertising campaign on this statement of objectives: "Our goal is to tell as many people as possible that camping is fun for the whole family as well as inexpensive and easy." Evaluate.

5. Why must benchmarks be stated? How can they be derived?

6. Evaluate the procedure used by General Motors in determining advertising strategy for the Watuni.

7. The advertising manager for a firm manufacturing a new type of home laundry presoaking agent has $6 million to spend. Present levels of awareness for this new product are approximately 11 percent in most markets. She is faced with the problem of ascertaining how much of an increase in awareness can be generated with expenditure of her budget. How can this problem be solved?

8. What can be done to ensure that attainment of a communication objective will, at some point, also have a positive influence on sales and profit?

9. A leading public relations practitioner made the following statement: "You people in advertising just don't understand the problems we face. We have to do your dirty work. Whenever you blow it, we have to mop up and make the customer happy again. We have to try to make the company look good in the community. We have to tell them that we are concerned about product quality, water pollution, abatement of slums, etc. Your job is easier. Don't tell me I can set goals for what I do. There just isn't any way we can measure performance." Evaluate.

CHAPTER 11

The Promotional Budget

The question of how much should be spent for promotion represents one of the most perplexing problems facing management today. Unfortunately, the answer is not easily found. At best, available methods of budgeting are only rough approximations of an ideal expenditure level.

In approaching this subject, it is important first to understand something of the economist's notion of the optimum expenditure. With this background it is possible to analyze existing budgeting procedures, to grasp the extent to which these methods approximate the ideal, and to analyze the potential of newer methods. Because advertising gives rise to the most perplexing problems in the promotional budget, most of the chapter focuses on problems inherent in advertising budgeting.

THEORETICAL FOUNDATIONS OF THE BUDGETING PROBLEM

The outlay for advertising or any demand stimulation effort ideally is approached in the manner shown in Figure 11–1, using the fundamentals of marginal analysis. The horizontal axis in Figure 11–1 refers to the number of units produced, and the vertical axis represents dollars per unit allocated for particular purposes, in this case advertising. Notice that price remains constant over the entire range of production; this assumption correctly designates that price is seldom changed during any short-run planning period. Moreover, per unit production costs (marginal costs) are assumed to be constant at .20 over nearly the entire range of output.

FIGURE 11-1
Short-Run Determination of Advertising Outlay by
Marginal Analysis

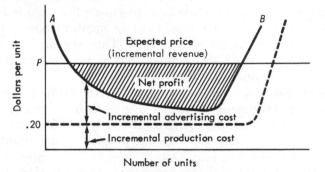

Number of units

Source: Reproduced by permission of Prentice-Hall, Inc., from Joel
Dean, *Managerial Economics* (Englewood Cliffs, N.J.: Prentice-Hall,
1951).

The per unit production cost sharply rises, however, at the point where
certain limits on plant capacity are reached. Costs of physical distribution
of products are included in production cost per unit.

It may be somewhat difficult at first glance to determine which line
represents advertising cost per unit. These costs are shown by line *AB*,
and the amount per unit at any given level of output can be read off
the vertical axis by extending a horizontal line from *AB*, reading the
dollar figure at that point, and subtracting the .20 allocated for production
costs.

It also may be puzzling why line *AB* is represented as a curve which
first declines, then is constant, and later rises at an increasing rate. On
careful analysis it is apparent that a promotional campaign will usually
involve a substantial expenditure, and if only a small number of units
is produced, the costs per unit will be high. In Figure 11-1 these costs
are even represented as exceeding the price per unit at low levels of
output. This cost line soon drops, however, as top prospects are won as
customers and the values of repeated messages and resulting learning
strengthen consumer response. At a later point returns diminish because
fewer prospects are being attracted, and the cost per "conquest" necessarily rises. Costs also may rise after a certain point because quantity discounts from media become less and the efficiency of invested dollars
declines.

The important question now becomes how much should be spent on
advertising and other forms of promotion. Notice that net profit is represented in Figure 11-1 as a diagonally striped area. Whenever promotion
costs per unit drop below the price per unit, a profit results. In other
words, when the total of production and advertising costs per unit is

less than the price per unit, a profit results. Profit continues to be earned until cost line *AB* once again exceeds the price per unit. *Therefore, the firm should continue to advertise until the costs of new business exceed the sales revenue per unit.* This point is reached when line *AB* equals the price line *P*. At this point, the marginal return from advertising equals marginal revenue, and it does not pay to invest more dollars. Thus the advertising and selling costs needed to reach this point would be totaled, and this sum would represent the promotion budget.

The value of marginal analysis is to detect when inefficiencies set in and to direct the investment of dollars to that point where gains are offset by costs. Unfortunately, marginal analysis is little more than a textbook exercise at this time. Consider the problem of determining the advertising response per unit sold. Does it drop in the manner depicted by line *AB,* or does it assume some other shape? Moreover, sales response is not the only relevant factor, for much advertising is directed toward attitude change, changes in awareness, and other strictly communication objectives. What will be the shape of response curves for these factors? Marginal analysis assumes full knowledge of the shape of the response function, but in reality only educated guesses can be made.

The short-run marginal analysis also overlooks the fact that promotion dollars continue to work for a period in the future. The result of this continued effect is that past efforts affect the response in the future and the dollars spent today will continue to pay off for an undetermined future period. This "lead and lag" effect is not represented in the short-run response curve.

Granted the validity of these problems, marginal analysis truly is the ideal approach to budgeting. It focuses on profit, which is the ultimate measure of a business activity. Nevertheless, it can only be crudely approximated by existing budgeting methods. Some newer operations research techniques have been used which appear to offer some promise. As yet, however, the most practical procedure is to use existing methods in combination. This chapter focuses on a procedure to approximate marginal analysis with existing tools.

TRADITIONAL APPROACHES TO BUDGETING

The traditional budgetary methods are: (1) arbitrary allocation, (2) percentage of sales, (3) return on investment, (4) competitive parity, (5) all you can afford, and (6) objective and task. In reality no method is used to the exclusion of others. Each is examined below, prior to suggestion of a composite approach.

Before examination of these procedures, it is interesting to note who are the biggest national advertisers in the USA and in what media they expend their advertising dollars. Figure 11–2 presents this information

FIGURE 11–2

Top 100 National Advertisers in 1980 (six media total, $000s)

Rank	Company	Total	News-papers	Genl. mags.	Farm pub.	Spot TV	Net. TV	Spot radio	Net. radio	Out-door
Airline:										
55	Trans World Corp	$ 52,760.4	33.3	5.8	—	21.8	27.0	12.0	—	0.1
59	UAL Inc.	49,286.2	33.0	7.5	—	25.2	17.2	16.5	—	0.6
71	American Airlines	42,105.2	41.5	9.7	—	26.0	2.5	19.0	—	1.3
76	Eastern Air Lines	40,340.2	50.0	11.4	—	15.7	4.9	13.2	—	4.8
87	Delta Air Lines	35,172.6	58.0	2.3	—	13.1	—	22.9		3.7
Appliances, TV, radio:										
33	RCA Corp.	77,297.3	32.5	31.4	—	8.0	25.7	0.2	1.8	0.4
35	General Electric Co.	74,296.3	16.3	22.1	—	11.3	44.4	1.9	3.7	0.3
Automobiles:										
4	General Motors Corp.......	295,968.4	17.6	18.7	0.7	6.4	41.7	10.9	1.3	2.7
6	Ford Motor Co.	247,310.5	9.9	14.5	1.0	12.8	50.8	7.9	2.3	0.8
9	Chrysler Corp.	165,451.4	12.8	9.9	0.6	7.1	39.5	29.8	0.2	0.1
34	Toyota Motor Sales	75,128.0	9.3	9.3	—	44.0	30.5	4.8	—	2.1
49	Volkswagen of America	59,720.3	8.3	36.3	—	21.7	32.5	0.2	—	1.0
53	Nissan Motor Corp.	54,365.7	12.6	13.6	—	28.3	33.4	10.8	—	1.3
65	American Motors Corp.	45,896.3	4.5	21.4	—	34.7	38.6	0.7	—	0.1
89	American Honda Motor Co.	34,910.7	8.1	30.5	1.2	3.7	44.8	7.5	0.9	2.3
98	Mazda Motors of America ..	30,116.0	1.9	20.9	—	9.2	67.5	—	—	0.5
Chemicals:										
62	Union Carbide Corp.	47,831.1	7.3	3.2	5.4	8.8	66.4	8.0	—	0.9
66	American Cyanamid	44,947.3	0.4	14.6	9.0	30.1	42.9	3.0	—	—
70	DuPont	43,104.4	1.5	50.3	5.4	5.5	36.5	0.6	0.1	0.1
Communications, entertainment:										
26	Time Inc..................	86,773.5	12.6	41.0	—	35.0	10.1	0.4	0.8	0.1
46	CBS Inc.	63,493.5	23.6	47.0	—	13.8	8.2	0.2	5.4	1.8
60	Warner Communications ...	49,104.5	3.5	7.9	—	19.0	64.0	4.9	0.1	0.6
78	MCA Inc..................	40,142.9	17.7	4.1	—	24.0	39.8	12.2	0.9	0.7
81	ABC Inc	37,931.1	31.5	47.5	—	13.0	—	0.5	5.4	2.1
85	Columbia Pictures Industries	36,432.2	0.8	3.2	—	14.1	74.4	7.4	—	0.1
Drugs:										
28	Sterling Drug	83,517.4	0.5	13.9	0.2	6.5	68.8	2.0	8.0	0.1
38	Richardson-Vicks	72,242.5	0.5	6.5	—	17.9	69.1	4.6	1.3	—
50	Schering-Plough Corp.	59,108.4	0.4	19.0	0.5	9.4	59.6	2.1	6.7	2.3
68	Miles Laboratories	44,116.5	0.1	4.6	—	12.5	81.2	0.4	—	1.2
72	Squibb Corp.	41,807.6	1.0	9.2	0.7	9.3	60.8	3.1	15.9	—
84	SmithKline	36,438.8	0.1	19.9	1.4	10.4	61.8	0.1	6.3	—
90	A. H. Robins Co.	34,726.7	0.2	6.5	—	93.2	0.1	—	—	—
96	Pfizer Inc.	30,712.2	0.1	10.4	5.2	4.8	79.1	0.2	0.1	0.1
Food:										
2	General Foods Corp.	338,717.0	2.9	10.1	—	24.6	59.5	1.6	1.2	0.1
10	General Mills	161,142.7	2.1	9.3	—	40.6	47.0	0.7	0.2	0.1
14	McDonald's Corp.	130,862.1	—	1.8	—	54.0	41.0	0.7	0.1	2.4
18	Dart & Kraft Inc.	122,841.5	5.4	22.4	—	27.1	39.2	4.5	0.9	0.5
21	Ralston Purina Co.	114,887.7	1.9	11.8	0.6	17.5	63.8	4.3	—	0.1
24	Pillsbury Co.	96,895.1	3.2	5.3	—	32.9	55.0	2.9	0.3	0.4
25	Kellogg Co................	90,486.2	4.6	4.9	—	21.0	66.1	2.8	0.6	—
30	Consolidated Foods Co. ...	82,571.0	2.1	15.3	—	26.4	52.4	2.2	1.3	0.3
36	Norton Simon Inc.	73,264.2	7.5	23.6	—	27.1	36.5	1.8	0.4	3.1
37	Nestle Enterprises	72,949.6	5.5	7.1	—	35.1	49.4	1.2	1.4	0.3
41	Quaker Oats Co.	68,575.1	1.4	13.8	—	16.4	68.0	0.4	—	—
44	Esmark Inc.	64,819.1	3.2	13.9	—	14.2	64.6	1.9	2.1	0.1
45	Nabisco Inc.	63,923.4	2.1	15.0	—	20.8	61.2	0.9	—	—
61	H. J. Heinz Co.	47,995.7	5.4	10.3	—	32.3	51.5	0.5	—	—
63	MortonNorwich	46,895.2	3.6	6.8	—	15.3	66.5	0.2	7.4	0.2
79	Campbell Soup Co.........	39,997.5	7.0	18.2	—	23.6	41.0	2.8	7.3	0.1
82	CPC International	37,429.9	1.8	13.8	—	32.4	51.3	—	—	0.7
86	Borden Inc................	35,820.7	5.0	12.4	0.5	21.6	49.0	6.7	4.4	0.4
94	Beatrice Foods Co.	31,493.3	8.1	13.5	3.0	46.8	17.0	9.4	1.8	0.4
97	Standard Brands	30,137.4	12.7	18.1	—	35.3	19.7	12.7	—	1.5
100	Carnation Co..............	29,201.8	7.5	2.3	1.0	10.4	78.2	0.1	—	0.5

FIGURE 11–2 (concluded)

Rank	Company	Total	News-papers	Genl. mags.	Farm pub.	Spot TV	Net. TV	Spot radio	Net. radio	Out-door
Gum, candy:										
39	Mars Inc.	$ 70,290.5	4.0	0.4	—	42.0	52.2	1.1	0.3	—
57	Wm. Wrigley Jr. Co.	51,143.5	1.1	1.2	—	26.4	66.7	1.7	2.9	—
88	Hershey Foods Corp.	35,081.8	2.2	8.8	—	26.0	60.8	2.2	—	—
Photographic equipment:										
52	Eastman Kodak	54,474.9	6.0	20.4	—	5.9	63.8	0.5	2.8	0.6
83	Polaroid Corp.	37,194.9	2.5	13.8	—	2.4	80.2	—	1.1	—
Retail chains:										
13	Sears, Roebuck & Co.	143,265.9	—	22.4	—	10.9	60.7	1.8	3.7	0.5
67	K mart Corp.	44,311.0	—	22.4	—	41.7	11.4	19.3	4.9	0.3
80	J. C. Penney	38,894.0	—	13.1	—	37.7	47.8	0.4	0.8	0.2
Soaps, cleaners (and allied):										
1	Procter & Gamble	545,723.2	1.4	6.8	—	24.8	66.1	0.8	—	0.1
16	Unilever U.S.	129,329.1	1.3	11.2	—	29.8	57.3	0.2	—	0.2
32	Colgate-Palmolive Co.	79,336.1	2.6	9.0	0.2	29.8	50.5	7.8	—	0.1
56	Clorox Co.	52,509.3	0.1	7.4	—	7.9	84.6	—	—	—
75	S. C. Johnson & Son	40,411.6	3.6	24.5	—	8.5	57.7	2.6	2.4	0.7
Soft drinks:										
11	PepsiCo Inc.	160,869.9	1.1	1.8	—	36.0	55.2	5.4	—	0.5
15	Coca-Cola Inc.	129,481.7	4.2	3.1	—	36.9	44.7	7.7	1.1	2.3
Telephone service, equipment:										
7	American Telephone & Telegraph Co.	180,665.6	10.6	19.1	—	28.1	31.8	6.7	3.3	0.4
47	International Telephone & Telegraph Co.	63,159.9	6.5	13.8	—	48.6	28.9	1.2	0.1	0.9
Tobacco:										
3	Philip Morris Inc.	319,594.7	24.2	24.8	—	7.1	30.5	3.5	—	9.9
5	R. J. Reynolds Industries	294,124.1	38.5	40.3	—	2.8	3.7	0.2	—	14.5
31	B.A.T. Industries Ltd.	79,457.0	17.2	41.3	—	8.5	—	0.1	—	32.9
40	American Brands	69,598.9	24.2	49.2	—	2.1	8.5	0.1	0.4	15.5
95	Liggett Group	31,386.4	12.0	39.9	—	11.0	30.6	—	—	6.5
Toiletries, cosmetics:										
8	American Home Products Corp.	180,288.2	0.8	5.2	0.3	20.2	68.7	2.9	1.9	—
12	Bristol-Myers Co.	150,996.3	1.7	12.2	—	13.9	70.2	1.8	—	0.2
19	Johnson & Johnson	120,409.1	4.2	15.3	0.2	4.1	75.1	0.5	0.6	—
22	Loews Corp.	112,785.2	40.8	34.2	—	1.4	3.9	0.3	—	19.4
23	Warner-Lambert Co.	98,202.0	2.9	5.8	—	21.7	64.3	0.1	5.0	0.2
27	Gillette Co.	85,981.7	1.4	14.0	—	15.3	69.2	—	—	0.1
42	Chesebrough-Pond's	68,428.7	2.8	16.6	—	8.8	71.7	0.1	—	—
48	Revlon Inc.	61,897.9	1.1	17.7	—	36.1	40.9	1.7	2.5	—
54	Beecham Group Ltd.	54,364.5	0.1	8.9	0.9	10.0	80.0	0.1	—	—
77	Noxell Corp.	40,193.2	0.3	22.4	—	7.4	69.8	0.1	—	—
92	Jeffrey Martin Inc.	33,408.1	0.4	0.7	—	34.1	42.5	—	22.3	—
Wine, beer, liquor:										
17	Anheuser-Busch	127,661.6	1.3	4.0	—	19.0	51.2	21.5	2.0	1.0
20	Seagram Co.	117,339.9	15.4	60.2	—	4.6	9.6	0.3	—	9.9
29	Heublein Inc.	82,959.3	6.1	19.8	—	21.6	36.5	7.7	—	8.3
58	Jos. Schlitz Brewing Co.	50,443.7	0.9	2.9	—	34.5	49.2	11.7	0.1	0.7
93	Brown-Forman Distillers Co.	31,466.9	8.7	46.4	—	11.3	15.9	—	—	17.7
Miscellaneous:										
43	U.S. Government	67,862.1	10.7	27.6	1.1	8.4	27.4	18.7	4.8	1.3
51	Mobil Corp.	55,377.1	10.7	5.0	3.5	59.8	15.6	5.2	—	0.2
64	Gulf & Western Industries	46,114.1	7.0	12.3	—	27.0	49.2	3.2	0.9	0.4
69	Greyhound Corp.	43,732.5	5.1	7.1	—	21.7	55.2	5.8	5.1	—
73	American Express Co.	41,578.8	6.7	14.8	—	27.3	45.0	3.9	2.2	0.1
74	Kimberly-Clark Corp.	40,527.9	3.8	22.7	—	24.4	44.7	0.8	3.6	—
91	Mattel Inc.	33,563.9	3.7	6.2	—	46.2	43.4	0.1	—	0.4
99	Levi Strauss & Co.	29,947.2	1.0	13.2	—	15.7	50.0	18.9	1.2	—

Source: *Advertising Age,* September 10, 1981, p. 12 with permission. Leading National Advertisers, Broadcast Advertisers Reports. Copyright 1982, Crain Communications, Inc.

organized by industry. Note that this Figure does not include local advertising by these advertisers (in newspapers, and so forth). The top 10
are Procter & Gamble, General Foods, Philip Morris, General Motors,
R. J. Reynolds, Ford Motor, AT&T, American Home Products, Chrysler,
and General Mills. If local newspapers were included Sear's expenditures
would be about $450 million, K mart $300 million, and J. C. Penney
$260 million.

Arbitrary Allocation

It goes without saying that allocation by arbitrary methods without
careful analysis has always been common. The shortcomings of such an
approach are numerous. For example, advertising frequently seems to
serve as a vent for executive emotion and personality traits. One authority
puts it this way:

Noneconomic, or psychological, criteria by which management evaluates advertising also need to be understood . . . the function of advertising is highly cathartic,
it is the focus of many strong emotional needs and drives relating to "self-expression" or aggressiveness . . . executive decisions on advertising philosophy and
budget often may reflect as much the executive's psychological profile as they
do the familiar economic criteria. The advertising philosophy and budget may
be determined as much by personality as by profit maximization , , , each type
of executive personality has a characteristic mode of feeling toward advertising
in the light of this association of advertising with self-assertiveness or aggressive
tendencies. Those who have either naturally or compensatorily induced strong
self-expressive tendencies clearly tended to budget more for advertising. The
latter tended to have wider swings in "intuition" or feelings of satisfaction or
dissatisfaction.[1]

Moreover, the budget may in no way be relevant for promotion tasks.
Proper management obviously focuses on profit maximization to the fullest extent possible.

Percentage of Sales

A commonly used method is the percentage of sales approach. This
technique involves nothing more than calculation of the proportion of
the sales dollar allocated to promotion in the past and application of
this percentage to either past or forecasted sales to arrive at the budget.
A fairly common variation is to allocate a fixed amount per unit for
promotion, and then the budget is obtained by multiplying this amount
by the forecasted unit sales. The percentage of sales invested by advertisers

---

[1] Melvin E. Salveson, "Management's Criteria for Advertising Effectiveness," *Proceedings,
5th Annual Conference* (New York: Advertising Research Foundation, Inc., 1959), p. 25. Quoted
with special permission of the Advertising Research Foundation.

188

FIGURE 11–3

Estimates of Average Advertising to Sales Ratios for Selected
Industries for 1980

Industry	SIC*	Advertising/sales
Motion picture	7810	10.7
Cosmetics, health and beauty aids	2844	8.8
Drugs	2830	7.8
Retail furniture	5712	7.8
Beer	2082	6.5
Tobacco/cigarettes	2111	6.3
Retail mail order	5961	5.9
Soft drinks	2086	5.7
Retail household appliances	5722	4.7
Canned foods	2030	4.4
Pens, pencils, etc.	3950	3.6
Radio, TV sets	3651	3.4
Restaurant and fast food chains	5812	2.9
Hotel and motel chains	7011	2.1
Airlines	4511	1.6
Consumer finance companies	6140	1.4
Automobile vehicles	3711	1.7
Petroleum	2911	0.2
Industrial organic chemicals	2860	0.0

* Standard Industrial Classification four-digit code.
Source: *Advertising Age*, August 17, 1981, p. 38. Reprinted with permission. Copyright 1981, Crain Communications, Inc.

on average in a great many industries is reproduced in Figure 11–3. It should not be inferred, however, that firms in these industries determine budgets through use of the percentage of sales approach. Also, individual company expenditures may be quite different from these averages.

Two studies of company practices disclosed that many firms use the sales ratio as a fixed guideline for their budgeting.[2] The base figure is the sales volume projected or forecasted for the period that the budget will cover. Many reported that the percentage used remains constant from year to year, and in some cases industry averages are taken as the point of reference. Variable ratios find favor with some companies, especially when new products are to be introduced.

The percentage of sales approach is in wide use for several basic reasons. It is simple to calculate, and it is almost second nature for management to think of costs in percentage terms. Because it gives an illusion of definiteness, it also is easy to defend to management, to stockholders, and

[2] David L. Hurwood, "How Companies Set Advertising Budgets," *The Conference Board Record*, March 1968, pp. 34–41; and Andre J. San Augustine and William F. Foley, "How Large Advertisers Set Budgets," *Journal of Advertising Research* 15, no. 5 (October 1975), pp. 11–16.

to other interests. In addition, it is a financially safe method because expenditures are keyed to sales revenues, thereby minimizing the risk of nonavailability of funds. Finally, when it is widespread throughout the industry, advertising is proportional to market shares, and competitive warfare is made less probable. This competitive aspect is especially appealing to those who give strong credence to the human inclination to resist change.

It should be clear to the perceptive reader that the advantages of the percentage of sales approach are illusory. Most important is the inherent fallacy that budgeting for promotion as a percentage of past sales views advertising as the *result and not a cause* of sales. This logical deficiency is widely recognized, and forecasted sales rather than past sales are more widely used. The use of forecasted sales, however, is fraught with circular reasoning, because how can sales be forecasted without knowing how much is to be invested in sales-generating efforts? Basically, the fundamental and perhaps fatal weakness is that the focus is not on the promotional job to be done; deceptively simple and arbitrary means are substituted for the comprehensive analysis which must, of necessity, be undertaken to approximate the goals of marginal analysis.

The percentage of sales method, then, is seldom an adequate tool unless the environment is almost totally static and the role for promotion is unchanging from period to period—a highly unusual situation. This method should be used only as a starting point to calculate how many dollars would be allocated if conditions remain the same. Then the promotional objectives must be examined to fine tune the budget to the job to be done. More is said later about this use of percentage of sales.

Return on Investment

Advertising may be viewed as an investment, in much the same manner as additions to plant or other uses of funds. Since dollar flows are not unlimited, advertising should compete for its share in the same fashion as alternative investments. This method seems to be especially logical for institutional advertising, which frequently is considered as an investment.

This type of analysis obviously is only an appealing exercise in logic, because, management can do little more than guess at the probable return from dollars invested. Nevertheless, it is true that payout analysis for other forms of investment is frequently as inexact, so his purpose no doubt is to admonish management to think of promotion in terms of larger organizational objectives. It is probable, however, that estimates of the return on dollars spent for promotion relative to other investments will be an impregnable barrier for some time to come.

Competitive Parity

Dollars are sometimes allocated through emulating competition and spending approximately the same amount. The data in Figures 11–2 or 11–3 could easily be used for this purpose, and similar data are available from many sources, including advertising periodicals, the U.S. Internal Revenue Service, and various trade associations.

Competitive parity offers the advantage that competition, a major component of the environment, is specifically recognized and adaptation to it is sought. In this sense, at least, it represents a small step past the percentage of sales method. It also offers the advantage that competitive relationships are stabilized and aggressive market warfare minimized.

Aside from coping with the variable of competition, however, this technique in no way recognizes other components of the promotion task, and the most gross oversight is total lack of emphasis on the buyer. It also is assumed that all competitors have similar objectives and face the same tasks—a most dubious assumption. It is further assumed that the competitor or competitors matched spent dollars with equal effectiveness; however, identical expenditures seldom imply identical effectiveness. Finally, the only data available to management, short of outright collusion or competitive espionage, are past expenditures. These data become useless, however, if the competitor changes its promotional mix. Future spending plans are seldom known, so the ability to match competitor expenditures will always be limited by available information.

In all fairness it must be stated that few companies rely on competitive parity as the sole means of budgeting. It should not be rejected totally as a budget approach, because competitive efforts can be the dominant variable to be met in the promotional environment. The firm's objectives may by necessity be largely defensive in nature. While it seldom is practical to match the competitor to the degree implied in competitive parity, this consideration often will weigh heavily in promotional strategy.

All You Can Afford

Occasionally it is reported that some firms budget largely on the basis of available funds.[3] It is not unusual for the need for satisfactory profits in a given year to limit advertising expenditures. Also, upper limits are sometimes based on customary ratios between total advertising expenditure and forecasted sales revenue. When these are exceeded, the budget will be pared. In other words, management spends as much as it is felt that company can afford without unduly interfering with financial liquidity.

---

[3] Hurwood, "How Companies Set Advertising Budgets," and San Augustine and Foley "How Large Advertisers Set Budgets."

It cannot be denied that liquidity is an important consideration. Assume the situation shown in Figure 11–4. With successive deduction of margins and other costs and a planned profit of 6 cents per unit, a residual of 13 cents remains for advertising, taxes, and other expenses. Assume further that it is determined that 10 cents will be allocated to advertising and that forecasted unit sales are 100,000. Then the advertising budget cannot exceed $10,000, unless funds are available from other sources. Management may be hard put to counteract financial necessity unless compelling reasons exist for expansion of the budget by borrowing or other means, although management may, with considerable justification, propose "payout planning," a procedure to be discussed later in connection with new-product budgeting.

FIGURE 11–4
Computation of Promotion Cost per Unit

Selling price	$1.00
Retailer margin 30%	−0.30
Wholesalers' selling price	$0.70
Wholesalers' margin	−0.11
Manufacturer's price	$0.59
Manufacturer's production cost	−0.40
Revenue minus costs	$0.19
Specified 6% profit (on retail price)	−0.06
Residual for selling and other costs	$0.13

It is apparent that the $10,000 budget may in no way be related to objectives in that it may lead to either underspending or overspending. For this reason it is seldom relied upon exclusively except possibly in the case of new products or in situations where it is grossly apparent that the firm has underspent in the past and that any amount of funds within reason will still generate a positive marginal return. Regardless of the situation, however, liquidity will always be an important factor, and management must be prepared with convincing arguments to justify requested increases.

Objective and Task

No method discussed thus far stands up under close scrutiny, either because of failure to focus on the job to be done or because of the assumed availability of virtually unobtainable data. This leads to the last major method of budgeting, objective and task. Of all those discussed, it clearly has the most merit and does have moderate use in practice.[4]

---

[4] San Augustine and Foley, "How Large Advertisers Set Budgets."

The objective and task approach is simple to describe. All that is necessary is to spell out objectives realistically and in detail and then calculate the costs necessary to accomplish the objectives. Often financial liquidity will enter as a constraint on the upper limit of the budget. It is assumed that research has been done to specify the tasks necessary to attain the objectives, and all that remains is to put dollar estimates on these efforts.

On the face of it, one cannot argue with this approach. Truly it epitomizes the thinking of marginal analysis in that it forces a striving for the intersection of marginal cost and marginal return. It avoids the arbitrary thinking and the illusory certainty of other approaches and generates research-oriented analysis consistent with a modern philosophy of promotional strategy.

No matter how compelling the advantages, it must be stated that management frequently has no conclusive idea of how much it will cost to attain the objective or even whether or not the objective is *worth* attaining. What is the best way, for example, to increase awareness by 20 percent next year? Should a combination of network television, spot radio, and newspapers be used with hard-sell copy, or should these variables be changed? Obviously all possible combinations of efforts cannot be evaluated, and it is perhaps impossible to isolate the *best* promotion mix. Nevertheless, what other alternative exists for profit-oriented management? There is no shortcut to experimentation and other forms of research, if scientific management is to be implemented.

A realistic goal is to find an approach that seems to work well on the basis of research, estimate the costs, and then accumulate a budget by this means. It may not be the best mix of efforts, but it no doubt will excel that arrived at by percentage of sales or other arbitrary means. Measurement of results then will permit the accumulation of data which, over time, should provide an invaluable source of information for future budgeting with the objective and task method. The difficulty of the method cannot continue to be a barrier to its practice. More suggestions for implementation will be given later in the chapter.

Conclusions on Approaches to Budgeting

Of the budgeting methods discussed, the objective and task approach most nearly approaches the ideal as provided by marginal analysis. Yet implementation of this approach is fraught with the difficulty of estimating the tasks necessary to accomplish objectives, to say nothing of costs. It requires a great commitment related to researching the shape of an individual brands advertising response function as it relates to the objective of interest (awareness, sales, etc.). In general, this response function has been found to exhibit decreasing returns as advertising expenditures are increased.[5] However, to make specific brand decisions on budget, specific research is necessary. The primary objective is to guarantee promotional accountability. Many companies have introduced semiannual, quarterly, or monthly reports for the purpose of reviewing decisions and introducing modifications where necessary. Procter & Gamble, Quaker Oats, Bristol-Myers, and North American Philips are all reported to have instituted this type of system.

IMPLEMENTING THE TASK AND OBJECTIVE APPROACH

The ideal approach to budgeting builds upon the concepts inherent in marginal analysis. The logical procedure would be to establish objectives and then to experiment until that level of expenditure is found which most closely approximates the optimum. It is not uncommon for larger firms to follow this procedure, although it can be time-consuming and expensive.

In one three-year test experiment a major petroleum company divided a large number of cities into three test groups and one control group. One test group received half as much advertising as normal; expenditures were twice the normal rate in another group, and three times the rate in the third. It was found that a 50 percent reduction had no great effect, whereas the greatest sales increases were in the double-expenditure markets. A tripling of the budget led to only minimal further increases. Similarly, a six-year research program at the Anheuser-Busch Company comprising advertising variations in 200 geographical areas showed that it was possible to reduce advertising expenditures and still increase sales. Many feel, as a result, that experimentation is the only feasible approach, given management pressures for greater promotional efficiency and accountability.

Experimentation obviously is not feasible for most firms because of time and cost constraints. Therefore, some combination of the procedures mentioned above usually must be employed. A logical approach encompasses the following steps:

1. Isolation of objectives.
2. Determination of expenditures through a "built-up" analysis.
3. Comparison against industry percentage of sales guidelines.
4. Comparison against a projected cost figure based on percentage of future sales.

---

[5] For a review of this literature see Julian L. Simon, and Johan Arndt, "The Shape of the Advertising Response Function," *Journal of Advertising Research* 20, no. 4 (August 1980), pp. 11–28.

5. Reconciliation of divergences between built-up costs and percentage of sales figures.
6. Establishment of a payout plan where appropriate.
7. Modification of estimates in terms of company policies.
8. Specification of when expenditures will be made.
9. Establishment of built-in flexibility.

Isolation of Objectives

The first step in building a budgetary plan is to estimate the total market for the product category. These figures may be available from governmental sources, trade publications, or from market research firms such as A. C. Nielsen or the Market Research Corporation of America. Then it is necessary to estimate the share of the total market that the firm most likely can attain. Factors underlying this estimate are:

1. Product uniqueness—the advantages relative to competition and the ease with which they can be duplicated.
2. Number of competitors—it is difficult to obtain a large share in a highly fragmented market.
3. The spending pattern of competition—a large share is more feasible where competition has not been aggressive and is unwilling and (or) unable to become so in the future.

Estimated market share becomes significant in that it is possible to approximate necessary spending levels based on past industry performance, as is discussed later.

In addition, of course, communication objectives must be specified. These objectives should be combined into a comprehensive and specific statement upon which a detailed plan of efforts producing measurable results can be built.

Expenditure Estimation through Built-Up Analysis

Once objectives have been specified, the next question concerns what is required to accomplish these tasks. This analysis, in turn, should encompass mass media expenditures (advertising and public relations), direct selling costs, and costs of stimulating reseller support.

Advertising and public relations. If the objective, for example, is to saturate the teenage market through repetitive advertising, it is clear that a large budget will be required for continued advertising in media which reach this market segment. In more technical terms, media strategy would be established to achieve *frequency*. On the other hand, the task may call for reaching as large a market as possible, in which case a wide variety of media would be utilized to attain *reach*. Reach and frequency requirements, therefore, are instrumental in determination of the required budget. The basic approach is to "build up" or select the necessary media.

The analysis underlying media selection, which is complex, is the subject of Chapter 13. It is recognized that media analysis lies at the heart of the task and objective approach; in fact, Roger Barton, a widely quoted authority, does not even mention percentage of sales and other approaches in his discussion of budgeting.[6] It is his contention that the final budgetary figure is based upon: (1) definition of the types of media to be used, (2) the costs of individual media, (3) frequency of insertions, (4) the media mix, and (5) other related considerations. This analysis, in turn, is common to both advertising and public relations, although much publicity is achieved at no cost to the firm.

Direct selling costs.   Next it is necessary to determine the required selling activities and resulting costs to reach wholesalers and retailers and stimulate their promotional support. Computations are usually made by territory or other subunits of the firm where environmental situations are known to differ. Judgment armed with research data is the only tool available. Recourse must be made to historical records detailing efforts under similar sets of alternatives in the past and the costs which were incurred. In the absence of appropriate records, experimental research may be required.

The costing of efforts raises problems which require some discussion. A first step always will be to determine the total of fixed selling costs, because, in all probability, they will change only slightly from period to period. A similar relationship may be found for semivariable costs which, for all intents and purposes, are fixed over large ranges of output. The problem comes in estimating variable costs, and detailed historical records are required for the estimates to have any meaning.

The problem of variable costs is clarified considerably if standard costs can be constructed for each activity. A cost standard is a predetermined norm for an operation intended to represent the costs under usual operating conditions. Standard costs frequently are based on time and duty analysis whereby time intervals required to perform an activity are translated into monetary terms. The availability of standard costs then permits the computation of a sales budget on the basis of estimates of the functions to be performed, multiplied by the appropriate cost standard for each function. It might be discovered, for example, that the standard cost per sales call in territories 1, 7, and 9 is $10 and the best estimate of calls required during the coming year is 1,000, 1,200, and 870 respectively. The budgeted costs then would be $10,000 in territory 1 (1,000 × $10), $12,000 in territory 2, and $8,700 in territory 3.

---

[6] Roger Barton, *Media in Advertising* (New York: McGraw-Hill, 1964), pp. 15–19.

The two most widely used cost standards are cost per sales call and cost per dollar of net sales. Standards also are established frequently for the salaries and expenses of home office sales administration, the expenses of field supervision, costs of home office and field office clerical efforts, and other related functions.

Even though standard costs are a significant aid, the applicability of standards is highly dependent on the nature of the tasks performed. Clerical activities, of course, are routine, and it is not difficult to establish standards such as cost per invoice line posted. Creative selling, on the other hand, may be far from routine in that a sale may not be made until many preliminary customer contacts are completed. In such instances, it may be impossible to establish reasonable standards.

The tasks of calling upon wholesalers and retailers, however, are frequently more routine than they may appear at first glance. A regular schedule of calls is typical, and the selling job itself may be little more than order taking. In such instances cost standards can be set and followed for both budgeting and cost control.

Cost standards, then, should be used whenever possible. In addition, conferences should be held at all management levels with those directly involved in the execution of planned efforts, to utilize combined judgment. The result hopefully will be a realistic estimate of marginal returns from sales efforts.

Stimulating reseller support. The departure point of analysis is the history of trade efforts in the product category. What is the ratio of trade expenditures to advertising of major competitors? In most product categories it is necessary to be competitive, or support will be lost. Costs will be incurred in the form of product sampling, couponing, margin manipulation, cooperative advertising, provision of displays, and so on.

Comparison against Industry Percentage of Sales Guidelines

It is frequently found that *share of industry advertising,* called *share of voice,* is a primary criterion of success, especially in marketing a new product. The advertising share of most successful products, for example, generally exceeds sales share by 1.5 or 1.6 to 1 in such product categories as household needs, food products, and proprietary medicines. It would of course vary somewhat from one product area to another. This would indicate that the firm should advertise, on the average, at a 45 percent rate to attain a 30 percent sales share. A strong brand might reduce this ratio somewhat, whereas a brand in second or third position may have to advertise in the range of 2 or 3 to 1. Also the quality of advertising will make a difference. Therefore, this type of ratio can only be a rough guideline.

Comparison against Projected Percentage of Future Sales

It was suggested earlier that the percentage of sales devoted to promotion in the past is a useful starting point in budgeting. These figures are readily available in conventional accounting statements, and breakdowns can be provided for sales territories and products.

The application of percentages to forecasted sales involves circular reasoning to the extent that it is difficult to forecast sales without knowing the investment in promotion. As a result this is not a sufficient basis for budgeting, but it does provide an estimate, all things being equal, of what would be spent if proportions were not altered to meet changed objectives. Thus it serves as a benchmark against which to compare the built-up budgetary sum.

Reconciliation of Divergences between Built-Up Costs and Percentage of Sales Figures

Once the projected percentage figures for both the industry and company and built-up expenditures figures are available, the focus can be on reconciling differences. If a 1.6 to 1 ratio is reasonable given past industry experience in the product category and projected spending is far in excess of the ratio, it may be necessary to revise premises, assumptions, and other factors in order to ascertain whether the projected figure is reasonable. The budgetary analysis is a continuing process of this type, because only by accident will a sum be arrived at which clearly is the optimum appropriation.

Payout Planning

It frequently is desirable to extend the budgetary period, especially when new products are introduced, because one calendar year may not be sufficient to accomplish objectives. Strategy may encompass three to five years, and the appropriation must be viewed in that time perspective. Moreover, profitability may not be realized until the end of the period. In other words, the payout from the expenditures is expected to occur at a later point in time, and this extension of the planning period is frequently referred to as payout planning. Because this is most frequently used in introducing new products, further discussion is reserved for the next section of the chapter.

Modification of Estimates in Terms of Company Policies

It is also pertinent to fine tune the appropriation figures to make the sums consistent with the overall framework of company policy and dollars invested in other functions. Financial liquidity must always be considered, for there are bound to be financial constraints which cannot be exceeded, even in payout planning, regardless of logic or compelling necessity. Moreover, *too much can be spent* for promotion in view of the entire company situation. There is the possibility that advertising and selling can easily disturb orderly flows of manpower, inventory, and cash by borrowing sales from the future and introducing unwarranted fluctuation in other flows. It must never be overlooked that the company is a system of related flows, and dollars must be invested to maximize the response of the *system* and not the *function* itself. The danger to be avoided is suboptimization, which results when management loses sight of the system in which it lives.

Specification of When Expenditures Will Be Made

Another requirement for a good budget is designation of when dollars will be expended during the budgetary period. This is to permit forecasting of cash flow requirements by the company comptroller to ensure that funds are available when needed.

Building in Flexibility

The budget should never be viewed as a perfect map to be followed without variation. The dangers of inflexibility are analyzed at length in the management literature, and there is compelling logic for building in sufficient flexibility to allow for changing conditions. Markets are becoming more volatile, product planning deadlines are shortened, and there are many possibilities of tactical shifts by competition. This flexibility may be provided by a 10 to 15 percent reserve sum which is not allocated until needed.

Adaptation to change, of course, requires maintenance of detailed records of results. More and more companies are now establishing a new management post—the advertising controller. He or she is appointed to be a watchdog over spending, with the result that there may be a more or less continual review of performance. Records also are useful as guides to future strategy decisions. Unfortunately, this type of record frequently is not kept on any systematic basis, and this lack can serve as a real impediment to the application of the philosophy of marginal analysis.

Comments on the Suggested Approach

This section has not been presented with the objective of providing a formula which can be automatically followed. Rather, a step-by-step procedure has been suggested to approximate marginal analysis through the task and objective approach, and it must be adapted creatively and analytically to each situation. The final result should never be construed as being ideal, because there always may be good reasons for major changes throughout the planning period. Also, the tendency to use the budget as a screen to hide inefficiencies must be guarded against. This danger can be avoided if top management insists on measurement of results and evaluates the competence of personnel in performance terms.

A decision that faces management once the total budget has been determined is how to allocate it to various parts of the country. This so-called *geographic allocation* is an important issue if the best returns for the money expended are to be realized.

GEOGRAPHIC ALLOCATION

Geographic variables often provide a useful basis for allocating promotional budgets. To use these variables it is necessary to determine the *relative sales possibilities* from one geographic area to the next. For example, if a product is sold nationwide, should twice as much effort be placed in the Chicago market as in Detroit, Michigan? Or should Detroit receive an equivalent allocation of promotional funds? Such questions can be answered only when *market potentials* are computed, for as a general rule efforts are allocated in proportion to potential, all other things being equal.

Several different potentials might be computed for a given product:

1. Volume attainable under ideal conditions, i.e., if all efforts were perfectly adapted to the environment.
2. The relative capacity of a market to absorb the products of an entire industry, such as the major appliance industry.
3. The relative size of market for a company's type of product, i.e., sales of color television sets versus stereo sets.
4. The actual sales a company can expect.

The last category, of course, is the equivalent of the sales forecast for a firm, or the sales volume which can be expected if the firm continues on its present course. Potential, on the other hand, refers to sales possibilities rather than expected sales, and it is of greater significance for purposes of demand analysis. Although forecasting is necessary in determining allocations and budgets, it is beyond the scope of this book.

The measure of potential which is generally found to be most useful comprehends either category 2 or category 3—market strength (capacity) for industry products or types of products rather than the specific products of a firm. This is not to say, however, that potential is the sole basis for allocation of resources, because potentials for industry sales do not reveal the competitive structure of a market or the firm's ability to make inroads. Detroit, for example, might appear to offer high potential, whereas in reality competitors are so entrenched that inroads would be impossible. Ideally, then, potentials must be augmented with information about the competitive structure as well as the firm's previous experience in the market. The goal, of course, is to make an optimum allocation of resources to alternative markets, and this never can be done with great precision without a reliable estimate of the impact of a given level of promotional expenditure on market share. Nevertheless, an array of markets in terms of potential provides a workable estimate of the probability of response to sales efforts.

The methods used to compute potentials include: (1) a corollary products index, (2) market surveys, (3) test markets, (4) industry sales, (5) general buying power indexes, and (6) custom-made indexes.

Corollary Products Index

At times it is possible to use the sales of another product as an indication of potential. Presumably the corollary product and the product in question are related in some way. If such a product can be found and its sales are available, these data may be used as clues of expected variations in sales patterns of one's own product from one market to the next.

Residential building permits, for example, should be a realistic indication of the sales potential for bathroom fixtures. The danger, of course, is that association between one product and another does not mean that the two sell in direct proportion in different areas. As a result this method should be used with caution, and in many instances it will be found to be inapplicable.

Market Surveys

When the problem is to introduce a new product to the market, there may be no alternative to a direct survey of the intentions of prospective buyers. Prospective buyers are asked what their purchasing plans are relative to the product, and the stated intentions of the sample are projected to the entire market as the measure of potential. Obviously there can be a divergence between stated intentions and actual purchasing behavior, with the result that this method should not be depended upon to produce a highly reliable index of potential. Yet it is better than no measure at all.

Test Markets

The test market is an important step past the market survey in that it measures actual buyer behavior in one or more specially chosen areas. The test market consists of an experiment where every attempt is made to study behavior without the expense of marketing efforts in all areas. The shortcoming, of course, is that test marketing can be time-consuming (six months or more) and expensive. In fact, where considerable investment is required in fixed assets of various types before a test can be made, it may not be feasible at all.

Industry Sales

In this method use is made of sales of the industry or a major portion of it as the measure of potential. It is thus possible to clarify areas where the industry has made maximum penetration. The advantage is that it takes the experience of all competitors into consideration and avoids the error of considering only the circumstances peculiar to an individual firm. From the industry sales it is relatively easy to compute the share of market possessed by the firm and thereby arrive at a measure of sales possibilities.

Assume, for example, that industry sales are available and that a firm is discovered to derive 1.3 percent of its sales revenue from Connecticut versus 3.4 percent for the total industry. It is clear that remedial steps are needed, and it is probable that a larger share of promotional dollars should be allocated to this state, all other things being equal. It is thus possible to capitalize on areas where industry products sell strongly and to avoid excessive promotion in the weak markets.

One limitation of this method is the frequent unavailability of industry sales data. In some circumstances (automobiles and motorboats are examples) license or tax records are a good source. Trade associations such as the National Electrical Manufacturers Association also make such statistics available to their members.

Sales data, however, reflect only *what is,* not what *might be.* In other words, there is no certainty that resulting data measure untapped market opportunity for both the industry and the firm. Moreover, it is assumed that past experience is a good measure of the future. In some industries producing staple commodities, this may be true. It is doubtful, for example, that total sales of men's shirts vary drastically from year to year. In dynamic markets, however, the probable existence of untapped demand makes this an unsafe assumption. As a result, other types of indexes may be preferable.

General Buying Power Indexes

The index of relative buying power in various localities is a good indication of potential for many products. A number of data sources are used for this purpose, among them magazine circulation. This index is based on the assumption that those reading magazines have money to spend. No doubt this is often true, especially among subscribers to special-purpose periodicals. A manufacturer of fishing reels, for example, might find the circulation of *Sports Afield* to be a reliable criterion; similarly, manufacturers of photographic equipment selling to skilled amateurs could use *Popular Photography* for this purpose.

Total retail sales in various markets also are used for a buying power index. Census of Business data are issued periodically and are updated annually by *Sales and Marketing Management* and other publications for this purpose. This measure should not be used, however, unless it is clear that there is a high correlation between variations in total retail sales and variations in sales of the product under analysis.

Usually the most accurate indexes are those which are constructed using several factors in combination. The best-known combination index is the *Sales and Marketing Management Survey of Buying Power* published annually. This index is derived by weighting population by two; effective buying income by five; and total retail sales by three. If the state of Illinois, for instance, were found to have 5 percent of effective buying power, a manufacturer using this index would allocate 5 percent of his promotional dollars to that state. Regardless of absolute sales volume, this state should generate about 5 percent of the total. Data also are provided by counties and cities so that a more precise allocation can be made.

A buying power index offers several advantages: (1) it is available in published form and can be used directly without additional computations, (2) the indexes are issued frequently and in considerable geographic detail, and (3) they may be used when other data which might be of greater use cannot be procured. A general index of this type, however, is not always appropriate. It is assumed that demand varies directly with this index, but this is likely to be correct only for those products whose demand rises or falls with purchasing power, regardless of other considerations. The demand for milk should not vary with buying power, and the use of snow tires is more associated with climatic conditions than anything else.

Custom-Made Indexes

It may be necessary to construct an index unique to a given product. In order to do so, it is necessary to isolate the important factors affecting demand, obtain data on these factors, and combine them into one index, with appropriate weights assigned to those with greatest influence. These factors may include any of the data mentioned previously. Buyer studies may be helpful, but the method usually depends more on informed guess than on scientific procedure.

To take an example, a large manufacturer of high-style belts, braces, garters, and jewelry found that the *Sales and Marketing Management* buying power index did not reflect the urban concentration of demand for its product. As a result, it used urban population (with a weight of three), retail sales (weight of three), and disposable income (weight of four). The result was a more precise indication of potential. Similarly, a brewery used the *Sales and Marketing Management* index to compute new-product potentials and found that sales in metropolitan areas did not meet expectations based on the index. It was discovered that total retail sales have little relation to the sales of beer, and the important determinants instead were found to be the number of people over age 18, social class, and per capita consumption of malt beverages.

Such an index is often constructed in somewhat arbitrary fashion by selecting and trying those factors that seem to be relevant. A more sophisticated procedure is to experiment with a greater variety of factors and choose those that are found to have the greatest relationship to sales through use of multiple correlation analysis. Correlation analysis measures the extent to which two or more variables are related by assessing the variation in one variable (say industry sales) which is accounted for by the association between this variable and others (say disposable income and housing starts).

The task of computing measures of multiple correlation once was formidable, but electronic computers have greatly simplified the procedure. Once various combinations have been tried, they may be readily compared. Assume that five series are tested and found to have coefficients of correlation with sales of .66, .81, .91, .84, and .87. The third (.91) obviously is the best of the five, since a correlation of 1.0 is ideal. In reality, however, it is doubtful that a correlation of .91 will be found because this is an exceptionally high degree of relationship.

Probably this procedure is the most acceptable of all of those discussed in this section, but it also has its disadvantages. First, the correlation may be spurious—a coincidence rather than a cause and effect relationship. Moreover, it is assumed that past industry sales success will hold in the future, and it is obvious that this might not be so in a volatile industry in early stages of its growth. Finally, the data needed may not be attainable or may be of questionable accuracy. Regardless of the problems, it does focus on finding the combination of factors which offers the best relationship to sales, and as such it is likely to be superior to a more general index under most circumstances.

BUDGETING FOR NEW PRODUCTS

There are some special considerations which enter into the budgeting process for new products, in addition to those that have been mentioned. Payout planning assumes particular importance, and experimentation with quantitative methods is providing some interesting new insights.

Payout Planning[7]

A payout plan is a procedure which extends the planning period for longer than one year, and it has proved especially useful in evaluation of the proper course of action in introducing new products. Most often it covers three years, but in the case of slow-maturing products such as proprietary medicines or where large initial expenditures are necessary, the payout plan may be extended to cover four or five years. The stages in payout planning are: (1) estimation of market share objectives, (2) assessment of needed trade inventories, (3) determination of needed expenditures, (4) determination of the payout period, and (5) evaluation.

Estimation of share objectives. It was previously mentioned that the first step in budgeting is to estimate the total market for the product category and then to assess the probable share to be captured by the firm. It should be noted that most new products reach their peak share and then decline to a lower level. Share builds slowly as distribution is achieved, promotion pressure is applied, and consumer trial is generated. Usually a brand will hit its peak share approximately 6 to 12 months after introduction in a new area, and then level off or decline. It is then necessary to recycle the brand through product improvement.

This short life cycle for most consumer products makes it important to accelerate trial through heavy advertising expenditures in the first few months. Products are only new once, and this is the most important period in the life of a brand. The higher the peak share, the greater the probability that the brand will be a success.

Assessment of needed trade inventories. The company also makes money on what is sold to the trade, so the goods necessary to "fill the pipeline" must be added to consumer sales to get the total volume for the manufacturer. There are two general guidelines to follow.

1. The larger the projected volume, the shorter the number of weeks supply necessary in trade inventories.
2. Most products lose inventory in the second year through resellers' cutbacks unless share is climbing; this exerts a negative force on sales in that year.

Determination of needed expenditures. There are several guidelines to be followed in arriving at the proper budget level based on experience:

1. The first-year budget should permit a heavy introductory schedule (13–26 weeks) followed by a sustaining schedule at least equal to the second year advertising budget.
2. A good rule of thumb is that expenditures for the introductory sched-

---

[7] This section was contributed by Robert Sowers, formerly senior vice president, Ogilvy & Mather, Inc.

ule should be about twice the rate currently spent by competitors who have shares equal to the company objective.

3. Carefully check expenditures on a per unit basis against competitors. The brand with the highest shares usually has a lower cost per unit, and vice versa.

Determination of the payout period.   In today's competitive marketplace, the trend is toward shorter payout plans. Most product development can be duplicated by competition in a short time. There is also reason to believe that brand loyalty is not as great as it once was. Finally, there is a high rate of new-product failures. Long payouts are justified only when the projected life cycle of the product is very long and the potential rewards are very big.

Two payout plans are shown in Figures 11–5 and 11–6. Notice that the new food product considered in Figure 11–5 was projected to return a loss in the first year and payout in the second year. The drug product considered in Figure 11–6, on the other hand, was not expected to payout until the fourth year. In the former example, the total promotional budget was highest in the first year so that maximum impact could be made, whereas the opposite is the case with the drug product, which matures more slowly.

Evaluation.   In evaluating the soundness of a payout plan, management usually directs attention to the first year (the year of heavy investment) and to the first year after payout is achieved. This latter year gives management an opportunity to assess the long-term rewards of the investments they have made in the other years. By comparison with other opportunities and other competitive products, it is possible to make an experienced judgment on the wisdom of the investment. Of particular

FIGURE 11–5
Payout Plan for a New Food Product (000s)

	Theoretical marketing years		
	First	Second	Third
Total market (units)	50,000	52,000	54,000
Market share (percentage)	5.0	5.2	5.0
Volume (units)	2,500	2,704	2,700
Pipeline (units)	400	(50)	—
Total volume (units)	2,900	2,654	2,700
Total sales (@ $9)	26,100	23,886	24,300
Gross profit (@ $4)	11,600	10,616	10,800
Advertising ($)	6,500	4,000	4,000
Promotion to the trade ($)	8,000	2,000	2,000
Total advertising & promotion ($)	14,500	6,000	6,000
Gross trading profit ($)	(2,900)	4,616	4,800
Profit (percentage of sales)		19.3	19.8
Cumulative gross trading profit ($)	(2,900)	1,716	6,516

FIGURE 11-6
Payout Plan for a New Drug Product (000s)

	First	*Second*	*Third*	*Fourth*	*Fifth*
			Theoretical marketing years		
Total market (units)	200,000	211,000	223,500	235,500	246,000
Market share (percentage)	2.0	3.3	4.4	5.6	6.7
Volume (units)	4,000	6,963	9,834	13,188	16,482
Pipeline (units)	700	750	780	800	800
Gross sales ($)	4,700	7,013	9,864	13,208	16,482
Gross margin (percentage)	7	7	7	7	7
Gross profit ($)	3,290	4,909	6,905	9,246	11,537
Advertising ($)	4,400	4,200	5,000	5,760	6,000
Promotion to the trade ($)	1,500	700	800	900	1,000
Total adv. & prom. ($)	5,900	4,900	5,800	6,660	7,000
Gross trading profit ($)	(2,610)	9	1,105	2,586	4,537
Profit (percentage of sales)	—	—	16.0	27.9	39.3
Cumulative gross trading profit ($)		(2,601)	(1,496)	1,090	5,627

importance are examination of profit margins and the financial implications of an investment of this size. Additionally, the net present value of cash flows may be calculated to determine the investment viability of the expenditures.

Adaptation. It must be emphasized that a payout plan is a theoretical financial plan calling for a national introduction at one specific point in time. Management has the option of making the plan fit overall company fiscal goals more closely by, first of all, picking the most propitious time to introduce a product. For example, introducing at the end of a fiscal year could fatten company profit for that year by accumulating the profits from heavy initial trade sales, while deferring the heavy introductory advertising expenses until the next fiscal year.

Companies frequently choose to introduce in waves. They might introduce in 20 percent of the market to start, and then 20 percent in the next two months, and so on. This has the effect of lowering the deficit position at any one point in time. There are other advantages, such as leveling production schedules and correcting errors found in the first regions. The disadvantages are that it may result in shortening lead time over competition and that it might be necessary to pay a premium to do regional advertising instead of national advertising.

Evaluation of payout planning. Payout planning is being followed by an increasing number of firms. An assumption is made, of course, that environmental conditions existing during the first year will not change greatly during the planning period. Competition might enter and drastically change the competitive environment, to mention only one possibility. Also, it is assumed that the effect of promotional expenditures on sales can be estimated with some accuracy. Nevertheless, payout planning encompasses a managerial philosophy which has merit, for a realistic attempt is made to implement the task and objective method without imposing arbitrary restrictions on funds in any given year.

New-Product Models

The new-product decision may be conceived of as consisting of four stages: (1) search for new product ideas, (2) screening of ideas to eliminate those that obviously are unsuitable, (3) analysis of remaining alternatives, and (4) implementation of the marketing plan. A number of quantitative models have been proposed for use at the various stages, and considerable experimentation has been undertaken to relate a product's marketing variables in such a way that quantitative expressions can be derived to predict the sales effects of marketing strategies. Models of this type are most useful in the analysis stage of the new-product decision.

The starting point for a demand analysis will be estimates of sales, given a forecast of the market and competitive environment and certain assumed levels of expenditure for various areas of the marketing mix. Then the quantitative demand model describes how sales change if the marketing mix changes. It may be felt, for example, that advertising affects awareness and that awareness, along with reseller efforts, determines trial rate for the product. Then trial rate, competition, and price would determine sales. One new-product model, DEMON, assumes that advertising dollars affect media weight, which in turn specifies advertising awareness. Then promotion, distribution, and awareness determine trial rate, which, in turn, determine usage rate.[8] Once these linkages are specified it is possible to predict the effects, given a certain level of expenditure on advertising and other efforts. The advantage in budgeting is obvious in that the probable effects can be predicted.

Awareness is often assumed to be the contribution of advertising to overall demand stimulation. As part of the new-products model used at Batten, Barton, Dusstine & Osborn (BBD&O), Albert J. Martin, Jr., predicted the following relationship between awareness and advertising level.[9]

$$A_j = KA_{j-1} + (A_m - A_{j-1})(1 - e^{-\Sigma\, n_j}),$$

where

[8] See David B. Learner, "DEMON New Product Planning: A Case History," in *New Directions in Marketing,* ed. Frederick E. Webster, Jr. (Chicago: American Marketing Association, 1965).

[9] Albert J. Martin, Jr., "An Exponential Model for Predicting Trial of a New Consumer Product," doctoral dissertation, Columbus: The Ohio State University, 1969.

> j = Time period determined by the timing of data collection
>
> A_j = Level of awareness at the end of time period j
>
> A_m = Maximum expected level of awareness
>
> e = Base of the natural logarithm
>
> Σn_j = Cumulative average number of exposures delivered by the media schedule from $j = 0$ to the end of time period j
>
> A_{j-1} = Level of awareness at the end of the previous time period $(j - 1)$
>
> K = The fraction of A_{j-1} remembered at the end of the time period j.

An empirical test of the model proved that it can give an accurate prediction of actual levels of awareness for a new convenience item. Assuming that the necessary input data can be collected and that a level of desired awareness has been specified, it then is possible to solve the equation to determine the level of advertising exposures needed to attain the desired awareness.

The ASSESSOR new-product model which is built off of laboratory experimentation, in what is called a simulated test market, goes even further by predicting market share.[10] In this model advertising impacts through its ability to obtain awareness for the new brand, and to affect both attitude and preference structure. ASSESSOR is too complex to explain in detail here. However, its predictive power is reported to be excellent,[11] as has that for similar models run by the firms of Yankelovich, Skelly and White, and Elrick and Lavidge.[12]

SUMMARY

This chapter began with a brief review of the theoretical model underlying the budgeting decision. It was then pointed out that the idealized marginal approach to budgeting can only be crudely approximated by the existing methods. The task and objective procedure is most suitable, and a nine-step process was suggested whereby a realistic budget estimate can be made, given a statement of objectives. Geographic allocation was also discussed.

It is no doubt apparent that the ideal of marginal analysis never will be attained with the precision specified by economists. Nevertheless, utilization of the systematic approach suggested here will in time provide a reasonable approximation, especially as a backlog of documented results

[10] A. J. Silk and G. L. Urban, "Pre-Test Market Evaluation of New Packaged Goods: A Model and Measurement Methodology," *Journal of Marketing Research* 15 (May 1978), pp. 171–91.

[11] Ibid.

[12] For a detailed description of these models, and ASSESSOR see Yoram J. Wind, *Product Policy: Concepts, Methods, and Strategy* (Reading, Mass.: Addison-Wesley, 1982), pp. 422–27.

becomes available. Even with the use of quantitative methods, however, judgment will never be eliminated—it will only be sharpened.

APPENDIX TO CHAPTER 11: APPLICATION OF QUANTITATIVE METHODS

The limitations of existing budgetary procedures have caused increasing interest in quantitative techniques. Much has been said regarding the potential of these methods, but many claims are commercially motivated. Therefore it is necessary to examine several of the most widely publicized approaches with the objective of ascertaining whether existing methodology has been augmented in a meaningful way. Obviously it is only possible to give a brief introduction in these few pages. The reader interested in further details must turn elsewhere.[13]

The General Approach

Nearly all models include a mechanism for relating the effects of expenditures on sales. This mechanism usually is referred to as the *sales response function*. Then data are collected on promotional decision variables of the firm and its competitors. It is the purpose of the sales response function to relate these variables in a meaningful way. Finally, a decision model is developed to generate optimal promotional expenditures.

The quality of the model, of course, is dependent initially upon the sales response function. In turn, its usefulness is determined at least in part by the way in which decision variables are related to sales, especially with respect to underlying assumptions which must be satisfied. Many of the models reviewed in these pages cannot be considered as especially useful from a practical point of view, yet progress is being made.

The Sales Model

In the simplest case, advertising is the only variable affecting sales in the current period. Profit therefore is expressed as:

$$Pr = pq - A - C(q)$$
$$= pf(A) - A - C[f(A)],$$

where

$$p = \text{Unit price}$$
$$Pr = \text{Total profit}$$
$$A = \text{Advertising}$$

---

[13] For example see Leonard J. Parsons, and Randall L. Schultz, *Marketing Models and Econometric Research* (New York: North-Holland, 1976), chaps. 1, 2, and 7–12.

$q =$ Quantity sold

$C(q) =$ Cost of producing and marketing

If there are decreasing returns to advertising at some level of A, then optimization procedures may be used to determine the profit-maximizing budgetary level. It is obvious, however, that this equation generally is an oversimplification of reality in that it fails to comprehend all factors which affect the budgeting decision. Its primary value is in specifying one possible relationship between advertising and profit.

Dynamic Models

In reality, advertising undertaken in previous periods will affect the current period; in the same sense current advertising will have future effects. To take this carry-over effect into consideration, dynamic models are required. There have been several published dynamic models; one is presented here to illustrate something of its variables and potential usefulness.

One approach combined the following factors into a mathematical model describing sales response to advertising.[14]

1. *The sales response rate*—the relative case of moving people toward purchase.
2. *The saturation level*—the maximum sales that can be achieved in a given campaign period.
3. *The response constant*—the sales generated by advertising.
4. *The sales decay rate*—the extent to which countervailing forces erode brand preference in the absence of advertising.

The basic equation is:

$$\frac{dS}{dt} = rA\frac{M-S}{M} - \lambda S,$$

where

$S =$ Sales rate at time t

$r =$ Response constant (sales generated per dollar of advertising when $S = 0$)

$A =$ Rate of advertising expenditure at time t

$M =$ Saturation level (the maximum sales for a given campaign)

$\lambda =$ Sales decay constant (sales lost per time interval when $A = 0$).

In words, this equation states:

---

[14] M. L. Vidale and H. B. Wolfe, "An Operations-Research Study of Sales Reponse to Advertising," *Operations Research* 5 (June 1957), pp. 370–81.

The instantaneous rate of increase of sales at any time, $t =$

$$\frac{\text{Response}}{\text{constant}} \times \begin{array}{c} \text{Rate of} \\ \text{advertising} \\ \text{at time } t \end{array} \times \frac{\text{Saturation level} - \text{Sales rate at time } t}{\text{Saturation level}}$$

$$- \text{Sales decay constant} \times \text{sales rate at time } t.$$

This model and others like it have been tested in the real world through estimating the various parameters in test market experiments.[15] If it is an accurate statement, it says, in effect, that the sales response per advertising dollar times the number of dollars spent, reduced by the percentage of unsaturated sales plus sales lost through decay, are the factors which result in the increase in the rate of sales.

This approach still needs much testing before it can be accepted as valid. Also, it is apparent that it may be difficult, if not impossible, to estimate such factors as response constant, saturation level, and sales decay constant without almost prohibitively expensive test market experimentation. In other words, it is often easy to assume that such variables are known and then specify an equation which relates them in a functional way. Nevertheless, this model does relate some important factors in sales response to advertising and hence should be viewed as a meaningful step forward in the search for new analytical methods.

Competitive Models

None of the models discussed thus far explicitly take competitive factors into consideration. Game theoretic models, building on the classic work of John von Neumann and Oskar Morgenstern, explicitly focus on this vitally important factor.[16] The basic assumption is that all players are interdependent and that uncertainty results from not knowing what the others will do. Strategy then is devised to reduce and control uncertainty. This requires use of the principle of minimax, in which each competitor acts as the "cautious pessimist," fully expecting the worst to happen and trying to minimize competitive inroads. In the game it would be, by assumption, irrational to try to maximize and produce the largest reward, because the competitor following the minimax strategy theoretically will always win.

It has been suggested that the theory of games is potentially applicable to the problem of budgeting for promotion. While the mathematics of complex solutions is beyond the scope of this book, it is possible to

---

[15] See Parsons and Schultz, *Marketing Models*, pp. 223–35 for a review of tests of more recent models.

[16] John von Neumann and Oskar Morgenstern, *Theory of Games and Economic Behavior* (Princeton, N.J.: Princeton University Press, 1944).

convey the basic nature and strategies of game theory through a comparatively simple example.

Assume that four possible advertising strategies are available to the two dominant competitors in an oligopolistic industry:

1. An expenditure of $250,000 on hard-sell copy using network and spot television.
2. An expenditure of $300,000 on soft-sell "image" type advertising using consumer magazines in four colors.
3. An expenditure of $500,000 on mixed hard- and soft-sell copy using local spot television and newspapers.
4. An expenditure of $500,000 on a mixture of network television and three consumer magazines using hard-sell copy.

Assume further that the revenue produced by competitor A following three strategies in light of expected retaliation by competitor B is that appearing in Figure 11–7. This payoff matrix indicates, for example, that if A follows strategy 1 and B does so also (cell $A_1 - B_1$), the return to A would be $2 million. However, if it follows strategy 1 and B uses strategy 4 (cell $A_1 - B_4$), $500,000 would be lost. The problem, then, is to arrive at the proper minimax strategy for both competitors, simultaneously behaving as cautious pessimists.

FIGURE 11–7
Conditional Returns to Competitor A, Given Retaliation by Competitor B ($000s)

A's strategies	B's strategies			
	B_1	B_2	B_3	B_4
A_1	$2,000	$2,000	$4,000	−$500
A_2	1,500	1,400	200	400
A_3	1,200	1,000	1,000	800
A_4	3,500	1,000	500	0

In the above example A will reason that it wants to make the maximum gain *assuming the strongest retaliation from* B. Hence, it will follow the strategy which gives it the *best of the minimum returns*. This strategy is determined by listing the minimum return under each strategy and following the strategy with the maximum minimum return, or the *minimax* solution. A would thus list the minimum value in each row in Figure 11–8 and designate the maximum minimum value. This value is $800,000, which is achieved by following strategy A_3.

In turn, B would follow the same reasoning, and its best decision is arrived at by consulting the payout matrix, determining the *maximum* return in each column, and choosing the minimum value. The maximum value in each column, of course, represents the worst that can happen

FIGURE 11–8
Computation of the Minimax Solutions ($000s)

A's strategies	B's strategies				Row minimums
	B_1	B_2	B_3	B_4	
A_1	$2,000	$2,500	$4,000	−$500	−$500
A_2	1,500	1,400	200	400	200
A_3	1,200	1,000	1,000	800	800
A_4	3,500	1,000	500	0	0
Column maximums...............	3,500	2,500	4,000	800	

to it (in that A makes its greatest gain), so naturally it will play the strategy which minimizes its losses. This solution will be optimum for it. The best B can do is to play strategy B_4, which gives A its smallest maximum return.

The minimax solutions for the payoff matrix in Figure 11–7 are computed in Figure 11–8. A return of $800,000 is the maximum A can expect, assuming competitive retaliation, and this return is produced by strategy 3. In turn, B can clearly see that it minimizes A's inroads by playing strategy 4, which gives A the smallest return of $800,000 and enables B to maintain its position.

Notice that the solution is the intersection of A_3 and B_4. This unique intersection is called the "saddle point," and neither competitor gains at the expense of the other, as would easily happen if this intersection had not been produced. Because no competitive gain results, this is called a "zero-sum" game. Not all games have a unique saddle point or a zero-sum solution, in which case mixed strategies are used to arrive at the actions which give the greatest *probability* of a minimax solution. Space precludes discussion of these complexities. Game theory has some intuitive appeal in that competitors must, of necessity, second-guess each other in oligopolistic markets. Perhaps modification might be introduced to permit more practical applications.

Stochastic Models

Several attempts have been made, using the laws of probability, to attack the budgeting process, the most notable being Markov chain analysis and the Stochastic learning model.

Markov chain analysis.   A. Markov, a Russian mathematician, first developed an extension of probability to analyze the movement and distribution of gas particles in a container. Using this approach, now called Markov chain analysis, it is possible to predict the concentration of particles at one point in time through knowledge of the concentration in the preceding time period. The data required are the location of particles at one point, called state 1, and the probabilities (called transitional probabilities) that the particles will either remain stationary or move at later states.

It became apparent that Markov analysis might be used to advantage to predict the movement of buyers from one brand to another; brand loyalty is an important consideration in promotional strategy. The required data are estimates of the probability that buyers will stay loyal to a given brand or move to another brand. These data can be estimated through survey research or, more often, educated guesses by management.

The Markov model potentially can be utilized to advantage to predict the movement of market shares a product may have, given an empirical estimate of the probabilities that buyers will either stay with a given brand or switch to another. Assume that the transitional probabilities of brand switching shown in Figure 11–9 have been discovered from survey research. Notice that the rows all add to one, indicating that all possible actions have been itemized. Of A's customers, for example, the probabilities are that it will retain 55 percent, B will gain 30 percent, and C will take the remainder (reading across the rows). In turn (reading down the columns), A will capture 20 percent of B's customers and 10 percent of C's.

FIGURE 11–9
Transitional Probabilities of Brand Loyalty and
Brand Switching

	Switch to Brand		
From Brand	A	B	C
A	.55	.30	.15
B	.20	.70	.10
C	.10	.10	.80

Let it be assumed further that the current market shares are: A—20 percent, B—50 percent, and C—30 percent. This provides sufficient data to calculate market shares in the future, *assuming that the transitional probabilities remain constant.* Through use of matrix multiplication it is apparent that A's share of the market in the next period will be 24 percent (.55 × 20% + .20 × 50% + .10 × 30%). That is, it will retain 55 percent of its present market share, gain 20 percent of B's, and gain 10 percent of C's. These computations may be carried on for as many periods as is desired. The resulting market shares are listed in Figure 11–10.

Notice that market shares ultimately stabilize at 25 percent, 37.5 percent, and 37.5 percent, respectively. The shares in period n, or the "steady

FIGURE 11–10
Market Shares in Ensuing Periods Given Transitional Probabilities

Period	Market shares		
	A	B	C
1	20%	50%	30%
2	24	44	32
3	25.2	41.2	33.6
4	25.46	39.76	34.78
5	25.4333	38.948	35.619
.	.	.	.
.	.	.	.
.	.	.	.
n	25%	37.5%	37.5%

state," are calculated using the Markov formulation with the tools of either matrix algebra or difference equations. The mathematics required is not difficult, and computer programs are available.

The concern here is not with the computation of solutions but with the uses to which this type of analysis might be put. Comparatively little of substance has appeared in the published literature, but Markov analysis has been found useful in two related ways: (1) projection of market shares period by period into the future and (2) analysis of the steady-state solutions resulting from experimental manipulation of promotion variables.

Analysis of probable market shares in coming periods may give useful information for strategy. A high probability of movement from one brand to another may indicate, for example, that advertising claims are exaggerated and have led to disillusionment. A change in strategy is clearly called for. Moreover, exceptionally high probabilities of brand loyalty are a good sign of promotional invulnerability, and strategy may then turn to means of strengthening loyalty of existing consumers instead of emphasis upon making inroads on competitors' shares. The reader no doubt could easily provide many similar examples.

Of more importance for budgeting is analysis of a family of steady-state solutions resulting from experimental studies of variations in the promotion mix. By steady-state solutions are meant the outcome of market shares at period n—the theoretical ending point of change, often referred to by mathematicians as infinity. DuPont has used this approach successfully. Assuming that brand loyalty is a function of promotion and price, variations are introduced in promotion in various matched test and control markets. Consumer interviews are conducted to detect resulting changes in brand usage, and the changed probabilities of purchasing one brand versus another are projected to predict market shares at the steady state. The various resulting steady-state solutions are then compared to detect the effectiveness of changes in the advertising mix. The strategy resulting in the largest market share at period n would then be utilized more extensively by the firm. This approach clearly isolates the monetary values of changes in brand loyalty through promotion, and valuable information is provided to implement the objective and task budgeting approach.

There are several difficulties, however, which will impede the widespread application of Markov experimentation:

1. It is assumed that the purchase of a brand in a coming period is correctly mirrored by the purchase in the last period, but empirical analysis has challenged this assumption. It has been found that prior purchases earlier in the purchasing history tend to strengthen a buying response in the future, as one might expect, and much switching occurs from one period to another without permanent changes in brand loyalty. Therefore, the probabilities based only on the last purchase may be inaccurate.

2. It is also assumed that the transitional probabilities remain constant. Such an assumption, of course, is unrealistic in a volatile competitive world, and this becomes especially crucial if much reliance is placed on projections of shares for a few periods into the future. In analysis of steady-state solutions, however, this assumption is not crucial. No one expects the steady state to result. The intent is only to isolate what *would* happen, given changed transitional probabilities.

3. It can be exceedingly expensive to procure necessary data. Continuing studies are required to generate the probabilities, and experimentation with changed probabilities resulting from promotional expenditure requires elaborate experimental designs (the difficulties of experimentation are analyzed further in another chapter).

4. The analysis becomes virtually impossible with products other than certain convenience goods with fairly regular purchase rates. A durable good purchased infrequently tends to defy analysis of this type.

The learning model. Alfred Kuehn has specifically attacked the assumption of Markov analysis that repurchase is dependent only on the last purchase.[17] The effect of prior purchases appears to carry over into the future in the form of an exponential curve, with the result that considerable residual influence from past buying action tends to remain. This conclusion is very similar to that found in psychological learning experiments. Kuehn modified a stochastic learning model of the Bush-Mosteller type for computational purposes, basing his model on household brand shifts in grocery product purchases. Price, changes in product, and distribution factors are specifically introduced, as well as advertising policy.

The sales revenue earned by a company in a given period is assumed

---

[17] Alfred L. Kuehn, "A Model for Budgeting Advertising," in *Mathematical Models and Methods in Marketing,* ed. Frank M. Bass et al. (Homewood, Ill.: Richard D. Irwin, 1961), pp. 230–41.

to be generated by a combination of brand shifts by buyers and the functions of advertising, price, product characteristics, and distribution. Assuming that advertising effectiveness is independent of dollars spent, the model introduces advertising costs in terms of both present and discounted future return for dollars spent, and the result is an optimal solution maximizing a brand's market position. The unique contribution is that the profitability of an advertising expenditure is related to future sales, and, as such, it provides a rich basis for experimentation and empirical investigation.

While the Kuehn model will generate an optimum advertising expenditure, it requires a considerable body of data, including the following:

1. The rates of decay of brand loyalty (which are assumed to be constant over time).
2. The percentage of purchasers staying with a brand due to loyalty.
3. Net growth of industry sales per time period.
4. An estimate of the lag between placement of advertising dollars and sales results.
5. The percentage of consumers who are impervious to marketing effort.
6. The share of brand shifters attracted by price, product, distribution, and advertising.
7. An index of advertising effectiveness.

This list could be extended, and it is clear that such data are usually unattainable except by the most tenuous of estimates. The difficulties are magnified greatly when many brands are compared.

While the difficulties of application are enormous, the importance of Kuehn's contribution should not be minimized. He has systematically implemented economic analysis by relating marketing-mix variables to empirical brand shift data to derive a mathematical model which yields an optimum promotional expenditure. The model obviously needs considerable refinement and extension as it now stands, to say nothing of sharpening the means of deriving the necessary input data. But the growth in the practical utility of computer models has been phenomenal, and it may be that the problem of budgeting is at last yielding to practical and significant new approaches.

Simulation

Various attempts to simulate the behavior of a market on a computer have appeared in the literature in recent years. All have in common the representation of the behavior of a sample of consumers stored in the computer so that the probability of consumer response in a certain way, given the input of marketing efforts, can be assessed. One of the most interesting simulation models has been designed to permit evaluation of advertising budget strategies.[18]

This model, referred to by the acronym NOMAD, is a combination Monte Carlo and analytic demand model designed to forecast purchase behavior of 500 consumers in a well-defined market containing up to 10 major brands. The model can be used to predict awareness, initial trial, peak purchase rates, sales for a new product, and demand for existing products. The individual consumer is described statistically. Three types of data are needed: (1) consumer panel purchase histories, (2) records of advertising by all leading brands in a product category, and (3) survey and market test data. There are then three principal initial values related to choice behavior for each consumer, based on records of past purchase behavior: (1) revealed brand preferences, (2) revealed store preferences, and (3) satisfaction level.

Inputs are then introduced to modify brand choice behavior. NOMAD has been validated in two product categories, and there was a close fit between actual and simulated purchases for each brand in these situations. Given this fit, attempts were then made to experiment with different advertising budget levels. Some statistically significant effects on market shares and purchase sequences were found, thus giving rise to the prediction that this type of simulation can prove useful in arriving at the optimum expenditure level.

Obviously, this type of model is still largely untested. It does, however, offer the realism of assessing the effects of advertising under competitive circumstances. It offers the advantages of providing essential information quickly and at low cost. As a result, simulation may in the future find widespread use as management strives to implement the marginal approach to promotional budgeting.

Conclusions on Quantitative Methods

This has by no means exhausted the literature on potentially applicable quantitative models. Others which might have been described if space allowed use simultaneous equations or adaptive models which are continually updated with inputs of new information.

Have quantitative methods remedied the deficiencies of traditional budgeting tools? The answer at the present time unfortunately is not clear, because there are some problems which have not been resolved. In the first place, the information required often is virtually unobtainable at a reasonable cost. Second, and perhaps more crucial, is the limitation that

---

[18] Jerome Herniter, Victor Cook, and Bernard Norek, "Micro Simulation Evaluation of Advertising Budget Strategies," working paper published by the Marketing Science Institute, Boston, Mass., 1969.

most of the models described here make budgetary recommendations based on the assumption that advertising is the only variable. Interdependencies within the marketing mix are ignored, and this causes the models to be highly unrealistic under most circumstances. Finally, many of the assumptions of the models themselves tend to be arbitrary, although it cannot be denied that the traditional tools of budgeting, such as percentage of sales, are also built on assumptions which frequently are even more unrealistic.

Review and Discussion Questions

1. What is the basic idea of the theoretical approach to determining the advertising appropriation as presented in Figure 11–1? Can this approach be used in the business firm? Why, or why not?

2. What are the cost or expense items which should be included in the advertising budget? Why does it often become a catchall for irrelevant items?

3. Sears, Roebuck & Company spent $143,000,000 on national (as opposed to local store) advertising during one year, making it the second largest advertiser. This figure amounted to about 2.4 percent of sales. Assume that you are assigned the responsibility of determining the next advertising budget. What role would you assign to the percentage of sales figure? What other factors would enter into your decision?

4. The Kellogg Company spends about 4.4 percent of its total sales for advertising, whereas the International Telephone & Telegraph Company spends about only 0.5 percent of its sales for advertising. Why is there such a difference?

5. It is said that the 1980s will be characterized by vigorous emphasis on advertising accountability on the part of top management. How will this influence budgetary practice?

6. What is meant by a built-up analysis? How does it fit into the task and objective approach?

7. Assume that the advertising share of successful products in the soft drink industry exceeds sales share by about 2.1 to 1. You are the advertising manager of Twink, a new dietary soft drink. Would you abide by this customary ratio? What size budget would result if first-year sales were estimated at $8 million? What factors might lead you to depart from the customary ratio?

8. How might one determine how to allocate promotional dollars to various parts of the country?

9. The president of a large advertising agency, a man who has long been considered by many to be a leader in the industry, made the following statement: "Our experience has shown that the operations research people have just sold us a bunch of hogwash. It sounds good but they cannot deliver the goods when it gets down to the final analysis. As far as I'm concerned, leave the computers for the eggheads in the universities." Evaluate.

10. Some feel that simulation is the quantitative method which offers the most promise in advertising budgeting. What might this be? Do you agree? Why, or why not?

11. What is payout planning? How can you explain its widespread use in new-product introductions? What possible dangers must be faced?

PART FOUR

Management of Advertising and Sales Promotion Efforts

The topic of management of program elements will be approached first with consideration of the issues involved in using advertising and sales promotion as two of the most significant parts of the promotional program. Chapter 12 surveys the array of available advertising media, and Chapter 13 considers the basic aspects of media strategy.

Media selection, however, is only part of advertising. Design of the message perhaps offers the greatest challenge to the decision maker. Chapter 14 reviews what is referred to in the trade as "creative strategy." No attempt is made to present rules or practices in message design; rather the focus is on more fundamental considerations and trends. Such detailed issues as design of headlines and television commercials are discussed in the Appendix to this book.

The tools of marketing research find considerable use in advertising strategy. Chapter 15 analyzes procedures used to pretest the message before it is run in the media, as well as the methods utilized to analyze the actual sales and communication effectiveness of the campaign.

Finally Chapter 16 discusses the management of sales promotion activity.

CHAPTER 12

Analysis of Mass Media Resources*

The investment of dollars in the mass media to reach the desired audience with a minimum of waste and a maximum of efficiency requires careful quantitative and qualitative analysis and selection of media vehicles. Selection and use of the mass media is the subject of the next several chapters. In this chapter the concern is with media resources—types of available media and their characteristics. Sources of information and media strategy are covered in the following chapters.

EXPENDITURE TRENDS

In 1981 the total volume of advertising in the United States exceeded the $61 billion mark for the first time in history. As the data in Figure 12–1 comparing U.S. advertising volume in 1980, and 1981 show, all of the media gained in overall revenue.

It should be noted that the real increase in advertising volume is concealed by the increased cost of units of advertising. If inflation is taken out, there was about a 4 percent annual gain from 1968–81. Additionally, we should note that the number of physical advertising units placed in

* The authors wish to thank Mr. Bernard Guggenheim, vice president of Campbell-Ewald, for his assistance in the preparation of this chapter. Also, we wish to thank the Media Department at Leo Burnett Advertising for providing data and other assistance.

FIGURE 12–1

Advertising Volume in the United States in 1980 and 1981

Medium	1980 ($ millions)	Percent of total	1981 ($ millions)	Percent of total	Percent change
Newspapers:					
Total	15,541	28.5	17,420	28.4	+12.1
National	2,353	4.3	2,729	4.4	+16.0
Local	13,188	24.2	14,691	24.0	+11.4
Magazines:					
Total	3,149	5.8	3,533	5.8	+12.2
Weeklies	1,418	2.6	1,598	2.6	+12.7
Women's	782	1.4	853	1.4	+ 9.1
Monthlies	949	1.8	1,082	1.8	+14.0
Farm publications	130	0.2	146	0.2	+12.2
Television:					
Total	11,366	20.9	12,650	20.6	+11.3
Network	5,130	9.4	5,575	9.1	+ 8.7
Spot	3,629	6.0	3,730	6.1	+14.1
Local	2,967	5.5	3,345	5.4	+12.7
Radio:					
Total	3,702	6.8	4,212	6.9	+13.8
Network	183	0.4	220	0.4	+20.0
Spot	779	1.4	896	1.5	+15.0
Local	2,740	5.0	3,096	5.0	+13.0
Direct mail	7,596	13.9	8,781	14.3	+15.6
Business publications	1,674	3.1	1,841	3.0	+10.0
Outdoor:					
Total	578	1.1	650	1.1	+12.5
National	364	0.7	419	0.7	+15.0
Local	214	0.4	231	0.4	+ 8.0
Miscellaneous:					
Total	10,744	19.7	12,087	19.7	+12.5
National	5,663	10.4	6,410	10.4	+13.2
Local	5,081	9.3	5,677	9.3	+11.7
Total:					
National	30,290	55.6	34,280	55.9	+13.2
Local	24,190	44.4	27,040	44.1	+11.8
Grand total	54,480	100.0	61,320	100.0	+12.6

Source: *Advertising Age*, March 22, 1982, p. 66. Reproduced with permission. Copyright 1982, Crain Communications, Inc.

various media have increased substantially.[1] Using 1968 as a base, the number of commercial placements on television has grown about 55 percent for spot television (local TV station buys), and about 40 percent for network television. The number of different brands advertised on television has grown about 50 percent during the same period, mostly in the spot market. Spot radio commercial units are up about 60 percent,

---

[1] Based upon Bernard Guggenheim, "What the Research Shows about Actual Growth in Ad Volume," *Media Decisions*, March 1978, p. 90, and updates from various advertising agency media guides through 1982.

and network radio about 40 percent since 1968. Since 1973 magazine pages of advertising are up about 10 percent for national editions, and 35 percent for special (regional or demographic) editions. Outdoor poster showings are up almost 40 percent since 1969, and newspaper advertising pages about 20 percent since 1960. This increase in units placed means that the fight to get consumers attention is becoming more difficult. It is hard to get noticed.

The trend toward increased spending is expected to continue. Total yearly advertising expenditures are expected to reach between $80 and $90 billion by 1990, depending on the rate of inflation. However, advertising as a percentage of gross national product (GNP), has declined from 2.20 percent in 1963 to a low of 1.97 percent in 1976. In 1980, this percentage rose to about 2.03 percent.

NEWSPAPERS

Newspapers have long maintained first place among all media in terms of combined national and local advertising revenues. Newspapers are for the most part a local medium with daily circulation confined to the city of publication and immediately surrounding areas. The circulation of Sunday newspapers, however, frequently is much greater, often extending beyond state boundaries.

The syndicated Sunday supplement is a distinct exception of the local flavor of newspaper editorial content. *Parade* and *Family Weekly* in effect are national sections inserted in more than 400 Sunday papers. Other supplements are local in editorial content and advertising. Some offer regional editions to permit insertion of advertising in a group of cities rather than purchase of the entire circulation.

Characteristics of Newspapers

Advantages. The use of newspapers as an advertising medium has the following advantages:

1. *Broad consumer acceptance and use.* Newspapers are truly a unique way of life to most Americans, according to studies. (See Figure 12–2 for details.)

a. Daily newspaper readership is high. Newspapers are read by 68 percent of all U.S. adults, and within the top 300 markets, newspaper coverage includes 87 percent of households. Over one week's time, the daily newspaper has a cumulative reach of 89 percent of all U.S. adults. (See Figure 12–2, part B.)

b. Readership is 79 percent for college graduates, 53 percent for grammar school graduates.

FIGURE 12–2
Newspaper Statistics

A. Cost and coverage cumed by top market groups*

Metro market	Number homes (000)	Metro circulation (000)	Open line rate-B/W	Cost per page B/W
Top 10	17,862	16,575	$132.72	$278,158
Top 20	25,431	23,631	184.46	400,303
Top 30	31,126	24,072	225.30	492,151
Top 40	35,210	25,174	251.45	556,919
Top 50	38,312	27,941	277.63	623,794
Top 60	40,934	30,238	297.90	671,338
Top 70	43,164	32,241	318.03	718,816
Top 80	45,110	33,996	334.42	757,748
Top 90	46,835	35,493	347.45	790,495
Top 100	48,336	36,809	361.95	824,280

* Daily newspapers in each market are included on the basis of circulation rank, until the combined circulations exceed 50 percent coverage of the market.
Source: Circulation 1981/82.

B. Newspaper readership (Average weekday)

	Adults	Men	Women
Total	68%	69%	68%
Age:			
18–24	59%	63%	55%
25–34	63	63	63
35–44	71	69	72
45–54	75	75	75
55–64	75	77	74
65+	69	73	67
Education:			
Graduated college	79%	80%	77%
Attended college	71	72	70
Graduated high school	69	68	69
Attended high school	65	64	66
Did not attend high school	53	56	49
Household income:			
$35,000+	79%	81%	79%
$25,000+	76	77	77
$20–24,999	71	68	72
$15–19,999	65	63	65
$10–14,999	64	63	65
Less than $10,000	54	56	52

Source: Simmons Market Research Bureau, 1981.

C. Newspaper reach (Adults—average market)

Total daily GRPs	Reach by type of schedule—five weekdays		
	1 paper	2 papers each day	2 papers (1 per day)
25	34	30	50
35	47	41	67
45	60	52	82
55	73	63	—
65	85	73	—
90	—	90	—

Sources: Leo Burnett estimates; Newspaper Advertising Bureau.

FIGURE 12–2 (concluded)

D. Newspaper readers per copy

	Average daily paper		Sunday/average weekend paper	
Age	Men	Women	Men	Women
18–24	.19	.16	.20	.20
25–34	.24	.24	.28	.28
35–44	.19	.19	.21	.21
45–54	.18	.18	.21	.19
55–64	.17	.17	.19	.18
65+	.16	.20	.15	.20
Total	1.13	1.14	1.24	1.26

Source: Simmons Market Research Bureau, 1981.

E. Newspaper readership by section

	Percent of readers opening average page	
	Men	Women
All sections (average page)	91%	86%
General news	85	91
Sports	81	70
Business	73	77
Society	82	90
Editorial	81	92
Amusements	78	82
Radio—television	83	89
Comics	77	90
Advertising only	75	78
Classified	72	79

Source: The Media Book, 1979.

Source: *Leo Burnett 1982 Media Costs and Coverage*, pp. 14–15. Used with permission.

 c. Newspaper reading increases with income. Of those making $35,000 plus, 79 percent read newspapers daily, compared to 54 percent of those earning $10,000 or less.

 d. Of the readers, most claim thorough readership.

 e. Because so many readers go through newspapers on a page-by-page basis, the average page has a 91 percent for men and 86 percent for women chance of being opened. (See Figure 12–2, part E.)

 f. Weekend readership is also high.

 2. *Short closing times.* Closing times refer to the deadline prior to publication by which advertising copy must be submitted. For daily newspapers, this period seldom exceeds 24 hours, thus giving the advertiser the opportunity to make last-minute changes. Closing dates for Sunday supple-

ments, however, are generally much longer, usually ranging from four to six weeks.

3. *Improvements in color reproduction.* Standard newspaper color printing (ROP or run-of-paper color) has become widely available. Papers accounting for about 90 percent of total circulation offer black and white plus one ROP color; about 70 percent offer black and white and three ROP colors. Fine shadings and pastels are now possible but, because of the porosity of newspaper stock, truly fine color reproduction is difficult. The average costs for a full-page ad with black and three colors run about 31 percent above those for black and white.

Since high-quality color is so hard to achieve with ROP, increasing use is made of preprinted color advertisements on a heavier stock of paper. This procedure, called Hi-Fi color, is available in about 90 percent of the markets and usually runs about $29 per 1,000 circulation above the cost of black and white. The chief disadvantage is that Hi-Fi methods require preprinting on a continuous roll of paper, and it is impossible to have the cuts coincide with the end of the copy. Creatively, this usually requires a wallpaper type of design. This problem may be eliminated, however, by the use of still another process called Spectacolor, available in approximately 25 percent of the papers and costing little more than Hi-Fi. Preprinted inserts can be prepared either on ROP stock or rotogravure or other high quality printing processes. These inserts are provided to papers, and the advertiser pays a special rate. Again the advantage is reproduction control.

4. *Increased geographic and market flexibility.* Newspapers are increasingly recognizing that one edition for a large market is not adequate to provide full local coverage. As a result many papers now offer zone editions. The *Chicago Tribune,* for example, offers several zone variations and supplements corresponding to suburban areas. In addition, special-interest newspapers are becoming more established. While many underground newspapers started during the latter part of the past decade have folded as U.S. society has changed, others have continued to flourish and have become more commercialized.

Perhaps the most significant trend, however, is the growth of community and suburban newspapers and the further segmentation of large central-city newspapers. Also a selling company called U.S. Suburban Press, Inc. (USSPI) has organized about 1,300 suburban papers in over 40 markets into a one-order/one-bill package, thus simplifying the buying process.

5. *Communication advantages.* The printed page is often believed to offer greater prestige and believability, perhaps based on the adage that "seeing is believing." There is no convincing research to verify this claim, but it is known that print induces superior retention of complex factual material when compared with oral presentation. Also it is thought that print

forces the reader to become more involved in the subject matter through groping to understand and to evaluate. Such involvement is less evident when material is presented in spoken form.

6. *Reseller support.* Of all media, newspapers are most used for the following purposes: (*a*) cooperative plans whereby dealers share costs, (*b*) identification and promotion of the local dealer, (*c*) promotion of quick action through coupons, and (*d*) other means to enlist dealer support. Dealer enthusiasm for this use of advertising dollars often runs high.

Disadvantages.   Newspapers also have disadvantages as an advertising medium, including the following:

1. *Rate differentials.* National advertising linage in newspapers has not realized as rapid gains as local advertising has. This lag is due in part to wide differentials between local and national (nonlocal) rates, in favor of local advertisers. As might be expected, rate differentials have been under fire. Defenders of the differentials in rates claim several justifications:

a.   National volume is not as dependable as local retail volume and therefore costs more to handle.
b.   The national competitor will have a large edge over his local counterpart and hence should be penalized.
c.   National advertisers are requesting more merchandising assistance in the form of special promotion to dealers, assistance in advertising plans, and other services.
d.   It costs more to handle national advertising. Newspapers claim that these costs are from 20–25 percent higher because the 15 percent discount is granted to agencies (this is the standard method of agency compensation), a cash discount is given, and representatives must be paid to solicit nonlocal advertising. This latter charge is also incurred for local advertising.

The first three claimed justifications have little basis in fact. The widespread use of newspapers by many national advertisers on a continuing basis largely removes the charge of lack of dependability; the national and local firms seldom are competitors and in fact it is more common for the national advertiser to work in partnership with local dealers; and, finally, local advertisers seldom use an agency and therefore are prone to request more in the way of special services than the national firm. The payment of agency commissions, however, and the other costs are valid reasons for a nominal differential. The problem is that the usual differential is far in excess of this justifiable amount, and most newspapers at this point seem to be unwillingly to change the status quo.

A Federal Trade Commission-initiated lawsuit almost affected this. *The Los Angeles Times* was charged with price discrimination in advertising rates between local advertisers. Specifically, they were charged with offering lower rates to large local merchants than those available to smaller local merchants. If the government had won this case, then the differential between national and local rates would also seem to be in jeopardy. However, the FTC by unanimous vote of the Commissioners withdrew from the case in 1982 citing possible raising of advertising rates and uncertain benefits.[2]

2. *Costs of national coverage.* The costs of reaching a national market through newspapers can quickly become excessive. National coverage through this medium often requires an additional expenditure of 80 percent or more in comparison with network television and magazines. However, newspapers do provide better intensity of coverage of households.

3. *Short life.* Newspapers usually are not retained in the home for extensive periods of time. As a result, little opportunity exists for repeat exposure to advertisements. This disadvantage is shared by all media, however, with the exception of magazines.

4. *Reproduction problems.* Newspapers, of course, are printed on an absorbent paper stock resulting in an inability to offer fine reproduction. In addition, the speed necessary to compose a daily newspaper prevents the detailed preparation and care in production which is possible when time pressures are not so great.

5. *Small "pass-along" audience.* Generally speaking, newspapers do not generate larger audiences through sharing of issues by purchasers, often referred to as pass-along readership. The pass-along audience of magazines may be substantial. (See Figure 12–2, part D.)

Buying Newspaper Space

Newspaper rates are usually quoted in detail in volumes published periodically by the Standard Rate and Data Service (SRDS). The basic space unit for strictly local advertising is usually the column inch. The national rate, however, is quoted in terms of agate lines (14 lines represent a column inch). The newspaper page consists of from six to nine columns, approximately 300 lines deep. The total number of lines is approximately 2,400. The tabloid page consists of about 1,000 lines with five or six columns.

Published rates vary if special treatment is specified. Color, of course, always carries a premium, as does location in a specific part of the paper. Unless otherwise specified, copy will be inserted on an ROP (run-of-paper) basis.

For local advertising, gross space rates are usually converted to a com-

---

[2] "FTC Bows Out of Ad Rate Foray in 'Times' Case," *Advertising Age,* July 12, 1982, p. 2.

mon basis for purposes of comparison. The milline rate, widely used for this purpose, is calculated as follows:

$$\frac{\text{Line rate} \times 1,000,000}{\text{Circulation}}$$

Rates are compared, then, in terms of costs of the circulation which is achieved. Otherwise an extremely low line rate might be deceptive if it fails to generate adequate circulation and advertising exposure. Also, milline rates are rarely used by national advertisers. They prefer to use a rating point measure, which is the reach of the paper times the frequency of insert, relative to cost.

Recently there has been an attempt by newspapers to develop "standard advertising units" (SAUs), as a way of simplifying national advertising buys. The American Newspaper Publishers Association has been the leader in this area. They have proposed 25 different SAUs. Most major newspapers have indicated a willingness to use such a system.[3] SAUs represent different sizes of ads. Thus a national advertiser could prepare one ad for insertion in over 1,300 newspapers and have rates quoted on this basis.

Also the Newspaper Advertising Bureau has developed a "Newsplan" program whereby national advertisers obtain discounts in newspapers. Eight out of 10 newspapers are cooperating in this plan.[4] Both SAUs and Newsplan await effective implementation for easy use by national advertisers.

The Future of Newspapers

There can be little doubt that newspapers will continue to be vitally important as a local advertising medium. Two major trends will probably continue.

First, and most vital to the survival of the newspaper, is the development of increased technological sophistication. More than one half of the total newspaper copy in the United States is now printed on offset presses. The use of electronic technology is also increasing. Among the new systems is one which basically consists of a typesetting computer linked to a visual display. It can be used for classified and display advertising as well as news copy because previously entered copy can be recalled directly from memory files, plus do pagination.

The second major trend is the segmentation and diversification of the

---

[3] "Industry Gears for Standard Advertising Ad Units," *Marketing & Media Decisions*, March 1981, pp. 59–62, 120–30.

[4] "8 out of 10 Newspapers Offer Newsplan Discounts," *Marketing & Media Decisions*, August 1979, pp. 64–65, 94–96.

newspaper industry with the growth of suburban and community newspapers and the publication of different sections of large central-city newspapers.

Chain controlled newspapers are also expected to grow in importance unless the federal government decides otherwise. Other newspapers are expected to expand into national distribution, like the *Christian Science Monitor*. However, there are logistical problems. For example *The Wall Street Journal* transmits copy to local plants via satellite, as does the national edition of the *New York Times. USA Today* was recently started by Gannett as a national newspaper.

Of special concern are newsprint shortages and rapidly increasing costs. For example, the price of newsprint has increased from $175 to over $560 per ton in just 10 years. One solution of that problem which has been foreseen by many is broadcast of the local newspaper over two-way cable television. Hard copies could be made of items of particular interest through the use of a facsimile printer linked to the set. This appears to be a long time off.

Additional future concerns and prospects for newspapers include:

1. The acceptance of SAUs, and associated growth in obtaining national advertising dollars.
2. Improvement in audience research. (See Chapter 13 for more details.)
3. The potential display of newspaper pages on television screens in homes through cable hookups or direct transmission.

AT&T has moved to offer such a service, much to the objection of newspaper publishers.[5] Some fear the demise of the newspaper as we know it.

TELEVISION

Television, a marvel of the electronic age, grew into a dynamic marketing force in less than 20 years. The type of television under consideration makes a difference in any discussion; network program advertising differs substantially from advertising on local television stations. We will center first on the characteristics of television in general and then on the use of network program advertising versus spot announcements.

In 1981, there were 1035 operating television stations in the United States. The breakdown is as follows: 522 commercial VHF stations, 244 commercial UHF stations, 107 noncommercial VHF stations, and 162 non-commercial UHF stations. Most commercial stations are network affiliated with only about 200 operating as independents.[6]

---

[5] "AT&T, Publishers' Battle on Five Fronts," *Advertising Age,* May 4, 1981, p. 22.
[6] *Broadcasting Cablecasting Yearbook, 1981,* p. A–2.

General Characteristics of Television

Advantages. The advantages of television as an advertising medium include:

1. *The combination of sight and sound.* Television, through its combination of sight and sound, provides audiences with a unique sense of participation and reality approximating face-to-face contact. As such it commands full attention from viewers. While it is not clear that information is retained better following television exposure than through the use of other media, it is reasonable to expect a high degree of emotional involvement and impact.

The combination of sight and sound also is advantageous because of the creative flexibility offered to the advertiser. Full opportunity exists for product demonstration and the amplification of selling points with audio presentation. In addition, color telecasting has the advantages of greater emotional impact and presentation of appetite appeal. Of the more than 81.5 million U.S. households now equipped with television, about 88 percent have color sets. About 71 million color sets are now in U.S. households, including some households with more than one color set. Of all television households, 47 percent have more than one set.[7] Twenty-eight percent of television households receive cable television programming.[8] The total number of sets in the United States exceeds 130 million, with almost 12 million color sets and almost seven million black and white sets bought in 1980 alone.[9]

2. *Mass audience coverage.* Television is now in 99 percent of all 83.1 million plus U.S. households.[10] Recent studies indicate that during an average day, 92 percent of these households will be exposed to television programming, and in the space of a week, this percentage reaches 98 percent. The average viewing time per day per television household is six hours and 45 minutes.[11] During an average week the average television viewing time per television household is over 48 hours. Television is truly a *mass* medium.

Figure 12–3 presents a more detailed look at television viewing by providing data on some demographic characteristics of viewers by times of the day. Note that viewing is slightly less in higher income groups, and among working women relative to other women.

3. *The psychology of attention.* The television viewer is in a sense a captive before his or her set. Most viewers give way to inertia and watch commercials rather than exert the effort to change the set to other program mate-

---

[7] Ibid.

[8] *Leo Burnett 1982 Media Costs and Coverage,* p. 5.

[9] *Broadcasting Cablecasting Yearbook, 1982,* p. B–200.

[10] Ibid.

[11] A. C. Nielsen, *National Audience Demographics Report,* October 1981.

FIGURE 12–3

Television Viewing (hours of TV usage per week)

	7-day, 24-hour total	Monday–Sunday		Monday–Friday	
		8:00 P.M.– 11:00 P.M.	11:30 P.M.– 1:00 A.M.	10:00 A.M.– 4:30 P.M.	4:30 P.M.– 7:30 P.M.
All households	48.07	13.06	2.92	8.29	6.86
Households $20M+	49.83	14.05	3.24	7.74	6.87
Households $30M+	47.02	13.48	3.23	6.73	6.57
Total men	28.26	9.39	2.02	2.57	3.78
Men 18–49	26.01	8.59	2.15	1.95	3.18
Men $20M+ HH	25.88	8.95	1.96	1.82	3.36
Total women	32.13	10.08	1.89	6.01	4.46
Women 18–49	29.33	9.28	1.93	5.43	3.69
Women $20M+ HH	29.27	9.81	1.92	4.91	3.77
Women employed	27.21	9.58	1.74	3.41	3.50
Women w/children	30.95	9.53	2.05	6.53	3.77
Teens 12–17	19.44	6.28	.96	2.02	3.20
Children 2–11	23.70	5.90	.21	3.09	5.01

Source: A. C. Nielsen, National Audience Demographics Report, October 1981. From *Leo Burnett 1982 Media Costs and Coverage*, p. 6. Used with permission.

rial. From this it can be inferred that they will be consciously exposed to a majority of advertising messages, with the result that at least one hurdle to promotional response is cleared. It must not be overlooked, however, that exposure by no means infers favorable response, because of the mechanisms of selective perception and retention discussed earlier. The low-involvement learning discussed in Chapter 7 assigns television advertising even more power due to its ability to affect cognitive structure.

4. *Favorable consumer reaction.* Television appears to have lost very little of its tremendous popularity that was evident in the extensive nationwide survey by Gary Steiner in 1960, when 60 percent considered it to be the greatest invention in 25 years to make life more enjoyable.[12] Another nationwide survey done two decades later by the Roper organization substantiates the still high popularity of television. Some of the major findings of these surveys are:[13]

a. That 65 percent of the U.S. public turns to TV as the source of most of its news and that 51 percent rate it as the most believable news source. Some media researchers have become concerned about these types of conclusions, and argue that the way one asks questions of people about these matters can affect the reported results. It is the authors' view that a safer conclusion is that television is the main source of daily world news and national political news. Radio is the main source of news during the daytime and the first source of news

---

[12] Gary A. Steiner, *The People Look at Television* (New York: Alfred A. Knopf, 1963).

[13] The Roper Organization Study as reported in *Broadcasting Cablecasting Yearbook 1982*, p. A–2.

in the morning. Newspapers give strong in-depth coverage of news and cover local and community news and affairs. Magazines are the main source of information about specific product categories for which they have designated themselves authorities.

b. That the better educated viewers reported less enthusiasm for television programming and different motivations for watching than others did, but these feelings actually made surprisingly little difference in actual television-watching behavior. The only exception was Educational Television (ETV) stations, which have a larger percentage of those with some college training in their audiences than do regularly programmed commercial stations. (See Figure 12–3 for income related support for this.)[14]

c. Commercials still are widely accepted as necessary.

Disadvantages.   Television also has certain disadvantages which affect its choice as an advertising medium:

1. *Negative evaluations.* There has been a growing tendency for programs to include more explicit sexual behavior and dialogue, more realistic violence and free use of curses and vulgarity. Even more recently violence has been decreasing, and seemingly replaced with sex. While some have praised this trend as greater freedom in realistic programming, others have condemned it as the product of a morally degenerate society. Some religious groups have organized boycotts of sponsors they believe are supporting these shows. The result has been a greater tendency to produce specialized programs and consequently more selective viewing, especially on the part of children. Groups such as Parents Against Advertising to Children have attacked the nature of children's programming, and the whole idea of advertising on television to children at all.

The question of bias in television news coverage becomes more acute as the proportion of Americans dependent chiefly upon television as their source of news becomes greater.

These are obviously issues which go beyond a particular communications medium, but they do have great significance in terms of television, and they are likely to be hotly contested for some time to come. The reaction of advertisers has largely been to seek a middle course, avoiding either extreme. Television still represents the least selective of the electronic and print media, and programs on the extremes are likely to offend a number of watchers. This could well bring negative as well as positive results to the advertisers on a particular program. The result is that truly unique programs winning critical acclaim may not survive because of failure to draw a large audience.

---

[14] For additional support for this conclusion and other aspect of television viewing see: Ronald E. Frank and Marshall G. Greenberg, *The Public's Use of Television* (Beverly Hills, Calif.: Sage Publications, 1980).

2. *Nonselectivity.* Though there may be growing selectivity among television watchers, it is still difficult to reach precisely a small market segment using television as the medium. Variations in program content and broadcast time will obviously achieve some selectivity, especially through children's programs, sports programs with masculine appeal, or late-night talk shows, but more precise segmentation in terms of age, income, and interest is practically impossible on broadcast television. Cable television (CATV) may eventually allow for such segmentation if it continues to develop, as many expect it will. This is discussed further in the section on the future of television.

3. *Fleeting impression.* The television message crosses the viewer's consciousness only momentarily and then is lost. If for some reason the message did not register, the promotional opportunity has been lost. The opportunity does exist for reexposure, however, through multiple commercials over a period of time.

4. *Commercial clutter.* Once a problem chiefly in spot television, the growing use of 30-second commercials and even split 30's, along with participatory buying by advertisers have resulted in a greater number of different commercial messages in each program. The competition in each commercial break combined with the shorter time used in developing and communicating the message has many advertisers worried about the persuasive effectiveness of the commercial—the fear of being lost in the crowd.

5. *"Promo" clutter.* Another aspect of the general clutter problem relates to the increased amount of hyping of their own shows undertaken by the networks. Again, getting one's message through to the consumer is made more difficult.

The Network Television Program

Networks are dominant in television for the reason that they originate most of the popular programs. The networks are confederations of stations in which each one is compensated at the rate of 30 percent of the gross commercial rate for programs carried in its area. While it is assumed that each station will air most network shows, the station is free to originate local programming if a greater profit can be made.

Several smaller networks also offer shows on a regional or selective programming basis. The Hughes Sports Network makes available to subscribing stations coverage of sports events not covered by the major networks. The Christian Broadcasting Network, with headquarters in Portsmouth, Virginia, includes several stations nationwide which operate on a nonprofit basis to broadcast a wide variety of religious programming. Metromedia owns six television stations which compete with the major networks in New York and several other large metropolitan areas.

A recent development in the use of transmission by satellite was made by Turner Broadcasting's WTBS Atlanta, WGN Chicago, and WOR New York. They are transmitting their own shows to cable systems in other regions of the country, and have earned the name "superstations." Further, Home Box Office (a division of Time, Inc.), transmits "pay" movies and other events via satellite to cable operators for sale to connected households.

Advantages of purchasing network time.   The advantages of network television programming as a medium for advertising include:

1. *Excellent time availabilities.* The networks have virtual control over the prime-time programming (8–11 P.M. New York time). FCC rulings regarding access to prime time put some limitations on network programming during that period, but the advertiser who wishes to reach a truly vast, nationwide audience at one time must necessarily buy time from the networks during prime-time hours.

2. *Simplicity of arrangements.* The time purchase is greatly simplified when network television is used. The mechanics of purchasing spot time can become exceedingly cumbersome and costly.

Disadvantages of purchasing network time.   The disadvantages of network time also must be considered:

1. *Costs.* Network television advertising is precluded for many because of the costs involved, although local spot announcements often can be purchased in network service times. In addition, commitments must be made well in advance, and modifications can be made only with great difficulty.

2. *Availabilities.* Even if smaller companies could come up with the money to buy prime time on network television, they might find it quite difficult to find time available, especially on high-rated programs. The virtual end of sole sponsorship of any program by a single advertiser may have eased this situation to some extent, but competition for the best programs still exists.

3. *Programs mortality.* The rate of program mortality is traditionally high each season. There is no good way of determining in advance the probable success of a program, and time buys too often must be made on the basis of educated guesses. This represents another reason why sponsorship of a single program has been largely replaced by time buying on a participating basis. The now-common network practice of program stunting in which great use is made of specials and mini series (for example, "Shogun"), have made the estimating process even more difficult.

4. *Variations in program popularity.* A program with a rating of 36 in one market (36 percent viewership) may produce a rating of only 10 in another. The advertiser's market potential would match variations in program popularity only by accident, with the result that dollars can become allocated in such a way that market potentials are not paralleled. A similar situation can result when program popularity does not parallel distribution. Occa-

sionally it is possible to purchase only part of the national coverage of a program, but this flexibility is the exception rather than the rule. To help deal with this problem, the Campbell-Ewald advertising agency developed a computer based timesharing system to facilitate the analysis and auditing of alternative network television schedules on a market-by-market basis.[15]

Buying Network Time

Network time is quoted at varying rates, depending upon the time of the day and season of the year. Prime-time rates are most expensive, of course. Approximately 65 percent of all stations are members of the National Association of Broadcasters (NAB), which permits its members to air commercials within the following guidelines:

1. *Commercials*—9½–12 minutes per hour in prime time and 16 minutes per hour in nonprime time. 12 minutes per hour on children's weekend programs.
2. *Number of interruptions:*
   a. Prime time—two per 30-minute program; four per 60-minute program; and five per 60-minute variety show.
   b. Nonprime time—four per 30-minute period; one per 5-minute period; two per 10-minute program; and two per 15-minute program.
   c. Number of consecutive announcements—four for program interruptions and three per station break.
3. *Multiple-product announcements.* There is a 60-second minimum on multiple-product announcements unless they are so well integrated as to appear to the viewer as a single announcement. Local retailers are excluded from this rule. The NAB guidelines are usually followed, although NBC added three minutes of commercial time to the "Tonight" show and 20 additional commercial seconds between 10 of its prime-time shows, to allow 62-second station breaks.[16]

The standing of the NAB code has been put in an uncertain state by a 1982 Federal district court ruling in the *United States* v. *National Association of Broadcasters* case. The government challenged four major NAB code provisions:[17]

A limit on the amount of commercial material per hour.

A limit on the number of commercial interruptions per program.

[15] Bernard Guggenheim, "Is There a Hole in Your Umbrella?" *Media Decisions,* November 1976, pp. 82–82.

[16] The Code Authority of the National Association of Broadcasters.

[17] Marianne M. Jennings, "Court Decision to Prompt Revision of NAD Ad Code," *Marketing News,* June 11, 1982.

A limit on the number of consecutive announcements per interruption.

A prohibition on the advertisement of two or more products in a single commercial if the spot is less than 60 seconds.

The court ruled that these provisions were a violation of the conspiracy to restrain trade provisions of the Sherman Act. Rather than appeal this ruling, NAB agreed with the Justice Department in November 1982 to drop their guidelines. However, in the short run, major changes in commercial time and placement are not likely to occur, as networks and local stations enforce their own codes that resemble the NAB guidelines.

Because of the escalating costs of advertising, most television time is purchased on a participating plan by which program costs are shared by other advertisers. The 30-second commercial dominates, comprising over 90 percent of all network advertising (up from 20 percent in 1970 and only 7 percent in 1967). The average 30-second prime-time network television time slot in 1982 cost about $100,000, and daytime slots cost about $13,000. A 30-second slot on a top-rated prime-time series cost $175,000, whereas low-rated slots averaged $45,000. A 30-second slot on the 1982 Super Bowl cost $345,000.[18] Obviously, these latter slots are not for the weak of budget. A widely used method of cost comparison is cost per 1,000 homes (CPM), which is based on the cost of the commercial time and the program ratings. Comparative numbers are presented in Figure 12–10 at the end of the chapter.

Spot Announcements

Many of the disadvantages of network television can be overcome through use of spot announcements on local television stations purchased on a market-by-market (nonnetwork) basis. Time availabilities generally range from 10-second IDs (station identification breaks) to a full 60 seconds, although 30-second spots predominate.

Spot television was given its greatest impetus by the well-known success story of Lestoil. This product was introduced in Springfield-Holyoke, Massachusetts, in 1954 using spot announcements, and the investment was extended market by market. Four years later a $60 million sales volume was generated by an investment of $9.5 million in spot time on 114 stations with 2,472 spots per week.[19]

Advantages of spot television. The use of spot announcements on television has some advantages for the advertiser:

1. *Geographic and time flexibility.* A key problem of purchasing network program time is the commitment to appear in nearly all markets where the program is aired, even though market potentials may differ. Spot

---

[18] *Broadcasting Cablecasting Yearbook, 1982,* p. A–2.

[19] "Short and Sweet, with the Accent on Sweet," *Printers' Ink,* June 14, 1963, p. 262.

announcements are an effective alternative when the creative advantages of television are desired. Total costs are usually reduced through minimization of waste coverage.

2. *Reseller support.* Spot television also offers one of the advantages of newspapers in that it can be used effectively in cooperative advertising programs, for identification of local dealers, and in other ways to achieve dealer support.

Disadvantages of spot television. The disadvantages of spot announcements include:

1. *Chaotic buying procedures.* When local time is purchased, the buying situation can become chaotic. There is little uniformity in rates or in quantity discount plans. In addition, favored advertisers receive desirable time periods, and a personal relationship and difficult negotiations may be necessary to achieve the best time purchase. Firms representing many stations, such as the well-known Katz Agency, simplify these problems, but the difficulties remain so great that there is no shortcut to long experience in time buying.

2. *Commercial clutter.* An excess of commercials seems to be a problem for television in general, but the volume of nonprogram material appearing in station breaks is a real headache for the industry. Talent credits and announcements appear as trailers on network programs, several commercials are aired in the station break, and time still must be left for station identification and introduction of the next program. Not surprisingly, lower recall of brand advertising occurs when station-break commercials are used.

3. *Viewing at station-break periods.* It is well known that the number of viewers declines during station breaks. Some leave the room, and the attention of those who remain is frequently attracted elsewhere. The total audience and viewer attention at station breaks may not be optimum.

Buying Spot Time

The purchase of network time involves only one contact; arrangements are considerably more difficult when local stations are used. The buyer either writes, teletypes, or telephones the station or its representative to request information on available time slots. These availabilities then are checked and communicated to the buyer, usually within 24 hours. The local station formerly guaranteed protection, in that advertisements for competing products normally will not be aired within 15 minutes of each other, but this practice is rapidly disappearing.

The listing of availabilities is always in writing, and a guarantee is given that the first buyer to make a request gets the time slot. Once the decision is made the order is usually submitted by telephone and later verified in writing.

Costs are always quoted on a spot by spot basis usually related to the time of day. Prime evening time usually carries the highest price and runs from 8:00 to 11:00 P.M. in all areas except the central time zone, where all classifications are one hour earlier. Stations affiliated with the network also quote fringe evening time from 6:00 to 7:30 P.M. and from 11:00 P.M. to 1:00 A.M. Daytime runs from sign-on to 5 P.M., Monday through Friday. In addition, it is common to quote a lower rate if the buyer is willing to run the risk that a competing buyer may later preempt the time spot. If one pays the full price, however, the buyer is guaranteed the time, and it is becoming increasingly common to reserve and hold desirable times over long periods by this means.

Most stations later verify, based on the program log, that the commercial actually was run. Following submission of this affidavit, the time bills become due. Also there are third party monitoring organizations such as Comtrac which tape the broadcast to provide verification.

It is obvious that spot-time buying can be complex, and most agencies have specialists in this field. In addition, these complexities have been instrumental in the formation of specialized media-buying services. In order to manage the paperwork, many agencies are utilizing the computer, their own and service companies such as Donavan Data Systems.

The Future of Television

Several specific issues promise to bring about changes in television programming and advertising: (1) the growth of cable television (CATV), (2) video cassette recorder/players, video disc players, and video games, (3) changes in network programming, and (4) overcommercialization. These issues are discussed below.

CATV. The continued growth and sophistication of cable television may well have a dramatic effect upon the television industry, dependent upon the rulings and guidelines created by the FCC. The major function of CATV in its early days was to bring the regularly scheduled programs of commercial stations to areas beyond the range of their broadcast signals. Subscribers who formerly had poor reception and limited channel selection could, with cable hookups, receive clear pictures and a wide variety of channel selections. Now cable serves as an alternative to standard television by offering specialty channels such as: movies, sports (ESPN—the sports network), Turner Broadcasting's 24-hour Cable Network News (CNN), music etc. (See Figure 12–4, part C.) A 1982 FCC ruling will also allow the established broadcast networks (NBC, etc.) to enter the cable television business, with as yet unknown consequences.

In 1982, there were about 4,500 operating systems reaching over 22.1 million subscribers, or 27 percent of television households.[20] Another 3,700

---

[20] *Broadcasting Cablecasting Yearbook, 1982,* p. G–3.

franchises are approved but not built. It is obvious that unless CATV can expand its services beyond the improved reception of signals from other stations, expansion in major metropolitan areas is limited. CATV's attempts to penetrate the major metropolitan markets has not at this point been extremely successful. The key to the success of CATV appears to lie in its tremendous potential in providing services, pay television, and programming not offered by network affiliates or independent stations. A number of systems now offer in-home movies, and specialty shows. See Figure 12–4 for additional facts on cable systems including penetration, cable networks and superstations, and the top-ten cable systems.

Further expansion of the services of CATV seems to be assured by the ruling handed down by the Supreme Court in March 1974. This decision overturned a lower court ruling which, in effect, prevented the importation of distant television signals by a cable system. In overturning this decision, the Supreme Court held that importation of these signals was not in violation of the copyright law when the program also served as a carrier of commercial messages. Briefly stated, since consumers in all areas of the United States paid the costs of advertising through the purchase of advertised products, the extension of television coverage by CATV to those who would not otherwise see a "free" broadcast does not constitute a violation of the law.[21]

The FCC, however, will not allow CATV to import all its programming. Consequently, CATV will have to become more competitive in creating original programming. The FCC has ruled that new CATV systems in the 100 major markets must have a minimum capacity of 20 channels, one of which must be devoted to original programming. There must also be at least three public service channels, one of public access, one of educational TV, and one for local government.[22] Efforts at original programming in most cases have provided poor alternatives to the programs of broadcast stations. If any original programming of high quality is to be provided, much greater efforts to this end must be made by CATV. Over 1,845 systems accept advertising on local originated channels, but most earn less than 5 percent of gross revenues from advertising.[23] And cable networks are aggressively seeking advertisers.

A more attractive proposal to CATV operators is pay television, which involves a mechanism attached to the subscriber's set which makes certain broadcasts impossible to view without the payment of a separate fee beyond the monthly subscription charge. This system would make possible truly specialized programming, since only those subscribers who spe-

---

[21] "Cable TV Ruling Says Ads Hike Prices," *Advertising Age,* March 11, 1974, p. 1.

[22] "Ogilvy and Mather Pocket Guide to Media," Ogilvy & Mather, Inc., 1973, p. 30.

[23] *Broadcasting Cablecasting Yearbook, 1982,* p. G–3.

FIGURE 12–4
Cable Television Facts

A. NTI sample: cable penetrations by market divisions

	Cable	Pay cable
Total U.S.	35%	17%
County Size		
A	20	14
B	38	22
C & D	51	17
Nonadults .		
None	35	14
Any	37	22
Age of head of household		
Under 50	36	35
50+	20	14
Household income		
Less than $20M	33	13
$20M+	39	22

Source: NTI, Cable Status Report, July 1981.

B. Cable and pay cable penetration

Year*	Number of systems	Cable TV homes		Pay cable homes	
		MM	% U.S.	MM	% U.S.
1960	640	.7	1.0	—	—
1970	2,490	4.5	7.5	—	—
1975	3,560	9.2	13.2	—	—
1980	4,225	17.7	22.0	7.6	9.8
1981†	4,400				
Feb.		19.7	25.3	8.4	10.8
May		21.3	26.5	9.6	12.3
July		21.9	27.3	10.6	13.6
Nov.		23.1	28.3	11.9	14.6

* November of each year.
† Change in Nielsen method for estimating cable homes.
Sources: A. C. Nielsen Company and CableVision.

C. Satellite-fed cable services

Superstations:
  WTBS, WGN, WOR
Pay Cable:
  Home Box Office, Showtime, The Movie Channel, Cinemax, Home Theatre, Galavision, Escapade, Bravo, Disney Channel (1983), Home Theatre Network Plus, Las Vegas Entertainment Network.
Basic Cable:

News:	Cable News Network 1, Cable News Network 2, Satellite News Channels 1 (Launch: 2nd Qtr, 1982), Satellite News Channels 2 (4th Qtr, 1982)
Sports:	ESPN, USA Network
Women:	Modern Satellite Network, Satellite Program Network, USA Network, Daytime (1st Qtr, 1982)
Children:	Calliope, Nickelodeon, Kid Vid Network (2nd Qtr, 1982)
Older People:	Cinemerica (TBA)
Ethnic:	Black Entertainment Television, Spanish International Network
Culture:	ARTS, CBS Cable, Satellite Program Network
Music:	Music Television, Nashville Network (1st Qtr, 1983)

FIGURE 12–4 (*concluded*)

Shopping:	Home Shopping Show, UTV Cable Network (2nd Qtr, 1982), Times Mirror Shopping Channel (1st Qtr, 1982)
Education:	American Educational TV Network, Appalachian Community Service Network
General Entertainment:	CBN Satellite Network, UTV Cable Network (2nd Qtr, 1982)
Health:	Cable Health Channel (2nd Qtr, 1982)
Weather:	The Weather Channel (2nd Qtr, 1982)
Religious:	CBN Satellite Network, Christian Media Network, PTL*, National Jewish TV, Trinity*, Episcopal TV Network*, Eternal Word TV Network*, National Christian Network*

* No advertising.
Source: CableVision.

D. Top ten cable interconnects

	Number of cable systems	Number of subscribers
Gillcable Bay (San Francisco-Oakland)	23	470,400
Cox Cable San Diego	3	315,000
Connecticut	8	273,000
International Cable (Buffalo)	3	190,000
Boston	5	183,000
Seattle	5	173,000
Orlando	3	126,000
Syracuse	5	125,000
Norfolk	3	120,000
Tulsa Cable	1	95,000

Source: Eastman CableRep.

Source: *Leo Burnett 1982 Media Costs and Coverage*, pp. 12–13.

cifically decide to watch a particular program and are willing to pay a fee to do so will be in the viewing audience. If commercial time is made available, the segmentation potential could be at least equal to that of the magazine. Even without pay television, more precise segmentation should be possible once CATV begins to produce its own programs. Pay cable is on about 3,000 systems and reaches 7.5 million subscribers in 50 states. Most pay systems have about 30 percent penetration of their potential subscriber count.[24]

Theater owners and broadcasters have been most opposed to the growth of pay television. Broadcasters fear that the additional options open to their audience would result in more selective viewing, lower ratings, and therefore lower revenues. Theater owners fear that if first-run movies are made available on pay television their business may just collapse altogether. The film makers, on the other hand, are excited about the possibilities of pay television because of the increased revenue it would bring. Subscriber fees vary but typical fees seem to be about $8–$9 per month for movies, with additional fees for other programming.

---

[24] Ibid.

Perhaps the most interesting recent development in this area is the Qube system which is currently in test in Columbus, Ohio. Qube, which is owned by Warner Communications, offers the standard CATV services, plus special stations with all-day childrens' programming, live nightclub shows, concerts, theater and a 24-hour news station. In addition, Qube is set apart by offering viewers the ability to react to programs through the pressing of a button on an in-home control panel. At a designated moment viewers push specific buttons to vote to rate shows, or guess what play a football coach will call, and so forth. The results are put on the screen within 10 seconds. The potential to display ads and have viewers order products from their homes is also being developed.

The net result of the growth in CATV will be a fragmentation of the network and spot television audience, plus a decrease in audience size, with potential negative consequences on advertising revenues. However, for the cable networks to survive, they must also draw advertising revenues. To get these revenues they must provide audience measurement numbers. Recently, ESPN and CNN have both made use of A. C. Nielsen's Home Video Index to establish their audience sizes. The development of audience measurement techniques for CATV will be a major thrust of media researchers in the next few years.

Video cassette recorders/players, video disc players, and video games. The use of video cassettes based on the same operating principles as cassette tape players are now common. Many companies are now marketing video cassette machines. In 1981, over 1.6 million video cassette recorder/players were sold up from 43,000 in 1976. The video recorder releases viewers from the fixed time schedules for programs. It is expected to greatly affect television viewing habits, and cause great problems for those attempting to measure the size of audiences of television programs. A show may be watched at any time using this system, since the viewer can automatically record any program even if he or she is not at home. Prerecorded video tapes of movies and sports events are also available at prices between $50 and $100, or rental in the $4–$7 range.

The only major difficulty with this product is a copyright infringement suit filed by MCA's Universal City Studios and Walt Disney Productions against Sony, several retailers, and some Sony Betamax owners. The suit charges that they are guilty of duplicating copyright material, films, and TV programs. In 1981, the U.S. court of appeals in San Francisco ruled against the recorder manufacturers. The case is being appealed, plus there is the potential that Congress will pass legislation to clarify this issue. The possibility of a royalty payment being added to the price of recorders and blank tapes is one proposed solution. Whatever the outcome, it is unlikely that the impact of recorders will be lessened.

Also potentially impacting on television audiences is a video disc system developed by MCA. The basic playing unit would be similar to a record player and could be attached to present television equipment. This device cannot record. The discs themselves would be packaged much like long-playing phonograph records, and are expected to sell for from $12–$15. RCA, Pioneer, and others now market similar systems.

As these systems reach widespread use, broadcasters might well be forced to provide more specialized entertainment and to concentrate on live coverage which, of course, would not be available on prerecorded discs or tapes.

Video game usage will also decrease the total audience size available to broadcast television, as will video recorders and disc players. In fact, these devices and cable offerings have already shown up in smaller standard television audiences.

Changes in network programming. All of the developments discussed above would have a bearing on network programming. The major trend created by the pressures of CATV and disc or tape systems would be toward more specialized programming, which would be necessary to fit into more selective viewing patterns. It has been predicted that the time spent watching television will continue to grow with increases in the number of television sets within each household. Since virtually all family members will have their own set, however, each will seek to watch a program conforming to his or her own interests. The decision will no longer have to be a compromise of family interests. Television ratings on individual programs will drop as the audience becomes segmented, and eventually television programming may well become similar to that of radio. Due to a more highly segmented audience, the cost per thousand individuals will probably increase, but the cost per thousand *prospects* should remain about the same or decline. There will be movement in this direction for the next few years, but broadcasting as it is today will probably persist for quite some time. Eventually, however, broadcasting may come to be referred to as "narrowcasting" to a highly segmented audience.

Overcommercialization. Many individuals feel that overcommercialization is already a very serious problem, expecially during station breaks and local programming. With the growing use of 30-second commercials, split 30's, participating sponsorship, and multiple-product announcements, the situation on network television has also rapidly grown more cluttered. Clutter will probably be reduced through a growth of new stations and multiset ownership which fosters expansion of local programming to segment target audiences, commercials customized to local market needs, and local service programming. For a while, though, the advertiser is going to have to compete with a clutter of other commercials to gain viewers' attention.

Overall, the future of television is one of great changes brought on by technology. The impact on advertising will be great in the long run.

RADIO

Radio, once considered to be a dying medium following the rise of television, has come back to exert a dynamic and vigorous competitive challenge. To underscore the extent of change, it has become almost totally a local medium, whereas it was dominated by networks prior to the onset of television. Moreover, there are more than four times more stations on the air today than in 1945. Radio networks came to exist primarily to feed newscasts to local stations and a limited variety of additional programs. Recently however, network radio has come back to attain high listening levels. (See Figure 12–5, part C.) The number of networks has grown from four in 1970 to 18 in 1982. In addition, FM, an unknown in 1945, has risen to over 90 percent penetration of U.S. homes and offers a new resource to the advertiser.

Characteristics of Radio

Advantages.   Radio as an advertising medium has a number of advantages, including the following:

1. *The mass use of radio.* In 1980, consumers purchased 28.1 million radios for home use and 9.6 million more for use in the car.[25] The overwhelming majority of these radios have both AM and FM capability. Almost 99 percent of U.S. households have at least one set, and the average household has 4.3 sets in the house and 5.5 overall including car radios.[26] In addition about 98 percent of cars have radios. Of the over 457 million sets in use, 118 million are car radios, and 339 million are in homes. Over 40 million are transistors. In January 1981 there were 4,628 commercial AM stations, 3,343 commercial FM stations and 1,116 noncommercial FM stations.[27]

The availability of transistorized portable sets has enabled radio to become a medium which can be used anywhere. Within one week's time, radio will reach 95 percent of all people 12 and over in the United States. (See Figure 12–5, part C for details and other radio listening facts.) In fact, during a single week, radio will reach well over 90 percent of all sex and age demographic segments of the United States. The exception is 6–11-year-olds, where reach is about 70 percent.

2. *Selectivity.* Radio has become a selective medium because local stations have differentiated the program formats to appeal to various consumer segments. As a result it is possible to reach nearly any class of consumer in most markets. Of course geographic flexibility has long been a strength of radio, as is true of all local media.

---

[25] *Broadcasting Cablecasting Yearbook, 1981,* p. C–368.
[26] *Leo Burnett 1982 Media Costs and Coverage,* p. 5.
[27] Ibid.

248

FIGURE 12–5
Radio Listening Facts

A. Percent listening during average quarter hour (Monday–Sunday)

	Men		Women		Teens
Daypart	18+	18–49	18+	18–49	12–17
6 A.M.–10 A.M.	21%	21%	24%	22%	15%
10 A.M.–3 P.M.	21	23	22	22	11
3 P.M.–7 P.M.	18	20	18	19	19
7 P.M.–midnight	10	12	10	10	17
Average 6 A.M.–midnight	18	19	18	18	15

Source: RADAR, Fall 1981.

B. Percent listening by location (Monday–Sunday)

	In-home			Out-of-home		
Daypart	Men	Women	Teens	Men	Women	Teens
6 A.M.–10 A.M.	52%	78%	80%	48%	22%	20%
10 A.M.–3 P.M.	35	60	57	65	40	43
3 P.M.–7 P.M.	38	61	74	62	39	26
7 P.M.–midnight	62	74	81	38	26	19
Average 6 A.M.–midnight	45	68	74	55	32	26

Source: RADAR, Fall 1981.

C. Potential radio audience (Reach)

Monday–Sunday, 6 A.M. to midnight

	Cumulative audience			Avg. quart.-hr. audience		
	Men	Women	Adults	Men	Women	Adults
Total radio:						
Number (000)	72,055	78,231	150,286	13,107	14,577	27,684
Population percent	96	94	95	18	18	18
Network radio:						
Number (000)	59,651	61,466	121,117	7,145	7,487	14,632
Population percent	80	74	77	9	9	9

Source: RADAR, Fall 1981.

Source: *Leo Burnett 1982 Media Costs and Coverage*, p. 11. Used with permission.

While many still consider FM radio as reaching a somewhat richer and better educated segment than AM, the distinction is much less clear now than it was five to eight years ago. The rapid growth of FM radio has resulted in a change from the widely used classical and symphonic formats to almost as much diversity as AM radio. Music, however, still appears to play a greater part in programming FM broadcasts than it does for AM. Many FM stations have also been more guarded than AM stations in the percentages of time given to commercial messages.

3. *Speed and flexibility.* Of all media, radio has the shortest closing period in that copy can be submitted up to air time. This flexibility has been capitalized upon by many advertisers. For example, quite a few travel-related companies found the radio to be of help in keeping their potential customers aware of the effects of the fuel shortage and encouraging them to still use their services.

4. *Low costs.* For an expenditure of under $100 in most markets, any advertiser can purchase air time. Of all media, its cost per time unit ranks among the lowest.

5. *Favorable psychological effect.* While the evidence is not unequivocal, there is some basis to the claim that there may be less resistance to persuasion over radio because many activities are directed by spoken word. Radio has also been found to produce greater retention of simple material than print, especially among the least educated. Finally, radio is easily attended to with little psychological resistance, but this casual attention can be a disadvantage when radio serves as musical background for other activities.

6. *Reseller support.* Radio, along with newspapers and spot television, is also used on occasion with effective results to stimulate dealer cooperation and selling support.

Disadvantages.   Counteracting the advantages of radio as an advertising medium are these disadvantages:

1. *The nature of the message.* Of course, radio permits only audio presentation, a disadvantage for products requiring demonstration, the impact of color, or the other features of visual media. Furthermore, the impression made is momentary, and, as with television, it is impossible to reexpose the prospect except through multiple commercials over a period of time.

2. *Chaotic buying.* Spot radio and television share the disadvantage of chaotic and nonstandardized rate structures and the bookkeeping problems connected with the purchase of time. Once again, however, large-station representatives have simplified arrangements.

3. *Costs for national coverage.* As with all local media, the costs of national coverage can become substantial. Use can be made of course, of network radio, and mass coverage is hereby achieved much more economically.

4. *Station fragmentation.* Unless substantial investments are made, it is difficult to achieve high levels of reach among mass audiences because of multiple-station fragmentation.

Spot and network radio rates are published by Standard Rate and Data Service. For stations subscribing to the code of the National Association of Broadcasters, 14 minutes of commercial time are permitted for each hour computed on a weekly basis, and the number of commercials is never to exceed 18 per hour or five per 15-minute segment. Many stations do not subscribe to the code, however, and offer a greater frequency of commercial time, much to the dismay of the advertising critics. This may be limited in the future by the FCC, which is now taking the position that licenses will not be renewed when stations broadcast commercials more than 18 minutes per hour for more than 10 percent of the broadcast day.

As in television, radio rates are differentiated into prime and secondary time. In radio, however, prime time covers the morning wake-up period and late afternoon drive-home time, when the most sets, especially car radios, are in use. The units of time available range from a few seconds to 60 seconds, thus affording great flexibility.

The cost per thousand homes reached is computed in a manner similar to that described for television. Although the accurate computation of network program ratings used to be difficult, RADAR (Radio All-Dimension Audience Research) was established in 1967 to help alleviate this problem, and the information available regarding radio available through RADAR is not too much different from the Nielsen television ratings. Market-by-market audience information is available from the Arbitron Company. (See Chapter 13 for details.)

The Future of Radio

Radio may be characterized in the future by increasing network participation, more specialization, and further growth of AM and FM stereo. Network radio appears to be making somewhat of a comeback. CBS has recently started the CBS Mystery Theater, and others of the old programs are growing increasingly popular when aired over local stations. Though this particular trend may be part of the overall mood of nostalgia, network radio is again exerting a greater influence through news and public affairs programming and giving advertisers more of a chance at national coverage.[28]

Radio is one of the most segmented of the media. The ABC radio network is actually a combination of four basic networks: contemporary, information, entertainment, and FM. Almost every major market has an all-news station such as WBBM, Chicago, and some advertisers expect that eventually there will be nationally recognized frequencies where anyone in the major market areas of the country could turn for news, weather, or public affairs.

The growth and specialization of FM is expected to continue. AM-FM radios are already standard equipment on some automobiles, and the commercial production of radio sets which will only handle one band is expected to decrease rapidly. FM stereo is expected to achieve a much better market share over AM radio than its present 61 percent, providing

---

[28] "The Booming Sound of Network Radio," *Marketing & Media Decisions,* December 1980, pp. 62–63, 116–18; and "The Revival of Network Radio," *Marketing & Media Decisions,* November 1981, pp. 191–206.

the economy remains in relatively good health.[29] This has caused a major thrust among AM stations to ask the FCC to allow them to broadcast in stereo. It is expected that such approval will be given in the not too distant future.

It is also expected that cable television may draw some audience away from radio in two ways:[30] (1) new cable network will compete for some of radio's selective audience; (2) music-oriented cable presentations will also compete.

MAGAZINES

Magazines have long been a significant medium and continue to show vitality, in spite of problems with paper shortages and postage rates. Magazines today reach nearly all market segments and cover a variety of special interests such as boating and photography. Some mass circulation periodicals continue to exhibit health despite the problems they face. There are about 1,700 consumer/farm magazines, and 3,600 business magazines.[31]

Characteristics of Magazines

Advantages.   The advantages of magazines as an advertising medium include:

1. *High geographic and demographic selectivity.* Once a nonselective mass medium, consumer magazines have attained a high degree of geographic selectivity. It is now possible to purchase one or more of 145 regional or demographic editions of *Better Homes and Gardens,* 301 editions of *Time,* 81 editions of *TV Guide,* and 70 editions of *Reader's Digest.* Twelve different consumer magazines with circulations ranging from 1.8 to 18.8 million offer 50 or more regional and demographic editions. Out of 76 of the best-known consumer magazines in the United States, only 24 do not have any regional or demographic editions.[32] Small premiums are usually charged for regional or demographic advertising, but the increased efficiency of the advertisement in reaching prospects usually is worthwhile. The magazine also becomes more of an option for advertisers such as banking institutions which serve only a limited regional market.

Demographic flexibility has long been a major virtue of consumer magazines. Appeal can be made to distinct groups of buyers with special interests, and virtually any segment of the market in terms of age, income,

---

[29] Leo Burnett media department research estimate, 1982.

[30] "Radio to Feel Cable's Impact on Ad Sales," *Advertising Age,* July 19, 1982, p. 47.

[31] *Leo Burnett 1982 Media Costs and Coverage,* p. 5.

[32] "Media Pocket Piece," Compton Advertising, Inc., New York.

or other demographic variables can be reached with a minimum of waste circulation. The editorial content of the publication also is tailored to the interests of the audience being reached so that the advertising is usually received by the consumer in a receptive mood. Figure 12–6 presents a description of *Time A⁺*, a demographic edition of *Time*. One may also buy so-called magazine networks, which are groups of magazines. One example is the City News Urban group composed of *Newsweek, Time,* and *Sports Illustrated.*

2. *The receptivity of magazine audiences.* Magazine readers appear more receptive to advertising than do television viewers. Younger segments of the audience also find magazine advertising more believable than what they see on television. In the business press area, readers often read ads to stay on top of new developments in products.

3. *Long life of a magazine issue.* Syndicated research indicates that there are between three and four adult readers for the average magazine issue, that the reader takes over three days to read the magazine, and devotes 60 to 90 minutes to do so.[33]

Other advantages include (1) the selection of editorial content to match the nature of the advertising message, and (2) the ability to reproduce ads in high quality color.

The increased reading of magazines by those on upper income and educational levels is well established in survey findings and widely accepted as fact. The reach to prime prospects can be maximized by using the right publication for the purpose or, in some cases, a demographically selective edition of a popular magazine reaching many different groups of people.

Disadvantages. The disadvantages of magazines include: (1) the inability to demonstrate the product in action, (2) its unintrusiveness relative to television and radio, (3) its limitation on geographic flexibility relative to television and radio, (4) its inability to display sound and motion, and (5) the lower levels of reach that go with repeated buys in a group of magazines relative to newspaper, television, and radio.

Magazines can also be expensive. For example the cost of a four-color page in the following magazines in 1982 is: *National Geographic,* $95,575; *People,* $34,800; *Scientific American,* $21,000; *TV Guide,* $76,000; *Business Week,* $25,745; *Time,* $61,665; *Good Housekeeping,* $58,020; *Self,* $15,500; *Vogue,* $18,000; *Road & Track,* $18,775; and *Sports Illustrated,* $49,465.

The Future of Magazines

The immediate future should see the continued growth of special-interest and special-audience magazines and continued difficulties on the part

---

[33] Simmons Market Research Bureau at different years.

FIGURE 12–6
Example of a Special Edition of a General Magazine

TIME A+

600,000 circulation, $54,000 average subscriber household income. In a class by itself.

When we tell you that TIME A+ is a brand-new advertising edition from TIME with a business/professional circulation of 600,000 and a b&w page rate of only $9,975, it sounds a little like some other magazine advertising buys you can make. Right?

But when you hear that TIME A+ subscriber households have an average income of $54,000, that 93% of its household heads have been to college, and that 100% qualify as professional/managerial, you'll probably begin to agree that TIME A+ must be in a class by itself. Nowhere else can you find comparable circulation with comparable subscriber demos.

Many advertisers will find in TIME A+ a splendid vehicle to reach decision makers in business (over 60% of its subscribers happen to be in top management). Others will find it a most effective consumer medium—say for an expensive car or an exotic fragrance. Because TIME A+ subscribers are in two positions to buy, whether it's a second factory or a second home. Whatever your market, you'll find that CPMs for TIME A+ compare most favorably with under-a-million-circulation magazines you might now be using.

TIME A+: among other things it stands for Affluence, Achievement, Action. And a great way to make your mark. Get all the facts. Write Jack Higgons, Associate Advertising Sales Director, Time & Life Bldg., N.Y., N.Y. 10020. Or call him at (212) 556-7811.

TIME A +		Subscriber Characteristics	
Circulation:	600,000	Average HH Income:	$54,000
B&W Page Rate:	$9,975	Attended College:	93%
4-Color Page Rate:	$15,560	Professional/Managerial:	100%

There's a right TIME for every advertiser.

of magazines for general readership. The growth of the special-interest magazine is reflected in the number of new magazines in this area. From January 1980 to September 1981 91 new special-audience consumer magazines were introduced, including the science magazines *Discover* and *Technology Illustrated,* and women's magazines *Vital,* and *Everywomen.*[34]

The list of magazines ending publication during the past years, however, includes such former giants as the *Saturday Evening Post, Look,* and *Life.* Recently a new publisher has revived *Life.* The outcome remains to be seen. Recent advertising figures also show the decline of the general-interest magazine and the rise of special interest and audience magazines. In 1963, general-interest magazines claimed 42 percent of magazine advertising dollars, while special interest and audience magazines received the remaining 58 percent. By 1972, however, the general-interest magazine's share had decreased to only 14 percent, and has declined slightly more into the early 1980s.[35] Figure 12–7 demonstrates how magazines compete for special interest markets.

The result of this trend for the advertiser will be a higher cost per thousand readers, because of decreasing circulation. This will be offset by the ability to isolate a narrow marketing segment for whom the commercial message would have relevance.

The magazine industry is not without its problems, basically in the form of rising postage, production, and labor costs and paper shortages.

Partly as a result of the shortage and partly due to inflation, production costs have risen steeply. Labor, paper, and ink costs have risen significantly. Magazines have continually passed these increases on to their readers and advertisers. Compton Advertising predicts that these higher magazine prices will result in a drop of 5 million in circulation in the top 50 magazines by 1990.[36]

Finally, postal rates continue to climb, with the latest increase in effect in March 1981. A growing number of new magazines such as Time-Life's *People,* their new general interest magazine, may be designed chiefly for distribution through newsstands and retail outlets. Not only are postal costs thus avoided, but the cost of maintaining a subscription department also can be avoided. The main problem is building and maintaining a consistent circulation. Most magazines, however, have no real alternative to the U.S. Postal Service at this time, and it appears that higher postal rates will just have to be survived. Attempts by a confederation of magazines to have their own mail service are just beginning to take shape. The success of this plan remains to be seen. Others such as *Better Homes*

[34] "New Consumer Magazines, 1980–81," *Marketing & Media Decisions,* December 1981, p. 70.

[35] *The Gallagher Report,* April 16, 1973, p. 4.

[36] Joel Fisher, "Compton's View of Magazines—Part One: How Healthy?," *Marketing & Media Decisions,* May 1982, pp. 102–4.

FIGURE 12–7
Intermagazine Competition

& Gardens seem committed to avoiding the Postal Service if possible in that it uses private delivery services in 13 cities. All this has made the competition for shelf space at supermarket checkout areas more intense. One retailer noted that: "the supermarket is the newsstand of today."[37]

OUTDOOR ADVERTISING

Outdoor advertising is the oldest of all the media; outdoor signs were found in Pompeii and elsewhere in ancient times. It still is an important medium for certain specific purposes, and outdoor service is offered in most cities and towns. Approximately 270,000 standardized signs are available for use.

Characteristics of Outdoor Advertising

Advantages. Several unique advantages are enjoyed by outdoor advertising.

1. *Flexibility.* Outdoor advertising may be readily tailored to create a truly national saturation campaign or to highspot in selected markets or even in parts of markets. The frequency of exposure also can be varied from market to market to adapt precisely to variations in potentials.

2. *A mobile audience.* The buyer views outdoor advertising while on the move, and many of those exposed will be purchasers of the product within a short time after viewing. This last-minute promotion thus may serve as a link between previous advertising messages and a probable purchase, as a reminder of a need, or as the required trigger for a pending sale.

3. *Relative absence of competing advertisements.* For the most part, outdoor signs stand alone and are not subject to the competition of other messages. Thus one source of distraction is removed, although it is apparent that outdoor surroundings substitute yet another and potentially more important source of distraction.

4. *Repeat exposure.* The opportunity for repeat exposure is great. It was found that a unit of sale reaches over 80 percent of all adults in the market in the first week. At the end of the month 89.2 percent of the adults will have seen the message an average of 31 times.[38] These reach and frequency figures rise as income rises, in that exposure to adults in high-income households is higher than average, and the average recall of message content is approximately 40 percent.[39] Thus the advantages of repetition are clearly achieved.

---

[37] "The Magazines' Counter Attack," *Business Week,* March 29, 1982, p. 170.

[38] "Reach and Frequency of Exposure of Outdoor Posters," study conducted by W. R. Simmons and Associates Research, Inc., for the Institute of Outdoor Advertising, Inc.

[39] "This Is Outdoor Advertising" Institute of Outdoor Advertising, New York.

Disadvantages. There are also certain disadvantages to the use of outdoor advertising:

1. *Creative limitations.* The fleeting expression permitted by exposure to a mobile audience limits copy to a few words or a single powerful graphic. Thus little more can be accomplished than a reminder or repetition of a brand name. When longer copy is required, outdoor cannot be used effectively.

2. *Mood of the viewer.* The consumer on the move is subject to many distractions, and his prime attention is usually directed elsewhere. Furthermore, he may be faced with the inescapable irritations of heavy traffic, heat, and dirt, and the opportunity for a successful advertising impact is therefore diluted.

3. *Public attack.* Outdoor advertising is under attack from many sources. The terms of the Highway Beautification Act, passed in 1965, authorize the federal government to require states to provide control of outdoor advertising and junkyards on interstate and primary highway systems.[40] Title I of this act requires effective control of signs, displays, and devices within 660 feet of the right-of-way on interstate and primary systems. Other provisions restrict outdoor advertising in commercial areas and check proliferation of signs.

The major effect of this act on the outdoor advertising industry, which actually supported its passage, has been the elimination of posters in small towns and the forced merger of small plants into larger ones to assure financial survival. The clutter of business signs which is a major concern of environmentalists is not an aspect of outdoor advertising, since the owners of the respective business establishments have these signs constructed on their own property.

The industry is not guiltless in the unwise placement of signs, but it maintains that violations of good taste and of a strict professional code are the actions of an irresponsible minority, and the majority is in agreement with the need to prevent abuse.[41] To the credit of the industry, some positive action has been taken. A fairly extensive study was undertaken to assess the effects of the presence of billboards on people's reaction to the environment they see.[42] It was found that the majority of those who were vociferous about outlawing billboards were unaware when billboards were removed from a stretch of highway viewed in a laboratory. In addition, the presence or absence of billboards on the routes used did not prove to be critical in achieving "environmental quality"; the effect of removing utility poles was double the effect of removing bill-

---

[40] Phillip Tucker, "State Implementation of Highway Beautification Act," Outdoor Advertising Association of America, 1968.

[41] "This Is Outdoor Advertising."

[42] "Measuring Human Response to the Urban Roadside," summary of a study conducted by Arthur D. Little, Inc., published by the Outdoor Advertising Association of America.

boards. However, it would be unwise to conclude on the basis of these limited results that consumers are indifferent to the presence or absence of billboards.

A San Diego law went further to mandate the removal of all but "on-premise" advertising structures. Over 1,300 boards would have been lost and two companies put out of business had the Supreme Court not ruled in July 1981 that this law was unconstitutional.[43] Unreasonable bans on outdoor advertising are thus not possible.

Purchasing Outdoor Space

Outdoor space is purchased directly from each outdoor plant or from media buying services specializing in outdoor, such as Out of Home Media Services, Inc. (OHMS). It gathers cost data and prepares estimates for any combination of markets, performs field inspections, and does the contracting.

Not all advertising agencies use OHMS, as they have complete departments equipped to handle outdoor contracts and billings. Space may be purchased also from any of the 700 individual outdoor companies, of course.

Space rates are published by the OHMS. Quotations have always been made on the basis of the desired showing. A 100 showing, for example, is supposed to provide enough signs to reach 93 percent of the population an average of 21–22 times in a 30-day period; a 50 showing is supposed to provide sufficient signs to reach 85 percent an average of 10–11 times in this same period.[44] A 100 showing may require only one or two signs in smaller areas, but costs for some of these signs can run as high as $20,000 per month in larger localities. Unfortunately, in practice a 100 showing is usually what the plant operator says it is. This is one of the reasons why the advertisers are searching for other rating devices.

Though the quotation based on showings is still used most often, the Outdoor Advertising Association of America (OAAA) has been promoting among its members a new rating system based on gross rating points. The OAAA maintains that this new system will give advertisers a more accurate basis for comparing outdoor advertising with the other media. Gross rating points are calculated by considering the number of "impression-opportunities" on the average weekday, regardless of repeat exposures, as a percentage of the entire market. Therefore, if the locations of signs during a campaign allowed for 400,000 impression-opportunities (calculated through the use of government traffic reports) daily in a market of 500,000 the plan would deliver 80 gross rating points daily.

---

[43] Pete Riordan, "Judgment from Babel," *Media & Marketing Decisions,* October 1981, pp. 87–92.

[44] Estimates provided by Ogilvy & Mather, Inc.

Standardized outdoor poster panels are approximately 12 feet high and 25 feet long, with a copy area of roughly 10 × 23 feet. Copy is printed in 10 to 14 sections. Painted signs represent about 10 percent of all outdoor structures, although they account for more than 30 percent of total space billings. Recently much small poster panel, 8-sheet so-called junior panels, have made an impact on streets in large urban areas.

The Traffic Audit Bureau (TAB) is the auditing arm of the industry and is responsible for traffic counts underlying the published rates. Effective circulation is computed as the average daily traffic having a reasonable physical opportunity to see the panels. Total gross traffic is therefore reduced as follows to arrive at effective circulation: 50 percent of all pedestrians, 50 percent of all automobile passengers, and 25 percent of passengers on buses or other forms of mass transit. Thus the 100 showing is based on *effective* circulation.

Several other organizations within the industry provide services to its members and to advertisers. The OAAA is the primary trade association; its members operate more than 90 percent of outdoor facilities in the country. One of the services of the OAAA is the Institute of Outdoor Advertising, a central source of information which also develops research, creative ideas, and methods for using the medium more effectively.

The Future of Outdoor Advertising

At least temporarily, outdoor advertising appears to have successfully withstood the attacks of the environmentalists. Its major problem is one it shares with most U.S. citizens—the probable extent of any future energy crisis. If auto traffic is significantly decreased in favor of public transportation, especially on trains and airplanes, outdoor advertising will be weakened. Continued growth is uncertain in the light of such developments. The attempt to develop small panels for urban use is one response to these potential problems.

TRANSIT ADVERTISING

Transit advertising has more than doubled its billings since 1969 and expectations are for an annual volume of about $90 million by 1985. Though it is still seen basically as a supplement to large advertising expenditures elsewhere, it is becoming an attractive option to many advertisers that have not used it previously.

Characteristics of Transit Advertising

Advantages.   Among the advantages of transit advertising are the following:

1. *Opportune exposure.* Of those riding buses and subways, about half reported that their last use of transit was for purposes of shopping.[45] Moreover, 52 percent indicated some recall of inside vehicle advertising, and more than 80 percent of those named specific products.[46] Thus this type of advertising can serve as an effective last-minute stimulus to a purchase.

2. *Geographic selectivity.* As a strictly local medium, transit offers the advantage of placing dollars in proportion to local market potentials. It also is used to provide extra advertising weight when required.

3. *High consumer exposure.* Exposure figures vary, of course, from transit system to transit system. It is believed that at least 40 million Americans ride transit vehicles every month. The New York Transit Authority alone claims over 152 million rides monthly.[47] A recent study of the Toronto transit system revealed that during one week the unduplicated audience represents 52.4 percent of the total market and that, in the space of a month, the reach encompasses 67.5 percent of the market. The individuals comprising this 67.5 percent coverage average 11 rides monthly.[48]

4. *Economy.* Transit advertising claims to be the least costly of all media. The cost per thousand inside-car exposures in the markets served averages between 15 and 20 cents, and for exterior exposure as little as 7 cents per thousand.

Disadvantages. Transit advertising also has some disadvantages:

1. *Weak coverage of portions of the population.* Although advertising is now available on the outside of vehicles, it is apparent that nonriders will not be exposed to the transit advertising on the inside of vehicles.

2. *Creative limitations.* The basic inside poster sizes are 11 × 28, 11 × 42, and 11 × 56 inches. With such small areas little opportunity is provided for creative presentation other than short, reminder-type messages. Greater opportunities are presented by the use of outside displays, where it is possible to purchase the king-size poster, 2½ × 12 feet in size. The standard exterior board is 30 × 144 inches. Creative opportunities are being expanded through the placement of exterior displays and such innovations as "Moods in Motion," in which an advertiser will purchase all the space in the interior of the vehicle and place his advertising in a setting he hopes will motivate the rider. Displays placed in transportation depots and terminals are also a part of transit advertising.

3. *Mood of the rider.* The usual bus or subway is frequently crowded, riders are uncomfortable, and attention often is directed toward reaching

[45] "The Transit Millions," New York Transit Advertising Association, and "Toronto Transit Rider Study," Daniel Starch Ltd.

[46] "The Transit Millions."

[47] "Transit Advertising Prospers."

[48] "Toronto Transit Rider Study," p. 4.

the destination as quickly as possible. It is doubtful that such an environment is ideal for advertising exposure, but little has been published to verify or refute this possibility.

4. *Availabilities.* Transit space is decidedly limited in quantity, and some satisfied advertisers use long-term contracts for space. The availability of space, then, may be unsatisfactory at times for the potential user.

Purchasing Transit Space

Published space rates are available in the appropriate SRDS listing. Costs are based on a system of showings similar to that used in outdoor advertising, though transit authorities are also monitoring closely the success of gross rating points as an alternative. The New York Subways Advertising Company will place an 11 × 28 card in all its 6,600 vehicles for a month for about $28,700, though discounts are available for contracts of longer periods. Exterior displays (30 × 144) are available on 400 New York City buses for about $31,000 monthly. Purchases may be made from either the individual companies or from centralized sources such as Metro Transit Advertising, a division of Metromedia.

The Future of Transit

The future of transit advertising is indeed bright. The energy crisis which may prove hazardous to outdoor advertising can only add to the already healthy billings of transit advertising. The United States is growing increasingly conscious of its need for effective mass transit. Present systems are being enlarged, new ones such as the Bay Area Rapid Transit System (BART) of San Francisco are being completed, and use of mass transit is growing rapidly. As mass transit grows, so will transit advertising.

THE NONCOMMISSIONABLE MEDIA

All of the media discussed thus far offer a 15 percent commission to advertising agencies, the standard means of agency compensation. Certain media do not provide this discount, however. These include direct mail, point-of-purchase advertisements, and advertising specialities.

Direct Mail

Direct mail is the third largest medium, ranking behind only newspapers and television and grossing over $8.5 billion in 1981, although this figure includes both direct mail *selling* and *advertising*. The most widely used forms are personal letters, booklets, brochures, catalogs, circulars and fliers, and mail cards.

Direct mail offers several distinct advantages to the advertiser: (1) preconditioning prospects in advance of a personal sales call, (2) stimulation of selective local store patronage, (3) extreme flexibility in pinpointing prospects with desired timing, (4) no limitations on space or format, (5) little competition from other advertising messages, and (6) personal nature of the appeal, among others. A Postal Service survey revealed that 63 percent of all pieces of direct mail are opened and read and 14 percent are set aside to read later. With direct mail that is expected by the consumer, immediate readership jumps to 70 percent and eventual readership to 85 percent.[49] Another USPS survey showed that 63 percent of the population purchased a product or service as a result of direct mail advertising.[50]

These disadvantages also must be considered, however: (1) high cost per thousand, (2) the difficulty of obtaining and maintaining a list of names, (3) the poor reputation of so-called junk mail, and (4) the creative skill required to create high readership. The high cost per thousand can be partially offset by the great selectivity offered, but in any event average production and mailing costs of 24 to 42 cents per unit (higher for first-class mail) cannot be avoided. The problems with mailing lists can be minimized by renting lists from brokers, publishers, and various advertising media.

Direct mail is used widely by small businesspeople, retailers, book and record clubs, catalog houses, magazine publishers, and the pharmaceutical industry. Insurance companies also use it to identify prospects and serve as sales leads, and it is a common medium for coupons, product samples, and other forms of "direct response" advertising.

Point-of-Purchase Advertisements

Most advertising reaches consumers when they are not near a store and in no mood to buy. Point-of-purchase (POP) stimuli reinstate earlier advertising and serve as final links in a purchase sequence. For this reason, point of purchase is an important medium. The largest users are manufacturers of soaps, packaged drugs, gasoline, beer, and liquors.

The roles of point-of-purchase advertising are:

1. It can trigger latent or postponed purchases.
2. It persuades shoppers to indulge in a treat.
3. It can trigger a desire to buy something special for family members.

---

[49] "The Direct Mailstream," *Advertising Age*, November 21, 1973, p. 119.

[50] "USPS Studies Ad Mail, Finds 63% Have Bought," *Advertising Age*, May 7, 1973, p. 2.

4. It can break a pattern of shopping intent and release a flood of un-planned purchases.
5. It can evoke a feeling that items are on sale.

Some innovative point-of-purchase efforts have included recorded advertisements played over a store's public address system, special sales of 5 to 30 minutes announced over the public address system which are identified by such devices as flashing lights mounted on dollies so they can be moved from place to place, video cassettes to aid in making the sale of major purchases such as automobiles, and even motorized signs mounted on wires which travel around the store above the heads of the shoppers. These and other POP devices do increase sales. This is well documented.[51]

The importance of good point-of-purchase advertising can hardly be questioned. The difficulty, however, is stimulating retailers to use the many displays and banners they receive each month. Since this is a problem in working with resellers, it is discussed in depth in Part Five.

INTERMEDIA COMPARISON

The media types discussed in this chapter compete with each other vigorously for the advertisers' dollars. The basis on which they compete is essentially to sell their own advantages while trying to highlight other media's disadvantages. Figure 12–8 presents an example of intermedia competition at a trade association level (the Radio Advertising Bureau). Individual media vehicles also present themselves against other media types as well as other vehicles within their class. Figure 12–9 presents an example of this latter type of activity.

One of the most fundamental bases on which media compete is cost. Figure 12–10 presents a comparison of media costs prepared by the media department at the Leo Burnett advertising agency. It indicates that television costs have increased the most over the period 1971–1981, and consumer magazines and spot radio the least (on all of total cost, and CPM bases).

Care must be taken in interpreting these CPM numbers as they are calculated on a *total* audience basis. Also outdoor audiences are measured in terms of total people while others are stated in terms of adults, and television is stated in terms of households whereas magazines are given by gross circulation, etc. Of more interest to marketers is the CPM on *target* audience of the advertising program. Thus, for example, for a particular target audience, the CPM for a specific television time could be higher

---

[51] For example see Gary F. McKinnon, J. Patrick Kelley, and E. Doyle Robison, "Sales Effects of Point-of-Purchase In-Store Signing," *Journal of Retailing* 57, no. 2 (Summer 1981), pp. 49–63.

264

FIGURE 12–8
Intermedia Competition

Drivetime. Walktime. Anytime is radio time.

It's the age of the headset phenomenon. People listening as they jog, walk, ride the train, play or shop. Hearing only the sounds of their radio. Hearing your message with no distraction. Catch someone like that on the way to shop, and you can get immediate buying action. Some trick in today's economy.

Add this growing audience to radio's big drivetime audience: 85 percent of all commuters who go to work by car.

Radio is big at home, too.

Surprise. Almost 60 percent of all radio listening is done at home. And the average household has 5.5 radios. It's no wonder radio reaches more adults in a day than television, magazines or newspapers. Even busy working women listen to radio an average of almost four hours a day—that's more time than they give any other medium.

Radio hits all lifestyles.

Radio goes with more people, more places, than ever before.

Young, old and in-between. In their cars, their homes, even on top of their heads.

Don't let your potential customers walk on by. Get your message into the streets. Get it on radio. For more information, call (212) 599-6666. Or write Radio Advertising Bureau, 485 Lexington Avenue, New York, NY 10017.

RADIO Red hot because it works.

FIGURE 12–9

An Advertisement by *Newsweek* Attempting to Compete with Spot Television

Newsweek
Now Offers 20 Top ADI's
as Metro Editions

Effective at once, and exclusively among the newsweeklies, Newsweek offers this new service to advertisers, agencies, and their media planners. The following twenty Newsweek Metro editions now have been realigned to conform closely to standard ADI configuration:

	Arbitron ADI Market Ranking		Arbitron ADI Market Ranking
Atlanta	16	Miami	15
Baltimore	19	Minneapolis/St. Paul	14
Boston	5	New York	1
Chicago	3	Philadelphia	4
Cleveland	9	Pittsburgh	10
Dallas/Ft. Worth	11	St. Louis	12
Detroit	7	San Francisco	6
Houston	13	Seattle	18
Indianapolis	20	Tampa/St. Petersburg	17
Los Angeles	2	Washington, D.C.	8

The ADI (Area of Dominant Influence) is widely recognized as a standard marketing tool. Now applied to the circulation and audience of Newsweek Metro editions, it enables advertisers to compare *inter*-media efficiencies, coverage, demographics, product usage patterns; achieve more accurate market planning and media selection.

With these 20 ADI Metro editions,* Newsweek now places a wealth of metro market information at the disposal of planners. For example, with the help of Major Market Index, data comparisons are now available between Newsweek and leading metropolitan dailies. With Media Market Guide, comparisons can now be made between a Newsweek metro buy and spot TV—by cost, average rating, cost per rating point.

All the many reasons for using Newsweek's metro editions: as an add-on to a national campaign; to heavy-up market emphasis in one or more target areas; to take advantage of seasonal variations in product usage; to test a campaign idea or introduce a new product; as a high quality medium for a local advertiser, or as any advertiser's alternative to rising TV costs or

diminishing TV availabilities—all become all the more logical with the advent of these Newsweek ADI Metro editions.

In addition, the "Top Ten" ADI Metro editions are available as a package, at a considerable saving under what the rates would be if the editions were bought individually: New York, Chicago, Los Angeles, Philadelphia, Boston, San Francisco, Detroit, Washington, Cleveland, and Pittsburgh.

The "Top Ten" buy will qualify for regional and national frequency discounts. And the remaining ADI metro editions (as well as Newsweek's 20 Metro Group II editions) can be added to the Top Ten package in which case, based on total circulation of the buy, the additional markets earn a minimum 16% discount.

A booklet is ready giving complete information on Newsweek's ADI Metro editions: rate bases, counties wholly or partially covered, key demographics, issue dates, rates. Contact your nearest Newsweek advertising office for a copy—or write or call Chuck Kennedy, Advertising Director, Newsweek, 444 Madison Avenue, New York, N.Y. 10022. (212) 350-2552.

*In no case is there any significant geographic variation between the Newsweek ADI metro and the corresponding ADI market area. Seven of the Newsweek editions represent more than one Arbitron ADI, but in every case a contiguous area. These are: Chicago/South Bend; Cleveland/Toledo; Detroit/Lansing/Flint; Miami/West Palm Beach; Philadelphia/Harrisburg; Pittsburgh/Johnstown; San Francisco/Sacramento.

Newsweek

Headquarters for media information

FIGURE 12–10
Media Cost Trends

A. Network television—1971 to 1981

Prime time	Average cost/ commercial (:30)		CPM homes	
	$000	Index	$	Index
1971	$27.6	100	$2.29	100
1972	30.5	111	2.32	101
1973	34.5	125	2.72	119
1974	39.0	141	2.93	128
1975	37.8	137	2.88	126
1976	49.4	179	3.49	152
1977	58.0	210	4.13	180
1978	62.6	227	4.41	193
1979	76.6	278	5.06	221
1980	74.3	269	4.94	216
1981	78.8	285	5.23	229

Daytime	Average cost/ commercial (:30)		CPM homes	
	$000	Index	$	Index
1971	$ 3.7	100	$0.80	100
1972	4.5	122	0.89	111
1973	4.6	124	0.93	116
1974	5.3	143	1.04	130
1975	6.2	168	1.35	169
1976	7.4	200	1.49	186
1977	9.0	243	1.96	245
1978	9.3	251	1.96	245
1979	10.7	289	2.14	267
1980	10.8	292	2.22	277
1981	11.4	308	2.35	294

Source: A. C. Nielsen, NAC Cost Supplement, October 1981.

B. Spot television—1971 to 1981
Top 20 markets

Prime time	Average cost/ commercial (:30)		CPM homes	
	$	Index	$	Index
1971	$14,161	100	$3.33	100
1972	14,198	100	3.32	100
1973	14,650	103	3.46	104
1974	17,078	121	3.50	105
1975	17,825	126	3.84	115
1976	22,516	159	4.86	146
1977	27,180	192	5.90	177
1978	30,330	214	6.42	193
1979	32,063	226	6.88	207
1980	37,371	264	7.35	221
1981	41,226	291	8.15	245

FIGURE 12–10 (*continued*)

Daytime	Average cost/ commercial (:30)		CPM homes	
	$	*Index*	$	*Index*
1971	$1,660	100	$1.32	100
1972	1,861	112	1.34	102
1973	1,701	102	1.24	94
1974	1,744	105	1.18	89
1975	1,647	99	1.36	103
1976	2,248	135	1.60	121
1977	3,024	182	2.17	164
1978	3,035	183	2.05	155
1979	3,344	201	2.12	161
1980	3,637	219	2.21	167
1981	4,159	251	2.63	199

Source: TvB Spot Television Planning Guide, 1981/82.

C. Network radio—1971 to 1981

	Cost per adult rating point		CPM adults	
	$	*Index*	$	*Index*
1971	$1,389	100	$1.01	100
1972	1,538	111	1.10	109
1973	1,564	113	1.10	109
1974	1,576	113	1.09	108
1975	1,671	120	1.14	113
1976	2,105	152	1.39	138
1977	2,358	170	1.55	153
1978	2,558	184	1.64	162
1979	2,904	209	1.84	182
1980	3,186	229	2.00	198
1981	3,473	250	2.24	222

Source: Media Decisions, August 1981.

D. Spot radio—1975 to 1981
Top 50 markets

Daytime	Average cost/ commercial (:60)		CPM adults	
	$	*Index*	$	*Index*
1975	$2,448	100	$1.52	100
1976	2,652	108	1.68	110
1977	3,078	126	1.86	122
1978	3,460	141	2.20	145
1979	3,984	163	2.57	191
1980	4,100	167	2.90	191
1981	4,305	176	3.04	200

FIGURE 12–10 (*continued*)

E. Spot radio—1975 to 1981

Drive time—morning	Average cost/ commercial (:60)		CPM adults	
	$	Index	$	Index
1975	$3,267	100	$1.51	100
1976	3,521	108	1.64	109
1977	4,039	124	1.87	124
1978	4,435	136	2.10	130
1979	5,071	155	2.43	161
1980	5,848	179	2.78	184
1981	6,140	189	2.91	193

Source: Katz Spot Radio Planning Guide.

F. Consumer magazines—1971 to 1981
Ten selected magazines

	Cost/page 4C		CPM-circulation	
	$000	Index	$	Index
1971	$370.1	100	$4.33	100
1972	388.9	105	4.43	102
1973	404.6	109	4.48	103
1974	425.6	115	4.75	110
1975	443.1	120	4.94	114
1976	452.2	122	4.91	113
1977	478.9	129	5.24	121
1978	539.9	146	5.90	136
1979	576.8	156	6.33	146
1980	625.4	169	6.97	161
1981	666.6	180	7.69	178

Source: S.R.D.S., June of each year.

G. Daily newspapers—1971 to 1981

	Line rate		Line cost/ MM circ.	
	$	Index	$	Index
1971	$406.41	100	$6.53	100
1972	419.57	103	6.71	103
1973	446.66	110	7.07	108
1974	508.08	125	8.21	126
1975	561.78	138	9.26	142
1976	620.30	153	10.17	156
1977	655.42	161	10.66	163
1978	714.29	176	11.61	178
1979	743.66	183	12.00	184
1980	802.00	197	12.89	197
1981	899.71	221	14.46	221

Source: Editor and Publisher Yearbook.

FIGURE 12–10 (*concluded*)

H. Syndicated supplements*—1971 to 1981

	Cost/page 4C		CPM-circulation	
	$	Index	$	Index
1971	$103,200	100	$4.00	100
1972	109,900	106	4.12	103
1973	117,845	114	4.21	105
1974	136,600	132	4.68	117
1975	161,505	156	5.46	137
1976	161,295	156	5.45	136
1977	173,480	168	5.64	141
1978	194,870	189	6.05	151
1979	215,500	209	6.45	161
1980	235,095	228	6.98	175
1981	266,480	258	7.81	195

* Parade and Family Weekly only.

Source: S.R.D.S., June of each year.

I. Outdoor—1970 through 1981

	Cost/month*		CPM
	$000	Index	Index
1970	$1,776.8	100	100
1971	1,924.2	108	105
1972	2,070.8	117	109
1973	2,215.9	125	114
1974	2,357.7	133	114
1975	2,602.1	146	123
1976	2,943.4	154	127
1977	2,964.9	167	134
1978	3,273.1	184	146
1979	3,608.9	203	155
1980	3,969.8	223	169
1981	4,354.9	245	185

* 100 GRPs in all markets.

Source: Institute of Outdoor Advertising.

Source: *Leo Burnett 1982 Media Costs and Coverage*, pp. 2–5. Used with permission.

than for a particular magazine. The use of the CPM target audience concept will be discussed in Chapter 13.

SUMMARY

The purpose of this chapter has been to condense a wealth of material on media characteristics, advantages, disadvantages, possible uses, and other factors which must be understood before discussing the media selection process itself. Of greatest importance is the way in which each of the media discussed is adapting to the current environment, because the changes have been great. Understanding of these changes makes it possible to discuss meaningfully the methods by which media should be analyzed and selected.

Review and Discussion Questions

1. The nationally distributed Sunday supplement seems to be losing ground in comparison with other media. What reasons can you see for this trend? Can it be reversed? Why?

2. The differential between local and national line rates is said by many to be triggering an exodus of national advertisers from local newspapers. Given this fact, what reasons can be advanced for continuation of the differentials? Why, in your opinion, has there been so little change?

3. Contrast the milline rate and cost per thousand formula. What advantage is gained by their use? What possible dangers could you see?

4. One of the distinct trends in the television medium is the rapid rise of CATV. What effects will this have on both local and national advertising in the future?

5. What are the implications for advertisers of the consumers' increasing acceptance of video recorder systems and video games?

6. Advertisers are showing a growing concern with commercial clutter in television and radio broadcasts. If clutter is allowed to continue, what might be the effects in terms of the consumer, as well as on the advertising copy and format?

7. The FCC is authorized to refuse to renew local station licenses if they fail to operate within broad guidelines of public interest. What are the advantages and dangers of this policy? What factors should the FCC consider in deciding license renewal?

8. Under what conditions might a 60-second television commercial be worth twice the cost of a 30-second version?

9. Radio continues its growth in advertising dollars. Do you think this steady upward trend will continue? Why?

10. What steps might be taken to save *Reader's Digest* from the same fate as *The Saturday Evening Post,* and *Look?*

11. In what sense can it be said that magazines are a highly flexible medium?

12. With a 100 showing, over 80 percent of all adults are reached with an average frequency of 31. What do these terms mean? Does this mean that outdoor advertising has unique advantages in terms of reach and frequency when compared with other media? What are the advantages of gross rating points as a substitute system of measurement?

13. There are frequent outcries that billboards should be removed entirely from the public roads. What arguments could you advance to refute this position?

14. For what types of products is transit advertising most suitable? Can it be used as a substitute medium for television or magazines?

15. Critics of direct mail advertising claim that the junk mail received in homes today is so excessive that government should step in to outlaw unwanted

use of the mails. Would this be in the consumer's interest? Why, or why not?

16. It is sometimes said that point of purchase is the untouched "promised land" of advertising, the presumption being that it frequently is neglected. What roles can point of purchase play?

CHAPTER 13

Media Strategy*

The two main problems faced in media strategy are selection of media vehicles and preparation of a media schedule. Factors which are fundamental in media selection are discussed in the following pages: (1) the requirements of creative strategy, (2) reaching the proper audience, (3) the requirements for reach versus frequency, (4) competitive factors, (5) cost efficiency, (6) qualitative factors, and (7) distribution requirements. Also discussed are media scheduling, with emphasis upon geographical and seasonal scheduling, and the use of the computer in media decisions.

THE REQUIREMENTS OF CREATIVE STRATEGY

The advertising requirements for the product often can easily favor or eliminate certain media candidates. For example, it has been a long-standing agreement among broadcasters subscribing to the Code of the National Association of Broadcasters that liquor will not be advertised on radio or television. Moreover, the product may be so sensitive that good taste calls for its exclusion from certain media. A good example is the virtual absence of women's intimate apparel displayed on models on television, both as a result of the NAB code and a keen awareness that such products should be advertised with discretion in printed media only, so as not to offend prospects or nonprospects.

* The authors wish to thank Mr. Bernard Guggenheim, vice president of Campbell-Ewald, for his assistance in the preparation of this chapter.

The product personality also will dictate media choice. The promotion of expensive French perfumes in *Mad* would clearly be inappropriate. The match between product prospects and media audiences would be poor, of course, but of even greater importance, association of the product with these media could affect its image adversely.

Finally, the requirements of the message may dominate the media decision. An automobile advertisement featuring acceleration and passing power will require a medium which dramatizes action for maximum creative impact, and where movement is required television or sales films are the only possible choices. Color might be specified to provide a more realistic representation of an automobile and to strengthen emotional impact. The finest color reproduction is available in magazines, although acceptable color can be purchased in both television and newspapers. Finally, the required use of sound eliminates substantially all media except radio and television (although some direct mail promotions contain small recorded discs). There are many other similar examples.

REACHING THE PROPER AUDIENCE

The pivotal consideration in media strategy is to select media vehicles which reach the target audience with a minimum of waste coverage. This is often referred to as *selectivity*. Computers make it possible to undertake selectivity analysis with considerable precision conditional, of course, on the accuracy of available data. This means, of course, that the analyst must have a grasp of the nature, scope, and uses of available sources of audience data. Audience data is discussed in some detail here, before focusing on the use of these data in media planning.

Media Audience Data

All practical considerations aside, most agree that it would be useful to have at least six categories of data for media planning and evaluation. The essential categories are (1) media distribution—the number of copies of a magazine in circulation or sets available to carry the advertising; (2) media audiences—people actually exposed to a medium; and (3) advertising exposure—people exposed to advertising units. In addition, data are also useful on (4) advertising perception—people aware of the message; (5) advertising communication—people affected by advertising; and (6) consumer response—people who make additional purchases.

The difficulty is that the roles of the medium and the message itself intermix in categories 3–6. In these categories it is difficult to determine whether people's awareness of the message is more attributable to layout, design, and wording than to the medium itself. Thus only the first two stages focus on the medium itself, and media audience data are largely confined to these levels, as our discussion also will be. A number of trade association and research supply companies are in the business of providing media audience data. The sections that follow will discuss some of these organizations.

Media distribution. Data in this category have long been available from such organizations as the Audit Bureau of Circulation (ABC). This organization is sponsored by national and local advertisers, advertising agencies, and publishers. It makes available sworn and audited statements of newspaper and magazine audiences. A publication must have at least 70 percent paid circulation (copies purchased at not less than one half the established prices) to be eligible for membership and listing. Most publishers meeting this qualification are members of ABC.

Publications which distribute to special groups, perhaps on a free basis, are audited by the Business Publications Audit of Circulation (BPA). The functions performed by BPA closely parallel those of ABC.

The notion of total physical distribution of media vehicles quickly loses its significance when one moves out of the publications field. While the Advertising Research Foundation has published a *National Survey of Television Sets in U.S. Households,* the most useful data on television and other media are confined largely to categories 2 and 3, with even very little audience measurement data available on category 3.[1]

These data are useful primarily in providing a verified audit of circulation claims. The figures sometimes are used as a guarantee for the rates established in magazine space contracts, but the data are of little additional use because there usually is a wide difference between physical distribution and audience exposure.

Media audiences. Media audiences refer to the actual number of people exposed to a medium on both one-time and repeat bases. The methods of audience measurement are complex, as the discussion below indicates.

In fact the Advertising Research Foundation (ARF), a nonprofit industry organization, is almost always studying this subject.

Magazine audiences. The accepted definition of the audience of a given magazine is the number of people claiming to recall looking into an average issue. This definition is supported by evidence which indicates that those looking into a magazine tend to be exposed to most of its contents. It should be apparent, however, that the problems of response distortion in survey research are often encountered. For example, it is not unusual for a respondent to deny reading a magazine which would appear to place him in a bad light in an interviewer's eyes or to claim readership of a prestigious publication. To underscore these dangers, we mention the report that the number of those who claim to be readers of a well-

---

[1] Published periodically by the Advertising Research Foundation, Inc.

known prestige magazine can be more than 15 times the number of copies printed.

It is obvious that methods used to measure actual readership must be designed to minimize response distortion. The most commonly used approach, the editorial interest technique, encompasses an attempt to make respondents feel that they are helping editors to evaluate the appeal of various editorial features. No attempt is made at the outset to determine whether or not the respondent actually read the issue. The question is usually reserved until the end and is often worded as follows: "Just for the record, now that we have been through this issue, would you say you definitely happened to read it before, or didn't read it, or aren't you sure?" Questioning at the end of the interview and this careful wording are effective devices to guarantee a minimum of overclaimed or underclaimed readership.

Another approach used to assess magazine readership is to interview different samples of respondents every day for a period of time regarding "yesterday's reading." Confining the interview to yesterday's reading is intended to prevent memory loss. Extension of the interviewing period also permits useful estimation of the total readership of a given magazine over time. It is well known, for example, that issue life (the time in which it continues to be read) may run into months.

It is difficult to say which method gives the more accurate estimate of readership. In one study it was found that the readership generated by the editorial interest technique was 2.5 percent lower than that produced by an unaided recall procedure.[2] It also has been reported that claimed readership overestimates the audience for monthly magazines and underestimates the audience for weeklies and biweeklies.[3] Another expert feels that the best approach is use of simple direct questions such as "Which magazines do you read?" The first step is to determine the probability that claimed readership is accurate, through benchmark studies using several techniques. From then on it would be possible simply to ask respondents, "Do you read this magazine usually, regularly, quite often, seldom, or never?" and to modify the answers given by the probabilities of accuracy found from previous surveys.[4] This approach offers an admirable degree of simplicity. Guggenheim concluded that much de-

---

[2] "An Experimental Study Comparing Magazine Audiences as Determined by Two Questioning Procedures," study conducted by Alfred Politz Media Studies for *Life* magazine.

[3] Donald G. McGlathery, "Claimed Frequency versus Editorial-Interest Method of Repeat Magazine Audiences," *Journal of Advertising Research* 7 (1967), pp. 7–15. See also W. R. Simmons, "A New Look at Reach and Frequency," *Proceedings, 15th Annual Conference* (New York: Advertising Research Foundation, 1969), pp. 13–23.

[4] Jean M. Agostini, "The Case for Direct Questions on Reading Habits," *Journal of Advertising Research* 4 (1964), pp. 28–33.

pends on how one asks the questions.[5] Box A of Figure 13–1 contains some of the different versions of the questions that are often used in magazine research. The diversity of questions all trying to measure the same thing is clear. Also important is the use of different interview types. Box B of Figure 13–1 shows results from a 1967 study. We note the differences in results for magazines A through O under personal interviews and different types of mail procedures. This problem is also highlighted by the 1976 Simmons Study of magazine readership. They attempted to determine which households were primary purchasers of 15 magazines. They used a series of questions to determine those households or individuals within households who either subscribed and/or purchased specified magazines. The projected number of claimed primary households were then compared to Audit Bureau of Circulation figures. Box C of Figure 13–1 indicates that substantial differences were found. Over claiming ranges from 109 percent for *Sports ·Illustrated* to −1 percent for *Reader's Digest*.[6] These types of results complicate the use of media research data.

It is useful to distinguish four types of magazine readers. Figure 13–2 provides a basis for classification of reader types. The classification relates to the source of the copy—whether purchased or picked up, and the location of reading—whether in-home or out-of-home. We define:

1. Primary readers in cells A and B,
2. Pass-along readers in cells C and D.
3. Out-of-home readers in cells B and D,
4. In-home readers in cells A and C.

Audiences can be measured also in terms of primary readers only (the person or household purchasing the magazine) or primary readers plus pass-along readers. Once there was a tendency to look with favor upon magazines with high percentages of pass-along readers, no doubt on the assumption that this premium is gained without extra cost, but survey evidence is disputing this assumption. The Advertising Research Foundation Printed Advertising Research Methods study (PARM) showed higher advertising recall in primary households.[7] Moreover, a Roper study for *Woman's Day* indicated that the average pass-along reader may be 35 to 40 percent less responsive to advertising than primary readers.[8] A *Reader's Digest* study by Alfred Politz, based on 5,062 interviews, disclosed that

[5] Bernard Guggenheim, "It Depends on How You Ask It!" *Media Decisions*, July 1977, pp. 82, 84, 89, 90.

[6] Ibid.

[7] Darrell B. Lucas, "The ABC's of ARF's PARM," *Journal of Marketing* 25 (July 1960), p. 14.

[8] Paul M. Roth, "What Is the Value of Pass-along Magazine Audience?" *Media/scope*, November 1963, pp. 84–87.

FIGURE 13-1
Magazine Audience Research

BOX A
Five ways to ask for consumer magazine readership

1. Which of the magazines listed below have you read or looked into in the past month?
2. Which of these magazines do you read regularly, that is at least three out of four issues?

Magazine	Read or looked into (past month)	Read regularly (3 out of 4 issues)
A	☐	☐
B	☐	☐
C	☐	☐
D	☐	☐
E	☐	☐
F	☐	☐
G	☐	☐
H	☐	☐
I	☐	☐
J	☐	☐

3. What magazines do you read regularly, that is, at least three out of four issues? (Please write in the names of the magazines.)

_____   _____   _____

_____   _____   _____

4. Next, the monthly publications. Next to each magazine, please check the box that describes how many different Issues of the magazine, if any, you personally have *read* or *looked into* for the first time in the *last 4 months*.

Monthly magazine	Do not read magazine	Read now and then but not in last 4 mos.	In the last 4 months, I read			
			1 Issue	2 Issues	3 Issues	4 Issues
A	( )	( )	( )	( )	( )	( )
B	( )	( )	( )	( )	( )	( )
C	( )	( )	( )	( )	( )	( )
D	( )	( )	( )	( )	( )	( )
E	( )	( )	( )	( )	( )	( )
F	( )	( )	( )	( )	( )	( )

5. For each of the magazines listed below, will you please check:
   (a) Whether or not *you personally* read the *most recent issue?*
   (b) Whether or not *you personally* read the *issue before that one?*

	Did you read the most recent issue? (please check "Yes" or "No" for EACH)		Did you read the issue before that one? (please check "Yes" or "No" for EACH)	
	Yes	No	Yes	No
A	☐	☐	☐	☐
B	☐	☐	☐	☐
C	☐	☐	☐	☐
D	☐	☐	☐	☐
E	☐	☐	☐	☐

FIGURE 13–1 (*continued*)

	Did you read the most recent issue? (please check "Yes" or "No" for EACH)		Did you read the issue before that one? (please check "Yes" or "No" for EACH)	
	Yes	No	Yes	No
F	☐	☐	☐	☐
G	☐	☐	☐	☐
H	☐	☐	☐	☐
I	☐	☐	☐	☐
J	☐	☐	☐	☐

BOX B
ABP test of percent who read average issue

	Personal interview editorial interest		Mail-aided recall					
			Check-off reproduced covers and titles		Check-off title typed on list		Mail-open end	
	Percent coverage	Index	Percent coverage	Index	Percent coverage	Index	Percent coverage	Index
A	22.0	100	20.2	92	23.8	108	9.9	45
B	13.0	100	15.5	119	10.3	79	8.0	62
C	*	*	8.6		12.3		5.6	
D	14.0	100	14.4	103	15.4	110	5.6	40
E	14.0	100	8.5	61	12.5	89	4.9	35
F	10.0	100	15.2	152	13.7	137	2.4	24
G	20.0	100	13.0	65	9.1	45	3.9	20
H	18.0	100	11.5	64	6.9	38	4.5	25
I	12.0	100	12.0	100	5.6	47	4.9	41
J	11.0	100	11.5	105	5.4	49	5.3	48
K	2.0	100	11.2	560	11.0	550	0.6	30
L	8.0	100	9.7	121	7.6	95	1.4	18
M	4.0	100	5.3	133	9.6	240	1.9	48
N	10.0	100	7.9	79	5.6	56	0.4	4
O	10.0	100	4.8	48	5.1	51	1.3	13
(Sample size)	(100)		(165)		(203)		(174)	

*Not surveyed.
Source: ABP Business Marketing Laboratory Study—Phase II Report November 1967.

FIGURE 13–1 (*concluded*)

BOX C
Claimed versus actual magazine buyers

Magazine	Percent claimed primary audience over (under) "actual" primary audience
Sports Illustrated	109%
Good Housekeeping	71
U.S. News & World Report	68
Newsweek	41
Time	39
Better Homes & Gardens	37
Family Circle	33
Woman's Day	29
McCalls	24
Ladies' Home Journal	22
Redbook	13
National Geographic	11
T.V. Guide	9
Playboy	5
Reader's Digest	(1)

Sources: 1976 Study of Primary and Pass-along Readers of 15 Major Magazines, Simmons Media Studies. Bernard Guggenheim, "It Depends on How You Ask It!" *Media Decisions*, July 1977, pp. 84, 89, 90.

pass-along audiences are of less value to advertisers than primary readers because:

1. They spend less time reading.
2. They read on fewer occasions.
3. Readership often takes place outside of homes, in waiting rooms and elsewhere.
4. Less satisfaction is reported from reading.
5. These readers are in lower brackets of income and education.

FIGURE 13–2
Classification of Readership Audiences

Source of copy	Location of reading	
	In-home	Out-of-home
Purchased	A	B
Picked up	C	D

6. Pass-along readers would be less disappointed if magazines suddenly ceased publication.[9]

In practice many agencies discount out-of-home, and pass-along audiences.

Two major organizations are active in the measurement of total magazine audiences, each using a different measure of reader.[10] The first is the Simmons Market Research Bureau (SMRB). SMRB samples about 15,000 individuals annually. The readership measurement method is the "through-the-book editorial interest method." In this approach respondents are shown logos of magazine titles, and asked to "pick out those you might have read or looked into during the last six months, either at home or at some place else." This is verified again later in the interview, after the respondent goes through a stripped down version of each magazine.

SMRB also provides audience estimates for newspaper supplements, network television, and national newspapers. Also collected is usage patterns for products, brand loyalty, and some demographic and psychographic measures. A major competitor is Mediamark Research, Inc. (MRI). MRI draws a sample of about 30,000 individuals (15,000 in the spring and fall) and measures audience size with the "modified recent reading method." Here respondents are given a list of about 160 magazines and are asked to note the ones they have read during the most recent publication interval. This is done in two steps. First, a deck of cards containing magazines are sorted by the respondent to indicate those read in the last six months. The cards for the read magazines are then sorted to indicate those read in the last publication interval. With differences in the methods of audience measurement, and some differences in sampling procedures, it is little wonder that SMRB and MRI report different audience sizes. The result of this is a great controversy as to which is the correct estimate.

In one reporting period MRI's audience estimates were as high as 161 percent and as low as 34 of those reported by SMRB among the 104 magazines reported in common.[11] The Advertising Research Foundation investigated this controversy and noted that the differences resulted from the methodological differences in the studies and not from execution problems. Ways to make the results of MRI and SMRB adjustable to each other are currently being investigated.

Newspaper audiences. The measurement of newspaper audiences involves essentially the same procedures as those reported for magazines. For exam-

---

[9] "Digest Finds 'Total Audience' Idea Fallacious," *Advertising Age,* April 13, 1964, p. 3 ff.

[10] This section follows a discussion in Thomas C. Kinnear and James R. Taylor, *Marketing Research: An Applied Approach* (New York: McGraw-Hill, 1983), chap. 24.

[11] "Does MRI Have The Answer?" *Marketing and Media Decisions,* November 1979, p. 66.

ple, a reader is defined as someone who has read a part of the medium being analyzed, and the time period covered generally does not exceed one day.

The Audit Bureau of Circulation's Newspaper Audience Research Data Bank (NRDB) is one approach to obtaining such data. NRDB is based on data provided by cooperating newspapers in the top 100 markets. The data are collected by the newspapers themselves and made available to NRDB. To be part of NRDB, the study must meet both methodological and format standards. In general, advertisers must rely on newspaper-collected audience data.

Another source of newspaper audience data is Three Sigma which was formed in 1974 and conducts surveys on 180 newspapers to measure audience size and demographic profile. These studies are done every few years, with the last report issued in 1980 and another one due in late 1982. Three Sigma is subscribed to by all major dailies and about 40 major advertising agencies. In 1981, it became part of Simmons Marketing Research Bureau.

Television audiences.   Television audience data are most frequently collected by means of a diary in which viewers record shows they have watched over a period of time. Several syndicated research services are widely used for this purpose, including A. C. Nielsen and American Research Bureau (ARB) for national audiences and Arbitron for local audiences. Use also is made of the audimeter which automatically records the number of television sets tuned to a particular channel. Finally, there is some use of coincidental telephone recall in which a sample of people is contacted by telephone during programs to establish listening or viewing patterns.

There is some controversy surrounding the accuracy of reports generated by panels of viewers using either the diary or the audimeter. It is possible that the act of recording what is listened to or viewed will lead to atypical patterns of behavior. The extent of this conditioning of panels is not known, but attempts are made to minimize it through panel turnover.

The ratings firms have been attacked also for the adequacy of samples used. It is well known that A. C. Nielsen and the other rating services faced serious criticism in the early 1960s by members of the Harris Investigation Committee in Congress and by the Federal Trade Commission. A number of irregularities were found, but this matter is now history in view of the substantial changes that have been made. Some problems do remain and the ratings are still somewhat controversial early into the 1980s. Specific issues relate to the fact that meters only measure whether the set is on or off, not if someone is watching. Diaries always need substantial weighting and editing. Nonresponse is as high as 50 percent in local ratings. Also substitutions are made on a judgment basis to replace randomly selected panel members, thus raising serious questions about the projectability of panel results to the country. Finally, panel members may be conditioned to behave differently just because their behavior is being recorded. Despite these problems most advertisers do use program rating data with relatively great confidence that sample data can be projected, within known error limits, to the entire population.

Radio audiences. A unique problem is presented by the fact that radios are used everywhere; hence, diaries and audimeters have not proved to be adequate radio audience measures. Until recently this problem appeared to defy solution, but RADAR (Radio's All Dimension Audience Research) now is the accepted measurement procedure for network audiences.

In this measurement technique, two telephone panels are established, one in the spring and one in the fall. Each household is telephoned eight different times on consecutive days during the survey period and is questioned about radio listening habits for each quarter hour for the preceding 24 hours. Respondents also complete a standard questionnaire which gives such characteristics as age and sex. This permits a reporting of all radio listening and weekly cumulative audiences by subgroup within the population. At the local level Arbitron dominates the ratings business using a mail diary method. During the measurement period of a week, respondents are called twice to reinforce the proper completion of the diary.

Audiences of other media. Other media such as outdoor and transit advertising provide no information regarding this dimension of audience evaluation, since the total audience of the medium and potential for advertising exposure coincide. Research measures for these media are discussed in the next section.

Audience profiles. Up to this point discussion has been confined to total audiences. Such data, however, are a poor indication of the characteristics of the individuals reached. Today most media data are also classified in such terms as age, income, occupation, sex, geographical location, and product purchases. It is commonplace for the media planner to receive many such reports. In fact, the volume of information has grown to the point that computer storage facilities are a virtual necessity.

Formerly it was necessary to consult research reports published by individual media when profile data were needed. This is no longer necessary because of the widespread use of the syndicated research services which report audience profiles for television and magazines, the two leading national media.

Comments on media data. Ideally, it would be possible to estimate the third category of data on *advertising exposure* (not simply media audiences) for all possible media. One researcher underscores the gap in audience information in this way:

Our problem lies in the sad truth that we are stuck with a great mass of media statistics that relate (at best) only to superficial media vehicle exposure and really tell us nothing about the ability of the medium to help communicate what we are trying to say. It is in this area that we need all the help that research can provide. Past and current inter-media studies only hint at differences that may exist between individual media.[12]

In addition, as was pointed out in Chapter 8, market targets can be defined in terms that go far beyond the usual demographic classifications. However, media profiles have not expanded to this same extent. There is an obvious need to enrich the data base through provision of data on the activities, interests, and opinions (AIO scores) of media audiences. Fortunately, there is every reason to anticipate that this will be done in the near future.

Finally, data must be provided which go beyond numbers to consider the fifth and sixth categories of data, on advertising perception and consumer response. Leo Bogart's conclusions in this respect are still valid:

Audience research in the future must go further in the task of examining the *quality* of media experience rather than the numbers who experience it, and distinguish among different kinds of communications experiences which are not included together under the heading of Total-Audience Figures. A serious attempt along these lines will lead inevitably to an emphasis on analysis rather than measurement as the proper preoccupation of advertising research.[13]

Using media audiences data. The central task of media selection is to achieve a media mix which reaches the target audience with a minimum of waste coverage and delivers exposure to the advertising unit in a proper frame of mind, apart from media content, so that the advertisement can perform its role. The most demanding task is to match the target market with media audience, and this obviously requires a good data base.

With available data and computer technology it is possible to utilize a number of characteristics of both the market target and media audiences in media selection. Thus, there is little excuse for failure to make use of audience research in building a media schedule, all other things being equal.

REACH AND FREQUENCY

Once determination is made of the extent to which a media schedule reaches the desired target market, it is important to determine both *reach* and *frequency*. Reach is defined as the number (or percentage) of *different* homes exposed to the advertising schedule during a given period of time (usually four weeks). Frequency is the number of times that the *average home reached* was exposed during that same period. A very useful summary measure referred to as *gross rating points* (GRP) combines both of these

---

[12] Stern, "Ad Communication Effects," p. 72.

[13] Leo Bogart, *Strategy in Advertising* (New York: Harcourt, Brace & World, 1967), pp. 245–46.

considerations; GRP is the product of reach times frequency. It is widely used as an indication of advertising weight or tonnage generated by the media schedule. Essentially, GRPs represent the operationalization of the communication objective. Buyers use them as a ready reference point to determine what a buy is worth.

It is important to note that reach and frequency cannot be both optimized at the same time. When one goes up the other must go down, if the budget is held constant.

An example will promote understanding of these concepts. Figure 13–3 represents the television viewing record over four weeks in 10 homes. Notice that all homes but home I were reached during the four weeks. This gives a reach figure of 90 percent. There were 26 total exposures. If 26 is divided by the nine homes reached, this gives a frequency of 2.9 percent. GRP (reach times frequency) then is 261.

FIGURE 13–3
Reach and Frequency Patterns for Ten Television Homes over a Four-Week Period

Week	Message	A	B	C	D	E	F	G	H	I	J	Total exposures
1	1	x				x			x			3
	2	x		x								2
	3		x		x		x	x				4
2	4			x							x	2
	5					x						1
	6					x						1
3	7	x					x	x				3
	8				x							1
	9		x		x							2
4	10				x	x		x				3
	11					x					x	2
	12		x								x	2
Total exposures		3	3	2	4	5	2	3	1	0	3	26

Source: Media Department, Ogilvy & Mather, Inc.

The Problem of Audience Duplication

Reach was defined above as the number of different homes exposed. A given media schedule could fail to achieve reach by delivering multiple exposures of the same audience. If intensive coverage of the same group is the objective, it is desirable to select media that reach essentially the same people; an opposite strategy is required to maximize reach. Therefore, *duplication* of audiences is an important factor.

In Figure 13–4 the audiences of media A, B, and C are depicted. The circle for each represents its audience, and the area within the boundaries of all three (the union) is the total audience reach of these media used

FIGURE 13–4
Audience Duplication in Three Media, A, B, and C

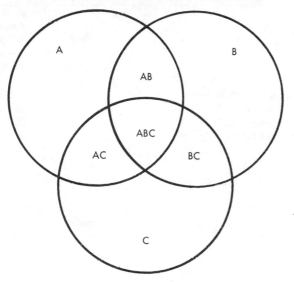

in combination. The area within the intersection of each circle represents the overlap between each media pair. Area AB, for instance, is the overlap or duplication between media A and B. Area ABC represents duplication among all three media.

In practice, the problem lies in estimating the extent of duplication present within a media schedule. Data for this purpose are far from ideal, although some estimates are provided by the various syndicated audience data services. The difficulty arises when a number of media are utilized, because available data sources then are inadequate. A partial answer has been provided by various mathematical formulas which are providing useful estimates without the vast data inputs that otherwise would be required.

Using Reach, Frequency, and GRP Measures

The starting point is to establish a media objective, usually in terms of desired GRP levels. For example, 100 gross rating points a week is a relatively heavy advertising schedule. In a highly competitive market, it is not unusual to invest at this level or even higher levels. The media planner must specify the media GRP levels desired. Then the media buyer can fit together an appropriate schedule.

For example, the media plan for a food product called for at least 200 gross rating points and maximum reach using prime-time television commercials. The media plan depicted in Figure 13–5 delivered 205 GRP

FIGURE 13-5

Reach, Frequency, and GRP Levels Produced by a Media Plan for a Food Item

	Total announce- ments	Average rating per announce- ment
Four-week schedule:		
1 announcement per week on "Hill Street Blues"	4	20.0%
1 announcement every other week on "Benson"	2	18.8
1 announcement every other week on "Dallas"	2	25.0
1 announcement every other week on "Wide World of Sports"	2	18.7
Reach—78.6 percent of all TV homes	10	
Frequency—2.6		
GRP—205.0		

Frequency distribution:

Number of announcements	Percent of homes	Cumulated percent
0	21.4	—
1	21.6	21.6%
2	22.4	44.0
3	15.4	59.4
4	10.0	69.4
5	4.8	74.2
6	2.9	77.1
7	1.2	78.3
8	0.2	78.5
9	0.1	78.6
10+	0.0	78.6

Source: Media Department, Ogilvy & Mather, Inc.

with a reach of 78.6 percent of all television homes. Hence it was entirely satisfactory, all other things being equal. Notice, by the way, that an equivalent GRP level could also be generated with much lower reach and higher frequency. Therefore it is necessary to specify both desired reach and GRP.

Guidance also is provided on which of several alternative plans would be most effective. Consider the data in Figure 13–6, which show the reach and frequency analysis for a luxury item. The best media plan includes monthly magazines; this is especially evident when plans 1 and 2 are compared. Also, plans 2 and 3 show that spot television is probably optional, since the effects on reach and frequency are not great.

Finally, reach, frequency, and GRP measures can be an excellent guide to estimation of budget levels through the built-up analysis discussed in Chapter 11. The data in Figure 13–7 Part A, for example, give a general indication of the reach and frequency levels achieved by from 100 to 300 GRP in a four-week period with a television schedule. To take just

FIGURE 13-6
Reach and Frequency Analysis for a Luxury Product

Plan 1	Plan 2	Plan 3
Spot People	Spot People	No Spot People
newsweeklies	newsweeklies	newsweeklies
no monthlies	monthlies	monthlies
Schedule (2x)	(1x)	
1 Spot *People*	1 Spot *People*	2 *Time*
		1 *Newsweek*
2 *Time*	1 *Time*	1 *U.S. News*
2 *Newsweek*	1 *Newsweek*	1 *New Yorker*
2 *U.S. News*	1 *U.S. News*	1 *Sports Illus.*
2 *New Yorker*	1 *New Yorker*	1 *Business Week*
2 *Sports Illus.*	1 *Sports Illus.*	1 *Sunset*
2 *Business Week*	1 *Business Week*	1 *Esquire*
		1 *Fortune*
	1 *Sunset*	1 *Nat'l. Geo.*
	1 *Esquire*	1 *Holiday*
	1 *Fortune*	1 *Harper's*
	1 *Nat'l. Geo.*	1 *Atlantic*
	1 *Holiday*	1 *Reporter**
	1 *Harper's*	1 *Town & Cntry.**
	1 *Atlantic*	1 *Status/Diplo.**
	1 *Reporter**	1 *Commentary**
	1 *Town & Cntry.**	1 *Venture**
	1 *Status/Diplo.**	1 *Réalités**
	1 *Commentary**	2 *Wall St. Journal*
	1 *Venture**	
	1 *Réalités**	
	2 *Wall St. Journal*	

User Groups	Reach	Frequency	GRP
Plan 1			
Total men	37	2.9	107
Own luxury, intend to buy	46	3.2	149
Income of $15,000+	65	3.5	229
Plan 2			
Total men	53	2.0	103
Own luxury, intend to buy	61	2.3	142
Income of $15,000+	77	2.9	225
Plan 3			
Total men	53	2.2	115
Own luxury, intend to buy	60	2.5	154
Income of $15,000+	77	3.3	249

*Tabulated by *Business Week*.
Source: Paul M. Roth, *How to Plan Media* (Skokie, Ill · Standard Rate & Data Service, Inc., 1968), p. 9–4. Used by special permission.

one illustration, 100 GRP in daytime network television will reach, on the average, 45 percent of all television homes with a frequency of 2.2 times in a four-week period. The objective for a media plan for a convenience food item calls for 61 percent reach with a 3.3 frequency in the top 100 spot television markets using daytime placement. The 200 GRP

FIGURE 13–7
Reach (R) and Frequency (F) Estimates and Costs at Various GRP Levels

A. Network TV reach and frequency (4-week period—households)
Averages for schedule in which the number of commercials is about twice the number of different programs. Evening estimates are for one or two network schedules; daytime estimates assume more than one network and show type.

	Evening		M-F day	
GRP Levels	Reach	Frequency	Reach	Frequency
100	62	1.6	45	2.2
150	74	2.0	55	2.7
200	81	2.5	61	3.3
250	85	2.9	66	3.8
300	88	3.4	69	4.3

Source: Leo Burnett U.S.A., Reach and Frequency.

B. Spot television (costs cumed by top market groups)

Markets	% U.S. TV households	Prime time, cost/rtg. point	Daytime, cost/rtg. point	Early fringe, cost/rtg. point	Late news, cost/rtg. point	Late fringe, cost/rtg. point
Top 10	32	$2,282	$ 710	$ 841	$1,558	$1,211
Top 20	45	3,378	1,061	1,322	2,330	1,837
Top 30	54	4,036	1,298	1,616	2,831	2,257
Top 40	61	4,484	1,483	1,858	3,165	2,533
Top 50	67	4,846	1,635	2,046	3,432	2,764
Top 60	72	5,137	1,742	2,177	3,670	2,969
Top 70	76	5,419	1,856	2,299	3,889	3,158
Top 80	80	5,632	1,945	2,401	4,057	3,305
Top 90	83	5,824	2,018	2,490	4,199	3,421
Top 100	85	6,023	2,089	2,572	4,334	3,538

Source: Media Market Guide, Fall 1981.

Source: *Leo Burnett 1982 Media Costs and Coverage.* Used with permission.

level thus would be adequate. Figure 13–7 Part B indicates that the gross cost for one GRP point in the top 100 markets on daytime television is $2,089. This would then yield a needed budget level of $417,800 (200 × $2,089).

Historically, reach and frequency were measures confined only to television and magazine audiences. Now data sources and computer technology permit estimates *across media* and between various market segments. Therefore, these measures are finding widespread use in media planning. Note in Figure 12–10 that media cost were reported on both a CPM and cost per rating point basis.

COMPETITIVE CONSIDERATIONS

Competition can assume major significance in media decisions. At times the advertising objective will call, for example, for maintenance of "share of voice." This is especially likely in a situation where the boundaries of a total market are more or less static and a number of competitors are offering essentially similar products.

The rationale underlying a share-of-voice objective is that market share will roughly parallel advertising share. In such situations it is necessary, therefore, to analyze market share, share of total advertising expenditures, and share of advertising messages actually reaching prospects. Consider the data in Figure 13–8. The first column depicts share of market for competing brands, and the next column reveals the best estimate of share of advertising spending for television. Brands A and B are spending in proportion to market share, whereas the management of brand C apparently feels that a dominant position can be maintained with a smaller proportional investment. Brand D apparently is a new product and is spending to attain an anticipated share.

The third column in Figure 13–8 may be somewhat more puzzling. It provides an estimate of the *efficiency* of spending and is not necessarily equivalent to total dollar levels. With available data sources providing information on media audience, program ratings, and so on, it is possible to estimate the probable advertising exposure delivered by each firm's media schedule. Here brand A is highly efficient in that an 8 percent

FIGURE 13–8
Competitive Marketing and TV Advertising Shares of Nine Leading Brands

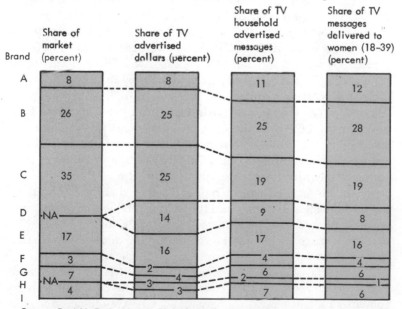

Source: Paul M. Roth, *How to Plan Media* (Skokie, Ill.: Standard Rate & Data Service, Inc., 1968), p. 6–2. Used by special permission.

share of spending delivers 11 percent of total messages. Brand C on the other hand apparently is choosing media which do not reach its prospects in that it has attained only a 19 percent share as compared with a 25 percent dollar share. These figures become especially significant when they are related to the key segment, messages delivered to women, appearing in the fourth column.

Obviously the quality of the advertising and other factors will affect the figures, but the data are quite revealing. It would appear, for example, that the brand A schedule will lead to an increase in share of voice as well as a probable gain in market share. Brand B probably will remain stable, but brand C may be in trouble. All other things being equal, it will be difficult to maintain market share with spending levels which lag competition to this extent. Finally, brand D should be watched closely, because it should achieve significant market inroads.

It should be stressed that this example represents a situation in which competition is a major factor, and this is not always the case. Nonetheless, competition is relevant in the majority of instances.

COST CONSIDERATIONS

Space and time costs are always important factors in media selection. These data usually will appear in the volumes published by the Standard Rate & Data Service (SRDS). However, in practice, network TV and radio cost must be obtained from the network. Spot television and radio cost in SRDS is a guide but of little value for real planning or buying since buys are negotiated in terms of price. Because of this problem of actual prices being different from SRDS, two new services have developed. Conceptual Dynamics, Inc. publishes *Media Market Guide* which among other things includes the cost for typical ad units by market. The second service is Spot Quotations And Data, Inc. (SQAD). This service provides real "street" prices for spot television in the top 51 markets. The measure provided by SQAD is the cost per household rating point (CPP) for a 30-second spot. SQAD averages the cost data from several unidentified agencies, plus combines this with the average of Nielsen and Arbitron audience measure for each market to give the CPP.

It will be recalled from Chapter 12 that there are formulas (cost per thousand readers or homes and the milline rate) which permit comparisons of the cost efficiency of various media. The logic of these formulas is that gross space costs must be refined by the audience reached per dollar spent before useful comparisons can be made across media.

The media planner then must obtain CPMs for target audience for every media vehicle under consideration. The computer can be used to combine audience measurement data, target audience designation, and the cost of an insertion to generate such figures. Figure 13–9 presents computer output from a run using Simmons data for magazines. Note that the CPM target audience varies substantially depending on the target market specified. With computer technology, CPM's target audience can easily be calculated for many different target audience designations. Most of these programs allow *subjective* weighting of audience data to take into account the media planner's judgments about growth trends since the audience data were collected (see weight of 111.20 for *People*), and to

FIGURE 13–9
Computer Output of CPM Target Audience Figures for Selected Magazines

Total Adults 1976/1977 Simmons

Target Market:
$15M+ Age 18–34
Population—6665 (000)
Percent of Base—4.47

Rank		Cost	WGT	Reach (000)	Percent covg.	Percent comp.	CPM
1.	People	13,475	111.20	1243	18.6	9.7	10.84
2.	Time	24,705	60.00	1317	19.8	10.6	18.76
3.	Time	24,705	55.00	1207	18.1	10.6	20.47
4.	Time	24,705	50.00	1098	16.5	10.6	22.50
5.	Newsweek	38,160	100.00	1687	25.3	9.5	22.62
6.	Playboy	40,745	100.00	1684	25.3	10.6	24.20
7.	Time	53,195	100.00	2196	32.9	10.6	24.22
8.	Sports Illustrated	34,010	100.00	1147	17.2	9.1	29.65
9.	Business Week	18,760	100.00	547	8.2	14.3	34.30
10.	Esquire	14,000	100.00	408	6.1	8.8	34.31
11.	U.S. News & World Report	26,420	100.00	691	10.4	8.2	38.23

Target Market:
$15M+ Age 35–49
Population—6635 (000)
Percent of Base—4.45

Rank		Cost	WGT	Reach (000)	Percent covg.	Percent comp.	CPM
1.	Time	24,705	60.00	1162	17.5	9.4	21.26
2.	Time	24,705	55.00	1065	16.1	9.4	23.20
3.	People	13,475	111.20	571	8.6	4.4	23.60
4.	Business Week	18,760	100.00	753	11.3	19.6	24.91
5.	Time	24,705	50.00	968	14.6	9.4	25.52
6.	Newsweek	38,160	100.00	1438	21.7	8.1	26.54
7.	Time	53,195	100.00	1937	29.2	9.4	27.46
8.	Sports Illustrated	34,010	100.00	1144	17.2	9.0	29.73
9.	U.S. News & World Report	26,420	100.00	733	11.0	8.7	36.04
10.	Esquire	14,000	100.00	287	4.3	6.2	48.78
11.	Playboy	40,745	100.00	831	12.5	5.2	49.03

FIGURE 13–9 (concluded)

Explanation of output

1. For each run a "target market" is defined by the user based on some demographic variable; for example, the first run specifies 18–34 year olds earning $15,000 and over as the target.
2. "Population" refers to the number of U.S. adults in this target; for example, there are 6,665,000 adults in the target market.
3. "Percent of base" refers to the ratio of population as defined in (2) to the total U.S. adult population; for example, 6,665,000 is 4.47 percent of the total U.S. adult population (over 18).
4. Cost refers to the four-color, full-page cost of a magazine.
5. "Reach (000)" refers to the number of target market readers of an average issue of a magazine in thousands.
6. Percent coverage (percent covg.) refers to the ratio of reach to population; for example, for *People* magazine it is 1,243,000/6,665,000 = 18.6 percent.
7. Percent composition (percent comp.) refers to the ratio of target audience readers of a magazine to total readers of a magazine; for example, 9.7 percent of *People* readers are in the 18–34—$15,000 and over target audience.
8. "CPM" refers to cost per thousand target audience readers.
9. Weighting (WGT) allows the user to adjust the audience figures for a magazine. A WGT of 100.0 means that the data on file are used as is in the calculations. *People* has been weighted up due to estimated expanded readership since the Simmons data were collected. Four different *Time* weights are presented. The 100.0 is the regular *Time* magazine. The other three weights for *Time* are for *Time Z*. This is so because Simmons surveys only measure readership on a national basis. Thus all special advertising editions of magazines (for example, *Time Z, Newsweek Executive, Business Week Industrial*) cannot be measured directly. What all publishers and users do in estimating readership is to simply take a percentage of the total readership when measuring demographic editions. *Time Z* is computed here by taking 50 percent, 55 percent, and 60 percent of regular *Time*. It was usual to use the 50 percent figure for $15,000 plus income and the 60 percent figure for $25,000 plus income.

Source: Kenneth L. Bernhardt and Thomas C. Kinnear, *Cases in Marketing Management* (Dallas, Texas: Business Publications, Inc., 1978), pp. 336–37.

allow the analysis of special editions (note three different special versions of *Time* in the output; each is subjectively assessed in terms of weight).

As useful as the CPM formula can be, it is often abused. First, it may be assumed that costs are the dominant consideration in media selection, whereas any of the other considerations mentioned thus far could be of great importance, especially selectivity in reaching target markets. Furthermore, notice that the denominator of these formulas is circulation, readership, or viewership, none of which is modified to ascertain the number of prospects reached. A CPM of $2.83 could easily be a CPM for prospects of $20 because of inefficient coverage of the target market. Thus formulas of this type should be used only when the denominator is refined to generate *cost per thousand prospects reached* as it is in Figure 13–9.

Finally, it can be difficult to interpret CPM figures under certain circumstances, as Bogart points out:

As it is conventionally calculated, cost per thousand represents an average which treats all impressions alike, regardless of whether they are delivered to different people or repeated to the same people. So long as the value of a repeated message is assumed to be equal to that of a message which is delivered for the first time, cost per thousand automatically gives an apparent advantage to a medium which reaches a concentrated audience over and over again.[14]

It is possible, for example, to arrive at the same CPM with 10 percent of the people reached 10 times, 100 percent reached once, or 1 percent reached 100 times.

It can be concluded, therefore, that CPM must be used with caution. Cost efficiency is a useful criterion *only* when the other considerations mentioned in this chapter have also entered into the analysis. Even then it is only one criterion of an adequate media schedule, not the ultimate criterion, as many falsely assume.

QUALITATIVE MEDIA CHARACTERISTICS

The term *qualitative characteristics* has come to assume several possible meanings. It is confined here to the role played by the medium or vehicle in the lives of the audience and with the positive or negative attitudes toward it and its advertising created by the medium or vehicle in its audience. This definition stresses the meaning of the medium to its readers, viewers, or listeners.

Qualitative values defy precise measurement and analysis, and existing data are sparse. Yet it should be clear that these characteristics form the mood in which advertising is received, and the resulting significance can exceed that of other factors which enter into media strategy. For instance, favorable attitudes toward a television personality can increase the effectiveness of advertising on that program.

As yet there are no continuing data sources which can be used to assess the qualitative media characteristics across media classes. Rather, the analyst must rely on isolated research reports and his or her own judgment. Judgment, moreover, frequently will suffice. It is intuitively obvious, for instance, that the editorial environment and subjective values of the reader of the *Atlantic Monthly* are such as to be incompatible with the advertising of washday detergents. In other situations, however, the qualitative considerations will not be obvious, and the need exists for more and better data. Fortunately, in this situation also, there is no serious methodological barrier to needed research.

A prime illustration of avoiding certain media environments is the recent action by some advertisers to remove their sponsorship from television shows or a specific episode featuring too much violence. Numbered

---

[14] Bogart, *Strategy in Advertising*, p. 257.

among these companies are Procter and Gamble, General Motors, General Foods, McDonalds, and Joseph Schlitz Brewing Company. The decline in the number of violent television shows is no coincidence.

DISTRIBUTION REQUIREMENTS

Distribution geography and stimulation of reseller support are considerations which easily can become dominant in certain situations.

Distribution geography refers to the density of distribution. Strictly national media would not be utilized if distribution were spotty across the country; local newspapers, radio, or television would represent a more economical media array. Promotional strategy also may call for heavy emphasis upon dealer cooperative advertising whereby the dealer places local advertising paid for in part by the manufacturer. Media choices in these cases are confined to local media by necessity, for the market reached by national media usually would substantially exceed that of the dealer. An identical situation is present when the manufacturer places advertising over the dealer's name without reliance on cooperative sharing of costs.

Promotional strategy will at times dictate heavy reliance on personal selling to gain retail distribution, and advertising may be used as a door opener. It is often very effective for the company salesperson to point out to the retailer that the product has been nationally advertised in a prestigious medium; the pulling power of the advertisement thus becomes secondary to its role as a selling point to dealers. The sponsorship of network television programs and placement of advertisements in large-circulation magazines are popular strategies for this purpose.

Finally, it frequently is appropriate to advertise in consumer media for the sole purpose of stimulating dealer efforts. The Pepsi-Cola Company, for instance, sponsors such television spectaculars as the Miss America Pageant solely to serve as a rallying point for bottlers and a stimulus for greater efforts on their part.

SCHEDULING

Once the media to be used have been selected, it is necessary to determine the timing and allocation of advertising insertions. Of special importance are (1) scheduling by geographical region, (2) seasonal scheduling, (3) flighting (concentration of efforts in restricted time periods), and (4) scheduling within a chosen medium (size and location of insertions).

Geographical Scheduling

When the determination of geographical market potential was discussed in Chapter 11, it was indicated that it is necessary to determine

FIGURE 13-10
Geographical Selectivity of the Media Plan for a Convenience Food Item

County size	Percentage in sample studied	Percentage of users	Index of brand use (base 100)	Geographical selectivity of media plan*
A	39.5%	52.0%	132	130
B	26.1	28.0	107	100
C	18.0	15.0	83	100
D	16.4	5.0	30	40 .

* Combination daytime television and three women's magazines.

an *index of relative sales possibilities* on a market-by-market basis. This index in turn serves as the foundation for geographical allocation of advertising dollars. The general principle is to allocate in proportion to market potential, all other things being equal. However, the "noise level" in major markets is higher than in smaller ones. Thus, more advertising weight relative to potential is usually placed in the larger markets.

Figure 13-10 presents the geographical selectivity of the media plan for a convenience food item. Notice that allocations were made so that the schedule closely paralleled the index of brand use by county size.

The data in Figure 13-10 provide only a very general indication of geographical selectivity. In addition, the agency utilized a computer program which permits media selection in proportion to market potential for each major metropolitan market. In this case the projected percentage of sales in a given area became the target figure for total advertising impressions as well. Estimates were made of the necessary impressions for the entire fiscal year. These figures then were converted into gross rating points per week, from which required dollar expenditure levels were estimated. In some cases judgmental modifications were made when it was deemed advisable to ensure that certain markets should receive greater media weight than others. Finally, a computer printout compared original objectives for advertising impressions with actual media delivery. Some of the results were as follows:

Market	Target impressions	Media weight
Portland, Maine	1.7	1.5
Albany, New York	2.2	1.9
Milwaukee, Wisconsin	2.5	1.8
Los Angeles, California	11.2	11.9
Toledo, Ohio	0.9	1.1

Notice, first of all, that there was not an exact correspondence between target objectives and actual media weight, but the differences were so small as to be negligible. Also, the media schedule was evaluated in terms of GRP delivered, not the number of dollars spent. The dollar figure is not necessarily a good measure of *advertising message weight,* which can only be estimated from audience ratings.

Seasonal Scheduling

Because many products show seasonal variations in demand, the advertiser is compelled to introduce appropriate modifications in the timing of advertising throughout the year. In some instances media weight is placed immediately prior to a seasonal upsurge so that maximum sales are generated at the beginning of the season. The promotion of air-conditioning or heating equipment is a good illustration. In other instances funds are allocated so that increases or reductions coincide closely with sales patterns.

In the convenience food example, there were some slight seasonal variations in sales of the product. As the following data show, the media plan coincided closely with seasonal patterns:

Quarter	Percentage of sales		Percentage of media weight	
June	26%	}55%	34%	}57%
September	29%		23%	
December	24%	}45%	22%	}43%
March	21%		21%	

Flighting

At times media planners are forced to concentrate dollar allocations in certain time periods while cutting back at other times. This is referred to as flighting, and it is done to avoid spending at an inadequate level throughout the year. The objective is to achieve higher reach and frequency levels in a more limited period with the hope that the impact generated will carry over in the remaining periods.

Consider, for example, the data in Figure 13–11. Substantially higher reach and frequency levels are generated when the advertising is concentrated in 26 weeks rather than spread over 52 weeks.

Flighting offers the following advantages:

1. There are media rate and purchasing values such as better prices or discounts to be gained by concentrating ad dollars rather than spreading them.
2. There are communications values in concentrating advertising impact. A consumer awareness threshold may be crossed which is impenetrable at light advertising levels.

FIGURE 13–11
Effect of Flighting on Reach and Frequency Levels

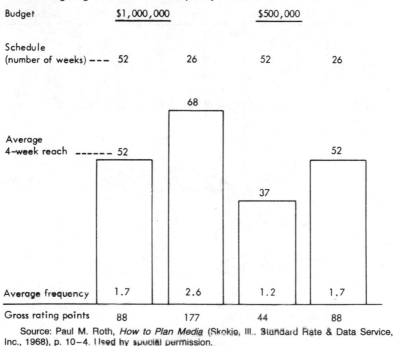

Budget	$1,000,000		$500,000
Schedule (number of weeks) − − −	52 26	52	26
Average 4-week reach − − − − − −	52	68	37 52
Average frequency	1.7 2.6	1.2	1.7
Gross rating points	88 177	44	88

Source: Paul M. Roth, *How to Plan Media* (Skokie, Ill.: Standard Rate & Data Service, Inc., 1968), p. 10–4. Used by special permission.

3.   The availability of greater funds in shorter periods of time opens up new media strategy possibilities.[15]

The first claimed advantage is rather apparent in that discounts increase in proportion to the concentration of dollars within a medium in a limited time period. Similarly, the third advantage can be a significant consideration in that a greater variety of media opportunities often can be presented. The second point, however, is more debatable. Obviously a greater short-run impact can be made, but this may be at the sacrifice of continuing reinforcement during the interim periods. The net effect, therefore, can be the opposite of what is intended, especially if competitive efforts are strong.

Flighting is probably most useful when available funds are inadequate to sustain a continued effort at adequate levels. Indeed, at times it may be the only feasible strategy when it is considered that spending at an unduly low level may result in little or no impact in view of competitors' efforts.

There are many different flighting patterns (sometimes called pulses)

---

[15] Roth, *How to Plan Media*, pp. 10–16.

FIGURE 13–12
Classification of Advertising Timing Patterns

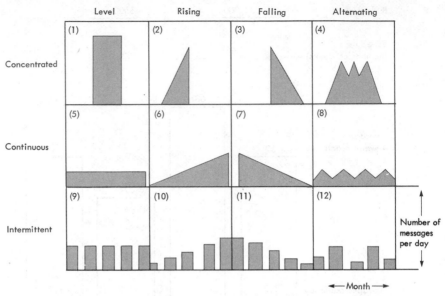

Source: Philip Kotler, *Marketing Management: Analysis, Planning and Control,* 3d ed. (Englewood Cliffs, N.J.: Prentice-Hall, 1976), p. 366.

available. Kotler has suggested one scheme for classifying these patterns (see Figure 13–12).[16] But which pattern is best? Kotler provides some guidance.

The most effective pattern depends upon the advertising communication objectives in relation to the nature of the product, target customers, distribution channels, and other marketing factors. Consider the following cases:

A *retailer* wants to announce a preseason sale of skiing equipment. He recognizes that only certain people will be interested in the message. Furthermore he recognizes that the target buyers only need to hear the message once or twice to know whether they are interested. His objective is to maximize the *reach* of his message, not the *repetition*. He decides to concentrate the messages on the days of the sale at a level rate, but varying the time of day to avoid the same audiences. He uses pattern (1).

A *muffler manufacturer-distributor* wants to keep his name before the public. Yet he does not want his advertising to be too continuous because only 3 to 5 percent of the cars on the road need a new muffler at any given time. He has therefore chosen to use intermittent advertising. Furthermore, he recognizes that Fridays are paydays for many potential buyers, and this would influence their interest

[16] Philip Kotler, *Marketing Management: Analysis Planning and Control,* 3d ed. (Englewood Cliffs, N.J.: Prentice-Hall, Inc., 1976), p. 366.

in replacing a worn-out muffler. So he sponsors a few messages on a midweek day and more messages on Friday. He uses pattern (12).[17]

General rules should be used with care as promotion is a very situation specific activity. A firm must be willing to experiment with its flighting pattern in order to attempt to determine the best one.

Scheduling within Media

In media scheduling it is necessary to specify both the size of the space or time unit to be purchased and the location within the medium. These issues have been extensively researched, and it is now possible to advance a number of generalizations.

Size of the advertisement. The numerous studies of size of the advertisement on the printed page have made it clear that doubling size will not double results. In fact, readership increases roughly in proportion to the square root of space increase.[18] This does not mean, of course, that a half page should necessarily be preferred over a full page. Size offers real advantages in greater power of attraction, more flexibility in layout arrangement, and greater opportunity for dramatic use of space elements. Moreover, the impact of larger space units on *attitude* may be greater, although existing evidence is not clear on this point.

The relative advantages of variations in the length of television or radio commercials defy generalization, although it is well known that longer commercials are often preferred for the reason that creative presentation is simplified when time pressures are not acute. The shorter commercial is usually more demanding to produce, but the rising costs of television time in particular have forced many advertisers to abandon the longer advertisement. The shorter commercial can be equally effective if proper care is taken to prepare a direct and convincing appeal. In fact, 30 seconds can be *too much* time for some messages, and the shorter 10-second commercial can be more effective.

Position of the advertisement. From the numerous studies documenting the role of position on the page in printed media, the following generalizations have emerged:

1. It makes little difference whether the advertisement appears on the left- or right-hand page in either newspapers or magazines. The analysis of readership of the Million Market Newspapers, for example, presents this conclusion unmistakably. In fact, Starch has concluded from 40 years of research that the primary factor in readership is the advertisement itself—what it says and how it says it.
2. In magazines, the greatest readership is usually attracted by covers

---

[17] Ibid.

[18] Barton, *Media in Advertising*, p. 109.

and the first 10 percent of the pages, but beyond this the location of the advertisement is a minor issue.

3. Page traffic is high in nearly *all* parts of a newspaper, and position within the paper is of little significance.

4. Although position does not appear to be a crucial factor, some advantage accrues to the advertiser if the copy is located adjacent to compatible editorial features. Most newspapers and magazines attempt to ensure compatibility, and it can be specified by the advertiser for extra cost.

5. Thickness of the magazine has been found to exert only a slight effect on coupon returns and advertising recognition and recall.

6. A number of other generalizations result from a series of analyses of newspaper readership:

   a. Position in the gutter (the inside fold) is no different from position on the outer half of the page.

   b. Position on the page has little effect except when competing advertisements become especially numerous.

   c. Some advantage accrues if the upper right-hand position is purchased.

   d. There are known differences in readership by sex and age of different editorial features such as general news and sports.

It thus appears that position on the newspaper or magazine page and location within the issue are minor considerations. There can, of course, be significant exceptions to these generalizations, but the advertisement itself appears to be the determining factor in high readership or coupon return.

Position in broadcast advertising has been researched to a lesser degree, at least insofar as published literature shows. It is known from the meager published evidence, however, that commercials frequently perform better when inserted as part of a regular program rather than at the station break, which often becomes cluttered. Location within a program seems to be especially advantageous for longer commercials. It also is felt by many that commercials at the beginning and end of a program are placed at a disadvantage because of the clutter of program announcements, production and talent credits, and other distracting nonprogram material. If this disadvantage appears to be important, the sponsor purchasing time on a participating basis would do well to specify insertion within the program. Others feel that program commercial position is of no consequence, and not enough data exist to support either position.

COMPUTER MODELS IN MEDIA SELECTION

Since the early 1960s increasing attention has been directed toward the potential uses of computer models in selection of advertising media.

Unfortunately the overly optimistic claims of certain early proponents of the computer have introduced a marked note of skepticism within the industry that persists as of this writing. It is fair to state that the payout from use of the computer has not lived up to initial expectations. Nonetheless, considerable progress has been made, and it is the purpose of this section to cover the nature and application of three types of computer models which have seen the greatest use: (1) linear programming, (2) iteration, and (3) simulation. Others such as dynamic programming, nonlinear programming, and heuristic programming also have been utilized experimentally but appear to offer less promise insofar as application to media strategy.

Linear Programming[19]

In 1963 Batten, Barton, Durstine & Osborn placed full-page advertisements stating that "Linear Programming showed one BBD&O client how to get $1.67 worth of effective advertising for every dollar in his budget." At the very least this was a gross overstatement, but considerable interest has been generated in the linear programming (LP) model, and it is examined here in greater depth than iteration and simulation.

The LP model. Linear programming is intended to derive maximum values for a linear (straight-line) function, given certain constraints on the decision space. When applied to media selection, the model takes the following general form:

Maximize:

$$\text{Total exposure} = \sum_{i=1}^{I} R_i X_i$$

Subject to:

$$\sum_{i=1}^{I} C_i X_i \leq B$$

Where:

$X_i \leq L_i$

$X_i \geq 0$ for $i = 1, 2, \ldots, I$

X_i = Number of insertions in medium i

C_i = Cost per insertion in medium i

B = Total advertising budget available

L_i = Physical limit on insertions in medium i

R_i = Rated exposure value of a single insertion in medium i

---

[19] For a detailed worked example see Anthony F. McGann, and J. Thomas Russell, *Advertising Media* (Homewood, Ill.: Richard D. Irwin, 1981), pp. 275–82, and 295–308.

The computation routine consists first of dividing each R_i by C_i to derive the rated exposure value per dollar. Then the objective is to select the medium which returns the highest rated exposure value per dollar (R_i/C_i) and purchase as much as is possible, given the limits imposed by B (advertising budget) and L_i (the total number of possible insertions, say, 12 issues of a monthly magazine). Then the solution proceeds to the medium with the next-highest rating and continues until a media schedule is chosen which maximizes the objective function, subject to the constraints imposed.

The steps in a well-conceived LP media allocation procedure are as follows:

1. Establishment of a target market objective.
2. Procurement of data on the audience profiles of various candidate media.
3. Application of an effectiveness rating procedure encompassing at least two phases: (1) audience profile match and (b) analysis of qualitative considerations.
4. Determination of the objective function in terms of rated exposure values per dollar.
5. Quantification of all constraint conditions, including budgetary limits, limits on media availability, and judgment, with respect to the maximum number of insertions desired in certain media.
6. Application of an LP computational routine.
7. Analysis of the resulting media plan to determine its sensitivity to changes in the constraint condition which are applied as well as changes in the rated exposure values of various candidate media. This will require a series of LP computations so that resulting changes can be isolated.
8. Selection of the final media plan on the basis of judgment as to which solution seems most appropriate in terms of stated objectives.

Advantages of linear programming. The LP approach described above is valuable because it:

1. *Forces definitions of markets to be reached.* Instead of guesses or hunches, data must be developed which characterize markets along several dimensions. The computer, in other words, forces a precise definition of markets, which should be done in any event.

2. *Requires quantification of qualitative factors.* Editorial climate and related considerations are subjective factors, yet they cannot usually be disregarded in media selection. The LP approach specifically requires management to cope with these considerations.

3. *Establishes a clear need for audience data.* It was previously mentioned that media audience data were only fragmentary, prior to the use of computers in media selection. Once LP came into use, however, the need

for good data became painfully evident, and today's sophisticated media data services are a manifestation of that need.

4. *Can be applied to problems with a variety of media.* There is no reason why LP cannot be applied to all media, assuming the availability of data. This makes it possible to consider a greater number of candidate media at any given time than would be the case without use of a computer.

5. *Allows the blending of many factors.* As one authority points out:

In the past we have worked at it with stubby pencils and people, many people. However, no matter how much time and how many people, we have had too many factors to contend with. The real advantage of an electronic computer to us then—its principal purpose—is to give us an opportunity to change these relationships, to juggle with them, to work with them while at the same time keeping all of them in the forefront of the operation and to end up with an effort that examines the whole, not individual pieces of media . . . the way, incidentally, our customers view the campaign that we're putting together.[20]

Limitations of linear programming. The following limitations of linear programming should be recognized:

1. *The assumption of equal effects for repeat exposures.* It is assumed that successive purchases in various media all contribute the same response value. Is it reasonable, however, to expect that the response to the 19th exposure is equivalent to the 1st? In all likelihood the response by the prospect will diminish after many exposures, thus introducing nonlinearity into the response function. Strictly speaking, LP is no longer applicable unless it is reasonable to assume that the response function is linear. It is possible to make the objective function nonlinear through a procedure called piecewise approximation, but this has not found widespread use.

2. *The assumption of constant media costs.* At the present time LP must be used on the assumption that media costs are constant and that no discounts are granted for multiple space or time purchases. This is unreasonable, in that earned discounts can be considerable. Introduction of discounts, however, would make the cost function nonlinear, and LP then would not be applicable.

3. *The danger of fractional time or space purchases.* The Simplex method, the basic LP computer algorithm, will not guarantee the purchase, for example, of full pages in magazines. What is the advertiser to do when the answer calls for 5.31 pages in *Ladies' Home Journal?* Is he safe in rounding the figure to 5.00 or 6.00? What will this do to the media schedule insofar as maximizing the objective function is concerned? Probably it is reasonably safe to round the answer to the nearest integer. The only feasible way to guarantee nonfractional purchases, however, is through use of

---

[20] Herbert Maneloveg, "Linear Programming," paper from the 1962 Regional Conventions, American Association of Advertising Agencies, 1962.

integer programming, which, to the authors' knowledge, has yet to be successfully applied in media strategy.

4. *Solutions determined without consideration of audience duplication.* Obviously one cannot be certain that the solution given by the computer is optimal in terms of unduplicated audience. There is no way in which the problem of audience overlap can be handled with present computer algorithms.

5. *The illusion of definiteness.* The resulting solutions can give a misleading illusion of definiteness. It must never be overlooked that the solution is only as good as the data and the assumptions on which it is built. The computer will only compound any inherent weaknesses.

Evaluation of linear programming. In a thorough analysis of the practical problems associated with the use of LP in media selection, Frank M. Bass and Ronald T. Lonsdale concluded that "Linear models are crude devices to attempt to apply to the media selection problem. The linearity assumption itself is the source of much difficulty. Justifying an assumption of linear response to advertising exposures on theoretical grounds would be difficult."[21]

The linearity assumption thus introduces a distinct note of artificiality into the media selection generated. Some have felt that the resulting solution still is superior to any that can be chosen strictly on the basis of human judgment without the aid of a computer. Others have abandoned LP in the hope of finding more fruitful approaches. There have also been some modifications which have reduced the disadvantages cited here.

Iteration Models

Media scheduling has made limited use of iteration models, in which the approach is to bring one medium at a time into the solution, depicted in the flow diagram in Figure 13–13.

Notice that the medium with the lowest cost per thousand prospects is selected first. Then remaining media vehicles are adjusted to show net unduplicated audience from the vehicle or vehicles already selected. The process continues until the budget is exhausted. Among the models embodying this approach are the high assay model of Young & Rubicam, and the media schedule iteration model of the Standard Rate & Data Service.

While the iteration model is not hampered with the linearity assumption of LP it has the disadvantage that it cannot guarantee an optimum or "best" solution, given stated constraints. This is because the computer algorithm is progressively limited as each medium is chosen. It cannot compute the value of different combinations of media because of the

---

[21] Frank M. Bass and Ronald T. Lonsdale, "An Exploration of Linear Programming in Media Selection," *Journal of Marketing Research* 3 (May 1966), p. 179.

FIGURE 13–13
Flow Diagram for the Iteration Model

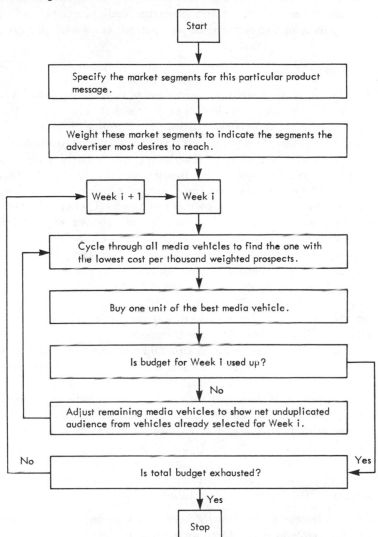

Source: Used by special permission from Dennis H. Gensch, "Computer Models in Advertising Media Selection," *Journal of Marketing Research*, vol. 5 (November 1968), p. 416.

necessity of starting with the highest rated medium and proceeding to the next accordingly. While the first vehicle in the solution might be optimum, there is no guarantee that an optimum solution will result with two or more media candidates.

There are certain other limitations which also should be noted: (1)

the model does not specify the timing of advertising, (2) the criterion function is too limited for a general model, (3) the model does not make use of integrated television and magazine audience data, and (4) there is no way in which advertising in past periods can be taken into account.

Simulation

Simulation models are designed to assess how a given media schedule or group of schedules will affect a target market. The approach in effect consists of storing the characteristics of a number of individuals in the computer and then evaluating their probable response to the media input. Three different approaches to simulation are in fairly widespread use: (1) the CAM model, (2) the Simulmatics model, and (3) COMPASS.

The CAM model. In 1964 the London Press Exchange began operational use of its Computer Assessment of Media (CAM) model.[22] It simulates the process by which individuals are exposed to both magazine and television advertisements. Viewing data are provided in four-week segments by Television Audience Measurement Ltd., and the data are converted into probabilities of viewing over the period of a year. Similar steps are taken on magazine data supplied by the National Readership Survey. Then the individuals in the two samples are carefully paired off so that television viewing and magazine reading patterns are assigned to each individual. These data are then stored in a computer.

Next a target audience for a campaign is selected and weighted. A perception value is assigned to each media vehicle, which attempts to assess the impact an advertisement will have on the viewer or reader in terms of exposure. This is further weighted by variations in prestige and influence from one publication to another. A final series of weights called impact weights is then assigned to assess the impact of the message on the person who sees or views it.

The model makes use of a single score which describes how much advertising an individual will receive. The probability of receiving an impression (PRI) is computed as follows:

PRI = Adjusted probability of seeing or viewing the media vehicle
× perception × selectivity × impact.

Media schedules then are run, and a single score is produced from the simulated response of the sample of individuals which serves as the criterion for choosing between media schedules.

The Simulmatics model. The Simulmatics Corporation stores information on nearly 3,000 imaginary individuals representing a cross section

---

[22] Simon R. Broadbent, "A Year's Experience of the LPE Media Model," in *Proceedings, 8th Annual Conference* (New York: Advertising Research Foundation, 1962).

of the U.S. population four years of age and over. Data are included on socioeconomic characteristics as well as media exposure habits. As with the CAM model, the simulated audience is exposed to an actual media schedule. Modifications are introduced to account for habit formation, saturation with too many of one type of medium, and so on. The summary statistics depict the probable viewing or listening audience and the extent of their exposure.

COMPASS. Ten large advertising agencies have retained a consulting firm to develop a simulation model referred to as COMPASS (Computer Optimal Media Planning and Scheduling System). No details have been made public.

Evaluation of simulation. Simulation offers the unique advantage of realism in that an attempt is made to depict the actual behavior of an audience when exposed to a media schedule. It is possible to include data on forgetting, duplication, discounts, nonlinear responses, and so on. Thus, at least conceptually, simulation is a meaningful forward step.

One of the main difficulties, however, is that knowledge of actual advertising response is so fragmentary that these models may be assuming an unrealistic degree of precision and exactness. In other words, actual media exposure habits may deviate substantially from those that are assumed to exist.

Another limitation is that results are confined only to exposure (i.e., reach and frequency). There is no way to measure the probable persuasive response. This, of course, is a disadvantage shared by all computer models. Finally, simulation models cannot generate an optimum solution. It is possible to evaluate a given set of schedules, but the number of trials necessary to generate an optimum would be excessive. Therefore, an assist is provided in determining only a satisfactory but not optimum media schedule.

The Role of the Computer in Media Strategy

Many agencies and advertisers are making effective use of the computer in storing and retrieving audience information. For the first time it is possible to make sophisticated use of data on reach, frequency, gross rating points, cost per thousand prospects and so on, for a wide variety of media. While this is largely a data processing function, the payoff in more precise media selection has been great indeed. In practice, to date, most computer analysis is for intramedia comparisons. The qualitative difference across media cannot be reduced to numbers very well.

Another advantage has been the growing demand for more and better audience data. The media information services have in large part experienced greatest growth since the advent of the computer.

Finally, there is every reason to expect that the computer models discussed here and others yet to be devised will overcome many of the present limitations.

SUMMARY

This chapter has investigated a number of factors which enter into media strategy, including requirements of creative strategy, audience selectivity, reach and frequency, competitive considerations, cost efficiency, qualitative factors, distribution requirements, and scheduling.

Clearly, it is impossible to present a conclusive set of steps leading to successful media selection in every problem. To do so would be to oversimplify relevant issues to an unrealistic degree. Media selection requires *research thinking* in that information must be sought at many points in the analytical procedure and utilized creatively and imaginatively. The considerations outlined above represent most of the major variables shaping the selection problem. A myriad of solutions is possible, depending entirely on these situational requirements. Fortunately, computer methods can now come to the aid of the media planner.

Review and Discussion Questions

1. In what ways, if any, can ABC and BPA data be used in the media selection process?

2. What are the advantages of having continuing data on advertising exposure across media? What are the difficulties faced in providing such data?

3. Here are the gross rating point levels delivered by three different media plans: 267; 192; and 400. What do these figures mean? All other things being equal, which of the three plans probably would represent the best media buy?

4. The advertising agency for the Crummy Candy Company has submitted a media plan with the statement that "this plan is designed to achieve maximum frequency; reach is of little importance." The campaign is aimed at the market under 25 years of age, and the product being advertised is a popular chocolate bar which now has second place in market share in most local markets. Is frequency a desirable strategy for this type of product?

5. How can the media plan mentioned in question 4 be designed so as to achieve maximum frequency? What changes might be necessary if greater reach were desired?

6. For what types of products is "share of voice" likely to be an important consideration?

7. Magazine A gives a cost per thousand of $4.91; magazine B, $7.12; and magazine C, $8.38. Which of these magazines is the best media buy for the Simmons Mattress Company?

8. For what types of products is geography of distribution likely to be a significant consideration in media choice?

9. Under what circumstances would it be appropriate to allocate media *not* in proportion to the index of relative geographic sales possibilities?

10. Flighting is often used when introducing new products. What advantages are offered? What are the disadvantages?

11. The problem of commercial clutter has caused many to leave television for other media. What can the television industry do to overcome this problem?

12. What is meant by the linearity assumption of linear programming? Describe in detail the effects this assumption has on the applicability of this technique in media strategy. Are there any ways in which it can be overcome?

13. How would you answer the claim that linear programming gives $1.67 worth of value for each $1.00 invested in advertising"?

14. What is meant when it is said that iteration and simulation are not optimizing models? Is this an advantage or a disadvantage?

15. Evaluate the various computer models and state which, if any, you feel offers the greatest future promise. Why? What questions remain to be answered?

CHAPTER 14
The Advertising Message

Because this text is concerned with basic considerations in promotional strategy, relatively little attention has been focused on methods of *execution* of that strategy. This is because execution generally is based on decision rules which are unique to a given set of circumstances. In keeping with this philosophy, this chapter is not intended to instruct the reader on how to design advertisements and write copy. In the first place, there are few if any general rules to be advanced for this purpose. Second, those responsible for determination of strategy may not be writers or designers, who are specialists employed for their ability to execute the strategy in written and verbal form. Much of their skill is an intuitive creative ability that those responsible for basic marketing and promotional strategy usually do not possess to the same degree. For those who are interested in methods of execution, the appendix to this book provides a brief overview of approaches to copy and layout.

This chapter begins with a review of the basic considerations in what is referred to as creative strategy. Then the subject of creative execution is approached by (1) examining the search for decision rules, (2) positioning the role of the behavioral sciences, (3) categorizing different advertising approaches, and (4) outlining one scheme for selecting an advertising approach. The chapter concludes with a discussion of procedures for pretesting advertising messages.

CREATIVE STRATEGY

Creative strategy is based on: (1) proper definition of market target, and (2) a statement of message content.

Definition of Market Target

Definition of market target is the key to media selection, as has been stressed in the preceding chapters. It also enters into creative strategy in a significant way, since it is necessary to inform writers and designers of the types of people who are expected to be exposed to the message. This is especially critical in that those who must execute the message are usually not a cross section of the consuming public they set out to persuade.

A statistical definition of the market, however, is not a sufficient guide for creative strategy. It is of relatively little value, for example, to tell the copywriter that the user of Salvo detergent makes over $20,000 a year, lives in a metropolitan area, has fewer children than average, and is a working wife. But it is necessary to document users' lifestyles. What are the interests which compete for the time of the working woman? How does she view the time spent in doing the family wash? It was an analysis of activities, interests, and opinions which led the Procter & Gamble Company to initiate the "active woman" campaign which stresses the convenience offered by Salvo.

Statement of Message Content

It also is necessary to specify the basic substance of the message to be communicated. This often is stated in fairly broad terms so that artists and writers can determine details. This type of statement is referred to as the *creative platform* or purchase proposition.

The creative platform generally is based on research which answers the following types of questions:

1. What are the features that are unique to the product or brand?
2. What criteria are used by consumers in evaluating alternative brands?
3. What is the brand image in comparison with competitors—i.e., what are the brand's strengths and weaknesses?

The platform itself should feature first the basic promise (the product benefits). It also must provide support for the product claims, making certain that the unique benefits of the brand are featured, as the following examples indicate.

Kero-Sun.[1]   The energy crisis of the late 1970s formed the basis for

---

[1] Gay Jervey, "Kero-Sun Gets Warm Feeling of Success," *Advertising Age,* December 28, 1981, p. 15.

Kero-Sun to use advertising to create a market for kerosene space heaters. The copy platform was built on the product's main benefit—energy cost savings. Ads used testimonials by satisfied consumers. For example, one ad stated: "We heated six classrooms for $2.40 a day." Kero-Sun's sales have doubled every year since it began in 1976 and should reach over $100 million in fiscal 1981/82.

Apple Computer.[2] In order to develop a market for personal computers for both personal and business use, Apple developed an application-oriented copy platform. These ads used real people to show the benefits of an Apple computer for such applications as keeping the family budget, saving inventory costs, and so forth. One business ad featuring a fitness center read: "Cut fat with an Apple. Now you can shape up your business without even working up a sweat." Sales of Apple computers grew from a few million dollars in 1975 to $335 million in 1981.

Evaluation of cases. Obviously no precise formula was followed to arrive at these successful but very different creative platforms. Rather, insight was gained from knowledge of how the product is used, the desires satisfied, unique product features, competitive claims, and so on. The result was a strategy which differentiated each product and supported its claim with clarity.

CREATIVE EXECUTION

While a correct strategy is essential to advertising success, this research in itself will never prove to be sufficient. There comes a point at which the strategy must be executed into the message. It is here that the creative ability of the writer or designer comes to the fore.

What is creativity? According to Webster, something is created when it is produced, formed, or brought into being. True creativity is *not* undisciplined imagination. Controls and discipline may be highly subjective, personal, perhaps subconscious, almost secret or covered up with a facade of "absolutely no control," but this does not mean that they do not operate powerfully in the creative personality. Creative work is largely conscious, deliberate, and *disciplined.* It is disciplined by the objective toward which it is directed and by the information and experience upon which it is based. First the creator hunts for new information and details and arranges them into a pattern through discipline of thought processes. The creative process at each step is the same, whether the discovery is made as a contribution to science, music, technology, art, advertising or some other area of interest. Rules or syntax can be developed, thereby keeping imagination within its most productive bounds.

Real communication does not occur until the message is attended to

---

[2] "Apple's Personal Touch," *Marketing and Media Decisions,* Spring 1982, Special Issue, pp. 77–84.

and correctly comprehended, retained, and acted upon by members of the target market in the manner specified in the statement of advertising objectives. Results which fall short of this signify that true creativity was not achieved in the execution process.

This is not to deny the significant role played by the intuition and skill of the writer and designer. Comprehensive objectives provide the boundaries for creative work; they do not guarantee advertising success any more than staying within the sidelines of a football field guarantees a winning performance. Indeed, intuition and imagination are required, and it is this subjective element which differentiates ordinary advertising from great advertising.

The Quest for Decision Rules

What distinguishes between a well-conceived and executed advertisement and those that are ineffective? Are there decision rules which can be followed? This question is of fundamental importance, and the answer can best be provided by consideration of some of the trends of recent decades.

As recently as the 1930s little attempt was made to measure advertising effectiveness, and there obviously were no decision rules. The Great Depression led to demands for research, however, and industry settled for methods which documented readership or listenership (attraction of attention and, to a lesser extent, comprehension and retention). This gave rise to the "readership-listenership era" (1940–60).

One generalization which quickly loomed above all others was that highest readership is captured by advertisements which resemble the editorial matter of the publication in which they appear. Since *Life* magazine dominated the 1940s, this meant that highest readership resulted when messages paralleled its easy-to-read short copy and predominantly visual style. Other appeals found to be highly effective were emphasis on service (i.e., provision of recipes, information on health and disease, and so on), humor, emotional writing, before-and-after demonstrations, and cartoon strips.

From the vast body of findings on readership and listenership, a number of so-called creative rules have been developed. Some of these appear in Figure 14–1. Much was learned from the research into readership and listenership that still is finding use today, but nevertheless some problems remain. In the first place, some who misinterpreted the proper use of research guidelines produced advertising copy which was routine, stilted, and stereotyped. At the same time, a proliferation of competing brands began to hit the market, especially after World War II, with the result that competition through advertising became intensified. Finally, there were some who wrongly assumed that attracting and holding attention

FIGURE 14-1
Representative Findings Based on Readership-Listenership Studies

Headlines
1. Headlines should appeal to reader's *self-interest*, by promising her [or him] a benefit. This benefit should be the basic product promise.
2. Don't worry about the *length* of the headline—12-word headlines get almost as much readership as 3-word headlines.
3. Inject the maximum *news* into your headlines.
4. Include the *brand name* in every headline.

Copy
1. Don't expect people to read leisurely essays.
2. Avoid analogies—"just as," "so to."
3. Make the captions under your photographs pregnant with brand name and sell.
4. Be personal, enthusiastic, memorable—as if the reader were sitting next to you at a dinner party.
5. Tell the truth—but make the truth fascinating.

Visualization
1. Put "story appeal" in your illustration.
2. To attract women, show babies and women; to attract men, show men.
3. Illustrations should portray reward.
4. Use photographs in preference to drawings. They sell more.

Television Commercials
1. Make your *pictures* tell the story. What you *show* is more important than what you say. If you can't *show* it, don't say it.
2. In the best commercials, the key idea is forcefully demonstrated.
3. Repeat the brand name as often as you can.
4. Make the product itself the hero of the commercial.
5. Start *selling in the first frame.*
6. Use close-up pictures instead of long shots.

Source: David Ogilvy, "Raise Your Sights! 97 Tips for Copywriters, Art Directors and TV Producers—Mostly Derived from Research" (internal publication, Ogilvy & Mather). Reproduced with special permission.

was a sufficient condition for persuasive success. For these reasons and others, concern was increasingly focused on the persuasive impact of the message itself.

The 1960s saw the onset of the tendency to challenge any social rule or tradition. Openness to change and emphasis on "doing your own thing" began to be reflected in all phases of life, and advertising was no exception. To the surprise of many, it was discovered that many of the established rules could be violated with outstanding results.

Rules can place undue constraints on creative imagination if they are followed in rigid fashion. Because this was recognized by many artists and writers, they were open to approaches which were suited to changing times.

The Behavioral Sciences

Prior to and during the readership-listenership era, teachers and academic researchers in advertising turned to the behavioral sciences in the hopes of finding new insights. The propaganda studies during World War II and the intriguing communication research at Yale under C. I. Hovland and his students made the prospects seem indeed good. Evidence was rapidly accumulating, for example, on the effects of a one-sided versus two-sided presentation, fear appeals, primacy versus recency, rational versus emotional appeals, source credibility, persuasibility, and a host of other areas.[3]

DeLozier has prepared a useful summary of these behavioral findings.[4] It is reproduced in Figure 14–2.

Not surprisingly, nearly every marketing and advertising book from the late 1940s until the present has dutifully quoted this evidence. The presumption is that important clues are provided for advertising practice. The only problem is that few advertisers have come to the same conclusion. In fact, this body of evidence has, for the most part, been unused. Does this imply a kind of naive provincialism on the part of the advertising industry? The authors do not think so. Instead, we feel that the naiveté is on the part of those academics who so glibly assessed the "implications" of this research without proper critical analysis.

An example may indicate the difficulty of borrowing from this type of research. In 1953 Irving L. Janis and Seymour Feshbach indicated that a communication stressing the unfavorable consequences of not following a suggested course of behavior (a "fear appeal") can have an adverse effect on attitude change if this fear appeal is too intense.[5] This early study stimulated well over 100 additional studies, most of which have produced a contradictory result, thus indicating that a fear appeal perhaps can be a good strategy.[6] This even led to a *Journal of Marketing* article chiding the advertiser for overlooking fear appeals.[7]

How should an advertiser of, say, fire insurance view this evidence? Should a fear appeal be utilized? The evidence cited scarcely would support such a conclusion, for a number of reasons:

1. Most of the underlying research has been undertaken in artificial laboratory circumstances in which exposure to the message is nonvol-

---

[3] For a review see M. Fishbein and I. Ajzen, "Attitudes and Opinions," in P. H. Mussen and M. R. Rosenzweig (eds.), *Annual Review of Psychology*, vol. 23 (Palo Alto, Cal.: Annual Reviews, Inc., 1972), pp. 188–244; also James F. Engel, and Roger D. Blackwell, *Consumer Behavior*, 4th ed. (Hinsdale, Ill.: Dryden Press, 1982).

[4] M. Wayne DeLozier, *The Marketing Communications Process* (New York: McGraw-Hill, 1976), pp. 224, 226–27.

[5] Irving L. Janis and Seymour Feshbach, "Effects of Fear-Arousing Communication," *Journal of Abnormal and Social Psychology* 48 (1953), pp. 78–92.

[6] This literature is thoroughly reviewed in Brian Sternthal, "Persuasion and the Mass Communication Process," unpublished doctoral dissertation, The Ohio State University, 1972, chap. 4.

[7] M. Ray and W. Wilkie, "Fear: The Potential of an Appeal Neglected by Marketing," *Journal of Marketing* 34 (1970), pp. 59–62.

FIGURE 14–2

Summary of Behavioral Science Findings Related to the Effectiveness of Advertising Messages

---

Facilitating retention: An application of learning theory to advertising communications

In advertising:

1. Unpleasant messages are learned as easily as pleasant messages.
2. Meaningful messages are learned more easily than unmeaningful messages.
3. Ideational learning is faster if massive advertising is followed by distributed advertising.
4. Products requiring mechanical skills are learned best if demonstrated in the ad as though the consumers were doing the task themselves.
5. Product benefits are learned best when presented at the beginning and end of a message.
6. Messages which are unique or unusual are better remembered than common-place advertisements.
7. Rewarding the consumer who attends to a message enhances learning of the message.
8. Learning by consumers is enhanced when they are told the benefits they will receive from using the product.
9. Active participation in the message enhances learning.
10. Message learning is faster if previous or following messages do not interfere.
11. Repetition increases the strength of an older idea more than a newer idea.
12. Messages presented closer in time to an intense need are learned faster than those which are presented when the need is weaker.
13. The greater reward a consumer perceives from viewing (or listening) to an ad message, the faster his learning of the message.
14. The less effort required to respond to an ad, the faster learning occurs.
15. The more complex an ad message is, the more difficult it is to learn.

Gaining conviction: Guidelines for persuasive advertising communications

In general, the source of an advertising message is more persuasive on consumer attitudes and opinions if the consumer:

1. Is perceived by his audience as highly credible (prestigious, expert, honest, etc.).
2. Initially expresses some views held by his audience, then presents his appeal.
3. Is perceived by his audience as similar to themselves.
4. Is perceived as powerful or attractive to his audience.
5. Is low in credibility, but argues against his own self-interests.
6. Has no perceived intention to manipulate his audience or has nothing to gain from what he advocates.

In general, an advertising message is more effective in creating or changing consumer attitudes and opinions in the desired direction if the message:

1. Is one-sided and is presented to consumers who (a) initially agree with the position advocated in the message, (b) are poorly educated, and (c) are not expected to see or hear subsequent counterarguments.
2. Is two-sided and is presented to consumers who (a) initially disagree with the position advocated in the message, (b) are well-educated, and (c) are likely to hear counterarguments.
3. Uses the *anticlimax* order for consumers who have a low level of interest in the product.
4. Uses the climax order for consumers who have a high level of interest in the product.
5. Uses a *primary* order for controversial, interesting, and highly familiar products.
6. Uses a *recency* order for uninteresting or moderately unfamiliar products.

FIGURE 14–2 (*continued*)

7. Arouses a need first, then offers the product as a means of satisfying the need.
8. Draws a conclusion by suggesting the correct action to take.
9. Uses strong fear appeals when they pose a threat to the consumer's loved ones, or are presented by a highly credible source, or concern topics somewhat unfamiliar to the consumer, or are directed at consumers high in self-esteem.
10. Actively involves the audience in the advertisement.
11. Uses highly affective language to describe the product.
12. Associates the product with popular ideas.
13. Arouses feelings of aggression, followed by suggestions of how the product can reduce those aggressive feelings.
14. Associates highly desirable ideas or feelings with the product.
15. Uses nonverbal communications to enhance the product's meanings, especially nonverbal cues which elicit positive consumer feelings and emotions.

Consumers exhibiting certain personality traits are more persuasible than others. In general, consumers who would be expected to be more easily persuasible are those who:
1. Are low in self-esteem and require social approval for their behavior.
2. Exhibit social withdrawal tendencies.
3. Inhibit aggressive feelings.
4. Are low in anxiety.
5. Are high in rich-imagery and fantasy.
6. Are women (in our society).

The persuasibility of certain consumer personality types depends upon the characteristics of the message and the message source. In general, it would be expected that:
1. Consumers who have authoritarian personalities are more susceptible to messages attributed to anonymous sources than those attributed to authority figures.
2. Consumers who have nonauthoritarian personalities are more susceptible to messages attributed to anonymous sources than those attributed to authority figures.
3. Consumers who have highly dogmatic personalities are more likely to be persuaded by authority figures whom they trust than by authority figures whom they do not trust.
4. Consumers who are open-minded are persuaded more by the merits of the advertising message than by who delivers the message.
5. Consumers who have the ability to draw valid inferences are influenced more by logical argumentation than by a message based on irrelevant and unsupported generalities.

Consumers also possess characteristics which make them resistant to persuasion. In general, consumers are resistant to the persuasive attempts of an advertising message which:
1. Attacks one of a consumer's centrally held beliefs.
2. Attacks one of a consumer's "derived" beliefs (i.e., those tied to centrally held beliefs).
3. Attacks a belief to which a consumer is strongly committed.
4. Is contrary to the norms of the group to which a popular or prestigious person belongs.

Consumers are influenced in their purchase decisions by the groups to which they belong. Some useful principles of persuasion in advertising communications are the following:
1. Advertising communications which appeal to culturally learned behavior are more persuasive than those which run counter to such behavior.
2. Advertising communicators are more likely to be successful when appealing

FIGURE 14–2 (*concluded*)

to specific subcultural group attitudes and norms than when appealing to broad-based cultural attitudes and norms.

3. Because the vast majority of family income in lower-income groups is for routine household purchases, advertising messages directed toward these groups should be aimed toward the wife.

4. Marketers who define their target market as "young marrieds" should design and direct their advertising messages toward both husband and wife. (They exhibit more joint-purchase decision making.)

5. Advertising messages which emphasize instrumental functions of a product should be directed toward the husband in a family, whereas those emphasizing the aesthetic features should be directed toward the wife.

6. Product advertising directed toward family purchase should consider the family's stage in the life cycle.

7. When product or brand purchase decisions are not influenced strongly by reference groups, the advertising message should emphasize brand features, intrinsic qualities, and benefits over competing brands.

8. When a reference group influences consumer purchase decisions, the advertising message should emphasize the kind of people who use the brand and reinforce these stereotypes in the minds of consumers.

9. For *new* products, advertising communications should stress the relative advantages of the new brand over existing brands, show how it fits into the consumer's present ways of doing things (i.e., be compatible), demonstrate the product's ease of use (i.e., reduce perceived complexity), and show the results of using the product (observability).

10. Some advertising messages should be designed to help consumers reduce post-purchase doubt. This task can be accomplished by (*a*) providing the consumer with a way to rationalize his decision and (*b*) providing the consumer with additional evidence to support the wisdom of his decision.

11. Where opinion leaders for a product can be identified and for whom media habits are somewhat homogeneous, the advertising communicator should direct a substantial portion of his communications effort toward this group, so that they might, in turn, favorably influence their followers.

Source: M. Wayne DeLozier, *The Marketing Communications Process* (New York: McGraw-Hill, 1976), pp. 224, 226–27.

untary. Hence there is little or no correspondence of the findings to real-world situations.[8]

2. The purposes of these studies usually were significantly different from those of the advertiser. Often the goal was to find better ways of indoctrinating people using face-to-face procedures. Furthermore, the topics considered usually deviated substantially from those in the domain of the advertiser.

3. The citation of evidence and "implications" in the marketing literature often overlooks important limitations and qualifications. In the case of fear, for example, what differentiates a fear appeal from a nonfear appeal? This question seldom has been addressed, and it leaves the

---

[8] Carl I. Hovland, "Reconciling Conflicting Results Derived from Experimental and Survey Studies of Attitude Change," *American Psychologist* 14 (1959), pp. 8–17.

comparability of findings open to challenge. Furthermore, most marketing writers have overlooked the latest evidence that the effects of fear are moderated by source credibility. That is, fear has a positive effect on attitude only if the communication source is perceived as credible.[9] From earlier chapters it should be obvious that advertising rarely has the necessary degree of credibility. For these reasons alone it is unwise to claim that advertisers have an "overlooked opportunity."[10]

One could extend this type of analysis to the primacy versus recency issue or any of the other areas of investigation mentioned above. The basic conclusion is that the majority of this evidence is devoid of empirical support under realistic field conditions, and therefore it is unwise to generalize from such a shaky base. The most that can be gained is a tentative indication of a persuasive approach that *might* work under certain circumstances. This is not to suggest that the behavioral science literature is of no value. Rather, it makes a plea for proper interpretation and applications. The advertiser must see what relationships hold in his or her specific circumstances. The results in Figure 14–2 are useful hypotheses, but no more. The need for research for real-world and product-specific situations should be obvious.

Is there then no aid for the reader who wants to develop a better understanding of types of advertising approaches and some guidelines for when each is appropriate? The next section presents one possible framework to guide the reader with this interest. Like all such schemes it is too simple, sometimes misleading, and not researched enough. However, we believe that the insights presented are useful and interesting.

A USEFUL GUIDE TO CREATIVE ASPECTS

Creative aspects of advertising hold a veto power over the effectiveness of a campaign. Good decisions in other areas can be wasted without meaningful copy, themes, presentation, and so forth. The marketing manager is likely not to be involved directly in the formulation of creative plans. This aspect is typically performed by the advertising agency. The manager is required, however, to approve and suggest changes in their creative efforts. To properly carry out this function he or she needs a framework related to what constitutes good advertising. The purpose of this section is to lay out a framework that has considerable practical usefulness. This framework is based on the writings of Simon.[11]

---

[9] See Sternthal, "Persuasion and Mass Communication."

[10] Ray and Wilkie, "Fear."

[11] Julian L. Simon, *The Management of Advertising* (Englewood Cliffs, N.J.: Prentice-Hall, 1971), pp. 174–206.

The framework is based upon developing links between product-market characteristics and advertising characteristics. To do this, one must first develop a classification scheme for both products and advertisements.

Alternative Advertising Approaches

The characteristics of ads that are important here relate to the way in which they attempt to activate buyers to action. Simon classified a number of activation methods. Some of them are:

1. *Information:* This type of ad presents straight facts. These facts are not presented in argumentative form nor is the relevance of the facts explained. Classified and yellow pages ads are prime examples of this type of advertising, but many other examples exist, such as: "round steak now 89 cents per pound," or "City Center Motors announces the arrival of the new models." Figure 14–3 presents an example of an information ad.

2. *Argument or reason-why:* This type of ad is structured in the form of a logical argument. The reasons utilized in the argument may be either facts or expected benefits to the consumer (social standing, and so forth). Figure 14–4 presents an example of an argument ad.

3. *Motivation with psychological appeals:* This type of ad makes use of emotional appeals. They try to enhance the appeal of the product by attaching pleasant emotional connotation to it. The ads create a mood. Selling points are then both explicit and implicit. Cosmetic, cigarette, and beer and liquor products are heavy users of mood commercials. Figure 14–5 presents an example of this type of ad.

FIGURE 14–3
An Information Ad

FIGURE 14–4
An Argument Ad

FIGURE 14–5
A Motivation with Psychological Appeals Ad

4. *Repeat-assertion:* This type of ad constitutes the hard-sell approach to activation. The statements made in these ads are usually unsupported by facts, and so are the reasons why the statements hold. Two examples of this form are "Rolaids absorbs 20 times its weight in excess stomach acid," and "the little tablet is the more effective." The assumptions here are that people will believe a statement if they hear it enough and that they have no intrinsic interest in the product message. One is, then, just interested in getting across the line to remember. Nonprescription drugs are heavy users of this type of ad. Figure 14–6 presents an example of a repeat-assertion ad.

5. *Command:* This type of ad orders us to do something. For example: "when you drink don't drive," "give the United Way," or "drink Coca-Cola." The intent is to remind us to do something. The assumption is that the audience is suggestible. Command ads probably work best for products that are well known and are generally well thought of by the audience. Figure 14–7 presents an example of a command ad.

6. *Symbolic-association:* This type of ad is characterized as a more subtle form of the repeat-assertion ad. The intent is to get across one piece of information about the product. Here the product is linked to a person, or music, or situation that has particularly pleasant connotations. The product and the symbol then become highly interrelated. Can anyone look at a picture of Gibraltar without thinking of what's-their-name? This type of appeal is obviously similar to emotional appeals. For example, beer is often associated with "good times with friends," a very emotional appeal. Both the emotion and the symbolic association are there. The first page of the color insert presents the classic Marlboro ad as an example of this approach.

7. *Imitation:* This type of ad attempts to present people and situations for the audience to imitate (using our product of course). The assumption is that people will imitate people who they wish to be like or admire. Hence, we note the use of famous people in testimonials, status appeals, a group of young friends drinking beer, and so forth. Figure 14–8 shows this type of approach with Lynda Carter saying: "Your make-up can help hide a wrinkle. Mine can help prevent one."

We note that information, argument, and motivation are all directed at the conscious, "reasoning" parts of the mind. The others are more directed at more emotional parts of the mind.

Choosing an Approach

Simon also notes a number of dimensions on which products and their markets may be classified. The positioning of a *product-market situation* on each dimension logically suggests an activation procedure.

1. *Industrial or consumer good:* The information and argument types of

324

FIGURE 14–7
A Command Ad

DON'T SPEND SUMMER SPINNING YOUR WHEELS.

Northern Illinois winters taught us to make the most of northern Illinois summers.

But you have to work at it. Because the minute the air conditioner goes on, those little dials on the meter start moving faster. Sending most electric bills higher than in any other season of the year.

Partly, because air conditioning naturally eats up a lot of electricity. And partly, because summer rates are higher than in any other season of the year.

It's been that way since 1979, when we stopped using the old, uniform, year-round rate. Raised it in the four summer months when electricity costs more to make. And lowered it the other eight to compensate.

Obviously, one of the big benefits was getting you to conserve. To help cut back on the growing demand for electricity every summer.

It's not impossible. Far from it. Those little dials don't have to move so fast. In fact, we know of at least a hundred things you can do to slow them down.

They're listed in our Waste Watcher's Guide, which is yours free.

(Write: Department AV, Box 767, Chicago, IL 60690.)

It'll help you conserve electricity, so you can save your money.

And spend your summer.

Commonwealth Edison
Don't take tomorrow for granted.

FIGURE 14–8
An Imitation Ad

ads are prevalent in industrial advertising. The complexity of the products, the dollar value of purchases, the risks of choosing a faulty product, and so forth, all dictate ads that provide facts and present logical arguments. The second page of the color insert presents an example of an industrial, argument ad.

For consumer goods any one of the activation methods may still be appropriate. We must examine other dimensions before a more definitive answer can be reached for consumer goods. Then, for consumer goods we look at:

2. *What word best characterizes the product:* "Style," "mechanical," "sensory," "service," or "hidden benefit." If "style," tend to use imitation, motivation, and symbolic-association. For example, the advertising of fashion goods or beauty aids (see the third page of the color insert and Figure 14–8). If "mechanical," tend to use information and argument. Note the use of statistical data in automobile and computer advertising (see Figure 14–9). If "sensory," tend to use symbolic-association motivation and imitation. These kinds of products appeal to all senses and need an appeal that goes beyond just words. Note the use of well-known people in cosmetic ads. For example, Chaz uses Tom Selleck and Chanel No. 5's use of Catherine Deneuve is a classic (see the last page of the color insert). If "service," tend to use information and argument. People need to know that the service exists and rationally why they should partake of it (see Figure 14–10). If "hidden benefit," tend to use information, argument, and motivation. Lots of products have hidden benefits. For example, nonprescription drugs, all kinds of insurance, and foods to name just a few. Buyers must be informed of these benefits, persuaded that they are important either with argument or through emotion (see Figure 14–11).

3. *Is it a necessity, a convenience or a luxury good:* If a luxury product we would likely use symbolic-association or imitation. Luxury products are designed to give prestige and so we must create the aura of prestige in the ads. Also, the farther away a product is from being a necessity, the more likely we will have to create a demand for the product class. Motivational methods are, then, likely to be useful (see Figure 14–12 as an example of a luxury good ad). The more necessary a product the more likely activation methods other than motivation will be appropriate.

4. *Stage of product class acceptance:* The newer the product class the more people need information about it and reasons to buy it. We would then tend to use information, argument, and motivation (see Figure 14–13). As the product progresses through the lifecycle, people become less interested in hearing information about it. We then turn to use repeat-assertion, imitation, symbolic-association or command.

5. *Stage of brand acceptance:* Even in an established product category, new brands must provide information, and therefore the early lifecycle meth-

FIGURE 14–9
A "Mechanical" Product Using an Argument Approach

Victor's Desktop Business Computer System.

Businesses today face a basic dilemma when it comes to selecting a computer.

So-called "personal" computers have limited power and capacity. They're just too small to be useful to most businesses.

And the larger minicomputers are more expensive.

Victor has a solution to that dilemma.

The Victor 9000 Business Computer is priced under $5,000. Like a "personal."

Yet the Victor 9000 has a capacity that rivals the expensive minis.

A close look at the chart below shows you just how the Victor 9000 compares.

The Victor gives you the kind of memory and storage capacity business applications demand. Much more than the IBM Personal Computer, the Apple III or their competitors.

To get the whole story of just how the Victor 9000 can solve your business computer dilemma, call Victor at **(800) 621-5559**. In Illinois **(800) 972-5858**. We're open 24 hours a day,

7 days a week. Or write Victor Business Products, P.O. Box 1135, Glenview, IL 60025.

VICTOR BUSINESS PRODUCTS
Subsidiary of Kidde, Inc.
KIDDE

MAKE & MODEL	Victor 9000	IBM PC	Xerox 820	Apple III	Radio Shack TRS80 Model II
Processor Type	8088	8088	Z80A	6502	Z80A
Word Length	16 bits	16 bits	8 bits	8 bits	8 bits
Memory Size (Internal)	128-896KB	16-256KB	64KB	96-256KB	32-64KB
Storage Capacity on 2 Floppies	1200KB (5¼")	320KB (5¼")	160KB (5¼")	280KB (5¼")	960KB (8")
CRT Display Standard Format	80 x 25	80 x 25	80 x 24	80 x 24	80 x 24
Alternate Format	132 x 50	None	None	None	None
Graphics Resolution	800 x 400	640 x 200	None	560 x 192	None
Communications Built-in Serial Ports at no extra cost	2	0	2	1	2
Built-in Parallel Ports at no extra cost	1	0	2	0	1
Human Factors Keys on Keyboards	94-104	83	96	74	76
Detached Keyboard	Yes	Yes	Yes	No	Yes
Tilting Display mechanism	Yes	No	No	No	No
Swivelling Display mechanism	Yes	No	No	No	No
Desk Area Required (Approx. Square In. with 2 floppy disks)	310	420	470	361	500
Operating System Supplied Standard	CP/M-86 MS-DOS	None	None	Apple DOS	TRS DOS

NOTE: Chart based on manufacturer's information and Dataquest, Inc. available as of April 4, 1982.

VICTOR®
Serving American business for 65 years.

FIGURE 14–10
A "Service" Product Using an Argument Approach

TIME WAS WHEN YOU COULD HARDLY MANAGE YOUR INVESTMENTS WITHOUT YOUR ACCOUNTANT, YOUR BROKER AND YOUR POSTMAN ALL GETTING INVOLVED.

THEN MERRILL LYNCH INVENTED CMA.™

It used to be a hassle to switch investments around—and keep track of them. Your broker handled some...but not if you invested in late 19th-century European oils or a lakefront property.

And even after talking to your broker, there was that wait for the mail. **Now, instant flexibility.** The revolutionary Merrill Lynch Cash Management Account* financial service eliminates all that.

At the heart of CMA™ are a Merrill Lynch brokerage account and an experienced Merrill Lynch Account Executive.

Don't lose interest. The CMA service also makes sure your money keeps earning money virtually all the time, at current money market rates. Your cash balance is invested in your choice of three professionally managed money market funds, with dividends reinvested daily.

If you need extra cash, just write a check or use your special VISA* card— both provided by Bank One of Columbus, N.A. You may automatically borrow up to the *full margin value* of your securities in the account.

An accountant's delight. At the end of each month, you receive a single, comprehensive statement that keeps track of everything you've done through your CMA. *Everything.*

How to get started. To join the 600,000 investors who already have put more than $30 billion to work through CMA, all you need is a minimum of $20,000 in securities and/or cash.

For more complete information, including a prospectus containing all sales charges and expenses, call 1-800-526-3030 Ext. 559 (in New Jersey, call 1-800-742-2900 Ext. 559). Read the prospectus carefully before you invest or send money.

THE MORE YOU DEMAND OF YOUR MONEY, THE MORE YOU NEED CMA.™

Merrill Lynch
Merrill Lynch, Pierce, Fenner & Smith Inc.

A breed apart.

CMA™ is not available in all states. The Cash Management Account program is proprietary to Merrill Lynch. U.S. Patents Pending. © 1982 Merrill Lynch Pierce Fenner & Smith Inc. Member SIPC

FIGURE 14–11
A "Hidden Benefit" Product Using Argument and Motivational Approaches

A GOOD HUSBAND SHOULD PREPARE HIS WIFE TO END UP ALONE.

Even if you have insurance on your life, you could be leaving your wife and children only half protected.

Here's what often happens: Upon the husband's death, a wife receives the proceeds of his Whole Life Policy. Now she should have insurance on her own life as new head of the family. However, she may not want to spend that money now. Or she may find insurance unaffordable because of her age, or unavailable because of her health. She's uninsured and the children now are unprotected.

But Metropolitan and you can keep that from happening to your wife.

We are introducing a "Surviving Spouse" rider available with Metropolitan's Whole Life *Plus* policy. So your wife would not only get the full proceeds of your policy, she would then automatically receive term coverage on her own life equal to what you had on yours. She would have that coverage until age 65, at no extra cost to her and regardless of her state of health.

You can take this step for only about

$15 a year, plus a premium of generally less than a dollar for each thousand dollars of term coverage.

Call a professional Metropolitan representative soon. Let Metropolitan make sure your wife is better prepared than most.

METROPOLITAN REALLY STANDS BY YOU.
Life/Health/Auto/Home/Retirement

©1982 Metropolitan Life Insurance Co., New York, N.Y.

FIGURE 14–12
A Luxury Product Using a Motivational Approach

Sources: Doyle Dane Bernback Advertising Agency and General Wine and Spirits Company.

FIGURE 14–13
A Product in a Newer Product Class Using Argument and Motivation Approaches

ATARI® HOME COMPUTERS BRING A WORLD OF INFORMATION, EDUCATION
AND ENTERTAINMENT INTO YOUR LIVING ROOM.

Press a few buttons and you're creating beautiful music. Or learning French. Or evaluating your investments.

The ATARI Home Computer is designed to be so simple, a child can use it—but so brilliant, it does a world of wonderful things for you.

Learn everything—languages, history, psychology, algebra....

Tap into almost limitless sources of information—news services, airline schedules, the Stock Exchange....

Invent your own games,

© 1981 Atari, Inc. "Trademark of Taito America Corporation.

create your own art, make your own discoveries.

Play your favorite computer games, including Space Invaders," and Asteroids."

The ATARI 400™ Home Computer is the perfect way to enter the computer age—affordable, easy to use, and versatile.

The ATARI 800™ Computer is for more advanced applications, but it's just as easy to use.

For more information, write: Atari, Inc.

Computer Div., 1196 Borregas Ave., Dept. Y, Sunnyvale, Calif. 94086. Or call in U.S.: 800-538-8547; Calif.: 800-672-1430.

ATARI® HOME COMPUTERS.
We've brought the computer age home."

ods are again appropriate (see Figure 14–14). The older brands utilize the later lifecycle methods.

6. *Price range:* If a high-priced item, tend to use information, argument and motivation. People need reasons for spending so much (see Figure 14–15). The smaller the dollar amount, the more impulsive is the purchase and so symbolic-association, command, repeat-assertion, and so forth become more viable (see Figure 14–16).

7. *Closeness to competing brands in objective characteristics:* A brand with great physical differences from its competitors allows the advertiser to say a lot about the physical product (see Figure 14–17). It can therefore make use of information, argument, and motivation. Brands that have few differences must rely on other methods (beer, cigarettes). For an example see Figure 14–18.

8. *Repeatability of purchase:* Products with short repurchase cycles (for example, soap, coffee, and so forth) utilize symbolic association, command, repeat assertion, and imitation much more than those with long repurchase cycles (for example, appliances). Information and argument become old hat for the former but are critical for the latter. Note the difference between Figures 14–18 and 14–15.

9. *Method of consummating sale:* The more direct-action oriented the ad (for example, mail order houses, Book-of-the-Month Club) the greater the need for argument and motivation methods. These types of ads must do the complete selling job and therefore can use many activation methods (see Figure 14–19).

10. *Market share held by brand:* If a brand holds a dominant position in a market, it has a lot to gain by expanding the whole market. One would, then, use information, argument or motivation, the methods we associated earlier with early stages of the product life cycle (see Figure 14–20).

Simon then suggests that we identify the most important product-market dimension, and keep this in mind when selecting an activation method. What we do is characterize our product on the dimensions given, note the most important dimensions, and select the activation method that seems most appropriate. Think of the ads you have seen lately, say, for beer and watches. Pick a brand and work through Simon's procedure. We think you'll be impressed with the usefulness of the framework.

Within any of these advertising approaches there are millions of different ways to create the ad. The words, colors, and graphics of the ad can be used in infinite variety. Further, such things as humor can be used, or a well known spokesperson (see Figure 14–8), or a "slice of life" presentation (see Figure 14–13). Thus, Simons' scheme can aid our understanding but does not reduce the need for creativity. We still should expect to find different brands of the same product using different types of ads, as Figure 14–21 demonstrates.

FIGURE 14–14
A New Brand Using an Argument Approach

FIGURE 14–15
A High-Priced Product Using an Argument Approach

What's behind our no-fingerprint doors.

Porcelain-enameled steel interior.
Durable. Easy to clean.

Ice and water dispensers.
Just push a bar and your glass will be filled automatically. No more ice trays to bother with. There's even a built-in night light.

Humidity sealed crispers.
Help keep foods extra fresh. Special lighting helps you see the foods you want.

Adjustable rollers.
Help compensate for uneven floors. Let you move the refrigerator easily for cleaning.

Heater control switch.
Lets you save energy during times of low humidity.

Adjustable tempered-glass shelves.
Not only look beautiful, but help prevent spillovers from dripping through.

Serva-Door® design.
Our special door-within-a-door design lets you get the foods you use most often without opening the whole refrigerator.

Adjustable slide-out utility tray.
Slide it out for easy access to items at the back. Lift it out for use as a serving tray.

A lot of people bought our refrigerators just because of the way their doors help hide fingerprints. But there's more inside. So much more. The kind of quality, the kind of convenience that makes Whirlpool... Whirlpool.

Whirlpool
Home Appliances

Quality Our way of life

FIGURE 14–16
A Low-Priced Product Using a Repeat-Assertion Approach

Source: Copyright © 1978 General Foods Corporation. Reproduced with permission of General Foods Corporation, owner of the registered trademark Sanka.

Marlboro

Warning: The Surgeon General Has Determined That Cigarette Smoking Is Dangerous to Your Health.

17 mg "tar," 1.0 mg nicotine av. per cigarette, FTC Report Aug.'77

A Symbolic-Association Ad

Shhhhhh

At some of the nation's busiest suburban airports Citations are the only jets judged quiet enough to land late at night

Some of the nation's busiest and most convenient airports are surrounded by people's homes. Several, consequently, have set nighttime curfews for all jets— all except Citations.

That's because Citation I and Citation II are the world's quietest business jets.

Citations operate far below the sound limits set by the FAA. They could be four times louder and still comply. And they're already way below the stricter noise limits proposed for 1979.

Some business jets are fully twice as loud as a Citation. And most turboprops will virtually drown out Citation's quiet engines.

And your Citation isn't just a blessing for your fellow man below. It's hours of peaceful flight for *you*. Because the quietest jets outside turn out to be the quietest *inside*, too.

For a quiet talk about Citation's many *other* advantages, call J. Derek Vaughan at (316) 946-6056. Or write him at Dept. BW7, Box 7706, Cessna Aircraft Company, Wichita, Kansas 67277.

cessna/CITATION I

An Industrial Product Using an Argument Approach

"I'm more comfortable in blue jeans than a designer dress. I'm more comfortable in jewelry that's right for me, too. That's why I like Accents. They complete my look, not compete with it. Accents let me shine through."

Accents by Hallmark Cards

Exclusively at shops featuring Hallmark cards. From $3.50 to $12.50.

A "Style" Product Using an Imitation Approach

A "Sensory" Product Using an Imitation Approach

FIGURE 14–17
A Physically Different Product Using an Argument Approach

YOU ALREADY OWN HALF OF THE WORLD'S MOST ADVANCED HOME ENTERTAINMENT SYSTEM.

You're already halfway to Magnavision* right now. Because all you have to do is plug it into your present color TV set.

Magnavision is a turntable. A *video* turntable as well as an audio one. It plays discs that show pictures on your TV. With stereo sound capability.

And what pictures. Magnavision delivers a picture that's clearer and crisper than video tape TV, even TV itself. And the Magnavision picture lasts, because the discs are impervious to wear.

See the buttons on the front of the Magnavision unit? They give you total control over what you watch and how you watch it. Consider the possibilities: Reverse. Slow motion. Individual frame-by-frame indexing. More. And you can exercise control from anywhere in the room, since Magnavision Model 8005 (shown here) gives you a full-feature remote control.

AMAZING: PICTURES WITH <u>STEREO</u> SOUND.
Magnavision even gives you high-fidelity stereo sound.

Just run it through your present stereo system and choose from one of the many stereo videodiscs (concerts, musicals, shows). You can't get stereo with video tape, and stereo TV is years away. Imagine, now you can see Liza Minnelli* for example, as well as hear her in stereo concert!

All of this wonderwork comes from Magnavision's laser-optical scanner. It is a beam of light that works like an audio player's "needle." But Magnavision's laser-optical scanner has none of the archaic limitations of a needle.

Magnavision is full of ideas. It can be a learning machine as well as an entertain-

ment source. Many of the discs are interactive. You can carry on a dialogue with them. *How To Watch Pro Football†, The First National Kidisc†*—games, puzzles, questions and answers for your children, *The Master Cooking Course†,* and *Jazzercise†* are just four examples.

You can put as many different kinds of programs on your television screen with Magnavision as you can imagine. Choose from over 120 videodisc albums now. They range from classic movies to new releases. From sports instruction to art gallery tours. From cartoons to concerts. And new programs are continually being developed exclusively for videodiscs.

So put your half of the world's most advanced home entertainment system together with Magnavision soon. *For the name of your nearest dealer, please call toll-free 800-447-4700 (in Illinois, 800-322-4400).*

© 1981 N.A.P. CONSUMER ELECTRONICS CORP.
A NORTH AMERICAN PHILIPS COMPANY
"Liza In Concert© Pioneer Artists" †Optical Programming Associates©

MAGNAVISION

MAGNAVOX
The brightest ideas in the world are here today.

FIGURE 14–18

A Product Not Very Different from Its Competitors Using a Motivation Approach

THE DICKIES JEAN. WILL IT CHASE THE BLUES AWAY? TWILL! TWILL! TWILL!

Let's face it. Blue denim is getting boring. That's why The Dickies Jean is now seen on more than *twenty million legs.* They're the Terrific Twills that chase the Blues and bring you Azure! Chocolate! Beetroot! And seven other delicious colors. Priced *lower* than the Blues, but look like they cost more. Get all the jeans fit, and more jeans fun. Look for the famous Dickies horseshoe, and get the Twill of a lifetime. A terrible pun, but wonderful jeans from the Williamson-Dickie Apparel Mfg. Co. of Ft. Worth, Texas.

FIGURE 14–19
A Direct Action Ad Using Argument and Motivation Approaches

Dear Debbera,
   I want to tell you about my study. At the end of last year I was announced as best student. My school report is very satisfactory. I got a present from school. How about you, Debbera? Are you still studying? I hope you are successful in your studies. I stop my letter now. I give you all my love. From your sponsored child,

Tristaca

Dear Tristaca,
   I was so pleased to get your letter. That's quite an honor to be first in your class. I'm very proud of you. I'm still teaching, but the only classes I'm taking now are ballet. Did you get all the postcards I sent? It was a great trip. I'm looking forward to the holidays now—hope to do a lot of skiing this winter. Take care now and write soon.

Debbera

P.S. I love you.

   Tristaca and Debbera, though they've never even met, share a very special love. Tristaca lived in extreme poverty. Her mother has tried to support her family herself, but she can only get menial jobs that pay almost nothing.
   Tristaca was a girl without any hopes, without any dreams. Then Debbera Drake came into her life.
   Debbera sponsors her through the Christian Children's Fund for $15 a month. Her money gives Tristaca food and clothing and a chance to go to school. It gives her hopes and dreams once more.
   You can give a child hope. Become a sponsor. You needn't send any money now—you can "meet" the child assigned to your care first. Just mail the coupon. You'll receive the child's photograph and background information. If you wish to sponsor the child, simply send in your first monthly check or money order for $15 within 10 days. If not, return the photo and other materials so we may ask someone else to help.
   We have thousands of children like Tristaca on our waiting list right now who desperately need sponsors. Let one of them share something special with you. Love.

For the love of a hungry child.

Dr. Verent J. Mills, CHRISTIAN CHILDREN'S FUND, Inc., Box 26511, Richmond, Va. 23261   NNWK87
I wish to sponsor a ☐ boy ☐ girl. ☐ Choose any child who needs help. Please send my information package today.
☐ I want to learn more about the child assigned to me. If I accept the child, I'll send my first sponsorship payment of $15 within 10 days. Or I'll return the photograph and other material so you can ask someone else to help.
☐ I prefer to send my first payment now, and I enclose my first monthly payment of $15.
☐ I cannot sponsor a child now but would like to contribute $_____.

Name_____

Address_____

City_____ State _____ Zip_____
Member of International Union for Child Welfare, Geneva. Gifts are tax deductible.
Canadians: Write 1407 Yonge, Toronto, 7. Statement of income and expenses available on request.

Christian Children's Fund, Inc.

FIGURE 14–20
A Dominant Brand Using an Argument Approach

Thanks to Crest, millions of kids have gotten less than they expected.

Crest with its fluoride strengthens a child's tooth enamel and makes it more resistant to decay.

We know Crest helps fight cavities because we have over 20 clinical studies that prove Crest reduced cavities better than the same toothpaste without fluoride. And millions of mothers know Crest works because their children have the good checkups to prove it. Of course, Crest can't promise everyone only one cavity, but we can promise most people good checkups.

So take your kids for regular checkups, have them cut down on treats and brush regularly with a toothpaste that's proved it fights cavities. Crest.

Crest. Proof, not promises, in the fight against cavities.

"Crest has been shown to be an effective decay-preventive dentifrice that can be of significant value when used in a conscientiously applied program of oral hygiene and regular professional care." Council on Dental Therapeutics, American Dental Association.

© 1976, The Procter & Gamble Company

FIGURE 14-21
Different Brands of the Same Product Using Different Types of Ads

THE FIRST BOAT SHOE DESIGNED TO PERFORM AS WELL ON LAND AS IT DOES AT SEA.

The boat shoe we're referring to is made by Timberland.® And it's the first one that takes into account this simple fact:

MOST PEOPLE WHO WEAR BOAT SHOES NEVER SET FOOT ON A BOAT.

The boat shoe, as we know it today, is actually a misnomer.

Because what started out as something worn exclusively by people who sail is now something worn by virtually everyone.

Today, boat shoes are as acceptable with a sport jacket and tie on Saturday night as they are with foul-weather gear that same afternoon.

The problem is, while their acceptance has improved tremendously, the quality of boat shoes hasn't.

THE TIMBERLAND® BOAT SHOE VS. THE SPERRY TOP-SIDER.®

When people think of boat shoes, one name always comes to mind. Sperry Top-Sider.®

We're about to change that. And we've started at the bottom.

The sole on Sperry's biggest selling boat shoe is made of a rubber compound. Timberland's is a long-lasting, rugged Vibram® sole.

Theirs is anti-skid, anti-slip; excellent on boats. So is ours.

But where Sperry's biggest selling boat shoe falls down is on land. Sperry's sole is stitched directly to their uppers. When the stitching breaks, Sperry's sole flaps. Timberland's sole is bonded to a mid-sole. Ours won't flap.

But the heart of a Timberland boat shoe isn't just the sole. Like Sperry's biggest selling model, Timberland's uppers are made only of full-grain leathers. Unlike Sperry's, which have an applied pigment

Timberland uses oil or silicone-impregnated leathers. They remain soft and supple for the life of the shoe. Sperry's biggest selling model has an applied pigment finish

Our laces are thick rawhide. Our eyelets are solid brass. Sperry eyelets are painted aluminum, which can chip and peel.

An abrasion count measures a sole's resistance to abrasion, a good indication of durability. The higher the number, the better. Timberland's count is 140, more than any other leading manufacturer.*

finish, Timberland's are silicone or oil-impregnated. Ours look more natural and feel softer than theirs.

We use only solid brass eyelets. They use painted aluminum ones.

The result of using only the highest quality materials and Timberland's unmatched handsewn moccasin construction is a boat shoe so comfortable, the breaking-in period ends the day you put

them on.

So what it comes down to is this: You can get a pair of boat shoes designed to hold up well just on a boat. Or a pair of boat shoes designed to hold up.

Timberland
The Timberland Company,
P.O. Box 370, Newmarket, New Hampshire 03857

*NBS abrasion tests conducted according to ASTM standards. Actual wear you get out of Timberland boat shoes depends on individual usage.

FIGURE 14–21 (*concluded*)

Some Creative Execution Issues

Some important creative execution issues that are important for marketing managers to understand are: (1) the use of likable and entertaining appeals, (2) provision of meaningful product information, (3) the use of comparative advertising claims, and (4) the avoidance of excessive repetition.

Likable and entertaining appeals.   An adage of an earlier era was that advertising does not have to be liked to be effective. Undoubtedly there is truth to this in that it is not the purpose of advertising to entertain. But it is equally erroneous to allege that what the consumer thinks of the message and its execution is irrelevant. Today's consumer is increasingly screening out advertising he deems to be obnoxious, irrelevant, or dull. Therefore, increasing attempts are being made to create likable and entertaining appeals.

It should be stressed, however, that a message does not have to be humorous to be entertaining. While there are some undeniable benefits to humor, a great many casualties have been due to it as well.[12] One of the most enjoyable campaigns, for example, was the prize-winning "Excedrin Headache" campaign. It was soon dropped and the company returned to a straight product benefit appeal for the reason that sales dropped severely. Humor can inhibit persuasion unless it is properly used. As a result, most authorities recommend against its use, except in unusual circumstances. A long running successful use of humor is presented in Figure 14–18.

Meaningful product information.   The volume of competitive products on the market has led consumers to become outspoken in their demands that advertisements provide information which is useful in product-buying decisions. Considerable use is made of all types of demonstrations and believable claims based on objective presentation of product benefits. The mere listing of product attributes is not enough, however. These attributes will be seen by the consumer as significant only when they are shown to meet the demands of his or her evaluative criteria for that specific decision. Mennen E deodorant for example, died an early market death for the reason that product attributes were not perceived as offering consumer benefits.

Comparative advertising claims.   One way in which some advertisers have attempted to provide meaningful product information is through the use of comparative advertising executions. This is where competitors are explicitly named and direct comparisons are made to the advertised product. The Victor ad in Figure 14–9 and the Intellivision ad in Figure 14–14

---

[12] Brian Sternthal and C. S. Craig, "Humor in Advertising," *Journal of Marketing* 37 (1975), pp. 12–18. See also Harry W. McMahan, "No Joking; Humor Sells!" *Advertising Age,* December 29, 1980, p. 19.

are examples of comparative ads. This type of advertising execution is currently very controversial. A study done by Ogilvy & Mather drew the conclusion that such ads are ineffective. This study concluded that comparative advertising: (1) increases awareness of competitors, (2) decreases belief claims, (3) increases misidentification, and does not increase brand identification.[13] A more recent Ogilvy & Mather study did allow that comparative ads can work "but only under very limited conditions," as a "short-term tactical weapon."[14] The research indicated that comparative ads work "only when a brand has a clear and important functional performance advantage over a larger competitor that can be visually demonstrated or otherwise clearly explained in advertising, and which the consumer will recognize when product trial occurs."[15] More academic research in this area gives mixed results.[16] A study by Shimp and Dyer concluded that noncomparative ads were demonstrably more effective by giving greater recall, being perceived as more believable, truthful, informative, and elicited more favorable reactions. Comparative ads were seen as more interesting, and equivalant on brand identification.[17] Another study concluded that comparative ads are no more or less informative than noncomparative ads.[18]

The FTC actively encourages comparative ads and holds that "comparative advertising provides valuable information concerning the performance, attributes, or costs of two or more competing products or services."[19] Indeed, comparative ads seem to have helped some brands such as: Savin copiers, Pepsi-Cola, Life Savers Care*Free sugarless gum, C&C Cola, and Comtrex cold capsules.[20] In using the comparative approach, the advertiser must be careful not to unfairly represent the competitor's product or lawsuits are likely to ensue.

Avoidance of excessive repetition. Repetition is a fundamental tenet of learning theory, and there is a large amount of evidence documenting the fact that repetition can enhance message reception (awareness and com-

---

[13] "Comparative Ads Ineffective: O & M Study," *Advertising Age,* October 13, 1975, p. 16.

[14] "Some Comparative Ads Work, O & M Concedes," *Advertising Age,* November 3, 1980, p. 6.

[15] Ibid.

[16] For an overview of the issues see William L. Wilkie and Paul W. Farris, "Comparison Advertising: Problems and Potential," *Journal of Marketing,* October 1975, pp. 7–15.

[17] Terence A. Shimp and David C. Dyer, "The Effect of Comparative Advertising Mediated by Market Position of Sponsoring Brand," *Journal of Advertising,* pp. 13–19.

[18] William M. Pride, Charles W. Lamb, and Barbara A. Pletcher, "The Informativeness of Comparative Advertisements: An Empirical Investigation," *Journal of Advertising,* pp. 29–35, 48.

[19] "Should an Ad Identify Brand X?" *Business Week,* September 24, 1979, p. 156.

[20] "Some Comparative Ads Work, O & M Concedes," *Advertising Age,* November 3, 1980, p. 6.

prehension), retention, attitude change, and behavioral change. Repetition, however, is one of the primary causes of consumer complaints, and there is no question that this strategy can be carried beyond the point of optimum response. When there has been undue repetition, the message is said to be satiated or worn out. Greater attention must now be paid to "wearout" to minimize the consumer revolt, and it is by no means easy to evaluate.

Each message performs in a unique manner, and no generalizations on the relationship between performance and wearout are possible. Some implications can be cited from the body of research findings, however, such as these:

1. Repetition aids consumer learning and hence can be effectively utilized at the start of a new campaign.
2. Repetition can help establish products or brands that are new to a particular medium.
3. A pool or group of commercials should not wear out as quickly as a single commercial, given the same frequency of exposure.
4. When it is not possible to produce a number of varied commercials, introduce several claims within the message to lengthen the learning process.
5. When several commercials are produced, introduce significant variations, or they are likely to be perceived as the same and hence wear out more quickly.
6. A commercial with humor or a single point wears out quickly.
7. Commercials for infrequently purchased products wear out more slowly for the reason that only a fraction of the audience are prospects at any given point of time.
8. The greater the time span between repetition, the longer a message can be run.
9. A message can be reintroduced after a period of absence from the air and hence be perceived as new.
10. Wearout is greatest among heavy television viewers.
11. If the budget is limited, a single commercial spread out over a period of time may produce greater learning than airing of a pool of commercials.
12. Commercials that involve the viewer wear out more slowly than those with a straightforward message.
13. Copy testing predicated on a single exposure can shed little light on wearout.
14. Performance must be tracked over time to assess wearout.
15. Only good commercials wear out—those that are ineffective to begin with will lose nothing.[21]

It is obvious that wearout must be monitored in the course of a campaign. This is easiest to do in terms of awareness. Once knowledge of, say, a brand name or product attribute peaks, serious consideration should

---

[21] A. Greenberg and C. Suttoni, "Television Commercial Wearout." Reprinted from the *Journal of Advertising Research* 13 (1973), p. 53. © Copyright (1973), by the Advertising Research Foundation.

be given to change. Changes in positive versus negative reactions can be monitored for the same purpose.

ANALYSIS OF THE MESSAGE

With all the millions of possible creative executions for an ad, the reader may conclude that it is impossible to differentiate a good advertisement from a poor one. Yet there comes a time when such a decision must be made so that time or space can be bought. In part this evaluation must be made on the basis of informed judgment, and some use also is usually made of copy tests (pretests).

Judgmental Analysis

This section will present some general criteria which can be used to evaluate both strategy and execution and then suggest some more detailed considerations which pertain strictly to execution.[22]

General criteria. The Levi's brand name is now used on many different types of products: jeans, men's jackets and slacks, women's slacks and tops, and so on. One television commercial designed to enhance the whole Levi's brand name is reproduced in storyboard form in Figure 14–22. This commercial cost $250,000 to produce. Without extensive testing how would one judge its effectiveness? What criteria should be utilized for this purpose?

The most important factor to consider is whether or not the commercial is "on strategy," that is, does it execute the creative strategy effectively in terms of appealing to the target audience and registering the message specified in the copy platform? The strategy here was to appeal to men and women 18–34 years old, and to reinforce the quality image of all Levi's products from jeans to sportswear. In general terms, the commercial appears to be "on strategy" very well. Quality is stressed in almost every frame on the board.

Evaluation of execution. An advertisement should be *memorable* in that it attracts and holds attention. It also must register its intended message and hence achieve its *persuasive* objective. The following types of questions are useful in assessing whether both memorability and persuasiveness have been achieved:

1. *Does the picture tell the story?* Given the large volume of competing advertising, no message has more than a fraction of a second to attract and hold the consumer's attention. Thus the visual portion of the message must register the message, without sole reliance on words.

---

[22] See Harry W. McMahan, "24 Questions to Help You Evaluate Your Commercials," *Advertising Age*, June 11, 1973, p. 49; also Roman and Haas, "Creative Secrets."

FIGURE 14–22
Levi's Trademark Commercial

FOOTE, CONE & BELDING/HONIG

Client: Levi Strauss & Co.
Product: Corporate
Title: "Brand Name"
Commercial No: LZMB 7621

MALE (VO): C'mon old Trademark, time for your walk. Where will you take me? Sure wish you could talk.

I know what you'd tell me. How your family began with

the same Levi's blue jeans worn by this man.

Hey, here come more Levi's; red, yellow and blue.

Free wheeling kiddos are wearing them, too!

And what a surprise! Look who's been window shopping for clothes.

Yeah, a gal in her Levi's instinctively knows of your special appeal. Enough of this kissing, little Register Mark.

Time that we meet some guys by the park. Dressed in your newest addition. Sums it up right there: Levi's Sportswear.

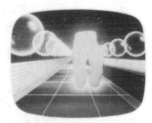

Hey, Trademark, this looks like the place where tomorrows begin.

Your family's future — sure looks like it should.

That's right, little Trademark —

Levi's don't have to be blue — just have to be good!

This ad is used by courtesy of Levi Strauss & Co.; the advertising agency is Foote, Cone & Belding/Honig; the commercial was produced by Bob Able & Associates.

2. *Are the words appropriate?* Do they communicate product benefits in terms that are meaningful to the target audience?
3. *Is one clear theme registered by the total advertisement?* Rarely will attention be held for a sufficient period to register more than one or two ideas, so the emphasis must be on a single-minded presentation of message theme.
4. *Is the brand name registered?* Many times the brand name is not stressed, with the result that the reader or viewer fails to associate message and product.
5. *Is the tone appropriate?* In other words, is the style of message appropriate for the product? Demonstrations are best used with unique product attributes that can be illustrated. When this is not the case, the tone or impression left may interfere with the intended message. Humor is more appropriate when no unique product benefits are present; other times it may be entertaining but ineffective.
6. *Is the advertisement distinctive?* Does it stand out from the noise? The dangers of novelty have been stressed, but a message must have an element of distinctiveness in view of mass media clutter.

The Levi's commercial meets these guidelines rather well. Its visualization stands by itself because words are not required to register the message. The words, however, focus on product benefits, and the result is a single-minded registration of the "quality" theme. The viewer is also attracted by the promise of benefits in the very first frame, and the brand name is registered quickly and repetitively without carrying repetition to excess. The tone is serious and authoritative. Finally, there is distinctiveness in the creative blending of real people and animation.

Thus not only is the Levi's commercial, generally speaking, "on strategy," but the execution appears to be effective. Obviously these conclusions are based on judgment, and there is considerable room for error. In the final analysis, the message cannot be fully evaluated apart from pretest research, and Levi's found that this was an effective commercial, registering one of the highest on the air scores (see Chapter 15) ever: a score of 59 versus a norm of 25.

Copy Testing

It is obvious that a point is reached where reliance on judgment is insufficient. For this reason, use is made of pretests (or copy tests, as they are more frequently referred to in the trade). This is a topic of discussion in Chapter 15.

SUMMARY

This chapter began with a distinction between strategy and execution. The fundamental issues concerned with creative strategy were reviewed in the first section, and the subject of creative execution then was approached through analysis of significant trends in types of appeals used and methods of presentation. It was stressed that there are no rules which can serve as conclusive guides to effective execution. Most of the so-called creative rules are based on ways to attract and hold attention, but this is only part of the task which must be accomplished by the message. It also must achieve its intended persuasive objective, and there is no way that rules can be established for this purpose.

It was also shown by a review of relevant literature that hypotheses and hard-and-fast rules are available from the behavioral sciences that can be utilized in designing and executing creative strategy.

The chapter ended with a brief review of the types of questions which can be raised in a judgmental evaluation of strategy and execution. While these guidelines can be used in differentiating a poor message from a good one, there is no substitute for pretesting through survey research.

Review and Discussion Questions

1. Is the description of market targets generally used in media selection also sufficient for use in determining creative strategy? Why, or why not?
2. What factors should be encompassed in the creative platform?
3. One authority states that the brand name should be stressed in every headline. Do you agree? Why?
4. Consult advertisements from past decades beginning in 1920. What changes do you observe? From these advertisements alone, what can be said about the social changes in these decades?
5. Assume that you have been selected as one of the judges who must select the 10 best from a group of 100 television commercials. What *two* criteria would you use for this purpose? Why?
6. Some contend that research hampers the creative person and constrains imagination. Comment.
7. What can be done, if anything, to stimulate greater use of research by advertising writers and artists?
8. Many critics contend that too much advertising today is "gimmicky" and "cute." The argument is that creative people are carried away with attention-attracting devices and are forgetting that good advertising must sell. How would you analyze this criticism?
9. In Figure 14–21 two ads are reproduced. Which do you think is more effective? Why?

CHAPTER 15
Measurement of Advertising Effectiveness

A persistent question is whether advertising effectiveness can be measured. The response in the past was mixed, but about 80 percent of advertisers utilize some type of effectiveness measurement.[1] Research orientation is becoming increasingly commonplace, largely because management is demanding proof that funds invested pay off. Measurement tools are being used with greater sophistication as new techniques are developed, although there is still room for substantial progress in the area.

Some feel that creativity and copy testing are incompatible. This justification has little merit, because creative imagination can produce *ineffective* copy. In reality, many artists and copywriters do not want to be held accountable for the productivity of their output. Part of the difficulty is that some managements use copy tests as a "report card." A better approach is to give artists and writers possession of copy-testing results with the option to use them as they see fit and to reveal or not to reveal the results.

The authors feel, on balance, that the arguments for copy testing outweigh the arguments against it. The objective is not to find a definitive measure of communication success. The presently available methodology

---

[1] Dik W. Twedt, *1978 Survey of Marketing Research* (Chicago: American Marketing Association, 1978), p. 41.

will not justify such a goal. Rather, all that can be provided is a good indication of whether or not copy will be comprehended and responded to as intended. While this does not guarantee production of a good advertisement, *it substantially lowers the risk of failure.* At the very least, copy tests will differentiate a poor message from a good one if properly used. What they cannot do definitively at the present time is to distinguish a *good* message from a *great* one. This type of fine discrimination awaits further methodological development.

Figure 15–1 is a classification of the most widely used measurement methods, classified first into those most useful in measuring response to the *advertisement* itself or its contents (awareness, comprehension, liking, and so on). The second classification differentiates actual impact of the

FIGURE 15–1

Classification of Advertising Effectiveness Measures

	Advertising related (*reception or response to the message itself and its contents*)	Product related (*impact of message on product awareness, liking, intention to buy, or use*)

Laboratory measures (*respondent aware of testing and measurement process*)	**Cell I**
	
	Pretesting procedures
	
	1. Consumer jury
	2. Portfolio tests
	3. Readability tests
	4. Physiological measures
	    Eye Camera
	    Tachistoscope
	    GSR/PDR
		Cell II
		
		Pretesting procedures
		
		1. Theater tests
		2. Trailer tests
		3. Laboratory stores

Real-world measures (*respondent unaware of testing and measurement process*)	**Cell III** *Pretesting procedures* 1. Dummy advertising vehicles 2. Inquiry tests 3. On-the-air tests *Posttesting procedures* 1. Recognition tests 2. Recall tests 3. Association measures 4. Combination measures	**Cell IV** *Pretesting and posttesting procedures* 1. Pre-post tests 2. Sales tests 3. Mini-market tests

Source: Adapted from the classification schema utilized by Professor Ivan Ross at the University of Minnesota.

message on *product* awareness, attitude, or usage. These data can be gathered under either *laboratory* conditions in which the respondents are aware they are being measured or *"real world"* conditions, in which there is no awareness of the measurement process. This chapter evaluates measures which are useful both in *pretesting* a message and in assessing its effectiveness following its placement in the media, as part of the whole advertising plan (*posttesting*).

CELL I: ADVERTISING-RELATED LABORATORY MEASURES

Under the category of advertising-related laboratory measures are those that yield data on attention, comprehension, retention or response to the message itself in a laboratory-type research situation, as opposed to measures under real-world conditions. A variety of approaches which primarily measure the ability of a stimulus to attract and hold attention are discussed. The usefulness of what are fundamentally copy-testing procedures is greatest in pretesting advertisements, as was pointed out in the previous chapter.

PRETESTING PROCEDURES

1. The Consumer Jury

Consumers frequently are asked to analyze advertisements and rate the probable success on the assumption that "if the layman is superior to the advertising expert in his conscious opinion as to the effectiveness of an advertisement, it is only because he is a better judge of what influences him than is an outsider."[2] Typically, 50 to 100 consumers from the target audience are interviewed either individually or in small groups.

In one method referred to as the order-of-merit rating, a member of the jury (usually a sample of from 50 to 100 representative consumers) is asked to rank in order a group of layouts or copy blocks usually presented in rough, unfinished form and often mocked up on separate sheets. The questions might ask, for example:

1. Which of these advertisements would you most likely read if you saw it in a magazine?
2. Which of these headlines would interest you the most in reading further?
3. Which advertisement convinces you most of the quality of the product?

---

[2] Charles H. Sandage and Vernon Fryburger, *Advertising: Theory and Practice,* 10th ed. (Homewood, Ill.: Richard D. Irwin, 1981), p. 537.

4. Which layout do you think would be most effective in causing you
    to buy?

The questioning progresses from the second best alternative to the worst.
The verdict presumably indicates the relative effectiveness of each alternative presentation.

Order-of-merit rating is of questionable value, for several significant
reasons:

1. It probably is asking too much of anyone to predict future behavior
    during and immediately after communication exposure.
2. Ranking of many alternatives can be exceedingly difficult, with the
    result that the ratings have little validity.
3. Some people have a tendency to rate one or two preferred alternatives
    high on all characteristics, just as they emphasize the good traits of
    a close friend while overlooking bad attributes. This distortion in
    judgment, called the halo effect, cannot be eliminated.

These problems are sufficiently serious that order-of-merit ratings usually
are abandoned for more precise approaches.

A better approach is to utilize some type of rating scale to elicit intensity
of preference for each stimulus. No attempt is made to provide a ranking.
In one example advertisements were developed to influence public attitudes toward the Prudential Insurance Company and to cause people to
think better of the company than of the insurance industry in general.
Twenty-five attitude scale statements were developed, focusing on aspects
of the company and its operation. Respondents were asked to rate on a
10-point scale the degree to which the statements applied to most life
insurance companies and then to the company whose advertisements they
were viewing in disguised form, with company identity blocked out. The
effectiveness of the advertisement was judged on the basis of the extent
to which it induced a change in the rating of the company to make it
more favorable than that for the industry. Meaningful differences were
produced, and it was possible to isolate the most effective creative treatment.

The advantages of the scale are that a basis is provided to isolate
dimensions of opinion; the technique is standardized and susceptible to
comparison over time; it is reliable and replicable; full allowance is made
for individual frames of reference; and problems of question phrasing
are eased. Also, norms giving average results by product class or even
the previous ads for the same brand can be calculated. Almost all major
copy testing services give norm scores. Furthermore, determination of
degrees of intensity of feeling provides a basis for ranking of alternatives
and assessment of how well each performs against predetermined norms.

Finally, the wording of questions reduces the danger that the individual will "play expert" and distort his or her reported opinion.

Consumer jury measures are widely used. Many experts feel that the artificiality of the questioning procedure introduces bias so that the ratings can have questionable validity. For this reason, more use is now made of the other measures discussed in this section as well as the real-world measures to be discussed later.

2. Portfolio Tests

The portfolio test method requires the exposure of a group of respondents to a portfolio consisting of both test and control advertisements. The principal criterion of effectiveness is playback of the content following exposure. The test advertisement that induces the highest recall of content presumably will be most effective in capturing and holding attention.

Portfolio tests are widely used, but vigorous attacks have been directed at the pretest use of this device. Critics contend that recall scores can vary from alternative to alternative for several reasons:

1. Variations can enter due to interviewing errors or memory defects, although this can be true of *any* research.
2. There may be legitimate differences between advertisements.
3. Differences may arise as a result of the consumer's interest in the products being promoted.
4. Also it is argued that recall scores are not appropriate measures for low-involvement learning situations. Recognition is a better measure in these circumstances.

Variation from the second source, of course, is the fundamental premise of the portfolio test, but it is felt by some that interest in the product, the third source, may be the most important factor. If so, the portfolio method clearly is not differentiating between advertisements on the basis of variations in creative treatment.

For the portfolio method to perform as claimed, scores on recall of the control advertisements should vary less from test to test than scores on the stimuli under analysis. Yet data have been reported to indicate this relationship does not hold true, and it appears that product interest dominates all other factors. Apparently interest in the product seems to affect memory of the advertisements viewed and thereby obscures real differences between the stimuli.

These arguments against the portfolio test are plausible. Perhaps momentary reexposure to the alternatives viewed in the portfolio would sharpen memory and minimize distortions entering from product interest.

Regardless of the danger of memory distortion, this test serves its purpose well if recall data correlate with readership scores following investment of funds in the campaign. Each user must be satisfied that the predictive power of this device is sufficient to warrant the costs of research.

3. Analysis of Readability

Procedures are available to permit analysis of the readability of copy without consumer interviewing. The foremost method was developed by Rudolph Flesch, whose formula is in wide use.[3] The Flesch formula focuses on the human interest appeal in the material, length of sentences, and familiarity of words. These factors are found to correlate with the ability of persons with varying educational backgrounds to comprehend written material.

Readability of advertising copy is assessed by determining the average number of syllables per 100 words. These factors are then substituted into the Flesch formula, the results are compared with predetermined norms for the target audience. It is usually found that copy is understood most easily when sentences are short, words are concrete and familiar, and frequent personal references are made.

Mechanical rules should not be observed to the extent that copy becomes stilted or unoriginal. The Flesch method is only a means to check communication efficiency, and gross errors in understanding can be detected and avoided. It should always be used, however, in connection with other pretest procedures.

4. Physiological Measures

Also within the laboratory-advertising related methods are a series of physiological measurement procedures.[4]

The eye camera. For many years it has been possible to track eye movements over advertising copy through use of the eye camera. The route that a person's eyes follow is then superimposed on the layout to determine which parts appear to capture and hold attention and whether or not various elements are perceived in the order intended by the creative person.

Eye camera results provide a guide to aid in designing the layout so that the eye follows the intended path, but the findings contain a large degree of ambiguity. In the first place, exposure is undertaken in highly unnatural conditions, and it is questionable that resulting eye movement patterns are similar to those expected when the consumer is not looking into a large apparatus. Furthermore, eye attraction does not necessarily reflect the person's thoughts or indicate success in capturing attention.

---

[3] Rudolph Flesch, *The Art of Readable Writing* (New York: Harper & Row, 1974).

[4] For a review of articles in this area see Paul J. Watson and Robert J. Gatchel, "Autonomic Measures of Advertising," *Journal of Advertising Research* 19, no. 3 (June 1979), pp. 15–26.

Lingering at one point may also indicate difficulty in comprehension. For these reasons, the eye camera has never achieved wide usage. However, one firm has argued that eye tracking will replace recall and persuasion tests in the 1980s.[5] To do this they will have to demonstrate the validity of their procedure.

The tachistoscope. This laboratory device is basically a slide projector with attachments enabling the presentation of stimuli under varying conditions of speed and illumination. The tachistoscope has come to be a useful tool for many advertising researchers especially in magazine and outdoor advertising. The Leo Burnett agency, for example, uses it to assess the rate at which an advertisement conveys information. The speed of response is recorded for various elements of an advertisement (illustration, product, and brand), and it has been found that high readership scores correlate with speed of recognition of the elements under analysis. Response to visualization seems to be especially important.

About 20,000 persons are tested with the tachistoscope each year at the Leo Burnett agency. The typical sample size is from 10 to 20, and no person is tested more than four times during any one year. As an indication of success, tachistoscopic measurement verified quick recognition of the Allstate Insurance Company name in an advertisement, a basic promotional objective, and the campaign built upon this finding was felt to be highly successful. All that Burnett researchers claim, however, is measurement of physical perception; response from this point on is solely a function of the copy.

GSR/PDR. Galvanic skin response (GSR) and pupil dilation response (PDR) measure different aspects of attention attraction. GSR measures first, the decline in electrical resistance of the skin to a passage of current and second, changes in the potential difference between two areas of body surface. When GSR elevates it is felt to be an accurate indicator of *arousal* in response to a stimulus. PDR, on the other hand, measures minute differences in pupil size and appears to be a sensitive measure of the amount of information or load processed within the central nervous system in response to an incoming stimulus. At one time it was widely claimed that PDR measured emotional response, and several published studies purported to document that it could isolate attitudinal reaction to marketing stimuli. The weight of current evidence, however, makes this interpretation highly questionable.

A series of studies was undertaken at The Ohio State University using both GSR and PDR with a variety of audio and print stimuli.[6] It was

---

[5] Bernie Whalen, "Eye Tracking Technology to Replace Day-after-Recall by '84," *Marketing News,* November 27, 1981, p. 18.

[6] These are reviewed in J. S. Hensel, "Physiological Measures of Advertising Effectiveness: A Theoretical and Empirical Investigation." (Ph.D. diss., Ohio State University, 1970.)

found fairly consistently that there is good short-term and long-term retention when both GSR and PDR are high in response to an advertisement. In addition, there is some tentative evidence that GSR also correlates with attitude change, but this finding needs further investigation.[7]

CELL II: PRODUCT-RELATED LABORATORY MEASURES

Some techniques can be utilized under laboratory conditions to determine the effects of the message on the product or service itself, such as awareness, attitude shift, changes in buying intentions, and so on. Included in this category are the theater test, trailer tests, and laboratory stores. These methods are again fundamentally pretesting procedures.

1. Theater Tests

Theater tests are a means whereby changes in consumer product preference after exposure to advertisements can be assessed. Typically, tickets are mailed to about 350–1000 respondent households, to yield a sample of 250–600. Respondents are also recruited by telephone and mall intercept. ARS and ASI Market Research, Inc. offer these types of test. The research format is essentially the same for all testing sessions: inviting people to view new television shows with commercials inserted in the usual place. A drawing is held before the showing, and each consumer is offered his or her choice of various products as gifts. Product choices are noted, and then the show and commercials are viewed. Another drawing and offer of gifts is held after exposure, and changes in stated brand preference are noted. Written comments are also solicited on the programs and the commercials.

At first glance it would appear that changes in stated preferences for gift products would in no way be related meaningfully to advertising exposure. Some rather dramatic conclusions, however, have been derived from the theater tests. Those campaigns rated as superior on the basis of changing product preferences tended to produce increases in sales as more dollars were invested in advertising. On the other hand, increased investment in inferior campaigns allegedly was found at times to *decrease* sales.

A definitive evaluation of the theater procedure must await disclosure of more details of research designed for purposes of validation. Many advertisers and agency executives have voiced dissatisfaction regarding its predictive ability, although it has been successfully used by a number of firms. On the other hand, a study reported by Robert D. Buzzell con-

---

[7] Unpublished studies at The Ohio State University under the direction of James F. Engel.

cluded that preference measurements were related to short-term changes in market share;[8] this would tend to substantiate the validity of the technique for this purpose.

Theater tests may tap a dimension of response which enables reasonably accurate prediction of advertising success, and for this reason it is in wide use. Respondents presumably are unaware that they are rating advertisements, and the tendency toward "buyer expertise" may thus be eliminated. There are also variations of this method in use.

2. Trailer Tests

Respondents may be brought to a central location, often a portable trailer or van set up in a shopping center, where they are shown several advertisements with or without surrounding editorial material or programming. Usually a comparative evaluation is made of two or more executions of the same theme. Respondents are told that the product can be made to different formulations and are shown copy describing each. Then they are asked to chose between the two formulations, and questioning reveals what the commercial communicates. While the technique is artificial, it is felt by many to be a useful way to measure comprehension of copy. Furthermore, it is quite inexpensive.

3. Laboratory Stores

The laboratory store is a variation on the theater technique described above. Respondents are exposed to advertising under various types of conditions and then are permitted to shop in a small store. Usually coupons or chits are provided which can be redeemed for actual merchandise. In this way actual product movement in response to advertising can be monitored.

CELL III: ADVERTISING-RELATED MEASUREMENT UNDER REAL-WORLD CONDITIONS

Procedures used in the second major category of technique depicted in Figure 15–1, real-world measures, usually involve exposure under real-world conditions such as would normally be encountered in the consumer's home. The greater realism provided is felt by most researchers to enhance the validity of the resulting data.

This section discusses the fairly extensive group of real-world measures of response to or liking for the message itself. Some are usually used for pretesting of the message prior to investment in time or space while

---

[8] Robert D. Buzzell, "Predicting Short-Term Changes in Market Share as a Function of Advertising Strategy," *Journal of Marketing Research,* August 1964, p. 31.

others are usually used for posttesting following airing or viewing. We begin our discussion by examining pretesting procedures.

PRETESTING PROCEDURES

1. Dummy Advertising Vehicles

Many testing organizations use a dummy magazine for purposes of pretesting, and accurate predictions of response are possible. Editorial features of lasting interest are permanent items in this magazine; the only variations in the five yearly editions are test advertisements. Each printing is distributed to a random sample of homes in various geographical areas. Readers are told that the publisher is interested in evaluations of editorial content and instructed to read the magazine in a normal fashion. A return interview focuses on both the editorial content and advertisements. Each advertisement is scored on recall, extent of copy readership, and whether or not the advertisement induces product interest.

The use of dummy vehicles is subject to the same criticisms as the portfolio test, but this procedure possesses the distinct advantage that advertisements are tested under completely natural surroundings—normal exposure in the home. Recall of content under such circumstances is likely to produce a more realistic indication of advertising success.

2. Inquiry Tests

Inquiry tests measure advertising effectiveness on the basis of return of coupons from advertisements run under normal conditions in printed media. Different creative treatments may be compared in several ways: (1) by running them in successive issues of the same medium, (2) by running them simultaneously in issues of different media, and (3) by taking advantage of "split-run" privileges offered by some media whereby alternate copies carry different versions of the message. The split-run procedure is more widely used, because all variables other than creative differences between stimuli are held constant.

The inquiry tests can focus on a number of creative variations: (1) one advertisement versus a completely different version, (2) variations in type or other elements of the same appeal, (3) summed inquiries compared over the total run of two or more campaigns, and (4) the effectiveness of different media when the same advertisement is run in each.

The advantages are apparent in that no interviews are required, and quantitative analysis of data usually presents no problems. As a result, the costs are not excessive. This approach, however, suffers from crucial limitations. First, the presence of a coupon attracts attention to the copy for this reason alone, and true differences in creative treatment can be obscured. Second, many people may read the copy and not return the coupon. Certain people are more prone to take this action than others, and "volunteer bias" can greatly overstate or understate the true effectiveness. One must constantly remember that the problem of pretesting copy is very different from the testing of individual elements. For example, the advertising manager of International Correspondence Schools has searched extensively for pretesting techniques that can accurately predict at least the relative inquiry pull of various ads. Just as there seems to be no relationship between scores and coupon returns, none of these methods, when tested, has yielded data that would indicate any useful predictive ability. Finally, coupon return bears no special relationship to advertising effectiveness, for attitude change, changes in awareness, the communication of copy points, and a host of additional responses are not tested.

It must be concluded that the disadvantages far outweigh the advantages of the coupon-return method for most purposes. The inquiry test should be used only when coupon return is the objective of the advertisement. When this is so, it is a completely valid measure of response.

3. On-The-Air-Tests

Some research services measure response to advertisements which are inserted into actual television or radio programs in certain test markets. The "on-the-air" test is an example. The advantages and disadvantages are identical to those encountered in the use of dummy vehicles. In television some of the best known services used are: Burke Marketing Services' Day-After Recall (DAR), Gallup and Robinson's Total Prime Time (TPT), and the Burke's AdTel cable system.[9]

DAR tests typically involve about 200 respondents who are contacted by telephone in any of 34 available cities and who claim to have watched a specific television show the night before. Measures are taken in both unaided and aided recall fashion. To begin with respondents are asked if they remember seeing a commercial for a product in the product class of interest. If they do not, then they are asked if they remember a commercial for the specific test brand. Those who recall the ad in either fashion are asked what they recall about the specific copy points of the ad. The DAR score for the Levi's television ad presented in Figure 14–22 was 57 percent recall against a norm of 25.

DAR tests dominate the television pretesting business, but do have some critics. Foote Cone & Belding, the advertising agency, recently released a study comparing DAR tests and their own method for creative

---

[9] This whole section is based upon Thomas C. Kinnear and James R. Taylor, *Marketing Research: An Applied Approach,* 2nd ed. (New York: McGraw-Hill, 1983), chap. 24.

executions that are "thinking" based and "feeling" based.[10] They proposed a *masked recognition test* (MRT) where they deleted all audio and video reference to the brand name in a commercial which respondents saw in its entirety the previous day. The respondent is then asked to identify the brand in the masked commercial. The reason for this approach is that DAR tests ask consumers to verbalize the advertising message, and it is believed that this is especially difficult when the appeal is emotional. All the MRTs so far have involved on-air cable audiences who have agreed in advance to watch the program in which the ad appeared. Scores for "feeling" ads are significantly higher for MRT than for DAR.

Additionally, a study conducted by J. Walter Thompson advertising, and supported by six major advertisers, indicated that a TV show's environment was an important influence on the effects of commercials on audiences, and that DAR scores should reflect this.[11] In one instance a brand recall was 41 percent on one show and 53 percent on another.[12] This raises questions about reported DAR norm scores, and comparisons scores of different ads that are tested on different shows. Burke has indicated that their methods of measurement are different than J. Walter Thompson's and that their research on this issue indicates: "that program has no effect on a commercial's related test score when Burke's standard procedures are followed. Burke is aware, however, of some broadcast situations which can affect a commercial score, and we advise our clients not to test in these situations."[13]

Total Prime Time (TPT) is a service of Gallop and Robinson (G&R) that can test commercials that appear in prime time. They survey about 700 men and 700 women in the Philadelphia area. Qualified respondents are those who have watched at least 30 minutes of network prime time the previous night. Another approach that is used is G&R's In-View. Here respondents are called in advance and invited to watch the show in which the test ad will appear. About 150 men and 150 women are used in In-View, again all from the Philadelphia area.

Measures taken for both TPT and In-View include:

1. Proved commercial registration (PCR)—percentage who can recall (from company or brand cues), and accurately describe the ad.
2. Idea communication—the percentage of recallers who can recall specific sales points in the ad.

---

[10] "FCR Says Masked-Recognition Test Yields Truer Remembering Measures than Day-after-Recall Test," *Marketing News,* June 12, 1981, pp. 1–2.

[11] "On-Air Ad Testing Misses Show Differences: Yuspeh," *Marketing News,* April 6, 1979, p. 4.

[12] Ibid.

[13] Ibid.

3. Favorable attitude—percentage of favorable comments about the brand offered by the respondent.

AdTel, a division of Burke, offers testing of alternative ads at the same time in the same show environment through the use of cable television. By using special dual-cable systems in selected test cities, AdTel can direct an "A" ad and a "B" ad to different cable subscribers who do not know the difference. Purchased diaries are kept by a panel of people who are in the A and B groups. Thus the measure of effectiveness is actual purchase.

POSTTESTING PROCEDURES

The following real-world tests on advertisements are usually done on a posttest basis.

1. Recognition Tests

The readership of printed advertisements has long been assessed using a standard technique called "recognition measurement" which was developed by Daniel Starch. In 1981, Starch Irra Hooper, Inc. measured about 100,000 ads in over 100 magazines and newspapers. The Starch method is described in detail because other related procedures are quite similar.

The nature of the Starch method. The Starch organization annually surveys approximately 30,000 advertisements in nearly 1,000 consumer and farm magazines, business publications, and newspapers. A national sample consisting of interviews in 20 to 30 geographical areas is chosen for each study. Although the sample is not a random selection, attempts are made to parallel the circulation makeup of each medium under analysis.

Interviewers are assigned a given number of readers over 18 years of age with certain demographic characteristics in terms of income and location. Studies usually include from 100 to 200 interviews per sex, and the quota for each interviewer is fairly small.

The interview is conducted in the respondent's home. The interviewer commences by asking whether or not the particular periodical has been read prior to the interview. If the answer is affirmative, the issue is opened at a page specified in advance to guarantee that the fatigue resulting from the interview will not unduly bias advertising appearing at the back of the issue. The respondent is then asked, for each advertisement, "Did you see or read any part of the advertisement?" If the answer is yes, he or she is asked to indicate exactly what parts of the layout and copy were seen or read.

Three principal readership scores are reported:

1. *Noted*—the percentage of readers who remember seeing the advertisement.
2. *Seen-associated*—the percentage of readers who recall seeing or reading any part of the advertisement identifying the product or brand.
3. *Read most*—the percentage of readers who reported reading at least one-half of the advertisement.

Several additional scores are also reported:

1. *Readers per dollar*—the number of readers attracted by the advertisement for each dollar invested in space.
2. *Cost ratios*—the relationship between readers per dollar and the median readers per dollar for all half-page or larger advertisements in the issue. A "noted cost ratio" of 121, for example, means that the copy exceeded the par for the issue by 21 percent.
3. *Ranks*—the numerical ordering of readers per dollar for all advertisements from highest to lowest.

Data are available on the readership of component parts of each layout, such as secondary illustrations, the company signature, or various copy blocks. Figure 15–2 presents an ad with readership scores placed on it. Note that this ad appeared in Chapter 14. Did you think then that it would score as highly as it did in effectiveness (recognition)?

The Starch method is a syndicated service, and other organizations offer similar features. In addition, individual advertisers and research consultants frequently conduct private specialized readership studies.

Analysis of the recognition method.   The recognition method, especially the Starch approach, is by far the most widely used means of measuring advertising readership. However, a growing number of criticisms of the technique have been published in recent years. These criticisms for the most part are based on significant methodological questions. The potential research pitfalls which have been reported involve (1) the problem of false claiming, (2) the reproducibility of recognition scores, and (3) sensitivity to interviewer variations.

The problem of false claiming.   The interview is conducted informally, with the respondent simply being asked to indicate whether or not he or she remembers seeing a given advertisement. It has been feared that the respondent could consciously or unconsciously give a completely false reply, because no means exists to check its accuracy. Research has brought this problem into sharper perspective.

The Advertising Research Foundation undertook the Print Advertisement Research Methods study (PARM). The Starch method, among others, was subjected to intensive impartial analysis. The syndicated services studied an issue of *Life* and reported readership as usual, and the PARM staff duplicated this research using a large randomly chosen sample. The

364

FIGURE 15–2
Starch Results for Metropolitan Ad

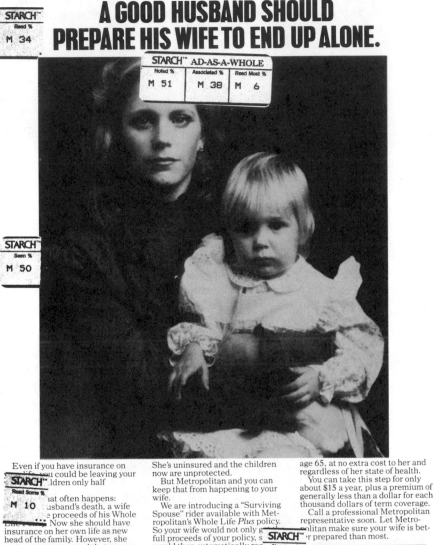

A GOOD HUSBAND SHOULD PREPARE HIS WIFE TO END UP ALONE.

STARCH™ M 34 Read %

STARCH™ AD-AS-A-WHOLE

Noted %	Associated %	Read Most %
M 51	M 38	M 6

STARCH™ Seen % M 50

Even if you have insurance on [your] life, you could be leaving your STARCH™ Read Some % M 10 [chil]dren only half [protected.]

[Here's wh]at often happens: [After a h]usband's death, a wife [receives th]e proceeds of his Whole Life Policy. Now she should have insurance on her own life as new head of the family. However, she may not want to spend that money now. Or she may find insurance unaffordab[le] STARCH™ Read % M 12 [because] of her age, or unavailabl[e because o]f her health.

She's uninsured and the children now are unprotected.

But Metropolitan and you can keep that from happening to your wife.

We are introducing a "Surviving Spouse" rider available with Metropolitan's Whole Life *Plus* policy. So your wife would not only g[et the] full proceeds of your policy, s[he] would then automatically rec[eive] term coverage on her own lif[e] equal to what you had on you[r life.] She would have that coverag[e to]

STARCH™ Signature % M 35

age 65, at no extra cost to her and regardless of her state of health.

You can take this step for only about $15 a year, plus a premium of generally less than a dollar for each thousand dollars of term coverage.

Call a professional Metropolitan representative soon. Let Metropolitan make sure your wife is better prepared than most.

✳ **Metropolitan**
Insurance Companies

METROPOLITAN REALLY STANDS BY YOU.
Life/Health/Auto/Home/Retirement

readership results were then compared, and additional analyses were undertaken to shed light on the meaning of readership data.

The analysis of recognition by the PARM staff showed a surprising tendency for scores to remain stable over time. In other words, the scores showed little variation as the interval between the date of the claimed readership of the magazine and the date of the interview increased. If the recognition score truly measures memory, the scores should exhibit a reliable tendency to decline over time. For example, the recognition of meaningful data was 97 percent after 20 minutes, as compared with 75 percent after two days. The failure of Starch scores to show this pattern indicates the possibility that factors other than memory are dictating research findings and distorting results.

Two researchers followed through on the PARM study and published findings which suggest that interest in the product leads to substantial overclaiming of readership.[14] In addition, the PARM study found that recognition of advertisements is significantly higher among owners of the advertised product. These results taken together suggest the strong possibility that product interest markedly distorts memory and leads to false advertising readership claims.

It has also been discovered that some people seem to have a kind of generalized trait which leads them to overclaim readership. In fact, for those claiming recognition of advertisements they could not possibly have seen, the average noted score for all advertisements was 75 percent! This is referred to by psychologists as a "noting set." It is related to multimagazine readership in that the greater number of magazines read, the greater the incidence of false claiming. There are several reasons for this tendency:

1. Respondents may genuinely feel that they have seen the advertisement, whereas in reality they have seen a similar version elsewhere.
2. Respondents may be saying, in effect, that they would expect to have seen such an advertisement in the issue, so they inadvertently give an incorrect report.
3. Readership may be either underreported or overreported to impress the interviewer, especially if the report is seen as indicating in some way social acceptability.
4. Interview fatigue can easily lead to underclaiming.

The Starch organization has issued a vigorous rebuttal of the research discussed above. In the first place, they claim that there is no reason to expect a dropoff in recognition scores over time. On this point the logic is not clear, and the argument is not completely convincing. They do present data, however, which indicate that false claiming declines markedly if the respondent is told that he or she may not have seen all of the advertisements presented to him or her; he or she may exercise greater

    [14] Valentine Appel and Milton L. Blum, "Ad Recognition and Response Set," *Journal of Advertising Research* 1 (June 1961), pp. 13–21.

discrimination if he or she is warned. Definitive research is obviously needed.

Perhaps all that can be done in the absence of further research is to utilize some type of controlled recognition procedure. In one of the most promising approaches, false advertisements are used to detect overclaiming, and respondents indicate the certainty with which they remember seeing and reading an advertisement. Overclaiming can be detected fairly reliably.

Reproducibility of recognition scores. The Starch organization, of course, uses a small national sample chosen by nonrandom means. Questions have arisen concerning the representativeness of this sample and the degree to which scores would differ if more rigorous sampling were used. The PARM study utilized a much larger randomly chosen sample so that these questions could be answered.

It was found that the average noted score in PARM interviews was 21.7 percent, as compared with the 26.4 percent average score reported by Starch. Although there is a small absolute difference, the coefficient of agreement was found to exceed .85 (1.00 is perfect). As a result of this close agreement, concern over the sampling procedure has abated.

Sensitivity to interviewer variations. Starch interviewers are trained not to point or to direct the respondent's replies in any way. Presumably such gestures could introduce bias. The PARM study analyzed the sensitivity of data to interviewer variations through using both experienced and inexperienced interviewers. Separate tabulation of results showed no significant differences in the noted scores produced by each group.

One might expect that the PARM results would be reassuring to the Starch organization, because a potential source of bias in recognition scores apparently is not present. They also challenge this finding, however, by noting that interviewers develop tendencies that produce either overly high or overly low claiming by respondents. It is their opinion that some of the studies criticizing the validity of Starch data have failed to control adequately for this factor.

Using recognition scores. Given the many unanswered methodological issues, what uses can be made of recognition data? Certainly the approach can be helpful in three ways:

1. Readership scores are at least a rough indication of success in attracting and holding attention, because it goes without saying that an advertisement must be perceived before advertising objectives are realized.
2. The relative pulling power of variations in creative treatment can be assessed from one campaign to the next or within the same campaign by controlled experiments.
3. The pulling power of competitors' campaigns can be measured.

These data are most useful if an entire campaign is analyzed rather than each advertisement one at a time. It is possible, for example, that the individual score can be biased by an unrepresentative sample for a given issue or other random variations. These variations become neutralized when many stimuli are compared over time.

Perhaps the least effective use of recognition scores is to test the pulling power of minor components within an advertisement. It is asking far too much of any reader to remember one's behavior in such minute detail.

Finally, these scores should not be projected to the entire market. The sample is not random, and for that reason no such projection can be made with measurable accuracy.

2. Recall Tests

Recall measures assess the impression of advertisements on the reader's memory through the extent and accuracy of answers given, without exposure to the stimulus.

Unaided recall. The purest measure of memory relies on no aids whatsoever. The respondent might be asked, for example, "What advertisements have you seen lately?" Such a question is obviously difficult to answer, because few respondents will retain such sharp recollections of advertising exposure that much detail will be recalled. Also, it is quite difficult to measure the impact of a specific campaign in this fashion, because answers will vary over a wide range of products. For these reasons, unaided recall is seldom relied upon as the only measure.

Aided recall. There is a practically limitless variety of means which can be used to jog the respondent's memory and thereby sharpen recall. One might be asked, "What automobile advertisements do you remember seeing in yesterday's paper?" or "What brand of coffee do you remember hearing about recently?" The recall of a specific brand is a strong indication of the strength of the advertising impression.

The Gallup-Robinson impact test. The Gallup-Robinson test, perhaps the best known of the aided recall measures, is offered as a syndicated service. Basically, the technique involves five steps:

1. The person interviewed must recall and describe correctly at least one editorial feature in the publication under analysis.
2. The respondent is then handed a group of cards on which are printed the names of advertised brands which appear in the issue, as well as some which do not. Respondent is asked to indicate which of these products are advertised in the issue.
3. For each advertised brand the respondent recalls from the issue, she or he is interrogated in depth to assess the strength and accuracy of recall.
4. The issue is then opened to each advertisement the respondent recalls. Respondent is asked whether this is the advertisement he or she has in mind and if it is the first time he or she has seen it. If respondent

has seen it before, the data are discarded in order to arrive at a "proven name registration" figure.

5. Information is gathered on the age, sex, education, and other details of the background of each person interviewed.

The interviewing usually commences on the day after the magazine appears. Responses are edited thoroughly to ascertain that the recall is genuine. The final score, *proven name registration* (PNR), is adjusted by size of the appeal, color, placement on the page, and the number of competing advertisements in the issue.

The PARM study referred to earlier also analyzed the Gallup-Robinson approach. The correlation between scores produced by the PARM staff and Gallup-Robinson was .82 for women and .61 for men. Therefore, this technique was not found to be as fully reproducible as the Starch approach.

Gallup-Robinson scores were found to show the expected pattern of dropoff as time between reading the issue and the interview increased. For this reason if no other, it is quite likely that two different interviewing organizations would produce different results, for only by accident would all respondents be in exactly the same stages of memory decay.

The PARM study also detected that the Gallup-Robinson measure is highly sensitive to interviewer skill. The more inexperienced interviewer produced scores which differed significantly from those of the interviewer with greater experience, thus underscoring the need for rigorous training and tight field control.

It has been concluded that the PARM test in general verified that the Gallup-Robinson test truly measures memory, as its proponents claim, with a minimum of distortion from other factors (unlike the Starch measure). However, unnecessary secrecy surrounds the procedures used to edit and adjust the proven name registration scores. It would be possible to interpret the data with more accuracy if these facts were available.

Evaluation of recall tests.   It is apparent that unaided and aided recall both offer minimum cues to stimulate memory, and it may be that memory is *understimulated*. The triple-associates and identification tests, of course, minimize this difficulty.

Understimulation of memory may not seem to be a problem. Consider the situation, however, when the advertised product is a convenience good and the objective is merely to register the name repetitively over a long period, or the situation involves low-involvement learning. In all probability, the respondent will not recall seeing the advertisement, but the objective still could have been attained. The point is that recall favors the distinctive appeals, especially those that are highly entertaining, and high-involvement products. The danger arises when one assumes that a low score always implies failure to attract and hold attention.

Recall and position in the issue. It has frequently been felt that the position of the advertisement in the issue will affect recall. For instance, it seems reasonable to expect that the advertisement close to the editorial section will be favored. It has been found, however, that the environment and location of the stimulus was not a factor in recall scores. The content of copy and the visualization seem to be the dominant factors.

Finally, it cannot be assumed that the true "impact" of the advertisement has been isolated. This observation is pertinent, because the Gallup-Robinson method is frequently referred to as "impact" measurement. If by impact is meant the stimulation of buying behavior or successful attainment of other advertising objectives, aided recall in no definitive way is an indication of success. All that can be said is that high recall scores (perhaps 5 percent or more) reflect that a strong conscious impression was made and that attention was successfully attracted and held.

3. Association Measures

A time-honored measure of message recall is the triple-associates test development by the late Henry C. Link. Respondents are asked the following type of question: "Which brand of gasoline is advertised as offering 'more miles per gallon'?" Two associates or factors are inherent in such a question: (1) the generic product (gasoline) and (2) the advertising theme ("more miles per gallon"). The third element, the brand name, is to be supplied by the respondent. The percentage of correct answers is thus a measure of the extent to which advertising has correctly registered a theme.

The triple-associates test can easily be modified to suit individual situations as long as it is confined to measurement of registration of a theme or a very abbreviated message. The communication of longer copy or advertising elements cannot be measured effectively with this technique. Also, registration of theme must not be taken as implying that advertising objectives have been achieved. All that can be said is that the advertisement communicated.

4. Combination Measures

It seems safe to observe that a recognition test *overstimulates* readers or viewers, while recall measurement *understimulates* them. It is possible, however, to combine these measures to capitalize upon the strengths of each.

A controlled combination. One of the authors combined the recognition and recall procedures by removing test advertisements from their editorial surroundings, exposing consumers to the copy for a controlled interval and asking for playback of copy and other features following exposures.[15] Respondents were first qualified as being readers of the issue in which the advertisements appeared, and they were then exposed to five advertisements, one by one, for a controlled short interval. The advertisement was then removed, and the respondent was asked to state whether or not he or she recalled seeing the advertisement. If the reply was affirmative, respondent was asked to state in detail one's recall of major features, copy points, illustrations, and other components. Finally, one of the five stimuli was an advertisement scheduled for appearance one month following the date of the interview, and it was used to detect false recognition claims. The extent of false claiming was found to be minimal.

This procedure minimizes the overstimulation inherent in the Starch method. The interval of exposure appeared to be long enough to jog the memory but not long enough to permit further reading of the advertisement and false claiming. Furthermore, the recall phase verified the accuracy of recognition claims. Thus this type of measure seems to be a more accurate indication of readership than either recognition or recall measures used separately.

The communiscope. The communiscope overcomes a disadvantage in the technique just described by mechanically controlling the interval of exposure. The communiscope is a portable tachistoscope which permits the presentation of stimuli at varying intervals of time. The advertisements are placed on slides and flashed at the correct interval. Playback of copy is then requested to verify the accuracy of readership claims.

The communiscope is sufficiently compact to permit use in a home under normal conditions. Because of the opportunity for precise stimulus presentation, its use should grow in the future.

CELL IV: PRODUCT-RELATED MEASURES
UNDER REAL-WORLD CONDITIONS

The most sophisticated and demanding of the various measurement approaches is field measurement of the effects of advertising. Sales test techniques, in particular, generally require considerable time and expense and hence are utilized mostly for purposes of posttesting the effects of an entire campaign. However, all of these procedures may be used on a pretest basis if one is willing to invest in a local tryout of a campaign (e.g.: test market a number of creative executions). The pre-post test is indeed widely used in pretesting.

---

[15] James F. Engel, "Are Automobile Purchasers Dissonant Consumers?" *Journal of Marketing* 27 (April 1963), pp. 55–58.

PRETESTING AND POSTTESTING PROCEDURES

1. Pre-Post Tests

When it is not possible to establish a clear-cut sales objective for advertising, the objectives usually are stated in terms of stimulation of awareness, attitude shift, or changes in preference. Whether or not the advertising has been effective requires a measurement approach which encompasses assessment of changes in response from the initial position of the members of the market segment. Therefore, both a before (pre) and after (post) measurement will usually be required.

Case studies of pre-post measurement. To promote understanding of this type of analysis we will first analyze several case examples in which communication effectiveness was measured. Then issues and problems in the use of the technique will be examined.

An association of tea importers and producers. The problem was an unfavorable attitude toward tea among many consumers, and the advertising goal was to generate a favorable attitude toward tea from a positive rating of 20 percent to 40 percent over five years. An attitude scale was developed, and studies were conducted annually to assess progress toward the goal. In each periodic assessment the same attitudes scale was used, apparently with a different sample of buyers.

A small overseas airline. The advertising objective of communicating the attributes of a luxury airline to an additional 20 percent in one year was established. Measurement consisted of mail questionnaires sent periodically to a representative sample of several hundred persons who were overseas-traveling customers of travel services in selected cities. The questions used were of the following type: "What airlines can you name that offer all-jet service to _____?" Survey costs were small (several hundred dollars), and a high return was produced because a free booklet of interest to travelers was given as an inducement. At the end of one year it was found that awareness of the company had increased 14 percent; the image of a luxury all-jet overseas airline was communicated to an additional 15 percent; and the proportion of those indicating they would seriously consider this airline for their next overseas trip increased 8 percent.

A pain reliever. The manufacturer of a leading brand of pain reliever previously had focused his advertising on the theme of "fast relief." Because leading competitors were also doing this, and it was decided that a new advertising objective should be to (1) hold the present level of message penetration on the headache-relief theme (35 percent) and (2) increase cold-relief message penetration from 15 percent to 25 percent in six months. This strategy was undertaken in test markets. The results showed that the headache message registration actually declined 2 percent at the outset but overall penetration reached 28 percent at the conclusion, thereby exceeding expectation.

Analysis of the cases.   The case examples discussed above have several aspects in common: (1) measurement of message penetration at the beginning of a period, (2) a clear-cut communication goal, (3) another measurement either during or at the end of the campaign period, and (4) assessment of ensuing changes.

In general, these examples are representative illustrations of research-oriented advertising management. There are problems, however, which may not be apparent to the reader:

1. What is the nature of the sample studied at the beginning of the period? Is it representative? If it is intended to focus on prospects, where is such a list obtained? It may not be possible to draw a random sample because of these problems, and, of course, the price paid for nonrandomness is inability to project the results to the universe being studied.
2. Were the people studied either in the interim or at the end of the campaign period the same as those chosen in the beginning? If so, the distinct possibility exists that the process of measurement may seriously bias later replies. The fact that respondents are asked for their opinions frequently causes them to think more deeply and change their opinions at a later time.
3. If the same people were not measured at a later point, were the samples studied clearly matched as to age, income, and other demographic variables? Even more to the point, is it known that the samples studied later possessed the same attitude at the beginning of the period as the sample used previously? Differences in any of these respects may vitiate the results.
4. Is it known what changes would have occurred in the interim without advertising? Even when there is no intervening advertising, some percent of respondents will change their attitudes or brand preferences. In the same sense, it is essential to determine what nonviewers or nonreaders would do before concluding that any changes are a result of advertising.

Until the above questions can be answered satisfactorily, conclusions cannot be drawn about the validity of the research. Basically, the only way in which these problems can be overcome is through utilization of an experimental design where attempts are made to control all the variables but one—in this case, the advertising used.

Experimental designs.   In a controlled experiment, the researcher intervenes, so to speak, to control for as many extraneous variables as possible. Usually it is necessary to use a test group and a control group.

One group is exposed to the advertising and the other is not. The design is represented thus:

A Simplified Experimental Design

	Experimental group	Control group
Premeasurement	Yes	Yes
Exposure to advertising	Yes	No
Postmeasurement	Yes	Yes

Changes which would have occurred in any event, without the exposure to advertising, presumably will be detected as differences between the pre- and postmeasurements in the control group. This change is subtracted from that noted in the experimental group, and the residual is the change attributable to advertising exposure.

However, the simple design above, sometimes called the "before and after with control group" design, may be grossly inadequate for this type of problem. As was mentioned before, the simple fact of asking people for their opinions is known to change the opinions later, and a very real source of bias is thus introduced by using the same experimental subjects for before-and-after measurement. One way to control for this factor is to use a four-group, six-study design, as illustrated below:

A Four-Group, Six-Study Design

	Experimental groups		Control groups	
	1	2	1	2
Premeasurement	Yes	No	Yes	No
Exposure to advertising	Yes	Yes	No	No
Postmeasurement	Yes	Yes	Yes	Yes

Notice that four groups are used, and a means now exists to detect the possible biasing effect of premeasurement. If, for instance, the effect introduced by advertising in experimental group 1 is much greater than that in the second group receiving no premeasure, it is quite probable that the premeasurement biased later responses. In that case the premeasurement of the first group under each heading would be compared with the postmeasurement of the groups receiving no premeasure.

No doubt the four-group, six-study design would represent the ideal means of isolating the communication effectiveness of advertising. It would be a mistake, however, to fail to point out the difficulties arising when one attempts to use this "textbook ideal" research method:

1. Is it possible to establish equivalent test and control groups, especially when two or more are used under each to create the necessary four

groups? Unless the answer here is yes, the research becomes question-able.

2. Is it possible to find equivalent groups, one of which is not exposed to the advertising? Where a saturation campaign is being used, this may be impossible. The individuals not exposed may be very different from those who are, and it may be exceedingly difficult to find typical groups of consumers who would qualify for this particular purpose.
3. Is the information gained worth the cost? The more elaborate the design, the greater the research costs. The basic issue, then, is the return for the investment relative to less ideal designs, and this question is exceptionally difficult to answer.

The problem of finding equivalent groups becomes somewhat less crucial when the numbers in each are large. Difference in various dimensions may then be offset by the force of large numbers. The second problem also may be overcome when the campaign is confined to a select group of media. For instance, assume that dollars are invested in one television program. It may then be possible to find equivalent exposed and unexposed groups, but it must never be forgotten that those who watch the program still may differ from nonviewers in psychological outlook and other characteristics. Finally, the last question is the most difficult of all. Little more than advance hunches regarding the return for an investment in research are possible until more is known about the strengths and weaknesses of various research methods.

Comments on pre-post tests. It should now be apparent that the examples above suffer from possible sources of bias, yet the application of experimental design also presents real problems. Probably it is safe to say that the kind of monitoring undertaken by the tea association and the airline is good practice if done on a routine basis. In other words, it is helpful to keep a running tally on the results of a campaign. This information, however, can never be a conclusive indication of success unless a control group of some kind is used.

The issue, then, once again revolves around the uses to which the research is put. Measurement without a control group provides a useful but rough indication of progress, and the strengths and weaknesses of the campaign can be pinpointed. If management uses these data with caution and fully recognizes that other factors in addition to advertising could be introducing change, the return of information for a minimum research expenditure can be worthwhile.

It is another matter, however, for management to take the results of uncontrolled research as a definitive indication of success or failure. The abandonment or continuation of a campaign theme involving millions of dollars should not rest on such a foundation. In this instance, experimental design procedures should be utilized. There are problems in methodology and possible sources of bias in experimental research, but the chances for error resulting from the research methods used or uncontrolled factors are substantially reduced.

2. Sales Tests

The question of whether the influence of advertising on sales can be measured has prompted much discussion in recent years, both pro and con. Consider, for example, the somewhat negative point of view expressed in the following quotation:

In essence, current sales figure are not the final yardstick of advertising performance unless one or more of these factors are present.

1. Advertising is the single variable.
2. Advertising is the dominant force in the marketing mix.
3. The proposition calls for immediate payout (such as in mail-order or retail advertising).
4. These conditions seldom prevail among so-called "nationally advertised" products.[16]

The point is that advertising is usually only one variable in the marketing mix, and it must pull together with the product, price, and distribution channel to produce sales. The contention is that the communication aspects of advertising are usually the only measurable results. As was noted in Chapter 10, this focus on communication has come to be referred to as DAGMAR (Defining Advertising Goals, Measuring Advertising Results).

DAGMAR, however, is referred to by some as a "philosophy of despair."[17] The argument is that communication goals are being substituted for the more relevant objectives of sales and profit and that communication comes from many sources other than advertising. Moreover, communication does not necessarily mean sales or profit, and examples are reported where one medium produced greater awareness or response but less sales or results than another. Therefore, there are some who advocate testing the influence of advertising on sales and attaining profit objectives rather than communication objectives.

It is useful to distinguish two distinct situations. The first is where one can directly attribute a sale to an ad. This is generally true in direct action ads, such as the Book-of-the-Month Club ad in Figure 15–3. A sales objective is relevant here and results are easily measured by the

---

[16] Russell H. Colley, *Defining Advertising Goals* (New York: Association of National Advertisers, Inc., 1961), pp. 10, 12.

[17] A. J. Vogl, "Advertising Research—Everybody's Looking for the Holy Grail," *Sales Management,* November 1, 1963, p. 42.

FIGURE 15–3
An Ad Where Direct Tracing Is Possible

level of sales obtained. The more general situation is where direct tracing of sales results to ads is not possible. Here a legitimate controversy exists.

The controversy over whether attainment of sales objectives is measurable has been briefly described. The authors do not take sides in the argument but feel it is pertinent to inquire into the possible ways in which the sales effectiveness of promotional dollars might be measured. These include the three discussed below: (1) direct questioning, (2) experimental designs, and (3) mini-market tests.

Direct questioning of buyers. On occasion it is fruitful to question buyers directly to define the factors that lead them to make a purchasing decision. For example, heavy television advertising for the *Living Bible* was undertaken in several test markets during the Christmas season. Direct questioning of buyers at point of purchase demonstrated high recall of television advertisements featuring Art Linkletter, although word of mouth was found to be the dominant influence on the decision.

The difficulties of direct questioning should be apparent. First, most people have great difficulty recalling the circumstances surrounding a decision. It is possible, of course, to minimize this difficulty by progressively taking the respondent back in time and asking him to restate the situation as well as possible. For example, one may associate the purchase of a new automobile with a particular time of year, with particular family discussions, or with other events. Questioning can help one to recall the situation, so that the influences on one's decision may come into sharper focus.

Even if the purchasing environment is clear in the respondent's memory, it still is doubtful that the role of advertising will be revealed. It seems to be natural for many to deny being influenced by advertising. Presumably this would be admitting in some way to being not rational in buying. Moreover, advertising often works in virtually undetectable ways. Awareness might have been stimulated years before, and it is impossible for the buyer to restate this influence by introspection.

These problems are potent barriers indeed. For this reason, introspection by the buyer is seldom relied upon to any great extent.

Experimental designs. There is no satisfactory substitute for an experimental design to isolate the influence of advertising from the influence of other elements in the marketing mix. The application of experimental design to this problem, however, is complex, and the problems to be faced are many. They include (1) selecting the appropriate design, (2) selecting test and control markets, and (3) analysis of these results.

The appropriate design for sales testing. The before-and-after with control group experimental design is applicable for sales testing. This design uses several test cities and control cities. The procedure can be outlined as shown in the following table:

A Before-And-After with Control Group Design for
Testing the Sales Effectiveness of Advertising

	Test markets	Control markets
Before measure of sales	Yes	Yes
Introduction of advertising	Yes	No
Postmeasure of sales	Yes	Yes

Sales usually are measured by auditing the inventories of a sample of stores, perhaps using the A. C. Nielsen store audit or a similar service. There is no need in this case for the more complex four-group, six-study design, because no interviews are being made. As a result, there is little chance that premeasurement of sales will bias the results.

A sales test usually runs from six months to a year, to permit time for advertising influence to be exerted. Several test and control markets should be used to minimize the danger that the markets chosen are later found to differ in some important aspect.

Selecting test and control markets. Every attempt must be made to assure that the markets chosen closely mirror the total market. In addition, the test and control areas must not differ in the following respects:

1. *Size*—Usually areas from 100,000 to 300,000 population are used. The areas must be large enough to encompass a variety of economic activities, yet not be so great that measurement and analysis of results is unduly costly.
2. *Population factors*—Areas with distinct and unique ethnic characteristics usually should be avoided. Milwaukee, Wisconsin, with its German stock, would be an unlikely area to test advertising for French wines. The more representative the area, the less likely it is to be rendered atypical by local disturbances such as strikes or layoffs. A one-industry town would be severely shocked by such an occurrence.
3. *Distribution*—The product must be readily available in retail outlets. If possible, retailers and wholesalers should not be informed of the test, in order to prevent unusual sales activity on their part which would severely bias the results.
4. *Competitive considerations*—Competition in the test and control areas should not deviate from that usually faced in the entire market. The competitive climate during the test must be carefully monitored, because any changes may render the test invalid.
5. *Media*—Full advertising media facilities must be available for use, or comparable media must be available in the test and control areas.

Analysis of results. If the results of the experiment are those shown in Figure 15–4, the results in the test city must be adjusted by the percentages for the control city to show the effect of advertising. Notice that

FIGURE 15–4
Comparison of Test City and Control City Sales Returns

City	Sales before test advertising (Feb. 1– Mar. 31)	Sales during test advertising (April 1– May 31)	Percentage increase or decrease	Adjusted percentage increase or decrease
Control City A:				
Dollars	$300	$270	−10.0	
Units	300	250	−16.7	—
Test City X:				
Dollars	$400	$480	+20.0	30.0
Units	400	460	+15.0	31.7

Note: For purposes of simplification, only one test city and one control city have been used in this example. In actual practice, at least three test cities and three control cities are used.

the control city showed a definite decline in sales. If conditions were similar in both areas, it is necessary to calculate what would have happened in the test city without advertising. A 10 percent decline in the test city would give dollar sales of $360, whereas in reality the sales were $480. Therefore, $360 must be subtracted from $480 to give a net increase of $120. Thus the actual net increase is 30 percent in dollar sales and 31.7 percent in unit sales. The actual meaning of these changes must be assessed, using statistical tests such as the t test or chi square analysis.

Notice that the results are predicated on the assumption that all other things are equal. Again it must be emphasized that variation in any factor, such as competition or retailers' efforts, that is present in the test cities and not in the control cities (or vice versa) will vitiate the experiment. If it appears that factors have not varied, however, the data should give a reasonably accurate measure of the influence of advertising on sales.

A multivariable experimental design.   In the above example only one variable has been measured—the advertising campaign in the test areas. It is possible to study more than one variable at a time and in so doing to reduce the cost of repetitive individual experiments.

Assume that the research assignment is to analyze the relative pulling power of four different media used individually and in combination. This problem would call for a factorial design. While the mechanics of factorial design are clearly beyond the scope of this book, an indication of a possible structure for the experiment is given in Figure 15–5. This design has been used at Ford Motor Company, where it was reported that the data have revealed a definite relationship between advertising and sales but no significant advantage for any of the media tested.

Multivariable designs are elaborate, and the difficulties of controlling variables are compounded. The data must be analyzed by analysis of variance, a statistical technique which permits delineation of the signifi-

FIGURE 15–5
Media Combinations in a 16-Cell Design

Combination	Area no.	Combination	Area no.
No media	1	Outdoor-radio	10
TV only	2	Outdoor-newspaper	11
Radio only	3	TV-radio-newspaper	12
Newspaper only	4	Outdoor-radio-TV	13
Outdoor only	5	Outdoor-TV-newspaper	14
TV-radio	6	Outdoor-radio-	
TV-newspaper	7	newspaper	15
Newspaper-radio	8	Outdoor-TV-radio-	
Outdoor-TV	9	newspaper	16

cance of sales differences resulting from individual variables or from variables in combination. In addition, sales frequently are lost in areas where advertising is reduced; costs become high when test advertising proves to be ineffective; and it is costly to undertake the necessary rigorous analysis and interpretation of data. As a result, experimental designs, especially of such great complexity, are usually the province of the large advertiser. This is not to say, however, that such designs cannot be tailored to the means of the smaller advertiser.

Comments on experimental designs. Even though the difficulties to be faced are great, there is no doubt that proper experimental procedures will permit measurement of the sales power of advertising. Du Pont uses experiments regularly. In one experiment, for instance, industrial advertising was undertaken in all but two states, which then served as the control, and changes in effectiveness were assessed in both sections. Similar examples are reported by others.

Obviously, more elaborate experiments will not be undertaken by the smaller advertiser with a local or regional market. The costs simply are too great at the present time. However, the experimental design need be only as elaborate as the problem being tested. In future years advertisers of all sizes no doubt will begin to experiment, and the effectiveness of advertising should increase markedly.

3. Mini-Market Tests

There are ways of undertaking full-scale experiments without the time and expense necessary for the market tests discussed above. One way is use of the so-called "mini-market." The leading research service providing this type of procedure is AdTel, a part of Burke Marketing Services, which utilizes a dual-cable CATV system and two balanced purchase diary panels of 1,000 households each. Because it is possible to control all variables except the one being tested over television, a precise measurement of effects is possible. (See earlier discussion of AdTel under on-the-air tests.)

RELIABILITY AND VALIDITY

Of course, the reliability and validity of any copy testing procedure need to be demonstrated. Unfortunately, all too many suppliers of copy testing services do not provide measures concerning these issues. Recently, 21 of the United States' largest advertising agencies endorsed a set of principles aimed at improving copy testing. These principles are called PACT (Positioning Advertising Copy Testing). These nine principles state a "good" copy testing system:[18]

1. Provides measurements which are relevant to the objectives of the advertising.
2. Requires agreement about how the results will be used in advance of each specific test.
3. Provides multiple measurements, because single measurements are generally inadequate to assess the performance of an ad.
4. Is based on a model of human response to communication—the reception of a stimulus, the comprehension of the stimulus, and the response to the stimulus.
5. Allows for consideration of whether the advertising stimulus should be exposed more than once.
6. Recognizes that the more finished a piece of copy is, the more soundly it can be evaluated and requires, as a minimum, that alternative executions be tested in the same degree of finish.
7. Provides controls to avoid the biasing effects of the exposure context.
8. Takes into account basic considerations of sample definition.
9. Demonstrates reliability and validity empirically.

These are important recommendations that should be followed. In doing so the reliability and validity of copy testing would improve greatly.

SUMMARY

This chapter has examined the assumptions, strengths, and weaknesses of the various techniques for measuring advertising effectiveness.[19] The use of some of these tools, however, does not shed light on the actual advertising response by the buyer. This may seem to be an obvious point,

---

[18] "21 Ad Agencies Endorse Copy Testing Principles," *Marketing News,* February 19, 1982, pp. 1 and 9.

[19] For a detailed discussion of experimentation, test marketing, and mini-markets see Thomas C. Kinnear, and James R. Taylor, *Marketing Research: An Applied Approach,* 2d ed. (McGraw-Hill, 1983), chaps. 12, 20, and 23.

but it frequently is forgotten by users of research. A high Starch score, for instance, may be a favorable indication of success, but high readership does not necessarily imply a strong response, nor does it indicate a rising sales curve.

At the present time, no area of advertising research methodology is without important unknowns and doubts. As a result, no method can be used with complete certainty that it will always give desired results. The need for additional empirical research and improved methodology is apparent, yet this need is growing more rapidly than it is being met. It is strange that management is willing to devote funds to new product development but is loathe to improve the tools with which advertising is measured.

Given the state of the art, it is essential to advance a strong warning against the quest for certainty. Everyone has a tendency to assume that a quantitative finding is absolute—something to be relied upon. The manager who relies upon research data religiously without a skeptical, questioning attitude is falling prey to the false god of certainty. This manager may be led into wrong conclusions that can be costly. Moreover, an unquestioning attitude implies intellectual inflexibility, which has no place in advertising today.

Review and Discussion Questions

1. What is the essential distinction between laboratory and real-world measures?

2. Describe and discuss the usefulness of the various measures of opinion used in a consumer jury test.

3. Studies often show that recall is the most widely used measure of communication effectiveness. Many refuse to measure other stages of the communication process, such as attitude change or purchase. Why does this occur? What arguments could you present on behalf of attitude and/or behavior measurement?

4. Do you agree that laboratory measures, especially those focusing on the physiological aspect of attention, will see more use in the future? Why or why not?

5. Describe the recognition method.

6. The Starch method for measurement of readership is widely used, as are other approaches. What precautions would you suggest in using findings of this type?

7. Unaided recall is rarely considered to be a powerful method to isolate advertising impact. Why?

8. The Gallup-Robinson impact test is one example of an aided recall measure. Describe and evaluate this procedure.

9. Recall tests often are hampered by "understimulation." What does this mean, and in what way is it a problem for researchers?

10. How does position in an issue affect recall of printed advertising messages?

11. What are combination measures? Are they an improvement over other approaches? In what ways?

12. Are measures of attracting and holding attention necessary to evaluate advertising success? Are they a sufficient measure for this purpose?

13. It is often overlooked that actual responses to advertising are more important in the final analysis than the attraction of attention. Why, then, is so much reliance placed on measures of attention attraction as opposed to more clear-cut indications of advertising effectiveness?

14. What are the major types of advertising response which can be measured?

15. Attempts to measure communications effectiveness are plagued with problems in research design. What are these problems?

16. Describe the experimental design approach to communications measurement. What problems are encountered?

17. What is the basis of the argument which claims that advertising effectiveness should be measured in terms of communication of a message rather than in terms of sales?

18. Can direct questioning of buyers isolate the effect of advertising on sales? Why, or why not?

CHAPTER 16

Management of Sales Promotion

Sales promotion has been defined by the American Marketing Association as encompassing "those marketing activities, other than personal selling, advertising and publicity that stimulate consumer purchasing and dealer effectiveness."[1] These activities occupy a gray area between advertising and personal selling possessing characteristics of each promotional tool. For example, if a premium were to be offered to induce buyers to try a new product and the premium offer was made in an advertisement in a national magazine, how would one classify the activity? A well-accepted view would be that the premium offer would be a sales promotion because of its nonrecurrent nature and because it was aimed at stimulating consumer demand in the short run. The communication of the offer itself in the national medium would be advertising.

Scope and Importance of Sales Promotion

Strang described sales promotion as including such activities as trade shows and exhibits, couponing, sampling, premiums, trade allowances, sales and dealer incentives, cents-off packs, consumer education and demonstration activities, rebates, bonus packs, point-of-purchase material and direct mail.[2]

---

[1] *Marketing Definitions: A Glossary of Marketing Terms,* American Marketing Association (Chicago, 1960), p. 20.

[2] Roger A. Strang, "Sales Promotion-Fast Growth, Faulty Management," *Harvard Business Review,* July–August 1976, pp. 115–24.

As can be seen from the diversity of activities subsumed by sales promotion lots of dollars are involved. Until recently there were few attempts to find out exactly what the magnitude of expenditures for sales promotion really were. The most interesting data were presented by Haugh who estimated expenditures in 1982 for sales promotion activities were in excess of $64.4 billion allocated as shown in Figure 16–1.

FIGURE 16–1
Estimated Promotion Expenditures 1981 and 1982 (by type)

Category	$1981*	Percent total	$1982*	Percent total	Percent difference '81 to '82
Meetings/conventions	$15.4	26.2%	$16.8	26.1%	9.1%
Premiums/incentives	10.8	18.4	12.0	18.6	11.1
Direct response	9.0	15.3	9.9	15.4	10.0
Display, POS†	6.4	10.9	7.1	11.0	10.9
Promo ads	5.0	8.5	5.4	8.4	8.0
Collateral	4.9	8.3	5.3	8.2	8.2
Trade shows	3.4	5.9	3.7	5.7	8.8
Coupon/refund	1.9	3.2	2.1	3.3	10.5
Specialties	1.1	1.9	1.2	1.9	9.0
All other	.8	1.4	.9	1.4	12.5
Total	$58.7	100%	$64.4	100%	9.7%

* Dollars in billions.
† Point of sale.
Source: Westport Marketing Group, Inc., as printed in Louis J. Haugh, "A Look Ahead: What's Hot and What's Not," *Advertising Age*, January 4, 1982, p. 32, with permission.

In another study reported by Strang and using data of Bowman, Young, and Adler, several interesting facts come to light. First, it appears that since 1969 (the base measurement year) expenditures for sales promotion have exceeded those for advertising. Second, the average annual growth rate of expenditures for sales promotion for the period 1969 to 1975 has been 9.2 percent. This rate is twice that of the rate of growth in advertising expenditures.[3] Both these overall trends have continued into the 1980s.

Using the reported rates of growth and assuming no major changes in the economic environment, it is likely that expenditures for sales promotion will reach $70 billion by 1985.

Sales promotion targets.   Given the scope and diversity of sales promotion activities, it is obvious that they have not all been developed to reach the same target audience or to achieve the same promotional objectives. Some of the activities have been developed to motivate the company sales force to provide extra selling effort during a specified period of time in order to make sure that the resellers are stocked with a new

---

[3] Russell D. Bowman, John C. Young, and John Adler, "Improving the Payout of the Advertising/Promotion Mix" (New York: Association of National Advertisers, 1975).

product prior to national introduction. Other activities were developed to gain added promotional support from resellers such as eye-level display in supermarkets to aid in the initial introductory promotional efforts. Lastly, certain activities may be used to stimulate consumer trial of the new product. These might include sampling, cash-rebates or premium offers. Approximately 59 percent of promotional money is spent on trade promotions, against 41 percent on consumer promotions.[4]

This chapter will concentrate attention on the last of these target areas; that of consumer promotion. Efforts aimed at the sales force will be considered in Chapter 18 while those aimed at resellers will be discussed in Chapter 21.

Consumer Directed Sales Promotion

This category of sales promotion activities includes those with which we are most familiar in our daily lives. They are those techniques and devices which sellers use to get us to try a new product or to increase our consumption of an established one. These are also the activities that must be coordinated closely with other elements of the promotional mix and especially with advertising if the full impact of sales promotion is to be realized.

Given the immediate nature of the economic environment or of competition, certain sales promotion techniques appear to be better suited to attain promotional goals than do others. The principal requirements for success seem to be that the chosen promotion be sufficiently different to attract consumer attention but not so unique that it scares people away. In addition, the technique or the approach must be well suited to the consumer needs and attitudes of the moment. For example, cents-off or other types of cash refund promotion seems to work well when the economy is depressed and people are trying to save money. In times of relative prosperity contests and premiums or other forms of nonprice incentives may be more effective. Regardless of the exact nature of the offering no sales promotion effort will achieve maximum success unless it fits well with the other elements of the promotional mix and is timed properly to reach the consumer.

Promotional Alternatives

In their excellent book Luick and Ziegler classify several promotional techniques in terms of objectives sought.[5] When new products are being

---

[4] Fred L. Lemont, "Room at the Top in Promotion," *Advertising Age*, March 23, 1981, p. 61.

[5] John F. Luick and William Lee Ziegler, *Sales Promotion and Modern Merchandising* (New York: McGraw-Hill, 1968), pp. 37, 65.

introduced they suggest that three major types of sales promotion effort may be utilized. These are (1) sampling, (2) couponing, and (3) money refund offers. When the goal is to increase sales of an existing product, major alternatives include: (1) price-off promotions, (2) premiums, and (3) consumer contests.

The remainder of this chapter will discuss these alternatives in some detail and will also consider the role of packaging as an important promotional tool.

Sampling.   Consumer sampling is an effective but rather costly means of introducing a new product. As a technique it is probably used more by large firms which produce broad lines of packaged consumer food or health and beauty items and engage in extensive advertising and personal selling on a national basis. When used as part of a coordinated promotional campaign to introduce a new product the catalytic effect of sampling upon trial usage and subsequent repurchase can be sufficiently strong to more than defray the expense of sampling.

The physical distribution of the sample either to resellers for redistribution to consumers or directly to consumers is a formidable task. Mail, house-to-house private delivery, distribution at point-of-purchase and inclusion in the package of another product are some of the ways suggested to get the sample into the hands of the prospective customer.

There is little doubt that the provision of a free sample can break through the noise level and stimulate a higher rate of trial than can other promotional efforts. Such trial is not gained without the expenditure of a lot of money and unless the trials translate into repurchase the sampling promotion cannot be deemed a success. Repurchase data may not be available for several weeks after initial distribution of samples and even if repurchase rates are high it is difficult to determine how much influence the sampling promotion had upon market results. What might be in order at this point would be a postintroduction market survey to determine how consumers were influenced to buy. Agree shampoo reached a leadership position in the market within six months of introduction, and eventually obtained over a 20 percent share of the market by using mass sampling. Over 31 million samples were distributed.

Because sampling is so expensive, research is recommended prior to the launching of a full-scale effort. Information can be gathered as to the proper size of the sample, the most effective means of distribution, and so forth. During the test marketing of Gainesburgers by the Post Division of General Foods, for example, a one-patty sample of dog food was distributed to consumers at supermarket checkout counters. Repurchase rates after trial were disappointing, and market research indicated that dogs were still hungry after eating the patty and that the image of the product was that it was not a complete meal but rather a snack or treat type product. The sampling strategy was changed so that two-patty packages of Gainesburgers were mailed to dog owners of record in the market area and the media advertising reinforced the idea that two patties were equivalent to one pound of canned dog food. Providing trial users with a sample adequate to supply a full meal to a dog and supplementing this trial with a copy platform of "Canned Dog Food Without the Can" resulted in a very high rate of product repurchase after introduction and launched a new product category which over the years has shown remarkable growth and profitability.[6]

In other situations sampling may not do the job. Customers will either disregard the sample or use it without switching their patronage. There can be many explanations for such a failure but the first hypothesis which should be investigated is that the consumer could find no demonstrable difference in the new product which would motivate him or her to buy. Sampling is most effective when the key product attributes that set the new product apart from its competitors are difficult to describe adequately in print or visual media. Scent, taste, consistency, balance, and the like are selling points which can be effectively communicated by sampling.

On occasion sampling will be used for other reasons. There have been some attempts to revive the sales of a slumping product, but the distribution of a sample rarely will reverse the downturn. The cause most often lies in some marketing deficiency which should be remedied first. Also, some large firms use sampling as a defensive weapon to blunt the effects of attempts by competitors to introduce new products through this means. Procter & Gamble, in particular, has utilized this strategy for decades, and its continuing domination in many product classes attests to the influence of its marketing muscle.

Generally the advertiser will not undertake the sampling effort but will retain one of the variety of service firms in this field. One of the largest is the Reuben H. Donnelley Corporation, which distributes samples through mass mailings, handouts, or door drops. It also is possible to confine distribution to more selective audiences through Welcome Wagon and other specialized service firms.

Price incentives. The use of a short-term reduction in price to encourage trial use of a new product or to stimulate demand for an established product is referred to as the offering of a consumer deal. Such deals are most frequently communicated to consumers by means of coupons and cents-off promotions. Figure 16–2 illustrates a deal in which the consumer can obtain a price reduction by presenting the coupon to the retailer at time of purchase. Notice that in this advertisement the major focus is to communicate the message that the product offering is superior to that of the competitor. The coupon and cents-off promotions are used to stimulate further consumer response in the short run.

[6] See "General Foods-Post Division (C)" case in Milton P. Brown et al., *Problems in Marketing,* 4th ed. (New York: McGraw-Hill, 1968), pp. 776 ff.

FIGURE 16–2
Example of a Consumer-Oriented Price-off Deal Implemented by a Coupon Included in a Magazine
Advertisement for Redemption by the Retailer

© 1981 The Nestlé Company. Courtesy The Nestlé Company and Leo Burnett Company, Inc.

A somewhat different approach is shown in Figure 16–3. Here we see a price reduction of two thirds of the retail value of the item being offered to those customers who will send the coupon together with payment directly to the manufacturer. In Figure 16–4 a price incentive is used in which a product other than the advertised one is the basis of the deal.

The objective of all of these sales promotions is to increase product trial among prospective customers. The best results are obtained in those product categories in which the rate of repurchase due to brand loyalty is low. Where brand loyalty is high, small price differences are unlikely to overcome the perceived advantage of remaining with a preferred brand. In the first place, brand switching often is seen as having a high degree of perceived risk, with the result that the psychological cost of trying an unknown brand is too high. Furthermore, a price-induced trial may last for only one purchase, and basic brand preferences may remain unchanged. Usually when loyalty is high, relatively large price reductions will be required.

There is always the danger that dealing will become the standard competitive tool, in which case no competitor really benefits. All engage in it for mostly defensive reasons, and the consumer wisely will adopt the strategy of purchasing the brand which offers the best deal at that point in time. No competitor really can gain differential advantage under these circumstances.

The consumer deal most likely will succeed under these conditions:

1. When the price incentive has been used only infrequently and at widely spaced intervals by the manufacturer.
2. When the manufacturer avoids dealing as a strategy to force the retailer to stock in the hopes of offsetting acceptance of a price offer by a competing brand.
3. When the brand is relatively new.
4. When deals are not used as a substitute for advertising.[7]

At all costs, deals should be avoided as a cure-all for declining sales. An ever-present tendency is to resort to the price incentive when the real problem lies elsewhere in deficiencies in the marketing mix. Careful analysis must be undertaken before embarking upon this strategy to ascertain that there is a favorable probability of increasing brand loyalty. Often this will require an actual market test. Great care also must be taken to maintain normal advertising support, and the trade must be approached in such a way that their cooperation is both solicited and maintained. The result otherwise may be a financially abortive strategy or, even worse, the triggering of unnecessary and ruinous competitive warfare.

---

[7] C. L. Hinkle, "The Strategy of Price Deals," *Harvard Business Review* 43 (July–August 1965), pp. 75–85.

FIGURE 16–3
Example of a Consumer-Oriented Price-off Deal Implemented by a Coupon in a Magazine with Redemption and Delivery of Merchandise by the Manufacturer

FIGURE 16–4

Example of a Coupon Promotion Advertised in a Magazine in Which a Premium Is Offered upon Return of Coupon with Modest Payment and Proof of Purchase to the Manufacturer

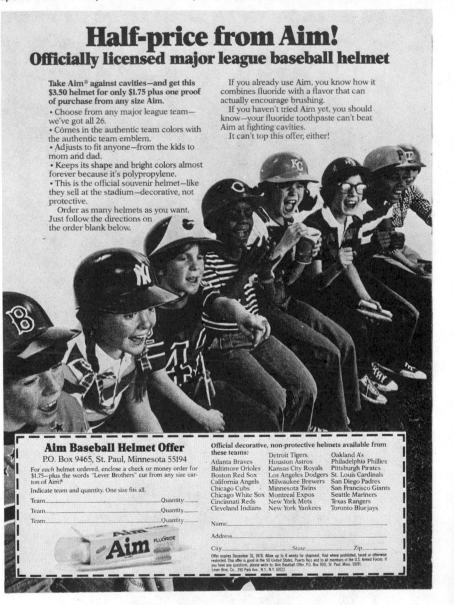

Couponing. The use of coupons as a means of sales promotion is very closely associated with price incentives. In fact, coupons are the major medium by which the manufacturer enables the consumer to take advantage of a price deal. In addition, if the coupon is to be redeemed at the retail store it is the vehicle which is used by the retailer and the wholesaler to gain reimbursement from the manufacturer.

The use of coupons as a sales promotion technique has increased dramatically in recent years. According to studies by A. C. Nielsen Company, 5.3 billion coupons were distributed in 1962. By 1975 35.7 billion coupons were distributed.[8] In 1980 90.6 billion coupons were distributed.[9]

The popularity of coupons is based on several advantages associated with their use. First, the use of coupons as a vehicle for a price reduction limits the granting of such an incentive to those customers who are sensitive to the price deal. All of the other customers continue to pay the regular price. Second, the use of coupons enables the manufacturer to specify the time frame for the promotion. This enables coordination with other activities in the promotional mix. In addition, the time limit induces more immediate response from consumers by pressuring them to act before the offer is terminated. Third, in this era when many products are losing their distinctiveness, the coupon offer may provide the differentiation which enables the manufacturer to develop a selective demand for his brand.

Coupons are distributed by a variety of media. Newspapers are the most widely used alternative accounting for over half of coupon distribution. The distribution breakdown is estimated to be: newspapers, 56 percent; Sunday supplements, 18 percent; magazines, 14 percent; and direct mail, 5 percent. Miscellaneous methods account for the rest. In addition to the utilization rates of the media alternatives, the manufacturer should be concerned with the percentage of redemptions associated with the use of a specific medium. Figure 16–5 presents redemption rate estimates by distribution method as supplied by three different research companies.

The cost of using a specific medium must, of course, be considered in relation to both the coverage offered and the redemptions expected. In addition, the financial liability associated with redemption of coupons seems to occur with differing time lags depending on the medium used. Nielsen research indicates that, "Newspaper offers redeem faster than either pop-up or on-page magazine coupons; and pop-up magazine offers come in faster than on-page magazine coupons."[10]

In order to compare various coupon plans and distribution alternatives, many companies calculate the estimated cost-per-redeemed coupon. Since

[8] "A New Look at Coupons," *The Nielsen Researcher,* no. 1 (1976), p. 2.

[9] Louis J. Haugh, "How Coupons Measure Up," *Advertising Age,* June 8, 1981, p. 58. Haugh is quoting Nielsen studies.

[10] Ibid.

FIGURE 16-5

Comparison of 1980 Redemption Rates Reported by Three Clearing Agents

Distribution type	Nielsen average	Nielsen middle half range	Donnelley median	MMS net effective redemption
Newspaper:				
R.o.p.* solo	3.1%	1.8–4.1%	2.2%	3.46%
Co-op (all)	3.4	2.3–4.8	2.5	3.8
Sunday:				
Magazine/supplement	2.1	1.1–3	2.6	3.56
FSI†	5.1	3.3–6.8	3.8	5.5
Comic section	1.5	1–2.2	1.2	nr
Comics co-op	nr	nr	nr	2.7
R.o.p.	nr	nr	nr	2.7
Magazine:				
On-page/r.o.p.	2.6	1.5–3.6	2.8	3.79
Pop-up	5.6	3.9–7.8	3.8	nr
Co-op	nr	nr	nr	8.2
Direct mail:	11.6	8.1–17.9	nr	nr
Co-op	nr	nr	10.6	10.52
Solo	nr	nr	10.4	10

Note: All data reported by A. C. Nielsen Company, Donnelley Marketing and Manufacturer's Marketing Services for most recent year available. Each redemption agent uses slightly different definitions for distribution type and in some instances no redemption estimate is reported (nr).
* R.o.p. = run of press—meaning the coupon appeared in all copies of one issue.
† FSI = free standing insert.
Source: Louis J. Haugh, "How Coupons Measure Up," *Advertising Age*, June 8, 1981, p. 58. Used with permission.

the redemption rates and distribution costs vary by method, each method will have a different cost per coupon. Figure 16–6 presents a procedure for doing this.

On average cost per coupon redeemed are estimated to be: newspapers r.o.p. solo, 55 cents; newspaper co-op, 37 cents; Sunday supplements, 75 cents; magazine on-page, 72 cents; magazine pop-up, 78 cents; and direct mail, 59 cents.

Although the couponing that we have been discussing in this chapter is consumer directed promotion, it is obvious that those strategies which require redemption at point-of-purchase cannot be executed without the cooperation of the retailers and wholesalers in the channel of distribution. The receiving of the coupons, their redemption and subsequent submission to the manufacturer for repayment is a costly process. Although most retailers receive a payment of about five cents per coupon handled, many complain that coupons cause more delay, expense, and general trouble than they are worth. The wise manufacturer makes certain that it doesn't overdo the use of coupons and that resellers are adequately compensated for their efforts when a coupon deal is used.

On the other hand, very often retailers are found to have engaged in misredemption practices in which customers are given price reductions when they have not bought the product. This is a cost that must be

FIGURE 16–6
Cost per Coupon Redeemed

1.	Distribution cost 10,000,000 circulation × $4/M	$ 40,000
2.	Redemptions at 3.1%	310,000
3.	Redemption cost 310,000 redemptions × $.15 face value	$ 46,500
4.	Handling cost 310,000 redemptions × $.07	$ 21,700
5.	Total program cost 1 + 3 + 4	$108,200
6.	Cost-per-coupon redeemed cost divided by redemptions	34.9¢
7.	Actual product sold on redemption (misredemption estimated at 20%) 310,000 × 80%	$248,000
8.	Cost-per-product moved— program cost divided by product sold	43.6¢

Source: Louis J. Haugh, "How Coupons Measure Up," *Advertising Age,* June 8, 1981, p. 58. Used with permission.

considered—see Figure 16–6. Until the computerized checkout using the Universal Product Codes becomes standard practice there is little the manufacturer can do but to press charges against those resellers who have been caught engaging in fraudulent practices such as misredemption.

Premiums. A premium is the offer of some type of merchandise or service either free or at a bargain price to induce purchase of another product or service offering. Although premium promotions vary greatly, their principal purpose is quite specific: to induce consumer change in purchase behavior. The goal may be to switch consumers from their present brand to that of the manufacturer in order to gain trial use and, hopefully, repeat purchase. Or the goal may be to induce present customers to increase their use of the brand or to purchase it in larger sized packages. Premium promotions are effective in that they appeal to the very human desire to get a bargain. Some evidence of how widespread is their use can be gained from industry figures which indicate that over $12 billion annually is grossed by those firms engaged in the supply and distribution of premiums.

Premiums may be classified in terms of whether they are offered free or are to some extent self-liquidating (see Figure 16–7). In the latter case the customer pays an extra amount which covers the manufacturer's out-of-pocket costs. Recent evidence indicates that with self-liquidating premium offers consumers are less concerned with the amount that they are required to pay than they are with whether or not they will be getting

FIGURE 16–7
Example of a Self-Liquidating Premium Offer

© 1980 The Nestlé Company. Courtesy The Nestlé Company and Leo Burnett Company, Inc.

a bargain. One of the most successful self-liquidating premium offers was the Kool Cigarette promotion in which a sailboat was offered for $88 with the enclosure of 10 empty packages as proof of purchase. Over 20,000 customers ordered this premium.[11]

Free premiums may range from toys offered for cereal box tops to towels packed in boxes of detergent. The item offered is carefully selected and often pretested to insure that it will be sufficiently appealing to induce purchase. In most cases the premium offered is not directly related to the main product as would be the case in a combination offer promotion.

Premium promotions differ by mode of delivery or redemption. The most widely used mode is the "free-in-the-mail" approach. The offer is communicated to the consumer by coupons or by media advertising. Requests for the free premium are mailed to the manufacturer or to a premium redemption specialist where they are processed and deliveries are arranged. This process is quite expensive.

The alternative strategy of placing the premium in or on the package of the basic product simplifies premium delivery and stimulates interest at point-of-sale. On-packaging has become increasingly popular as technology has enabled the use of blister or bubble packaging. With a blister pack, for example, the premium can be placed next to the main product without fear of detachment and loss. Yet, the plastic packaging material allows the premium to be seen at point-of-purchase thus stimulating consumer reaction. Of course, the use of the in- or on-pack modes of delivery require the support of the resellers. They must buy the promotional packs and place them on display so that they will be available when the national advertising communicates the promotion to the public. Closely associated with on-pack promotion is the use of the package itself as a premium. This topic will be discussed in the section on packaging.

The use of premiums is effective in gaining short-run trial use. However, unless the product offers distinctive advantage to the consumer, trial use will not translate into repeat purchase. Under these circumstances all that the use of a premium promotion will do is to provide a temporary boost to product sales. A better strategy would be to divert some of the promotional resources to product development activities.

Contests and sweepstakes. Promotional activities which involve consumers in the advertising and merchandising activities of the manufacturer by gaining their participation in games of skill or chance are known respectively as contests and sweepstakes (see Figure 16–8). Comparing these devices to other alternative means of sales promotion, they are

---

[11] Robert L. Uebele, "Premiums" in *The Tools of Promotion* (New York, Association of National Advertisers, 1975), p. 1.

398

considered to be potentially as strong as the strongest premium offer (in-pack) and stronger than the weakest premium offer (self-liquidating).[12]

A contest requires that the participant apply a skill in creating an idea, a concept, or an end product. Contests have been based on suggesting the best name for a new product, new uses for established products or as in the case of the Pillsbury Bake-Off Contest the creating and utilizing of recipes to produce outstanding baked good products. In contrast, sweepstakes are games of chance in which each participant has an equal chance of winning a prize from a rather extensive and expensive list of rewards. Care must be taken to prevent the sweepstakes from being considered a lottery, which is illegal in most states. Judicial review has indicated that the requirement that a sweepstake entrant buy the manufacturer's product is not a "consideration" which would make the event a lottery. Even so most firms that use sweepstakes allow contestants to use facsimiles of the box top or coupon rather than the original.

Contests and sweepstakes have many advantages including their ability to gain a high degree of consumer involvement in the manufacturer's advertising and merchandising program. In addition, they can help gain support from resellers and often add excitement or interest to a lagging product or advertising theme.[13]

The disadvantages associated with contests and sweepstakes flow essentially from the fact that it is impossible to test these devices in a limited market before using them on a national basis. Such testing cannot be done because it is not possible to allocate a portion of the total prize packages to a limited market without reducing the impact of the promotion. Because of the limitations on pretesting it is also difficult to determine how much advertising and other types of promotional support should be given to the contest promotion to maximize the effectiveness of the total program.

Finally, many persons who enter these contests or sweepstakes are professionals. It is difficult to weed them out, and their presence discourages entry by ordinary consumers who feel that their chances of winning the contest or sweepstakes are very limited.

Packaging

Although initially designed to provide protection for products as they move from producer to consumer, the product package has played an increasingly important promotional role in recent years. The recognition that the package is more than a protective container has boomed the packaging industry to an annual level of gross sales approaching $60

---

[12] Luick and Ziegler, *Sales Promotion,* p. 76.
[13] Ibid., p. 77.

billion. No small part of that expenditure is to obtain the sales stimulation that well-designed packages can provide. In spite of the large role that packaging plays in promotional strategy there is only a modest amount of literature on the subject. The remainder of this section will attempt to highlight what is available. The promotional aspects of packaging can be both long term (such as advertising) or short term (such as most sales promotions).

Promotional aspects. The prime promotional aspects of a package are the ability of a package to identify a product from an array of competing goods and upon its ability to convey information and meaning about the product. In those increasingly numerous situations in which consumer goods are sold with a minimum of clerk service or by self-service, the package is the salesperson. It plays the role of the attention getter or triggering cue which starts the sales process. It provides information about product attributes such as price, quality, quantity, instructions for use, warranty and so forth. In addition, the package conveys meaning of an emotional or psychological nature. It can aid in the creation of product imagery. Package color and shape are very important in this area.

Package color. The use of color is one example of the ability of a package to convey psychological meaning. White packages, for example, are usually utilized to suggest purity and cleanliness, green packages suggest association with nature and thus natural ingredients, blue packages indicate coolness, thus the use of blue on some menthol cigarette packs or on "Cold Water All" detergent. Red and yellow packages, in contrast, indicate a "hot" new product which demands consumer attention.

Package shape. The physical form of a package in addition to providing protection and convenience can also convey the psychological message which is deemed appropriate given the target market audience and the overall copy platform which is used in the advertising. For example, a successful promotion involved the packaging of a liquid cleaning compound in a container that was designed to be a miniature version of a 55-gallon industrial drum. The packaging and the TV advertising carried the message that the compound was strong enough to be used by a janitor engaged in commercial cleaning. The package design, needless to say, reinforced this message.

Another example of package shape is more Freudian in nature. It is the use of packages which are shaped as phallic symbols to create specific imagery for certain types of beauty aids. The general idea is to convey the emotional message that use of the product will increase one's appeal to the opposite sex. Look at the package shape for Pierre Cardin men's cologne, and Jōvan men's and women's cologne next time you are at the store.

Package size. By making different amounts of product available to different types of buyers, package size variation can increase the size of the market in many situations. Large size "economy" packages can attract heavy users while small size "trial" packs can provide an option for light users or can induce trial use. The experience of the Morton Salt Company in placing their product in picnic packs barely an inch in diameter and in table-size packages the size of a salt shaker greatly increased market share and made it possible to differentiate a rather homogeneous product on the basis of packaging innovation.

Reseller needs.   Most of the discussion to this point has been concerned with the role of the package in filling consumer needs. What must not be overlooked, however, is that packaging plays an important role in gaining the support of resellers. Without such support the product does not get the stocking and shelf position which is required if it is to succeed in the marketplace. In order to gain a fair chance of success in competition with thousands of other packaged items, three conditions must be met. First, the package must be durable and easy to handle by the reseller. Breakage, leakage and the like must be minimized in order to save the reseller time and expense. Second, the package must be so designed that it can be stacked and displayed with a minimum use of shelf or floor space. Third, the package must aid in the sale of the product to such an extent that in combination with the rest of the manufacturer's promotional effort the reseller's return per unit of space allocated will be in the acceptable range of profitability.

The case history of Sylvania's entry into the supermarket channel for sale of light bulbs is illustrative of how packaging design can gain support from resellers. Facing the problem of not having been in supermarkets previously and noting that although light bulbs were a high margin item, they were not looked upon with great favor by supermarket buyers because of the great difficulties involved in handling and displaying light bulbs, Sylvania created a packaging strategy that overcame reseller lack of enthusiasm for the product category. The company developed a shipping carton which not only protected the bulbs from breakage but also converted into a compartmentalized selling rack. In addition, bulbs of different wattages were color-coded by individual pack and placed in the appropriate compartment of the display. This use of packaging was most successful in gaining access to the supermarket channel for Sylvania.

The unique egg-shaped packaging and the specially designed display racks for L'Eggs panty-hose enabled Hanes to gain supermarket distribution for their product line. Again, attractive and attention getting packaging which is also protective and a display strategy which maximizes return per square foot of allocated space is the secret of success when reseller support is vital.

Packages as premiums.   As noted in a previous section, packages can be used as premiums. Instant coffee packed in containers which can be used as servers, cookies packed in jars which can be reused and the

FIGURE 16–9
Illustration of a Premium Offer in Which the Package Is the Premium

Source: Herman Davis, "Harness That Marketing Knowledge, and Let the Package Reflect It," *Advertising Age,* May 8, 1978, p. 45, reprinted with permission.

like are all examples of how packages themselves can be used as a form of premium promotion. Figure 16–9 illustrates a promotion in which a specially designed cannister was used to sell a product produced by Dunkin' Donuts.

Package Design and Evaluation

The package has been referred to in this chapter as a salesperson. Davis, however, describes the package as an advertisement and one that has to work hard in its environment.[14] In recounting the design objectives he sought to achieve in creating the package for a new toothbrush entry by Johnson & Johnson named "Reach," insight is gained into the nature of the process. Problems faced by the designer included the fact that the new product was of a completely unique design and looked very different than did a traditional toothbrush. Next, the toothbrush category was inundated by hundreds of brands and the challenge was to gain recognition in a mass display situation. Lastly, the package had to enable a close tie-in with the national TV advertising campaign which would be used to promote the introduction of Reach.

---

[14] Herman Davis, "Harness That Marketing Knowledge, and Let the Package Reflect It," *Advertising Age,* May 8, 1978, p. 45.

FIGURE 16–10
Package Design for a New Toothbrush Entry

Source: Herman Davis, "Harness that Marketing Knowledge, and Let the Package Reflect It," *Advertising Age,* May 8, 1978, p. 45, reprinted with permission.

Believing that the package should go beyond good design and make a statement like a print ad, Davis came up with the package illustrated in Figure 16–10. The Reach package integrates form and content and uses a photograph of the new product to illustrate the nature of the contents of the package. In addition, the photograph is placed upon a black background so that the package will stand out among the array of competitive products which are predominately packed in white to connote cleanliness. Davis notes that his design "sticks out like a sore tooth."[15]

Evaluation of the package.   It is not a simple task to evaluate a package proposal. Most marketing executives do not have the experience upon which to base their judgments. Test marketing is always feasible but quite expensive. Twedt has suggested four criteria which can be of considerable help in evaluating product proposals. He uses the acronym VIEW so that the approach might be remembered and he further suggests that adequate methods presently exist for measuring package performance in terms of the VIEW criteria.[16]

*V*isability is the first criterion. To determine how visable a package design is, tests can be made to see how quickly respondents can find a package in its natural environment; generally a mass display such as is found in a supermarket. The second criterion is *I*nformation or the ability of a package to communicate key product attributes to a consumer. Tests can be made to see how much information can be gained by a respondent in a limited time from the proposed package design. *E*motionally appealing is the third criterion. Tests can be made to see if the package communicates a "product personality." For example, does the package connote old fashioned or modern values, economy or luxury and so forth? Finally, *W*orkability or the criterion which considers how well the package performs its task of protecting its contents, how easily does it open, close and reopen, and how well does it preserve the freshness of its contents after it has been opened for the first time.

Twedt concludes by noting that few packages will score high on all

---

[15] Ibid.

[16] D. W. Twedt, "How Much Value Can Be Added through Packaging," *Journal of Marketing,* January 1968, pp. 61 ff.

of the criteria.[17] But by using these or similar guidelines the marketing decision maker will be able to select those designs best suited to the needs of the target market audience and which blend in best with the overall promotional strategy.

SUMMARY

This chapter has discussed some of those marketing activities encompassed by the term *sales promotion*. The growing importance of these activities was described and special attention was paid to such promotional alternatives as sampling, couponing, money refund offers, price-off promotions, premiums, and consumer contests. In conclusion, the role of packaging as a promotional tool was examined.

Review and Discussion Questions

1. Why is it so difficult to define "sales promotion"? How would you go about classifying a promotional activity as a sales promotion rather than advertising or personal selling?
2. What are the advantages of sales promotion over other promotional tools? The disadvantages?
3. Can you explain why the use of certain sales promotional activities seems to change over time?
4. What are some of the specific objectives for sales promotional effort?
5. When would the use of sampling be likely to be most effective?
6. What is a cents-off deal, and how does it compare with a cash refund offer?
7. What are the advantages of couponing?
8. What conclusions might you draw from the redemption data shown in Figure 16–5?
9. What is a self-liquidating premium?
10. Differentiate between a contest and a sweepstake?
11. What are the two main functions of a package?
12. Describe how package color, size, and shape can influence consumer behavior.
13. What is the VIEW approach to package evaluation?

---

[17] Ibid.

PART FIVE

Principles of Personal Selling

Our consideration of the stages in promotional strategy outlined in Chapter 3 has given considerable attention to the management of mass communication efforts, particularly the management of advertising efforts. The part will continue the discussion of management of program elements by considering problems inherent in managing the personal selling resources available to the firm. These resources provide for face-to-face contact with potential customers with the purposes of informing them of new product or service offerings and persuading them to buy.

Although personal selling is used at every level in business, from the manufacturer to the retailer, this section is primarily concerned with the use of a sales force by manufacturers to seek out new business by contacting end users or resellers. Many of the points discussed are applicable at all levels of the channel of distribution.

The first chapter in this section deals with personal selling as a special form of interpersonal communication and considers the nature of the selling task in considerable detail. The next two chapters discuss the management aspects of building, training, deploying, and motivating a sales force.

CHAPTER 17

Principles of Personal Selling

Personal selling is a special form of interpersonal communication. Its goal is to "bring to the prospect's attention information that will satisfy a need and that will elicit a response, hopefully in the form of a purchase."[1] Although personal selling is only one of several communication tools used by marketing managers, it is unique in that it is a form of dyadic communication. In this it is opposed to advertising, sales promotion, and publicity, which are mass communication forms. Moreover, business firms spend more money on personal selling activities than on the other means of persuasive communication. It has been estimated by one source that industry spends twice as much on personal selling activity as it does on advertising.[2]

Although the use of personal selling is quite large in the aggregate, when compared with the use of other tools, not all firms favor personal selling over alternate means of communication. There are, however, many instances in which personal selling is vitally important to the attainment of the firm's marketing objectives. This chapter is concerned with those instances and especially with those firms that use salespeople to seek out buyers. These are typically manufacturing firms, although wholesaler salespeople also spend part of their time locating and developing new customers.

---

[1] Kenneth R. Davis and Frederick E. Webster, Jr., *Sales Force Management* (New York: Ronald Press, 1968), p. 10.

[2] Ibid.

The first part of this chapter views personal selling as a communication process and considers how the nature of the firm's marketing strategy influences the role assigned to personal selling activities. The second part of the chapter discusses those tasks performed by sales personnel with special attention being paid to the skill of selling.

PERSONAL SELLING—A COMMUNICATION PROCESS

Modified Interpersonal Communication Model

A model of the interpersonal communication process was presented in Chapter 2 as Figure 2–1. A better understanding of personal selling as a communication process can be gained by examining a slightly modified version of this model. Figure 17–1 presents this modified model.

FIGURE 17–1
Personal Selling: A Communication Process

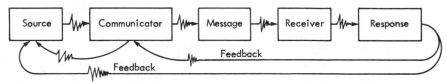

The source.   Note that the element "source" has been added to the model presented in Chapter 2. This addition is necessary because in the personal selling process a distinction must be made between the firm, which is the true source of the message, and the salesperson, who is the communicator of the message. This distinction is, of course, not needed in those instances where the source and the communicator are the same, as would be the case in casual nonbusiness-motivated conversation between two persons.

While the recognition that in personal selling activity there is a difference between source and communicator is self-evident, it is important nevertheless. Without such recognition one cannot fully comprehend the subtleties of the personal selling process. For example, when salesperson X representing company Y calls on a prospect, the response which may be elicited is a function not only of the prospect's reaction to the salesperson but also of the company he or she represents.

The communicator.   The salesperson is the communicator in the process; her or his message is the information that one transmits to the prospect. The channel in the case of a salesperson-delivered message usually consists of the spoken word, although as noted in Chapter 2 the importance of nonverbal communication such as the appearance or personality of the salesperson must not be overlooked.

The message.   In personal selling communication the message is the sales presentation or the series of attempts on the part of the salesperson to provide information to the prospect. The purpose of the message is to persuade the prospect that the salesperson's offering is useful. The ability of the salesperson to custom design a sales presentation to the perceived needs of the prospect is one advantage that personal selling has over advertising. In addition, the sales presentation can be altered in light of feedback received by the communicator or the source. More is said about this in a later part of this section.

The receiver.   The receiver of the message is the prospective customer or prospect. This is usually an individual, thus preserving the dyadic relationship. There are exceptions, however, and in both the industrial and consumer markets the salesperson may have to make a presentation to a buying group. In the former situation the salesperson might prefer to see each member of the buying group on an individual basis, while in the consumer market the saleperson of life insurance, a new home, or an automobile may prefer to have all the members of the group together when making a presentation.

In any event, the skill of a salesperson will be demonstrated by the ability to identify those individuals to whom the sales message should be directed and to decide whether the recipients should be seen individually or in groups.

The response.   Another element that has been added to the communication model of Chapter 2 is response. For communication to have taken place some type of response must have been elicited from the receiver. This response may be in the form of overt behavior such as a refusal to buy or, more positively, a decision to buy. Or it may be psychological, in which case the receiver's awareness and (or) comprehension of the message may be increased, with a resulting change in the receiver's attitudes toward the product offering. While not all personal selling activity is aimed at evoking immediate buying action, a widely sought goal is a sufficiently favorable attitudinal change on the part of the receiver so that buying action is likely to occur in the future.

Feedback.   The last of the elements to be considered in the communication process is feedback. This is a reverse flow of information. The receiver becomes the source and the response becomes the message, and either the salesperson or the source is the receiver. Feedback allows message modification by the salesperson during the period of interaction with the prospect. It also enables the firm to alter the content of its suggested sales messages to conform better to customer information needs, or to meet competition more effectively.

In the portrayal of the expanded communication model the connections between adjacent elements as well as feedback loops have been illustrated by means of jagged lines. These lines indicate that interference or "noise"

FIGURE 17–2

Sales Strategy as a Communication Process

	WHO says	WHAT	to WHOM with what RESULT?	
Elements of communi- cation	Communicator	Message	Receiver	Response
Elements of sales strategy	Salesperson	Presentation	Buyer	Objectives
Information needed— inputs to planning	Functions Selling Services Market informa- tion Number of accounts	Product appeals Order of presentation Handling objections Length of call Frequency of calls	Needs charac- teristics Location Buying pat- terns Potential Decision maker	Marketing objectives Sales forecast (Expected and desired results)

Source: Kenneth R. Davis and Frederick E. Webster, Jr., eds., *Readings in Sales Force Management* (New York: Ronald Press, 1968), p. 7.

may be present in the system. Such interference is anything which can obstruct or alter the message as it moves from source to receiver.

Feedback also serves the purpose of monitoring the level of noise in the system and of indicating how clearly the message is coming through. It must be remembered, however, that feedback is just as susceptible as the original message to interference from system noise.

Implications of the Communication Process

If the sales strategy of a firm can be viewed as a communication process, the requirements of such a strategy become easier to define, as does the function of the salesperson in carrying out the strategy. It has been suggested that the analysis of any communication process involves answering the question, "*Who* says *what* to *whom* with what result?"[3] It is further suggested that a sales strategy can be planned within the framework of the question, as is illustrated in Figure 17–2.

Personal Selling in the Promotional Mix

In order to understand better the nature of tasks performed by salespeople it is necessary to examine how the role that personal selling plays

[3] Kenneth R. Davis and Frederick E. Webster, Jr., eds., *Readings in Sales Force Management* (New York: Ronald Press, 1968), p. 7.

in the promotional mix changes with various product-market situations. One way of seeing how the type and extent of personal selling effort can vary is to consider three case histories detailing the experiences of a drug manufacturer, a computer manufacturer, and a provider of specialized welding services.

Proprietary drug manufacturer.   Imagine a situation in which a manufacturer is desirous of launching a new patent medicine through retail drugstores. Market research has indicated that the market is geographically dispersed and that a large percentage of present proprietary drug users are potential buyers of the new product. Cost analysis has indicated that national advertising by means of newspapers and radio and TV spots will provide the most economical coverage of the market. Accordingly, $2 million is appropriated for consumer advertising and $200,000 for personal selling effort. Why the disparity in budgeted amounts, and what is the role assigned to personal selling?

The answer to the first question is that the product type and the large and dispersed market present a situation in which advertising can stimulate demand more economically than can personal selling. The patent medicine has hidden qualities and appeals to emotions concerned with health and well-being. Moreover, the usage rate of the product promises revenues of sufficient size and continuity to sustain a costly advertising campaign. In brief, this situation is ideally suited to dominant emphasis on advertising.

Personal selling effort is utilized, however, at three different levels in the channel: manufacturer, wholesaler, and retailer. At the first of these levels the manufacturer uses his salespeople to call on large wholesalers and chain drug retailers. The advertising aimed at the household buyer is creating a "pull" effect, and the primary task of the salesperson is to make certain that resellers have ordered adequate stocks of the product. The selling task here is essentially order taking, with considerable time being allocated to supporting activities to ensure that wholesaler and retailer point-of-sales efforts are coordinated with the national advertising campaign.

The budget does not allow very much personal selling activity by the manufacturer, so whatever effort is available is directed to those customers that appear to offer the greatest potential. The great bulk of the orders are received by mail from interested wholesalers and retailers.

At the wholesale level a different type of personal selling activity is taking place. The wholesaler sales force is engaged in making routine calls on members of the wholesaler's customer group. These salespeople carry catalogs and price lists describing thousands of items. Their essential functions are of the order-taking variety. If, however, the demand for the new patent medicine is being felt at retail and the salespeople are aware of the promotional plans of the manufacturer, they may engage in some promotional selling aimed at getting the retailer to carry special stocks and to provide in-store promotional tie-ins.

Personal selling at the retail level is still another type of activity. In this case the retail clerk or the pharmacist may suggest the particular brand of product to those customers who ask for a remedy of the general type. If the situation is as highly advertisable as is assumed, it is more likely that the customer will ask for the remedy by name, thus reducing the personal selling task at retail to one of order filling. Retailer support, in this instance, is largely confined to providing ample display and counter space for the product.

Computer manufacturer. After several years of research and development, a manufacturer of personal computers located in California developed a portable computer of great power. Limitations of production capacity and the desire to have consumers given a great deal of personal attention at point-of-sale dictated a distribution policy under which only a few hundred dealers would carry the line. A modest advertising campaign directed to the trade as well as to end users was planned. The bulk of promotional effort, however, was to be in the form of personal selling at both the manufacturer and retailer levels.

The manufacturer must develop a highly skilled group of salespeople whose principal task is to get several hundred of the best computer retailers in the country to stock, display, demonstrate, and sell the new computer. This will not be an easy task because the product type is totally different in a technical sense from anything previously seen. The cost of the new product will be relatively high and the extent of demand is unknown. In this situation the manufacturer salesperson must be an order getter. Creativity and aggressiveness are necessary if the salesperson is to succeed in gaining the best quality retailers in each market area.

Selling effort at retail is also very important. A potential customer for the new computer must be given a very thorough demonstration of how it operates. Knowledge of the product and persuasive ability are required of the retail salesperson if a sale is to be made. The manufacturer's margin payment to the retailer must, therefore, include payment for the superior selling effort required.

Over time as the product moves along its life cycle and enters a more mature stage, the nature of the personal selling task will change along with the other elements of the marketing mix. The product itself will be better known by potential customers, distribution will be more intensive, price will be reduced, and the promotional mix will include a larger amount of consumer advertising and less personal selling effort.

From the manufacturer's standpoint the need then will be to gain more sales from present retail outlets rather than to increase the coverage of the market. The selling task will become more routine with greater emphasis on order-taking and service. Similarly, at retail the requirements for a creative selling job will have lessened. At all levels in the channel personal selling will give way to greater reliance on consumer advertising and price promotion.

Electron beam welding service.   As a third illustration of the determination of proper sales tasks, consider the promotional problems facing a small company offering an electron beam welding service to industry.[4] The electron beam technology, developed in the aircraft industry, had not gained widespread acceptance in the manufacture of industrial goods and consumer products, although it offered many advantages over conventional welding techniques.

The company hired a manufacturers' representative on an expenses-plus-commission basis to contact potential accounts within the market area. After two years the owners found, much to their dismay, that the sales rep was not producing enough business to cover his expenses. A reappraisal of promotional strategy was very much in order.

If the owners of this small company had analyzed their present customers in terms of informational requirements, they would have found that some customers required much more information input than others did. For example, buyers who had previously used the process or who had a relatively small job to be welded did not require a great deal of selling effort. On the other hand, those who were unfamiliar with the nature of electron beam welding or who had large and expensive jobs to complete required a great deal of information about the technical capability of the supplier, the price, and the delivery date for the finished work. In one case it took six months of inquiry and negotiation to close a sale.

From this type of analysis it would appear that although a manufacturers' representative might handle some of the routine buying situations, one would have neither the expertise nor the time to apply oneself to the more complex situations. Given such a set of circumstances, the owners would either have to hire another salesperson of their own to engage in the complex selling task or, if such an addition were not economically feasible, they would have to assume the responsibility themselves for the specialized personal selling effort required to make a sale.

Implications of the cases.   The three situations discussed above illustrate briefly how product and market influences affect the role played by personal selling in the promotional strategy mix. In the consumer area, as products mature, the role of personal selling is diminished, and advertising becomes more important. In the industrial market, as the product moves through its life cycle, personal selling is generally a more important element in the promotional mix than is advertising. But even in

---

[4] See the "Advanced Technologies, Inc." case in Stewart H. Rewoldt, James D. Scott, and Martin R. Warshaw, *Introduction to Marketing Management,* rev. ed. (Homewood, Ill.: Richard D. Irwin, 1973), pp. 220 ff.

the industrial market, as the information requirements of customers vary so does the extent and nature of the personal selling task.

What Do Salespeople Do?

As seen in the above case histories there can be wide variations in environmental or strategic conditions which influence the role assigned to personal selling activities by a given firm. Regardless of these variations, however, salespeople perform certain functions which can be identified and described. For example, they must seek out or meet prospective buyers, discover customer needs and attitudes and help the customer to buy the product or service best suited to the requirements. In this process of helping the customer to buy, the salesperson must be prepared to supply generous quantities of information about product or service characteristics. The salesperson must also persuade the buyer that a particular offering is best suited to the buyer's needs, and one must act decisively to overcome buyer uncertainty by sensing how and when to close the sale. Follow-up after the sale is also important to ensure that the buyer receives the fullest utility from the purchase and to prevent dissonance by assuring the customer that the correct choice has been made.

Thus the essential tasks of personal selling consist of (1) locating and (or) meeting prospective customers, (2) discovering customer needs and attitudes, (3) recommending a product package to fill the needs of the customer, (4) developing a sales presentation aimed at informing the customer of product attributes and persuading the customer to buy the recommended package, (5) closing the sale, and (6) following up to ensure total satisfaction with the purchase.

Of course, all salespeople do not place equal emphasis on the various components of the selling task. This may be the result of inadequate performance or simply because the selling strategy requires a different pattern of behavior. It is essential that the selling task be clearly defined so that the salesperson understands the nature of the job to be performed. Without a clear definition of what is to be done, evaluation of selling performance is impossible.

Salesmanship

T. F. Stroh has defined salesmanship as "a direct, face-to-face, seller-to-buyer influence which can communicate the facts necessary for making a buying decision; or it can utilize the psychology of persuasion to encourage the formation of a buying decision."[5] Another way of looking at salesmanship is to consider it as a set of skills which can make the personal

---

[5] T. F. Stroh, *Techniques of Practical Selling* (Homewood, Ill.: Richard D. Irwin, 1966), p. 7.

selling efforts of the salesperson more effective. Because these skills are so important to us in a noncommercial as well as a commercial setting, it is worthwhile to examine the subject area in some detail.

Whether or not we choose to make our career in some phase of personal selling activity or not we are all engaged in some aspect of selling in our daily lives. If we try to convince our parents that we should be able to borrow the family automobile, if we are trying to land a summer job, or if we are trying to gain the attention of a member of the opposite sex we are engaged in selling. Because we are continuously selling our ideas and ourselves to others, the question is not whether we shall be selling but how effectively shall we be selling.

Effective selling either in a commercial or noncommercial context requires a very clear understanding of the nature of dyadic communication when one party is attempting to influence the response of the other.

The buyer-seller dyad. There are a variety of influences which have an effect on how the buyer receives and interprets messages sent by the seller. The seller's appearance, personality, level of knowledge about the product or service offering all contribute to buyer reaction. In similar manner, buyer knowledge of the seller's company and familiarity with the seller on a personal basis are important determinants of how the seller's message is received and whether or not it is acted upon. Even the buyer's immediate state of mind or of health can have a major influence on the nature of the information-receiving and processing function.

Given the large number of operable variables, research has been undertaken to provide useful insights which might serve as a basis for formulation of an effective sales approach. In a study by Evans of buyer-seller dyads in the life insurance industry, for example, it was found that prospects who bought insurance knew more about the salespeople and their companies, and felt more positively toward them, than prospects who did not buy.[6] In addition, the greater the similarity between the salesperson and the prospect in terms of physical, demographic, and personality characteristics, the greater the likelihood that a sale would occur.[7]

Such findings may be the basis for selling strategies when the number of potential customers is small, when the individual sale involves a large outlay, and when there is some possibility of matching salesmen and prospects. It is doubtful that the strategy would be viable given large numbers of prospects, low value unit sales, and limited ability to match sellers and buyers across a given set of attributes.

Different selling situations. Recognition must be given to the fact that selling situations differ in degree of difficulty and that a selling strategy developed for one situation may not be suitable for another. For

[6] F. B. Evans, "Selling as a Dyadic Relationship—A New Approach," *American Behavioral Scientist,* April 1963, p. 78.

[7] Ibid., p. 79.

example, we may classify selling activities as having the goals of (1) order getting, (2) order taking and (3) supporting.

The "order getter" engages in "creative selling" and aggressively undertakes a campaign to seek out potential buyers and to persuade them to buy a specific product or service. The "order taker," on the other hand, operates on a more relaxed basis. Order takers make routine calls on customers to maintain a continuing relationship. Their approach is a low-pressure one designed to enable them to live well with their customer group for a long time. It is a mistake to compare order takers unfavorably with order getters, for the basic goals of the two types are different. However, if a salesperson who is supposed to be an order getter performs as an order taker, management must step in to assure that the proper emphasis is placed on creative and aggressive selling activity.

In the supporting category are found selling activities which do not in themselves aim at getting or taking an order; missionary selling, technical support, and assistance in management or promotion fall into this grouping. These indirect selling activities build goodwill for the seller and increase the ability of the order-oriented salespeople to close the sale.

It is obvious that the role of the individual salesperson in any of the three classifications will vary. Certainly the channel position of the seller has a profound effect on the nature of the selling job. Manufacturer salespeople selling to wholesalers or end users will play a role that differs from that of wholesaler salespeople selling to retailers or retail salespeople selling to people who enter their stores. Product characteristics as well as market characteristics are important influences on the nature of the basic selling task.

It is important, however, to recognize that the skill level required of the salesperson will vary considerably over the range of selling situations and that the quality of salesmanship required in order getting is considerably higher than that required to take orders to provide service after the sale.

Steps of a Sale

Many authors who have written on the subject of salesmanship break down the steps of a sale into discrete steps or stages. Although in reality the selling process is continuous with considerable overlapping of the steps, for explanatory purposes it is useful to consider the steps one at a time. In addition we shall consider those steps as described by Beach and others in writings which have endured the test of time.[8] These steps

---

[8] Frederick A. Russell, Frank H. Beach, and Richard H. Buskirk, *Textbook of Salesmanship*, 10th ed. (New York: McGraw-Hill, 1977).

include (1) prospecting, (2) the pre-approach, (3) the approach, (4) the presentation, (5) meeting objections, (6) the close, and (7) the follow-up.

Prospecting.   In this, the first stage of the selling process, the salesperson attempts to locate prospective customers who are likely to have a need or desire for the products or services offered. In addition the prospect must also be qualified to buy. The prospect must have the authority to enter into a purchase agreement and must be financially able to pay for the goods or services purchased. The goal of prospecting, therefore, is the location and qualification of individuals who have both needs and abilities to satisfy those needs with products and services offered by the salesperson and his or her company. The prospecting process is continuous as enough likely candidates to receive a sales call must be provided to utilize fully the salesperson's time.

The systems that are used in prospecting are varied and numerous. One such approach is termed the snowball technique in which every prospect, regardless of whether she or he has made a purchase, is asked to recommend one or two additional prospects who might be able to make use of the salesperson's offering. Leads may also be evoked through the placement of advertisements containing coupons requesting further information about the product/service offering or from direct mail activities in which prepaid postcards are enclosed allowing the prospect to request more information and thus providing a lead for a salesperson. When all else fails the salesperson may adopt the "cold canvas" approach in which one calls on a series of individuals knowing little more about them than their name and address. The cold canvas approach is the least productive of all the methods in terms of time and effort input. If the salesperson is not utilizing all of her or his time in planned prospecting and selling, then the marginal cost of cold canvassing is low and the benefits will generally exceed the costs.

Pre-approach.   Once a prospect has been identified and qualified the problem facing the salesperson is how to approach the prospect with the greatest effectiveness. Analysis of information on hand about the prospect's purchase behavior in the past, about the nature of current needs and about alternatives offered by competitors can lead to the development of an approach strategy. Thus information gathering, analysis, and the planning of the approach based on the analysis make up the key elements of the pre-approach step.

The approach.   This is the step in the selling process that is most easily identified in that it occurs when the seller first meets the buyer. Unfortunately, too many selling processes start at this step without sufficient prospecting or pre-approach effort. The approach must be carefully planned and this is especially true if the salesperson is meeting the prospect for the first time. The goal of the approach is to secure the interest and the attention of the prospect. If this goal is not met the selling process is stopped and the best that the salesperson can do is to exit politely so that he or she may return another day to try again.

Approaches are varied ranging from the most widely used and least effective one of presenting a business card to the prospect or the prospect's secretary to the more imaginative approaches in which the salesperson uses product samples, premiums, or intriguing opening statements to capture the prospects' interest. Careful prospecting and pre-approach planning should provide ideas for those approach strategies most likely to succeed with a given prospect.

The salesperson will know very quickly whether or not an approach is succeeding. If the prospect invites the salesperson to have a seat or to continue with the presentation the approach has worked. A polite suggestion that the salesperson leave as the prospect is very busy will indicate that the salesperson will have to try again at another time or with another prospect.

The presentation. The objective of this step is to create in the prospect's mind a desire for the product or service offered. In order to achieve this goal the salesperson must communicate as complete a story as possible about the product attributes and the benefits that the prospect will derive from the product. The salesperson must gain the prospect's confidence as a prelude to effecting a change in the prospects behavior. The seller must always be aware of the nature of the dyadic relationship in which one is involved. The seller must be the influencer; the prospect is the one that must act. To avoid making a decision most prospects will raise objections as the presentation continues or will attempt to side-track the seller with extraneous remarks. The skilled salesperson will know how to anticipate and overcome objections and will be able to steer the discussion back to the topic at hand.

Some sellers use "canned" presentations which have been carefully developed and memorized. This approach has the advantage of completeness as the presentation has been pretested to make sure that it covers the principal selling points. It lacks the spontaneity and flexibility of a noncanned approach, and thus except in rather standardized selling situations in which relatively unskilled salespersons are being used its use is not recommended.

Meeting objections. Closely allied with the presentation step is that of meeting objections. Indeed, one could make a good case for combining this step with the preceding one. But because this skill is so important to the salesperson, we will look at it a little more closely. Objections can be handled most effectively if the salesperson knows what the true purpose of the objection is. In some cases the prospect might object to some aspect of the physical design of the product and yet this objection may be a device used to cover up the fact that the prospect cannot afford to make the purchase at this time. Thus even if the salesperson overcomes the stated objection, the sale is not any closer to fruition. Perhaps continued probing by the seller would uncover the true nature of the problem and enable the seller to overcome the real blockage on the part of the prospect by discussing the possibility of extended terms or a leasing agreement.

In other cases the best way to handle objections is to treat them as requests for clarification of information already transmitted or for new information. The prepared salesperson will anticipate objections and be prepared for them. Indeed, in such cases the overcoming of an objection can move the sale closer to fruition.

Closing the sale. This is the step in which the goal of the salesperson is to obtain action, preferably a commitment on the part of the prospect to become a buyer. The skill of closing is perhaps the most important that a salesperson can possess but also the most difficult to master. A seller who cannot close has been described as a "conversationalist." Part of the skill of closing is knowing when the prospect is ready to buy. When the prospect's questions pertain to delivery dates or credit terms, it may indicate that the time to close is at hand. The salesperson who is uncertain that the time is right might attempt a "trial" close which can be pushed to a complete close if the prospect appears willing to act or it can be withdrawn if the prospect requires more information or more persuasion. Closing techniques differ widely ranging from those which simply ask for the order to those who promise to alter the offering to suit the specific needs of the buyer in order to gain the sale.

Closing is a skill and preplanning of the presentation and careful monitoring of the verbal and body language of the prospect can help the salesperson to develop that sixth sense which is so crucial to successful selling.

Follow-up. Many salespeople end their selling efforts when the order is signed. This is a very serious shortcoming because the aftersale or follow-up stage is so valuable for the removal of any feeling of dissonance the buyer may have and for making sure that the buyer is receiving the full utility from the purchase. The follow-up is the ideal time to suggest add-on sales of accessory equipment or maintenance items. The buyer is relaxed, is committed, and thus is fairly receptive to proposals to increase the investment to gain more advantages from the initial buy.

Even if no further business occurs during the follow-up, the effort made by the salesperson will be repaid many times over by the uncovering of problems that might have made future sales difficult and by the cementing of a relationship that make future sales very much more likely.

SUMMARY

This chapter has considered personal selling as a communication process and has examined salesmanship as a set of skills which are used by salespeople to improve their effectiveness. The steps of a sale presented above are based on a model developed by Strong in 1925 which has been described by the acronym AIDA, standing for *A*ttention, *I*nterest, *D*esire, and *A*ction.[9] Each step in the approach developed in this chapter has as its objective the movement of the prospect through the phases of buying readiness. Although there are many models which could have provided the motivation for the analysis, the Strong AIDA concept and the Beach, et al., steps in the selling process have withstood the test of time and are worthy of your consideration if you seek a career in personal selling.

Review and Discussion Questions

1. How does personal selling differ from advertising as a communication process?
2. Why do firms vary in their dependence upon personal selling as opposed to other tools of persuasive communication?
3. Describe the elements of a personal selling communication process in terms of their roles in achieving the firm's communication goals.
4. How does viewing sales strategy as a communication process help to define the nature of the salesperson's task?
5. What are the essential tasks of personal selling? Do all salespeople perform these tasks with the same emphasis?
6. How do product and market characteristics influence the nature of the selling task?
7. What is salesmanship? How is it related to personal selling?
8. Explain what is meant by a buyer-seller dyad.
9. What are the key steps of a sale?
10. What problems and opportunities are associated with the concept of "cold canvas"?
11. Why is the closing skill so important? How does one become proficient at closing a sale?
12. Why is the follow-up step so important? Relate follow-up to the concept of cognitive dissonance.

---

[9] E. K. Strong, *The Psychology of Selling* (New York: McGraw-Hill, 1925), p. 9.

CHAPTER 18

Management of Personal Selling I: Selection, Training, Assignment, Compensation, and Motivation of Sales Personnel

This chapter and the one which follows deal with the management aspects of personal selling. Topics covered include the building of a sales force through the steps of recruitment, selection, and training of those individuals who will represent the organization in the marketplace. Attention will also be devoted to those problems which concern the assignment, compensation, and motivation of members of the field selling force. The focus in Chapter 19 will be upon the evaluation and control of sales force performance.

BUILDING THE SALES FORCE

The building of an effective selling organization must begin with a clear understanding of the nature of the selling task. If, for example, the selling job is one of calling on wholesalers to get stocking and promotion of a relatively homogeneous line of products, the recruitment, selection, and training processes are different from a situation where the salesperson is faced with diversity in terms of types of customers to be contacted or products to be sold.

The important consideration is a clear grasp of overall promotional strategy by those in the company responsible for the recruitment, selection, and training of salespeople. The overall strategy determines the *kind* of selling that is required. The *kind* of selling, in turn, determines the personal qualifications needed by members of the sales force and the methods of training, compensation, and motivation.

Job Descriptions and Recruitment

Before recruiting activities for salespeople can take place, a clear exposition must be made with respect to the nature of the selling task. In writing, this exposition is the job description. It is necessary to have a carefully thought out and fully updated job description for every position on the sales force. Examples of job descriptions for different types of selling situations are shown in Figures 18–1, 18–2, and 18–3.

FIGURE 18–1
Example of a Consumer Hardware Sales Representative's Job Description, Hardware Division, The Stanley Works

Function:
Within the limits of Divisional Policy, promotes sales of consumer hardware products to attain the sales and profit objectives in the assigned territory.

Responsibilities:
1. Develops a thorough knowledge of products, merchandising and promotional programs and procedures concerning sales of consumer products.
2. Develops sufficient knowledge of each customer's business internally and externally, including usage of data processing to properly sell and service them.
3. Develops a thorough knowledge of the buying habits and motivations of the consumer market on our type products in the territory.
4. Develops and maintains a thorough knowledge concerning consumer distribution in the territory and implements plans to achieve proper market penetration.
5. Keeps informed on current competitive activities in the territory regarding products, merchandising programs, promotions, pricing, and terms.
6. Attends and participates in all meetings, as directed by the regional manager.
7. Actively participates in trade functions (conventions, shows, seminars, etc.) necessary to keep informed of activity of customers and prospective customers, and lends support to these activities for the purpose of increasing sales and market penetration.
8. Schedules sales time effectively so as to obtain maximum coverage of the assigned territory.
9. Plans sales presentations to customers and prospective customers, using products, merchandising programs, promotions, and sales aids made available and implements them as required.
10. Assists customers in increasing consumer sales through a joint effort.
11. Educates and assists customer sales representatives in selling consumer type products through joint retail sales calls and conducts sales meetings to increase knowledge of our line.
12. Carries out special assignments as directed by the regional manager.
13. Actively seeks new channels of distribution in consumer market.
14. Assists other hardware sales representatives when requested.

FIGURE 18–1 (concluded)

15. Actively makes retail sales calls on key retail accounts in the territory to increase full line support in consumer hardware.
16. Assists sales representatives of other Stanley Divisions when requested.
17. Submits an itinerary each week covering the following two weeks.
18. Submits a weekly call report on a weekly basis.
19. Submits an expense report weekly and stays within the allocated budget.
20. Submits a territorial report on a monthly basis.
21. Submits special reports as conditions warrant or when requested by regional manager or New Britain management.
22. Maintains records of *all* customers in the territory and administrative records as directed.
23. Maintains leased or company automobile assigned in accordance with automobile manual.
24. Recommends additions or deletions of customers in the territory.
25. Obtains approval from regional manager of any deviation from established pricing procedure.

Relationships:
1. *Regional manager*—Reports to, informs, consults, and obtains approvals as required.
2. *Divisional sales management*—Consults, informs, and obtains approvals as required.
3. *Customers*—Promotes and maintains good business-like relations.
4. *Public*—Promotes good Stanley image and maintains respectable position in his territory and his local community.
5. *Sales service department*—Furnishes factual information when requesting service. Maintains proper balance in representing company and customer.
6. *Marketing department*—Cooperates and assists as requested.
7. *Other divisions*—Communicates and cooperates as directed.

Source: Adapted from The Stanley Works, rev. March 1, 1982. Reproduced by permission.

Once the specific kind of selling job to be filled has been determined, the search for a likely employment prospect can begin. The ranks of currently employed salespeople, college campuses, and persons in business currently holding nonselling jobs make up the prime areas from which candidates for sales jobs may be sought. The recruitment process, however, is a difficult one, for personal selling is not as attractive a career choice to many of the more talented or better educated people as are other alternatives. The career image is one of long hours, frequent travel, and constant discouragement. The growing recognition of the value of the sales force as a resource of the firm has resulted in attempts by management to improve salespeople's working conditions and financial remuneration and to provide them with security for the future. Unfortunately, it takes time to change career images, and personal selling is still handicapped by such stigmas as "hucksterism" and the "Death of a Salesman."

In addition to the image issue, recruitment is also made difficult by the problem of turnover. Undeniably, not all people who attempt a career in selling are successful. Those who are poor producers either become discouraged and drop out or are eventually terminated by their employers.

FIGURE 18–2
Example of a Salesperson's Job Description, Grocery Products Division,
General Mills, Inc.

I. *Purpose*

To represent the Grocery Products Sales Division and to secure the maximum in profitable sales volume and product distribution through selling and merchandising the entire line of Grocery Products and assigned subsidiary products (within the limits of established policy and expense programs) to all assigned accounts within a specific territory.

II. *Accountabilities*

1. Achieve programmed volume deliveries by product and product categories.
2. Accomplish timely and productive execution of sales/marketing plans, promotions, and new product introductions.
   a. Secure trade support via display, ad feature, and/or pricing promotions at direct and retail levels.
   b. Ensure compliance with the terms and intent of trade activation plans, exercising proper control over volume and payments.
   c. Establish and execute chainwide or storewide sales events to assigned accounts, supported by proper display, ad feature, and/or pricing promotion.
3. Maintain coverage against both direct and/or retail accounts to ensure:
   a. Delivery of no less than programmed volume.
   b. Optimum distribution on new and established products.
   c. Correct shelf placement and holding power.
   d. Adequate inventories.
   e. Proper pricing.
   f. Good account relationships.
   g. Complete predetermined special retail assignments.
4. Communicate to region office and all affected sales personnel details relative to assigned account's or headquarter buying group's promotional activity, product distribution, and other pertinent information.
5. Maintain and/or develop sound customer relations and goodwill with all assigned accounts.
   a. Assure proper handling of all sales practices and Company policies, including GMI legal responsibilities with and to all accounts.
   b. Ensure proper and prompt handling of all customer problems/complaints and prompt payment of any amounts owed to the customer.
   c. Achieve full acquaintance with the organization chart and people at all levels of responsibility in all accounts, i.e., Management, Financial, Buying, Sales, Warehousing, Delivery, and Clerical.
   d. Firmly and diplomatically protect the company's interest in all credit and/or collection problems.
6. Secure and relate to management complete information on:
   a. Market and/or product problems with recommendations for solutions.
   b. Competitive activities.
   c. Market and product opportunities.
   d. Needs for addition and deletion of stores in coverage pattern to achieve maximum retail volume and distribution.
7. Operate assigned territory within established limits of approved expense program.

III. *Relationships*

This position reports and is responsible to the District Sales Manager.

Source: Adapted from General Mills, Inc. Effective June 1980. Reproduced by permission.

FIGURE 18–3

Examples of a Salesperson's Job Description, Household Products Manufacturer

Basic function
  To sell the budgeted quantities of the company's household and automotive products in assigned territory and to maintain distribution and promotion of these company products marketed through retail outlets.

Product knowledge
  Knowledge of the company's household, automotive, and insecticide line to:
  1. Demonstrate and sell these products in the assigned territory to direct retail outlets, chain outlets, and wholesale distributors in accordance with established sales objectives, policies, and programs.
  2. Carry out specific assignments, as assigned.
  3. Answer questions of a routine nature relative to uses and applications of household, automotive, and insecticide products and handle routine complaints.

Promotion
  1. Develop in-store merchandising techniques that increase the turnover of the household, automotive, and insecticide products.
  2. Conduct wholesale distributors' sales meetings as assigned to educate their salespeople and create enthusiasm and cooperation in the sale of household products.
  3. Engage in field selling with wholesale distributors' salesmen to demonstrate successful selling techniques.
  4. Arrange for advertising and promotion of household products by wholesale distributors, chain headquarters, and key direct retail accounts.
  5. Erect consumer displays in stores of direct retailers and post all advertising material supplied by the advertising department as assigned.
  6. Establish and maintain good will of the company with all its customers.
  7. Inform the area, district, or zone manager of any potential customers for company products other than those for which manager is responsible.
  8. Maintain a constant rate of turnover of wholesale distributors' stock through work in retail outlets.

Contacts
  1. Contact buyers and sales promotion personnel, advertising managers and sales managers of direct retail outlets, wholesalers, and chain outlets in the direct sale and promotion of household products.
  2. Contact wholesale distributors' salespeople to assist them in selling and to demonstrate successful selling techniques.
  3. Contact, as directed, local advertising media such as newspapers to arrange tie-in advertisements.

Planning
  1. Plan own work schedule within limits assigned by area or zone manager.
  2. Control expenses within the budget for the assigned territory.
  3. Maintain accurate sales coverage records according to plan and make changes in count by class of outlet.

Direction
  None

Personnel relations
  Assist the zone and area manager in the training of new salespeople according to Sales Training Plan.

Source: Adapted from Kenneth R. Davis, *Marketing Management* (New York: Ronald Press Co., 1961), p. 480. Copyright © 1961, The Ronald Press Co.

Successful salespeople, on the other hand, may shift to other companies to improve their positions or rise to a position in sales management in the same company. Regardless of the cause of turnover, the net result is that openings on the selling staff are frequent. Attrition because of failure or success by salespeople means that the recruitment task must be continuous and closely attuned to the future needs of the selling organization. A simple illustration of the effect of turnover on recruitment needs is seen in terms of a company with a sales force having an average strength of 200 people. Its separation rate is 20 people per year, or 10 percent. Thus the entire sales force must be replaced every 10 years!

Selecting Salespeople

Assuming that a continuing supply of applicants for selling positions is available, the next step in the process of building a sales force or adding to an existing organization is that of selection. This phase of the sales force building process is of great importance because success here can have a great impact on the effectiveness of the selling organization. Selection of qualified and motivated people means that more and higher quality selling activity may take place. It also reduces separation, either voluntary or involuntary. This in turn means less turnover and lower expense incurred by the firm.

Three tools are useful in the selection process: (1) the personal history statement, (2) psychological tests, and (3) the personal interview.

Personal history statement. The personal history statement or application form is designed to elicit information about the prospect which will be of use in initial screening. Conventional practice is to cover data such as:

1. *Personal data*—age, height, weight, marital status, and number of dependents.
2. *Education*—including a resumé of applicant's educational background with data on performance, extent of self-support, and extracurricular activities.
3. *Experience*—prior employers, types of jobs held, and reasons for leaving.
4. *References from several sources*—former teachers, employers, and current acquaintances who can provide information about specific traits or abilities.
5. *Personality and motivation*—general questions about interests in hobbies, organizations, sports, and so on. The applicant may also be asked to explain why he or she is interested in selling as a career and why he or she chose the specific company as a possible employer.

It is evident that a great deal of information about the job prospect can be gathered by means of a well-designed personal history form. Not only the specific information but its mode of presentation can give insight as to the type of person involved. If used as a preliminary screening device, great care must be taken to have the questionnaire designed to get the type of information *relevant* to the nature of the job to be filled. In addition, analysis and interpretation of the application form must be carried out by persons skilled in psychology, aware of the nature of the job to be filled, and involved in the design of the application form.

Psychological tests.   Perhaps the most controversial of the tools used in selecting salespeople are psychological tests. These devices are used to supplement the information gained from personal history forms and from the interview. It would, however, be very unwise to view them as a substitute for the other approaches used in the selection process.

Tests are designed to provide insights about the applicant's intelligence, personality, and interests. The intelligence tests are perhaps the least criticized of all of the tests, in terms of reliability and validity. The problem is not with intelligence tests themselves but rather with the relation of a given level of intelligence to probable success in the sales position. It is clear that a minimum level of intelligence is required of salespeople and that perhaps higher levels are needed for the successful performance of more technically oriented selling tasks. However, it is also suggested that too high a level of intelligence for a given selling job may result in boredom and subsequent job dissatisfaction.

It appears that the successful use of intelligence tests is predicated on screening out extremely low and high performers for further investigation. If some relationship can be found between a range of intelligence and success in a particular type of selling job, then of course the tests assume predictive value.

Tests of personality, interests, and aptitudes appear to have greater relevance than intelligence tests. These tests deal with human traits that are important in a sales situation. Unfortunately, they are not easily validated—that is, shown to be successful in predicting success in a given situation. As John A. Howard has noted, "Tests are designed to predict, but often it is not at all clear as to just what is being predicted."[1] What is required is that the user must analyze the nature of the selling job to be filled in terms of the personality traits most likely to lead to success. Then the seller must construct a test to measure the existence of such traits or use a standardized test of some sort and engage in sufficient experimentation to validate the test or, more likely, the battery of tests. The goal is to be able to predict which persons from a group of applicants are most likely to succeed in a given selling situation. It is quite clear that this goal requires personnel skilled in psychological testing proce-

---

[1] John A. Howard, *Marketing Management: Operating, Strategic, and Administrative,* 3d ed. (Homewood, Ill.: Richard D. Irwin, 1973), p. 289.

dures, time, money, and a sales force of sufficient size and turnover rate to provide opportunities for validation experiments. Smaller firms may utilize the services of testing consultants. It must be reemphasized, however, that without validation in terms of the particular selling task, testing should be considered only a small part of the selection procedure.

The personal interview. Another approach to selection is the personal interview. It is a flexible device and may be used for such diverse purposes as initial screening, as in college campus recruitment, or for final investigation prior to hiring.

The purposes of the interview include the discovery of traits not uncovered by the application or by testing, probing to find out more about interest and motivation, and evaluation of such characteristics as personal appearance and oral expression. The interview may either be structured through a questionnaire or unstructured, depending upon the preference of management. Regardless of the type of interview used, management must provide well-defined criteria which can be used to evaluate the person taking the interview as well as to validate the interviewing process. This provision of criteria is especially important when selecting salespeople because of the many ill-founded preconceptions about the personality attributes of a good salesperson which are held by interviewers.

In order to prevent interviewer biases or preconceptions from lessening the effectiveness of the interview as a selection device, many firms have the applicants appraised personally by several interviewers. Regardless of the method, the personal interview can be a useful tool if it can be validated against later sales success. Such validation, in turn, requires a standardized approach. Traits that are important to the selling task at hand must be identified, and all the interviewers must agree on how the existence of these traits is to be discovered and measured.

Training Salespeople

The third component in building a successful sales force is training. After recruitment and selection of new additions to the sales staff, effort must be expended to prepare these people to assume their selling responsibilities. However, training must not be limited merely to new personnel, because it is a continuing process encompassing all members of the sales force—old as well as new.

Training programs vary widely from firm to firm, and the type and extent of training required is a function of several factors, including:

1. The complexity of the product line and product applications.
2. The nature of the market in terms of buyer sophistication.
3. The pressure of competition and the resulting need for nonsales service.

4. The level of knowledge and the degree of the sales experience of the trainee.

   Goals of training.   Regardless of the type of program required in a specific situation, the objectives of a training program for newly selected salespeople are quite clear: To make the salesperson more productive; to enable the salesperson to reach a sales norm more rapidly; and to reduce the rate of sales force turnover.

   In terms of increasing selling productivity, training can:

1. Provide the product knowledge necessary for all beginning salespeople.
2. Introduce new products and new applications of old products to regular members of the sales force.
3. Point out opportunities in which the existing line can be used to satisfy customer needs.
4. Emphasize nonselling activities aimed at improving customer relations or cultivating selected accounts.
5. Increase salespeople's productivity by showing them how to utilize their time more effectively and how to engage in personal expense control.

   It takes considerable time for a new seller to become broken in on a territory. Not only is the learning process time-consuming, often it is several months before the new person has the feel of the territory and can develop sales volume consistent with sales potential. The training program must be viewed as a means of supplementing the role of experience in the learning process. Its goal is to shorten the time span required between introduction of a new salesperson to a territory and his or her attainment of a satisfactory level of sales volume.

   Because of the considerable expense involved in the process of building a sales force, each salesperson represents a large investment of the firm's resources. When salespeople leave for one reason or another the investment is lost. In addition, the replacement of an old salesperson by a new recruit results in a lag in sales volume until the new seller becomes experienced. Thus turnover, although inevitable to some degree, is expensive.

   Training, both initial and continuing, may be viewed as an additional investment made to reduce the rate of turnover and thus the related costs and losses of revenue. Proper training may help the individual salesperson to be more successful by teaching him or her new techniques and approaches. Perhaps of even greater importance is the supportive role training plays by indicating to the salesperson the concern of the company for his or her success. It thus has a motivational role which may be as important to the building of a successful selling organization as its informational role.

Assignment of Sales Personnel

After recruitment, selection and initial training at the home or district office, the new salesperson is assigned to a territory where he or she will come into contact with current or prospective buyers. In some situations the salesperson will be assigned to a senior salesperson who will provide guidance and instruction. In other situations the new seller may explore the new territory alone, although under the general supervision and tutoring of the sales manager in the district.

The importance of proper assignment cannot be fully understood without considering the concept of a territory. Although the term has a geographic meaning, it would be a mistake for a sales manager to think of a territory only in terms of its geographic boundaries. These boundaries are important in that they affect the distances that salespeople must cover and they provide a basis for collecting data used in estimation of sales potential or measurement of sales performance. More importantly, the territory is considered in terms of its customer content. The number and type of firms and their needs for various types of goods and services are the territorial attributes that are so important in making assignments. Envisioning the sales territory as a set of actual or potential customers aids in achieving the true goal of assignment which is to match the selling resources available as effectively as possible with the buying needs of the target group of customers.

To achieve this goal the assignment of new sales personnel must be well planned. Assigning a territory to an individual whose training and experience are insufficient to satisfy customer needs results in customer dissatisfaction and salesperson frustration. To avoid such problems many companies design their sales territories around clusters of customers with similar needs for information and service. The actual location of the customer is of secondary importance as long as there are transportation services which can minimize travel times.

When the skill level required of salespeople varies greatly among the firms in the cluster or even within each individual firm, assignment of new salespeople may be facilitated by providing them with back-up support. Thus when new salespeople encounter selling situations which require more skill and experience than they can offer, more experienced senior salespeople can be called in from the district or home office.

Regardless of how the assignment task is handled by sales management it is important that they recognize that it is not an easy task for a new person to start to sell effectively without continued support and on-going training. Careful matching of the skill levels of new salespeople with customer needs and the provision of back-up support when necessary can avoid excessive rates of turnover among new employees and can maintain high levels of customer satisfaction while new salespeople are learning the skills of their trade.

SALES FORCE MANAGEMENT—COMPENSATION AND MOTIVATION

In the actual management of an ongoing sales organization, it is assumed that the sales force has an acceptable rate of turnover and that new people are being added to fill vacancies caused by terminations or territorial growth or a combination of both factors. It is further assumed that a training program is available for the newcomers as well as a continuing program of retraining for the more seasoned members of the sales force. Given this type of situation, the next aspect of sales force management to be considered is that of compensation.

Compensating Salespeople

Company policies which determine the level and type of payment received by salespeople have an important influence on the effectiveness of the sales force. Policies that are fair in terms of recognizing variations in territorial sales potentials and reward individuals for a job well done attract a better caliber of applicant and help keep the more productive sellers satisfied with their positions. Thus well-designed and executed compensation plans can help to upgrade the quality of the selling force while reducing the turnover rate. This latter benefit means that the costs of recruitment and selection are lessened and the investment in training is utilized more effectively.

The goals of a good compensation plan have been stated in various terms, but most agree that the purpose is to gain the cooperation of the employees and further the interests of the employer. This is not an easy objective to achieve because individual self-interest on the part of a salesperson does not always coincide with the goals of the firm. Thus the most effective compensation plans are designed to provide an incentive for performance of those activities the employer deems most profitable. These activities include making sales, of course, as well as providing service, cultivating new accounts, and gathering market intelligence, not to mention many other tasks. The difficulty encountered in devising a good compensation plan is caused by the diverse nature of the typical selling job in terms of tasks to be performed as well as the breadth and heterogeneity of the typical product line or customer list. The complexity of the problem becomes especially evident when the dynamics of product-line development, customer turnover, and competition are added to this situation.

The starting point for appraising or redesigning a compensation plan is again the all-important job analysis. The particular selling task at hand must be analyzed in terms of the components of the task which, when well performed, lead to salesman success. These are the components the compensation plan must spotlight to get more and better performance from the sales force. Second, an income analysis of the salespeople involved must be made. Will the compensation plan proposed provide competitive levels of income to members of the sales force? Will any members of the force receive a reduced income if the plan becomes operative?

It is desirable to avoid instituting a new compensation plan which will cause major changes in the income of participants in the short run. Instead, it is preferable to change the rewards for performance of certain activities or for the sale of certain products over a period of time so that changes are evolutionary rather than abrupt.

After a careful job analysis, including a definition of objectives for the compensation plan, a tentative approach can be developed and discussed with the salespeople. This step provides an opportunity for feedback—a chance to pick up new ideas from the sales force as well as to hear their criticisms. It also allows management to explain the way in which the plan will operate and to anticipate and assuage fears the sellers may have about the impact of the proposed plan upon their well-being. The plan proposed may be modified in view of suggestions and fears brought to light in the meeting with the salespeople.

After preliminary analyses the plan is ready to be tested. A test can be simulated by utilizing past sales records to see what earnings would have been if the new plan had been in force. Or the new plan can be put into effect in specific territories representing a range of competitive conditions and employee skill and experience. The second approach is much preferred because it is impossible to tell how salespeople will react to a new plan until they actually work under it. Information from the test run can be used to improve the plan further and to indicate whether or not it should be fully implemented.

Components of compensation. The methods of compensation are: (1) base salary, (2) commission, and (3) bonus.

Base salary. The base salary is payment for certain routine activities performed by the sales force. It is a means of control by which management can require that a route be covered or that certain types of supporting activities be performed through guaranteed income. It also provides a cushion against too great fluctuations in employees' income caused by conditions beyond their control. Hence the greater the routinized selling activity or the larger the fluctuation in sales volume, the more the reliance is likely to be placed upon base salary in the compensation mix.

Commission. A commission or percentage payment associated with the sale of certain items in the line is used by management to direct selling

effort to specific items (or customers). Rates of commission may be periodically adjusted to reflect changes in product or customer profitability or
the market environment. The role of the commission form of compensation is determined by the incentive requirements and the stability of
sales volume. Customer needs for nonselling services place limits on the
degree of sales incentive which management can blend into the compensation mix. With too much emphasis on incentive compensation the salesperson becomes a "high-spotter," spending time with larger accounts and
neglecting smaller customers.

Bonus. Bonus compensation is a more diffused type of incentive payment. Generally bonuses are paid for exceeding a predetermined quota,
although they may represent some allocation of profits based on performance and length of service. A bonus is a means of letting a salesperson
share in the progress of the firm without making the payment as directly
related to performance as is the case with a commission. The bonus may
assume considerable importance in the compensation of technical representatives who back up salespeople by solving customer problems but
do not actually make sales.

An actual compensation plan may call for any combination of the
three components. The nature of the selling task and the requirements
of the market which determine the role of personal selling also suggest
the emphasis to be placed on salary, commission, and bonus payments.

Objectives of a good compensation plan. The following have been
suggested as four general objectives of a compensation plan:

1. To attract and hold good salespeople.
2. To stimulate the sales organization to produce maximum attainable
   volume by profitable sales.
3. To control selling expense, especially where there are major fluctuations in sales volume.
4. To ensure full attention to customer needs through complete performance of the sales job.

Although the general objectives are common to all compensation programs, the relative importance of each one may change with respect to
different firms or to individual firms in different stages of development.
For example, the small firm just starting out may find that expense control
is the most important objective of its compensation plan. On the other
hand, a more established firm might find that competition requires that
the compensation plan motivate the firm's salespeople to the complete
fulfillment of customer needs.

In addition to the general objectives there are more individualized goals
designed to achieve specific company marketing and sales objectives. The
following goals have been suggested:

1. To encourage solicitation of new accounts and development of new sources of revenue.
2. To encourage full-line selling.
3. To stimulate the sale of more profitable products.
4. To hold a salesperson responsible for the profit contribution on sales where she or he can influence margins.

The specific objectives listed above are by no means exhaustive. Neither are they common to all plans for compensating salespeople. A truly effective program will contain the means to reach goals common to all firms and, in addition, will be tailored to reach specific objectives which are an outgrowth of the resources, competitive environment, and particular promotional strategy of the individual firm.

Motivating Salespeople

The very nature of the selling job requires that special attention be paid to the proper motivation of personnel. The seller who works alone, often away from one's home, faces considerable discouragement in daily routine. The depressing effects of loneliness and rejection usually require some type of supportive action from management. For some personalities the selling task may be sufficiently intriguing to require little more in the way of motivation than a good incentive compensation plan and a new list of prospects. Such salespeople are rare, however, and the average member of the sales force requires some motivating efforts in addition to that provided by regular monetary compensation. The human traits of laziness and procrastination are as present among sellers as in any other group in society, and managers have learned from experience that effort expended to overcome human inertia pays off in increased sales productivity.

The types of motivating action which might be taken by management are varied. Essentially, they may be classified as: (1) additional incentive compensation, (2) career advancement, and (3) contests or other types of special sales stimulation promotions.

Additional compensation. This attempt at providing added motivation for the salesperson is predicated on the belief that monetary rewards are the most meaningful. The payment of special compensation in addition to the regular plan may be used to motivate salespeople to reach special short-run objectives in terms of sales volume, customer coverage, or product emphasis. Monetary rewards have the advantage of being direct, easily understood by employees, and readily administered. The question is simply this: Do they motivate salespeople to sell as well as other alternatives do?

Career advancement.   In this approach the better sales performers are offered transfers to more lucrative territories or invited to join the ranks of sales management. Thus the income advantage of job betterment is combined with the prestige of a rise in the organizational hierarchy. The motivating appeal of job advancement is less immediate in its impact than a direct monetary payment. But the reward, if achieved, has longer lasting benefits to the salesperson. The problem, of course, is the lack of immediacy of payoff.

Special activities.   Somewhere between the immediate and somewhat prosaic approach of direct monetary payoffs and the longer run approach involving job advancement lies a range of special activities including contests and other types of special sales promotions aimed at increasing salesman motivation. Contests are especially popular among sales managers for this purpose. They are viewed as a means of evoking extra effort to achieve short-run goals by means somewhat more dramatic than purely monetary payments. Contests may liven the competitive spirit of the salespeople, may involve wives and children, and may promise rewards such as travel or vacations with pay which may have more general appeal than mere money.

The dangers inherent in their use as motivators, however, are numerous. Contests, like any other form of stimulation aimed at getting extra effort in the short run, may lose their impact with continued use. The nature of some contests and other events may alienate the more serious and professionally oriented members of the sales force. Moreover, contests by their very nature engender rivalry among members of the sales organization and may thereby break down a close group relationship built over a long period of time. Thus they must be used with care and never as a substitute for effective activity in the other aspects of sales force management discussed earlier.

Methods of Communication

Because salespeople work at a distance from the home office and are usually on their own a great deal, management has a special problem in establishing lines of communication to them. Written messages going one way and reports from the field flowing in the other direction are found in almost all sales situations, but there is serious question as to the effect of this type of communication on employee morale or motivation. Certainly, a note from a superior congratulating a salesperson on a job well done will have a favorable influence on the salesperson's feeling of being recognized and appreciated, but a routine written pep talk too often has little or no effect on motivation.

Recognition of the shortcomings of written communication has led many sales managers to use the telephone instead of the memo. Of course, personal contact is the best method of communication between salesmen and their managers. Traditionally, the sales manager has attempted to build a personal relationship between self and individual salespeople. In fact, a psychiatrist, highly experienced in these matters, has indicated that sellers often view their sales manager as a parent figure and are quite disturbed emotionally when separated from this superior by transfer or promotion.[2]

Evidence indicates that the traditional person-to-person pattern of organization common to so many sales management situations may not be the best approach in terms of motivation and productivity. Because the problem of motivation is so closely related to the ways in which salespeople are paid, controlled, and supervised, some attention should be paid to the effects of management organization patterns on seller's performance.

Patterns of Organization for Sales

Research findings based on a large number of studies made during the past two decades have indicated that the pattern of management or organization may be an important factor in the motivation and productivity of sales organizations.[3] As indicated in Figure 18–4, given a manager with a well-organized plan of operation, high performance goals, and a high degree of technical competence, the method of supervision will affect (1) organizational morale and motivation and (2) organizational attainment. The findings as reported by Rensis Likert indicate that sales managers who supervise their salesforce in accordance with the principle of supportive relationships and by group methods will develop better adjusted and more productive sales organizations than will sales managers who use the traditional methods based on direct hierarchical pressure for results, including the usual contests and other practices of the traditional systems.[4]

The principle of supportive relationships means that the relationships between the sales manager and salespersonnel should be such that they build the ego of the subordinate and maintain and support values, both economic and noneconomic, that are deemed important by *the subordinate*. The principle has been stated as follows:

---

[2] Leonard E. Himler, M.D., "Frustrations in Selling Activities," in *Changing Perspectives in Marketing Management*, ed. Martin R. Warshaw (Ann Arbor: Bureau of Business Research, University of Michigan, 1962), pp. 81–82.

[3] Rensis Likert, *New Patterns of Management* (New York: McGraw-Hill, 1961).

[4] Rensis Likert, "New Patterns of Sales Management," in Warshaw, ed., *Changing Perspectives in Marketing Management*, pp. 1–25.

FIGURE 18–4

A Well-Organized Plan of Organization in Traditional and Newer Management Systems

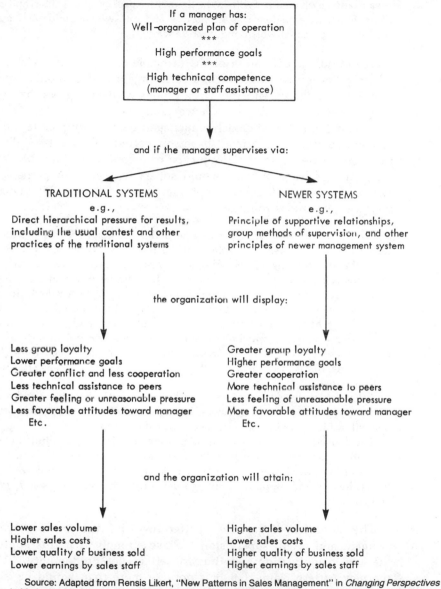

Source: Adapted from Rensis Likert, "New Patterns in Sales Management" in *Changing Perspectives in Marketing Management,* ed. Martin R. Warshaw (Ann Arbor: Bureau of Business Research, University of Michigan, 1962), p. 24.

The leadership and other processes of the organization must be such as to ensure a maximum probability that in all interactions and all relationships with the organization each member will, in the light of his background, values, and expectations, view the experience as supportive and one which builds and maintains his sense of personal worth and importance.[5]

In addition to utilization of the principle of supportive relationships, Likert believes highly productive sales organizations should consist of "overlapping, highly effective work groups with each group having high group loyalty and high performance goals."[6]

Thus in the newer approach to management the group pattern of organization replaces the person-to-person pattern. Figure 18–5 illustrates these two patterns. In the group type of organization (part b), the sales manager or sales supervisor would supervise a *group* of perhaps six to 12 salespeople by holding meetings once or twice a month. Likert describes a typical meeting as follows:

As a rule, the sales manager or one of his sales supervisors presides. Each salesman, in turn, presents to the group a report of his activity for the period since the last meeting of the group. He describes such things as the number and kinds of prospects he has obtained, the calls he has made, the nature of the sales presentations he has used, the closings he has attempted, the number of sales achieved, and the volume and quality of his total sales. The others in the group analyze the salesperson's efforts, methods, and results. Suggestions from their experience and know-how are offered. The outcome is a valuable coaching session. For example, if sales results can be improved through better prospecting, this is made clear, and the steps and methods to achieve this improvement are spelled out.

After this analysis by the group, each person, with the advice and assistance of the group, sets personal goals concerning the work one will do and the results one will achieve before the next meeting of the group.

The manager or supervisor acts as coordinator of the group but the analyses and interactions are among the sellers. The coordinator keeps the orientation of the group on a helpful, constructive, problem-solving basis and sees that the tone is helpful and supportive, not ego-deflating as a result of negative criticisms and comments.[7]

The supporters of the newer pattern, which involves supportive management and group supervision, believe strongly that this approach is the key to motivation and thus to better sales productivity. Critics of the new pattern claim that it is nothing more than would be expected of good management. They also point out that there are situations in

---

[5] Ibid., p. 6.
[6] Ibid., p. 6.
[7] Ibid., p. 16.

FIGURE 18–5
Person-to-Person and Group Patterns of Organization

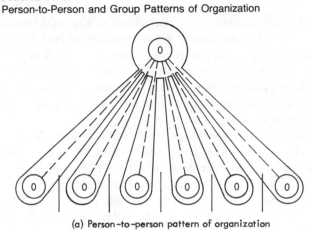

(a) Person–to–person pattern of organization

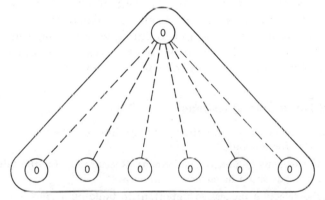

(b) Group pattern of organization

Source: Adapted from *New Patterns of Management* by Rensis
Likert. Copyright 1961, McGraw-Hill Book Co. Used by permission.

which group supervision of the sales force is impractical, such as when
salespeople are widely dispersed geographically.

Regardless of its applicability in all situations, the new pattern has
placed attention on the role of sales supervision as an important motivating
factor. There is little argument with the suggestion that noneconomic
motives such as ego enhancement should reinforce the more direct economic motives in order to increase salesman motivation. Research findings
indicate that the use of the principle of supportive relationships and group
supervision does provide for this reinforcement and thus leads to higher
morale, greater motivation, and higher productivity.

SUMMARY

This chapter has considered personal selling as a special form of inter-personal communication. Inasmuch as the salesperson is the key element in the communication process, the nature of his or her task was examined in some detail. In addition, the process by which a sales force is built into an effective promotional resource was examined. Furthermore, attention was paid to the compensation and motivation of the individuals who make up the selling organization.

In this chapter the sales force was treated in a manner similar to that in which advertising was approached—as a "controllable." This implies that the type, amount, and direction of promotional effort are subject to variation in the short run by marketing management.

The view of personal selling as a promotional input subject to control in the short run is generally sustainable. However, a really effective selling organization cannot be built overnight. Thus, although short-run control is possible in terms of type of effort, extent of effort, or direction of effort, the truly qualitative aspect of the effort is dependent on a continuing process of recruitment, selection, training, supervision, and control. Good management is vital at each of these stages if the firm is to get the best payoff possible from its personal selling effort.

Review and Discussion Questions

1. Why may it be said that the written job description is the foundation upon which a sales force is built?
2. Discuss the reasons behind this statement: Recruitment for the sales force is both a difficult and a never-ending process.
3. Why is the selection process so important in building a sales force? What tools are available to aid in this process?
4. What are the dangers of too great reliance on psychological testing to select salespeople?
5. What are the purposes of the personal interview? What dangers must be avoided in conducting such interviews?
6. What are the goals of a training program for salespeople? Can sales force training ever cease?
7. What are the goals of a good compensation plan for salespeople? Why is it so difficult to devise such a plan?
8. What guidelines should be considered in attempting to change a plan of compensation of salespeople?
9. Under what circumstances would you recommend greater reliance on base salary in the compensation plan?
10. Compare and contrast commission and bonus methods of compensation in terms of their objectives.

11. Why must management be concerned about sales force morale and motivation?

12. What role do contests play in motivating salespeople? What dangers are involved in their use?

13. What is a pattern of organization, and how might it influence seller performance?

CHAPTER 19

Management of Personal Selling II: Evaluation and Control of Sales Force Efforts

The evaluation and control of promotional effort which involves personal selling is a prime responsibility of marketing management. Promotional activities include those performed by the firm as well as those performed by members of its channel of distribution. This chapter pays special attention to the evaluation and control of the personal selling efforts of the firm. Evaluating and controlling reseller promotional efforts will be considered in Chapter 21.

The evaluation and control process encompasses four distinct steps: (1) the development of standards of performance, (2) the measurement of actual performance, (3) the comparison of actual performance with the norm or standard, and (4) the taking of corrective action to remedy substandard performance. The fourth step may involve a reallocation of effort and is discussed at some length.

PURPOSES OF EVALUATION

The general purpose of evaluation of sales force efforts is to ensure that the resources allocated by the firm to these efforts are being used efficiently and in such a way as to facilitate the achievement of the firm's profitability goals.

In the short run, evaluation can determine whether more specific objectives such as revenue goals and expense goals are being met. Without such evaluation management cannot take those steps necessary to improve sales force performance during the current period.

In the longer run, evaluation is necessary in order to make better decisions about such inputs as the number of persons to be employed at various levels in the sales force organization, the hiring and training requirements, and the development of the sales budget.

In addition to its evident impact on sales force productivity, such an evaluation program can improve the morale of individual salesmen by providing them with information as to what is expected of them and how well they are performing relative to expectations. Opportunities are thus presented to management to praise good performance and to provide help in improving substandard performance.

INFORMATION NEEDS

In developing a system of evaluation and control the manager is faced with the problem of what is to be measured. Of course, some information on individual performance is required in most situations. There are times, however, when information on group performance is also useful. This is especially true when the pattern of organization is such that a group participative approach is being used. In still other cases information about the performance of the entire sales organization will be required.

It is the responsibility of the manager to evaluate the relative costs and values of different types of information and to adjust information collection procedures accordingly.

THE EVALUATION AND CONTROL PROCESS

Developing Performance Standards

Considerable information about the firm and its market is necessary for the development of standards for sales force performance. The firm must develop its sales forecast from data on market potential or aggregate demand for a specific good or service. This forecast is the best estimate of sales to be expected during a given period, assuming a given set of environmental conditions and a specific marketing plan or program. The sales forecast is thus the basis for the promotion budget. It can, however, also be used as a starting point from which to develop sales goals or quotas for specific products, territories, or classes of customers. As such it is vital to the development of criteria for performance evaluation.

Measurements of sales potential, however, should not be the sole basis of performance standards. Special territorial characteristics such as terrain or dispersion of customers must be considered, as well as special attributes of products, customers, and the salesmen if meaningful performance standards are to be developed.

With respect to characteristics of individual salespeople, some consideration must be given to the fact that not all salespeople perform in the same way. For example, the high-pressure type may do very well in the short run if results are measured in terms of sales volume in relation to potential. These methods may, however, lead to a decline in sales in the long run as customers tire of that approach. On the other hand, the low-pressure type may not score well on the basis of short-run performance but over the years may show a rising sales trend with regular, repeat customers.

Because of the unique circumstances faced by each firm in terms of market potential, customer and product mix, competition, and qualitative characteristics of the sales force, the development of standards of sales performance must be closely related to the specific sales objectives previously planned. As stated by one source:

The standards of performance selected should facilitate the measurement of progress made toward departmental objectives, both general and specific. Although specific objectives vary from time to time in accordance with changes in the firm's marketing situation, they should always be reconcilable with the general goals of volume, profit, and growth.[1]

Standards of Measurement of Performance

Quantitative standards. The most commonly used standards are quantitative and are based on single ratios or combinations of ratios. Those expressed in quantitative form offer the advantages of ease of calculation and explanation to salespeople. This latter factor is most important, especially when the performance standard is being used for incentive purposes as well as for control. Some ratios or measures commonly used include:

1. Sales volume as a percentage of sales potential.
2. Selling expense as a percentage of sales volume.
3. Number of customers sold as a percentage of total number of potential customers.
4. Call frequency ratio, or total calls made divided by total number of accounts and prospects covered.

There are other measures in addition to those cited above, such as average cost per call and average order size, which can be used for this

---

[1] Richard R. Still, Edward W. Cundiff, and Norman A. P. Govoni, *Sales Management*, 3d ed. (Englewood Cliffs, N.J.: Prentice-Hall, 1976), p. 378.

purpose. The correct choice of the combination of measures to use is best set by the sales manager to meet the needs of a specific situation.

Profit contribution standards.   Most writers on the subject agree that the key measurement for setting standards is sales volume achieved in relation to sales potential. After all, the main objective of the sales force is to make sales, and without such sales, considerations of profitability cannot begin. However, more and more the norms of sales performance are being combined with those of expense control so that profitability standards may be set. Perhaps the best way to control and appraise sellers' performance is by the application of the techniques of distribution cost analysis. In this manner not only can relative profit contributions of individual salespeople be measured but standards can be set which reflect such diverse factors as gross profits, product mix sold, customer mix, direct selling expenses, and the amount of sales promotion assistance going into the territory.

In very simple terms a distribution cost analysis would be used to find out the gross margin contribution of each salesperson. This computation based on sales volume less cost of goods sold would give some idea of the *initial* profitability of the product mix being sold. From gross margin would be subtracted those expenses that can be allocated to the salesperson on a causal or benefit basis. This means that only those items that are *caused* by that person's activity or *benefit* him or her in terms of reaching goals (direct mail advertising, for example) should be charged against a personal gross margin contribution. The residual is the contribution to general overhead (not allocated to the territory) and to profit. This amount, often termed the "contribution margin," is an excellent measure of the *relative* performance of individual salespeople. But, equally important, the technique allows the development of both revenue and cost standards based on actual as well as desired performance. Several sources are available which discuss cost standards in greater detail than can be done here.[2]

The contribution margin can also be used as part of a return on investment analysis. For example, if a certain territory produced a contribution margin of $80,000 on sales of $1 million and if $500,000 of company assets had been employed in support of the territory, the following return on investment (ROI) calculations could be made:[3]

$$\frac{\text{Contribution: } \$80,000}{\text{Sales: } \$1,000,000} \times \frac{\text{Sales: } \$1,000,000}{\text{Investment: } \$500,000} = 16 \text{ percent ROI}$$

---

[2] See especially Charles H. Sevin, *Distribution Cost Analysis,* Economic Series no. 50 (Washington, D.C.: Government Printing Office, 1946), and Donald R. Longman and Michael Schiff, *Practical Distribution Cost Analysis* (Homewood, Ill.: Richard D. Irwin, 1955).

[3] See Michael Schiff, "The Uses of ROI in Sales Management," *Journal of Marketing* 27 (July 1963), pp. 70–73.

The use of two fractions rather than one (contributions over investment) is to illustrate that the ROI is a function of both the profitability of the sales volume and the turnover rate. Thus ROI can be improved in a given territory by increasing sales with investment held constant, by increasing profitability of sales, or by reducing the investment needed to sustain the present level of sales.

By indicating the relative ROI's of various territories, the analysis can be used to appraise how well the various salespeople are doing, given the assets at their disposal.

Qualitative criteria. The setting of quantitative performance standards, whether based on revenue, cost, or other considerations, has as its major shortcoming the inability to measure activities and traits which may pay off for the salesperson in the longer run. To make certain that these qualities are not overlooked in the appraisal process, many firms use a more subjective approach in order to develop norms of performance standards related to the qualitative aspect of the salesperson's job. In some cases the sales manager or supervisor uses personal judgment in appraising how well the salesperson displays the desired traits. In other cases, a more formalized merit-rating checklist may be used.

Comparing Sellers' Performance to Standards

It is inevitable that some attempts will be made to appraise sellers' performance. Appraisals are needed to indicate where performance is substandard and to provide evidence to support salary adjustments or promotions. Appraisal also provides a good check on how well the sales force building process—selection and training—is being carried out. Last, but very important, is the beneficial effect that a well-administered appraisal program has on seller morale and motivation.

The difficulties encountered are many. The selling task itself is quite complex, and short-run effort by salespeople may not have immediate results. In addition, some of the results may not be measurable or as a consequence of joint effort may not be separable.[4]

The appraisal process begins with a rather mechanical step. It is the comparison of the actual performances of salespeople or groups of salespeople with the performance standards previously developed. Data on actual performance may come from an analysis of company records or from special reports required of salespeople. Once the data are collected the evaluation process can begin.

---

[4] Salesmen rarely work alone. They are aided by other salesmen, supervisors, managers, or product specialists. The question of who is responsible for the sale is very difficult to answer. See D. Maynard Phelps and J. Howard Westing, *Marketing Management*, rev. ed. (Homewood, Ill.: Richard D. Irwin, 1960), p. 741.

A brief example may be helpful here.[5] Baker and Kent are two salespeople whose sales to date are $93,000 and $98,000 respectively. Their performances are to be measured primarily on the basis of sales in relation to sales potential, the latter being expressed as a quota figure, as follows:

	Sales in thousands to date		Increase or decrease	Quota (thousand)	Percentage of quota to date	
	This year	Last year			This year	Last year
Baker	$93	$ 80	+16%	$170	55	47
Kent	98	104	− 6%	200	49	52

If performance is measured on sales alone it might appear that Kent is outperforming Baker. In terms of quota, however, Baker is performing better. Indeed, if the trends from last year are considered, Kent appears to be slipping while Baker is improving his position.

Although the relatively sparse data presented above can provide for some important analysis, it cannot answer all of the questions required for a complete performance evaluation. For example, the appraiser would need to know the relative profitability in the short run of the sales volume recorded. An analysis of gross margins less allocable expenses would provide the answers needed in this area.

Seller activities performed in the current period which may have payoffs in the future require the use of different standards of performance. Evaluation may take place on the basis of effort expended to gain new accounts or to cultivate old ones. Regardless of the approach, the objective is to gain some feel for the way in which the salesperson is performing the nonorder-seeking portion of the job.

In addition to the quantitative evaluation of the salesperson's performance there is the appraisal of qualitative factors such as attitude, judgment, and appearance. Here the appraiser may use some sort of rating scale. It is good policy to have several people involved in subjective evaluation of salespeople to avoid bias on the part of those engaged in the rating process.

It cannot be stressed too strongly that the criteria, both quantitative and qualitative, used as the bases for appraisal must be consistent with the seller's task as *communicated by the written job description.* The selling job differs widely from firm to firm, and the appraisal process must be custommade to fit the specific needs and goals of the individual selling organization.

---

[5] Harold H. Maynard and James H. Davis, *Sales Management,* 3d ed. (New York: Ronald Press, 1957), pp. 476–77.

Corrective Action

If the preliminary stages of the control process have been handled correctly, the sales manager should have a good idea as to the relative performance of the salespeople under her or his supervision. The concept of relative performance is based on performance as compared with predetermined standards. In those cases where individual performances are well below the norms, the sales manager or supervisor can take corrective action. The philosophy underlying this action is that a better utilization of the resources (sellers) under one's control will increase the contribution of the sales organization to the goals of the firm. This philosophy might also provide the basis for remedial action in the case of salespeople whose performances are substandard. Essentially, this approach would involve helping the salesperson to utilize his or her most valuable resource—time—more effectively. After this type of remedial action has been undertaken, a second approach may be considered—the direction of activity to areas of greater opportunity.

Time and duty analysis. This approach to the better utilization of salesmen's time is an adaptation of the time-and-motion studies used by industrial engineers in the factory. A well-planned study by James H. Davis reported several pertinent conclusions about salespeople's time utilization.[6]

In brief, the findings show that there is a measurable relationship between selling time and sales volume. In addition, the actual amount of selling time available to a salesman in a typical day is very limited. In his study of wholesale drug salespersons Davis reported that city salespeople spent only 17 percent of their day in actually attempting to promote new merchandise, and 37 percent in all essential activities inside the retail store. Experiences of other companies in different industries have indicated about the same fraction of time available for promotional selling and essential activities.[7]

As a result of the recognition of the time-sales relationship and the limited time available to sellers, two points become apparent:

First, through careful training and scheduling, management should do all it can to increase the amount of time available for essential activities at the expense of nonessential ones. Second, the essential activities that management wants performed should be scrutinized carefully to see if they are, in fact, essential. For example, many companies ask their salesmen to perform some or all of the task of collecting in their territories. If this is really an essential one for the salesman, no further question need be raised. In many cases, however, it will be found to

---

[6] See James H. Davis, *Increasing the Wholesale Drug Salesman's Effectiveness* (Columbus: Bureau of Business Research, College of Commerce and Administration, The Ohio State University, 1948).

[7] Maynard and Davis, *Sales Management,* pp. 468–69.

be more nearly desirable than essential. In this event, the value of time spent in collecting should be carefully weighed against the value of the same time available for more direct selling activities.[8]

In addition to the recognition of the value of selling time and the suggestion that management attempt to maximize the availability of such time by careful planning is the question of how time is used by individual salespeople. It does little good to increase selling time at the expense of other activities when selling time is poorly utilized.

In the Davis study, activities of 70 wholesale drug salespeople were analyzed. It was found that when genuine sales arguments or reasons to buy were presented to prospects, sales resulted in 50 percent of the cases. A mere mention of an item resulted in a sale only 13 percent of the time.[9]

Of course, the selling argument or reason-to-buy approach is only one way in which the salesperson may make limited time available for selling more productive. The point is that management may be in a better position to correct substandard selling performance if it knows how much selling time is available and how well it is being used. Time and duty analysis is one way of getting this information.

Routing.   If about half of the salesperson's time is spent in contact with the customer (perhaps with ⅙ of time used for promotional selling and ⅓ of time engaged in nonselling activity), the other half is spent in traveling. Such time is totally nonproductive and bears a very high hourly cost. If careful routing and travel plans are made by sales management in those selling situations where such control is feasible, the savings in time may well be substantial. Thus improving total time utilization is an important step toward correcting substandard sales performance.

REALLOCATION OF EFFORT

The process of changing the nature of the seller's task or of reducing travel time to allow more opportunity for creative selling is in a very real sense a reallocation of resources. In this case time is the scarce item and attempts are made to provide more of it for selling and to improve the utilization of that which is available. In a way the type of action described above may be viewed as an attempt to optimize the performance of each individual salesperson in each territory.

From the standpoint of the sales manager viewing all of the territories under his or her control such efforts may be only one approach to improving overall performance of the sales force. Certainly, corrective action should begin at the level of the individual salesperson, but time utilization

---

[8] Ibid., p. 469.

[9] Ibid., pp. 470–71.

is only a part of the story. Time must be used effectively, but the chances of success are conditioned strongly by the sales targets chosen. If individuals are using their selling time effectively yet their performance is substandard, perhaps their effort should be reallocated to different products or to different customers. Further analysis of product types sold and customer classes covered may provide answers to the question of whether the product mix or customer mix can be changed to improve the performance of the subpar salesperson.

However, the sales manager has one other alternative to consider. Briefly, that is whether or not to reallocate selling resources to the various

FIGURE 19–1
Optimum Allocation of Selling Expense

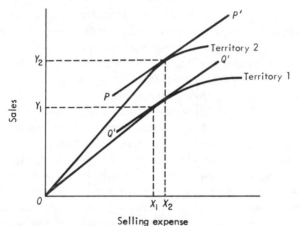

Selling expense

Note: The curved lines indicate the relations between sales and selling expenditures in two sales areas, territory 1 and territory 2. The optimum allocation of a given personal selling appropriation is to spend OX_1 in territory 1 and OX_2 in territory 2 because PP' and QQ', which are tangent to the respective territorial personal-selling-sales relations, are parallel.
Source: John A. Howard, *Marketing Management*, rev. ed. (Homewood, Ill.: Richard D. Irwin, 1963), p. 448.

territories which make up the market. Economic analysis provides the conceptual ideal for allocation of selling effort among territories. The rule for an optimum allocation is that the level of selling expenditures in each territory should be such that the incremental receipts per dollar of selling effort should be equal among all territories. Figure 19–1 illustrates this concept graphically.

Although the precise application of this approach probably cannot be made to the problem of reallocation of selling effort, a simplified version may be usable. This is the rule that for an optimum allocation the ratio of the variable cost of personal selling to sales in each territory should be equal.[10] This rule is illustrated in Figure 19–2, which shows a selling expense to sales relationship for two sales territories. The allocation of $2,000 to each territory results in total sales of $5,000 plus $20,000, or $25,000. If, however, expenditures are reduced by $1,000 in territory 1 and increased a like amount in territory 2, total sales will be $2,500 plus $30,000, or a net increase of $7,500 with no increase in total sales expense.

The marketing or sales manager must know *how much* of a shift in selling expenditures among the territories is necessary to achieve the optimum allocation. A mathematical method for answering the question can be constructed based on two assumptions: (1) relationships between total

FIGURE 19–2
Comparison of Two Allocations of Selling Expense

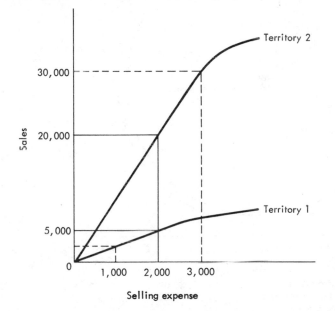

variable selling costs and sales in each territory are known from past experience and (2) underlying factors which determined the relationship in the past have not changed significantly.[11]

In contrast to the methodology described above is the more pragmatic approach of the field sales manager. It is useful to look briefly at the way he might approach the problem of redeployment of sales effort.

---

[10] J. A. Norden, "Spatial Allocation of Selling Expense," *Journal of Marketing* 7 (January 1943), pp. 210–19.

[11] See John A. Howard, *Marketing Management: Operating, Strategic, and Administrative,* 3d ed. (Homewood, Ill.: Richard D. Irwin, 1973), pp. 175–80.

A Case History

The director of sales of the Dow Chemical Company has provided valuable insights into how one company views the problem of reallocation or redeployment of the field sales force.[12] The corporate objective in this

FIGURE 19–3
Relationship of Marketing Effort to Corporate Profitability

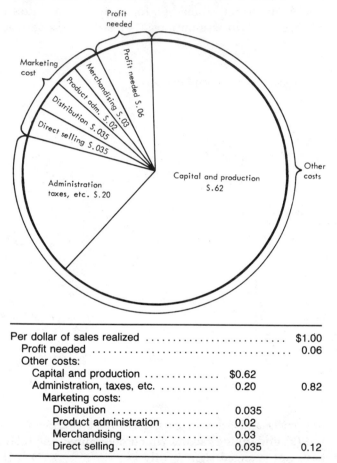

Per dollar of sales realized		$1.00
Profit needed		0.06
Other costs:		
Capital and production	$0.62	
Administration, taxes, etc.	0.20	0.82
Marketing costs:		
Distribution	0.035	
Product administration	0.02	
Merchandising	0.03	
Direct selling	0.035	0.12

example was to achieve a 6 percent profit on total sales dollars. The planned distribution of costs was as indicated in Figure 19–3. Of special importance to the problem at hand was the budgeting of approximately 3.5 percent of sales revenue to direct selling effort. The major question

[12] William R. Dixon, "Redetermining the Size of the Sales Force: A Case Study," in *Changing Perspectives in Marketing Management*, ed. Martin R. Warshaw (Ann Arbor: Bureau of Business Research, University of Michigan, 1962), p. 59.

FIGURE 19–4
Territorial Objectives
Territory Concerned with ───────────→ Accounts

		Present	Potential	Total
Product Sales Dept. Concerned with	Present	1. Hold 2. Grow with 70%	1. Seek new customers 2. Seek new uses 15%	85%
Product	New	3. Introduce 10%	3. Seek and introduce 5%	15%
	Total	80%	20%	100%

is not whether the 3.5 percent figure is correct but how direct selling resources can best be deployed, given this cost-revenue constraint.

Figure 19–4 illustrates the territorial objectives, which are clarified in the following statement:

In [Figure 19–4] we see that the field force is primarily concerned with the subject of accounts. The major efforts of a going field force are usually directed toward present accounts (column 1). The major job is to hold and grow with present accounts on present products of the company. We have indicated some approximations of the amount of effort going toward these objectives, with the field force which is under study. In a company with a complex product line like the Dow Chemical Company, we feel that the field force should spend a certain part of its time (10 percent for this group) introducing our new product lines to the present customers. Hence, we see about 80 percent of the field force's time spent with present customers. Likewise, we find that this particular field force should spend about 20 percent of its time with potential customers, seeking new customers for new products. As a by-product, we note that it is spending 85 percent of its time on present products and 15 percent of its time on new products. The mix of every organization is different, of course. In our other marketing groups we apply effort to these different objectives in varying magnitudes. Likewise, variation will be found from company to company. Yet we feel that any company which has a complex product mix and which is constantly creating new products will face some combination similar to this. My illustration shows a single territorial force of one marketing group in the Dow Chemical Company. We shall examine later some of the major methods that we use to arrive at this deployment of effort.[13]

Having recognized the constraints imposed by profit and cost criteria and having defined the territorial objectives, the next step was to ascertain the cost of keeping a salesperson in the field. Compilation of salary, fringe benefit, automobile, supervision, and other expenses resulted in a figure of about $30,000 per year per person of direct selling cost (or variable

[13] Ibid.

FIGURE 19–5
Analysis of Effort

Field salesperson
Salary
Fringe
Automobile
Travel and entertainment
Supervision
Stenographer
Office and supplies
Communication and other
       Total $30,000

Effort	÷	Effort/Results	=	Results
$30,000		.03		$1,000,000
		.035		850,000
		.05		600,000

---

cost). If this expense were to reflect the 3.5 percent of revenue average, then sales should be about $850,000 per person ($30,000/.035). The profit picture does not allow a performance of much below $600,000 or a 5 percent expense to sales ratio. Performances of over $1 million (3 percent expense to sales) raise the question of what an additional salesperson might do in the territory.

An analysis of effort and a review of current performance are shown in Figures 19–5 and 19–6. From the latter it appears that all is well. In 10 territories 42 salespeople sold $35.8 million, for an average of $850,000 per person. The cost-revenue relationship is 3.5 percent, or directly on target.

FIGURE 19–6
Present Performance

	Performance		
Territory	$ M Sales	Field salespeople	($ M/person)
1	10,000	9	(1,110)
2	6,000	5	(1,200)
3	4,500	5	(900)
4	3,500	4	(875)
5	2,500	3	(833)
6	2,400	4	(600)
7	2,300	4	(575)
8	2,000	4	(500)
9	1,800	3	(600)
10	800	1	(800)
	35,800	42	(850)

Closer inspection indicates that performance might be improved. Specifically, while in territories 1 and 2 sales exceed $1 million per person,
in territory 8 four salespeople are selling $500,000 apiece—quite a bit
below the minimum goal.

Figure 19–7 compares present performance against sales potential as
developed by market research. Some answers become evident here. In
those areas in which sales were high per salesperson, market penetration
in terms of potential was about 30 to 33 percent. In the areas where
volume per person was low, sales were at 50 percent of potential.

Analysis indicated that although Dow had started with a total penetration larger than the present 35.8 percent, sales lost to competitors were
greatest in the territories with the largest potential.

The immediate reaction might be to attempt to regain company position
in all territories. Such action might, however, be costly and might also
invite retaliation which would disturb revenue and profit contributions.
A crucial decision is, therefore, what *share* of market can Dow *profitably*
attain?

Assuming that the decision to try for 40 percent of the market has
been made, Figure 19–8 illustrates the plan to capture $40 million in
revenues. The basic philosophy underlying the plan is to increase effort
in those territories where (1) potential is large and (2) Dow participation
is small. Conversely, ground will be given in those territories where performance is close to marginal.

A closer analysis of individual territories gives a clear indication of
how many people might be profitably redeployed from one territory to
another. In territory 1, for example, nine people were selling $10 million
or 33 percent of the market. An analysis of customers summarized in
Figure 19–9 showed that 20 percent or 200 accounts were providing 90

FIGURE 19–7
Present Performance Versus Potential

Territory	$ M Sales	Field salespeople	($ M/person)	$ M	Perf./Pot.
				Potential	
1	10,000	9	(1110)	30,000	33%
2	6,000	5	(1200)	20,000	30
3	4,500	5	(900)	13,000	35
4	3,500	4	(875)	10,000	35
5	2,500	3	(833)	7,000	36
6	2,400	4	(600)	6,000	40
7	2,300	4	(575)	5,000	46
8	2,000	4	(500)	4,000	50
9	1,800	3	(600)	3,000	60
10	800	1	(800)	2,000	40
	35,800	42	(850)	100,000	35.8%

456

FIGURE 19–8
Analysis of Market

Territory	Potential $ M	Our sales $ M	Percent mkt.	Our plan Percent mkt.	$ M
1	30,000	10,000	33	40	12,000
2	20,000	6,000	30	40	8,000
3	13,000	4,500	35	35	4,500
4	10,000	3,500	35	45	4,500
5	7,000	2,500	36	36	2,500
6	6,000	2,400	40	40	2,400
7	5,000	2,300	46	40	2,000
8	4,000	2,000	50	45	1,800
9	3,000	1,800	60	50	1,500
10	2,000	800	40	40	800
	100,000	35,800	35.8	40	40,000

percent of the sales volume. It was decided to concentrate on those "target accounts" which brought in $9 million of business.

Figure 19–10 shows the call time needed to service each of the 200 target accounts in territory 1. Factors entering this analysis are the salesperson's itinerary, the location of the account, the nature of the purchasing influence in the company and—very important—the *desire of the customer* concerning frequency of calls.

A careful appraisal of the total call requirements of the 200 target accounts indicates that 1,800 man-days should bring in $9 million in sales, while $1 million of noncall business is likely to be generated because of the presence of an efficiently run sales office in the territory. Judgment indicates that an additional 360 labor-days would bring in $2 million in added volume. Thus the allocation of 2,160 labor-hours of effort to territory 1 should attain the goal of $12 million as planned. Dividing 2,160 by 180 (the average number of call days available to a salesperson after deducting vacation, holidays, meetings, travel, illness, etc.) indicates a need for 12 people in the territory. This effort should provide $12 million, or 40 percent of market within acceptable cost limits.

FIGURE 19–9
Territorial Account Analyses (Territory 1)

Number of accounts	Number (cumulative)	Percent	$ M	$ M (cumulative)	Percent
20	20	2	4.0	4.0	40
80	100	5	3.5	4.0	75
100	200	20	1.5	9.0	90
800	1,000	100	1.0	10.0	100
1,000			10.0		

FIGURE 19–10
Call Time Needed for Each Target Account

Target account	Planned calls per year	Travel and call time (days)	Labor days per year
	Majority 8–26	¼–½	
	Limits 6–52	⅛–1	
Acct. No. 1	6	½	3.0
Acct. No. 2	26	¼	6.5
Acct. No. 3	18	⅛	2.2
Acct. No. 4	20	⅓	6.7
Acct. No. 5	8	¾	6.0
Acct. No. 6	12	1	12.0
.	.	.	.
.	.	.	.
.	.	.	.
Acct. No. 200	52	⅛	6.5
Total 200			1,800

The same procedure shows that by reducing input in territory 8 from four people to two people, penetration will slip from 50 percent to 45 percent. But in sales volume the drop will be only $200,000, or from $2 million to $1.8 million. The important point is that two people are freed to be redeployed to territory 1.

The results of the total process are illustrated in Figure 19–11. The following conclusions resulted:

Let us now look at our general redeployment [Figure 19–11]. Here we see that by redeploying four men from offices in territories 7, 8, and 9, plus the expansion of our force from 42 to 46 men, we are able to increase our participation

FIGURE 19–11
Results of Redeployment

Territory	Present performance			Potential performance			
	$ M Sales	Field sales person	($ M/ person)	($ M/ person)		Field sales person	$ M Sales
1	10,000	9	(1,110)	(1,000)	+	12	12,000
2	6,000	5	(1,200)	(1,000)	+	8	8,000
3	4,500	5	(900)	(900)		5	4,500
4	3,500	4	(875)	(750)	+	6	4,500
5	2,500	3	(833)	(833)		3	2,500
6	2,400	4	(600)	(600)		4	2,400
7	2,300	4	(575)	(667)	—	3	2,000
8	2,000	4	(500)	(900)	—	2	1,800
9	1,800	3	(600)	(750)	—	2	1,500
10	800	1	(800)	(800)		1	800
	35,800	42	(850)	(870)		46	40,000

significantly in territories 1, 3, and 4. Despite the modest loss in territories 7, 8, and 9, our overall participation went up to $40 million.

Here is another very interesting point. You will note that in offices 1, 2, and 4, the new men who were added sold less than the men already there, as indicated in the middle two columns by the lower average sales per man. Despite the fact that these new men sold less than their predecessors, their performance in these particular territories, plus the moving of men from the marginal territories 7, 8, and 9, actually brought the sales per man in the entire sales force up from $850,000 to $870,000. It does not always work out this way. Nor is it always necessary to gain in sales per man in order to gain in profitability.

But this particular case illustrated a double effect of the fruits of redeployment. By concentrating on the areas of greatest potential *and* lesser Dow participation and by giving insignificant ground in marginal territories, we significantly improved our position and profitability. This improvement started from an original position which we thought in the beginning was pretty good.

We have covered a few aspects of decision making relevant to resizing a sales force. We have glossed over many. I certainly do not want to leave you with the impression that analysis is a substitute for that priceless possession of a successful sales marketing manager—judgment. However, I hope that I have left you with the impression that a philosophy of orderly planning and analysis is an essential prelude to the *best* judgment. If I may summarize the points which need to be considered in the redetermination of the size of your territorial sales force, they would be as follows:

1. Know quite clearly your territorial objectives.
2. Analyze your territorial market.
   a. Determine by market research the position of each territory.
   b. Determine the territories in which you are likely to gain the greatest return for the effort to be invested and, conversely, those territories which are marginal in respect to return on effort.
3. Analyze the sales effort needed.
   a. [Labor-days] for target accounts.
   b. [Labor-days] for potential accounts.
   c. The cost of this effort.
4. Relate the sales return expected to the cost of the effort.
5. Within your corporate profit objective determine the cost parameters within which you can profitably expand effort to gain a dollar's worth of sales.
6. Perform the above steps in a continuum. And remember that the constantly changing market environment as well as the changing environment within your own corporation require constant maintenance of this process.[14]

SUMMARY

The evaluation and control of sales force efforts requires diverse types of information input dealing with individual, group, and organizational performance. Actual performance is then compared with predetermined

---

[14] Ibid.

standards and appraisals are made by management on the basis of how well actual performances met the norms. The final step in the process is the taking of corrective action to improve and (or) reallocate sales efforts.

The short-run goal of the evaluation and control process is to meet more effectively the firm's revenue and expense objectives for the current period. In addition, the process can improve the productivity and morale of individual members of the sales force. The longer run and more general objective of the evaluation and control process is to ensure that sales force strength, training, and mode of deployment are such that it is making an optimum contribution to the overall profitability of the enterprise.

Review and Discussion Questions

1. What are the four basic steps in the process of evaluation and control of sales force efforts?

2. What are some of the purposes of the evaluation process in the short run? In the longer run?

3. What types of information input might be desirable in developing a system of evaluation and control of the sales force?

4. How does one go about setting sales force performance norms or standards? What are some quantitative standards?

5. What is a profitability standard? Why is its use superior to the mere application of sales volume standards?

6. What are qualitative performance standards, and why are they important in appraising seller performance?

7. What type of remedial action is available to the sales manager who finds some company salespeople with substandard performance records?

8. What is a time and duty analysis, and how might it be of use to sales management? Why is routing so important?

9. Of what aid, if any, is economic theory in solving the problem of allocation of resources to sales territories?

10. What are some of the lessons to be learned from the description of the Dow sales force redeployment analysis?

PART SIX

Reseller Support and Supplemental Communications

Our consideration of the stages in promotional strategy outlined in Chapter 3 has given considerable attention to the management of mass communication efforts, particularly the management of advertising efforts. This part will continue the discussion of management program elements by considering problems inherent in gaining the support of independent resellers in the channels of distribution. By examining the task resellers can be expected to perform given their economic role and their objectives as independent businesses, suggestions can be offered as to how manufacturers might stimulate reseller promotional activity or improve, supplement, or control reseller promotional efforts.

The concluding chapter in this section considers supplemental methods of communication, such as publicity and public relations, which serve to bridge the gap between the firm and its many publics.

CHAPTER 20

Resellers as Promotional Resources

In considering the various promotional resources available to the firm which make up the elements of the promotional program, we have emphasized communication with the consumer through the mass media. Except in cases where the manufacturer sells directly to the end user, however, the next owner of the good is not the ultimate consumer but a marketing intermediary such as a wholesaler or retailer. These intermediaries, often referred to as resellers, perform the vital functions of effecting exchange so that the goods produced by diverse manufacturers are available to buyers in usable assortments. The important implication for promotion, however, is that when the title to the goods passes from manufacturer to reseller, so does a large portion of the control a manufacturer can exert over how its goods are sold.

The situation is one in which the channel of communication to the ultimate consumer may be direct, but the path of ownership and control of the goods is indirect in the sense that marketing intermediaries are used. Thus the success of the entire program may depend on how skillful the manufacturer is in gaining the cooperation of its wholesalers and retailers and exploiting the tremendous selling potential inherent in the aggregate reseller organization.

To develop a promotional program which effectively utilizes reseller resources, an understanding of the role that a reseller can play in a manufacturer's marketing strategy is vital. Another requirement is that manufacturers know what resellers can do to stimulate demand and what they cannot do because of limitations arising from the nature of their economic role. If manufacturers are familiar with the nature of the promotional support which resellers can supply and understand how this support is allocated, then more effective programs to gain reseller support can be designed. To provide the insights necessary to develop such programs is the purpose of this chapter.

THE PROMOTIONAL ROLE OF RESELLERS

The promotional strategy of a manufacturer is a blend of the elements of advertising, personal selling, and sales promotion which is aimed at the attainment of specific marketing objectives. Given certain product characteristics and market situations, the optimal blend of promotional elements may allow for only a small promotional role for resellers. In contrast, in other product-market situations the manufacturer's mix might require a great deal of promotional support from resellers.

Regardless of the mix, the manufacturer concerned with gaining the maximum reseller support must know what the role of these intermediaries is to be under a given strategy. Only with this information can the manufacturer evaluate the selling performance of its wholesalers and retailers and consider ways to supplement or improve reseller performance.

The Impact of Manufacturer Promotional Strategy

Under certain product-market conditions, manufacturers place major emphasis on consumer advertising to stimulate demand. These conditions might include: (1) a rising primary demand trend for the product type, (2) an opportunity to develop selective demand for the particular product on the basis of differentiation, hidden qualities, or strong emotional buying motives, or (3) a turnover and margin combination sufficient to generate funds necessary to support the advertising expenditure. Products such as grocery and food specialty items, proprietary medicines, distinctive soap products, and cosmetics lend themselves especially well to strategy which relies on consumer advertising to "pull" the product through the channel of distribution.

The greater the manufacturer emphasis on pull-type strategy, the less the opportunity for resellers to engage in promotion. For example, a manufacturer of a packaged drug often faces a product-market situation which offers an excellent opportunity for stimulating sales through the use of consumer advertising. Here the selling role of wholesalers and retailers is at a minimum. Other than providing availability to drug outlets and performing the minimum exchange and storage functions, the wholesaler makes no selling effort. The retailer, in turn, is required to do little more than stock the product. The sale of well-known brands of aspirin is an example of this situation.

In the above extreme example the manufacturer's policy is to force the product through the channels at minimum margins for resellers, paying only for the costs of physical distribution. As long as availability is achieved through retail stocking, there is little that resellers can do to improve sales that could not be done better by consumer advertising. Therefore, switching funds from consumer advertising to personal selling or dealer promotion would result in a less effective program for the manufacturer. It should be pointed out, however, that this situation is rare, because resellers usually have a greater part to play in the overall strategy.

Product Evolution

In addition to the influences of product-market characteristics at any one time, changes in the promotional role of wholesalers and retailers occur as products mature. The process of product aging is described by the concept of the maturity or product life cycle, in which the life of a product is divided into stages. Although in Chapter 24 a five-stage product life cycle will be discussed, for purposes of illustrating the impact of the various stages on the promotional mix three basic stages will suffice. These stages have been described as (1) the introductory stage, (2) the competitive stage, and (3) the commodity stage.[1]

In the introductory or pioneering stage the demand for the product with respect to price is generally more inelastic than in the later stages of development. However, the manufacturer must make a considerable investment in promotion in order to educate consumers about the existence and uses of the product. In the competitive stage of the cycle the product is challenged by substitutes produced by other manufacturers. The selling task changes from stimulating primary demand to stimulating selective demand. Price becomes more important as cross elasticity of demand (the sensitivity of demand for a product to changes in the prices of close substitutes) increases. The final phase of the cycle is the commodity stage. When a product reaches the point where market shares are relatively stabilized, where brand preference is low or nonexistent, and where price reductions will produce more profitable volume than will promotion, the product is said to have reached maturity. It has, indeed, become a commodity like salt, sugar, calcium chloride, or copper wire, and little need exists for promotion.

Introductory stage. In the introductory stage of product development a great deal of special selling effort is required to acquaint consumers

---

[1] See Joel Dean, "Pricing Policies for New Products," *Harvard Business Review* 54 (November–December 1976), pp. 141–53.

with the new product type and to gain distribution at wholesale and retail. Some manufacturers sell directly to retailers in this stage, bypassing wholesalers until the need for special promotional effort has subsided. Other manufacturers use wholesalers but restrict distribution so that each wholesaler will be willing to engage in the special selling required. Distribution at retail may also be on a highly selective basis, to gain cooperation from individual retailers.

Competitive stage. As products pass from the introductory stage to the competitive stage, the manufacturer's selling task changes from building primary demand to stimulating selective demand. When the product reaches this stage in the cycle, the manufacturer must recognize that, unless special incentive is provided, wholesalers and retailers have little reason to push one brand of a product type at the expense of another. The reseller's task has changed from stimulating demand for a new product to the routine selling of an established one.

Commodity stage. In the final stage of the cycle during which the product reaches maturity, brand preference weakens, physical variation among competing products narrows, and methods of production stabilize.[2] At this stage manufacturer strategy puts a greater reliance on price rather than nonprice competition. As the price spread among different brands of the same type of product narrows, the opportunities for wholesalers and retailers to sell on the basis of their own patronage appeals increase. Therefore, service, delivery, and credit extension become the reseller's important selling points.

Implications of Resellers' Promotional Role

As the promotional programs of different manufacturers vary in response to individual product-market requirements, so does the nature of the selling task at wholesale and retail. In those situations where manufacturer emphasis is on the use of consumer advertising to pull the product through the channels, the selling role of wholesalers and retailers is at a minimum and is usually concerned with little more than order taking. As elements of push strategy enter the mix, however, the aggregate selling resources of the reseller family become of considerable importance to the manufacturer's program. Such importance increases in such cases as the appliance industry, wherein retailer appeal to the consumer often is more important than brand and the wholesaler can be the most effective agency to gain retailer support.

It is also important to note the changing nature of the reseller's task as products mature. From heavy need for primary demand stimulation in the introductory stages and selective demand stimulation in the com-

---

[2] Ibid., p. 149.

petitive stage, the emphasis shifts to price and patronage appeals as products become established commodities. If resellers are assigned some of the extraordinary selling activities required in the earlier stages of the maturity cycle, the manufacturer must be sure to offer extraordinary profit opportunities. But, on the other hand, if the product has matured, the manufacturer should recognize that the role of resellers in stimulating selective demand is limited.

The wise manufacturer takes the step-by-step approach of first analyzing his own promotional program to identify the selling task *resellers might reasonably be expected to perform in light of this program.* Only then is the manufacturer in a position to formulate policies for improving or supplementing reseller performance.

Wholesaler Performance of the Promotional Function

The promotional job that can be expected from a wholesaler involves a variety of selling tools, including personal selling, samples, and advertising. The success of the individual wholesale merchant, like that of any other business enterpriser, depends upon ability to distribute sufficient quantities of goods at margins high enough to cover costs and provide a profit. It is rare, indeed, for a wholesaler to reach a profitable volume level without exerting selling effort.

The general requirements of business usually determine what sales volume must be reached, but the merchant may also have to exercise considerable discretion in formulating a selling plan which will reach secondary objectives. These objectives may include attaining quotas set by manufacturers of franchised lines, exerting special effort to gain preferential treatment from manufacturers of certain lines, and building goodwill for his own establishment so that future sales will be achieved with less effort.

Selling tools. The problem facing the wholesaler is rarely whether to sell or not to sell; it is rather to determine the type, direction, and amount of selling efforts that will enable one to reach planned objectives. In planning selling effort wholesalers have access to most of the tools available to other marketing institutions. The emphasis of most wholesalers on local or regional markets, however, limits their utilization of media to those covering these market areas rather than those providing national coverage. The tools used include (1) personal selling, (2) samples, and (3) advertising.

Personal selling. Among service wholesalers personal selling is the most widely used sales tool. It has been estimated that approximately one third of all operating expenses of wholesalers is directed toward the delivery of a continuous sales effort. Further, the cost of engaging in personal selling has been judged to account for between 80 and 90 percent of the total wholesaler promotional expenditure. Personal selling, defined as an oral presentation of the sales message, is carried on mainly by the wholesaler's field salespeople, although counter salespeople are becoming increasingly important. The growing emphasis on inside selling is noted in such industries as auto parts and electronic parts, in which wholesale selling is exhibiting many retailer characteristics.

Personal selling encompasses a wide range of activities which may include some or all of the following: (1) checking the customer's inventory; (2) assisting in arrangements for advertising and merchandise displays; (3) helping to make adjustments on customer complaints; (4) providing advertising material, catalog information, and other dealer helps; (5) suggesting seasonal merchandise and advising the account on stock needs; and (6) providing technical assistance and advice.

Although the above activities are highly routinized, they account for an important portion of the personal selling effort expended by wholesalers. The remaining time is, of course, available for special activities or the kind of aggressive selling visualized by many manufacturer promotional programs.

Samples. The sales tool which ranks next to the almost universal use of personal selling is the use of samples. Ranging all the way from models, photographs, or visual aids carried by the salesperson to many trunks of merchandise displayed in hotel rooms, samples often constitute an important selling expense. They tend to increase the productivity of personal selling effort and are especially effective when the attributes of the product are difficult to describe and when the quality of the product is a decisive factor in its sale.

Advertising. Generally used as an adjunct to personal selling, advertising expenditures by individual wholesale establishments are small compared to those made for personal selling activities. Advertising expenditures have been estimated to run between 10 and 20 percent of the amounts wholesalers allocate to their sales forces. Advertising is used by wholesalers to pave the way for their salespeople, to inform customers of new products, and to promote the patronage appeals of the wholesale establishment.

The preparation and distribution of catalogs are also sizable items of promotional expense for the wholesaler. Because of the breadth of their product lines, salespeople depend heavily upon catalogs for information about the goods they sell. Although catalogs are prepared primarily for field and counter selling personnel, they may also be distributed to certain key accounts.

Other tools. Promotional activities such as displays, shows and expositions, demonstrations, and nonrecurrent selling efforts which serve to coordinate personal selling and advertising are supplementary tools used by the wholesaler. Another tool is publicity or nonsponsored commercially significant news. Although it is probably never free, publicity is an effective way for the wholesaler to promote itself as a key part of the local business community.

Factors Influencing Wholesalers Ability to Sell

Although wholesalers generally have access to the same array of selling tools, their individual selling programs may be quite diverse. Factors which account for the diversity and thus influence the type and amount of selling effort expended for the manufacturer include: (1) the product line at wholesale, (2) the character of the market served, (3) service requirements, and (4) the competitive environment.

The product line.   The composition of the wholesaler's line in terms of whether it is made up of standardized or differentiated items, low unit-value or high unit-value items, and other factors determines to a large extent the selling support provided for the manufacturer. Lines composed of standardized, relatively low unit-value supply items lend themselves to cataloging and routine personal selling. There is little need for the wholesaler to advertise these products, for such patronage appeals as availability, delivery, and credit extension weigh more in customer's minds than the brand of any particular product.

In contrast, wholesaler lines composed of products which are more highly differentiated or which have unique appeal suggest different kinds and amounts of selling effort. The history of an electrical distributor illustrates a situation in which a wholesaler was able to engage in active selling and promotion because of the nature of its product line. This particular wholesaler sold a line of industrial equipment which was less standardized and of higher unit value than the items sold by mill supply houses. It recognized that personal selling effort must locate customers, must grant important presale services such as cost and engineering estimates, and must reach the many people who influence the final decision to purchase. Furthermore, this wholesaler utilized direct mail and advertising in trade publications in support of its personal selling activities. Not to be overlooked is the important fact that it sold a line with a margin and turnover sufficient to provide the funds needed to support an ambitious program of selling and promotion.

Wholesalers of consumer goods often take a different approach to promotion. In the drug and grocery industries, for example, it is common to deal with numerous and differentiated products of low unit value with high rates of turnover. Because of the intensity of distribution required to sell these convenience goods and because of the importance of the economies of physical distribution, the wholesalers in these industries concentrate on gaining coverage and on selling themselves as efficient distributors. To ensure continued demands for their services they devote much of their effort to cultivating their retail customers rather than to stimulating demand for specific products.

The most striking characteristic of wholesaler lines is their breadth, and certainly one generalization is reasonable: *the broader the line, the greater the limitation on aggressive selling or promotion of an individual line or product.* Although aggressive selling is a routine part of the manufacturer's program, the wholesaler uses such selling sparingly when breadth of line is extensive.

Character of market served. In addition to product types carried and breadth of product lines, the nature of the market in which the products are sold also influences the kind and amount of selling support provided for the manufacturer. Wholesaler markets consist of either final users or other resellers. Within each of these classifications the kind and quantity of firms may vary. A mill supply house selling industrial operating and maintenance supplies to manufacturers may have a rather uncomplicated market situation. Even though its customers probably produce a variety of end products, they all are manufacturers who are purchasing for final use. In the consumer goods area an analogous situation might be one in which drug or grocery wholesalers are serving a relatively homogeneous market composed of single types of retail outlets specializing in the sale of drugs or dry groceries.

In contrast, there might be other situations in which wholesalers face a considerably more complex market structure. A paper wholesaler, for example, may serve both the industrial and consumer goods markets by selling to retail stationers for resale and to industrial and institutional users for final consumption. An electrical wholesaler selling primarily to the industrial market may also supply public utilities and large electrical contractors. An electric appliance wholesaler may sell only durable goods for resale to household buyers, but even within the market it deals with many kinds of retailers—radio, radio and appliance, music, hardware, dry goods, and department stores.

Variations in not only markets served but also in kinds of customers within each market explain why selling programs are so diverse. With only a given amount of resources available to the wholesaler for selling and sales promotion, the complexity of the market structure it faces influences its ability to provide concentrated selling effort to any one particular segment. This ability to concentrate selling effort is also related to the number of customers to be covered and to their location.

Wholesale selling programs are also influenced by varying needs to divert effort from the creation of present sales to the cultivation of potential customers who may provide future sales.

Finally, but not the least important, the profitability of the average order received from specific customers or kinds of customers determines, in great part, the frequency with which personal calls can be made or the amount of selling help which can be offered.

Service requirements.   Traditionally the services provided by wholesalers for their customers are buying, selling, transportation, storage, financing, risk taking, and market information and advice. However, wholesalers do not provide the same array of services or perform the same functional mix for each type of customer. These differences in what is needed to keep old customers or to gain new customers explain much of the variation in ability to grant specific kinds and amounts of selling effort.

The change in functional mix performed by wholesalers is most pronounced in the grocery industry. In order to help their retailer customers survive the price competition from integrated chains, grocery wholesalers shifted the performance of the routine selling function (actually order taking) to the retailer and assumed some of the management function which should have been, but was not, performed by the retail merchant personally. Specifically, they provide weekly order forms for their retailer customers which suggest retail prices and show gross margins. They plan promotions and help prepare newspaper display advertising. Wholesalers also provide management advice on store design and layout, accounting, and personnel relations problems.

The need for wholesalers to provide management services to retailers is not confined to the grocery industry. The same pattern of functional shifting is to be found in the sale of drugs and hardware. In fact, the concept of the "voluntary chain" is that the wholesaler grants management services and buying economies in exchange for the retailer's commitment of continual patronage. This guarantee of demand eliminates for the wholesaler the expense of sales solicitation.

The traditional service patterns which preceded those discussed above still are dominant in many industries. Traditional services include frequent calls in which product and market information are provided and orders solicited, holding large stocks in wholesale warehouses, speedy delivery, credit extension, and after-sale service, among others. These are all parts of the service mix. But providing these "bundles" of services, although necessary in some instances, is very costly. Any pressures on margins, from either the cost or the revenue side, causes the wholesaler to reexamine the quantity and quality of its functional performance. It is the provision of selling support for the manufacturer—perhaps because of the relatively easy manner in which it can be diluted and curtailed—which is most likely to be reduced in the face of cost or competitive pressure.

Nature of competition.   The kind of competition that wholesalers face has a major influence on their ability to provide specific kinds and amounts of selling effort. Competition bears down on the entire array of functions performed, but it is especially meaningful in terms of its impact upon ability to engage in promotional support. As discussed here, competition is defined as rivalry, of both the price and nonprice varieties, emanating from other resellers within the wholesale channel as well as from other channels.

The pressures of competition, no matter what their source or type, fall on wholesale margins. If the wholesaler protects its share of market against competitors by responding to price or nonprice moves of rivals, unit revenues go down as prices are shaved and unit costs go up as promotional effort is increased. Unless the end result of its action is greater volume, the wholesaler finds itself with a shrinking bundle of dollars to cover its costs of operation and to provide a return on its investment.

If it is caught in a margin squeeze, the wholesaler, like any other business firm, resists the change in its profit position, and it shows this resistance either by reducing expenditures for functional performance or by reducing investment in plant and inventory. The outward evidence of margin squeeze may, at first, be an attempt to shift the storage function back to the manufacturer. Thus greater dependence upon drop shipments and the practice of hand-to-mouth buying are indications that wholesalers are attempting to compensate for falling margins by increasing turnover. Selling support also may be reduced to compensate for increased price competition which must be met with increased discounts to its customers.

Economic Role of the Wholesaler

Although wholesaler promotional programs are quite diverse, they do share certain characteristics. These characteristics are an outgrowth of the wholesaler's economic role and have important influences on its ability to engage in promotional activity.

Wholesalers base their economic justification for being merchant resellers largely upon their abilities to reduce the total costs of physical distribution. Because of their specialized function and because of their ability to reduce the number but increase the scale of transactions necessary to effect intermediate exchange, wholesalers are able to provide distributional economies to their many sources and customers. Since these economies are derived from serving many firms, however, the inherent nature of the wholesaler's role usually prevents it from serving any one source or any one customer on an exclusive basis.

The economies of wholesale distribution result largely from performing efficiently the functions of physical distribution such as breaking bulk, storage, making of assortments, and the delivery of these assortments to customers. There is, therefore, an understandable tendency on the part of wholesalers to concentrate their efforts in that area rather than on promotional functions. When the wholesaler does have an opportunity to engage in other than routine order-taking activities, it finds it to its advantage to build up its own patronage appeals rather than to stimulate demand for the branded products of its suppliers. From its vantage point in the distributive structure, the most effective promotional strategy it can use is to develop a loyal customer group which will continue to patronize it. It reasons that its success is closely related to its ability to satisfy the desires of its customer group rather than those of individual manufacturer sources.

This orientation makes it difficult for the wholesaler to be concerned with the problems or requests of individual manufacturers whose promotional activities do not increase the size of the wholesaler's market but merely recut the pieces of the pie. The manufacturer, on the other hand, is necessarily concerned with selling its brand or product line. Its promotional strategy is directed toward stimulating a selective demand, exercising control over the methods of sale of its line, and accruing whatever goodwill arises from the use of its products. Its strategy, in essence, is oriented toward *brand.* This strategy is in marked contrast to that of the wholesaler, whose aim is to increase the sales of the *commodity* by building a loyal customer following.

The wholesaler finds that its profits lie in building a reputation for itself as a good house with which to do business. Prompt delivery, competitive prices, and convenient credit extension are but a few of the usual inducements the wholesaler uses in its sales message to its customers. When it does promote a specific product, it is generally the one that most benefits its customers in terms of ease of sale and subsequent profitability. Such promotion is consistent with the wholesaler's goal of increasing its patronage appeal. It is equally evident that if a wholesaler actively supports a product by applying extra effort to its sale, the manufacturing source will benefit. But if the wholesaler thinks that the expenditure of such effort is unwise or unprofitable in terms of its total program, it is quite likely to ignore the demands of any one manufacturer. This pattern of behavior is most characteristic of general-line, full-service wholesalers and is the cause of much disagreement and conflict between them and the manufacturers they represent.

It can be seen that the economics of wholesaling, as well as the divergence of promotional strategy common to firms occupying different positions in the distributive structure, explains several of the characteristics shared by wholesaler selling programs: (1) the inability of wholesalers to grant exclusive attention to any one of their suppliers, (2) the tendency among wholesalers to devote more attention to the performance of the functions of physical distribution than to those of a promotional nature, and (3) the wholesaler strategy of promoting their own patronage appeals rather than the products of specific manufacturers. Those characteristics are the common denominators in almost all wholesaler selling situations, and they account for the similarities in the promotional effort which wholesalers give their manufacturers.

Factors Influencing Wholesalers' Allocation of Selling Effort

The wholesaler's economic role, as well as the nature of its product line and market environment, influences its *ability* to put forth selling effort. There remains, however, the question of how the effort that can be expended is allocated to the individual products in the wholesaler's line. The answer to this question requires analysis of: (1) the objectives of wholesalers, (2) the division of the selling task, (3) the type and extent of manufacturer help, (4) the type and extent of competition, and (5) the adequacy of margin.

Objectives of wholesalers. The long-run economic goal of any wholesale establishment is, essentially, to maximize profits. As such it does not differ markedly from those of any other business enterprise. Individual wholesalers, however, may seek a wide variety of shorter run objectives which they hope will maximize profits in the long run. How the wholesaler *defines* these shorter run market objectives may influence its willingness to allocate selling effort to particular manufacturers. For example, if a wholesaler believes that its success and that of its customer group are based upon the ability to compete on a price basis, the allocation of selling effort will be heavily biased toward the promotion of private brands or the brands of those manufacturers that provide products with price rather than nonprice appeals. On the other hand, if the demands of the market indicate a preference for advertised brands, with low price being a secondary appeal, the wholesaler may allocate its support in favor of the manufacturer selling branded, nationally advertised lines.

It would appear that, given a range of short-run objectives *based on the market requirements of its customer group,* the wholesaler will allocate its selling and promotional effort to those manufacturers whose products and programs best fit the needs of this group. Admittedly this is a broad generalization, but here is a case in point: In the grocery industry prior to World War II, private brands were a major means by which wholesalers could provide their independent customers with merchandise which could undersell national brands at retail, retain goodwill for the distributors, and provide wider margins at wholesale and retail than would national brands. With the rapid growth of self-service among independent as well as chain grocers during the postwar decade, however, the household buyer's influence became more clearly felt. The desire to trade up in food, supported by rising national income, negated much of the price appeal of private brands. In addition, the self-service process gave advantage to manufacturer brands, especially those whose distinctiveness made possible the stimulation of brand preference through national advertising.

To meet this changing condition, wholesalers serving independents had to change their merchandising and promotional emphasis. Private brands often were consolidated or dropped, and renewed promotional support was given to those manufacturers that supplied well-advertised branded products. This is not to say that private brands are unimportant today, only to illustrate the influence of customer requirements on wholesalers' efforts.

Division of the selling task.   Essentially, the wholesaler faces the problem of allocating limited promotional resources over a broad product line. At the same time it must anticipate the needs of its customer group and carry and promote those products they find easy and profitable to sell. Thus in apportioning selling effort to specific products or product lines the wholesaler is greatly concerned with how much of the total selling job has been done by the manufacturer and how much remains to be performed by it and its customers.

With established products wholesalers can estimate the existing level of demand and thus determine the extent of the demand-stimulation task they must undertake if the product is to be properly handled. It should be recognized, however, that wholesalers are wary of diverting large amounts of efforts to demand-stimulation activities that may be necessary for the sale of particular products. The reasons for this hesitation are purely economic, for the diversion of selling effort from the bulk of a wholesaler's line to the promotion of one product may result in a less favorable profit position. Such a situation will occur if the loss of sales and profits in the area from which effort has been withdrawn is greater than the gain in revenues and profits resulting from the newly directed effort. Therefore, in order for an established product to receive a larger portion of the wholesaler's selling effort, its promotion must promise a net revenue and profit gain. The manufacturer who divides the total selling task between the firm and its wholesalers so as to make such a gain possible generally receives the needed selling support.

New products pose an especially troublesome problem for the wholesaler. Whereas in the case of established products some evidence of the level of demand is available, such information is often lacking for new products. The problems arising from the lack of information about demand are further compounded by the continual introduction of a wide variety and large number of new products by manufacturers, especially in consumer goods. One wholesale grocer reported that he received an average of 100 "new" items per week for its consideration.[3] (Many of these, however, were actually variations of old products.) Unless new items result in increased *commodity* sales, the result for the wholesaler is usually

---

[3] See "Abner A. Wolf, Inc. (A)," *Michigan Business Cases*, Marketing Series no. 41 (Ann Arbor: Graduate School of Business Administration, University of Michigan).

an increased investment in inventory and a further dilution of selling effort over an expanded product line. Acting rationally, wholesalers do not like to allocate effort if the new result is a shifting of market shares between manufacturers without a concomitant gain at wholesale. Therefore, they divert effort to new products and lines *only* when they feel that such diversion will provide profits in excess of those lost by the reduced selling effort allocated to the remainder of the line.[4]

The preceding analysis assumes that the manufacturer pursues a "push" type of strategy, in which the active selling support of the wholesaler is needed to gain sales to industrial users or retailers. If the manufacturer's product is highly advertisable, however, it might elect to utilize a "pull" type of strategy, in which heavy advertising to the final user (the consumer) pulls the product through the channel.

Wholesalers like some degree of pull, because the product thereby becomes easier to sell. But if the manufacturer resorts to "forcing" by pulling the product through the wholesale channel at lower than average margins, the wholesaler's attitude changes, in many cases, to one of open hostility. Under these extreme circumstances it may refuse to engage in any promotional program suggested by the manufacturer.

Type and extent of manufacturer help. Assuming that the manufacturer has decided on the general division of the selling task between itself and its wholesalers, it still must make adjustments to the needs of individual establishments. Recognition of this requirement by a manufacturer and its subsequent activities to give promotional assistance have great influence upon the willingness of the individual wholesaler to cooperate. Wholesalers are especially interested in the manufacturer providing such support as missionary salespeople (i.e., manufacturer salespeople who try to gain new customers for the line), training programs, cooperative advertising, and packaged promotions. These helps are discussed in greater detail in Chapter 21. At this point it is sufficient to note that the type and extent of assistance offered by manufacturers affects not only the wholesaler's promotional costs but its ability to perform its part of the distributive and selling task as well. Inevitably, therefore, the amount of help the manufacturer will give has a great deal to do with a wholesaler's decision as to where to allot its selling effort.

---

[4] Ibid. An interesting example of a new-product policy is noted in the Abner Wolf, Inc., case. This company, the largest dry grocery wholesaler in Michigan and one of the largest in the nation, served 100 chain supermarkets and 900 independents. Using the order book method, it supplied over 4,400 items to its retail customers. A products committee consisting of wholesaler and retailer representatives every week sifted through an average of over 100 new items which were presented for their attention by various manufacturers. Those products that showed promise were in turn presented to a merchandising committee which continually evaluated the performance of each of the firm's many merchandise departments. If the product suggested had merit and if the merchandising committee felt that it could be a profitable addition to a line or a replacement for an existing product, the buyer in charge of the department was granted permission to negotiate for its purchase.

Type and extent of competition.   When allocating promotional resources to specific manufacturers, wholesalers consider the type and extent
of competition they expect to face in selling a given product or product
line. They are concerned about the rivalry of other wholesalers handling
the same product, as well as that emanating from the direct channel.
Another aspect of the problem is whether the rivalry encountered will
be essentially of the price variety or whether it will assume nonprice
forms.

Wholesalers scrutinize that portion of manufacturer policy which determines selectivity of distribution within the wholesale channel for an indication of the possible intensity of intrachannel conflict. And they take
a good look at the manufacturer's past channel policies for some indication
of the interchannel competitive pressures they must be prepared to face.

The one area most closely examined is the manufacturer's direct sale
policy. Although excessive rivalry from resellers in other channels is not
to a wholesaler's liking, competition from the manufacturer is a severe
irritant. Wholesalers do not like to give support to sources that compete
with them for customers. The direct sale policy of a manufacturer, therefore, is of vital concern to wholesalers who must determine their allocation
of selective selling effort.

Adequacy of margin.   The adequacy of the spread between the price
at which they buy and the price at which they can sell specific products
is another major consideration influencing wholesalers in their allocation
of selling and promotional effort. The discussion of margin is placed last
in this section because margin is a meaningful criterion only in relation
to the extent of the total wholesaling job to be done. This job includes
the full range of functional performance in the areas of both physical
distribution and selling.

Inasmuch as a single margin payment must cover the cost of wholesaler
performance and provide a profit, any factors that affect the price at
which wholesalers can sell or the costs of functional performance result
in margin adjustments. (The extent of the selling job to be done at wholesale and the amount of help provided by manufacturers, for example,
influence costs. The intensity of the price competition it faces, on the
other hand, influences the price at which the wholesaler can sell.) The
truly unique nature of margin squeeze at wholesale, regardless of whether
the cause is from the cost or the revenue side, or both, is that *the effects
upon the wholesaler's willingness to perform fall unequally on different functional areas.*
The promotional functions appear to be much more amenable to dilution
or shifting than do the functions of physical distribution. Of course,
wholesalers attempt to shift the storage function back to their sources
by hand-to-mouth buying, relying more on drop shipments, and by carrying narrower assortments. Such shifts, however, are more quickly recognized than are reductions in the quality of wholesaler selling effort.

Wholesaler selling effort in general goes where it pays to go. It can go, however, where it is *paid* to go by manufacturers who desire more effort at wholesale than can be profitably provided by normal wholesale margins.

RETAILERS AS PROMOTIONAL RESOURCES

Retailers are those marketing intermediaries that resell commodities to final users, generally for household consumption. They compose the final link in the chain which begins with the manufacturer and ends with the household. Retailers perform those marketing functions that enable them to build assortments of goods which will appeal to their markets. In addition to making the goods available, they often must convince the target customers of the satisfaction to be obtained from them.[5]

Retailers are the most numerous of all types of business establishments. Recent census data indicate that there are about 1.9 million retailers in the United States, as compared with about 370,000 merchant wholesalers and 449,000 manufacturers.[6]

The economic basis of retailing is the ability of these many, often small, widely dispersed business enterprises to act as the buyer's purchasing agent by anticipating and satisfying wants.[7] In addition, retailers perform the typical mix of functions necessary to engage in intermediate exchange such as buying, selling, transporting, and storing.

Other than the generalization that retailers make most of their sales to the final buyer, there is not much else about them that falls in a very clear pattern. They vary enormously in terms of size of establishment, type of goods carried, functional mix performed, and ownership. Regardless of their size or type, they face intense competition because of ease of entry into retailing. Moreover, retailers have difficulty in building or maintaining a competitive advantage over other retailers of their own type or over newer forms of retailing organizations. Perhaps one other valid generalization is that retailing and retailers are in a constant state of change because of the competitive forces prevailing and because of the ever-changing tastes and desires of buyers. The implication of this dynamism for the marketing manager is quite clear. Continual careful monitoring of retail outlets in the pattern of distribution is essential to the success of a marketing program. Retail leaders of the not too distant past may be displaced very quickly by other entrants to the competitive scene.

---

[5] E. J. McCarthy, *Basic Marketing—A Managerial Approach,* 6th ed. (Homewood, Ill.: Richard D. Irwin, 1978), p. 335.

[6] Ibid., p. 322.

[7] William J. Stanton, *Fundamentals of Marketing,* 4th ed. (New York: McGraw-Hill, 1975), p. 339.

Classification of Retailers

A classification of retail establishments, for purposes of this text can be made in terms of (1) store types, (2) functional mix of marketing efforts, and (3) ownership.

Store types. Retail stores might be classified into three types: (1) convenience, (2) shopping, and (3) specialty.[8] A convenience store is one which customers patronize because of its excellent location or other factors which add to customer convenience. A shopping store is one which attracts customers on the basis of width and depth of assortments carried and which might also be in close proximity to other shopping stores. A specialty store is one which has developed a strong selective demand because

FIGURE 20–1
The Product-Patronage Mix

1. *Convenience store—Convenience good:* The buyer, represented by this category, prefers to buy the most readily available brand of product at the most accessible store.
2. *Convenience store—Shopping good:* The buyer selects a purchase from the assortment carried by the most accessible store.
3. *Convenience store—Specialty good:* The buyer purchases a favored brand from the most accessible store which has the item in stock.
4. *Shopping store—Convenience good:* The buyer is indifferent to the brand of product he bought, but shops among different stores in order to secure better retail service and (or) lower retail price.
5. *Shopping store—Shopping good:* The buyer makes comparisons among both retail controlled factors and factors associated with the product (brand).
6. *Shopping store—Specialty good:* The buyer has a strong preference with respect to the brand of the product, but shops among a number of stores in order to secure the best retail service and (or) price for this brand.
7. *Specialty store—Convenience good:* The buyer prefers to trade at a specific store, but is indifferent to the brand of product purchased.
8. *Specialty store—Shopping good:* The buyer prefers to trade at a certain store, but is uncertain as to which product one wishes to buy and examines the store's assortment for the best purchase.
9. *Specialty store—Specialty good:* The buyer has both a preference for a particular store and a specific brand.

Source: Adapted from Louis P. Bucklin, "Retail Strategy and the Classification of Consumer Goods," *Journal of Marketing* 27, no. 1, January 1963, pp. 53–54.

of its particular product, price, and service offering, as well as its location. Customers prefer to shop at this type of store for a variety of goods.

A really clear picture of how a consumer views alternatives at retail is gained if the classification of products and stores types is made jointly. Figure 20–1 illustrates the range of combinations. The implication of this type of classification for promotional strategy is clear: In those situations where the convenience appeals of the outlet dominate the specialty or patronage appeals, promotion must seek to gain maximum coverage of

---

[8] See Louis T. Bucklin, "Retail Strategy and the Classification of Consumer Goods," *Journal of Marketing* 27, no. 1 (January 1963), pp. 50–55.

the market for the manufacturer. In other situations, where patronage appeals of the individual outlets are stronger than selective demand for the product, the manufacturer's campaign must be aimed at getting distribution and promotional support from these key retailers.

Functional mix of marketing efforts. The marketing functions performed at retail are quite similar to those performed by wholesalers. They include buying, selling, storage, transportation, and the granting of credit, among others. Retailers far exceed wholesalers, however, with respect to the variety of ways in which they alter the relative emphasis placed on specific areas of performance. To illustrate the range of variation possible it is useful to consider several types of retail establishments in terms of the functions performed and the services offered to the consumer.

The department store (epitomized by Macy's, Field's, or Dayton-Hudson's) is an example of a full-service retailer that is analogous to the full-service wholesaler. It offers a wide variety of goods at different price-quality levels. In addition, such customer services as delivery, return privileges, credit, warranty, and service are offered. Of special significance to the promotion manager is the fact that department stores perform the selling function *in its entirety.* Local media advertising, personal selling, window and interior display, and special sales promotional events all are utilized to stimulate demand for the store and the products it carries.

In contrast to the full-service department store is the discount department store, which emphasizes price in its product-price-service offering. In order to reduce their operating expenses from the 38 to 40 percent of sales typical of full-service department stores to the 20 to 25 percent level needed to make a profit, given their lower gross margins, the discount stores must cut back on functional performance. Areas of customer service such as credit, delivery, and service are not offered on a "free" basis. In addition, in-store personnel selling activities are at a minimum, and the major burden of promotion is placed on display and advertising.

The supermarket is yet another type of retailer. Specializing in groceries, although carrying nonfood items to an increasing extent, supermarkets are a hybrid of the department store and the discount house. They emphasize price and convenience, and most are departmentalized. Personal selling by store employees is supplanted by self-service; the goods are left to sell themselves with the help of manufacturer and retailer advertising and retailer-allocated shelf space and position.

These are but three examples of literally thousands of combinations of ways in which retailers may perform their functions. The way in which selling is performed at retail is especially important for manufacturers that require retail selling support for their products. More is said about this later.

Ownership. Type of ownership influences the way in which retail stores sell. Census data indicate that about 90 percent of all retail units in the nation are independently owned and operated. These independent units account for about two thirds of all retail sales. Although chain stores account for only 10 percent of the total number of stores, their sales make up one third of the retail total, with the trend being in favor of greater penetration. In certain trades the chain stores account for a very large percentage of total volume.

Thus two distinct types of retailers serve the consumer market. The independents are usually, but not always, smaller than the chains. They generally lack the specialization of management possible with larger organizations. On the other hand, independents can build a strong patronage appeal based on the personality of the store owner who is a local resident. From the standpoint of the manufacturer's promotional strategy, a program must be developed that is acceptable to both claims and independents if full coverage of the market is required. Cooperative advertising plans, demonstrators, and point-of-sale displays suitable for independents may not fit in with the scheduled programs of the chains. The problem for the manufacturer is to coordinate promotional programs with diverse types of retailers.

Selling Effort at Retail

While recognizing the tremendous variation in selling which takes place in individual retail stores, according to the type of merchandise carried, store type, or store ownership, selling activities at retail can nevertheless be considered in general. An understanding of the qualitative aspects of retail promotion can be as important to the manufacturer as an understanding of wholesaler selling activities.

Personal selling. The activity of face-to-face selling in a retail store bears very little resemblance to the activity as performed at the manufacturer and wholesaler levels in the channel. The basis of retail selling consists of providing product information and taking orders. In many cases even these aspects of the selling task are poorly performed, for creative selling at retail is almost a lost art. The reasons for this decline in personal selling performance derive in part from the nature of the average retail salesperson's job. In addition to meeting customers and attempting to fill their needs from the assortments carried, the salesperson is also responsible for housekeeping duties dealing with stock, displays, or the sales book. These duties serve to keep the salesperson occupied while waiting for customers, but they are not highly productive efforts in terms of sales. When customers do come in, the average sale is small for the time consumed in making the transaction. In addition, customers tend to arrive in bunches, so the retail selling staff is often unable to handle them efficiently.

The economies of a situation in which the retailer is usually either overstaffed or understaffed to gain sales of modest magnitude results in low productivity and low wage levels. These wages do not attract the most gifted sales types into retail trade because the opportunities are greater for them as wholesaler or manufacturer salesperson. Of course, the preceding statement may not be true when the type of product being sold has considerable profit potential and requires some technical knowledge for its sale, as is the case with automobiles. But even among these situations there are many examples of poor-quality personal selling effort.

Attempts to improve retailer selling performance and to gain in-store selling support are discussed in a later chapter. For now it is sufficient to recognize the tremendous potential offered by sales personnel in the many retail outlets in a typical pattern of distribution. The low qualitative level of performance of the personal selling function by many retailers also must be recognized, however.

Advertising. The average retail merchant who engages in advertising utilizes the local newspaper, with perhaps some supplementary support from the local radio station. Newspaper display advertising is of the direct-action type and is aimed at informing the consumer of specific product and price offerings. Grocery retailers rely almost entirely on price promotion; their weekly advertisements are little more than published price lists. Stores of the shopping or specialty type generally limit their advertising efforts to the promotion of a small number of specific products or even to the patronage appeals of the stores themselves. In most cases where small independents are concerned, the advertising layout is planned with the help of the media representative or, in the case of groceries and drugs, with the assistance of the wholesaler salesperson. In almost all industries manufacturers provide standardized advertisements and layouts in the form of mats which can be cast into type by the local newspaper.

Radio advertising by retailers is generally limited to spot announcements which are used to publicize special promotional events or to supplement newspaper display advertising.

Display. One of the most potent tools available to the retailer is display—both window and point of sale. Display makes the buyer's searching task easier by indicating the type of merchandise carried by a store in terms of assortments and price-quality levels. It thus enables buyers to judge whether they are at a store where prices and assortments meet their requirements without the necessity of making an inquiry. In addition to its function as a locater and classifier, display also serves to trigger impulse buying. The shopper who enters a supermarket and leaves only with those items on a shopping list is a very rare case.

Because of its power to influence customers, display space at retail is valuable. The wise retailer uses its window and in-store display areas well by merchandising them carefully, keeping them neat and clean, and changing displays frequently to keep its store interesting to the consumer. Promotional programs of manufacturers often require retailer display co-operation. So great is the rivalry among manufacturers for limited window, shelf, or in-store display areas that often retailers sell space to the highest bidder. Even then there is little assurance that once display space is "pur-chased" by the manufacturer the retailer will cooperate for very long.

The allocation of display areas in supermarkets is being made on a more sophisticated basis. Progressive managers allocate space to products or groups of products in terms of their profitability. Such profitability is calculated by subtracting the costs associated with carrying the product in the line from the revenues brought in by the product. The relative size of the profit contribution made by various products or groups of products determines the size and location of shelf area assigned.

Other sales promotion. Retailers may also engage in special promo-tional activities such as providing in-store demonstrations, special selling events, or particpating in communitywide merchandising events such as bargain days or street fairs. The range of promotional activity is almost limitless. In fact, the variation in type, amount, and quality of activity available makes manufacturer development of a workable program a most difficult undertaking.

Factors Affecting Retailer Ability to Sell

The factors that influence the retailer's ability to engage in promotion are very similar to those affecting wholesalers. They include, among oth-ers, (1) the type of store, (2) the nature of the product line carried, and (3) the character of the market served. In considering these factors it is important to recognize the extreme variability among retailers. Even among retailers of the same type selling similar items to a common market, the qualitative and quantitative aspects of promotional efforts may be quite dissimilar.

Type of store. Given the classification of retail stores based on whether buyers view them as convenience stores, shopping stores, or specialty stores, a reasonable generalization is that those stores that are shopping or specialty types offer greater opportunity for promotional effort at retail than do the convenience stores. Location and broad assort-ments of competitively priced goods are the primary ways by which con-venience stores attract patronage. In contrast, the shopping store carries fewer lines of more costly merchandise and usually engages in a full array of promotional effort. This is also the case with specialty type outlets which have even narrower lines but engage in advertising, display, and in-store personal selling.

Product line. The product line carried by the retailer also influences his ability to engage in selling support. If items in the line are highly differentiated from others of a similar type, if they are profitable to sell, and if they add to the patronage appeal of the store, then they provide the opportunity for retailer promotion. On the other hand, lines composed of routine commodity-type items on which price competition is severe provide little opportunity for nonprice promotion at retail.

Segmentation of market. Because of the wide diversity in buyer wants and tastes, most retailers aim their merchandising programs at a particular segment of the market. The choice of such a segment by the retailer influences his ability to engage in promotional support. For example, if a retailer is serving a market composed of buyers who are very price conscious, its ability to engage in nonprice promotion is limited. In contrast, if its target segment is made up of those who want quality and are willing to pay for it, then there will be more opportunity and margin to support nonprice activities such as personal selling, advertising, and display.

Factors Affecting Retailer Willingness to Sell

Although retailer ability to engage in promotional activity varies widely, all retailers can do some promotion of the goods they carry. The factors that influence how the retailer allocates available selling effort to products of specific manufacturers are similar to those that guide wholesaler allocations. They include: (1) the strategies and objectives of retailers, (2) the division of the selling task and the margin payment, (3) the type and extent of manufacturer's help provided, and (4) the nature of competition.

Strategies and objectives of retailers. Retailers are, of course, in business to make money. They are agreed on the point that in order to make money they must carry assortments and provide services that suit the needs of a sufficient number of customers. Retailers are also convinced of the necessity of selling their stores as convenient, economical, and interesting places to shop. The one promotional strategy common to all independent retailers, therefore, is that of developing patronage appeals and of communicating these appeals to prospective customers.

There are many variations of the common strategy of building and promoting patronage appeals. In many instances the retailer emphasizes its own name and carries a large assortment of private brand merchandise. Macy's in New York or the A & P grocery chain illustrates this type of strategy. Given this strategy it is very difficult for a manufacturer to get promotional support for his product from retailers unless it fills an important gap in their product lines. In contrast, a retailer may feel that, given its type of business, the brand names of the manufacturers who supply it with goods are more meaningful to its customers than are its patronage appeals. If this situation prevails the retailer may promote the goods of specific manufacturers and indicate that such items are to be found in its store.

The way in which the retailer seeks to reach his objectives of growth and profitability in terms of emphasizing its own appeals or those of the goods of specific manufacturers thus is an important determinant of how it will allocate the effort it can expend. Essentially, the manufacturer whose brand appeal is stronger than the appeal of the retailer itself will get retailer support. This support will, however, be tempered by the other considerations to be discussed below.

Division of the selling task and the margin.   If the retailer feels that it must engage in selling support of the goods of a specific manufacturer to reach its business objectives, it still must choose from a large array of products. In attempting to maximize its return from expenditure of effort it could engage in rather detailed studies of product profitabilities to guide its allocation of effort. Many larger firms do just that. However, the bulk of retailers who, because of their size, lack specialized management use the margin payment as a criterion of profitability. Against this payment they weigh the extent of promotion undertaken by the manufacturer and the amount required of them. If the size of the task required seems reasonable in light of the manufacturer's efforts and margin payment, the retailer may allocate some of its limited resources to the promotion of a specific brand or product line.

Extent of manufacturer help provided.   In addition to the margin payment, the retailer also considers the type and extent of support it might receive from the manufacturer. Cooperative advertising allowances, display material, advertising layouts, and demonstrators are some of the supporting services or payments which might be provided. These, of course, have a monetary impact because they reduce the cost of selling for the retailer. The inherent danger is that the retailer may be persuaded to engage in promotion for a particular manufacturer, even though the product promoted has little appeal to the members of its customer group.

Nature of competition.   Promotion by retailers is expensive even if monetary support is provided by manufacturers. Retailers are therefore hesitant to invest their money unless they have a chance to recoup it with a profit. The type and extent of competition they face is a very important determinant of profitability and thus is a consideration retailers examine when deciding on allocations of promotional effort.

Retailers cannot hold manufacturers responsible for the presence of close substitutes for specific products. Such is a fact of life in many industries. They do hold manufacturers responsible, however, for competition they face from other retailers or from other channels of distribution handling the same product. If manufacturer distribution is very intensive, then, of course, many retailers in each market carry the line. Because volume is spread among so many outlets, profit potentials decrease for individual firms. With this decrease in profit potential comes a decrease in willingness to give the manufacturer promotional support.

Of even greater impact is the threat of interchannel competition. In this situation the retailer is faced with competition from other types of resellers or from the manufacturer itself. It is very difficult for a retailer (say a jeweler) to understand why a watch manufacturer asks for its personal selling support and then distributes through the local discount store which sells watches on a price basis. The less competition retailers face from both within and without their channel, the more willing they are to engage in selective promotion for a specific manufacturer. In general, they hesitate to build demand for specific manufacturers unless they themselves can have a good share of the benefits.

SUMMARY

In this chapter resellers were examined as promotional resources. A brief attempt was made to explain how their economic roles influence wholesalers' and retailers' ability to engage in selling support. In addition, consideration was given to those factors that influence resellers to allocate their promotional resources to specific manufacturers.

Chapter 21 discusses how manufacturers might gain reseller support for their programs. It is important to recognize, however, that any attempts to stimulate reseller promotional activity require an understanding of what resellers can and cannot do and how they view their roles as intermediaries in the distributive structure.

Review and Discussion Questions

1. Why does the development of a promotional program by a manufacturer require an understanding of reseller functions and motivations?
2. Discuss the statement: Wholesaling functions would exist even if there were no wholesalers.
3. In what ways are wholesalers promotional objectives similar to those of manufacturers? In what ways do they differ?
4. What factors influence a wholesaler's ability to engage in promotional effort?
5. What aspect of the wholesaler's economic role makes it difficult for it to support the program of an individual source?
6. Which factors appear to influence the wholesaler's apportionment of its selling support activity to various product lines?
7. Why do wholesalers pay close attention to a manufacturer's policy on direct sale to retailers or end users?
8. Is the margin offered the best indication of product profitability to a reseller?
9. Contrast the reseller segment composed of retailers with that composed of wholesalers in terms of numbers as well as degree of diversity.

10. Why is it useful to classify stores in terms of types as well as ownership?

11. Why is display at the retail level such a valuable tool for promotion? How do retailers allocate their display space to specific products?

12. What is meant by the term *interchannel competition?* How does this type of competition influence retailer willingness to engage in sales-supporting activities for the manufacturer?

Stimulating Reseller Support: Improving, Supplementing, and Controlling Performance

When the manufacturer has a clear idea of the role its resellers can be expected to perform, given the overall promotional program, and when it understands the ways in which its other reseller policies can influence wholesaler and retailer willingness and ability to sell, it can consider ways to improve or supplement their activities. With respect to *improving* the selling performance of wholesalers and retailers the manufacturer can consider: (1) training programs for reseller salespeople, (2) setting quotas for resellers, and (3) providing assistance to resellers with respect to their advertising and sales promotion efforts.

In terms of *supplementing* reseller activity the manufacturer might consider: (1) the use of missionary salespeople, (2) provision of display and selling aids, and (3) the scheduling of special sales and consumer deals.

Two means are suggested for *controlling* reseller activity: (1) selection of resellers and (2) vertical integration through ownership of reseller outlets or by means of contractual agreements.

IMPROVING RESELLER PERFORMANCE

Training Reseller Salespeople

One of the most effective methods by which manufacturers can improve reseller performance is to assume part of the responsibility for training wholesaler and retailer salespeople. One writer states bluntly, "Generally speaking you [the manufacturer] will benefit from your distributor relationships more or less in proportion to the effort you put into training the distributor's sales [people]."[1] A study made by the National Industrial Conference Board further affirmed the contention that training of dealer salespeople was a profitable undertaking for manufacturers. It was found that well-trained reseller salespeople built goodwill for the manufacturer as well as for their own houses by recommending the right product to satisfy the customer's needs and by keeping customers informed about the advantages and uses of new products. Moreover, well-trained dealers maintained more adequate inventories and had better service facilities than did untrained distributors. Finally, well-trained dealers required less of the manufacturer salespeople's time, so they could make more calls per day.[2]

Training at the wholesale level. Although the generalizations stated about the value of training are valid for both wholesalers and retailer selling personnel, there is a difference in the objectives and scope of programs aimed at these two levels. The training programs at wholesale are intended to improve the salespeople's knowledge of the line and his or her selling techniques, and often, to train one in addition, to assume the role of management counselors. For example, one manufacturer of major household appliances has an extensive program to train the field representatives of its wholesale distributors. Courses held at the factory are given in such diverse areas as product, business, and sales management; retail selling, handling of used merchandise; service training; and general supervision of a sales territory. There is no charge for the courses, but the distributors must pay transportation and living expenses for their people in the program. Courses run for up to five and one half days, and the trainees are worked hard. Heavy emphasis is placed on visual aids, and after factory training each distributor salesperson is equipped with a sound-film strip projector and a wide variety of training films. These films are made under factory supervision and are sold to distributors at production cost for use in their own training programs for retailer salesmen.

Thus the objectives of a program to train wholesaler salespeople may be twofold—first, to provide them with knowledge about the product line and how it may be sold most effectively, and second, to prepare wholesaler salespeople to provide management assistance to retailers. This assistance may include the training of retailer sales personnel.

---

[1] Carl C. Gauk, "Training the Distributor's Salesmen," *Development of Dealer and Distributor Cooperation for Greater Sales,* Marketing Series no. 80 (New York: American Management Association), p. 17.

[2] E. F. Higgins and J. F. Fogarty, Jr., *Training Dealers.* Studies in Business Policy no. 48 (New York: National Industrial Conference Board), p. 4.

Regardless of the exact content of the manufacturer's training program, it is clear that a program for training wholesaler salespeople fills a gap which in many cases *cannot be filled by the wholesaler itself.* Because of either the pressures of day-to-day business or the lack of specialized sales management in smaller distributor organizations, many wholesalers will not or cannot do an adequate job of training. Thus this is one form of assistance rendered by the manufacturer which helps the wholesaler where it cannot help itself. In those cases where the wholesaler does have its own training facilities and personnel, manufacturer assistance can make the program more effective and at the same time lighten the cost load.

Training at the retail level. Manufacturers' programs to train sales personnel at retail share many objectives in common with programs aimed at training wholesaler salespeople. Attempts are made to impart product knowledge to those who meet the public, as well as to improve their selling techniques. There are differences, however, because of the great dispersion at retail in terms of store size and location. A further complication is the Robinson-Patman Act, which requires the manufacturer to offer promotional allowances or services (including those for training) to retailers on a "proportionally equal" basis. More is said about this requirement later.

Regardless of the difficulties in developing training programs for retailers, the manufacturer must take the initiative when high-quality retail selling is vital to his success, as in the EMBA case.[3] An association of mink breeders had developed a promotional program encompassing both national advertising and point-of-sale activity. Unfortunately, the point-of-sale efforts were handicapped by a shortage of trained fur sales personnel. Moreover, even the largest retailers lacked the ability to develop a training program for their salespeople.

To remedy the situation EMBA commissioned the development of a retail sales force training program to accomplish the following purposes:

1. To make a retail sales force as competent in selling EMBA mink garments as they are in selling ordinary cloth garments.
2. To dispel doubts in the minds of sales personnel regarding the meaning and significance of the EMBA label.
3. To remove the fear that surrounds the sale of fur garments.
4. To emphasize the EMBA image of quality.

Nine stores agreed to participate in the first training session, which lasted three days and was held on the store premises. EMBA specialists conducted a class for the first 30 minutes of each day and then spent the rest of their time on the selling floor. The program was followed

---

[3] See "EMBA Mink Breeder's Association" case in Wayne F. Talarzyk, James F. Engel, and Carl M. Larsen, *Cases in Promotional Strategy* (Homewood, Ill., Richard D. Irwin, 1971).

up by the visit of a "mystery shopper" to each store who monitored sales procedures and offered suggestions for change when weaknesses were spotted.

Another situation of interest is the one faced by the Royal Worcester Porcelain Company.[4] This manufacturer of fine English bone china engaged in the selective distribution of its line through 1,500 jewelry and department stores. Although serving a national market, the company's sales volume could support a relatively small appropriation of $200,000 for advertising and sales promotion. Research studies had indicated that the retail salesperson was highly influential in the sale of china but that most were sadly lacking in product knowledge or awareness of the type of information consumers wanted from them. Moreover, retail sales personnel did not give Royal Worcester very much selling "push."

To improve the caliber of retail selling and to gain greater support for the product line, Royal Worcester developed a program for training retail sales personnel. It consisted of a 20-minute sound training film which was presented by Royal Worcester salespeople at meetings held for about 1,000 of their retail accounts. The film discussed fine china in general and was well received by sales personnel. To maintain continued contact with retail salespeople, the company developed a monthly sales bulletin which provides product information, selling tips, and information about sales contests and serves to inform retail salespeople of the national consumer advertising program.

These two examples of efforts to train retail sales personnel show that such a program is vital to the success of the manufacturer's promotional program when the product is of such a type that the buyer must seek information and advice from the salesperson. In addition, it is clear that very few retailers have the means or the volition to initiate training programs for the sale of specific types of goods. Thus the manufacturer must assume the responsibility and the cost of training retail personnel if it desires an improvement in the quality and quantity of retail support. Moreover, this assumption of responsibility must be on a continuing basis because of the high rate of turnover of retail employees.

Quotas for Resellers

The establishment of quotas, if properly planned and administered, is a device which can improve reseller performance. Although the use of quotas to measure the performance of salesmen is quite common in an integrated organization, the application of this technique to independent wholesalers and retailers is somewhat limited. One authority points out that:

---

[4] See "Royal Worcester Porcelain Company, Inc.," case in Talarzyk, Engel, and Larsen, *Cases in Promotional Strategy.*

. . . not all sellers set quotas for their resellers. This results from one or more causes: failure to recognize that there is an underlying need to measure performance; difficulty in setting accurate quotas, especially where sales results may be far removed in time from sales effort, as for instance is often the case with the sale of costly industrial machinery; or lastly a realization of the inability to take any action if the quotas are not consistently met, as would be the case with the manufacturer whose product line would be of little importance to a reseller.[5]

In an interview with officials of a home appliance manufacturer it was learned that quotas were used to measure the relative performance of independent wholesale distributors against sales branches. In addition, quotas were set for each sales division within the territory. Of course, in this situation the manufacturer was granting exclusive agencies and could exert considerable influence in requiring distributors to meet quotas. Persistent failure to make the quota could well mean loss of franchise.

In other cases when the manufacturer's line is less important to his resellers, the manufacturer's ability to encourage resellers to meet their quotas is weakened correspondingly. Even if the manufacturer cannot force distributors to meet quotas, however, the use of quotas to provide information on sales potentials can be a means of improving reseller performance. For example, the Atkins Saw Division of Borg-Warner Corporation makes available to its distributors at no charge a market analysis of distributor territory. The purpose of this service is to aid distributors in accurate measurement of their sales performance, to help distributors establish quotas for retail dealers, and to get the resellers to work for a larger share of the available business.

Advertising and Sales Promotion Assistance

In addition to training of reseller sales personnel and the setting of quotas for resellers, manufacturers can attempt to improve reseller efforts by assisting wholesalers and retailers in the planning and execution of their advertising and sales promotion programs. Such assistance may take the form of: (1) cooperative advertising programs, (2) promotional allowances, (3) merchandising the advertising, (4) in-store promotions, and (5) contests and incentive payments for sales personnel.

Cooperative advertising. A program under which a manufacturer pays a portion of his reseller's local advertising costs is commonly called cooperative advertising. (See Figure 21–1.) Usually the manufacturer shares the cost of local reseller advertising on a 50–50 basis up to a certain limit, often a percentage of reseller purchases from the manufacturer.

---

[5] Harry L. Hansen, *Marketing: Text and Cases*, 4th ed. (Homewood, Ill.: Richard D. Irwin, 1977), p. 475.

FIGURE 21–1

An Example of a Reseller-directed Promotion to Gain Dealer Use of Cooperative Advertising

New allowance deals from Quaker State.

Quaker State will pay you more than your ad space or time costs 3 ways!

How can our 1982 Retail Allowance Program pay back more than you've spent? Here's how. Say you have $1000 accrued in your fund and you place an $800 advertisement for Quaker State products. You can be paid 100% for that, plus a $200 bonus. Both...in a single check from Quaker State! Read on for more details: **125% allowance** for portion featuring Quaker State motor oil, filters, and/or anti-freeze in the same ad. **125% allowance** for portion featuring Quaker State products exclusive of competitive brands. **125% allowance** in initial Grand Opening ad for portion(s) featuring Quaker State exclusive of competitive brands. **100% allowance** for Quaker State portion in multi-brand ads. **Plus $25 allowance** for end cap or free-standing displays. For details, see your 1982 RAP Kit. **Plus 10% New Product Allowance** on cost of qualifying Quaker State products not purchased by you as an existing customer in the previous 12 months. One-time per year only. Minimum purchase $25. No ceiling. **Plus 10% Grand Opening Allowance** on the cost of the first order for a new automotive retail outlet, or a new building, featuring Quaker State products on the same premises. Advertising allowances are based on 5¢ a gallon for motor oils, transmission fluids and lubricants, and 10¢ a filter. For complete details, check with your Quaker State distributor or sales representative, or write Quaker State Oil Refining Corporation, P.O. Box 989, Oil City, PA 16301, Attention: Advertising Department. Have a terrific 1982 with the Big Q, America's quality Motor Oil.

Quaker State: Pipeline to profits.

If, for example, the agreement specified a 50–50 share up to 4 percent of purchases, a retailer who had purchased $2,500 worth of goods from the manufacturer would be able to spend $200 on advertising them and would receive a $100 rebate from the manufacturer. Thus the net cost to the retailer for this advertising would be $100.

An advantage of cooperative advertising to the reseller, in addition to the partial defrayal of his local advertising expense, is that under most programs the manufacturer furnishes a good assortment of advertising layouts and stereotype mats for reproduction in the local press.

There are also disadvantages for the reseller. First, there is a tendency to promote a line with more vigor than it deserves simply because the cost is being shared by the manufacturer. Moreover, the nature of the advertisements may stimulate selective demand for the manufacturer's brand without increasing the patronage appeal of the store.

From the manufacturer's point of view a well-planned cooperative advertising program can be useful. First, it involves the reseller financially. The wholesaler or retailer lays some of its own money on the line to promote a given item. Even though the sum expended is matched by the manufacturer, the reseller has made an investment in promotion, and to protect its investment the wise reseller will make sure of three things: (1) that it has a sufficient stock of the item on hand to back up the ad; (2) that the item (or items) receives adequate display at point of purchase and, perhaps, in the window; and (3) that the item (or items) advertised receives in-store selling support from the sales personnel. If a manufacturer's cooperative advertising program can get resellers to follow through in this manner, it is probably worth the trouble and cost of its administration.

A more detailed view of a cooperative advertising program is provided by consideration of the one sponsored by the Palm Beach Company, a manufacturer of men's summer weight suits. In one year, for example, Palm Beach spent about $1 million for printed media advertising, with 60 percent of the budget for company advertising and 40 percent, or $400,000, for cooperative advertising with retailers. The bulk of the company advertising (80 percent) was placed in newspapers, with the remainder going to magazines and to trade advertising.

The cooperative advertising plan paid 50 percent of a retailer's cost for newspaper space, radio and TV commercial time, and billboard and car card space. The dealer could spend up to 4 percent of the net wholesale price of merchandise shipped to him and would be reimbursed up to a maximum of 2 percent.

Palm Beach required that the ads include proper product labels and descriptions and be devoted exclusively to the promotion of Palm Beach products. The company also reserved the right to refuse reimbursement "to any retailer, subject to fair trade laws, who broke a valid fair trade price set by Palm Beach."[6]

The really interesting aspect of this program is the intensity with which the company promoted its cooperative program to the retail dealers. Strategy included the following:

1. A magazine-size booklet informing dealers of the Palm Beach line and promotional program for the coming year was mailed in the spring.
2. In addition, the retailer received a 17 × 25-inch cooperative advertising service book containing descriptive material, ad layouts, reproductions of available mats, and suggested radio scripts. Plates for four-color ads were also available at cost ($20–$35) to retailers who wished to advertise in color.
3. The 50-person Palm Beach sales force devoted a major portion of its time talking to retailers about tying in their local promotion with the Palm Beach national campaign. They also planned balanced promotional campaigns for retailers, including display, direct mail advertising, and newspaper advertising.

As a result of the program Palm Beach reported that 65 percent of available cooperative advertising funds had been used by retailers. Careful records were kept, and salespeople as well as top executives of the Palm Beach Company called on stores whose advertising usage was far below the potential permitted by their sales volume. Every attempt was made to convince these retailers to make full use of the cooperative advertising allowance.

The Palm Beach program illustrates a situation in which a high level of reseller support is vital to reaching the manufacturer's sales objectives. The manufacturer has placed a major emphasis on cooperative advertising to gain the reseller support required. Moreover, the program was carefully planned and coordinated with the national advertising campaign. To make certain that retailer participation in the program was as extensive as possible, the manufacturer engaged in considerable personal selling effort to get retailers to increase their advertising. While there are these advantages, there also are real problems, which are discussed later.

Promotional allowances.   In situations where retail promotion is crucial to manufacturer success, payments may be made for types of reseller support other than media advertising. Such promotional allowances or payments are very often used to gain display at retail. Display is of great importance when the product being sold is purchased on impulse or is unable to attract any "push" from retailers because of its limited contribution to overall retail profits.

---

[6] Clauses such as this are no longer operative since the demise of "fair trade" in 1976.

The Whitehall Pharmacal Company case is a good illustration of how one manufacturer of proprietary drugs attempted to improve reseller support effort for its products through the use of promotional allowances.[7] The company manufactures such products as BiSoDol antiacid mints, Kolynos dentifrices, and Anacin. Sales were over $25 million annually, with over $5.3 million being spent on national advertising. To supplement the heavy "pull" strategy, the company used 100 salespeople to call on retailers.

A research study had indicated that point-of-sale displays using about 2½ square feet of counter space were especially effective in increasing sales. The company embarked on a program to get as many retailers as possible to utilize the special display. The key to the program was an allowance to the retailer of 5 percent of its purchases if certain promotional activities were performed.

Problems faced by Whitehall were of two varieties. First, competitors offered equivalent allowances (or in some cases even higher allowances), and it was difficult to gain retailer support because of the tremendous demand for limited counter space. Second, most druggists took the 5 percent allowance, but not all followed through with the placement of the display. It was evident that some type of action was required to get drug retailers to participate in the display program and to make sure that they kept the display on the counter for as long as they were collecting the promotional allowance.

This case illustrates both the need of a manufacturer to gain display at retail and the difficulties faced in gaining such support. The promotional allowance is one approach to gaining special retailer support, but to insure its success special payments have to be backed up by the manufacturer's sales force. The competition for retailer display or advertising tie-in as well as the general inertia of most retailers required, in most cases, more than a mere payment. On the other hand, "push" from the manufacturer without special payment will not be as effective as "push" with a payment for special effort at retail.

Merchandising the advertising. Another approach to improving reseller demand-stimulation effort, especially at retail, can be illustrated by the program of the Speidel Corporation. This manufacturer of metal expansion watch bands and identification bracelets sold its line to about 250 jewelry wholesalers who, in turn, supplied 18,000 retail jewelers. Most wholesalers and retailers carried lines directly competitive with that of Speidel.

Although Speidel was spending over $2.5 million per year on advertising, it did not have a cooperative advertising program for its resellers,

---

[7] "Whitehall Pharmacal Company" in Hansen, *Marketing,* pp. 615–17.

nor were there any promotional allowances or payments. The company did, however, give the retailer "every possible aid in selling Speidel merchandise." This assistance included a comprehensive dealer display and dealer advertising program. Twice a year ads were placed in trade publications informing retailers of the availability of the latest merchandise and promotional material. Most important, the retail promotions were keyed to the national efforts in magazines and on radio and television. Eventually, TV became Speidel's major medium, and the company used commercials to sell specific items in the line.

Here is an illustration of an effective strategy to gain retailer selling support which does not utilize cooperative advertising or promotional allowances. (See Figure 21–2.) It is essentially a strategy by which the manufacturer creates selective demand for its product. Such demand makes the retailer's task easier so that the sale of the manufacturer's product becomes more profitable to it.

In-store promotions. Other types of manufacturer programs to improve reseller demand-stimulation support may not be on a continuing basis but aimed instead at reaching limited objectives in a short period of time. The in-store promotion is one program of this type. The Inco "Gleam of Stainless Steel Promotion" is illustrative of the use of such a promotion.[8]

Inco, a leading producer of nickel, felt that nickel usage would be increased if sales of stainless steel consumer products could be stimulated. A program was planned around department stores, because research had indicated that they were the most powerful influence on consumer buying habits in the major market areas. The objectives of the program were: (1) to spotlight stainless steel in the large stores, (2) to generate sales enthusiasm among retail sales personnel, and (3) to increase demand for stainless steel products and thus the derived demand for nickel.

The promotion was timed for February and was first run with 32 participating stores. Inco inserted a four-color, two-page ad in *Look* and *Saturday Evening Post* as well as local newspaper ads featuring the name of the cooperating department store in each of the 32 market cities. In addition, the stores ran 103 newspaper ads featuring stainless steel, and many devoted key window space to the display of stainless steel items. Several steel manufacturers supported Inco's national advertising effort.

Inco gained retailer cooperation by offering the campaign to each store on an exclusive basis. Nominal cooperative advertising allowances were granted, and each retailer was provided with a complete promotional kit. Sales training sessions provided for retail personnel featured a nine-minute training film produced for this purpose.

---

[8] See case of same name in Talarzyk, Engel, and Larsen, *Cases in Promotional Strategy.*

498

FIGURE 21–2
Reseller-Directed Sales Promotion Aimed at Merchandising the Advertising of the Manufacturer

SALES YOU CAN BANK ON. FRESH START® ANNOUNCES BIGGEST AD BUDGET EVER!

When you've got a winner, run with it. For the third straight year Fresh Start gives you more ad support than ever before.

- More Network TV
- More Spot TV
- More National Magazines

Promotions that make your sales happen.

- More exciting consumer trial programs
- More high-value coupon offers
- More sales per cubic foot than any other powder product
- Highly competitive deals
- Easier pack out
- Superior packaging—looks better, less damage

When your Colgate-Palmolive sales representative calls, ask about Fresh Start Laundry Detergent's exciting 1982 programs.

®1982 Colgate Palmolive Co.

1/4 Cup Powder!

Fresh Start

1/4 Cup Concentrated Laundry Detergent

Give your sales a Fresh Start!

Courtesy Colgate Palmolive Company

The results were so favorable that the in-store promotion was continued for three more years. Modifications in the program were minor, but retailer and industry participation increased greatly in each succeeding year.

A similar type of effort on behalf of Hilton Hotels was seen in the Hilton "Follow the Sun" campaign.[9] Tie-ins were made with airlines and with the leading retailers in 15 target areas. The campaign sought to relate the Hilton Hotels' vacation and honeymoon facilities to the bridal promotions of the retailers. The promotion was built around a contest in which registrants might win a free honeymoon in the Caribbean or Hawaii. The participating stores were given a format around which to develop their bridal promotions and also benefited from the store traffic generated by the chance to win a free honeymoon.

Regardless of the method used by the manufacturer, in-store promotion must offer the retailer a *quid pro quo,* or else it will not succeed. Few retailers will put themselves out to support a specific manufacturer unless doing so promises a reasonable payoff. See Figure 21–3. Although an in-store promotion does offer a retailer a profit potential worthy of its effort, it still must be carefully planned by the manufacturer, and the execution of the program must be guided through to the end if best results are to be obtained. Once a manufacturer has concluded a successful in-store promotion on a modest scale, it is easier to expand the number of participants the next time it is run. Retailers have an effective grapevine which informs them on how their counterparts in other markets did with a specific promotion.

Contests and incentives.　To stimulate or improve the selling effort at retail, manufacturers may devise contests or provide special incentives for retail sales personnel. A contest or incentive plan is generally a part of a larger program and is aimed at motivating salespeople to participate in the selling campaign with enthusiasm. In the Royal Worcester case, for example, communication with the salesperson was established through the issuance of monthly sales bulletins.[10] Shortly after the bulletin was first issued it was used to announce a monthly contest based on the theme "How I Made a Royal Worcester Sale." Prices were awarded to the senders of the best letters received each month; the grand prize was a trip to England. Retail clerk participation in the contest was unusually high and served to focus the attention of many salespersons on the overall Royal Worcester campaign to gain retailer support.

Contests or incentive payments developed by the manufacturer can get out of hand. Too frequent use of contests can orient the salesperson's attention to a payoff to be received for good sales performance at the cost of making him overlook the merits of the product line itself. Salespeo-

---

[9] Described in personal correspondence with one of the authors.

[10] See Royal Worcester Porcelain Company case in Talarzyk, Engel, and Larsen, *Cases in Promotional Strategy.*

FIGURE 21–3
Reseller-Directed Sales Promotion Aimed at Gaining Use of Instore Display

We're pitching the first perfect All-Star game. Again.

Gillette's newest All-Star promotion is the perfect tie-in to the giant popularity of baseball. And that means you can expect capacity crowds at All-Star time.

Leading off, all of your customers have a chance to win a Grand Prize of $25,000. Or they could walk home with one of 1,000 Sony Walkman Stereo Cassette Recorders.

To play, they simply fill out an All-Star ballot and drop it into the ballot box contained in every display. And after they vote, they'll scoop up plenty of Gillette products. Because we're putting coupons good for 50¢ off right on packages of Atra razors.

The display stand teams up these three winners: Atra, the #1 selling pivoting razor; Atra 5's, the #1 selling pivoting cartridges; and Trac II 9's, the #1 selling twin blade cartridges.

We'll be backing our All-Star promotion with hard hitting advertising and Sunday Supplement 20¢ store coupons on Atra and Trac II blades that'll reach 53 million fans. So you know they'll be ready to play.

For you, there's a free All-Star tote bag (a $19.95 value) when you send in  the dealer coupon from the floor stand display. Special promotional allowances also are available.

So order your All-Star display right away. It's a promotion with so much going for it, you're bound to come out a winner.

Gillette
The Leading Edge.

Courtesy The Gillette Company

ple begin to sell items because *they,* rather than the customers, will profit most from the transaction. This orientation, while perhaps giving the manufacturer a temporary increase in volume, does not necessarily provide a lasting benefit unless the product itself is superior. Too many manufacturers use incentive payments and contests for retail salespeople to push products which are inferior to those offered by competitors.

Moreover, contests and incentive payments for retail sales personnel may conflict with the desires and objectives of retail management. Some retailers refuse to allow their employees to participate in manufacturer-sponsored contests or to accept incentive payments from manufacturers because they want to maintain control over their selling activities. For a manufacturer program of contests or incentives to succeed, obviously, it must have the approval of retail management. In addition, the program should serve as an attention getter to interest salespeople in the product line and the overall promotional campaign. Finally, it should be viewed as a short-run effort to support the overall program and not as a long-run substitute for product attractiveness or utility.

Legal problems and other issues.   The use by the manufacturer of cooperative advertising programs, promotional allowances, and other forms of assistance is not without its problems. Of an especially serious nature are those imposed by law. Sections 2d and 2e of the Robinson-Patman Act have perhaps the most relevance to the area of promotional allowances and services as granted by sellers to resellers.[11]

These sections of the act define, in rather loose terms, the conditions under which nondiscriminatory payments or services can be made to members of a reseller group. Such payments or services are legal if they are granted on a "proportionally equal" basis. That is, the dollar value of the payments or services rendered by a seller to various resellers must be in proportion to the size of their purchases from the seller. For example, a reseller buying $10,000 worth of goods a year from a manufacturer should be entitled to 10 times the value of payments or services received from the manufacturer, as compared to the reseller whose purchases totaled only $1,000.

Moreover, the seller's program must allow participation by all interested resellers. The nature of the seller's promotional strategy must not exclude competing resellers on the basis of size, geographical location, or other characteristics.

Revised guidelines for the use of cooperative advertising were issued by the Federal Trade Commission on June 1, 1969. These guidelines make many new demands on both manufacturers and retailers who use cooperative plans. Key items include the following:

---

[11] Public Law no. 92, 74th Cong., H.R. 8442, June 19, 1936.

1. All competing customers, whether wholesalers or retailers, must be informed of the availability of a co-op plan. This may be done through notices in trade publications, announcements, or in the container or package. The manufacturer may transfer the responsibility for notification to the wholesaler but must still make spot checks to see that the information is being received.
2. A given co-op plan must be "functionally available" to all competing customers on proportionally equal terms and must include more than one way for various kinds of customers to participate.
3. A section called "third party liability," which deals with double billing, bars any advertising medium from quoting higher rates than are actually charged in order to allow customers to claim greater payments than they are entitled to as part of a co-op plan. Under this section the customer is required to reveal and refund any deferred rebates on the cost of its advertising in newspapers and other media.[12]

Additional legal restrictions on the use of cooperative advertising or promotional allowances are those limitations imposed by reseller misuse. For example, many resellers do not run cooperative advertisements correctly. Poor composition, inadequate copy, and poor timing all mean that funds are not as well used as they might have been if more care had been taken in preparation.

Similar abuses are also common with respect to payments made to obtain display space or to gain in-store promotion. Monies are diverted to margin rather than to specific promotional activities.

Finally, there is a wide variance in reseller attitudes toward cooperative selling ventures which makes the manufacturer's task difficult indeed. In some cases resellers may engage in "blackmail," threatening to buy from another source unless special allowances or services are forthcoming. In other situations they may show little interest in even the most generous program, preferring to push their own private brands over those of the manufacturer.

SUPPLEMENTING RESELLER PERFORMANCE

In those situations where *improving* the quality of quantity of reseller performance of selling activity is not sufficient to reach manufacturer promotional objectives, more direct action must be taken to *supplement* reseller effort. The manufacturer must assume some of the responsibility for selling and sales promotion at wholesale and retail levels. The utilization of missionary salespeople is one method of gaining greater activity

---

[12] Adapted from *Washington Report* (Washington, D.C.: American Advertising Federation, January 28, 1970).

at reseller levels in the channel of distribution. Provision of selling aids and price incentives are other methods.

Missionary (Specialty) Selling

The use of manufacturer salesmen to supplement the personal selling activities of resellers is known as missionary or specialty selling. In the sale of consumer goods, missionary salespeople are employed by manufacturers to contact both wholesalers and retailers. They check wholesalers periodically to determine if adequate stocks are being held. They call upon retailers to inform them of new products, to arrange window and in-store display, to provide advice on selling, to answer questions posed by the retailer and, in general, to build goodwill. If they take orders for merchandise they usually turn such orders over to wholesalers for filling.

In the sale of industrial goods, missionary salespeople train distributor salesmen, demonstrate effective selling techniques by accompanying distributor salespeople on their calls, secure introductory orders from users, and assist distributor salesmen in closing those sales that demand greater technical knowledge or selling skill than the distributor salesperson has.

Two short case histories will illustrate what missionary salespeople can and cannot do to supplement reseller demand stimulation effort.

Paint manufacturer.   A company which manufactured a broad line of varnishes, lacquers, enamels, and other paint products had a product line consisting of over 250 separate items which was sold to the consumer market through exclusive wholesale distributors, who in turn sold to selected retailers. Thirty-five company salespeople called on the wholesalers and spent a great deal of their time with wholesaler salespeople, performing missionary selling activities such as soliciting orders from retailers for the wholesalers' accounts. Paint company executives felt that the salespeople were providing excessive missionary support and that such activity should be curtailed.

In commenting on this case, a consultant pointed out that:

The fact that such cooperative sales work was needed to maintain sales when the distributors were granted exclusive territories suggests there was a basic weakness somewhere in the company's marketing plan—as to just where the weakness lay no clues are furnished by the statement of the case. The weakness may have been in the company's advertising, in the merchandise itself, in the type of retail distribution sought, or in the management of the wholesale distributing firms.[13]

Thus, although the belief of company executives that missionary selling support should be curtailed was probably correct, attention should have been directed to finding out why so much missionary selling support was needed by wholesalers who were exclusive agents.

---

[13] See "Nancock Varnish Company," *Harvard Business Reports,* vol. 9, p. 26.

Cereal manufacturer. A manufacturer of cereals which distributed through wholesalers to retail grocery stores had a regular sales force which called upon wholesalers and another group of salespeople, known as specialty people, which called upon retailers to solicit orders that were turned over to the wholesalers to fill. Wholesalers were allowed the same gross margin on orders, whether obtained by them or by the manufacturer's specialty sales force.

The primary duty of the specialty salespeople was to expand the market coverage. In many situations specialty men used the orders they received from retailers to "force" wholesalers to stock the line or to carry new products. Wholesalers were antagonistic toward the manufacturer's missionary selling because of forcing but also because they felt that it would be an easy step for the manufacturer to establish wholesale branches and to circumvent the wholesalers entirely.

The board of directors of the manufacturer considered the discontinuance of the missionary selling program, but the general manager was able to persuade the board that such effort was needed to sustain sales volume.

This case illustrates the problem faced by a producer of a relatively narrow line who has to obtain intensive retail distribution. The manufacturer needs wholesalers for their coverage but also requires aggressive selling effort beyond the ability of wholesalers to provide. In this situation manufacturer supplementation of wholesaler personal selling activity by means of a special sales force is perhaps the best solution to the problem.

Implications. Missionary effort is advisable when the product being sold requires more personal selling effort than the wholesaler can afford to give. For example, if a product or product line represents a relatively small portion of the wholesaler's line but yet requires extensive retail distribution, point-of-sale display, or the acquisition of shelf space, the manufacturer can use missionary selling effectively to achieve these objectives. Such a situation was illustrated by the case of the cereal manufacturer.

On the other hand, the use of missionary salesmen probably is not wise when, as in the case of the paint manufacturer, other elements of the promotional program are weak. It is an expensive undertaking for any manufacturer, and its use to cover up defects in other elements of the marketing mix can be an unnecessary financial burden.[14] In addition, excessive dependence on missionary selling can generate wholesaler resentment. When missionaries assume tasks such as routine order taking or delivery that could be performed by wholesalers, the wholesaler may feel that there is just a short step to his total circumvention. The net result is a fall-off in promotional support. Even if circumvention is not

---

[14] It has been estimated that the use of missionary salesmen adds between 10 and 15 percent to the cost of goods sold by them.

the issue, wholesalers may resent the missionary salespeople infringing on the time of their sales forces. A general-line wholesaler carrying the products of hundreds of suppliers may feel that missionary salespeople interfere with the most effective allocation of his salespeople's time.

Certainly, correct use of missionary salespeople can improve or supplement wholesaler selling effort. The problems which arise from missionary selling seem to be caused by using missionaries to *supplant wholesaler efforts where supplementation would suffice,* or from poor management of missionary selling effort. As one authority concludes:

Missionary selling . . . in large measure substitutes direct action on the part of the manufacturer for cooperation, which would otherwise be needed, on the part of wholesalers. Still, unless handled judiciously, such selling can be productive of a lack of cooperation in other selling activities, even of unwillingness to handle a manufacturer's products. Missionary salesmen have often been accused, and with some justification, of overstocking dealers, selling to poor credit risks and then expecting wholesalers to fill the orders, of playing one wholesaler against the other by shifting orders between them, of offering special terms or rebates to certain dealers in the name of the wholesaler, and of other similar activities. Wholesalers may believe that missionary sales work is the first step toward direct sale and that it is just another way of decreasing the wholesaler's independence. Also, when missionary salesmen accompany wholesaler's salesmen on their calls, a conflict of personalities may arise which creates ill will.[15]

Display and Selling Aids

Manufacturer provision of display material for point-of-purchase use, mailing pieces for reseller distribution, dealer identification signs, and similar incentives are other ways to supplement reseller efforts. Manufacturer use of these promotional devices has the dual purpose of stimulating demand for the product and getting an increased share of the dealer's promotional effort placed at the manufacturer's disposal.[16]

The manufacturer usually has great difficulty in getting resellers to utilize the display material and selling aids made available. Based on the volume of material distributed to resellers, it appears that manufacturer response to nonuse of material is to double the quantity made available. Because resellers often do not know what to do with this great flood of material, it is not uncommon to find a great deal of it in the refuse box in unopened cartons.

Several approaches are available to the manufacturer who requires some degree of display or other activity by retailers, for example. The payment

---

[15] D. Maynard Phelps, *Sales Management* (Homewood, Ill.: Richard D. Irwin, 1953) p. 514.

[16] D. Maynard Phelps and J. Howard Westing, *Marketing Management,* rev. ed. (Homewood, Ill.: Richard D. Irwin, 1960), p. 465.

of promotional allowances for display, the use of the sales force to obtain display and in-store promotion, and charging resellers a total payment for materials are all methods which may help gain better point-of-sale display or selling effort.

Perhaps the most effective approach is that of pretesting dealer aids. An executive of General Foods reported the following:

We made several field surveys . . . on the use to which our point-of-sale material was being put, and we reached some disappointing conclusions. We learned, for example, that on several campaigns last year, only half the material shipped out to the field was being used effectively. . . . It has not been checked with the field to predetermine its acceptance. .We now have a continuous program . . . for periodic surveys of the grocery stores regularly contacted by our salesmen. . . . This system afforded us an accurate picture of the types and amounts of material which could best be used in these stores. . . . We àre convinced that it is a waste of time, effort, and money to send point-of-purchase material to the field if we cannot demonstrate how it will work for the benefit of the store operator. . . .[17]

The Whitehall Pharmacal Company case noted above illustrates the difficulties of using promotional allowances to gain point-of-sale display. Because research had indicated that a new type of display had increased sales as much as 150 percent in those stores in which it was used during a 60-day period, Whitehall developed a bonus plan for its salesmen. This plan could result in a salary increase of as much as one third for those salesmen who were able to get the stores in their territories to utilize the new point-of-sale displays. The extent of the payment to salesmen indicates the value of display to the company. This situation is of special interest because Whitehall was spending over $5 million annually, or 20 percent of sales, on national advertising. It appears, therefore, that even with extensive "pull," point-of-sale display is an important element of strategy.

Consumer Deals

When the manufacturer wishes to blend some price promotion into its promotional mix to increase sales at retail, it may offer the buyer a temporary price reduction. Such reductions are known as consumer deals or, more explicitly, price deals. They can be contrasted with deals to the trade in that consumer deals attempt to create "pull," while trade incentives are aimed at getting reseller "push." Regardless of the target, a price deal is an attempt to exploit price sensitivity of demand. The

[17] W. P. Lillard, "Point-of-Purchase Promotion," *Proceedings, 6th Annual Advertising and Sales Promotion Conference,* Ohio State University Publications, College of Commerce Conference Series no. C–65 (Columbus, 1950), pp. 55–57.

strategy of such deals is clarified in a study of the Chicago market in which the findings included the following:

1. Off-season price reductions seem to be more profitable.
2. A high frequency of price promotions tends to make consumers overly price-conscious.
3. Deals do not seem to be a good way to counter new brands offered by competitors, and they are not necessarily more effective if accompanied by product or package innovations.
4. Price dealing is more effective for new brands than for established ones, and it is almost always more effective if kept in proper balance with advertising.
5. No brand—even a well-established, nondealing, luxury brand—is invulnerable to price-deal competition if it has basic marketing problems, and price-deal promotion is never a cure for marketing problems.
6. When special promotional campaigns fall short of expectations, the manufacturer will do better to question his own planning and policy making than to blame the failure on "intractable" retailers.[18]

The last point above has special relevance to the stimulation of reseller performance because the use of price deals to buyers may hinder rather than help reseller cooperation. Poor scheduling, inadequate trade incentives, excessive frequency of deals, and the like may cause wholesalers and retailers to rebel. Interviews with several retailers indicated, for example, that the pressure on grocery retailers to shift inventories back to the manufacturers has been increased in part by the extra confusion and expense caused by a multiplication of deal merchandise.[19]

CONTROLLING RESELLER PERFORMANCE

The control of reseller promotional performance is considerably more difficult for the manufacturer than is control of its own sales force. First, the chain of command which exists in an integrated organization is replaced with a relatively unstructured network of communication connecting independent intermediaries. Through this network flows a series of suggestions and persuasion rather than commands. (Of course, the greater the selective demand for the products of a given manufacturer, the greater the weight its suggestions will carry with resellers.) Second, resellers are both geographically dispersed and operationally diverse. No two wholesalers (or retailers) are really alike because each serves the market in a unique manner in terms of location, assortments carried, and demand-stimulation mix utilized. Thus the combination of manufacturer loss of direct authority due to passing of title of goods sold to resellers and

---

[18] Charles L. Hinkle, "The Strategy of Price Deals," *Harvard Business Review* 43, (July–August 1965), pp. 75–85.

[19] Ibid., p. 82.

reseller geographical dispersion and operational diversity makes manufacturer control of reseller activities a most difficult undertaking under ordinary circumstances.

The degree of control over reseller performance which manufacturers can exert is, of course, a function of the importance of the manufacturer's line to the individual wholesaler or retailer. When the manufacturer engages in highly selective or exclusive agency distribution and has limited market coverage to make its line more important to its selected resellers, some degree of control over these resellers may be expected.

Selected Resellers

The control process, as discussed earlier in this text, consists of formulating standards of performance, measuring performance, comparing actual results with the standards, and then taking action to correct substandard performances. If resellers are selected wholesalers or retailers for the line of a given manufacturer, the basis for control may be contained in the franchise agreement. In situations where the manufacturer's franchise is extremely valuable (as in the sale of automobiles), the reseller may contract to supply data on sales volume, inventory levels, and general operating expenses. Such information may be used by the manufacturer to measure reseller performance against a variety of standards. Commonly used criteria include share of market, sales growth over time, and the reaching of goals or quotas. In addition, attention may be given to size of sales force, expenditures of advertising and sales promotion, and similar items.

Once arrangements have been made to monitor the reseller's performance in a quantitative sense (and, hopefully, incorporated into the franchise agreement), attention can be paid to the qualitative nature of reseller performance. This aspect of reseller control does not usually require a contractual arrangement. A perceptive manufacturer's salesperson generally can report on how resellers are using promotional materials furnished by the manufacturer or whether resellers have effective training programs for their sales personnel. Moreover, the manufacturer or an independent agency such as the Advertising Checking Bureau can audit the reseller's media advertising for control of cooperative advertising payments or to measure degree of support being provided the manufacturer's line. Similar checking may measure reseller activity in getting point-of-sale display or in setting up demonstrations or special selling events.

Nonselected Resellers

When coverage requirements are such that broad distribution through many resellers is required, the manufacturer's problem of control is intensified. There is a limit to what the manufacturer may expect from any one reseller in terms of furnishing data or following a specific recommendation to improve performance. Measurement and control of reseller performance thus becomes less concerned with individual reseller performance and concentrates instead upon the performance of groups of resellers.

The manufacturer may attempt to classify the many resellers carrying its line by type of institution, location, size, ownership, and other criteria. Then a distribution cost analysis may be made to show the relative profitability to the manufacturer of different groups of resellers. One such study, made by a manufacturer of major electrical appliances, indicated the relative profitability of sales made through diverse channels of distribution and retail outlets. The important lesson to be learned from examples of this type is that, given a situation in which many resellers are used, measurement of reseller performance may help the manufacturer control *its utilization of specific groups of resellers,* rather than the performance of individual resellers.

There are, however, some devices for the measurement and control of resellers under a policy of selective distribution which are also usable with broad, intensive distribution. For example, manufacturer's salesmen may be used to arrange for retailer use of point-of-sale display and to check back with retailers to see if displays have been properly placed. Such a program is seen in the case of Whitehall Pharmacal Company.

Manufacturers may also take elaborate steps to check on cooperative advertising efforts of resellers. They can monitor reseller participation by means of a special department or use outside agencies to supplement internal activities.

Knowledge of the levels of reseller inventories is vital to many manufacturers who engage in intensive distribution through many resellers. Unable to use their salespeople to take shelf and storeroom counts of goods on hands, the manufacturer may avail itself of the services of an independent research agency to collect data on how rapidly products are moving off the retailer's shelves.[20] Without such information the manufacturer might mistake an inventory accumulation by resellers for steady or rising consumer demand for the line.

Vertical Integration

Because of the limits on the control that manufacturers can exert over independent intermediaries, many producers have chosen to vertically integrate their channels of distribution through ownership of either all or part of the channel intermediaries. Through ownership the manufacturer gains maximum control over the manner in which its goods are

---

[20] The A. C. Nielsen Company's Retail Store Audit is the best known of these approaches.

physically distributed and promoted through all of the channel stages.

Vertical integration by means of ownership can be a very expensive undertaking. Not only are the capital commitments enormous, but unless the producer's product line is broad and sales volume is high, unit distribution costs will generally be greater than if traditional channels were used. For those firms engaging in vertical integration by means of ownership, the higher costs of physical distribution are accepted as a tradeoff against the higher levels of promotional activity and customer service that can be provided by closely controlled resellers.

Only a few firms engage in vertically integrated distribution by owning their intermediaries, but those that do have greatly increased their share of market. Thus the vast majority of firms that do not have the economic capability to own their resellers find themselves in an increasingly severe competitive struggle with their integrated rivals. To counteract the advantages associated with vertical integration and avoid having to make the needed financial commitments, many of these firms are adopting a strategy of "distribution programming," in which an integrated marketing system is developed by contractual agreements between a manufacturer and members of the reseller organization.

Distribution programming.[21]   The development of a planned, professionally managed distribution system utilizing independent resellers enables manufacturers to increase the effectiveness and efficiency of their distribution activities. McCammon defines distribution programming as "the development of a comprehensive set of policies for the promotion of a product through the channel."[22] These policies are formulated as a joint effort between the manufacturer and the individual reseller as an attempt to negotiate a relationship that will give both parties some of the advantages of vertical integration, without the need for the manufacturer to purchase resellers.

Recent investigations have indicated that planned vertical marketing systems are "rapidly displacing conventional marketing channels as the dominant mode of distribution in the American economy."[23] Planned systems are taking over because they avoid the loose relationships, autonomous behavior, and diseconomies associated with traditional channels of distribution. In addition, they do not require the capital investments associated with ownership systems. Yet, these planned systems, being "professionally managed and centrally programmed networks, pre-engineered to achieve operating economies and maximum market impact,"

---

[21] This section is based on an excellent article by Bert C. McCammon, Jr., "Perspectives for Distribution Programming," in *Vertical Marketing Systems,* ed. Louis P. Bucklin (Glenview, Ill.: Scott, Foresman, 1970), pp. 32–50.

[22] Ibid., p. 32.

[23] Ibid., p. 43.

FIGURE 21-4
A Frame of Reference for Distribution Programming

Manufacturer's marketing goals

Based on a careful analysis of:
    Corporate capability
    Competition
    Demand
    Cost-volume relationships
    Legal considerations
    Reseller capability
and stated in terms of:
    Sales (dollars and units)
    Market share
    Contribution to overhead
    Rate of return on investment
    Customer attitude, preference
        and "readiness-to-buy" indices

Manufacturer's channel requirements

Reseller support needed to achieve marketing goals (stated in terms of):
  Coverage ratio
  Amount and location of display space
  Level and composition of inventory
    investment
  Service capability and standards
  Advertising, sales promotion, and
    personal selling support
  Market development activities

Retailer's requirements

"Compensation" expected for required support (stated in terms of):
  Managerial aspirations
  Trade preferences
  Financial goals
    Rate of inventory turnover
    Rate of return on investment
    Gross margin (dollars and percent)
    Contribution to overhead (dollars
      and percent)
    Gross margin and contribution to
      overhead per dollar invested
      in inventory
    Gross margin and contribution to
      overhead per unit of space
    Nonfinancial goals

Distribution policies
"Price concessions
Financial assistance
Protective provisions

From *Vertical Marketing Systems,* edited by Louis P. Bucklin. Copyright © 1970 by Scott, Foresman and Company. Reprinted by permission of the publisher.

can compete effectively with systems which are vertically integrated through partial or complete ownership of channel intermediaries.[24]

The first step in the formulation of a strategy of distribution programming is the careful analysis of manufacturer marketing goals, manufacturer marketing requirements, and the needs of retail (and wholesale) resellers. These goals and requirements are outlined in Figure 21–4. Note that both

---

[24] Ibid., p. 43.

the goals and requirements can be stated in quantitative terms, thus eliminating the danger of misunderstanding during subsequent negotiations between the manufacturer and individual resellers.

After the completion of the analysis, specific distribution policies can be formulated. McCammon suggests that the policy alternatives available, although quite numerous, fall into three major categories: (1) those that offer "price" concessions to resellers, (2) those that provide financial assistance, and (3) those that provide some form of protection for resellers.[25] Selected policy alternatives classified under the three headings are illustrated in Figure 21–5.

Using the mix of distribution policy alternatives available, and based on the prior analysis of goals and requirements, a "programmed merchandising agreement" must be developed for each type of outlet utilized in the pattern of distribution. This agreement, the result of joint deliberation between the manufacturer and a reseller, is essentially a comprehensive plan to distribute and promote the producer's product line for a period of six months or longer. An outline of such an agreement is to be found in Figure 21–6. Of special interest is the completeness of the agreement. After a clear delineation of quantitatively measurable goals, it is concerned with plans for inventory requirements, merchandise presentation, personal selling, and advertising and sales promotion. Finally, the responsibilities of both parties are enumerated, together with a schedule of dates when certain performances are due.

In describing the application of such agreements McCammon has suggested that:

Programmed merchandising agreements are fairly widespread in the following product categories: garden supplies, major appliances, traffic appliances, bedding, sportswear, cosmetics, and housewares. Manufacturing organizations currently [1970] engaged in programmed merchandising activities include: General Electric (on major and traffice appliances); Baumritter (on its *Ethan Allen* furniture line in nonfranchised outlets); Sealy (on its *Posturepedic* line of mattresses); Scott (on its lawn-care products); and Villager (on its dress and sports wear lines).[26]

SUMMARY

Manufacturers' policies developed from diverse selling strategies influence the role of resellers in the overall promotional program. Inasmuch as personal selling activities make up the largest portion of promotional activity at wholesale and retail (with the exception of self-service stores), the maximum use of reseller potential can be made when the manufacturer emphasizes a push strategy. Regardless of the selling activity expected,

---

[25] Ibid., p. 37.
[26] Ibid., p. 48.

FIGURE 21–5
Selected Distribution Policy Alternatives

I. "Price" Concessions
   A. Discount structure:
      Trade (functional) discounts
      Quantity discounts
      Cash discounts
      Anticipation allowances
      Free goods
      Prepaid freight
      New product, display, and advertising allowances (without performance requirements)
      Seasonal discounts
      Mixed carload privilege
      Drop shipping privilege
      Trade deals
   B. Discount substitutes:
      Display materials
      Premarked merchandise
      Inventory control programs
      Catalogs and sales promotion literature
      Training programs
      Shelf-stocking programs
      Advertising matrices
      Management consulting services
      Merchandising programs
      Sales "spiffs"
      Technical assistance
      Payment of sales personnel and demonstrator salaries
      Promotional and advertising allowances (with performance requirements)

II. Financial assistance
   A. Conventional lending arrangements:
      Term loans
      Inventory floor plans
      Notes payable financing
      Accounts payable financing
      Installment financing of fixtures and equipment
      Lease and note guarantee programs
      Accounts receivable financing
   B. Extended dating:
      E.O.M. dating
      Seasonal dating
      R.O.G. dating
      "Extra" dating
      Post dating

III. Protective provisions
   A. Price protection:
      Premarked merchandise
      Fair trade
      "Franchise" pricing
      Agency agreements
   B. Inventory protection:
      Consignment selling
      Memorandum selling

FIGURE 21–5 (*concluded*)

> Liberal returns allowances
> Rebate programs
> Reorder guarantees
> Guaranteed support of sales events
> Maintenance of "spot" stocks and fast delivery
> C. Territorial protection:
>   Selective distribution
>   Exclusive distribution

From *Vertical Marketing Systems,* edited by Louis P. Bucklin. Copyright © 1970 by Scott, Foresman and Company. Reprinted by permission of the publisher.

FIGURE 21–6

Outline of a Programmed Merchandising Agreement

1. Merchandising goals
    a. Planned sales
    b. Planned initial markup percentage
    c. Planned reductions, including planned markdowns, shortages, and discounts.
    d. Planned gross margin
    e. Planned expense ratio (optional)
    f. Planned profit margin (optional)
2. Inventory plan
    a. Planned rate of inventory turnover
    b. Planned merchandise assortments, including basic or model stock plans
    c. Formalized "never out" lists
    d. Desired mix of promotional versus regular merchandise
3. Merchandise presentation plan
    a. Recommended store fixtures
    b. Space allocation plan
    c. Visual merchandising plan
    d. Needed promotional materials, including point-of-purchase displays, consumer literature, and price signs
4. Personal selling plan
    a. Recommended sales presentations
    b. Sales training plan
    c. Special incentive arrangements, including "spiffs," salesmen's contests, and related activities
5. Advertising and sales promotion plan
    a. Advertising and sales promotion budget
    b. Media schedule
    c. Copy themes for major campaigns and promotions
    d. Special sales events
6. Responsibilities and due dates
    a. Supplier's responsibilities in connection with the plan
    b. Retailer's responsibilities in connection with the plan

From *Vertical Marketing Systems,* edited by Louis P. Bucklin. Copyright © 1970 by Scott, Foresman and Company. Reprinted by permission of the publisher.

if the *quality* of the selling performance by wholesalers and retailers is less than is desired by the manufacturer, it may lend assistance to *improve* reseller performance.

Training programs for reseller salesperson seem to be one effective way in which manufacturers can upgrade the caliber of wholesaler personal selling effort. Such assistance is especially desirable when the product sold requires demonstration, installation, or a high degree of technical competence on the part of the reseller salesperson. Training is not recommended in cases where the volume potential of the manufacturer's line is small in relation to the costs involved in setting up a suitable program.

Providing market information beyond what the reseller can gather for itself seems to help it allocate its selling efforts more effectively. Such information can point out where sales opportunities are not being exploited. It can also indicate to the reseller how its performance measures up against that of other members of the reseller organization.

If the *quantity* of reseller effort is less than is deemed necessary to achieve manufacturer objectives, assistance may be provided in the form of missionary salespeople. These manufacturer efforts have as their objective the *supplementation* of reseller activity. When carefully supervised, such assistance can greatly increase the extent of sales effort aimed at wholesaler customers.

Under appropriate conditions cooperative advertising programs are a very effective form of advertising assistance. They are especially helpful when, as with selected distribution, it is necessary to identify local retail sources of supply. Further, by getting distributors to invest their own funds in the local promotion of the manufacturer's brand, cooperative advertising programs may predispose resellers to carry better assortments of stock and to push the products advertised.

Manufacturer contributions which help resellers to do a better selling job themselves or encourage reseller promotion, such as display material or special deals, must be carefully integrated into the overall strategy, with special attention being paid to making these aids or deals fit the requirements of the *resellers.*

The manufacturer must be careful not to confuse his objectives and attempt to supplement wholesaler performance when efforts to improve it would suffice. Larger than necessary promotional costs are then incurred by the manufacturer. Conversely, if additional selling effort is needed at wholesale or retail, manufacturer programs to improve the quality of current reseller performance will probably not fill the gap.

Manufacturer efforts to supplement or improve reseller performance may grow to take over typically reseller functions. Such functional shifting should not be permitted by the manufacturer unless his analysis and experimentation have indicated that efforts to supplement or improve reseller performance will not do the job. Taking over tasks historically performed by wholesalers and retailers may suggest that the manufacturer is considering their ultimate circumvention. The reseller who harbors such a suspicion is not likely to offer its selling support willingly.

The control of promotional activities by the manufacturer is much easier when the agency being controlled is under the manufacturer's direct supervision. Such is the case with manufacturer control of the sales force. Control becomes more difficult when the agencies performing the efforts are independent middlemen who have purchased the manufacturer's product line for resale. Regardless of the degree of difficulty involved, the control process in either case is identical and consists of setting standards, measuring performance in light of these standards, and taking corrective action where actual performance is substandard.

The extent of control over resellers is a function of the importance of the manufacturer's line to them. Thus efforts to create selective demand through advertising or to reduce intrachannel rivalry by means of selective distribution should result in heightened manufacturer ability to control reseller efforts. If resellers are uncooperative for one reason or another, the manufacturer may use independent specialists to check on their performance. The manufacturer can always control its own channel strategy by careful selection of resellers, even if it cannot control their individual performance.

If a level of control is needed beyond that which can be expected from independent channel intermediaries, the manufacturer may engage in partial or complete ownership of its resellers. Because of the long-term financial commitments associated with vertical integration through ownership, an increasingly utilized alternative is vertical integration by means of contractual relationships between manufacturers and individual resellers. The resulting distribution system provides many of the advantages of a system owned by the manufacturer, without requiring a heavy investment in ownership. It also preserves the independence of the intermediary and allows it to provide the distributive economies which result from its carrying the lines of several manufacturing sources.

Review and Discussion Questions

1. Why is it important for manufacturers to assume some responsibility for training the personnel of their resellers? Why must this be a continuing responsibility?

2. Why is it so difficult to enforce quotas for resellers? Of what value might a properly set quota be to a seller?

3. What advantages may accrue to a manufacturer who offers a cooperative advertising allowance to its resellers? What are some possible disadvantages?

4. Why are promotional allowances by themselves usually insufficient to gain reseller cooperation? What else can a manufacturer do to supplement promotional allowances to resellers?

5. When might a contest for retail clerks be useful in furthering a manufacturer's promotional program? Why are many retail managements against contests for their employees?

6. What types of reseller abuse may limit the effectiveness of manufacturer programs to stimulate reseller promotional efforts?

7. Explain the difference between improving and supplementing reseller performance. Why is it so important that the manufacturer make this distinction?

8. What tasks should a missionary salesperson perform? What tasks should he not perform? Why do some resellers resent manufacturer missionary activity?

9. Why does so much of the display material sent retailers end up unused in the refuse basket? What steps might a manufacturer take to prevent this waste?

10. What is the manufacturer's strategy in offering a temporary "price deal"? What reactions might it expect from its resellers?

11. What is the principal danger faced by a manufacturer who attempts to supplement the performance of its resellers?

12. Why is control of reseller performance so difficult for a manufacturer?

13. What roles do selection of resellers play in gaining some degree of control over their activities? What factors limit the extent of control that manufacturers can exert over their resellers?

14. What are the advantages and disadvantages of a policy for vertical integration of channels of distribution through ownership?

15. What is distribution programming, and how does it differ from traditional efforts to work with resellers?

16. Mention some of the areas that might be covered by a programmed merchandising agreement. How would you expect that compliance be monitored under such an agreement?

CHAPTER 22
Public Relations

Public relations is that communication function which "evaluates public attitudes, identifies the policies and procedures of an individual or an organization with the public interest, and executes a program of action to earn public understanding and acceptance."[1] Its purpose thus is to secure mutual understanding and goodwill, and it can be an important part of the promotional program of an organization.

Figure 22–1 provides an overview of the target markets for public relations and some of the tasks which can be accomplished through this form of communication. Communication is both internal within the organization and external to its various publics. The media utilized can be any combination of print, oral, or audio-visual. Included are the functions of corporate advertising and publicity.

Because public relations is a communication function, it should be undertaken to accomplish specific communication goals, using the procedures discussed in preceding chapters. Much of the detail of management problems can be omitted here, therefore.[2] Our intention is to build an understanding of the role of both internal and external public relations, and to this end several case histories are cited.

---

[1] Bertrand R. Canfield and H. Frazier Moore, *Public Relations: Principles, Cases, and Problems,* 7th ed. (Homewood, Ill.: Richard D. Irwin, 1977), p. 5.

[2] See Canfield and Moore, *Public Relations,* and E. J. Robinson, *Communication and Public Relations* (Columbus, Ohio: Charles E. Merrill Publishing, 1966).

FIGURE 22–1
Target Markets and Representative Objectives for the Public Relations Function

Ultimate consumers
  Disseminate information on the production and distribution of new or existing products
  Disseminate information on ways to use new or existing products
Company employees
  Training programs to stimulate more effective contact with the public
  Encouragement of pride in the company and its products
Suppliers
  Providing research information for use in new products
  Dissemination of company trends and practices for the purpose of building a continuing team relationship
Stockholders
  Dissemination of information on: (1) company prospects, (2) past and present profitability, (3) future plans, (4) management changes and capabilities, and (5) company financial needs
The community at large
  Promotion of public causes such as community fund-raising drives
  Dissemination of information on all aspects of company operations with the purpose of building a sense of unity between company and community

INTERNAL COMMUNICATIONS

Internal communication is designed to let employees know what management is thinking, as well as to facilitate communication in the reverse direction. At one time organizations were sufficiently small that this could easily be done on a face-to-face basis, but this is no longer so in most situations, and the need often exists for a formal communication program designed for such purposes as information and morale building. Failure to provide such a program can have devastating effects on productivity, morale, and turnover.

Because the details of internal communication programs are beyond the scope of this book, only brief reference is made to the variety of media which can be utilized for this purpose. These are itemized in Figure 22–2.

An example of the use of internal communications is the program by which the Atlanta Gas Light Company introduced its new corporate symbol to employees.[3] Following a series of mergers, the company was faced with difficult communications and public relations problems caused by the use of three different names in different parts of the state of Georgia. A need existed to design a company symbol which was so distinctive and identifiable that it would immediately identify the "gas company" no matter where or when it was seen. Once the new symbol was designed

---

[3] Bertrand R. Canfield and H. Frazier Moore, *Public Relations: Principles, Cases, and Problems,* 7th ed. (Homewood, Ill.: Richard D. Irwin, 1977), pp. 70–75.

FIGURE 22–2
Media for Internal Public Relations

Print
Management letters to employees, employee newspapers and magazines, bulletin board announcements, annual and interim financial reports, employee handbooks or manuals, management bulletins for executives and supervisors, pay-envelope inserts, booklets explaining policies and procedures, daily news digests, reading racks, indoctrination kits, posters, and policy statements.

Oral
Employee and executive meetings, public address systems, open houses, plant tours, family nights, informal talks by key executives on visits to departments, new-employee orientation meetings, employee counseling, panel discussions, grievance and employee-management committees, recordings, and employee social affairs

Audiovisual
Motion pictures, color slides and film strips, closed-circuit television, sound slide film, flip charts, easel charts, posters, maps, flannel boards, and product exhibits

---

Source: Bertrand R. Canfield and H. Frazier Moore, *Public Relations: Principles, Cases, and Problems,* 6th ed. (Homewood, Ill.: Richard D. Irwin, 1973), pp. 60–61.

and adopted it was necessary to inform employees of the program and indicate how they could assist in building a more distinct public image. This took the form of stories in company magazines, letters to supervisors, and personal visits to key executives and operating staff.

EXTERNAL COMMUNICATIONS

As a part of the promotional plan, public relations is most concerned with external communications designed to enhance the image of the organization in the minds of its various publics—ultimate consumers, suppliers, stockholders, and the community at large. The image is the overall reputation or *personality* achieved by the organization in its public interface.

Image is of great importance for overall promotional strategy because it is the attitudinal background against which all organizational offerings are evaluated. If it is defective in important ways, a considerable competitive handicap results.

There is no denying the fact that many, if not most, business firms are facing a growing public credibility crisis. This has been caused, in part, by the attacks from consumerists, government, and other critics. It is also true, however, that public antipathy has been aroused by numerous examples of product failure, outright deception, and various other forms of irresponsibility.

Some firms, of course, by and large ignore their public image. Many others, however, are quite sensitive to their public interface, however, and make wise use of corporate advertising, customer relations programs, and publicity. Figure 22–3 illustrates the rich variety of media opportuni-

FIGURE 22–3
Media for External Public Relations

Mass Media
Newspapers, magazines, radio, television, annual and interim reports, correspondence, booklets, reprints of executive speeches, program kits and study materials for clubs, educational materials, library reference materials, manuals, and handbooks

Oral
Meetings with shareholders, consumers, dealers, suppliers; opinion leaders in plant communities, educators, and legislators; open houses; plant tours; business education days; speeches by employees and executives; visits to community institutions and suppliers; radio and television broadcasts; and community social affairs

Audiovisual
Displays and exhibits, motion pictures, sound slide films, charts, maps, posters, slides, television broadcasts, models and construction, and demonstration devices.

Source: Bertrand R. Canfield and H. Frazier Moore, *Public Relations: Principles, Cases, and Problems,* 6th ed. (Homewood, Ill.: Richard D. Irwin, 1973), pp. 60–61.

ties that is available for this purpose. Of special importance in the external campaign are (1) organizational symbols, (2) corporate advertising, (3) customer relations programs, and (4) publicity.

Organizational symbols. Organizational symbols and names are significant in identifying the organization and differentiating it from competitors. Each symbol in Figure 22–4 is a type of shorthand stimulus which calls to mind a constellation of meanings every time it is seen.

Concern over corporate image has prompted a rash of symbol changes in recent years. In part this has been brought about by mergers, as was the case with the Atlanta Gas Light Company. In other situations established symbols were felt by management to project an image which was no longer in keeping with the current environment or current organizational activity.

The symbol must identify the organization at a glance, or it has failed in its intended purpose. Most of those illustrated in Figure 22–4 meet this criterion well. If there are one or two which you cannot identify, then the corporate symbol may be too abstract.

While the identification value of the organizational symbol is obvious, many feel that changes have at times been instituted for the wrong reason. The sums spent for this purpose are often surprisingly high, and the minor changes introduced quite frankly usually do not justify the effort. In the final analysis the primary reason for the symbol change often is simply to gratify the egos of top management. It is not by accident that a symbol change frequently accompanies a major turnover of top-management personnel.

Corporate advertising. Corporate advertising differs from the types of advertising discussed previously only in that it usually does not focus

FIGURE 22–4
Organizational Image Symbols

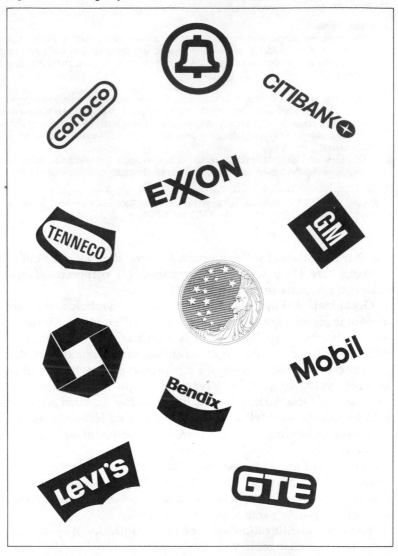

on specific products of the organization. Its purpose, instead, is to build awareness and favorable attitudes toward the firm. The problems of media selection and message design, however, are virtually identical.

The key question in a corporate campaign is what the company wants to be known for.[4] Corporate advertising can be of real significance in

---

[4] F. E. Webster, Jr., *Marketing Communication* (New York: Ronald Press, 1971), p. 617.

creating a coordinated overall image which can provide the background and setting for all other efforts.

Corporate advertising also is a useful means of reaching the public to fulfill such communication objectives as correcting mistaken impressions, announcing new programs, generating interest among the financial community, or attracting new personnel. In Figure 22–5, the Phillips 66 advertisement is a direct attempt to stave off criticism of the oil industry and the company, in particular during the early days of the energy crisis.

FIGURE 22–5
Examples of Corporate Advertisements

Who made the difference between oil that's waiting, and oil that's ready and waiting?

The North Sea. Treacherous. And violent. Beneath it, millions of barrels of crude oil—desperately needed to help solve the world shortage. Finding it was one thing. But getting it out is another. Frequent storms churn the North Sea and make it impossible for tankers to load. So the oil must wait.

Ekofisk One. A million barrel oil storage tank that enables production to continue in any weather. From the bottom of the North Sea, it reaches 36 stories—130 feet above the water.

Ekofisk One is built to withstand any storm. And it can store all the oil produced until the weather lifts and tankers can load safely.

Who was instrumental in the development of this million barrel marvel? The same company that makes fine products for your car.

The Performance Company: Phillips Petroleum Company. Surprised?

PHILLIPS **66** **The Performance Company**

Courtesy Phillips Petroleum Company

FIGURE 22–5 (*continued*)

"What's happened to the price of life insurance in the last 20 years?"

It's gone down.

One reason why the price of life insurance is lower is that people are living longer than they used to. Which means that companies can charge less.

Another thing that's helped reduce the price of life insurance is an improvement in the earnings from our investments. An improvement we've applied against the price of insurance.

And finally, we've done our level best to keep down the cost of doing business.

Because of these things, the price of life insurance is actually less today than it was 20 years ago. And these days that's something nice to know about.

We're bringing you these messages to answer your questions.

And here's what we're doing to help you know more.

We're maintaining a field force of over 200,000 agents, trained to answer your questions about life insurance. On the spot.

We'll send you a personal answer to any questions that you may have about life insurance or the life insurance business.

We'll mail you a free copy of our 20-page booklet, "The Life Insurance Answer Book". With helpful answers to the most frequently asked questions about life insurance.

Just send your card or letter to our central source of information: the Institute of Life Insurance, Dept. D-7, 277 Park Ave., New York, N.Y. 10017.

Your life insurance companies.

FIGURE 22–5 (*concluded*)

Some little-known facts explain why 9 out of 10 homes in America are built with wood.

Wood is man's most accepted building material. This isn't just because wood is available. It's because wood makes a better home.

Pound for pound, wood is stronger than steel. When wood sheathing is attached to wood framing, the structure becomes so strong it can withstand stresses better than other kinds of construction.

How well a wood house resists stress is best summed up by this fact: most wood homes survived the violent shaking of the 1971 Los Angeles earthquake without serious damage.

Wood also insulates 400 times better than steel; 1770 times better than aluminum. Tests made against masonry have shown that a wood frame house can save you money on heating and cooling bills.

If you're in the market for a new home, you owe it to yourself to demand wood. For more little-known facts and a free House Hunter's Guide, write **American Wood Council,** Dept. T, 1619 Massachusetts Avenue, N.W., Washington, D.C. 20036.

PHOTO: HIDDENBROOK, MILLER AND SMITH, MCLEAN, VA.

Courtesy American Wood Council

The message by the Institute of Life Insurance is an attempt to reduce public apathy toward life insurance and to point out a generally unrecognized point regarding price trends. The American Wood Council has a similar purpose.

Some objectives for corporate advertising are not at all obvious on the surface. Quite often a campaign will be undertaken to make a company or perhaps an industry appear to be competitive and thereby ward off potential antitrust and monopolistic behavior charges by government. Another purpose is simply to gratify executive egos. This may explain why corporation presidents so often appear in print in full color saying things which might be said more appropriately using other means.

Customer relations program. One response to the pressure of consumerism is the establishment of customer relations programs. These can be in the form of corporate advertising such as that by the Ford Motor Company illustrated in Figure 22–6. The low credibility assigned advertising by large segments of the public, however, limits the impact of this type of effort.

Other firms have instituted "hot line" response to complaints. A more effective strategy probably is to improve quality control programs and then offer stronger warranties. The improved warranty offered by American Motors Corporation and illustrated in Figure 22–6 must have had some impact because the other domestic auto firms are offering similar inducements to consumers.

Publicity. The role for publicity is to present "information designed to advance the interests of a place, person, organization, or cause and used by mass media without charge because it is of interest to readers or listeners."[5] It may come as a surprise that a large percentage of editors stated that up to 50 percent of the publicity material received is valuable for immediate or future articles in their publications, and more than one fourth would like to receive more.[6]

The principal types of publicity are business feature articles, news releases, financial news, new-product information, background editorial material, and emergency publicity. Any of these can be of real value in making the program of an organization known. For example, a series of articles was written about Dr. Kenneth N. Taylor, who paraphrased the *Living Bible* which now has sold over 11 million copies and was the fastest selling nonfiction book of 1973. A study of the influences on the decision to buy indicated that a *Newsweek* article, in particular, proved to be influential in stimulating initial awareness and interest in this new product.

---

[5] "Public Relations and Publicity," in *Marketing Handbook,* ed. A. W. Frey (New York: Ronald Press, 1965), pp. 19–25.

[6] Canfield and Moore. *Public Relations,* 7th ed., p. 136.

FIGURE 22–6
Customer Relations Corporate Advertisement

Everybody talks about quality, Ford people make it happen.

Our engineers create a design and specify materials that protect against wind noise and water leaks. People like Gary Lilley carefully fit weather stripping to provide a pleasing interior environment for driver and passengers in every Ford vehicle.

This dedication to quality at Ford Motor Company is paying off. Latest results show a 48% average improvement in quality over 1980 models as reported by new car owners.

Visit a Ford or Lincoln-Mercury dealer and take a close look at what total employee, management, union and supplier involvement can achieve.

At Ford Motor Company, Quality is Job 1!

Ford
Mercury
Lincoln
Ford Trucks
Ford Tractors

Courtesy of Ford Motor Company

FIGURE 22–6 (*concluded*)

TAKE A 5-YEAR FREE RIDE

5 years

2 years

Announcing Buyer Protection Plan® 5... and a $500 price reduction.

For 5 years/50,000 miles, a virtual "Free Ride" over the repairs you fear most.

The best part of American Motors' new Buyer Protection Plan 5 starts where Ford and GM leave off...after 2 years.

Buyer Protection Plan 5, on every Concord, Spirit and Eagle, includes: a full 12-month/12,000-mile warranty.

Plus, extended service coverage on major components for 5 years or 50,000 miles. (Owner pays first $25 for each repair visit.)

Plus, a 5-year No-Rust-Thru Warranty™...made possible by the exclusive Ziebart® Factory Rust Protection Program.

Plus, loaner car assistance.* And trip interruption protection, which covers extra food and lodging expenses up to $150 if you're 100 miles or more from home and warranty repairs take overnight.

Plus, a $500 price reduction on every Concord, Spirit and Eagle...but only until June 12.

At American Motors, wherever you go...Buyer Protection Plan 5 goes with you...all the way into 1987.

See us for warranty and rust program details. Aluminized exhaust warranted for 12 months/12,000 miles. Ziebart is a registered trademark of Ziebart International Corporation.
*If dealer has to keep your car overnight for warranty repairs, you'll get a free loaner car during the first year. And for the next 4 years, you'll get $15 a day toward loaner car expenses for up to 5 days.

AMERICAN MOTORS.

Only the Tough Americans give you more and charge you less.

Spirit, 4-wheel drive Eagle and Concord

Reproduced by permission of American Motors Corporation

CASE HISTORIES OF SUCCESSFUL PUBLIC RELATIONS

Two case histories which illustrate the basics of strategy and execution in a public relations program are presented here. They concern a professional association and a major airlines.

The Ohio Association of Osteopathic Physicians and Surgeons.[7] The public does not generally recognize that the Doctor of Osteopathic Medicine (D.O.) has the same basic training as the M.D., plus unique training in treatment of the muscular-skeletal systems. As a result, there is an untapped market opportunity for osteopathic medicine.

A study of 619 Ohio residents disclosed that the overall image of the D.O. in the state is low, primarily because of ignorance of his or her function. Most could not define the meaning of the term osteopath, for example. The least knowledgeable proved to be under 25 years old.

In addition, evaluation of the D.O.'s competence was low, especially as reflected in questions on the type of physician who would be used to treat a back ache and (or) severe stomach pain contracted in a strange city. Not surprisingly, preference for the D.O. was substantially higher among those who are knowledgeable about osteopathic medicine. Also, competence ratings were significantly more positive among those who were aware that the M.D. and the D.O. are equivalent in training, specialization of practice, and available hospital facilities.

These findings pinpointed some needed remedial efforts:

1. People must be informed about osteopathic medicine, especially those in the younger age brackets.
2. Present users are more knowledgeable than the public at large, but they frequently are not aware of the full scope of osteopathic medicine and hence (1) do not make full use of the D.O.'s services and (2) are not a positive influence on others.
3. The use of D.O.s would probably increase if the public were aware of (1) the equivalency of training between M.D.s and D.O.s, (2) the full range of specialization in practice offered by D.O.s, and (3) the excellence of facilities and care at osteopathic hospitals.

While there is not space to review the complete public relations program recommended to the Ohio Osteopathic Association, it centered primarily around a brochure designed with a distinct youth appeal stressing the nature of osteopathic medicine and the full range of services offered. The first target for dissemination of this brochure was present patients. The objective was to make the user a more enlightened patient so that she or he would utilize the D.O. for a broader range of illness and to

---

[7] "The Ohio Association of Osteopathic Physicians and Surgeons," in *Cases in Promotional Strategy*, eds. James F. Engel, W. Wayne Talarzyk, and Carl M. Larson (Homewood, Ill.: Richard D. Irwin, 1971), pp. 28–50.

provide the D.O. with more concrete information so he or she could inform others through word of mouth.

Another target was the high school student who is tomorrow's patient as well as osteopathic practitioner. Efforts were suggested in the form of assemblies, programs, and individual counseling to broaden the base of understanding of this form of medicine.

A third suggested target was the community at large. The profession as a whole is derelict in disseminating research findings and hence does not present a scientific image to the public. This can be changed easily. The individual D.O. was encouraged to make his or her office and facilities reflect a modern, up-to-date image. The D.O. was also urged to be active in community affairs. Increasing his or her visibility by this means should lead to an increase in patient load, to say nothing of presenting a more positive view of osteopathic medicine.

Notice that no mention has been made of paid advertising. It was felt that newspaper advertisements, for example, would only invite retaliation by the M.D., and costs would be excessive.

While definite quantitative objectives for the campaign were not stated because of the uncertainty of the amount to be funded by the Association, clear benchmarks were provided. Thus it would be quite possible to resurvey a comparable sample at a later period to ascertain changes in awareness and preference.

This case illustrates that public relations is a communication function and hence should be managed to attain communication goals. It is based on consumer research to the same extent as advertising and other forms of promotion. In this case a consumer survey led to (1) an indication of target markets for public relations and (2) determination of the informational content of the campaign. Accountability was facilitated by the utilization of known benchmarks.

Eastern Air Lines.[8]   In the early 1960s Eastern Air Lines faced a loss of nearly $20 million, mostly as a result of public antagonism to poor service. In fact, WHEAL (We Hate Eastern Air Lines) clubs had been informally organized by business travelers. Needless to say, the very survival of the airline was threatened.

A new management team instituted many changes, one of the first of which was to commission an image study. The Young and Rubicam agency conducted an attitude analysis of travelers in New York, Chicago, and Washington D.C., the primary service areas of Eastern. It was found, in summary, that the airline had a high awareness level, but its image was seriously deficient. Ratings of specific performance categories were

[8] "Eastern Air Lines: Attitude Change," in *Cases in Consumer Behavior,* eds. Roger D. Blackwell, James F. Engel, and David T. Kollat (New York: Holt, Rinehart & Winston, 1969), pp. 94–102.

the lowest among the various competitors. Businesspeople, in particular, flew on Eastern only because they had to.

One of the first areas for remedial action was to add to the jet fleet and to update all phases of service. An initial specific change was the design of a new Eastern symbol. Lippincott and Margolis, an industrial design firm, presented a bold new symbol intended to connote speed, modernity, and the jet age. A modern color scheme of "Ionosphere and Caribbean" blue was designed for all planes, and flight personnel appeared in new, smartly tailored uniforms.

Training films stressing the new look at Eastern were developed and presented to employees. The internal communications emphasized the marketing program of total customer satisfaction. Ticket agents and other support personnel were trained to give customers complete satisfaction.

The company also endeavored to be a good corporate citizen. One phase of this program was to improve employee satisfactions through compensation, recognition, pride, advancement, and labor peace. It improved relationships with the regulatory agencies by personal management appointments. The financial community also was the target of public relations through development of timely and factual reports. Improved relationships with society as a whole were achieved through participation in federal, state, and community affairs of all types. The company story was told widely through films and other means.

The extensive changes in the total product of the airline and these public relations activities succeeded in turning the corner and generating a profit.

THE IMAGE OF PUBLIC RELATIONS

It is clear that much can be done to improve organization image through external public relations. Unfortunately, often public relations is undertaken as "window dressing" to gloss over and distort the true facts. The result is that the public relations industry itself has a bad image in many quarters, a reputation that frequently is quite deserved. Organizational accountability demands credibility in dealing with the public. To use the vernacular, anything less than this is rightly termed a "corporate ripoff."

SUMMARY

This chapter has examined public relations as a supplemental form of communication. By means of public relations an individual organization can strengthen its interface with its various publics. Some efforts must be directed internally to employees and resellers. At other times it is necessary to address the consuming public, government, educators, and other influences in the external environment. The corporate symbol, corporate advertising, customer relations programs, and publicity were discussed in terms of their role in relating the firm to its externalities.

Review and Discussion Questions

1. Differentiate between internal and external public relations; between public relations and publicity; between public relations and corporate advertising.

2. How does corporate advertising differ from regular consumer advertising?

3. What justification can you advance for having the public relations department outside of the marketing department? Support placing it in the marketing department.

4. Based on current public attitudes toward business, politics, and other types of institutions at the time of your reading this text, what is your opinion of public response to public relations activities? Can it be strengthened? How?

5. One of the leading manufacturers of portable dictating equipment for home and business use has produced a model which, by experience, has spent more time in repair shops than on the job. Considerable hostility has arisen toward this otherwise reputable firm. You, as public relations director, are given the assignment of improving the corporate image. What would you do?

6. A leading public relations practitioner made the following statement: "You men in advertising don't understand the problems we face. We have to do your dirty work. Whenever you blow it, we have to mop up and make the customer happy again. We have to try to make the company look good to the community. We have to tell them that we are concerned about product quality, water pollution, abatement of slums, and so forth. Your job is easier. Don't tell me I can set goals for what I do. There just isn't any way we can measure performance." Evaluate the statement.

PART SEVEN

The Promotional Program: Other Topics

Having discussed management of the various elements of the promotional program, we will again assume the broader perspective of the framework for promotional strategy. Chapter 23 examines the subject of organization of promotion within the firm. Consideration is also given to the use of such outside resources as advertising agencies and media-buying services. Chapter 24 clarifies the management problems inherent in bringing about necessary coordination as the complete promotional program is implemented. Evaluation and follow-up, the final stages in the promotional planning program, are also discussed in Chapter 24.

The discussion up to the end of Chapter 24 has largely been from the vantage point of managerial strategy, although frequent reference has been made to broader social issues. Many questions remain to be examined, however, for no manager can escape the social, moral, and economic consequences of his or her actions. In this sense, Chapter 25 may well be the most important segment of this book. The authors have attempted to take a fresh look at opposing points of view without resorting to the defensive platitudes and self-serving value judgments so often advanced when marketing is placed under social scrutiny.

CHAPTER 23

Organization of the Promotional Program

Because the organization of promotional activities requires a proper marketing orientation, organizational relationships within the marketing department are the first topic of this chapter. Next is the division of effort between internal resources and outside service agencies. In the case of advertising, in particular, considerable use is made of advertising agencies and other types of specialized services. There are no clear-cut rules and procedures to guarantee an effective organizational pattern, however, and this chapter should be viewed primarily as an overview of the most important considerations.

ORGANIZATIONAL REQUIREMENTS AND STRUCTURES

This section begins with the requirements of a modern marketing organization and then evaluates common organizational patterns as they pertain to marketing in general and to promotion in particular.

The Requirements of a Modern Marketing Organization

Marketing has undergone a rapid evolution from its early position as a secondary business activity to its present status as the basic area for decision making in a firm. The need for an organizational structure consistent with the changing role of marketing in a marketing-oriented company has become apparent.

The following requirements are minimum for a modern marketing organization:

1. *A systems view of marketing by top management.* Success in today's business environment requires recognition by top management of a systems approach to marketing. Basic to the attainment of corporate goals is the conceptualization of the firm and its activities as a marketing system.

2. *The importance of a systems approach to marketing.* Good marketing performance is seldom achieved when the related functions are placed low in the corporate hierarchy. This means that (*a*) the marketing activities in a firm must be better organized, coordinated, and managed, and (*b*) the marketing executive must be accorded a more important role in total company planning and policy making than generally has been true in the past—marketing management is the marketing concept in action. The organizational structure should guarantee that the chief marketing officer reports directly to the primary operating executive.

3. *An organization consistent with marketing requirements.* No single form of organization is superior for all purposes, but there is a basic criterion underlying all adaptive organizational structures: responsibility must be delegated commensurate with authority to appropriate operating levels, and the capacity for quick-response decisions cannot be hampered by excessive reliance on top-management approval of all action. The capacity to move quickly to meet marketing opportunities is built into the structure through clear-cut, operating delegation of duties.

4. *Marketing strategy oriented toward a systems approach.* It may seem obvious to emphasize that all marketing efforts should be aimed toward attainment of common objectives, but there appears to be an inevitable tendency for strategy to branch out in unrelated directions. For instance, the advertising manager may sponsor a campaign featuring house-to-house sampling in the expectation of a strong increase in demand in a given area. The sales manager may be unaware of this strategy, so proper sales force efforts at the retail level are lacking. The problem here is a communication problem which may de due to the fact that the advertising and sales departments are located in different divisions in the firm. Marketing strategy can be unified when related activities are discussed and integrated in the organizational structure.

5. *A tailor-made promotional program.* Many companies still place the majority of the promotional effort in advertising. The result is that personal selling and reseller support often are deemphasized. Allocation of funds must be related to the tasks to be performed.

6. *Sophisticated use of outside resources.* Finally, it is a rare firm which is totally self-sufficient in all resource areas. For this reason, the advertising agency is used. The specialized agency can augment a firm's own resources

in specific areas. Moreover, it can bring an expertise and wealth of experience to bear on marketing promotional problems which may be difficult to match within the firm. In addition, there is much to be gained from the perspective of an outside source which presumably can analyze problems with greater objectivity. The development of a proper working relationship, however, requires considerable effort by both parties. This subject is discussed later in this chapter.

Organizational Structure

Types of structure. It is, of course, impossible to describe all of the organizational structures traditionally used in the business firm. The traditional form is the so-called *functional* structure illustrated in Figure 23–1.

The *product organization* form illustrated in Figure 23–2 originated in the consumer goods industries and has grown until it is the basic pattern of over 75 percent of *Fortune's* top 500 companies today. This reflects in large part the significant influence of product diversification since World War II. As Figure 23–2 indicates, it is common for the product (or brand) manager to report to a corporate vice president of marketing, although there are many variations in patterns of lines of authority.

Organization of promotion. A significant disadvantage of the traditional functional organization is that marketing decisions are made by several functional managers and finally coordinated by one of the marketing executives. This results in imposing too many management levels to be filtered before a final decision can be reached. The product organization is a significant step toward reducing these levels and maximizing the ability of the firm to act and capitalize upon profit opportunities.

The product manager is generally given responsibility for profit performance, but this responsibility, in the past at least, is not always backed by sufficient authority to act. Advertising strategy and execution, for

FIGURE 23–1
Common Form of Functional Organization

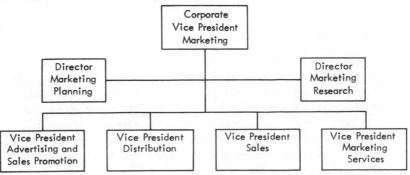

FIGURE 23-2
Product Organization Form

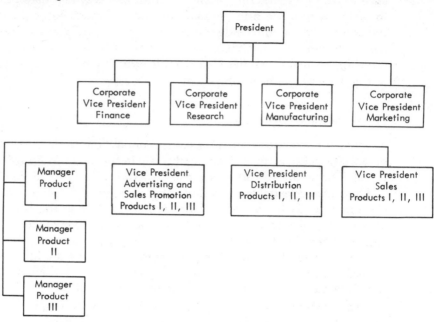

example, often reside with the advertising and sales promotion manager. Obviously this can create an intolerable situation, but there appears to be a trend now toward appropriating both the necessary authority *and* responsibility to the product manager. The product manager's role is more one of coordination and execution in less important areas of decision, whereas advertising decisions usually are made at the higher levels.

Unfortunately, full organizational coordination of promotional activities is a rarity. This is decidedly unfortunate, and it certainly inhibits the ideal of a systems approach to marketing management.

USING OUTSIDE SERVICES

Many large firms are staffed and equipped to perform the full range of their own promotional functions; Procter & Gamble is an example. However, it generally is not feasible for the smaller organization to develop the necessary expertise to do this, and they must utilize various outside services to carry out their promotional program. These include (1) media-buying services, (2) creative boutiques, (3) research services, (4) consultants, and (5) advertising agencies. Even Procter & Gamble makes extensive use of advertising agencies.

Media-Buying Services

The media-buying service initially appeared in the middle 1960s to provide help for smaller advertising agencies. A period of rapid growth has ensued, largely due to the growing complexity of media buying that has been brought about by the proliferation of specialized media to reach highly segmented markets. Today these organizations service both agencies and clients, who determine their own media strategies so that the sole role of the media-buying service is to execute the plan in optimum fashion. Historically there has been a concentration in broadcast media, but this is rapidly changing. Compensation plans vary, but most consist of some type of fee averaging from 3 to 5 percent.

The media-buying service has provoked controversy, much of it stemming from the traditional advertising agency, which has seen some departure of clients. Growth of this type of service has continued unabated, however, and it would appear that continued media proliferation will make for a bright future.

Creative Boutiques

The success of the media-buying service has encouraged the formation of specialized agencies whose sole function is to provide assistance in creative planning and execution. Media buying and other activities are left to the client. Compensation is a negotiated fee. The greatest use to this point has been for new-product development, print advertisements, and television commercials. Perhaps the most significant advantage is concentration of talent within one group which can be focused as needed on specific projects. The number of such groups has burgeoned, and continued growth seems assured.

Research Services

The significant role of marketing research has been stressed in this text, and expenditures for this purpose have increased dramatically during the past decade. The demands for technical expertise in this function have grown commensurately. Only a few advertisers have in-house capability for this purpose, and most make use of outside research agencies. These specialized organizations can provide services such as the following: interviewing and field supervision, sampling design, questionnaire construction, data analysis, specialized store audits, and so on.

ADVERTISING AGENCIES

Of all the outside services, the advertising agency is by far the most significant. For example, almost all leading advertisers make at least some use of the advertising agency. Figure 23–3 presents a list of the largest 30 advertising agencies in terms of world income. World billing along with U.S. gross income and billings are also presented. Billings refer to the cost of advertising time and space placed by the agency in media, plus fees for certain extra services, which are converted by formula (capitalized) to give an estimate of their magnitude which correspond to media billings. The agency does not receive the billing figure as income. In general, agency income is about 15 percent of billing.

Advertisements placed by a few large agencies to promote their own services are shown in Figure 23–4. Obviously, this is but a small part of agency efforts to obtain clients.

The existence and growth of specialized outside services such as the creative boutique have brought dramatic changes in both the use of the traditional advertising agency and management within it. It is no overstatement that the agency business is in real turmoil today, and the conventional wisdom which was true just a few years ago is no longer operative.

The nature and operation of the traditional full-service advertising agency is analyzed first. Then, to highlight the significant changes now taking place, the new type of agency which is emerging will be examined.

The Traditional Full-Service Agency

The advertising agency originally was a broker of space for advertising media, but there has been a dramatic change since this beginning over 100 years ago. Today most large agencies, at least, are equipped to provide full counsel on advertising strategy, media placement, research, development of package designs, determination of advertising budgets, the staging and managing of distributor and dealer meetings, design of sales-training programs and advertising presentations for sales meetings, and a host of related promotion functions.

Principles of the agency-client relationship. Through custom and years of trial and error, four basic principles have been established to serve as the foundation of the traditional agency-client relationship:

1. *Avoidance of a relationship with competitors.* It is traditional for an agency to refrain from handling the advertising of a firm which competes with a client. In turn, the client agrees not to engage a second agency. The issue of the agency retaining a competitor, referred to as account conflict, has largely been resolved by avoidance of *directly* competing accounts. Indirect conflicts between large accounts which *may* have some products in common are increasingly being overlooked. Clients, however, commonly retain multiple agencies, some of which handle only portions of the total account. Hence this operating principle has in essence been abrogated.

FIGURE 23–3

The Top 30 Agencies in World Income*

1981 World income rank	U.S. income rank	Agency	World gross income 1981	World gross income 1980	U.S. gross income 1981	U.S. gross income 1980	World billing gross income 1981	World billing gross income 1980	U.S. billing gross income 1981	U.S. billing gross income 1980
1	1	Young & Rubicam	353.0	340.8	222.8	200.0	2,355.0	2,273.0	1,490.0	1,334.0
2	3	J. Walter Thompson Co.	331.7	320.0	153.7	135.3	2,212.7	2,120.7	1,025.4	901.9
3	2	Ogilvy & Mather	286.5	245.9	157.5	125.5	1,933.8	1,661.9	1,050.3	837.1
4	12	McCann-Erickson	277.3	268.7	75.8	64.6	1,927.3	1,792.1	505.3	431.0
5	4	Ted Bates & Co.	236.7	210.6	129.1	108.1	1,578.1	1,404.1	860.4	720.3
6	5	BBDO International	205.2	175.6	127.9	105.8	1,400.0	1,305.0	858.8	806.4
7	6	Leo Burnett Co.	198.6	171.1	124.0	108.2	1,336.0	1,154.5	838.4	734.6
8	23	SSC&B	176.4	166.7	41.7	38.1	1,168.3	1,203.0	277.8	254.4
9	7	Foote, Cone & Belding	170.3	164.5	116.5	109.1	1,153.3	1,118.8	794.9	749.3
10	8	Doyle Dane Bernbach	165.0	150.7	115.0	98.1	1,150.0	1,004.0	800.0	671.0
11	13	D'Arcy-MacManus & Masius Worldwide	164.0	156.0	73.9	67.4	1,094.3	1,045.3	601.9	516.8
12	9	Grey Advertising	133.4	119.4	94.4	78.7	889.8	795.5	629.0	524.9
13	10	Benton & Bowles	127.5	118.5	81.4	73.8	870.0	806.0	541.0	492.0
14	19	Compton Advertising	118.9	94.5	59.8	51.2	812.6	640.0	420.4	350.9
15	16	Marschalk Campbell-Ewald	106.0	105.4	64.9	55.8	717.3	703.0	432.7	372.4
16	11	Dancer Fitzgerald Sample	85.2	76.3	76.4	70.3	599.6	558.4	520.0	505.0
17	14	N W Ayer Inc.	77.6	76.0	68.4	68.0	532.3	497.2	470.6	443.8
18	20	Needham, Harper & Steers	73.6	61.5	59.2	51.2	490.0	410.5	395.0	341.6
19	21	Marsteller Inc.	71.7	66.0	50.2	44.7	478.2	439.8	334.6	298.0
20	15	William Esty Co.	66.8	58.5	66.8	58.5	445.0	390.0	445.0	390.0
21	17	Wells, Rich, Greene	65.2	62.4	64.0	61.7	435.0	416.2	426.7	411.5
22	22	Kenyon & Eckhardt	63.1	56.0	48.1	41.0	412.0	379.1	311.9	279.1
23	18	Bozell & Jacobs	62.6	58.3	61.7	57.5	425.0	388.5	420.0	383.6
24	96	NCK Organization	56.7	54.5	4.9	9.3	378.0	363.0	39.2	62.0
25	24	Ketchum Communications	48.7	42.8	38.6	32.9	342.2	301.6	257.2	219.2
26	25	Cunningham & Walsh	36.7	31.3	36.7	31.3	283.0	240.8	283.0	240.8
27	26	Campbell-Mithun	31.5	27.7	31.5	27.7	210.0	184.3	210.0	184.3
28	33	Scali, McCabe, Sloves	27.2	21.5	19.0	15.8	185.6	143.5	131.0	105.6
29	27	Backer & Spielvogel	27.0	19.5	27.0	19.5	180.0	130.0	180.0	130.0
30	28	Creamer Inc.	25.0	18.3	25.0	18.3	167.0	122.0	167.0	122.0

* All figures in $ millions.

Source: *Advertising Age*, March 24, 1982, p. 10. Reproduced with permission. Copyright 1980, Crain Communications, Inc.

FIGURE 23–4
Advertisements by Advertising Agencies

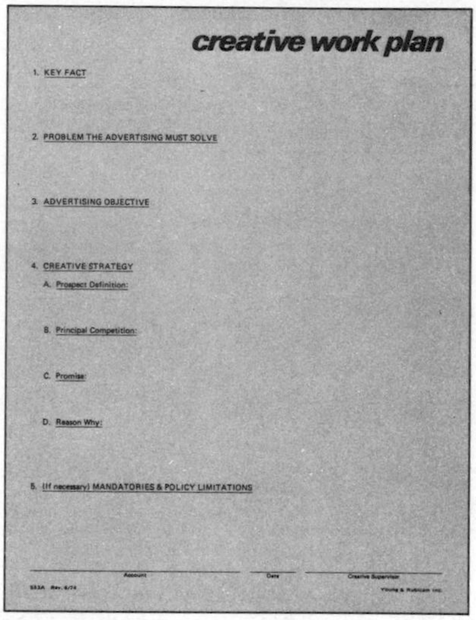

creative work plan

1. KEY FACT
2. PROBLEM THE ADVERTISING MUST SOLVE
3. ADVERTISING OBJECTIVE
4. CREATIVE STRATEGY
   - A. Prospect Definition:
   - B. Principal Competition:
   - C. Promise:
   - D. Reason Why:
5. (If necessary) MANDATORIES & POLICY LIMITATIONS

Account — Date — Creative Supervisor

Young & Rubicam Inc.

The most effective advertising doesn't begin with someone yelling "I've Got It!"

All of our advertising begins with the Creative Work Plan. And it's unique to Young & Rubicam. It is a disciplined, time consuming, sometimes agonizing exercise that we impose upon ourselves. We do it for a lot of reasons, primary among them; memorable advertising and increased sales for our clients.

We know that the most entertaining campaign in the world simply isn't worth the effort if it doesn't get results. Sure, we win our share of awards. But they're for very successful campaigns. They're for campaigns on cars like Chrysler Cordoba, our work on Manufacturers Bank and the public service work we do for people like the United Foundation and the Boy Scouts.

While the space at the bottom of the Creative Work Plan calls for the signature of a creative supervisor, we consistently utilize the talents of our marketing, media and account services people.

More importantly, we utilize the talents and input of our clients. When the exercise in discipline is over, and the Creative Work Plan is finally completed, we are at the point where a lot of ad agencies begin.

We believe that all that extra work helps us sell everything from cars to banking services to soda pop to Band-Aids . . . all around the world.

Perhaps it could help sell a lot of whatever you sell.

For more information, contact Joe Seregny, Executive Vice President and Office Manager, Young & Rubicam, Detroit, (313) 963-1345.

Y&R
DETROIT

FIGURE 23–4 (*continued*)

**General Motors • The Budd Company
Whirlpool Corp. • The Bendix Corp. • Pontiac
Motor Division • The Dow Chemical Company
The General Tire & Rubber Company • Kirsch
Company • Fruehauf Division • Cadillac
Motor Car Division • Detroit Diesel Allison
Division • Anheuser-Busch, Inc. • Ralston-
Purina Company • Brown Shoe Company
General Motors Parts Division • Ozark
Air Lines • Westinghouse Electric Corp.
Colgate-Palmolive Company • Uncle
Ben's Rice • Pfizer, Inc. • Red Lobster Inns
of America • International Telephone and
Telegraph Corp. • Lipton, Inc. • Sun Maid
Raisins • United States Air Force • Mars, Inc.
Lorillard Corp. • Helene Curtis Industries
Amoco Oil Company • The 3M Company
The Coleman Company • General Mills, Inc.
Kimberly-Clark Corp. • Litton Industries
Inc. • Hoover Ltd. • Standard Oil Company
(Indiana) • Rust-Oleum Corp. • American
Dairy Association • Ace Hardware • Bell
Scotch • Heineken's Brewery Ltd. • Scripto,
Inc. • Mentholatum Company • Heublein, Inc.
William Wrigley, Jr. Co. • Bankamerica Corp.
Universal Pictures • Wilkinson Sword, Inc.
Crown Zellerbach Corp. • Trans-Lux Corp.**

We made a name for ourselves by making a name for others.

D'Arcy-MacManus & Masius – Advertising

Bloomfield Hills (Detroit), Atlanta, Chicago, Los Angeles, Minneapolis/St. Paul, New York, St. Louis, San Francisco,
Adelaide, Amsterdam, Auckland, Brisbane, Brussels, Cape Town, Copenhagen, Hamburg, Helsinki, London,
Melbourne, Mexico City, Milan, Oslo, Paris, Pretoria, Stockholm, Sydney, Toronto, Vienna, Wellington, Zurich

FIGURE 23–4 (*concluded*)

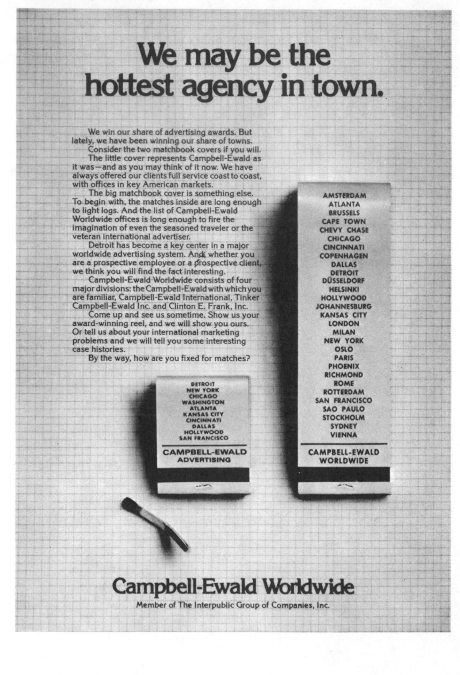

We may be the hottest agency in town.

We win our share of advertising awards. But lately, we have been winning our share of towns.

Consider the two matchbook covers if you will.

The little cover represents Campbell-Ewald as it was—and as you may think of it now. We have always offered our clients full service coast to coast, with offices in key American markets.

The big matchbook cover is something else. To begin with, the matches inside are long enough to light logs. And the list of Campbell-Ewald Worldwide offices is long enough to fire the imagination of even the seasoned traveler or the veteran international advertiser.

Detroit has become a key center in a major worldwide advertising system. And, whether you are a prospective employee or a prospective client, we think you will find the fact interesting.

Campbell-Ewald Worldwide consists of four major divisions: the Campbell-Ewald with which you are familiar, Campbell-Ewald International, Tinker Campbell-Ewald Inc. and Clinton E. Frank, Inc.

Come up and see us sometime. Show us your award-winning reel, and we will show you ours. Or tell us about your international marketing problems and we will tell you some interesting case histories.

By the way, how are you fixed for matches?

DETROIT
NEW YORK
CHICAGO
WASHINGTON
ATLANTA
KANSAS CITY
CINCINNATI
DALLAS
HOLLYWOOD
SAN FRANCISCO

**CAMPBELL-EWALD
ADVERTISING**

AMSTERDAM
ATLANTA
BRUSSELS
CAPE TOWN
CHEVY CHASE
CHICAGO
CINCINNATI
COPENHAGEN
DALLAS
DETROIT
DÜSSELDORF
HELSINKI
HOLLYWOOD
JOHANNESBURG
KANSAS CITY
LONDON
MILAN
NEW YORK
OSLO
PARIS
PHOENIX
RICHMOND
ROME
ROTTERDAM
SAN FRANCISCO
SAO PAULO
STOCKHOLM
SYDNEY
VIENNA

**CAMPBELL-EWALD
WORLDWIDE**

Campbell-Ewald Worldwide

Member of The Interpublic Group of Companies, Inc.

2. *Client approval of expenditures.* The agency is obligated to obtain approval for all expenditures made in the client's behalf. Obviously this is good business practice.

3. *Client obligation for payment.* The client is obliged to pay its bills for space or time purchased by the agency promptly. The space bill is received by the agency, which then forwards it to the client. If the bill is not paid promptly, the agency must make payment to the media, an unwarranted drain on cash reserves.

4. *Forwarding of cash discounts.* Most advertising media offer a small cash discount if bills are paid within a certain period. The agency is obliged to forward this discount to the client because it is, in effect, the client's reward for prompt payment of space and time bills.

Recognition of agencies by media.   The agency must be recognized by advertising media before orders for space or time will be honored. At one time this practice of recognition was so rigid that agencies were compelled to follow certain practices which were later found to be in violation of antitrust laws. The most troublesome criterion of recognition in terms of the Justice Department was compulsory agreement by the agency to accept compensation only through full retention of a 15 percent commission paid by the media to the agency on the total bill for space or time. In other words, agencies were required to agree not to rebate any portion of the commission. The net effect of this practice was to forbid, by arbitrary dictate, any price competition by agencies. A consent decree was signed by five media associations and several associations of advertising agencies in the 1950s, and commission rebating is no longer prohibited.

Media recognition is presently based on proof by the agency that it possesses sufficient financial resources to pay space or time charges if the client defaults on payment. Media may also request proof that the agency offers adequate personnel and facilities to service clients, but such approval is largely a formality.

As onerous as media recognition became prior to the consent decree, the procedure has been instrumental in improving agency practice. A tightening of standards through recognition led to major improvement in agency performance, and all members of the advertising business were beneficiaries.

Agency management and operation.   A traditional full-service agency needs personnel in such specialized fields as marketing research, media research, media planning, media buying, creative writing, creative design, and account management. The work usually is demanding, and considerable reliance must be placed on the imagination and resourcefulness of the individual. There are few routine tasks in the usual sense of the word; most agency employees are forced to be self-starters. Many agencies require a master's degree of new trainees. As a result, the pay for qualified personnel is higher than in most other fields.

The agency business has been tagged a "heart attack" business. There is some truth to this; pressure placed on the individual is great and may not be readily apparent. The agency organization chart is not deep; there are relatively few layers of management. The chief manager (called the account executive) for a given product will have several assistant account executives working with him or her. There are no lower levels of management as such. Tasks and responsibilities placed on most agency management personnel are therefore equivalent to those faced only by *higher management* in most manufacturing firms. Though pressures may be high, rewards are great. Independent, energetic, creative, and talented people are attracted to advertising agency work.

Agencies are organized in a variety of ways, but two forms are most common: (1) by group and (2) by department.

Organization by group. A group agency, in effect, is a cluster of individual agencies under one management. A complete team is assembled to prepare the promotion program for each large account or perhaps for several smaller accounts. The team typically is headed by a senior account executive with top management status, as well as several junior account executives. It will include artists, writers, promotion people, researchers, and others to provide needed services.

The group system concentrates efforts and skills on a related set of problems without dilution of managerial talents through assignments to other accounts. A high degree of specialization is thus attained.

Organization by department. The departmentalized agency provides a separate department for each agency function. Departments for media, copy, art, production, research, traffic (coordination), account service, and promotion each serve all clients. The account service department, composed of account representatives, assumes responsibility for service of accounts. Services of other departments are drawn upon as needed without the assignment of specified individuals on a permanent basis. One writer may be assigned to five accounts. Specialization is discouraged by this form of organization, but individuals can gain a breadth of experience not possible under the group system. Figure 23–5 illustrates this type of structure.

Top-management contact with agency output is paramount, whatever form the organization takes. In smaller agencies, top management can readily evaluate and approve the campaign as it develops. In larger agencies, day-to-day contact becomes impossible, and "plans boards" are established for periodic top-management review.

While the plans-board procedure may seem to be time consuming and unwieldy, it serves to detect loose thinking and questionable recommendations prior to presentation of plans to the client. Moreover, the

FIGURE 23–5
Departmental Organizational Structure of Advertising Agency

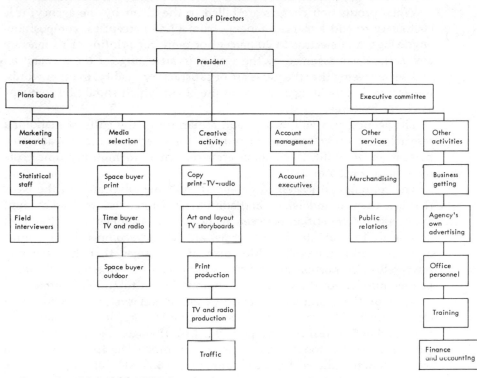

Source: Association of Advertising Agencies, Inc.

account group benefits from the insights of skilled professionals. There is a danger that the account team, being tempted to prepare the campaign only for plans-board approval, will forgo daring and imaginative recommendations. The board should be viewed as a valuable resource for ideas and guidance rather than as a court for evaluation of the performance of the account group.

Agency compensation. Rapid changes are taking place in agency compensation plans. Two basic plans are used: (1) the commission system and (2) the fee system.

The commission system. The great majority of advertising media are "commissionable" in that a traditional 15 percent discount is paid to the agency that places the advertising. This historically has provided the compensation for the agency.

The 15 percent commission is an arbitrary sum. Agreement must be made between client and agency enumerating the services to be provided under the commission and those for which extra fees will be charged. The planning, design, and preparation of advertisements are provided by the agency without additional compensation, but other services, including marketing research and publicity, are performed on a fee basis.

When production charges are billed to the client by the agency, it is customary to add a markup ranging from 17.65 percent for composition, engravings, and electros to 20 percent or more for printing. This markup covers the costs assumed by the agency in arranging for the preparation and guaranteeing that the items are of satisfactory quality. In other words, the agency is providing a service to the client which should be compensated for by a fee.

The agency also will usually add a markup to the costs of marketing research and other services to provide for overhead and a reasonable percentage of profit. A common arrangement is to multiply time costs by a factor of 2.5 or 3.0.

The commission system is defended by some advocates on the basis that it is easy to understand and administer. Moreover, its fixed amount avoids price competition between agencies. The argument is that an idea is difficult to evaluate in cost terms, and agency competition in terms of price is thus impossible. Moreover, it is claimed that the agency is rewarded in proportion to the use made of its ideas—the more the space or time purchased, the greater the commission in total dollar terms.

Most of these arguments for the commission system dissolve upon close analysis. The critical weakness is that a 15 percent commission may not be related to real services performed by the agencies, possibly being either excessive or too low. Consider this example: The 15 percent system would seem to indicate that an ad running in a $35,000-per-page magazine requires seven times the effort of an ad running in a $5,000-a-page magazine, and the commercials for a $10,000-per-program show. This is not the case.

Another important weakness is that the commission system has provided an excuse for some agencies not to utilize accounting systems to justify their charges. To a manufacturer, on the other hand, the absence of cost accounting is unthinkable.

Yet another limitation is the temptation for agency management to avoid placing dollars in noncommissionable media. Direct mail, point of purchase, and advertising specialties are only three of many useful media an agency may avoid rather than charge a fee to the client. Most agency spokespersons will emphatically deny that commissionable media are favored, but this temptation can be avoided completely through abandonment of the commission system.

The fee system. The 1960s and 1970s saw a strong movement toward compensation of the agency by fees, a movement given impetus by the fee arrangement between Shell Oil and Ogilvy, Benson, and Mather (now Ogilvy and Mather, Inc.) in 1960. In this agreement, the agency is compensated by a fee based on agency costs plus an appropriate markup, with all commissions from the media either rebated to the client or deducted from the fee.

In assessing the benfits of the fee system, one client stated:

> The arrangement calls for the client to decide the kind and extent of services appropriate for each product and, in turn, the agency will be compensated for these services as performed. . . . This new approach well may solve the twin problems of tailoring the amount and kind of service to the needs and stage of development of each product, while at the same time adequately compensating the agency for the services required on new products versus established ones.[1]

The agency also benefits, as one agency executive pointed out:

1. The agency can be totally objective in its planning and recommend noncommissionable media with no concern over agency compensation.
2. The agency knows it will be compensated for its services, and an incentive thus exists for provision of a total system of communication services.
3. Agency income is stabilized; sudden cuts in commissionable media will not spell financial disaster.[2]

The fee system requires the use of precise cost accounting. Account executives must keep accurate time records which become the basis for charges to the client. These reports provide an excellent record of profitability as well as a structure of costs.

It should be made clear that the fee system is difficult to administer; the exact fee is a matter of negotiation. Nevertheless it is more defensible than the commission basis, for compensation is geared to the tasks performed. A better basis is provided for a productive working relationship between both parties.

Agency and client allocation of effort.   There are many tasks involved in developing and placing advertising. Typically, the agency and client divide these tasks between themselves. Figure 23–6 presents a typical allocation. Note that the agency is involved in the early stage of setting advertising strategy, and that client approval is necessary at each step.

IN-HOUSE AGENCY

The traditional full-service agency is in real jeopardy unless changes are made. The root cause is that client organizations are shifting various promotional functions out of the agency. To some extent they are being transferred to media-buying services and creative boutiques, as discussed earlier. Furthermore, clients themselves are assuming an increased share of the task. When the entire function is assumed by the client (creative

---

[1] A. J. Vogl, "What's Behind the Big New Test of the Agency Fee?" *Sales Management,* November 15, 1963, p. 37.

[2] John Elliot, Jr., "The Pros and Cons of the Fee System," address given at the Association of Industrial Advertisers, July 1, 1964.

FIGURE 23–6
Major Steps in Developing and Placing Advertising

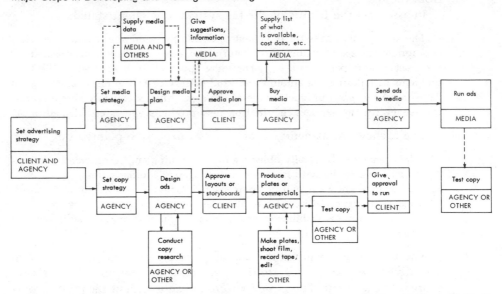

Source: Kenneth A. Longman, *Advertising* (New York: Harcourt Brace Jovanovich, Inc., 1971), pp. 30–31. © 1971 Harcourt Brace Jovanovich, Inc. Reprinted by permission.

design, media scheduling and placement, and so on) the client is often said to operate a "house agency." Probably a better term is *client management,* because most who do this use some combination of outside services as well as their own staff. Norton Simon, Inc., for example, is serviced by its own advertising-marketing organization, entitled Norton Simon Communications. It started with over $6 million in assignments from the Hunt-Wesson division, but it also makes use of advertising agencies and media services, all of which are compensated on a fee basis for certain products.

There are a number of reasons for this trend toward client self-sufficiency. Most stem from the various pressures for accountability which require closer control by client management over all of its activities. These pressures include, for example, increased costs of consumerism; costly documentation of advertising claims brought on by government review; market segmentation, with its requirements for specialized copy and media; and the lack of precise measures of advertising effectiveness. Promotion is increasingly viewed as more than just advertising, and more significance is placed on such facets as improved display, personal selling, and store demonstrations.

Development of a Productive Working Relationship

Good working relationships between client and agency do not just happen—a real dedication to this end must be manifested by both parties.

Experience has established a number of guidelines, some of the most important of which are discussed below:

1. *Maintain a top-level liaison.* Top-level client and agency executives should communicate regularly to air major issues arising as part of day-to-day operations. Most junior executives do not have sufficient status to modify operating policies. Minor misunderstandings can easily become magnified into major difficulties.

2. *Accept innovation.* The agency is a specialist in marketing communication. Its recommendations should not be constrained by client pressure for noninnovative strategy. The comments of one agency president in this context are:

Don't be afraid to try something new. Expect your agency to keep innovating. Don't feel obligated to continue a campaign which doesn't live up to hopes. Don't expect your agency to be right every time, but be sure that the chances for success are good always. Don't give up something which is good too soon. Don't ask for great ads; insist instead on great campaigns.[3]

3. *View marketing communication in proper perspective.* One of the danger signs often seen is undue reliance on advertising as compared with other elements of the communication mix. When advertising fails to perform as hoped, the agency frequently must assume blame. Once again, the importance of realistic communication objectives and a balanced promotion mix cannot be overstressed.

4. *Emancipate the agency from fear.* As David Ogilvy says:

Most agencies run scared, most of the time. This is partly because many of the people who gravitate to the agency business are naturally insecure, and partly because many clients make it unmistakably plain that they are always on the lookout for a new agency. Frightened people are powerless to produce good advertising.[4]

Some clients have achieved the reputation of being "agency hoppers," changing agencies every year or two. In many such instances the agency serves as the scapegoat for deeper troubles elsewhere in the client organization. In these instances, an agency change is seldom a permanent solution to the difficulties.

Procter & Gamble, one of the world's largest advertisers, rarely changes agencies. Other large firms such as DuPont, AT&T, Kraft, Kelloggs, Clairol, and General Mills follow a similar philosophy.[5] It is recognized that all agencies will fail at times to produce great campaigns, and evalua-

---

[3] William Marsteller, "How to Get the Most Out of Your Ad Agency," *Sales Management*, November 31, 1961, p. 36.

[4] David Ogilvy, *Confessions of an Advertising Man* (New York: Dell Publishing, 1963), p. 92.

[5] For a list of such companies and their agencies see *Advertising Age*, July 12, 1982, p. 41.

tion is based instead on the overall batting average. The agency is encouraged to do its best by knowing that one misstep will not be fatal.

5. *Permit the agency to make a profit.* The operating margin is sufficiently small that most agencies will cut costs and avoid utilizing top-managerial talent if a client demands such a volume of services that the agency cannot profit on the account. With no incentive to offer top-quality service, the agency may seek every opportunity to resign the account. The agency and the client must each make a profit. Good service will not be provided if unnecessary impediments are placed in the way of this complementary objective.

SUMMARY

This chapter has explored the subject of organization. The focus first was on organization structures which facilitate coordinated and integrated marketing strategy. Two forms of this organization were analyzed: functional and product. Because the product structure has become more common, greatest attention was paid to promotional management in this context. Then attention was directed to the division of functions between internal personnel and outside services. Five different types of outside services were reviewed: the media-buying agency, creative boutiques, research services, consultants, and the advertising agency. Because of the historically significant role of the advertising agency, an in-depth analysis was made of the causes and results of an important trend away from full-service operation to what is now known as modular or à la carte service.

There are no clear-cut rules and procedures guaranteeing effective organization. This chapter has offered insight into alternative patterns and the nature of the various outside services that can be utilized.

Review and Discussion Questions

1. Differentiate between the functional and product forms of organization. What differences are there in promotion management under each form?
2. It was noted that there is a disadvantage to the product form of organization in that advertising and other forms of promotion are assigned to personnel who may lack the necessary experience and expertise. What can be done, if anything, to minimize this disadvantage? Do the advantages of the product form of organization compensate for this problem?
3. What factors led to the growth of the media-buying service? Why do many experts predict that its role will be even greater in the future?
4. One authority feels that the creative boutique is only a passing fad which will disappear in favor of a return to the full-service advertising agency. Do you agree? Why or why not?

5. Evaluate the commission method of agency compensation. What are the reasons for its use? Is it likely to be replaced by the fee system?

6. It is said by some that the full-service agency as it has traditionally existed must change or it will be forced out of existence. What are the pressures for change? What must the agency do, if anything, to survive?

7. Some full-service agencies are adamant in opposition to offering modular or à la carte services. What reasons could you think of to explain this attitude? If you were called in as a consultant, what would your recommendations be to agency management with this attitude?

8. Some suggestions were given for development of a productive working relationship between client and agency. What guidelines, if any, would you add to this list?

CHAPTER 24

Program Coordination, Evaluation, and Follow-Up

Once the first four stages in promotional planning and strategy as outlined in Chapter 3—situation analysis, establishment of objectives, determination of budget, and management of program elements—have been completed, the next stage is coordination and integration of the program. This is the topic of the first part of this chapter, which includes a case history and an analysis of the PERT technique. The second major part considers evaluation and follow-up, the final stages in the promotional plan, with emphasis on the product life cycle.

COORDINATION OF PROGRAM ELEMENTS

Before dollars are actually invested in a program or campaign, a final review must be undertaken to determine whether each element has been properly designed to attain its stated objective. Next the program is scheduled so that each step is implemented as planned, without any activity getting out of phase. Achieving effective coordination is a difficult task, but the success of the campaign can be affected in a major way if it is not attained.

By way of illustration, the first part of this section is devoted to description and analysis of a campaign undertaken to launch the Kahala Hilton Hotel in Honolulu. This case history, which illustrates the way in which the various elements in the promotional mix are combined to attain communication objectives, should make apparent the magnitude of the need for achieving coordination and integration in promotional programs. The Program Evaluation and Review Technique (PERT) is later introduced as a promising solution to some of the difficulties encountered in the coordination attempt.

The Kahala Hilton: A Case History[1]

The Kahala Hilton in Honolulu, Hawaii, is situated on a somewhat remote site a short distance from Waikiki. Although it was destined to be one of the world's great resort hotels, the initial occupancy did not live up to expectations. The need for a crash promotion program became apparent, and McCann-Erickson, Inc., was given this assignment.

Situation analysis.   A prolonged situation analysis was not possible, but several basic issues soon became apparent. First, the Kahala Hilton was not designed to appeal to the mass market. While its prices are not excessive by U.S. standards, its location in Hawaii limits the potential market to those in the continental United States and elsewhere who have considerable discretionary income. Moreover, the costs of travel to Hawaii are least from the West Coast of the United States and Canada. Therefore, the market to be reached, for the most part, was greatest among those living in the western part of the United States and Canada with above-average incomes.

It was hoped that favorable publicity through word of mouth and other means would soon develop, but awareness of the facilities offered by the Kahala appeared to be low among prospective customers. Moreover, little was being generated in the way of support from travel agents and others who influence travel plans.

Objectives.   From the situation analysis, the objectives for the campaign quickly emerged. The target market was designated as prospective users located on the West Coast who, ideally travel extensively and can afford the expense of a trip to Hawaii from the U.S. mainland. The communication objective was to communicate the advantages offered by Kahala facilities in a striking and unusual fashion so that interest would be generated which was sufficient to bring occupancy figures past breakeven levels as quickly as possible. Travel agents were established as a promotional target with the goal of stimulating sufficient interest that they would actively encourage customers to patronize the Kahala.

Budget.   The exact procedure utilized to arrive at the budget was not disclosed, but it is known that it generally followed the task and objective procedure using the build-up method discussed in Chapter 11.

---

[1] Used with special permission of Hilton Hotels, Inc., and McCann-Erickson, Inc.

Basic strategy called for reaching a large mailing list with direct mail appeals as well as use of selected newspapers, in-store promotions, and other means. To support this program over a period of several months, at least $50,000 was required, and this figure was the final amount allocated.

In this instance, the entire campaign was planned and implemented by McCann-Erickson, whose previous work on similar problems furnished the background necessary.

Program elements. The promotional program was comprehensive, and prospective customers were approached in a number of ways. These included (1) direct mail, (2) newspaper advertisements, (3) a tie-in with an airline, (4) contacts by Hilton executives, and various specialized promotions.

Direct mail. Because of the sharply segmented market for this client, considerable waste would occur if the usual mass media were used. To reach the pinpointed potential customers in the western target market, a precisely aimed direct mail campaign was designed. The mailer focused on telling the recipient that the Kahala is an unspoiled resort property not yet discovered by the mass of travelers. This inside-story appeal was reinforced by enclosure of a four-color brochure describing the Kahala which was stamped "First Proof Not Color Corrected." (Reproduced here in black and white in Figure 24–1.)

The mailing list included over 150,000 members of Carte Blanche, Hilton's credit card subsidiary. The mailing was sent to all members located in Arizona, California, Colorado, Nevada, New Mexico, Oregon, Texas, Washington, and British Columbia. In addition, delegates to the Republican National Convention in San Francisco were included.

Newspaper advertisements. While the direct mailing reached an excellent potential market, it by no means exhausted the list of those who might be induced to visit the Kahala. Therefore, it was decided to run a series of small newspaper advertisements (224 lines) on the society pages of daily or weekly newspapers in wealthy communities in California, Arizona, Texas, and British Columbia. The complete media schedule is given in Figure 24–2.

Small space was used for the reason that large display advertisements are not required to attract attention in this type of paper. Moreover, space was purchased on the society page on the assumption that women serve as a kind of "family opinion leader" in formulating family travel plans. In the newspaper copy in Figure 24–3, it will be noticed that the same inside-story appeal was used. This advertisement was run four times during the months of June and July in most papers, and the total cost was $7,872.54.

Tie-in with Western Airlines. Western is one of the leading air carriers between the West Coast and Hawaii. A tie-in between the Kahala and Western offered substantial benefits to both.

FIGURE 24–1
Brochure Mailed

FIGURE 24–2

Newspaper Schedule for the Kahala Hilton

Publication	Date	Cost
Piedmont Piedmonter	July 3, 10, 17, 31	$143.40
Menlo Park Recorder	July 2, 9, 16, 30	143.40
Burlingame Advance-Star and Green Sheet (includes Palo Alto Times and Redwood City Tribune)	June 28, July 5, 12	383.04
Orinda Sun	July 3, 10, 17, 31	89.60
Ross Valley Times	July 1, 8, 15	80.64
Lafayette Sun	July 3, 10, 17, 31	89.60
San Marino Tribune	July 2, 9, 16, 30	98.56
La Canada Valley Sun	July 2, 9, 16, 30	134.40
Beverly Hills Times	July 3, 10, 17, 31	249.60
Palos Verdes News	July 2, 9, 16, 30	116.48
Arcadia Tribune	June 28, July 5, 12, 26	134.40
Millbrae Sun & Leader	July 2, 9, 16, 30	125.44
San Carlos Enquirer	July 1, 8, 15, 29	125.44
Walnut Creek Contra Costa Times	June 28, July 5, 12, 26	179.20
Fullerton News Tribune	June 29, July 6, 13, 27	134.40
Inglewood News	June 30, July 7, 14, 28	89.60
Los Gatos-Saratoga Times Observer	June 20, July 6, 13, 27	80.64
Newport Beach-Costa Mesa Orange Coast Pilot	June 29, July 6, 13, 27	179.20
Palm Springs Desert Sun	June 29, July 6, 13, 27	116.48
Monterey Peninsula Herald	June 29, July 6, 13, 27	161.28
Pasadena Independent Star News	June 29, July 6, 13, 27	331.52
San Diego Union Tribune	June 28, July 5, 12, 26	752.64
San Gabriel Valley Tribune	June 28, July 5, 12, 26	295.68
San Mateo Times & News Leader	June 29, July 6, 13, 27	206.08
San Rafael Independent Journal	June 29, July 6, 13, 27	197.12
Santa Barbara News Press	June 28, July 5, 12, 26	197.12
Santa Maria Times	June 29, July 6, 13, 27	134.40
Sunnyville Mt. View Standard Register Leader	June 29, July 6, 13, 27	107.52
Ventura County Star-Free Press	June 29, July 6, 13, 27	152.32
Whittier News	July 1, 8, 15, 29	134.40
Midland Reporter Telegram (Texas)	June 28, July 5, 12, 26	125.44
Dallas News (Texas)	June 28, July 5, 12	423.36
Houston Chronicle (Texas)	June 28, July 5, 12	501.90
Phoenix Republic Gazette (Arizona)	June 28, July 5, 12, Aug. 9	562.24
Tucson Star Citizen (Arizona)	June 28, July 5, 12, 26	358.40
Vancouver Sun Province (B.C.)	June 28, July 4	537.60

A mailing was sent to 10,000 customers in the target market states who had traveled on Western at some time in the past. The copy read in part as follows:

Here's a little secret—shared only with the private world of travelers. We've joined with another gracious host, the Kahala Hilton, to offer you an elegant new way to travel and enjoy Hawaii. It's a Western-Hilton holiday—a world apart, where comfort and good taste come first. Minutes from the frivolity of Waikiki, the quiet elegance of the new Kahala Hilton beckons discerning visitors. A secluded, pristine beach is your doorstep to the blue Pacific. Sunning, dining, cocktails—the life is an easy one. Send us the reply card, and we'll send you complete information.

FIGURE 24–3
Newspaper Advertisement for the Kahala
Hilton

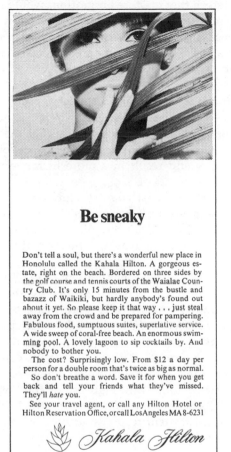

Be sneaky

Don't tell a soul, but there's a wonderful new place in Honolulu called the Kahala Hilton. A gorgeous estate, right on the beach. Bordered on three sides by the golf course and tennis courts of the Waialae Country Club. It's only 15 minutes from the bustle and bazazz of Waikiki, but hardly anybody's found out about it yet. So please keep it that way . . . just steal away from the crowd and be prepared for pampering. Fabulous food, sumptuous suites, superlative service. A wide sweep of coral-free beach. An enormous swimming pool. A lovely lagoon to sip cocktails by. And nobody to bother you.

The cost? Surprisingly low. From $12 a day per person for a double room that's twice as big as normal.

So don't breathe a word. Save it for when you get back and tell your friends what they've missed. They'll *hate* you.

See your travel agent, or call any Hilton Hotel or Hilton Reservation Office, or call Los Angeles MA 8-6231

Kahala Hilton
HONOLULU

A four-color brochure was enclosed describing the services and facilities of Matson and the Kahala.

Contacts by Hilton executives. It was felt that the Kahala would profit most through word-of-mouth advertising. Therefore, Hilton executives around the world were asked to write personal letters to their friends and relatives or to contact them in other ways to announce the Kahala and its services. Over 1,200 letters were written, and the response was felt to be excellent.

The newlywed market. The Luce Clipping Service was retained to collect all announcements appearing in West Coast papers during the promotion, beginning in August. Each bride-to-be received a letter mailed from Hawaii inviting her to honeymoon at the Kahala. An unusually receptive market was thus reached in an efficient manner.

In-store promotions. It was agreed that in-store promotions would provide excellent communication exposure. A complete store package was prepared and personal selling was utilized to solicit the cooperation of fashion department stores and specialty shops in a number of leading cities on the West Coast. This promotion got under way in August, with 30 cooperating stores as the target.

The basis of this promotion was display of a 22" × 28" poster costing $2.50. If a store agreed to use the display in a high-traffic window or in an inside department, a complementary gift of six nights at the Kahala was offered to management. Cooperation by a retail store beyond this specified minimum, of course, would result in a more lucrative reward. Display suggestions appear in Figure 24–4.

Contacting country clubs. The West Coast country club set was felt to be another promising market segment. Direct-mail solicitations were sent to 900 golf pros at various clubs and to 1,100 club officers during August. Stimulation of word-of-mouth advertising was the objective of this mailing.

Stimulating travel agent support. The travel agent, widely used by international travelers, was a prime target for personal selling by the Hilton International Division sales staff. Frequent calls were made by Hilton representatives, and each agent received a monthly sales letter including hotel brochures and selling tips.

Agents received the letter in Figure 24–5 along with a kit containing the full direct mailing sent to the Carte Blanche list. They were asked to publicize the Kahala to their customers through use of the hotel brochure and display material. Over 23 percent of agents returned the reply card requesting these items—an excellent response. Moreover, all agents whose cooperation was judged to be good were visited by Hilton sales representatives.

The Western-Hilton tie-in was promoted to the travel agent through direct mail and personal selling, although it was not begun until the above efforts had been completed.

Contacting other airlines. The Hilton sales force also called regularly on all airlines and other transportation companies. Every attempt was made to motivate airline sales offices to publicize the Kahala with brochures and display materials.

The outcome. The total expenditure for the promotion was approximately $50,000, the largest part of which was invested in direct mail advertising. Results of this direct mail effort are difficult to measure. On the basis of initial occupancy figures, predictions for the first year would not have exceeded 20 percent. Occupancy reached nearly 50 percent of capacity during and immediately following the campaign. Moreover, the

FIGURE 24–4
Display Suggestions Provided for the Kahala Campaign

Order these full-color
Kahala Hilton posters
for your own office
and display windows.

Each poster measures 28" wide
by 22" deep.

Bright, colorful parasols,
made of translucent paper,
show off smart swimwear
fashions. The poster is
in the foreground. On the
floor is an easel-backed
card which carries the
selling message. Fanned-
out Kahala Hilton brochures
are also shown.

The "big catch" of this window
design is travel luggage, shown
caught in a fisherman's net
suspended from a fishing hook.
Pineapples and tropical fruit,
sand and sea-shells, carrying
out the Hawaiian feeling,
surround the selling sign.
The poster is in the foreground.

payout over the long run should be considerable from vacation trips stimulated by the promotion.

Analysis of the Kahala program. This campaign was an apparent success for many reasons. Of primary importance was the fact that the situation was analyzed effectively in a short time, the market target was pinpointed, and realistic communication objectives were established and followed. To Hilton's credit were lack of rigid budgetary limits and willingness to invest in promotion necessary to reach the objectives.

Media selection was such that the target market was reached economi-

FIGURE 24–5
Travel Agent Promotion for the Kahala Campaign

Hilton Hotels International

CONRAD N. HILTON, PRESIDENT

CABLE ADDRESS
HILTELS.NEW YORK

THE WALDORF-ASTORIA · NEW YORK 22, N Y

TELEPHONE
212 MURRAY HILL 8-2240

Dear Travel Agent:

We've been talking directly to your clients and prospects about the stunning, new Kahala Hilton Hotel in Honolulu, Hawaii.

How? We've pinpointed that segment of the traveling public in your area that represents the best market for the Kahala Hilton -- and you! Yes, we've been pre-selling your clients and prospects on this fabulous new resort with a unique advertising and promotion program. This program included:

* Special mailings of the First Proof of the colorful Kahala Hilton brochure, with a reprint of a rave review by Lowell Thomas, to select lists of the top travel prospects in your community.

* Special window display program in key department stores and fine specialty shops throughout four western states.

* Special series of two advertisements directed to women, on the society pages of small community newspapers reaching high-income families in 39 markets in the West.

This entire promotion was directed to the best travel prospects in your area. They now know that the completely air-conditioned Kahala Hilton is a superb, secluded resort ... yet it is only a twelve-minute drive to Waikiki by free and frequent shuttle service ... that it is truly the pearl of the Pacific. Many of these prospects will be planning a Kahala Hilton vacation soon.

So take advantage of this tailor-made market for Pacific travel. Order the Kahala Hilton material contained in this folder in the quantities you need. Use the Lowell Thomas letters and "first proof" spread for your own direct-mail promotion ... the magnificent, full-color brochures for your other mailings and rack use ... and the beautiful, full-color poster for your office and display windows. Just fill out the postage-paid reply card and mail today.

Remember, they've all been planned to help you make the Kahala Hilton your first resort ... for profit!

Cordially,

HILTON HOTELS INTERNATIONAL

William F. Prigge
Director of Sales

WORLD PEACE THROUGH INTERNATIONAL TRADE AND TRAVEL

cally. The glamour of mass media was bypassed for face-to-face communication, in-store promotions, and interpersonal relations with travel agents and airline personnel.

An advertising message was formulated based on awareness of the motivation of international travelers to avoid tourist spots and to frequent hotels and resorts which do not appeal to the masses. The inside-story appeal clearly capitalized on this preference and presented the Kahala Hilton effectively. The brochure marked "Not Color Corrected" gave the reader the feeling of being part of a unique group getting the inside story in advance of others. This same appeal was played up to a lesser extent in newspaper advertising.

Point-of-sale communication through travel agents and in-store promotions was handled effectively. The response of travel agents was further evidence that campaign objectives were attained, for many apparently recognized and capitalized on a profitable opportunity.

Finally, the entire campaign was well coordinated and integrated. It was underway in all phases just three months after its inception, with no activity out of phase with any other. The direct mailing and newspaper advertising were timed to coincide, and displays were in position and travel agents' offices were aware sufficiently in advance to generate enthusiasm to follow through on the response to advertising by prospective travelers.

PERT: A Method for Coordinating Campaign Elements

Coordination obviously is necessary for campaign success, but it can be difficult to achieve in practice. A campaign is a complex undertaking in which many elements run simultaneously. Although the Kahala program was not an extensive one in terms of investment, duration, or geographical reach, it nonetheless was sufficiently complex that difficulties were encountered in meshing the various parts of the plan so that none fell out of phase with others. It was a task, for example, to ensure that all travel agents had received direct mail kits and had been called on prior to the starting date.

There is no substitute for a master planning schedule which spells out in detail what is to be done, who is to do it, and when it is to be done. Management, then, has an analytical tool which provides a complete picture of the campaign and facilitates a review of its progress at any point in time. The use of such an analytical method has been greatly enhanced since the advent of electronic computers. One such method, PERT (Program Evaluation and Review Technique), offers real potential in promotional planning.

The nature of PERT. The foundation of PERT is a graphic representation of activities and events required to accomplish a given task, with explicit attention given to interdependencies and interrelationships between activities. A sequential network of activities is constructed, and analysis centers upon realistic estimates of the time required for completion of necessary activities. This provides a comprehensive plan for program completion wherein the effects of delays in the completion of any activity upon the whole program immediately become apparent. This information provides the necessary data for realistic rescheduling.

A PERT network. The PERT network is a flow diagram consisting of activities and events required to accomplish stated objectives in which the interdependencies are graphed. An event is considered as a specific accomplishment which is apparent at a given point in time. Activities are defined as tasks which utilize available resources and lead to the events. Activities are the work to be done and the personnel and materials needed, and events are specific accomplishments or finished activities.

On a PERT network diagram, activities are represented by arrows between the events depicted numerically within circles. One such relationship is shown in Figure 24–6. Events 4 and 7 are functionally related. The activity connecting these events cannot take place until event 4 is finished, and, in turn, event 7 does not take place unless the connecting activity is completed. If several activities lead up to an event, all activities must be completed before the event comes into existence.

FIGURE 24–6
The Activity-Event Relationship

In Figure 24–7 the beginning activity in planning part of a campaign in an advertising agency is shown as the product group meeting. This meeting gives rise to three separate activities which lead to media, budget, and creative plans. These plans must be executed before the complete preliminary strategy statement (the final event) can be prepared.

Time estimates. Promotional planning and scheduling seldom is routine, and realistic time estimates present a real problem. PERT usually requires the following three time estimates for each activity:

1. *Optimistic time*—the least amount of time required to finish an activity.
2. *Most likely time*—the time which seems most probable as estimated by those responsible for completion of the event.
3. *Pessimistic time*—the maximum amount of time the activity could take if "the worst happened."

These three estimates are combined to derive "expected time," which is computed as follows

$$T_e = \frac{a + 4m + b}{6}$$

where

T_e = Expected time
 a = Optimistic time
 m = Most likely time
 b = Pessimistic time.

The critical path.   Assume that a PERT network has been graphed (with events numbered in circles) and expected times have been computed for each activity (indicated on lines connecting circles). At this point the greatest managerial usefulness of PERT becomes apparent, for it is possible to isolate the most time-consuming path or paths. This is referred to as the "critical path." Since the ending event cannot occur until all

FIGURE 24–7
PERT Network Diagram

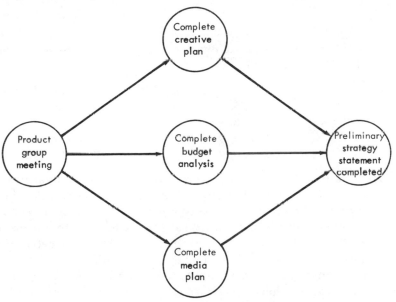

activities leading to it are completed, the critical path clearly controls the ending time for the entire project. A major advantage of PERT is that trouble spots are identified ahead of time, and special efforts may then be allocated to overcome various bottlenecks and delays in the entire project.

In the PERT network represented in Figure 24–8, the critical path is depicted by broken lines. There are nine events, and the expected time in weeks is indicated by the numbers above each arrow. The critical path is determined by adding the numbers of each possible path of activities between events 0 and 9. The path with the *greatest* amount of time required for completion is the critical path.

FIGURE 24–8
PERT Network Representing a Critical Path

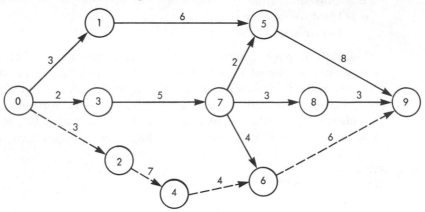

In this example there are five possible paths, with required times ranging between 13 and 20:

0, 1, 5, 9	17 weeks
0, 2, 4, 6, 9	20 weeks
0, 3, 7, 8, 9	13 weeks
0, 3, 7, 5, 9	17 weeks
0, 3, 7, 6, 9	17 weeks

Here path 0, 2, 4, 6, 9 is the critical path, with a total elapsed time required of 20 weeks. Therefore, it is the path that requires the greatest attention if the project is to be completed in less than 20 weeks.

Another way to view the critical path is to state that it has the least slack. By "slack" is meant, in effect, open or free time between the time required to finish the activities along a given path and the latest allowable time for these activities. Computation of PERT times using the concept of slack can be done using a standard computer program. One of the advantages of PERT is that resources can often be interchanged whenever slack exists along some path or paths in the network. That is, resources can be "traded off" and applied to the critical path to reduce the total time required for its completion and hence speed up completion of the entire project.

Application of PERT to promotional strategy. If a systematic planning approach has been followed for a promotional program, it is a relatively simple step to utilize PERT in scheduling and controlling. All that PERT involves is graphing these interrelated events, specifying the connecting activities, and computing expected times. Although the resulting network can be quite complex, the critical path or paths are easily isolated using computer procedures. The complexity of resulting networks should not be a deterrent to the use of PERT, for these complexities are a function of the *promotional requirements,* and they exist regardless of whether or not PERT is used. The advantage of PERT is that it enables management to depersonalize the complexities and bring them under objective, realistic control.

An example of the use of PERT in promotion appears in Figure 24–9. Notice that there are five network paths between events 1 and 12:

A. 1, 2, 5, 7, 8, 10, 11, 12
B. 1, 3, 6, 9, 12
C. 1, 3, 6, 8, 10, 11, 12
D. 1, 3, 4, 6, 9, 12
E. 1, 3, 4, 6, 8, 10, 11, 12

If the time values along each of the paths are added, the following results:

A. 8.8 weeks
B. 10.4 weeks
C. 8.0 weeks
D. 11.5 weeks
E. 9.1 weeks

The critical path is thus path D, requiring 11.5 weeks.

If this critical path time of 11.5 weeks would mean that the project will exceed its programmed finished time, then efforts may be aimed at speeding up performance along path D. For instance, it may be possible to reduce the activity time between events 6 and 9 by asking the plate maker to work overtime. The costs, of course, would be increased, and it must be determined whether or not the reduction in time is worth the increased costs.

PERT can be a truly valuable management tool, and *it is a logical extension of a systematic approach.* Thus it offers these advantages:

1. Systematic planning is guaranteed. PERT requires a systems approach to planning, and the technique imposes discipline on management thinking.
2. Responsibilities are clarified. The PERT network clearly defines what is expected from individuals responsible for each activity and with whom each manager is expected to coordinate his work.
3. Decisions can be pretested. Alternative networks can be graphed and expected times computed. Thus the outcomes of alternative approaches can be isolated with a clarity not previously possible.
4. Delays can be evaluated. Without PERT or its equivalent, management is prone to apply crash programs to all activities to speed up those few that are really critical. Crash programs on network paths with slack, however, are highly wasteful. PERT avoids this waste through

FIGURE 24–9
PERT Application to Promotional Strategy

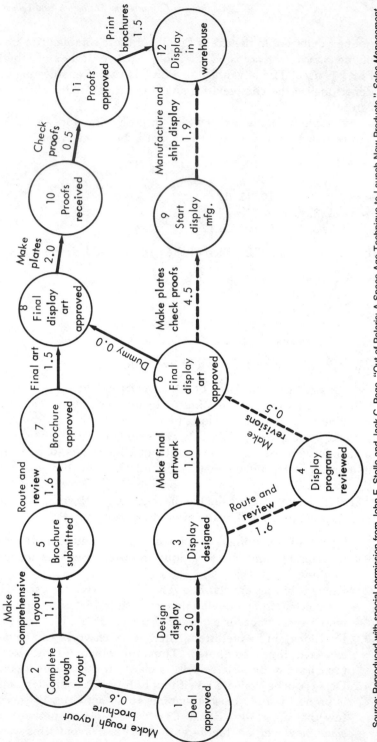

Source: Reproduced with special permission from John F. Stolle and Jack C. Page, "Out of Polaris: A Space Age Technique to Launch New Products," *Sales Management,* July 3, 1964, pp. 26, 27.

isolating the critical path or paths, so crash programs can be applied only at the trouble points.

EVALUATION AND FOLLOW-UP

There are two final stages in promotional planning and strategy which follow execution of the coordinated program. The first of these is measurement of effectiveness, which has been discussed in other chapters and will not be stressed here except as it contributes to the final stage, *evaluation and follow-up*. The steps in evaluation and follow-up are: (1) assessment of results against objectives, (2) postmortem appraisal, (3) assignment of accountability, and (4) assessment of future implications.

Assessment of Results against Objectives

It has been stressed that objectives must be *measurable*. If they have been stated in vague terms, evaluation and follow-up are impossible. Assume, for example, that the communication objective is "to interest people in buying tax-free municipal bonds." There is no way that results, no matter how precise, can be compared against this objective. Assessment is possible, however, if the objective is stated as: "to stimulate awareness so that 60 percent of those interviewed will mention tax-free municipal bonds when asked 'What are the names of the types of bonds you are familiar with?' " An appropriately designed pre-post analysis permits an accurate indication of whether or not this second goal has been attained.

Postmortem Appraisal

In the postmortem stage the question asked is: What did we learn from the results of this campaign? Assume that an actual advertising program fell 15 points short of the 60 percent awareness specified for the tax-free municipal bonds. An analytical look then should be taken at the campaign, step by step. Perhaps the message was unclear, inappropriate media were chosen, or the 60 percent awareness objective was unrealistic. In any case, the goal is to pinpoint the causes for the results.

Common sense would specify that the results of the postmortem analysis be written down and used in later planning. Chapter 10 described how difficult, if not impossible, it is to set objectives without some basis of experience. The postmortem thus provides invaluable data for the future.

Unfortunately, most organizations completely neglect the postmortem. In his study of leading advertisers, Victor P. Buell lamented that managers were repeatedly reinventing the wheel and making the same mistakes, both of which could have been avoided by relying on properly digested experience.[2] The obvious solution is to codify experience and extract the operating principles that emerge. One of the great managers of all time stated that "The wise man is glad to be instructed, but a self-sufficient fool falls flat on his face." (Proverbs 10:8, *Living Bible*.)

Assignment of Accountability

One result of the postmortem should be assignment of accountability to those who are responsible for the program's success or failure. One of the most pervasive human tendencies is to use every possible device to escape accountability. Anyone who has worked in complex organizations could find evidence of the effects of this practice. The senior author, for example, was a consultant for several years for one of the large oil producers of North America. It became obvious that postmortem analyses were never held, and each manager, once he was promoted and left that job, was careful to leave nothing tangible which could implicate him with failure and tarnish his career opportunities. Not surprisingly, rewards seemed to be given to those who played it safe, and incompetency was apparent at top-management levels.

Such situations must be avoided *at all costs*. A simple step is to assign precise job descriptions to each manager and measure his or her performance against these standards. If the product manager has failed to meet objectives, and *this pattern is repeated over time*, the obvious step is to take some sort of remedial action. Similarly, success should be promptly rewarded. Only then is it possible to get minimum benefit from systematic promotional planning.

Assessment of Future Implications

Throughout this book, the perspective has been on the short-term program or campaign by necessity, because most management decisions are of this nature. Evaluation and follow-up, however, demand that a broader viewpoint be taken to encompass the longer term. In particular, the focus must be on the *product life or product maturity cycle*, or that period of time during which the product will offer commercial payout sufficient to warrant its continued existence.

A model of the generalized product life cycle is given in Figure 24–10. It has the following phases:

1. *Development*—that period prior to the time the product is brought to market during which situation analysis and production tool-up are performed.

---

[2] V. P. Buell, *Changing Practices in Advertising Decision-Making and Control* (New York: Association of National Advertisers, 1973).

FIGURE 24–10
The Generalized Product Life Cycle and Typical Promotional Activity

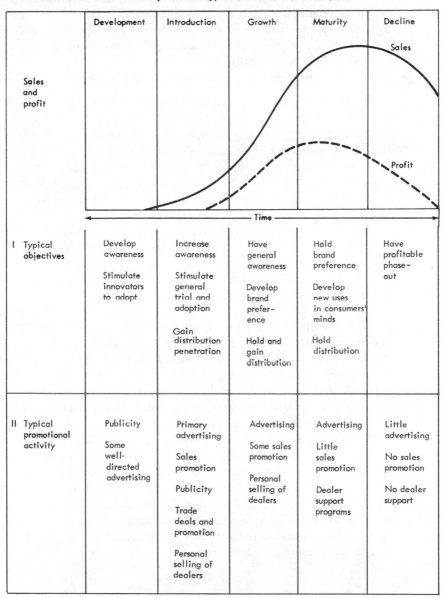

	Development	Introduction	Growth	Maturity	Decline
I Typical objectives	Develop awareness Stimulate innovators to adopt	Increase awareness Stimulate general trial and adoption Gain distribution penetration	Have general awareness Develop brand preference Hold and gain distribution	Hold brand preference Develop new uses in consumers' minds Hold distribution	Have profitable phase-out
II Typical promotional activity	Publicity Some well-directed advertising	Primary advertising Sales promotion Publicity Trade deals and promotion Personal selling of dealers	Advertising Some sales promotion Personal selling of dealers	Advertising Little sales promotion Dealer support programs	Little advertising No sales promotion No dealer support

2. *Introduction*—usually a period of slowly growing sales, during which the costs of introduction are greater than the return (refer to payout planning discussed in Chapter 11, which takes account of an explicit period in which a loss is deliberately incurred to launch a product).

3. *Growth*—demand accelerates, and the promotion problem shifts from stimulating awareness to stimulating trial of the product over those of competitors, which are now appearing.
4. *Maturity*—the market is now saturated by competitors, and competition shifts more to maintenance of "share of mind" (see Chapter 13) and price competition.
5. *Decline*—the product is losing appeal and is a candidate for deletion.

Figure 24–10 also presents typical promotional activity by life cycle stage for a consumer product. Thus the role for promotion changes over the product life cycle. The introductory campaign usually will require a larger than normal budget and will utilize high levels of both reach and frequency to build awareness and initial interest. Competitors usually appear quickly, however, and the emphasis shifts during the growth stage to stressing competitive superiority. Once maturity is reached, there usually are few if any real product differences. Hence the objective is to prevent share of mind from decreasing, and increased resort will be made to various forms of price competition. In the decline stage, active promotion usually ceases other than to guarantee that appropriate distribution still is achieved. The product is continued, other things being equal, only as long as it makes a contribution to profit.

The timing of the life cycle varies from product type to product type, but it is inevitable. As a result, management must be sensitive to signs that the present marketing program, and promotion in particular, is wearing out. Often it is necessary to introduce product changes or to stress in promotion hitherto untapped benefits in order to delay the onset of maturity and decline. An ability to sense the need for these changes and the appropriate timing is often what differentiates a consistently successful firm from an also ran.

When sales and profits are leveling off or turning down, however, it should not automatically be assumed that the problem lies in advertising or other aspects of promotion. It could be due to a number of other factors, and there is an inherent danger in changing a campaign and thereby sacrificing the awareness and momentum which have been built up. Dial soap and Crest toothpaste for example, have retained their positions as the top brands for over 20 years without a change in their fundamental advertising propositions.

SUMMARY

From the perspective of the total promotional program, this chapter has considered the coordination of the various program elements to meet the objectives of the plan. A case history illustrated the importance of coordination and integration, and it was shown how PERT analysis can be a powerful assist at this phase. Then attention was directed to evaluation and follow-up, which take place after the campaign has run its course. It was stressed that this is the appropriate time to learn from what has succeeded or failed, to codify this experience for future use, and to assign accountability to those responsible for performance. It was also pointed out that the evaluation phase should move from the short-run perspective to a longer run view which encompasses the total product life cycle and the changes in promotional strategy which must occur as a product approaches maturity and decline.

Review and Discussion Questions

1. Review the Kahala Hilton case history and prepare a PERT network of its various phases.
2. Would PERT analysis have helped management in the Kahala campaign? If so, how? What difficulties, if any, would be encountered in its application?
3. What is the significance of the critical path in a PERT network?
4. It was pointed out that the results of a postmortem analysis should be codified for use in future planning. What, in particular, should be written down and used? Be as specific as you can, using the Kahala case as an example.
5. Why does management seem to avoid accountability? What would you do if you were hired as marketing director and assumed responsibility over a group of product managers who had been permitted to escape accountability for many years? What problems would be anticipated?
6. What stage of the product life cycle do you think the following products have attained? Dial soap, Pepsi-Cola, Amana Radar-Range ovens, knit clothing, Vitalis hairdressing, video tape television systems, home/personal computers?
7. How would the promotional strategies of each of the above products differ? What factors account for your judgment?

CHAPTER 25

The Economic and Social Dimensions of Promotional Strategy

In the past it was customary for textbooks on advertising and selling to devote one chapter to social and economic considerations, mostly because it was felt to be the proper thing to do, not because anyone was really interested. A body of conventional wisdom thus took shape which was dutifully quoted and rarely challenged. Today, however, the social justification of promotion has become a primary concern. Many are advocating radical change, even to the point of abolition of the profit motive and business as it is now known.

The authors have not hesitated to discuss these broader dimensions throughout the text. There are some as yet unaddressed issues, however, which touch upon very sensitive nerves and which affect the ultimate survival of a way of life.

This chapter begins with a review of the traditional justification of promotion. Reference is made most frequently to the economic and social role of advertising, for the reason that it usually represents the front line of critics' fire. It should become apparent, however, that the points of controversy underlie all forms of promotion in common. Then these traditional arguments are challenged, and the need for some drastic revisions in basic premises is made evident. The chapter concludes with an assessment of the fundamental meaning of socially responsive promotional management in a rapidly changing world.

PROMOTION IN A FREE ENTERPRISE ECONOMY

Two fundamental and highly significant premises underlie any discussion of the role of promotion in a free enterprise economy. First, and probably most important, it is assumed that a *high and rising standard of living is a valid social goal.* Second, *profit is assumed to be an accurate measure of the extent to which a business organization has succeeded in meeting consumer desires and thereby contributing to a rising living standard.* Promotion then becomes defensible to the extent that it performs the following functions: (1) motivation of the consumer to increase standard of living and provision of useful information toward that end, (2) provision of a stimulus for firms to produce new products at lowered prices, and (3) prevention of monopoly and strengthening of competition.

Each of these points will be examined. The effects of the three basic functions of promotion will be discussed first, followed by reevaluation of the two basic premises regarding the role of promotion in our present economy.

Effects on Consumer Behavior

Motivation to increase standard of living.   It is assumed that motivational influences on the buyer are not sufficient to induce people to work, to produce, and to distribute the necessary goods. Some stimulus is required to influence buyers to attain higher incomes and to spend these funds on a rising inventory of goods and services. Leo Bogart defends advertising in this way:

Apart from what a specific advertising campaign does for a specific product, there is a broader combined effect of the thousands of advertising exhortations that confront every consumer in America each day, a constant reminder of material goods and services not yet possessed. That effect at the level of individual motivation is felt as a constant impetus toward more consumption, toward acquisition, toward upward mobility. At the collective level, it is felt in the economic drive to produce and to innovate which fuels our economic system.[1]

There is no denying that promotion (advertising in particular) performs this role, yet its impact should not be overstated. Advertising is not a major *causative* factor in the remarkable level of affluence in Western societies. The original settlers in America were forced to conquer a hostile environment, and this work orientation was perpetuated and reinforced through the doctrine of individual effort inherent in the Protestant religion (the Puritan ethic). In addition, a unique orientation toward the future resulted from a conscious revolt against the traditions of parent countries.

---

[1] L. Bogart, "Where Does Advertising Research Go from Here?" *Journal of Advertising Research* 9 (March 1969), p. 10. Reprinted from the *Journal of Advertising Research,* copyright 1969, Advertising Research Foundation, Inc.

Therefore, striving toward improvement of standards of living is intrinsic in this country, and it is doubtful that such a desire is in any way established by advertising. It is more probable that advertising reinforces these values and directs them toward specific products and services so that their production and sale become feasible. Therefore, demand stimulating activities do indeed exert an indirect effect on national income, as alleged, but it should not be concluded that advertising and selling are the cause of high and rising living standards.

Provision of buying information. It is the traditional defense that advertising offers benefits to the consumer through providing information which is useful in buying decisions.[2] One economist claims that:

> . . . advertisements provide the information that the brand advertises. This is useful information for the consumer to have. Advertisers have an incentive to advertise winners rather than losers. In consequence simply by responding to advertising the consumer can expect to get a better product than he would get otherwise. . . . Advertising helps consumers by directing them to the better brands.[3]

Certainly it is true that advertising *can* provide useful information, especially when a deliberate effort is made to discover the buyer's evaluative criteria and to build awareness along these dimensions. This role becomes especially significant in a world characterized by rapidity of change. An apt illustration is provided by the study which documented that educated housewives spending more than the average amount of time in shopping failed to pick the most economical item almost 50 percent of the time.[4] They were unable to make the best choice because there were so many models, sizes, and choices. Hence, the consumer must be helped in the choice process, and advertising can be of real value in this regard.

The actual performance of industry in meeting the information needs of consumers, however, falls far short of the ideal. Consider this example, which is just one of hundreds which could be cited. The late naturalist Euell Gibbons was retained by General Foods in 1973 to advertise its long-established product, Post Grape Nuts. Gibbons claimed that "natural ingredients are important to me . . . its naturally sweet taste reminds me of wild hickory nuts. I call Grape Nuts my back-to-nature cereal." The unfortunate fact is that Grape Nuts is fortified with vitamins and minerals and hence does not qualify as a true natural food, in contrast to recent offerings of competitors. But what will be comprehended by the consumer? It should be obvious to the reader, as Weiss points out,

---

[2] See George J. Stigler, "The Economics of Information," *Journal of Political Economy* 69 (1961), pp. 213–25.

[3] P. Nelson, "The Economic Consequences of Advertising," unpublished paper, State University of New York at Binghamton, 1973, p. 2.

[4] E. B. Weiss, "Markets Fiddle while Consumers Burn," in *Marketing and Social Issues*, ed. J. R. Wish and S. H. Gamble (New York: John Wiley & Sons, 1971), p. 276.

that this is a subtle evasion of fact.[5] This can hardly qualify as advertising which "helps consumers by directing them to the better brands."

This is just one example of the type of competitive behavior which has given rise to the consumerism movement. What has the response of business been to the pressures generated by Ralph Nader and others? Some light was shed by A. G. Woodside's study of advertisers' willingness to document their advertising claims when queried.[6] Most manufacturers were unwilling to provide any justification whatsoever. Only a minority replied affirmatively, leading Woodside to conclude that a typical response was "We do not propose to debate our advertising with you." There were some outstanding exceptions, however, such as the following reply from Charles Hearnshaw of the 3M Company with respect to advertisements in *Time* for Scotch Brand cassette tape:

> As the manufacturer of a quality product, we welcome the opportunity to provide our customers with information of a nature more detailed than that which could be included in a one-page ad. Being proud of our accomplishment, we are eager to share the full story of its superiority. Our only regret is that we so seldom are given the opportunity to completely explain the details of the product's excellence to a willing ear.[7]

In a broader study of company response to consumerism, F. E. Webster, Jr., reports that planned, coordinated programs of response to these pressures are the exception rather than the rule.[8] The usual response is more one of tokenism, and there seems to be a widespread tendency to regard consumerism as a passing fad which "affects the other guy."

Given the pervasiveness of public disenchantment with business veracity today, one is not likely to win a debate by taking the affirmative on the informative role of advertising.[9] All that can be concluded is that advertising *can* and *does* perform this role when it is managed responsibly and is conditioned by a genuine consumer orientation. Unfortunately the exceptions speak so loudly that the public is skeptical.

Effects on New Products and Price

New-product development.   It is claimed by the apologist for advertising that buyer interest does not attain sufficient intensity in the absence of promotion to justify investment by manufacturers in new products.

---

[5] E. B. Weiss, "Does Consumerism Show Signs of Giving up the Ghost?" *Advertising Age,* April 30, 1973, p. 47.

[6] A. G. Woodside, "The Documentation of Advertising Claims," *Scan* 21, no. 4, p. 18.

[7] Ibid.

[8] F. E. Webster, Jr., "Does Business Misunderstand Consumerism?" *Harvard Business Review,* September–October, 1973, pp. 89–97.

[9] See for example T. P. Hustad and E. A. Pessemier, "Will the Real Consumer Activist Please Stand Up," Paper no. 345, Herman C. Krannert Graduate School of Industrial Administration, Purdue University, March 1972.

Advertising, it is said, provides that stimulus, along with a quick and economical way of reaching a mass market with product information and persuasive communication. It is contended that the rapid rate of new-product development that is so characteristic of the American economy would be substantially reduced without advertising.

Does advertising, in fact, influence the rate of product development? Most would answer in the affirmative. Buyer adoption of new products is slow and, as a result, advertising and selling contribute to the quick establishment of large-scale demand which is necessary to serve as a profit incentive for the producer.

Advertising stimulates product development in other ways as well. Producers in oligopolistic markets compete largely on a nonprice basis, and competitive advertising can be self-defeating unless the producer can somehow claim its product is superior. Such pressures provide incentive for product differentiation and improvement.

Mass selling contributes to product quality in yet another (often overlooked) manner. Producers seldom enter the market for a one-shot, hit-and-run sale. The profitable manufacture and sale of an advertised brand requires continued satisfied use by a mass market of buyers, and maintenance of quality is essential for repeat purchase. The buyer is not likely to repurchase unless personal demands are satisfied. Therefore, both the buyer and the producer can be served simultaneously. This relationship is not unique to Western societies; it was found, for example, that the incidence of shoddy merchandise and buyer deception declined sharply in the Soviet Union after producers were encouraged to identify their products.[10] Customer loyalty cannot be generated unless quality is maintained.

Effect on prices. One of the alleged economic contributions of promotion on a mass scale is to lower the costs of production and distribution through facilitating economies of scale. According to this argument, promotion permits producers to offer goods to the public at lower prices than would otherwise be possible. Advertising can affect price also by reducing distribution margins on brands. This can happen for two reasons: (1) goods are caused to turn over so rapidly that they can be sold profitably at a smaller markup, and (2) product identity is created which permits the public to compare prices between stores, thus setting a limit on the retailer's pricing freedom.[11]

There is, in fact, no current definitive evidence to contend that advertising either lowers or raises price.[12] It should be pointed out, however,

---

[10] Marshall Goldman, "Product Differentiation and Advertising: Some Lessons from Soviet Experience," *Journal of Political Economy* 68 (August 1960), pp. 346–57.

[11] R. Steiner, "Does Advertising Lower Consumer Prices?" *Journal of Marketing* 37 (1973), pp. 19–26.

[12] Ibid.

that production and selling costs can be reduced only when firms have excess capacity which can be utilized if sales volume is expanded. When this does not exist, there are no economies of scale to be generated. This fact may help explain some of the ambiguities in the evidence. But even if costs are reduced, it is by no means clear that the gains will be passed on to buyers as lower prices. While the most intensively advertised product categories have, in fact, shown smaller increases in price than their less heavily advertised counterparts since World War II, the differences in price levels are not large.[13]

It is also possible to argue plausibly that advertising can *raise* prices. In the first place, some contend that advertising is inherently wasteful for the reason that rival appeals cancel one another.[14] The only price effect of advertising then is to add to the costs of each firm, and ultimately to the level of prices. It is undeniable that this argument has a substantial measure of truth. When competitors are advertising to gain market share, efforts often are offsetting. No competitor will succeed unless one has some skill or product advantage not possessed by the others. This can, of course, be a powerful incentive for product innovation.

Others allege that advertising affects price adversely by encouraging competition to achieve product differentiation, which enables the firms to develop a high level of brand loyalty. This brand loyalty in turn renders demand less responsive to changes in price, with the result that firms thereby avoid price competition and, at times, charge higher prices than would otherwise be possible.[15]

While advertising can affect brand loyalty as the critics claim, it is dangerous to argue that brand loyalty in itself permits a firm to engage in anticompetitive behavior. The evidence supports an opposite conclusion, because brand-share stability is often lower for the most heavily advertised product categories.[16] In reality, high advertising levels frequently result from the introduction of new products to counteract consumer dissatisfaction with existing brands. Therefore, advertising outlays often are the result of brand *disloyalty* rather than *loyalty*. Advertising itself is incapable of maintaining consumer acceptance of an unsatisfactory product.

It is true that price competition is avoided in certain industries, but once again it is false to assign the causative role to advertising. The indus-

---

[13] Jules Backman, *Advertising and Competition* (New York: New York University Press, 1967), p. 144.

[14] See Donald F. Turner, "Advertising and Competitors," address to Conference on Federal Controls of Advertising-Promotion (1966).

[15] See for example Colston E. Warne, "Advertising: A Critic's View," *Journal of Marketing* 26 (October 1962), p. 12.

[16] L. G. Telser, "Some Aspects of the Economics of Advertising," *Journal of Business* 41 (April 1968), p. 169.

tries usually referred to by critics are oligopolies characterized by a few large firms producing similar products. It is not economically feasible to engage in price competition because price changes are promptly met by competitors. The net result can be ruinous for the entire industry. Therefore, it is to be expected that nonprice competition will prevail.

Granted that nonprice competition is prevalent in many industries, this does not necessarily mean that advertising under such circumstances is socially detrimental. First it must not be overlooked that few markets are truly static. There always are new customers entering, so advertising can perform a broader function than merely shifting the boundaries of market share. Moreover, it should be apparent to any observer of the economic system that companies seldom succeed under oligopoly if an unchanging product-service mix is maintained for long. Powerful incentives exist to expand market share through product improvement, and the companies remaining on top do so through innovative marketing. The buyer, of course, is a beneficiary.

To mention yet another point in rebuttal, there are powerful counter-effects to the long-run avoidance of price competition. Distributors quickly enter mature markets with private brands at lower prices. Furthermore, firms past the peak of a product lifecycle seldom can reverse the downturn with advertising, and, as a result, turn to price as an alternative.

Effects on Competition and Market Structure

The defender of mass promotion often bases much of the argument on the premise that it facilitates and strengthens competition. Incentive is generated for product improvement so that the firm has unique benefits to feature in its advertising. By this means any given competitor is deterred from attaining a monopoly position. Without this incentive for innovation it is contended that market shares of existing firms would stabilize, and there would be general stagnation insofar as product improvement is concerned.

The issue of competition and market structure has long drawn the critics' fire. Two types of rebuttal to the argument of the beneficial effects of promotion are offered: (1) large companies drive weaker competitors out of business through sheer financial power, and (2) the necessary volume of advertising creates barriers for entry of new firms into a market. Many feel that large firms have acquired such a degree of advertising power that competition is eliminated and market shares are concentrated within a limited number of firms in the industry. The U.S. Supreme Court, arguing from this point of view, ordered the Proctor & Gamble Company to divest itself of the Clorox Company on the grounds that Clorox had gained an unfair advantage over competitors. The FTC has since followed this same line of reasoning in several other cases.

If advertising truly reduces competition in this manner, as contended, then there should be high levels of advertising in those industries in which leading firms have a large share of the market, and vice versa. While this is true in some industries (soaps, cigarettes, and others) it is untrue in others such as drugs and cosmetics.[17] Furthermore, advertising power alone does not ensure permanence of market share; in fact only 13 of 50 industries had the same top four companies in both 1947 and 1958.[18] This trend has continued into the 1980s.

Insofar as the second argument is concerned, the following is a typical statement from those who contend that high level of advertising expenditure creates a barrier which prevents the entry of new firms into the market:

. . . the second most disturbing feature of advertising . . . lies in the area of monopoly power it has placed in the hands of the most substantial spenders (that is, investors in advertising). The national advertising outlay is not evenly divided among contenders for customers. It bulks with a very heavy weight at the top. It appears difficult, if not impossible, today to launch a new brand of food or drug without the outlay of as much as $10 million. If this is true, then what we face is a fantastic tax upon freedom of market entry.[19]

It is futile to deny that the heavy marketing investment necessary to survive in most markets today is a deterrent to entry. Moreover, existing firms have built brand loyalty, which prevents newcomers from finding an easy foothold. Once again, however, advertising is assigned a burden which it does not bear alone. Large capital outlays, investment in inventories, the establishment of distributive networks, and other components of successful marketing all are deterrents to entry. In fact, high concentration in many industries developed *without* advertising. Perhaps it is more realistic to state that the requirements of a large scale of operation are the fundamental deterrent to entry, and advertising is only one manifestation.[20]

If advertising does create barriers to entry, this should be demonstrated by a correlation between levels of advertising and profit rates. The evidence on this point is mixed. The strongest negative evidence comes from the food industry, where it was found that profits are highest among the heaviest advertisers.[21] This was not found in an analysis of the 100 leading advertisers, however.[22]

Even if advertising does help to contribute to entry barriers, this does

[17] Telser, "Aspects of Economics of Advertising," p. 169.

[18] Backman, *Advertising and Competition*, p. 113.

[19] Warne, "Advertising: A Critics View," p. 12.

[20] Backman, *Advertising and Competition*, p. 79.

[21] *Advertising Age*, May 11, 1970, pp. 1 ff.

[22] Backman, *Advertising and Competition*, p. 154.

not necessarily imply absence of competition within the industry. As Jules Backman points out: "That competition is both vigorous and intensive among companies already in the market is clearly apparent from the marked increases in the number of products available and the significant changes that continue to take place in the market shares in most industries."[23]

To sum up, available evidence does not support the case of either the advocate or the critic of the influence of advertising on market structure. There is undoubtedly a complex of other causative factors, of which mass promotion is only one.

The Validity of the Fundamental Premises

It is difficult indeed to make a strong case for large-scale advertising and selling using the traditional arguments. The case has not been conclusively disproved by its critics, but neither has it been proved by its advocates.

However, consider the implications of a successful challenge of the two fundamental tenets stated above, that a high and rising standard of living is a valid social goal and that profit is an accurate measure of business performance. The effects of the basic functions of promotion could become almost irrelevant, because the foundation of the case would have been removed. This section, which questions the validity of these premises, therefore deserves careful consideration.

Is a high and rising standard of living a valid social goal? The basic premise contends that society should work toward the goal of a continually higher standard of living. This premise is the target of formidable challenges from two sources: (1) environmentalism and (2) historical precedent.

Environmentalism. The world is beginning to awaken to the fact that its basic resources are not inexhaustible. Unfortunately Western societies, the United States in particular, have proceeded as if air, water, minerals, and other resources were free goods that could be used without restriction. Ownership of these resources has been viewed as a common property right to be used by all with the cost to be borne by society as a whole. The fallacies of such thinking were placed in sharp perspective in 1972 when Meadows and colleagues warned that the quality of life inevitably will decline in the face of unchecked population growth, pollution, and exploitation of natural resources.[24]

These concerns are the rallying cry of a movement which has come to be known as environmentalism. Environmentalists would broaden soci-

---

[23] Ibid., p. 8.
[24] D. H. Meadows, et al., *The Limit to Growth* (New York: Universal Books, 1972).

etal consensus beyond consumer satisfaction to focus on maximization of *life quality*. They reject a marketing concept centering only on filling consumer needs and add the dimensions of societal and ecological considerations. Make no mistake about the muscle exhibited by this movement because many an industry has been hit by regulations forcing concern about the ecological properties of product and packaging.

What this all comes down to is that a marketing system cannot be evaluated simply on the basis of what it does to enhance materialistic desires. Environmentalists are forcing the use of yet another criterion reflecting fears about the very survival of a way of life. Meadows et al. use the analogy of a pond which contains a crop of lilies that doubles in quantity every two days and will totally consume the pond and cause it to die in 30 days.[25] On the 29th day the pond will only be half covered, and there is just one day remaining to prevent disaster. In their opinion, the world is either at or approaching the 29th day.

Historical precedent.   A second type of challenge may be even more devastating. This comes from the careful student of history. There is no convincing historical precedent that an increase in standard of living means true social progress in any basic sense. Quite to the contrary, a generalized quest for personal wealth and economic attainment often has been symptomatic of a society in the last stages of decay. Consider the observations of Will and Ariel Durant:

Caught in the relaxing interval between one moral code and the next, an unmoored generation surrenders itself to luxury, corruption, and a restless disorder of family and morals, in all but a remnant clinging desperately to old restraints and ways. Few souls feel any longer that "it is beautiful and honorable to die for one's country." A failure of leadership may allow a state to weaken itself with internal strife. At the end of the process a decisive defeat in war may bring a final blow, or barbarian invasion from without may combine with barbarism welling up from within to bring the civilization to a close.[26]

It may well be that present-day Western societies mirror ancient Rome's free-living days before its ultimate fall generated by decay from within. As materialism and economic achievement were carried to extremes, they contributed, along with other factors, to the eventual collapse of one of the most advanced civilizations to date. It is possible that promotion is only accentuating the very forces which may be bringing our civilization to its knees.

Is profit a valid measure of business responsibility?   It has traditionally been held that profits are an objective measure of the social values of ideas and that the national consensus is found in market performance.[27]

---

[25] Meadows, et al., *The Limit to Growth.*

[26] Will and Ariel Durant, *The Lessons of History* (New York: Simon & Schuster, 1968), p. 93. Reproduced with special permission.

[27] Joel Dean, *Managerial Economics* (Englewood Cliffs, N.J.: Prentice-Hall, 1951), p. 10.

In other words, motivation to attain a long-run profit results in service to society because profit will not result unless buyer needs and desires are served in a satisfactory manner. If this contention is true, profit will be the reward of the firm that has been most successful in following the marketing concept which embodies at its heart adaptation to the desires of the consumer.

For most of the period since World War II, there has been some validity to this point of view because, on the whole, the firms that have been most successful have been those with the most responsive marketing programs. *Assuming a high and rising standard of living to be valid,* the consumer has been served materially by the firm which continually strives to gain a competitive edge through marketing innovation. It was quite acceptable in 1960 to allege that "A manager can say he is putting 'fairness' or 'the good of society' ahead of profits, but the suspicion arises that he is merely escaping from accountability into the realm where there are no checks on his power."[28]

But does a striving for profit allow for a restraint which takes account of environmentalism and other issues concerned with survival of a way of life? Kenneth Boulding has observed that there is a marked distinction between the profit system as an organizer of economic life and the profit motive in the "bad" sense of unadulterated lust for selfish gain.[29] Many now agree that the profit system functions successfully only if the profit motive is tempered by altruism or by a sense of public responsibility and identification with the individual in a larger community.[30] In the final analysis, profit must be defined to encompass more than mere financial attainment. Without such a broadened conception, business practices may be considered justifiable which, from the perspective of history, might be counter to the public interest. In reality, the premise underlying profit orientation is that business must be *accountable* for its performance— accountable to owners and stockholders in the traditional financial sense but also to consumers and to society at large.

Are there any solutions? It should be apparent that the conventional wisdom regarding the economic and social role of promotion is open to challenge. An increasing number of voices are uniting to advocate some sort of radical change in the free enterprise system. All involve some type of constraint on traditional economic forces motivated by profit.

John K. Galbraith, for example, has long been concerned with the viability of an economic system that operates with unrestrained self-

---

[28] "Have Corporations a Higher Duty Than Profits?" *Fortune,* August 1960, p. 108 ff.

[29] Kenneth Boulding, "Ethics and Business: An Economists' View," in *Marketing and Social Issues,* pp. 91–97.

[30] See for example H. M. Williams, "Why and How Are We Losing the Free Enterprise Battle," *Advertising Age,* November 26, 1972, p. 34 and W. C. Engs, "Needed: New Rules for Industrial Managers," in *Marketing and Social Issues,* pp. 228–32.

interest.[31] His writings have evolved over the years, and he now advocates an equalization of power between planning and marketing systems.[32] He calls for a freeze of prices, costs, and incomes. The wealthier members of the "technostructure," for example, would not be permitted to grow more affluent, and the gains from economic productivity would go largely to increasing the incomes of poorer segments of the population. Profit motivation as well as individual materialistic acquisition thus would be sharply curbed in the interests of restoring a balance of power between the various economic groups and entities. Presumably greater income equality and a better quality of life would evolve.

There is some undeniable appeal to such proposals, especially given the excesses and abuses discussed above. Yet, it is necessary to consider some basic premises of this viewpoint. Would our materialistic striving change if the economic and social environment is radically changed? There is an all-important yet unexpressed assumption that man enters the world with no inherent predisposition to become self-centered and hence materialistic. These strivings then are shaped by the environment in which we live.[33] If this premise about the nature of humans indeed is true, then the logical solution lies in changing the environment through radical reform if necessary. We then will change, and a more utopian world can be achieved.

There is, however, a diametrically opposed view of the nature of man which would lead to quite a different conclusion as to the most appropriate course of action to be taken in order to achieve social change. After a lifetime study of history, the Durants conclude that:

> . . . the first biological lesson of history is that life is competition. Competition is not only the life of trade, it is the trade of life—peaceful when food abounds, violent when the mouths outrun the food. . . . we are acquisitive, greedy, and pugnacious because our blood remembers millenniums through which our forebearers had to chase and fight and kill in order to survive, and had to eat their gastric capacity for fear they should not soon capture another feast.[34]

They go on to point out that this basic nature of humans does not change: "nothing is clearer in history than the adoption by successful rebels of the methods they were accustomed to condemn in the forces they deposed."[35]

---

[31] In his earlier writing, Galbraith contended that advertising does nothing more than build a system that cannot meet its basic survival needs. See John K. Galbraith, *The Affluent Society* (Boston: Houghton Mifflin, 1958).

[32] John K. Galbraith, *Economics and the Public Purpose* (New York: Houghton Mifflin Co., 1973).

[33] This is the widely accepted point of view articulated most convincingly by B. F. Skinner. See *Beyond Freedom and Dignity* (New York: Alfred A. Knopf, 1971).

[34] Durant and Durant, *Lessons of History,* p. 19.

[35] Ibid., p. 34.

According to this view we are constrained by human nature to live a self-centered life, according to the dictates of our ego. Thus excessive materialism, war, moral decay, and so on are *symptoms of a problem inherent within man himself,* with the result that a change in the environment would not strike at the heart of the problem. This is also the Judeo-Christian view, which proceeds from the premise that we are incomplete within ourself, that we are sinners and cannot bring about fundamental internal change apart from a faith in a personal god and total commitment of one's life to that god.

The Durants, proceeding from their premise about our acquisitive and competitive nature, have concluded that profit is an inevitable necessity:

The experience of the past leaves little doubt that every economic system must sooner or later rely upon some form of the profit motive to stir individuals and groups to productivity. Substitutes like slavery, police supervision, or ideological enthusiasm prove too unproductive, too expensive, or too transient. Normally and generally men are judged by their ability to produce—except in war, when they are ranked according to their ability to destroy.[36]

If the Judeo-Christian view is true, then the changes must come from within ourselves as a result of the exercise of our volition, *not* from changes in the environment. How such a change takes place, of course, raises spiritual questions which are beyond the scope of this book. A real dilemma thus faces the individual. Each reader must decide the issue personally as we take our place in a complex world.

Can the Present System Be Made to Work?

The authors do not believe that radical social reform is necessary, for we feel that the system can be made to work. We agree with Boulding when he says that there is nothing inherent in the profit system per se which requires a narrow selfishness and lack of identification with the broader concerns of mankind.[37] The key is to adopt a proper attitude with respect to social and ethical responsibility.

Social responsibility is less demanding in that it embodies accepting an obligation for the proper functioning of the society in which a firm exists. It involves accountability for those activities through which the firm can reasonably be expected to contribute to the society. Often it requires little more than obedience to existing laws and norms.

More is required than social responsibility, however, as one businessman colorfully points out:

If the law as written gives a man a wide-open chance to make a killing, he'd be a fool not to take advantage of it. If he doesn't somebody else will. There is

---

[36] Ibid., pp. 54–55.
[37] Boulding, "Ethics and Business."

no obligation on him to stop and consider who is going to get hurt. If the law says he can do it, that's all the justification he needs. There is nothing unethical about that. It's just plain business sense.[38]

In this context, a produce manager in a supermarket who gets rid of a lot of half-rotten tomatoes by including one with its good side exposed in every pack is doing nothing socially improper. After all, it *is* legal.

This kind of short-sightedness cannot contend with the current critical challenges to our way of life. Whether he likes it or not, the businessperson must also wrestle with *ethical responsibility*—determination of *how* things should be, pursuit of the right course of action, and doing what is morally right. This responsibility requires a finely developed sense of values which provides a real code for behavior. It must be assumed that one choice is better than others when many options are available. The major perplexity is to develop a value system so that the best choice is made, given the complex of influences on management today.

ORGANIZATIONAL RESPONSE TO A CHANGED ENVIRONMENT

The pressures on today's manager are multifaceted. Decisions must be made which satisfy not only traditional monetary profit criteria but also the pressures from consumers, labor, government, and a host of other sources. Old rules are obsolete; times have changed. The question is no longer whether changes *will* occur in business practice but rather *how these changes will occur and what form they will take.* Those who long for an earlier more comfortable era and cling to "business as usual" have no place in today's world.

The Organizational Mission

It has traditionally been assumed that profits are an objective measure of the contribution of a business organization to society. The shortcomings of this point of view were explored above. Profit is just one form of *accountability;* as Peter Drucker points out, all institutions must now hold themselves accountable for the quality of life and must make fulfillment of basic social values, beliefs, and purposes a major objective of their normal activities.[39]

Financial accountability. Frequently the financially successful firm is viewed as suspect, especially if it has gained at the expense of its competitors. It must be recognized, however, that buyer desires for new and improved products are met through competition, and firms cannot compete without some emerging as victorious and others suffering losses.

---

[38] A. C. Carr, "Is Business Loving Ethical?" in *Marketing and Social Issues*, p. 107.

[39] Peter F. Drucker, "Management's New Role," in *Marketing and Social Issues*, pp. 24–28.

Moreover, it is often overlooked that successful businesses are managed to enhance the long-run survival of the organization. The firm, especially if it is incorporated, outlives any individual set of managers, and successful management must of necessity be oriented toward survival on a money-making basis. It cannot afford to extract a momentary gain from shoddy merchandise, because reliance must be placed on repeat sales. Repeat sales, in turn, will not be made to dissatisfied customers, so the firm is forced to serve the customer's interests.

Accountability to consumers. A "Guide to Consumerism" stipulates that the consumer is entitled to "(1) Protection against clear-cut abuses . . . (2) provision for adequate information . . . (3) protection . . . against themselves and other consumers.[40] Consumerism has arisen because management has been guilty of *one-way communication with the buyer; it is not listening to what is being said in reply.* Of course, most firms give lip service to the marketing concept, but does it really pervade their corporate missions? A survey of 250 leading corproate executives revealed that over two thirds of them are having difficulties with consumer activists, but the vast majority feel that the cause is *failure of business to publicize its good side!* And nearly 80 percent evidenced a belief that the current negative attitude toward business is not justified.[41]

It is difficult to sympathize with the kind of shortsighted management that cannot grasp the true causes of consumerism. The fact is that business is falling short of a consumer orientation. No amount of publicity will correct this situation. If service to the consumer is not a part of the organizational mission, a commitment backed up by action, then there is little hope that voluntarism will work. Government must step in to compel the firms to ensure the legitimate rights of the buyer.

Accountability to society as a whole. "It is increasingly recognized that business must divert some of its profits to help solve social problems or it may face upheavals as serious as those which have swept the college campus." These are the sentiments of the president of Hunt-Wesson Foods, in a speech made to an industry group.[42] Hunt-Wesson is acting on these convictions in many ways, such as improved medical care facilities in the ghetto. It is only one of a number of companies that recognize a broader responsibility, beyond that of financial returns to stockholders. Indeed, survival, the basic goal of any business enterprise, may demand expenditures and efforts directed to basic social problems.

It is obvious from this discussion that profit, in the narrow sense of financial return, can no longer be a complete measure of the contribution of a firm to society. Accountability, on the other hand, is a more realistic

---

[40] G. S. Day and D. A. Aaker, "A Guide to Consumerism," *Journal of Marketing* 17 (1970), pp. 12–19.

[41] *The Gallagher Report* 20 (November 20, 1972).

[42] Quoted in *Advertising Age,* February 23, 1970, p. 191.

criterion, because it encompasses financial return as well as contributions to broader social issues. As this point is recognized and acted upon responsibly by management, there is reason to hope that many of the most flagrant abuses will be corrected and steps taken toward solution of unresolved social problems.

Phasing accountability into strategy.   Most organizations now assign reward to individual managers on the basis of sales performance, regardless of how much publicity they give to social responsibility. As H. M. Williams notes:

> Such an environment does not encourage any activity that does not maximize current profits. Nor does it recognize or penalize shoddy but temporarily profitable marketing and advertising practices. We do not make, nor in many cases do we know how to make or desire to make, estimates of the nonquantifiable or of the social and political implications of achieving plans.[43]

This is accentuated in the product form of organization, which decentralizes corporate and divisional responsibilities.[44] Social concerns tend to be centralized at the headquarters level but do not find their way to those levels at which decisions really are made and implemented. The solution is for top management to initiate appropriate social and ethical considerations, to make compliance a part of the reward and punishment system, and to provide staff help in implementation at decentralized levels.

Cooperative Efforts

Because social and ethical responsibilities will never be met completely by individual organizations, a need exists for cooperative efforts. Certainly as a very minimum an industry should provide a means for curbing false advertising as well as practices which are deceptive or unethical. Unfortunately there are numerous codes of practice that represent nothing more than unenforced platitudes. Such superficial efforts, often undertaken to keep government at bay, do more harm than good in the final analysis, because they are nothing more than a band-aid placed over an open wound.

It is sometimes said that it goes against the grain of free enterprise to make cooperative codes of ethics compulsory, and to an extent we must agree. Nonetheless, it must not be overlooked that the mass media are intended for public use and are not the sole province of the advertiser. Government can present a convincing case for expanded activity to protect the public interest if self-regulation does not suffice. As never before,

---

[43] Williams, "Free Enterprise Battle," p. 34.

[44] R. W. Ackerman, "How Companies Respond to Social Demands," *Harvard Business Review* 51 (1973), pp. 88–99.

the advertising industry is faced with a challenge in this respect which cannot be ignored.

Cooperative efforts have taken the following forms: (1) Better Business bureaus, (2) policing by advertising media, (3) cooperative improvement efforts, and (4) public service.

Better Business bureaus. Local Better Business organizations are sponsored by business firms to eliminate unfair methods of competition. They work with the national Better Business Bureau, which, among other things, publishes *Do's and Don'ts in Advertising Copy* to help advertisers steer clear of legal and ethical hurdles.

Individual customers or business firms initiate complaints to Better Business Bureau offices, and the action taken varies .from publicity to legal action. The volume of advertisements and sales claims investigated each year is said to substantially exceed that processed by governmental enforcement agencies.

Policing by advertising media. The media also have taken some positive steps in the form of industry self-regulation. Magazines and newspapers frequently turn down advertising which in their opinion violates good taste or is deceptive in its claims.

Most of the larger television and radio stations belong to the National Association of Broadcasters (NAB). The NAB issues a seal of approval to stations subscribing to the NAB Code of Good Practice. This code is fairly rigorous in its provisions; it bans, for example, payoffs, rigged quiz shows, and deception regarding product characteristics. This is not to say that all areas of public responsibility are comprehended in this code. There have been numerous attempts to establish the NAB as a more definitive voice within the industry, and support for such an action may be growing.

Cooperative improvement efforts. Industry associations of various types attempt to induce their members to adhere to ethical codes. The Proprietary Drug Association of America, for instance, enforces a code of ethics for its members, who handle over 80 percent of all packaged medicines sold in the United States. Similarly, the Toilet Goods Association operates a board of standards to which members submit advertising copy. The board ensures that the copy is consistent with provisions of the Food, Drug, and Cosmetic Act and other legislation.

One encouraging cooperative effort is the National Advertising Review Board (NARB) sponsored by the Council of Better Business Bureaus and other organizations. Its organization and functioning were discussed in Chapter 9. As noted previously, the council's national advertising division receives and evaluates complaints against advertising. If an agreement cannot be reached, reference is made to the NARB for study by a panel.

Some have contended that NARB efforts have been too few and that its machinery grinds too slowly. There may be merit to this criticism, but hasty judgments also would be unwise. Further assessment of the NARB record must await longer service.

Industry public service. Some members of the business community have long been sensitive to their role in serving the public sector of the economy. The War Advertising Council was the first formal manifestation of this awareness; it was set up during World War II under the sponsorship of advertisers, agencies, media, and trade associations. The primary purpose was to stimulate the sale of War Bonds, and this objective plus others was given a real assist by the industry. This organization was later superceded by the Advertising Council.

The variety of public causes given support by the Advertising Council is impressive. Among the better known organizations and social issues given backing are: (1) aid to higher education, (2) the American Red Cross, (3) United Community appeals, (4) the Radio Free Europe Fund, (5) the Youth Fitness program, and (6) the Smokey the Bear campaign to stamp out forest fires. Costs are underwritten by advertisers, media, and agencies, for the council has only 50 full-time employees.

Further cooperative efforts. There are many additional unmet needs which require cooperative efforts, one of the most crucial being research directed toward a greater understanding of the process of promotion. The barriers of limited information which hinder the effective management of advertising and promotion have been noted throughout this book. Steps have been taken in recent years to dispel these barriers, but they are only a beginning. Basic research is needed into all phases of promotional decisions. Because the pressures of day-to-day management virtually preclude the necessary research efforts by individual firms, a cooperative industry research program is required.

In addition, industry can continue to meet its obligations through expansion of its activities on behalf of public causes. The tools of mass communication are ideally adapted to stimulating public awareness of unmet needs, and the Advertising Council has done excellent work in this respect.

Finally, industry codes of ethics must become more than just platitudes stated for public consumption. Unless real enforcement provisions are established, little purpose is served. If business is serious about cleaning its own house, it must do so through incisive action.

The Individual Manager

If the spirit of social and ethical responsibility discussed here is to be made operative, a commitment to this end is required of individual managers. This commitment, however, often requires a type of personal courage and sacrifice that many are not prepared to give because too many obstacles must be faced.

A 1973 study by the American Management Association found that a majority of the almost 3,000 executives questioned felt under pressure to compromise personal standards to meet company goals.[45] Pressures for profitable performance have been markedly stepped up rather than abated. It is small wonder that 85 percent of all managers face a deep personal conflict when they discover that their youthful ideals and goals run counter to business operations that seem to be low on principle and high on expediency.[46] This conflict is most severe between the ages of 34 and 42, and it often is manifested by unwillingness to take on new problems and a desire to minimize the total demands of a job on one's life.

What is the individual to do when one finds his or her own personal goals to be in conflict with organizational expectations? Researchers at the California Institute of Technology gave this advice: "take a tranquilizer, conform to the system, and realize that there are problems beyond your ability to solve."[47] In other words cop out and conform. This is also the advice of an executive who noted the contradictions he faced but concluded that it is necessary to "play by the rules of the game" if one is to accumulate much money or power.[48]

Are increased salary and advancement really worth that sacrifice? More and more are answering a resounding no to that question and dropping out of the system rather than compromising their convictions. This is sometimes a necessary action, but the end result if all who are similarly in conflict drop out could be disastrous.

Obviously, ethical concerns can no longer be swept under the rug; they must be acted on if a way of life is to survive. This demands people who *dare to be different*—who are willing to seek solutions and act upon their convictions regardless of personal cost. When such a spirit of innovation is absent, there is little basis for optimism about the survival of a way of life whose vitality stems from the exercise of individual initiative.

There are increasing examples of managers who indeed are daring to be different. Creative people in advertising agencies are demanding factual backup of advertising claims from their clients. Younger managers are not hesitating to voice their dissatisfaction with insulting advertising. Executives at all levels are refusing to give in when forced to behave illegally or unethically. The authors are personally familiar with a number who have successfully taken their stands. Others, unfortunately, have taken their stands and paid the price of dismissal, but their personal integrity remains intact.

It must be assumed that each individual has arrived at a workable

[45] *Business Week*, September 15, 1973, p. 178.
[46] *Sales Management*, May 1, 1969, p. 20.
[47] Ibid.
[48] Carr, "Is Business Loving Ethical?"

code of ethics. Some see no problem with subtle deception and other forms of legal but basically immoral business behavior. This speaks volumes about the content of their ethical codes. Far too many conclude that they will do what is necessary for themselves, regardless of the consequences, as long as they do not get caught. This is not the kind of ethical code which will make a real difference in today's world.

Ultimately everyone must come to grips with the eternal question of whether or not there are standards of truth which can govern behavior. Some say no—that truth is illusive and behavior should be based on the whims of the moment. Others place their roots deeply in religious conviction and guide their lives accordingly. Is religion out of place in the business firm? Some may say yes, but others are coming to a commitment that real ethics and morality pervade *all of life,* including life on the job.

Those who have found themselves—who have a workable philosophy of life—have a place to stand from which they can dare to be different. Those who have not come to this point have little choice but to cave in when the pressures become great.

Will Voluntary Self-Regulation Work?

The issue of voluntarism versus governmental control which was raised at the outset of this section must be addressed again. Hopefully, business people, individually and collectively, will be able to meet the challenges of today without intervention by government. Quite honestly, the authors join those who express their doubts. Over half of 1,000 advertising executives indicated that they do not feel the industry can effectively regulate itself.[49] Few advocated more governmental restriction, but they seemed to be without any suggestions for necessary change.

All that need be said in conclusion is that the pressures for sweeping change will not abate. If the industry does not respond, it has only itself to blame when government steps in.

SUMMARY

This chapter has been devoted to a critical analysis of the economic and social role of promotion. The criticisms of this economic activity are far-reaching, and the pros and cons were discussed in terms of their effects on prices, competition, consumer choice, and standards of living.

For the most part, the claimed social benefits of promotion are based on the premise that a high and rising standard of living is valid. Once this premise is disavowed, the issues become more sharply focused, be-

---

[49] *The Gallagher Report* 20 (June 5, 1972).

cause the materialistic society of today's Western world may be sowing the seeds of its own destruction. It was pointed out, however, that the economic system is merely a reflection of the basic motivations of its members, and the ultimate solution lies outside of business itself.

Nevertheless, there is much that can be done through a philosophy of business management which stresses financial accountability to owners and stockholders as well as accountability to consumers and to society as a whole. Some suggestions were given which centered around the corporate mission, collective activities, and the role of the individual manager.

Review and Discussion Questions

1. Many critics of marketing claim that advertising creates impediments to workable price competition. The premise is that greater price competition would enhance consumer welfare. Do you agree?

2. Is the absence of price competition a sign that a business firm has established a monopolistic position?

3. Can the blame for development of economic concentration within a few firms in an industry be attributed to advertising? Why, or why not?

4. In the early 1960s a detergent in tablet form, Vim, was introduced for a short period and then removed from the market because of unsatisfactory sales. Assume that the company could come into possession of unlimited financial resources. Could increased advertising expenditures have saved this product?

5. A well-known student of consumer affairs made the following statement to a group of home economists at a national meeting: "One of the greatest problems consumers face is lack of adequate information in making a purchase decision. They lack the know-how to be rational buyers, and business is not about to do anything to help them. The only hope is for government and other agencies to step in and give the consumer the information she needs." Comment.

6. Are the mass media, in your opinion, influenced by advertisers to present editorial content compatible with vested interests? If so, what suggestions can you make for change?

7. William Lazer has argued that marketing should work toward the end of helping the consumer to accept self-indulgence, luxurious surroundings, and nonutilitarian products. Do you agree?

8. Many proposals are advanced to reform the practice of advertising. Some have as their intent the elimination or reduction of the volume of advertising and hence a reduction of the socially detrimental effects of undue materialism. In your opinion, will this type of reform be a meaningful step in solving the basic underlying problems?

9. What is consumerism? What are some of the ways that business can adapt meaningfully to the pressures being generated?

10. The president of Hunt-Wesson Foods proposes that business must divert some of its profits to help solve social problems. However, this may serve to reduce the financial rewards to stockholders, thus giving rise to what might become a conflict of interest. Can this conflict be resolved?

11. In what sense are many criticisms of promotion really a criticism of poor management?

12. Congress has enacted into law safety standards for automobiles. Should this legislation have been necessary, or can cooperative industry efforts suffice for such purposes?

Designing and Producing the Mass Communication Message

INTRODUCTION

This section is written for those who are charged with the responsibility for doing the creative work required for the production of a variety of mass communication messages. It is for practitioners and students who have to put together the various components of the creative mix and eventually have to look at the messages and say yes or no.

There are several objectives for this appendix. First, it is the intention of the authors to bring together various types of production treatments from a number of sources. Second, sets of operational guidelines have been outlined at numerous points to suggest techniques, procedures, or methods for managing the creative aspects of advertising messages. They should not be considered as rules made for the obedience of fools but rather as suggestions for the guidance of wise people in the advertising business.

The language of advertising is very much like the language of war: campaigns are "launched" for new products, messages are "aimed" at "target" audiences, and advertising "strategies" employ certain "offensive" and "defensive" "tactics" in order to reach marketing goals. In this respect the process of producing advertising is akin to the one generals might employ in working out battle plans or determining goals for the achievement of military objectives.

In discussing the design and production of the mass communication message we will not repeat the materials presented earlier which suggest the ways in which a product or service is positioned. This takes into account the various parts of the marketing mix that help determine the marketing strategy and the tactics to implement in execution. In various chapters suggestions were given on how to build different strategies and the steps that can be taken to carry them out. Here is a summary:

1. State the marketing objective or objectives.
2. Make the strategy or strategies fit the marketing plans.
3. Put the strategies in writing.
4. Make the objectives and strategies reasonable.
5. Be single-minded; great plans can be carried out when they are not fragmented by multidirectional goals.
6. Check your competition.
7. Determine whether your increased business may come from someone else's business.
8. Understand your target audience.
9. Make a meaningful promise to the buyer.
10. Support your promises with convincing evidence.
11. Make your product unique; set yourself apart.
12. Agree on what is most important about your product.
13. Think ahead, don't underestimate your competition.
14. Keep your strategy up to date.
15. Have a good product or service to offer.

THE HEADLINE

The headline is often considered to be "what would be said if only one or two lines of space were available for the message." It must put forth the main theme or appeal in a few words. Considered in this context, there is no reason to make it less than a powerful selling message.

Without doubt the headline shoulders a large part of the task of attracting the reader's attention. It should tell the whole story, including the *brand name* and the *promise* to the buyer. Otherwise the advertiser is wasting his money. Research shows that four out of five readers never get farther than the headline. The illustration also aids in attracting and holding attention, but readership studies repeatedly demonstrate that the headline is the major component in attracting attention. If it is not powerful, many good prospects will never get far enough into the ad to read the message.

Classifications of Headlines

Headline information serves various purposes. It may (1) provide news, (2) state product claims, (3) give advice, (4) select prospects, (5) arouse curiosity, or (5) identify product or company name.

News. This type of headline plays a role similar to its counterpart in the news story, for it often summarizes the point of highest interest in the copy. To command attention and arouse interest, such a headline must be pertinent and timely. It dispenses with cleverness and gimmicks and uses a direct, straight-selling approach. "Chevrolet Wins the Mobil Economy Run" is an example.

Product claim. Featuring a product claim can be a good attention-getter in that it appeals to the reader's self-interest. The claim should be significant and believable. A headline that says "This Tire Will Give You Good Mileage" would have less impact than one that says "This Tire Gives 30% More Mileage Than Competitively Priced Tires." One might expect many brands of tires to give good mileage, but 30 percent more is something worth looking into.

While there are many examples of successful headlines that make claims, the use of this approach has been somewhat weakened by advertising that makes irresponsible statements. You should proceed on the assumption that the reader will be dubious. To ensure believability, care should be taken to provide ample supporting evidence in the copy.

Advice. Advice given in a headline may be followed by a promise of results from product use. Such a headline is "You Owe It to Yourself to Try Slimmo Reducing Tablets," with a secondary headline featuring a claim: "Use Slimmo Ten Days and Lose Ten Pounds." A properly conceived advice headline appeals to the reader's self-interest in that it is aimed at helping him solve a problem or prevent its occurrence.

Prospect selection. Because very few products are of interest to everyone, the advertisement should appeal only to potential customers. The headline is a principal device in the process of selecting prospects from among readers. Copy striving to reach everyone is usually so generalized that its effectiveness is lost. A headline that says "New Drug Aids Those Who Suffer from Asthma" would be a combination of *news* and *selectivity*. In other situations the headline may be purely selective in purpose, as in the headline that says "Attention, June Graduates." The great majority of headlines are selective to some extent, regardless of emphasis.

Curiosity. Sometimes referred to as the provocative approach, the curiosity-oriented headline attempts to arouse interest through appeal to the unusual. It is hoped that the reader will be stimulated to read the copy text to find the answer to a "riddle" that is posed.

The curiosity approach can be used when some aspect of the product is of such genuine and timely interest that the reader is predisposed to seek information. A headline that asks "Are Your Protected from Atomic Pollutants?" would arouse interest on the part of many people and induce them to read the text for more information. Volkswagen has made effective use of this approach. In one of the most memorable advertisements in its campaigns the headline read, "Lemon." Then the copy proceeded to explain the quality control procedures which prevent the customer from getting a "lemon."

The curiosity headline gives the copywriter great freedom in the use of his or her imagination, and its use can be tempting. However, some experts caution against the use of this approach in situations in which a direct-selling headline would be more appropriate. The curiosity type of headline too often is used for the sake of novelty alone, and, as was pointed out in Chapter 14, novelty without meaning is not creativity.

Product or company name. Occasionally the name of the product or company is used as the headline. This approach might be effective when the product is of such timely interest that the mere mention of the name is sufficient to arouse interest. In World War II a headline reading "Tires" would have attracted real attention from consumers in a market of scarcity. Substantial interest among many ethnic and racial groups can be obtained today by giving recognition to integrated racial relationships.

Some Guides for a Persuasive Headline

A fair amount of published research is available which delineates the characteristics of headlines that are effective in attracting attention. Although there is general agreement on certain of these characteristics, they can be violated successfully in many situations. There is a real difference, however, between violating a known criterion intentionally and violating it through ignorance.

Researchers at Marplan have found that confining the headline area to a small portion of the advertisement and using only one or two lines of type will produce the highest readership.[1] In addition, David Ogilvy mentions the following criteria:

1. On the average, five times as many people read the headline as read the body copy. If you haven't done some selling in your headline, you have wasted 80 percent of your client's money.
2. Headlines should appeal to the reader's *self-interest,* by promising a benefit. This benefit should be the basic promise of the product.
3. Inject the maximum news into your headlines.
4. Include the *brand name* in every headline.
5. Write headlines which force the reader to read your subhead and body copy.
6. Don't worry about the *length* of the headline—*twelve*-word headlines get almost as much readership as three-word headlines. Headlines in the six-to-twelve-word group get the most coupon replies. Better a long headline that sells then a short one which is blind and dumb.

[1] "Basic Readership Factors," internal publication of Marplan Division of the Interpublic Group of Companies, Inc., New York.

7. Never change typeface in the middle of the headline; it reduces readership.
8. Never use a headline which requires readership of body copy to be comprehensible.
9. Never use tricky or irrelevant headlines.
10. Use words to select your prospects—like MOTHER and VARICOSE VEINS.
11. Use words which have been found to contain emotional impact.

KISS	DARLING	INSULT	HAPPY
LOVE	ANGRY	MONEY	WORRY
MARRY	FIGHT	FAMILY	BABY[2]

It is also generally accepted that the headline must be simple and easily understood. Moreover, it must join with the other message elements in presenting a unified and coherent message.[3]

COPY

During construction of the headline, ideas flow toward the next step—writing the body copy. An idea put aside as inadequate for the headline often becomes a subhead, a copy block lead line, or the lead for successive copy paragraphs. The copy reinforces the headline and delivers the sales message.

Whatever writing form the copywriter chooses to express the selling points, he will find that there is an ever-increasing demand for facts. It is a naive copywriter who does not include hard information on the product and its benefits throughout the message.

Classification of Copy Approaches

It is useful to classify copy approaches by manner of presentation.[4] In *direct-selling news* copy, for example, the message is presented in a straightforward manner similar to the informative content of newspaper articles. New-product messages are typical examples. In contrast, *implied suggestion* gives the reader an opportunity to draw conclusions from the facts which are presented. Usually the facts are obvious enough to direct the reader to a favorable conclusion about the product or service.

In *narrative description,* the copywriter starts with an account of some human experience that presents a problem and the solution in terms of favorable orientation toward a product. In a related copy type, the *story form,* human experience also is used in a straightforward account of product

---

[2] David Ogilvy, "Raise Your Sights! 97 Tips for Copywriters, Art Directors and TV Producers—Mostly Derived from Research" internal publication of Ogilvy, Benson, & Mather, New York. Reproduced with special permission.

[3] Hugh G. Wales, Dwight Gentry, and Max Wales, *Advertising Copy, Layout and Typography* (New York: Ronald Press, 1958), p. 155.

[4] Ibid., pp. 189–200.

use by a purchaser. It also may involve an analogy between a storybook use and the product itself.

One effective approach is to use *monologue* and *dialogue.* The monologue is a single subject, such as a person (or an animal) reporting on personal reactions to certain goods and services. The dialogue presents a conversation between two persons (or animals) who elaborate on the merits of the product. This often can be in the form of a *testimonial message.* One benefit of the testimonial is the implied opportunity for the reader to emulate or imitate the person giving the testimonial. The testimonial is also employed to provide a means of stating authoritatively that certain benefits can be found in using a product or service by following the exemplary behavior of the person or persons giving the testimony.

Humor can be very effective if the entertainment value of the presentation has real selling appeal to those who are exposed to the message. Messages that deal with food, drinks, and entertainment generally find this an appropriate form. More is said shortly about the use of humor.

Finally, some use can be made of the *comic strip* or *continuity* forms. These have found growing use because of the popularity of children's television programming and fictional characters, but its effectiveness is limited by mechanical problems in production of the comic strip.

Some Copy Problems

The use of humor. As mentioned above, considerable use is made of humor, but this should not be regarded as an index of its effectiveness. Many agree with Ogilvy's statement: "Humorous copy does not sell. It is never used by the great copywriters—only by amateurs."[5]

Others would not take such a strong stand, but research findings seem to support the conclusion that humorous commercials generally are less effective than their nonhumorous counterparts. The Schwerin Research Corporation reports that commercials featuring *all* humor (less than 4 percent of all advertisements) seldom prove to be as effective as other approaches. However, some use of humor, in general, will help the commercial to perform better than a commercial with no humor whatsoever.[6] The conclusion, then, is that humor at its best is used sparingly.

The purpose of advertising is *not* to entertain. Few advertisements can entertain and sell simultaneously; both elements are combined only through use of great skill.

Answering competitors' claims. Perhaps it is human nature for an advertiser to react defensively when attacked by a competitor. While direct competitive derogation is seen infrequently, many advertisers indi-

---

[5] Ogilvy, "Raise Your Sights!"

[6] *Schwerin Research Corporation Bulletin,* vol. 10 (October 1964).

rectly attack competitors through their own strong claims of superiority.

There is real danger in a direct counterattack. If a competitor makes the claim, for example, that its make of automobile is the "quietest on the road," it has in effect appropriated that claim for itself. If it is answered by a counterclaim stating that "we also are quiet," the earlier statement is reinforced. Lindley Frazer has concluded from his study of propaganda in World War II that propaganda always must be offensive, not defensive.[7] If an appeal is answered, this lends credence to it.

Direct-action copy. Much advertising copy is designed to activate those in the final stages of their decision-making process as they move toward purchase. Similarly, the copy may serve to lead those now preferring a brand to purchase it more frequently and in greater quantities.

Among the many direct-action approaches are samples, contests, coupons and price offers, premiums, and combinations of related products. Some of the objectives to be attained are:

1. To obtain new triers and convert them into regular users.
2. To introduce new or improved products.
3. To increase brand awareness or awareness of a new package.
4. To increase readership of advertising by using coupons as attention-attracting devices.
5. To stimulate reseller support.

Success with the direct-action approach is most likely where brand loyalty is low. A buyer may actively seek a special incentive to buy, such as a price reduction. In addition, the direct-action method can be highly effective when the product or service being advertised possesses no distinct competitive advantage. For this reason, coupons and other incentives are a basic competitive tool among manufacturers of soaps, breakfast foods, cake mixes, and other items where no single firm can claim uniqueness and where brand loyalty is not especially strong.

The direct-action or "forcing" approach must be used with caution. When all competitors use this type of stimulus the result cannot help but have a diminishing effect for any individual firm. Moreover, the person may buy only for the incentive and return to a preferred brand later, in which case a costly promotion has failed.

Experience indicates that the forcing approach should seldom be used when strong appeals can be made to product superiority. The Scott Paper Company abandoned couponing for this reason and was successful in its stress on the product line itself and its unique advantages for the buyer.[8] Moreover, a strong stimulus to buy will have a lasting effect through increasing market share only if the product clearly demonstrates

[7] Lindley, Frazer, *Propaganda* (London: Oxford University Press, 1957), p. 99.

[8] "Coupons: ANA Study Cites Dangers," *Printers' Ink*, May 18, 1962, pp. 25–28.

its differentiation in use. Many new products have been successfully introduced by direct-action means but sales of an existing product with no apparent superiority are not likely to be affected greatly.

The direct-action stimulus clearly has a legitimate role when it has been indicated through research that a significant number of buyers require an additional stimulus for purchase action. The danger is that it may be used simply as a competitive fad. Thus the importance of sound product strategy based on consumer research is again apparent.

Slogans. A slogan is a small group of words combined in unique fashion to embody the selling theme. In general it will be short and to the point and feature the product name whenever possible. Through repetition it hopefully becomes associated with the product and its benefits, thereby provoking prompt recall of the advertising message.

Some slogans emphasize product performance, and the mention of the generic name is all that is needed to bring a powerful association to mind. Others are designed to emphasize product quality, such as the ageless slogan for Ivory Soap: "99 and 44/100 Percent Pure." A manufacturer may employ a slogan to minimize substitution of a competitor's product and stress confidence in quality. "You Can Be Sure if It's Westinghouse" became a well-known quality slogan.

Legal protection for slogans was granted in the Lanham Act of 1947. If the slogan is registered and certain additional requirements are met, legal protection is ensured. The detailed requirements of the act are explained in most basic marketing texts.[9]

Some Guides for Persuasive Copy

Imagination, of course, must be disciplined to generate creative and persuasive copy. While there is no universal set of steps to be followed, there is substantial agreement with many of the following points mentioned by Ogilvy:

1. Don't expect people to read leisurely essays.
2. Go straight to the point; don't beat about the bush.
3. Avoid analogies—"just as, so to."
4. Avoid superlatives, generalizations, platitudes. Consumers discount them—and forget them.
5. Be specific and factual.
6. Be personal, enthusiastic, memorable—as if the reader were sitting next to you at a dinner party.
7. Don't be a dull bore.
8. Tell the truth—but make the truth fascinating.

---

[9] For a summary see Theodore N. Beckman, William R. Davidson, and James F. Engel, *Marketing*, 8th ed. (New York: Ronald Press, 1967), Chap. 3.

9. Use testimonials. Celebrity testimonials are better than anonymous ones.
10. Don't be afraid to write *long* copy. Mail-orders advertisers never use short copy—and they know exactly what results they get.
11. Make the captions under your photographs pregnant with brand names and sell.[10]

One could, of course disagree with some of these points. Some advertisers never use testimonials. Notice the several important basic criteria that are set forth. Persuasive copy should be (1) specific, (2) interesting, (3) believable, (4) simple, and (5) relevant.

If the copy surrounding an illustration or several illustrations does not make it apparent as to what the product's use or contribution to the buyer's benefits may be, a caption must be included underneath it. Research has generally found that the readership effect of a series of pictures with captions can be twice as great as body copy.

Nothing can lose a reader's attention more quickly than a general claim insufficiently supported by specific facts. "Chevrolet gets good gas mileage" is much less effective than "Chevrolet delivers 23.9 miles per gallon in the Mobile Gas Economy Run." Furthermore, the copy must contain relevant, meaningful information if it is to interest—not bore—the reader. Even interesting copy generally should not demand complex mental reasoning by the reader. It is much more effective if it focuses on a single theme.

The wording has much to do with the effect of the message on the recipient, for clumsy wording can violate the criterion of simplicity. Such words as "new," "wonderful," "powerful," "time-saving," and "finest" have lost their impact through overuse by advertisers, and the consumer is likely to reject them as being irrelevant. Good copy in most advertisements should amplify the headline, offer proof of what the headline claims, explain the product's advantages, and make clear what the reader is expected to do. It should in most cases end with an appeal to action, such as "visit your dealer now."

VISUAL ELEMENTS

The visualization of the basic theme is of such importance that one authority has suggested it be prepared before any other elements.[11] According to this view, the most graphic, poignant, and appealing picture should be made of the theme; then the words are added. This is substantiated by a number of studies that demonstrate that the illustration is of critical importance in attracting and holding attention.[12]

---

[10] Ogilvy, "Raise Your Sights!"

[11] Beatrice Adams, "What's the Big Idea?" *Creativity—Methods and Techniques,* Proceedings, American Association of Advertising Agencies, 1958, pp. 1–20.

[12] "Why People Will Read Ads Through," *Printers' Ink,* December 6, 1963, pp. 23–29.

A number of methods can be used in creating the illustration—line drawings, cartoons, photographs, and artistic renderings of subjects. Photographs provide the most realism, but an artist's drawing may create a subtle mood or highlight an attribute of a product in use which may not be possible with photographs. In large part the choice of the method will be made on a subjective basis by the creative team.

Classification of Visual Forms[13]

Visual forms can be classified according to their features or techniques.

The product alone.   Perhaps the simplest form of illustration is one in which the product is shown without background or setting. This method may prove powerful when the product has intrinsic characteristics which command attention. Precious jewels, high-priced automobiles, and similar distinctive items can attract attention without the use of background. At times, in fact, a background may distract from the product's impact.

The product in a setting.   Not many products are of such distinction that they can be shown without background. The setting is chosen to show the product to advantage and, in many instances, the objective is to have the reader associate the quality of the setting with the product. In other situations the setting may imply the pleasant and satisfying uses of the product; Figure A–1 is an example.

The setting must be chosen carefully, for an incongruous background can lead to violation of the important criterion of believability. The low- or medium-priced car, for example, should not be shown in exclusive surroundings, because the product would seldom be found in such an environment.

The product in use.   This is perhaps the most widely used method of visualization. The power of suggestion is stimulated by this means, because the reader immediately identifies self with the product user and becomes the recipient of its benefits. Figure A–2 provides an excellent example of this approach.

Benefits from product use.   This method features the positive results derived from product use. It is hoped that readers will project themselves as ones who can benefit equally, especially if they have an acute need for the product. The reader with a headache clearly could grasp the benefits from the remedy advertised in Figure A–3.

Dramatizing need.   Frequently the need satisfied by a product is obvious, and little would be gained by illustrating it. In fact, such an illustration could be a trite and irrelevant visual treatment. In other situations, the

---

[13] Much of the discussion here is drawn from Wales, Gentry, and Wales, *Advertising Copy, Layout and Typography*, pp. 110–21.

FIGURE A–1
Distinctive Attributes Enhanced by Background

FIGURE A–2
Use of Product Coupled with Benefits Derived

FIGURE A–3
Showing the Benefits from Product Use

Calms anxiety
lifts depression
...*as it relieves*
headache pain

New Trend In Pain Relief:
When you have a headache you not only often suffer from pain but from anxiety tension and depression. Today's Anacin® now has a combined new action that actually calms anxiety and helps lift your depression as it turns off headache pain in minutes. You feel wonderfully relaxed and more cheerful again.

Anacin contains the compound doctors prescribe most for headaches. In fact, it's *twice as strong* in this as any other extra-strength tablet.

Only Anacin has this fortified combination of ingredients with a combined action that relieves pain, the underlying anxiety and helps brighten your spirits.

Next time try Anacin Tablets. See if Anacin doesn't work better for you.

Source: Used with permission of Whitehall Laboratories, Inc.

potential customer may not be aware that a need for the product exists until it has been illustrated. Moreover, effective visualization may dramatize an obvious and known need and thereby spur the reader to take action. Scouring pads, for example, are used mostly on pots and pans, but they also can be used to clean white-sidewall tires. The reader may have experienced difficulty in cleaning white sidewalls and may never have associated the use of scouring pads for this purpose. A dirty tire being made white through this product use can thus be a powerful illustration.

Explaining product uses. The illustration of a scouring pad in use serves another purpose—to dramatize multiple product uses. Frequently there is limited market knowledge of product capabilities, and customers may refuse to buy because they don't know how to use the product. If they do buy, they may use the product incorrectly and get poor results. The visual treatment can be helpful in showing details of methods of use or the procedures to be followed.

Featuring product details. Often the advertising theme will center around an improvement in some detail of the product or its operation. The detail may be dramatized by changing the perspective to make one part proportionately larger than others or by presenting the product from an unusual angle to call attention to that part. Other methods are to show a cross section of the product or print parts of it in color. Product details are clearly highlighted in the advertisement in Figure A–4.

Dramatization of evidence. Evidence is often the lifeblood of effective advertising. Unfortunately, advertising too frequently has been handi-

FIGURE A–4
Highlighting Product Details

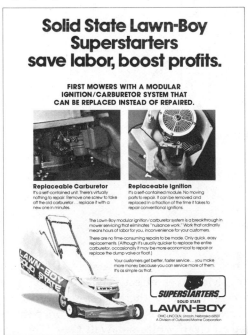

FIGURE A–5
Dramatizing Evidence Supporting Product
Claims

capped by the use of unsupported claims. Many effective illustrations
are created to support claims with factual evidence. Figure A–5 provides
an example.

The comparison technique. This method may be used to point out
certain product attributes that have competitive superiority. One variation
is to show the results of using the product as compared to the situation
existing before product use. The removal of carbon from engine valves
after using a brand of gasoline for 6,000 miles is an example. Another
method is to compare the results of using one product with the results
obtained from another.

Dramatization of the headline. The headline and illustration are usually closely related, and the illustration can effectively strengthen the
headline by communicating in a picture what the headline states in words.
This technique is effectively used in Figure A–6.

The use of symbolism. The winged feet of Mercury symbolize speed;
Uncle Sam signifies patriotism. Advertising may make effective use of
such symbols to associate the product or service with the basic idea con-
veyed. Notice how often the cross is used in advertising products with
Christian religious significance.

Some Guides for Persuasive Visualization

Studies on the use of visual elements to attract and hold attention
have disclosed that greatest effectiveness results when:

610

1. The illustration is placed in the upper part of the page instead of being positioned below the headline.
2. The illustration is the dominant element in the layout.
3. Photography is used instead of art work.
4. People or things are pictured in proper proximity.
5. The colors used are vivid.[14]

In addition, Ogilvy offers the following suggestions which can generally increase the probability of attracting and holding attention:

1. The average person now reads only four ads in a magazine; it is becoming increasingly difficult to find readers. That is why it is worth taking great plains to find a GREAT illustration.
2. Put "story appeal" in your illustration.
3. Illustrations should portray reward.
4. To attract women, show babies and women.
5. To attract men, show men.
6. Avoid historical illustrations; they don't sell.
7. Use photographs in preference to drawings. They sell more.
8. Don't deface your illustration.
9. Use captions that are written the way people talk.

_____
[14] "Basic Readership Factors."

10. Don't use a lot of illustrations—they look cluttered and discourage a reader.
11. Don't crop important elements in your illustration.[15]

Some advertising artists would disagree with certain of these points; others would state different ones. Each would react according to personal experience and working knowledge.

The use of color. There is no question that using color adds to costs of space or time, printing, and production. Advertisers have found, however, that the extra cost is well rewarded, for a number of reasons:

1. The attention-attracting and attention-holding power of the message may be increased sharply.
2. Contemporary social trends have encouraged experimentation in color in all phases of life, ranging from the factory to the home. Thus people have become responsive to innovative color stimuli.
3. Most products look better in color, especially food.
4. Color can be used to create moods ranging from the somber appeal to the freshness of greens and blues.
5. Color can add an image of prestige to the advertisement, especially if most competing advertisements are in black and white.
6. Visual impressions can be retained in memory, hence resulting in greater message recall.

Numerous studies have demonstrated the attention-attracting power of color. It is, for example, the one outstanding factor in stimulating high readership of newspaper advertisements.[16] The data in Figure A–7 are representative of the findings of many newspaper advertising studies. In television, color commercials have been found to be 55 percent more effective than black and white.[17]

Skillful use of color also can set the mood for the advertisement. Connotations of various colors include:

RED: Anger, action, fire, heat, passion, excitement, danger
BLUE: Sadness, cool, truth, purity, formality
YELLOW: Cheerfulness, spring, dishonesty, light, optimism
ORANGE: Fire, heat, action, harvest, fall
GREEN: Calm, wet, spring, youth, nature, ignorance, immaturity
BLACK: Mystery, mourning, death, heaviness
WHITE: Cleanliness, purity, virginity

Color reproduction techniques have reached a high degree of refinement in magazines, and newspapers have made major improvements in its use.

[15] Ogilvy, "Raise Your Sights!"
[16] "What Stirs the Newspaper Reader?" *Printers' Ink,* June 21, 1963, pp. 48–49.
[17] *Are Color Television Commercials Worth the Extra Cost?* (New York: Association of National Advertisers, 1966).

FIGURE A–7

Comparison of Readership of Black and White Advertisements and Color Advertisements by Size

Range of size lines	Number of ads	Average size lines (rounded to nearest 5 lines)	Men			Women		
			Noted	Seen-assoc.	Read most	Noted	Seen-assoc.	Read most
Black and white advertisements								
140–289	847	195	7%	6%	3%	26%	22%	11%
290–389	409	315	9	7	4	33	30	14
390–589	403	475	10	9	4	38	35	14
590–689	329	605	13	11	5	44	40	17
690–974	206	830	15	14	5	47	43	17
975–1089	341	1000	15	14	5	50	47	17
1090–1289	148	1200	20	18	6	51	47	17
1290–1589	45	1480	21	19	4	57	53	17
1590–2399	40	1940	26	23	7	54	51	16
1 page	20	1 page	37	34	10	60	58	20
Color advertisements black and one color								
1000–1089	262	1005	22	20	7	54	50	20
1090–1289	70	1205	24	21	7	57	54	25
1290–1589	47	1485	26	24	6	55	52	20
1590–2399	19	1875	30	29	8	59	57	20
1 page	36	1 page	40	39	11	64	64	23
Full color								
1000–2399	57	1160	31	29	9	59	56	21
1 page	119	1 page	42	38	11	72	68	29

Source: *Starch—Million Market Newspapers Adnorms Report,* Daniel Starch & Staff, Inc., Mamaroneck, N.Y.

Increasing use has been made of preprinted inserts for newspapers, and real advances are seen daily in standard newspaper color procedures (run of press color). Inks have been standardized so that the advertiser can order certain colors and expect the same result anywhere the message is run. Moreover, production improvements have served to lower costs significantly, and the differential for the addition of color is now from 5 to 10 percent in newspapers. There is little doubt that it will be used in increasing amounts in a wide variety of newspaper ads.

TYPOGRAPHY

An important element in the printed advertisement is the type to be used. There are few areas of the graphic arts of more interest historically and of greater importance in the development of civilization and culture than the creation of type printing surfaces, first used in printing the Gutenberg Bible in 1456. The first movable type was hand carved and crude in outline and impression, but its impact on literacy was startling as reading matter became available to more than a privileged few.

In place of the hand-carved, wood-block, one-design typefaces of medieval days, there now are hundreds of typefaces in many sizes. They are available as foundry type to be set by hand and matrices, which are brass-type molds from which single pieces of type, large or small, may be cast by machines operated by hand or computer and ejected as single letters, words, or lines of type.

These days even more typefaces are available from sophisticated typewriter-like equipment, machines that compose type photographically, and even devices that electronically create type on the face of a cathode ray (TV) tube at phenomenal speeds.

Type Structure and Measurement

Figure A–8 represents a single piece of foundry type and labels its components. Notice that each piece of type includes a face, neck, shoulders, and feet. The face is the design of the letter or symbol. It may contain serifs (the little lines at the top and base of the letters), but some forms of type do not have this characteristic and are called sans serif (without serif).

FIGURE A–8
Foundry Type Characteristics*

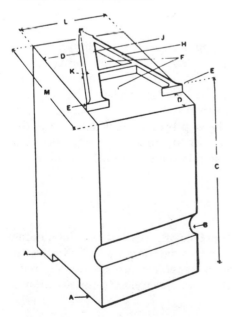

A. Feet. Type that is loosely spaced and leans over when printed is called "off its feet."
B. Nick. Helps compositor to place type right side up in stick. Keeps him from using wrong font.
C. Type-high, or height to paper, .918 inch or approximately $11\frac{1}{12}$ inch.
D. Shoulder. Nonprinting area surrounding a character.
E. Serif.
F. Counter or void.
H. Thin stroke of face.
J. Thick stroke of face.
K. Neck, beard, or drive. Made in matrix while casting, rest is made in the mold.
L. Set or set width.
M. Point size.

* In modern production methods, instead of foundry type, phototype methods are used.
Source: David Hymes, *Production in Advertising and the Graphic Arts* (New York: Henry Holt & Co., 1958), p. 66.

There are various classifications of type, according to:

1. *Type groups*—type families with similar characteristics. Such a group is Old Style, which has serifs. Another is more modern, without serifs.
2. *Type families*—typefaces with similar characteristics. These may carry the same name as their designer, as in Bodoni, or signify mood, as in Futura.
3. *Type series*—the typefaces designated on the basis of their size. Each type family has many series within it.

It is important to learn the terms used in designating type series. The following are of special importance:

Point = $\frac{1}{72}$ of an inch.

Pica = 12 points.

Inch = 6 picas or 72 points.

Em = Area occupied by a capital M. A 12-point em is 12 points wide and 12 points high and is equal to one pica in its linear measurement.

FIGURE A–9
Point Method of Type Measurement

The letters in Figure A–9 have 72 points to an inch, but the point measure does not reflect the exact size of any single letter. Rather, point size measures the height of a line of type, or the distance between the *descenders* and the *ascenders*. The width of a letter is measured by the pica, the pica unit equaling one sixth of an inch.

The standard unit for measuring the depth of a block of copy is the agate line. The line equals one fourteenth of an inch. Remember that the agate line or the column inch is the standard means of quoting newspaper space rates.

Selecting the Type

Selection of the most appropriate typeface or faces can be a demanding task. The two most important factors in this decision are legibility (readability) and mood. The connotations of typefaces are clearly different. You would not, for example, want to use an old-style face in advertising a new-model automobile.

There are other factors to consider as well:

1. *Type size in relation to use.* Headline type will be larger and perhaps of more weight than the type used in the reading matter.
2. *Number of words in the headline to be capitalized.* Words in the headline to be in all "caps" should be in typefaces whose capitals are easy to read, but it should be remembered that it is easier and more natural to read words set in "caps and lower case" (capitals and small letters).
3. *Number of words or word units in the headline.* The length of the headline or subheads will help determine the size of type to be used, as well as the number of words in each word group.
4. *Design of type in relation to use.* The design of the typeface may set the right mood, but script designs, for instance, tend to be more difficult to read than other faces.
5. *Amount of copy and amount of space available in the layout.*
6. *Uncontrollable factors.* The reader's ability to read cannot be controlled, but it would be folly to use very small type for older persons. The larger the type size the easier it should be to read under most lighting conditions.

The current trend in type size in magazine advertising is toward body type set in a size large enough so that the whole advertisement can literally be read with one sweep of the eyes. It may be that 24-point type will replace 12-, 13-, and 18-point for this purpose.

Greater reader interest can be assured by using space between the lines of set type. This is called leading; it can be done automatically in typesetting or by hand. The lines of type in the body of this text are leaded 2 points.

THE PRINTED ADVERTISEMENT

Layout

The layout is an arrangement of all elements of the advertisement in an integrated whole. Each element may be excellent by itself, but the finished advertisement will be unsatisfactory unless the elements are carefully blended in terms of the probable reaction of the reader.

Steps in preparing a layout. The elements of the layout are first assembled into what is usually referred to as the "rough." As can be seen in Figure A–10, lines are drawn in for the copy and the picture is only sketched. As rough as this first layout is, it permits an evaluation of the manner in which the elements combine to create a pleasing effect. The copy at this stage is usually prepared on separate sheets.

The layout then is refined into "semicomprehensive" form. The elements are drawn in with sharper clarity, and it is possible to pretest

FIGURE A–10
Illustration of a Rough Layout

for the holidays

store name

Source: Taken from *Advertising Copy, Layout, and Typography* by Hugh G. Wales, Dwight L. Gentry, and Max Wales. Used with permission of the Ronald Press Company.

the message at this stage to derive a preliminary indication of its probable effectiveness. If pretesting evaluation is favorable, it is common to prepare a final version referred to as the "comprehensive." Copy is not yet inserted, but the lines representing copy blocks are drawn precisely to represent the exact size of the space for copy. The layout at this stage is ready for approval by management, and a final buyer pretest may be necessary.

Roughs are made in miniature in the same proportions as the final advertisement. The reduction is one to two—the dimensions of the miniature sketch are one half the dimensions of the finished layout. An easy way to determine this size is to draw a full-dimension layout area and bisect it with a diagonal, as in Figure A–11. The line through *A* (the midpoint) drawn parallel to the top of the layout will strike the diagonal at *D*. A line dropped from the intersection *D* to the bottom of the layout, parallel to the vertical edge of the advertisement, will complete the miniature. Elements of the rough made in this reduced size will appear in the same proportions when the advertisement is produced in actual size.

Criteria of an effective layout. The layout of a printed advertisement usually is formalized along the lines of certain principles which recognize that the situation of the reader is more stable than that of the listener to the television or radio commercial. There is time for the reader to feel the presence or absence of unity, balance, good proportion, judicious

FIGURE A-11
Method for Determining Proportions in the Rough Layout

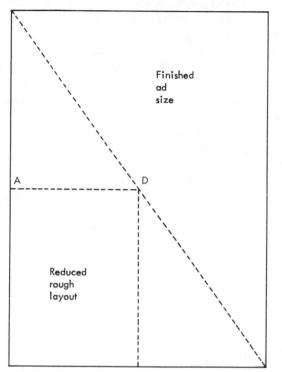

contrast, harmony, and eye direction. The television viewer or radio listener, however, is exposed to the message for only a short time, and attention may be fragmented. Layout principles of printed advertisements include (1) unity, (2) balance, (3) proportion, (4) contrast, (5) harmony, and (6) eye direction.

Unity.   Each element is first designed as a separate unit, but the completed layout should create a feeling of oneness. The headline should not stand out unduly from the remainder of the message, any more than the roof of a building should dominate the structure. Consistency in typeface, overlapping elements, and the use of such connecting devices as lines and arrows may serve to enhance unity.

Balance.   Balance has to do with the way an advertisement "feels," whether it is formal or informal. Balance occurs when elements of equal weight or substance are placed in proportion in reference to a given point. The focal point is the optical center—a point slightly above the center and to the left. The eye is most likely to be attracted to this spot at first glance.

When elements are placed in equal relationship on both sides of a center point, the resulting layout is said to be in formal balance. An example of formal balance is given in Figure A–12. If elements are placed at different distances from the center, the layout is in informal or asymmetrical balance. Figure A–13 is an example.

Formal balance obviously can create a somewhat uninteresting effect if it is carried to extremes. On the other hand, it does connote dignity and conservatism. Informal balance can be more interesting in its visual impression and create an impression of excitement. Carried to extremes, however, it can appear unnatural to the reader.

Proportion.   This principle is closely related to balance; it refers to the division of space among the elements to create a proper optical effect. Yet proportion also requires creating emphasis in terms of the size and shape of each element. There are some sales points or copy elements that deserve more weight and space than others, and proportion calls for allocation of space in these terms.

Contrast.   This attention-getting device is vital when an advertisement is competing with many others for the reader's attention, particularly among several advertisements on a magazine or newspaper page. Dramatic use of color, for example, may cause an advertisement to stand out. Also,

FIGURE A–12
Advertisement with Formal Balance

FIGURE A–13
Advertisement with Informal Balance

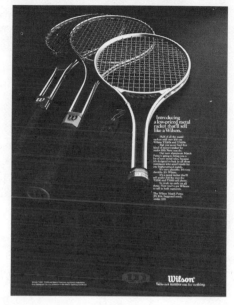

the background may be left uncluttered to create large areas of white space. White space is utilized effectively in Figure A–14 to create an unusual effect.

Harmony.   Harmony, like unity, has to do with the impression the whole advertisement makes on the reader. It is the reader's feeling that all is right in what he sees—the parts of the layout are related. There is nothing incongruous or unmatching, or, if incongruity is introduced, it has been so skillfully accomplished that the reader is not jolted into a negative reaction toward the presentation.

Eye direction.   As noted earlier, the reader's eyes are generally attracted to the optical center of the advertisement. From that point they may move in any direction, and it often is useful to employ various devices to direct this motion in a desired manner throughout the message.

The eye might be attracted from the optical center through heavy emphasis on color in other parts of the layout. In addition, arrows, lines, or other mechanical devices might be employed. Perhaps more common is the placement of elements so that the angle of the dominant elements will lead the eye in the desired direction naturally. Notice how the eye is drawn downward into the copy in the advertisement reproduced in Figure A–15. In addition, the direction of gaze of dominant figures depicted in the layout can be used for this same purpose. The use of gaze motion is illustrated in Figure A–16.

FIGURE A–14
Effective Use of White Space

Source: Used with permission of Eastman Kodak Company.

FIGURE A–15
Placement of Elements to Create Eye Movement

FIGURE A–16
Gaze Motion and Good Space Management

Even she knows what tastes good

There's much <u>more</u> <u>flavor</u> in

THIN KRISPY crackers

Source: Used with permission of Sunshine Biscuits, Inc.

Layout styles.   Just as artwork, photography, typeface choice, and hand-lettering design have gone through periods of "in" and "out," so has layout. The trend in the 1970s and early 1980s has been toward the space-dominating close-up of a model or the product, coupled with a headline and selling message set in the same type style, the headline often being the lead sentence in the copy and the size of the type diminishing only slightly after several lines. This style allows a sweep of the eyes to catch almost the complete pictorial and written sales message. Figure A–17 is an example.

There is also the "Mondrian" style, which was inspired by the delicately related size of rectangles in the style of the Dutch painter, Piet Mondrian. The area is divided by intersecting sets of parallel lines, and the elements of the ad are assigned to the various areas created by the intersecting sets of parallel lines. This style is the least costly for the illustrations used because each is finished as a rectangle. It is a style that is infallible in its dependency on the sound relation of spaces, but it has the inherent advantages and disadvantages of the standardized format. Limitations may be imposed by its inflexibility.

Frank Young's "white fence" method utilizes white space as a separating element. One element touches only once on all four imaginary borders

FIGURE A–17
Space-Dominating Close-Up Visualization and Layout Popular during the 1970s and Early 1980s

of the page, and each point is not equally spaced in relation to the others. Such conscious use of white space recognizes white space for what it is—an element of layout, to be dealt with as an element rather than as ample space to be filled up. Used as a design element, white space is particularly important in newspaper advertisements, where it is worth every bit as much as the space occupied by the illustration or the copy in its ability to isolate the elements of an advertisement from competing with news and other advertising matter. It can be an element of direction for eye movement, an element of control, and an element of contrast or emphasis.

Modern art has in no small way been responsible for some imaginative approaches to design in the graphic arts, industrial packaging, and advertising design. The informality of modern art has created its own formality—the dignity of unbalanced use of space. Its contrast with the formal pattern of spacing and weight of elements and the only slightly less inflexible informal balance that has prevailed has meant new horizons for creative talents in advertising. It has been felt in photography and in type, in the use of color and paper texture, and in an open discovery approach to layout elements and their relationships.

Producing the Finished Advertisement

Printing methods. The basic printing methods are: (1) letterpress, (2) lithography, (3) gravure, and (4) silk screen.

Letterpress printing. Use may be made of a platen press (two flat surfaces), a flatbed press (flat and curved surfaces) or a rotary press (two curved surfaces). Platen and flatbed presses are used for the printing of direct mail and product information enclosures as well as some smaller newspapers.

The majority of printed advertising is reproduced through the letterpress method. It is the oldest printing method, originating with the printing of the Gutenberg Bible. In the letterpress method, the impression of the type on the paper comes directly from the face of the type itself and from other typographical elements. The type may be set by hand, by a mammoth linotype machine that has a manually operated keyboard similar to a typewriter, or by a computer-controlled facility.

The traditional letterpress method uses hot, molten lead in which lines of type are cast. The main headline and subheads are often set by hand. The type which has been set is then assembled with the other elements, as outlined in a later paragraph.

One of the trends in the field of type composition replaces hot-metal casting with fast cathode-ray tube (CRT) phototypesetting. The unit may or may not be computer controlled, but in larger installations it is always either tape operated or computer controlled. With the increase in phototypesetting, the use of hot metal is decreasing, as it has for the past decade. Hot metal will probably continue to be used, but its percentage of use will undoubtedly decline year by year.

Even newspapers are turning to photocomposition, a natural method for papers printed by web offset. (Web offset refers to a lithopress which prints on both sides of a web or roll of paper in one operation.) Many of the letterpress newspapers are also moving to photocomposition. In such a case, the output of the phototypesetter is "stripped up" (the act of positioning or inserting copy elements in negative or positive film on a unit negative) to make a full newspaper page, which is then photographed to produce a negative. The negative is used to make a relief plate that is mounted on the press. A pattern plate is produced from the negative by using an emulsion on the plate. The plate is then used to make mats (a papier-mâché reproduction of the page), the mats are used to produce stereos (metal plates cast from the mats), and the stereos are attached to the cylinder or bed of the press so that printed copies can be produced.

The first step in letterpress printing is the marking of the printed materials and layout to give details of how the advertisement or printed page is to be set up and printed.

The compositor will assemble the type bars and illustrations and fasten them securely in a metal frame; will pull a proof to permit corrections, make the corrections, and will place the corrected metal frame in a page form which is the size of the finished page. If the copy is computer-set and assembled, all these steps are performed automatically. The last stage is to prepare the papier-mâché mat to be cast into the plate. The printing surface receives the ink, which is transferred to the paper under regulated pressure at high press speed and accuracy.

Lithography.   This is literally "chemical printing." The most common form of lithography is referred to as offset. The process basically involves impression of the design onto a metal surface, application of ink, transfer of the message to a roller, and final printing onto paper. The offset method provides high-quality reproduction of direct mail sales messages, catalogues, and booklets and is especially good for four-color reproduction.

A plate is prepared of the entire advertisement, including type and visual elements. The images on the plate are in the form of a greasy coating. Then the plate is dampened with water. The greasy images repel the water, while the uncoated or blank portions of the plate retain it. Then the plate is coated with an oily ink. The dampened, uncoated portions of the plate repel the ink, while the greasy image retains it for transfer to the paper.

Gravure.   This method of printing is often found in the special sections of Sunday newspapers featuring four-color advertisements. In addition it is widely used in printing magazines. The gravure procedure lays a heavy coating of ink on the paper, and it can always be felt by running a finger over the surface.

Printing is done from an engraved or depressed surface. Small cups are etched into the surface of a cylinder, representing type, pictures, and other elements. Acid etches the metal to sufficient depth to reproduce the tonal values. (Hence gravure which provides an infinite variation in tone and color reproduction is excellent.) The paper is then placed in contact with the printing cylinder, and ink is transferred to the paper in the desired pattern.

Silk screen.   The silk-screen process is widely used where printing runs are small and when other methods would be too clostly. No plates are required; printing is done from a silk screen stretched in a frame over the surface. A stencil is placed on the screen which blanks out areas that are not to take a printing image. Then ink is pressed through the uncovered areas of the screen and transferred to the printing surface.

Silk-screen printing is useful in color reproduction. It also is economical in print runs of less than 10,000 copies, for it eliminates the costly stages of preparation of plates. In addition, it can be used in combination with the letterpress or lithography methods.

Producing the illustration.   Reproduction of the visual elements of the message is a fascinating part of the graphic arts. Advertising agencies may use their art departments for hand-lettered renderings and for the rough layouts, but the comprehensive or finished layout is often sent out to art studios which are staffed and equipped to prepare illustrations for printing.

Line drawings, consisting of black lines and white space, with no grays or shading, are the simplest form of drawing to reproduce. A picture is taken of the copy. The film is then processed as a negative and is laid upon a thin metal plate. The plate is coated with an acid-resistant emulsion which clings to the areas which are photosensitive and is washed away from those that are not. When submerged in an acid bath, the unprotected areas are etched out, leaving raised areas which are the lines of the drawing. When ink is applied directly to this plate, the lines of the drawing will print, and the areas around the lines will not.

If shading is required it can be done on the original drawing through skillful use of black and white. Or it can be done on the finished copy through use of the benday method. Bendays are line and dot shadings available in many varied patterns that can be added directly to the original negative to produce the desired effect.

Photographs are reproduced by a different process called halftone. The picture is placed on a copy board before a camera, but a direct exposure is not made as it is in reproducing a line drawing. Instead a screen or grid is placed between the camera lens and the film. The result is that the mass of the picture is broken down into thousands of tiny dots, the fineness of the dots being determined by the printing requirements. For newspaper printing a 60-line screen is used, with 3,600 dots per square inch. The result can easily be seen with the naked eye. Newspaper stock is somewhat porous, so a fine screen cannot be used because the dots will blur together and ruin the reproduction.

Magazine reproduction demands a finer 120-line screen, giving 14,400 dots per square inch. The finished picture is reproduced with much greater clarity. If color is to be used an even finer set of screens is employed. Tonal values are broken down into 57,600 dots per square inch.

If the picture requires both line-drawing and halftone treatment, a combination plate is made of the line-drawing negative overlaid with a halftone negative. The engraving process is the same for both methods. Hand finishing may be required to make the picture sharper in detail or to highlight areas of the picture by removing some of the dots, leaving pure white space to "highlight" the objects.

Color reproduction. A refinement of the halftone process is used for this purpose. A separate negative must be made for each of the primary colors (red, yellow, and blue) and one for black (to give depth and perspective). A negative is made for each of the four colors by using filters which block out unwanted colors. Each color is photographed with a different screen, and the screen is turned a specified number of degrees so that the dots of each negative will fall beside those of the other negatives rather than pile on top of them. Individual plates are made, each of which prints its own color, and the plate must be perfectly placed on the press so that each dot will fall precisely where it should. The human eye then takes over, and the illustration will appear to be solid color.

Producing the complete advertisement using letterpress. In the engraver's composing room the elements of the advertisement are "locked up." A wax mold is made by placing a metal plate coated with wax over the type form and applying pressure that implants a deep and sharp impression in the wax. The wax sheet is placed in an electrolytic bath where by electrolysis copper is deposited on the wax to a required thickness. The copper is stripped from the wax, backed with additional metal, and mounted on a wood base to bring it to the proper height for printing purposes. The result is a finely etched plate called an electrotype.

Four-color process work utilizes lead instead of wax. The original plates are set, and the lead is molded under the pressure of hydraulic presses. The lead later receives the copper deposit, and the finishing process is the same from this point on. The resulting plate may be sent to the newspaper or magazine for direct use in their presses, but it is more common to use mats for this purpose.

LAYOUT AND PRODUCTION OF THE BROADCAST ADVERTISEMENT

Layout and Design

Layout in broadcast media seldom is formalized by utilizing principles such as those discussed for the printed message. There was greater formality in the early days of radio, when an opening commercial, two program breaks, and a closing commercial were commonly used. It was assumed that listeners were sitting at home with ears tuned to the radio. The informality and casualness of radio programming and radio listening habits has changed this, and the form of the broadcast advertising message has become quite varied to adapt to the nature of the listening situation.

The customary format of radio programs today provides a substantial number of hours devoted to music recordings during the 24-hour broadcast schedule. Often 12 minutes of each quarter-hour segment are given over to music, with from two to three minutes of news or weather. During this 15-minutes music-news-weather segment, there will be different radio commercials of varying lengths. Radio stations also schedule interview programs, which may be educational or entertainment segments.

The television message is somewhat more formalized, but the viewing of television is also casual. Thus there are few principles of layout per se to be followed in broadcast advertisements, other than to specify the importance of harmony among elements. Obviously, one element, such as the audio portion, should not dominate other portions if this can be avoided.

The layout of the television commercial usually is developed through use of storyboards, although a script may be used without direct rendering of the visual elements. The radio commercial uses only the audio script. The storyboard differs little in its nature from the rough layouts developed for printed advertisements, except that individual rough layouts are made for each major scene in the commercial. An example of a storyboard appears in Figure A–18. Notice that the audio elements are written beside a rough rendering of the visual ones.

Production of the Commercial

Radio commercials usually are produced in final form by the script department of the advertising agency, by an agency specializing in such script and dramatic writing, or by staff members at a radio station. The message elements are combined carefully and reproduced on tape. The "live" radio commercial is confined mostly to local radio advertising today.

The production of a television commercial entails greater complexity. For this reason, storyboards or trial commercials should be pretested before

FIGURE A–18
Television Storyboard

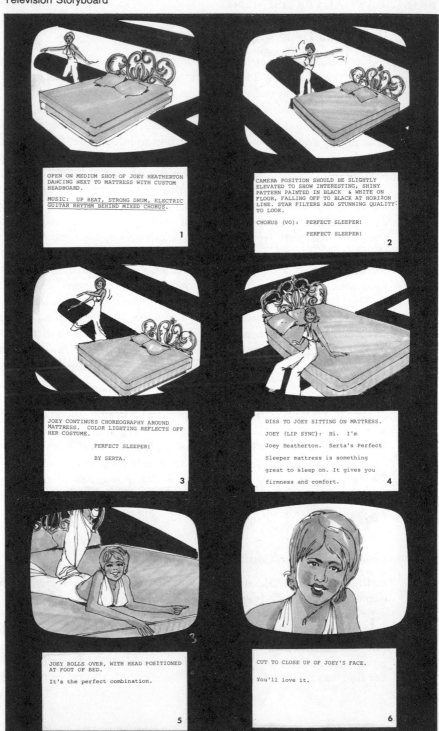

OPEN ON MEDIUM SHOT OF JOEY HEATHERTON
DANCING NEXT TO MATTRESS WITH CUSTOM
HEADBOARD.

MUSIC: UP BEAT, STRONG DRUM, ELECTRIC
GUITAR RHYTHM BEHIND MIXED CHORUS.

1

CAMERA POSITION SHOULD BE SLIGHTLY
ELEVATED TO SHOW INTERESTING, SHINY
PATTERN PAINTED IN BLACK & WHITE ON
FLOOR, FALLING OFF TO BLACK AT HORIZON
LINE. STAR FILTERS ADD STUNNING QUALITY
TO LOOK.

CHORUS (VO): PERFECT SLEEPER!

PERFECT SLEEPER!

2

JOEY CONTINUES CHOREOGRAPHY AROUND
MATTRESS. COLOR LIGHTING REFLECTS OFF
HER COSTUME.

PERFECT SLEEPER!

BY SERTA.

3

DISS TO JOEY SITTING ON MATTRESS.

JOEY (LIP SYNC): Hi. I'm

Joey Heatherton. Serta's Perfect

Sleeper mattress is something

great to sleep on. It gives you

firmness and comfort.

4

JOEY ROLLS OVER, WITH HEAD POSITIONED
AT FOOT OF BED.

It's the perfect combination.

5

CUT TO CLOSE UP OF JOEY'S FACE.

You'll love it.

6

FIGURE A–18 (*concluded*)

the finished commercial is made. The costs of production can be considerable—often $60,000 or more—and few companies can afford the risks of producing the commercial and *then* testing it.

Commercial production is largely the province of specialized firms. The commercial may be shot in a studio if the visual background permits the use of fixed sets. The costs, of course, are greatly minimized if this is possible. Often, however, it is necessary to "go on location" and make the commercial under natural settings. The costs then become considerable, especially if color is used.

Once the films are shot, the designers of the commercial spend considerable time viewing the film (often referred to as the rushes). Unusable footage is cropped out, and the finished commercial is then made by combining the visual and audio elements at appropriate places.

Until recently all television commercials were reproduced on 16-mm film. Substantial use is now being made of video tape.

MEDIA REQUIREMENTS AND THE ADVERTISING MESSAGE

Many of the topics discussed above require modification and qualification from medium to medium, for the media themselves impose requirements on the creative task. Requirements of the various media are discussed below.

Newspapers

Copy. Newspaper advertising often attains a high degree of readership, for it is frequently used as a source of buying information. Because much newspaper copy is oriented toward stimulating visits to dealers and other forms of direct action, there is need for concise wording using such appeals as economy and urgency.

Production. A newspaper is severely limited in quality compared with other printed media. Layouts cannot depend for their effect on fine-screen reproduction, for example. Under no circumstances should a plate used for a magazine illustration be used in newspapers, or vice versa. Line drawings may prove to be more effective because they offer greater clarity and eye appeal.

All reading matter must be designed to attain high legibility. Newspapers, as a rule, are read quickly, and there is competition from other advertisements and editorial matter. Moreover, distracting typographical elements should be put aside in favor of layouts that provide highly controlled eye movement. The directional movement created by judicious placing of elements plays a large role in overcoming the distracting effect of competing advertisements and news features.

Magazines

Copy. Magazine copy frequently can be longer than newspaper copy, for the reader generally spends more time on each page and may be exposed to the message more than once. The elements must combine to separate prospects from nonprospects, and a heavy burden is placed on the copywriter to produce a headline that will successfully generate reader selectivity. More time is probably spent on writing the headline than on any other element of the message.

Because the magazine will typically reach a relatively select audience by the nature of its editorial content, copy must be closely tuned to the motivational determinants of the prospects. The selected audience frequently is a critical audience, not likely to be satisfied with a general claim that might be successful with larger consumer groups. In addition, the audience of a special-interest magazine (say a photography magazine) is likely to be sensitive to the product and highly interested in important facts. The copy may, as a result, be more technical and take more space. More illustrations are often used to depict details of product construction or use.

Production. Most magazines offer colors, high-gloss paper for fine-screen halftone reproduction, placement on certain pages, and a wide range of typefaces. Even though it may add to costs, it usually is advisable to make the total advertisement as much in character in all respects with a given publication as the budget will allow.

A decision must be made on whether or not to use "bleed"—the technique of laying out photographs or other materials in such a way that they will extend to the edge of the page without the usual white border. Bleed usually costs 15 percent extra, but it often is necessary for proper visualization of the product. Frequent use is made of two facing pages to provide more space for arranging the elements in a dramatic combination.

Billboards

Copy. The poster depends almost entirely on the power of the illustration to attract attention. Color and size are two of the most widely used devices to attract attention, as are animation and various illumination devices. Copy usually will be brief, and it may be in the form of a slogan. The fleeting moment for reader attraction and attention requires the use of highly legible type in very large sizes.

Production. Poster space is usually referred to in terms of "sheets," ranging in size from 82 × 48 inches to 104 × 234 inches. The finished layout will consist of many sheets which are printed by silk screen or lithography.

Direct Mail

Copy. Much effort is devoted to creating a personalized message. Procedures exist so that what appears to be a hand-typed letter can be reproduced by mechanical means, personalized, and sent to a long list of potential customers. It is human nature to be flattered by personal attention, and the object is to make the reader become personally involved in the mail piece.

The headline or lead paragraph bears the burden of holding attention unless an illustration or graphic feature is used. The advertiser may want the person to read a letter or accompanying enclosure; the person may be urged to send in a coupon or make some other form of direct response. In any event, direct mail usually calls for the reader to do something and do it now before he puts the mailing down, even if it is just to mark the calendar for a coming event.

Direct mail copy by its very nature will be more personal than any other form of advertising writing. Often this personalization requires a unique skill, and it may be wise to use specialists for this purpose. In any event, authorities have offered these useful suggestions:

1. Know exactly what you want your mailing to do for you. What are you trying to accomplish? Do you want an order? Or an inquiry? Or a chance to have one of your salesmen call?
2. Address each mailing piece (correctly) to an individual or company who can buy the product or service you have to sell. . . . The mailing list is the absolute foundation of successful direct mail. Solicit your list as often as it pays off.
3. Write your copy so that the recipient will know what your product or service will do for him! Have you appealed to his or her selfish interests of have you used all your white space talking about yourself, your president and your beautiful new factory?
4. Make the layout and format of your mailing tie in with your overall plan and objective. Have you used black-and-white when four-color printing is indicated? Have you used a typewritten letter when mimeographing would fit the picture better? . . . The appearance of your mailing must be in keeping with the overall job you're trying to do.
5. Make it easy for your prospect to send you an order or an inquiry. Have you included in your mailing an order form for direct business, have you listed the places where your product is available?
6. Test every mailing you make. Never take anything for granted in direct-mail advertising or selling. Don't even trust your own experience. . . . Test everything—even the ideas that seem sure to fail as well as the ones that are bound to succeed. Test media. Test ad size. Test position. Test color against black and white.
7. Tell your story over again. Very few salesmen make a sale on their first call. Even the best of them call back many, many times before turning a

prospect into a customer, and it isn't reasonable to expect a single mailing to produce a large return.

8. Include several pieces in any direct mail package, such as advertising about several products, coupons, and certificates. Every product offered should be measured in terms of profit. The weak must go—or at least take less space in the catalogue or sheets. For example, every year over 200 new items are tested in separate mailings by the Shell Oil Company as candidates for inclusion in the Shell Merchandise Catalogue.

9. Don't be afraid of long copy. If your headline or mailing selects the audience and offers them a worthwhile promise, they will read on—and frequently buy. For example, a six-page letter for Mercedes-Benz sold approximately 1,000 diesel cars in one month. Since this model sold at $4,400 each, the letter produced over $4 million in sales.[18]

Layout and design. The form of the direct mail piece will determine its layout in part. The usual form is a letter, but it also may be a card or catalogue, to mention only a few possible variations. Direct mail is unique in that for a moment or longer it may have the sole attention of the reader. There is no competition from news or other media stimuli. Special burden is thus placed on the layout and visual elements to hold attention. Type is varied, and color is introduced at various points to hold and direct the eye through the entire message.

Radio and Television

Copy. The discussion to this point has been concerned with printed advertisements. It is to be expected that broadcast advertising differs in certain details. Radio has become perhaps the most informal of all media, and this informality has permeated its advertising requirements. Frequently the commercial is not written down word for word, but an outline is given to the announcer, who then provides words and style. Heavy use may also be made of humor and whimsy.

Ogilvy makes these suggestions for the television commercial:

1. It is easier to double the selling power of a commercial than to double the audience of a program.

2. Make your *pictures* tell the story. What you *show* is more important than what you *say*. If you can't *show* it, don't say it.

3. Try running your commercial with the sound turned off. If it doesn't sell without sound, it's a feeble commercial. Words and pictures must march together, reinforcing each other. The words in your titles must be identical with the words spoken.

4. In the best commercials the key idea is forcefully demonstrated. But in the poorest commercials there is little or *no* demonstration.

---

[18] Edward N. Mayer, Jr., "7 Cardinal Rules for Direct-Mail Success," *Printers' Ink,* May 30, 1957, p. 38, and David Ogilvy, "Raise Your Sights!" Reproduced with special permission.

5. The best commercials are built around one or two simple ideas—*big* ideas. They are not a hodgepodge of confusing little ideas; that is why they are never created in committee. The best commercials flow smoothly, with few changes of scene.

6. The purpose of most commercials is to deliver the selling promise in the most persuasive and memorable way. State your promise at least twice in every commercial.

7. The average consumer sees ten thousand commercials a year. Make sure that she knows the name of the product being advertised in your commercial. Show the package loud and clear. Repeat the brand name as often as you can. Show the name in at least one title.

8. Good commercials rely on simple promises, potently demonstrated. But promises and demonstrations can be made tedious and indigestible by logorrhea [excessive talkativeness]. Don't drown your prospect in words.

9. Make the product itself the hero of the commercial.

10. In *print* advertising you must start by attracting the prospect's attention. But in television the prospect is *already* attending. Your problem is not to attract her attention, but to *hang on to it.*

11. *Start selling in your first frame.* Never warn the prospect that she is about to hear a "friendly word from our sponsor." Never start your commercial with an irrelevant analogy. Never start with an interrupting device.

12. Dr. Gallup reports that commercials which set up a consumer problem, then solve it with the product, then prove it, sell four times as much merchandise as commercials which simply preach about the product.

13. Dr. Gallup also reports that commercials with a news content are more effective than the average.

14. All products are not susceptible to the same commercial techniques. Sometimes there isn't any news; you cannot always use the problem-solution gambit; you cannot always demonstrate. Sometimes you must rely on *emotion* and *mood.* Commercials with a high content of emotion and mood can be very potent indeed.

15. To involve a person emotionally you should be human and *friendly.* People don't buy from salesmen who are bad-mannered. Nor do they buy from phonies or liars. Do not strain their credulity. Be believable.

16. Movie screens are forty feet across, but TV screens are less than two. Use close-up pictures instead of long shots. You have a small screen; get some *impact* on it.

17. You cannot bore people into buying your product. You can only *interest* them in buying it. Dr. Gallup reports that prospects are bored by "sermon" commercials, in which the announcer simply yaks about the product.

18. Television commercials are not for entertaining. They are for *selling.* Selling is a serious business. Good salesmen never sing. The *spoken* word is easier to understand than the *sung* word. Speech is less entertaining than song, but more persuasive. Persuasive commercials never sing.

19. The average consumer sees more than two hundred commercials a week, nine hundred a month, ten thousand a year. For this reason you should give your commercial a touch of singularity. It should have a *burr* that will

cling to the viewer's mind. But the burr must not be an irrelevance. And it must not steal attention away from the PROMISE.
20. Whenever you write a commercial, bear in mind that it is likely to be seen by your children, your wife—and your conscience.[19]

Design and production.   Production procedures were discussed earlier and will not be repeated here, other than to stress the growing importance of film and videotape over live commercials. Most network telecasting now is in color. There is no question but what the greater realism pays off in strengthened ability to hold attention. In addition, many feel that the persuasive effectiveness of the commercial is greatly sharpened.

SMALL SPACE: A SPECIAL CREATIVE PROBLEM

Small space is a relative term: a quarter page or less in a magazine; a few column inches in a newspaper; the ten-second commercial; the two- or three-foot highway sign; the direct-mail piece of less than standard letter size. Small space offers a special challenge to creativity, for it is usually easier to say what you have to say in large space. Nevertheless, small space also offers unique advantages.

The short commercial (often called the "ID") is growing in popularity on radio and television because prime time may be purchased at a much lower cost per commercial. Research has shown that viewers much prefer the shorter commercial. The persuasive effectiveness (based on the Schwerin measure discussed in Chapter 15 is nearly as great as the 60-second message, brand name recall is virtually identical, and playback of specific sales points from the 20-second spot is 71 percent as effective as playback from its 60-second counterpart.[20] In addition, many feel that the "shorty" can do almost any advertising task. One television expert puts it this way: "There is hardly a product that cannot be successfully advertised with 20-second commercials. We've found that's time enough to allow for adequate demonstration and good registration of the product name. And, a 20-second announcement can be made just as colorful and exciting as a longer one."[21]

Research data also document the effectiveness of small space in printed advertising. While larger advertisements do produce a greater number of readers, the gain in readers is not in direct proportion to size.[22] Unique creative use of the small space can more than offset the advantage of the larger unit.

---

[19] Ogilvy, "Raise Your Sights!" Reproduced with special permission.
[20] Robert M. Hoffman, "The 20-Second Commercial," *Media/Scope*, July 1963, p. 74.
[21] Ibid., p. 74.
[22] "What Is the Best Size for a Newspaper Ad?" *Media/Scope*, July 1965.

The emphasis, of course, is on brevity. The headline may carry the entire burden, and there seldom is space or time enough to develop lengthy copy. As a result it is common to take one selling idea at a time and develop it over time through a series of integrated messages. Each advertisement in the campaign will have common elements such as visual treatment, slogan, or background music. Integrated 10-second commercials for Sprite utilized a common background jingle effectively, and many other examples could be given of this technique.

SUMMARY

This appendix has focused on design of the various message elements, with special emphasis on the printed advertisement. Most of the discussion, however, applies to advertising in *all* media.

While a number of guides or criteria were advanced, it cannot be emphasized too strongly that there is no universal set of rules. These criteria were included to provide the foundation for proper disciplining of the imagination to produce a persuasive message. To these would be added many more gained from experience and research. Moreover, they must be modified and adapted to fit each individual situation.

Many technical details of design and production have only been highlighted. However, the complexity should be apparent. Art and production specialists are employed for these various tasks, and the interested reader is encouraged to consult appropriate books to augment his background.[23]

[23] One useful source is Wales, Gentry, and Wales, *Advertising Copy, Layout and Typography.* Another is Hugh Wales, John McNamara, and Hal Johnson, *New Product, Brand Name, Consumer Packaging and Advertising Philosophy* (DeKalb, Ill.: Northern Illinois University, 1972).

Index

This book has been set VideoComp in 10 and 9 point Compano, leaded 2 points. Part and chapter numbers are 14 point Compano Semi Bold. Part and chapter titles are 18 point Compano Semi Bold. The size of the overall type area is 30 by 46 picas.